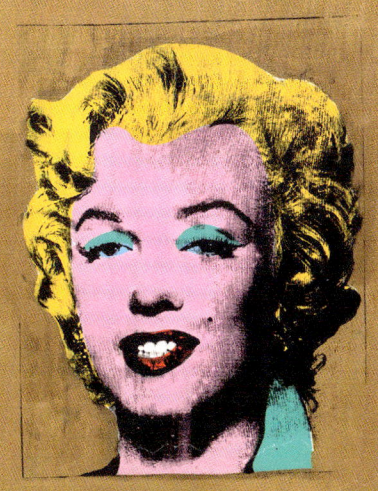

"Art evokes the mystery
without which the world would not exist."

RENÉ MAGRITTE

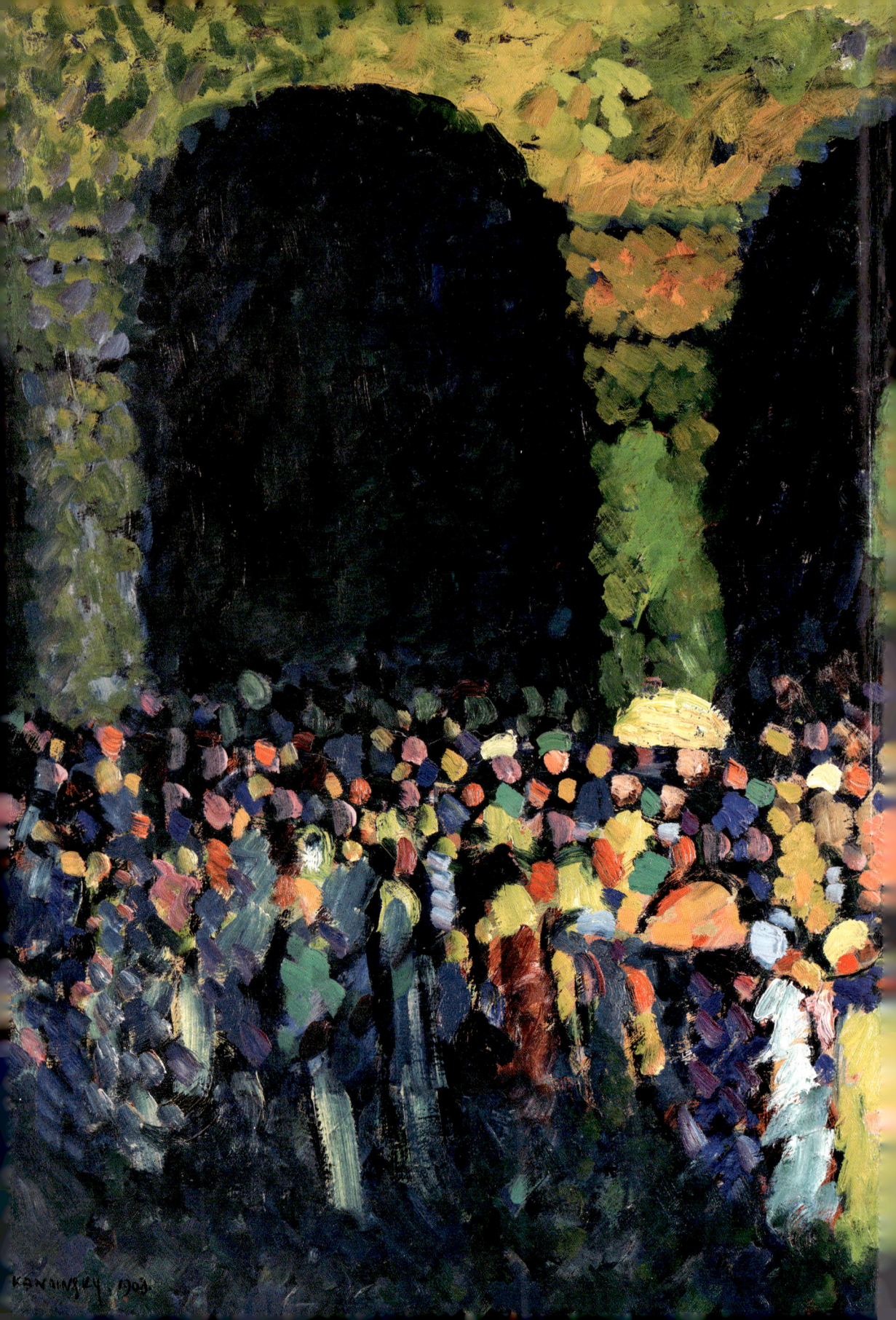

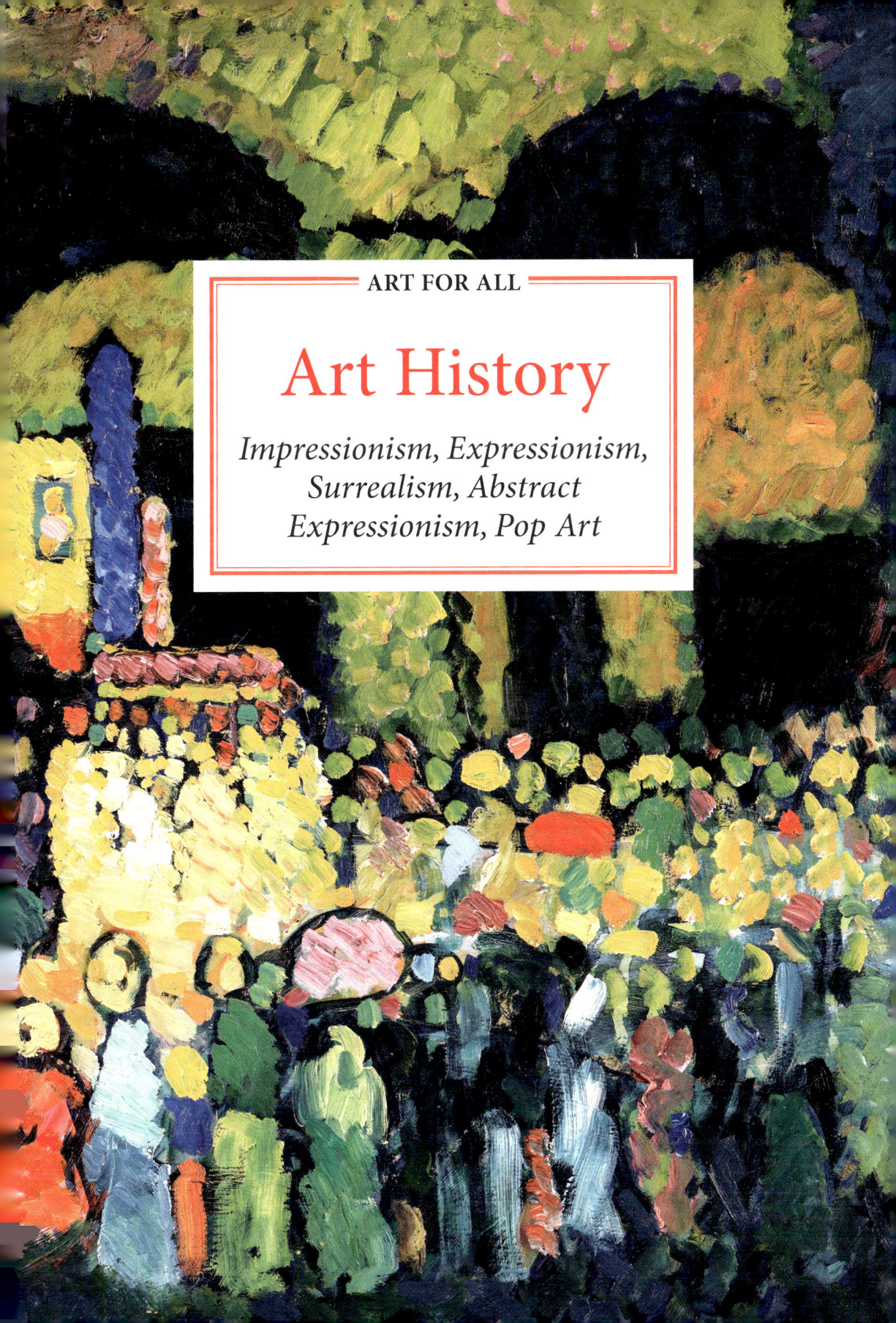

ART FOR ALL

Art History

Impressionism, Expressionism, Surrealism, Abstract Expressionism, Pop Art

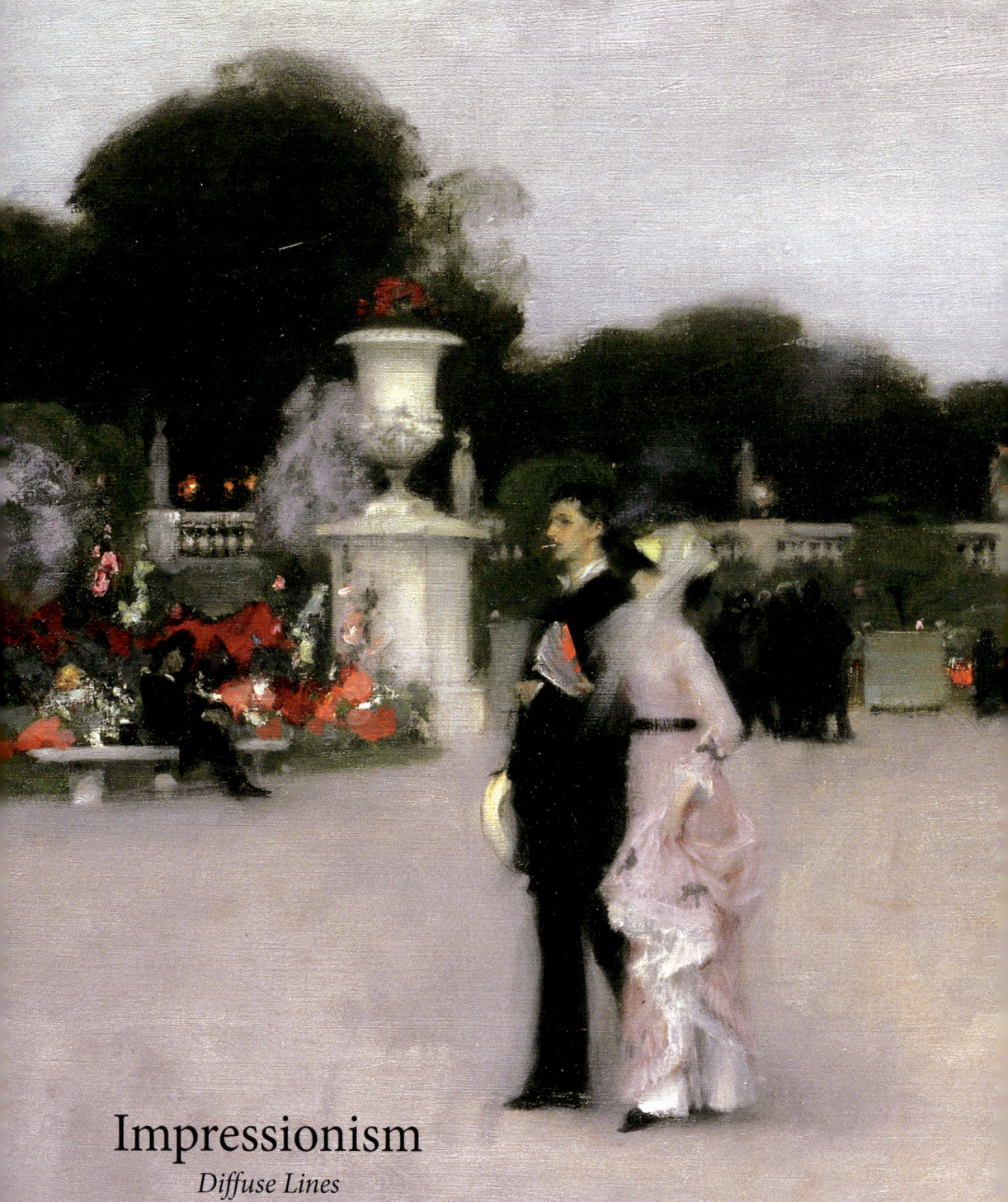

Impressionism
Diffuse Lines
Karin H. Grimme
6

Expressionism
This Visceral Life
Norbert Wolf
102

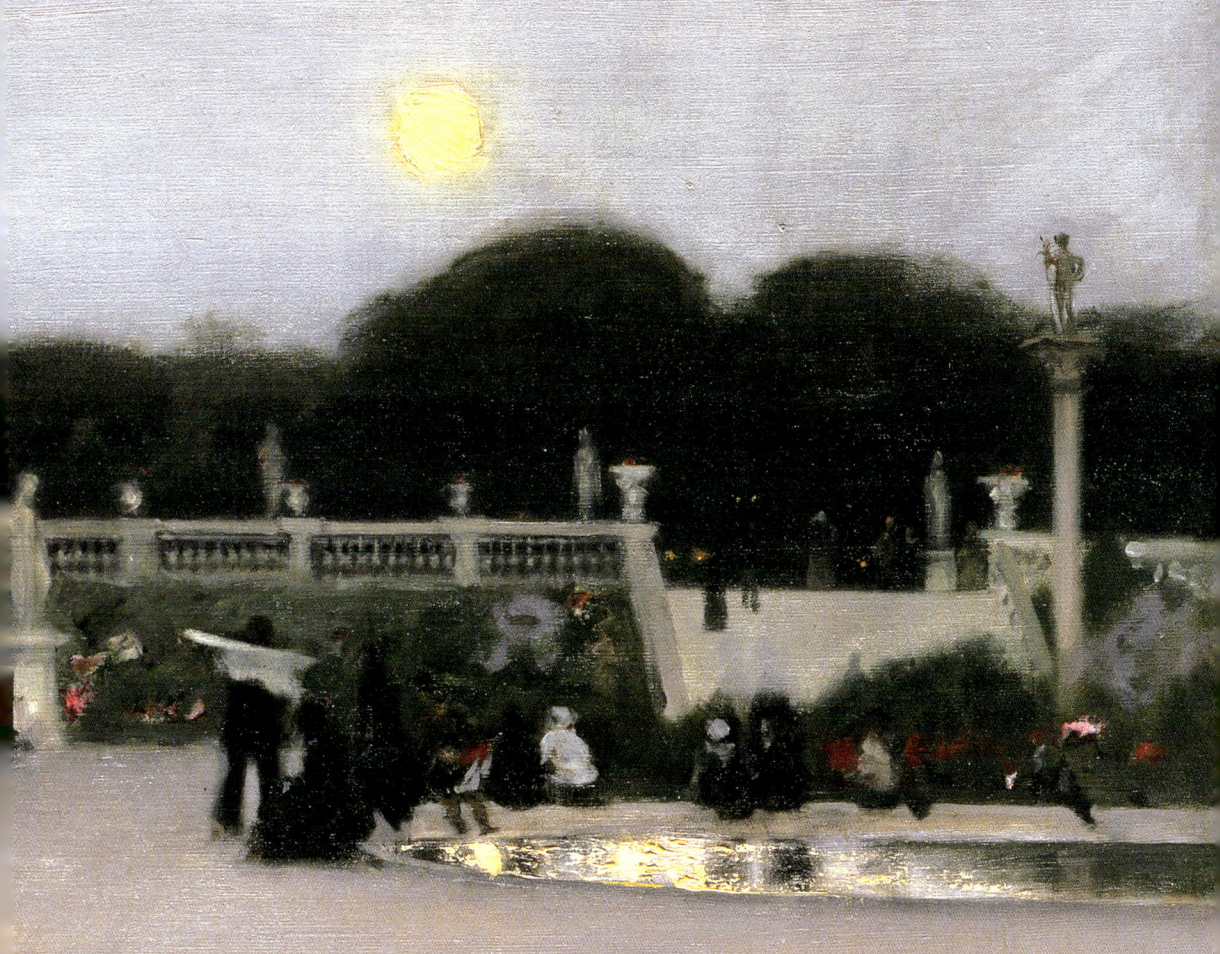

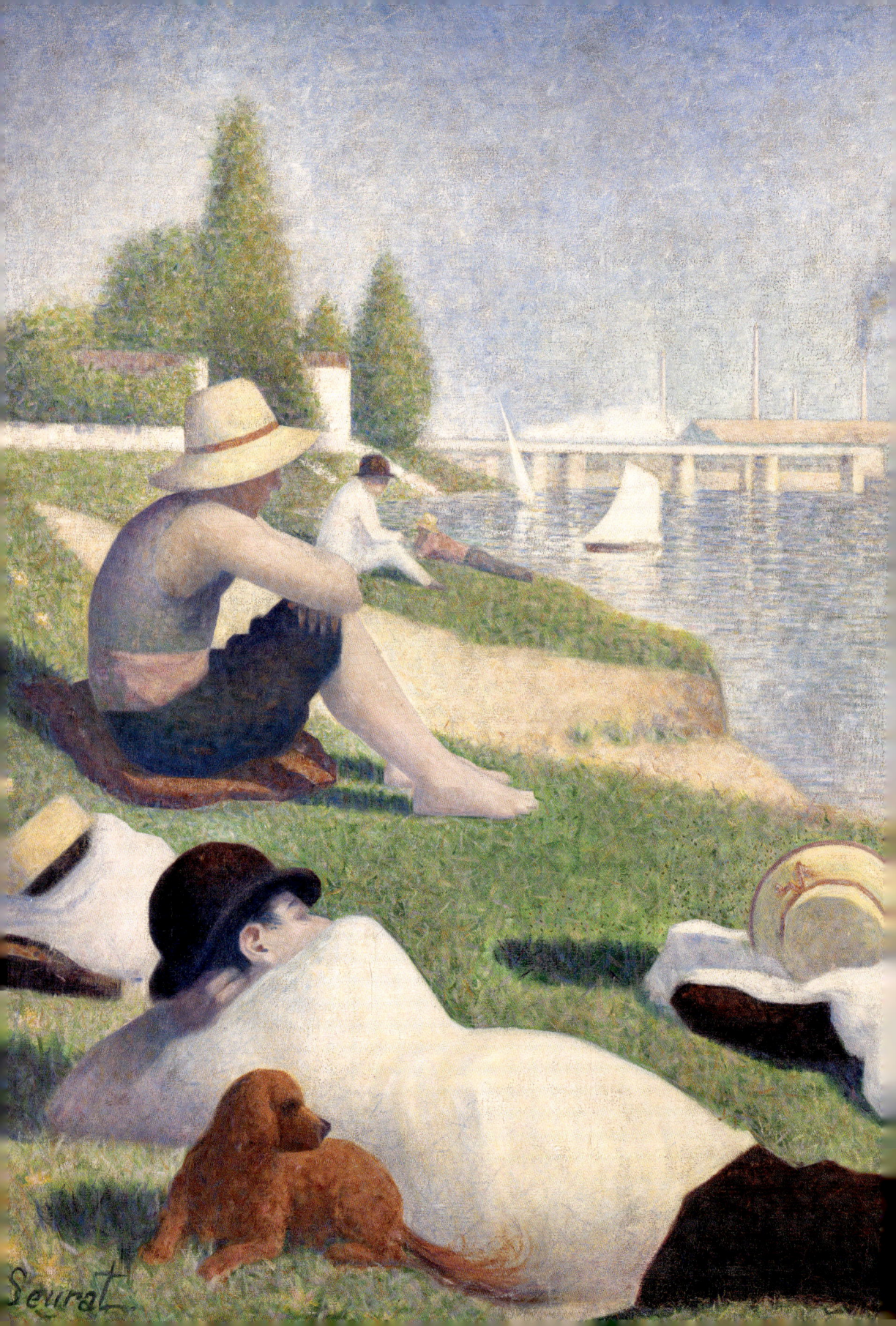

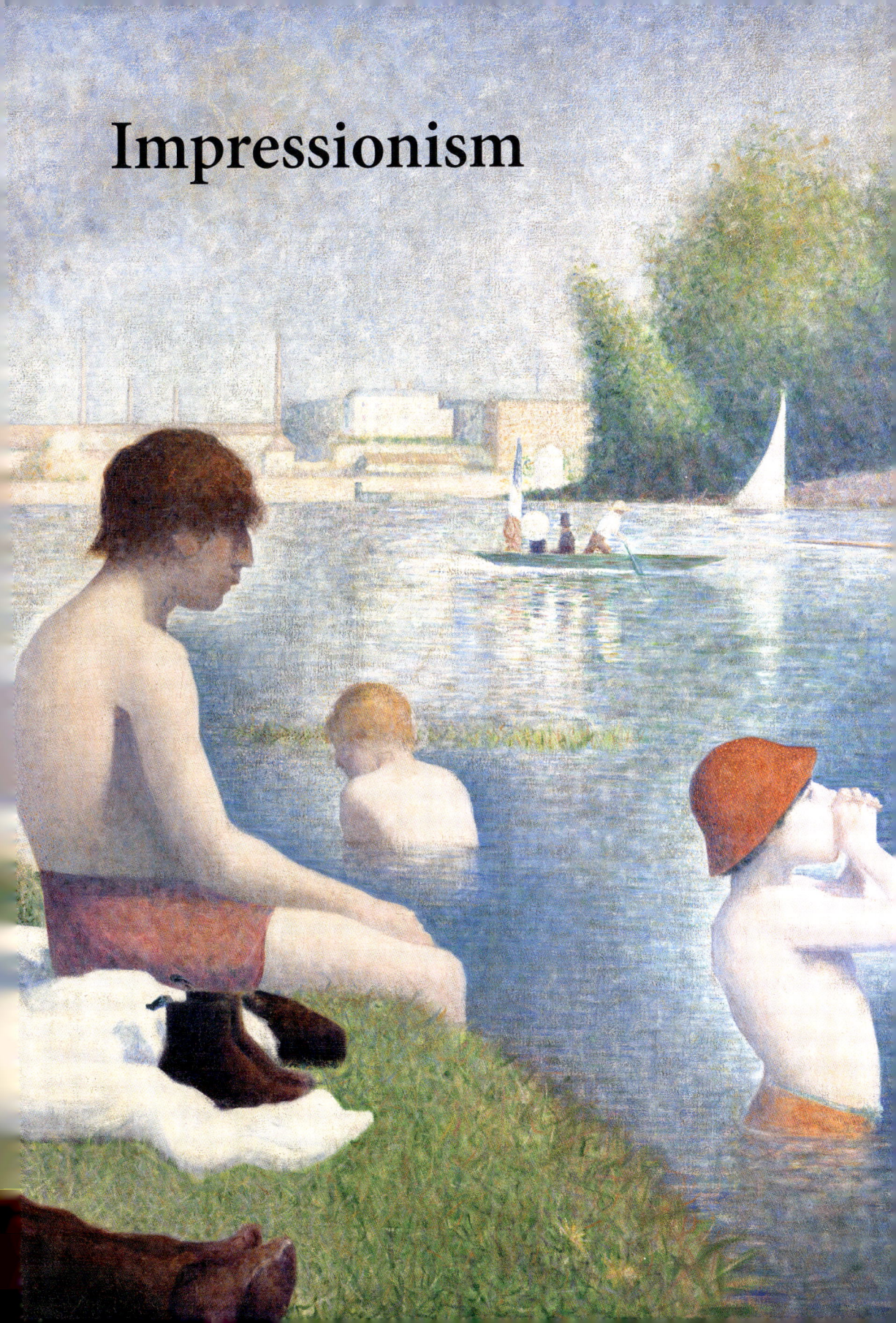

Impressionism

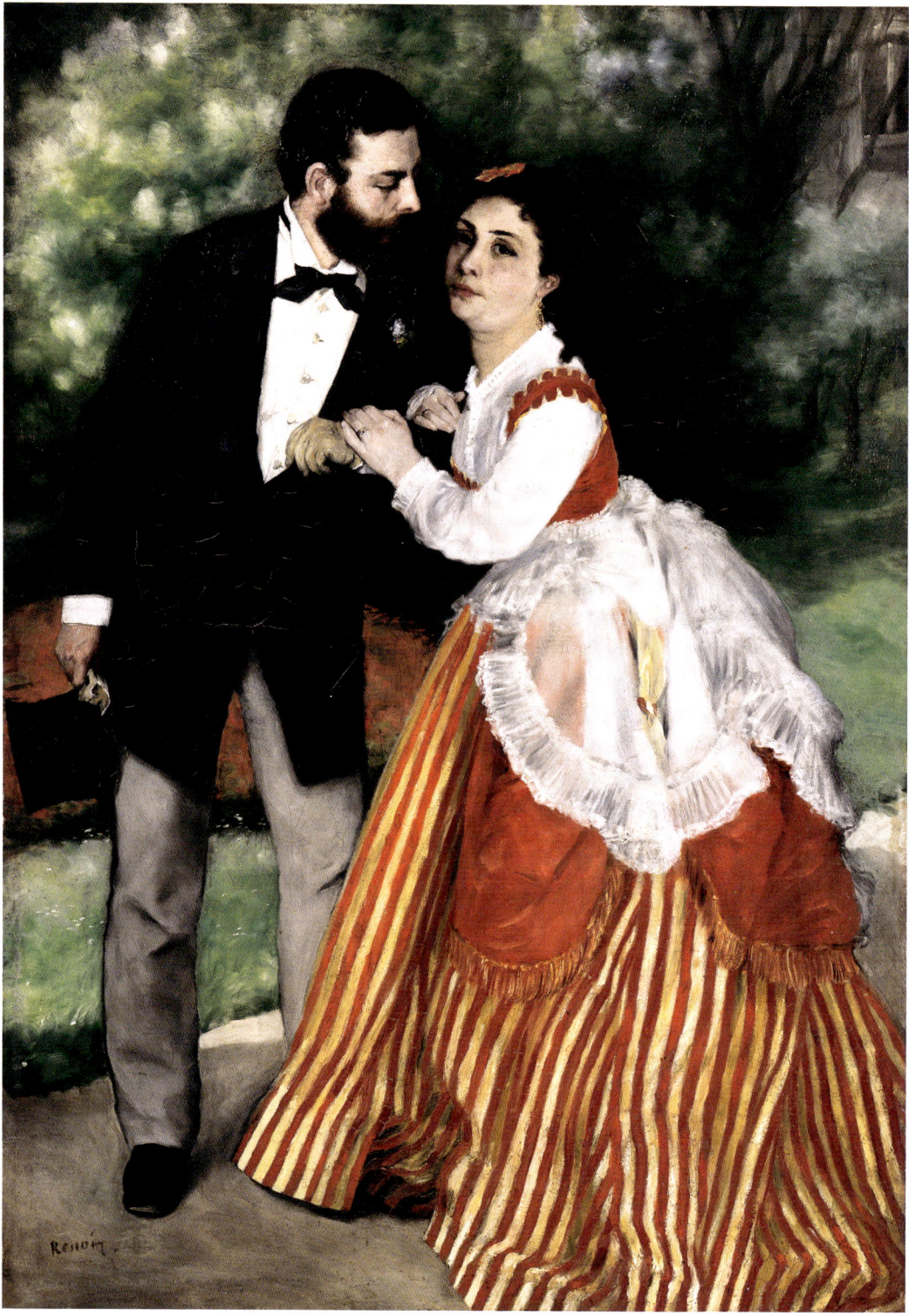

Karin H. Grimme
Norbert Wolf (Ed.)

Impressionism

Diffuse Lines

"Impressionism: it is the birth of light in painting."
Robert Delaunay

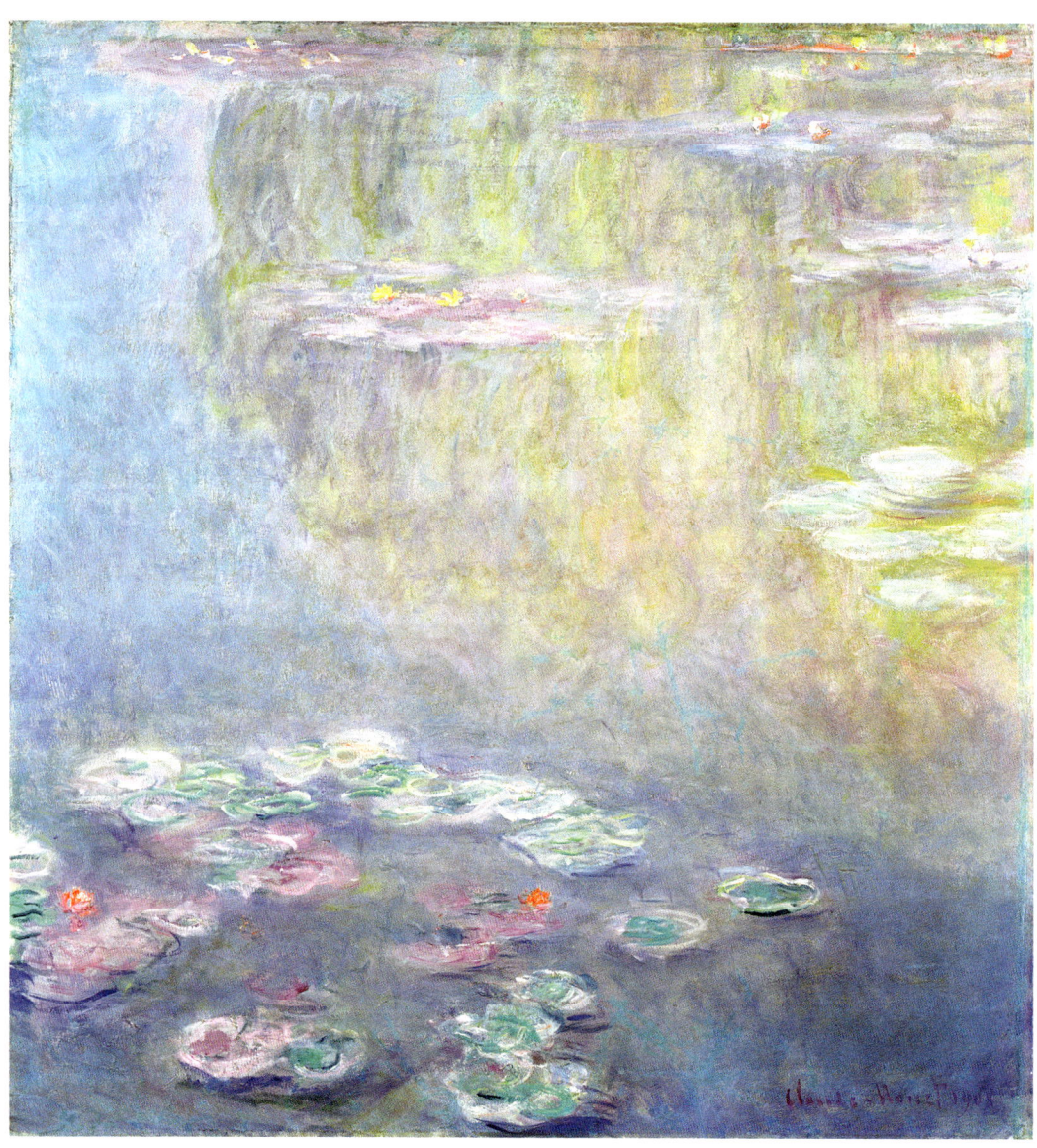

Contents

Pictures Created from Light and Colour

12

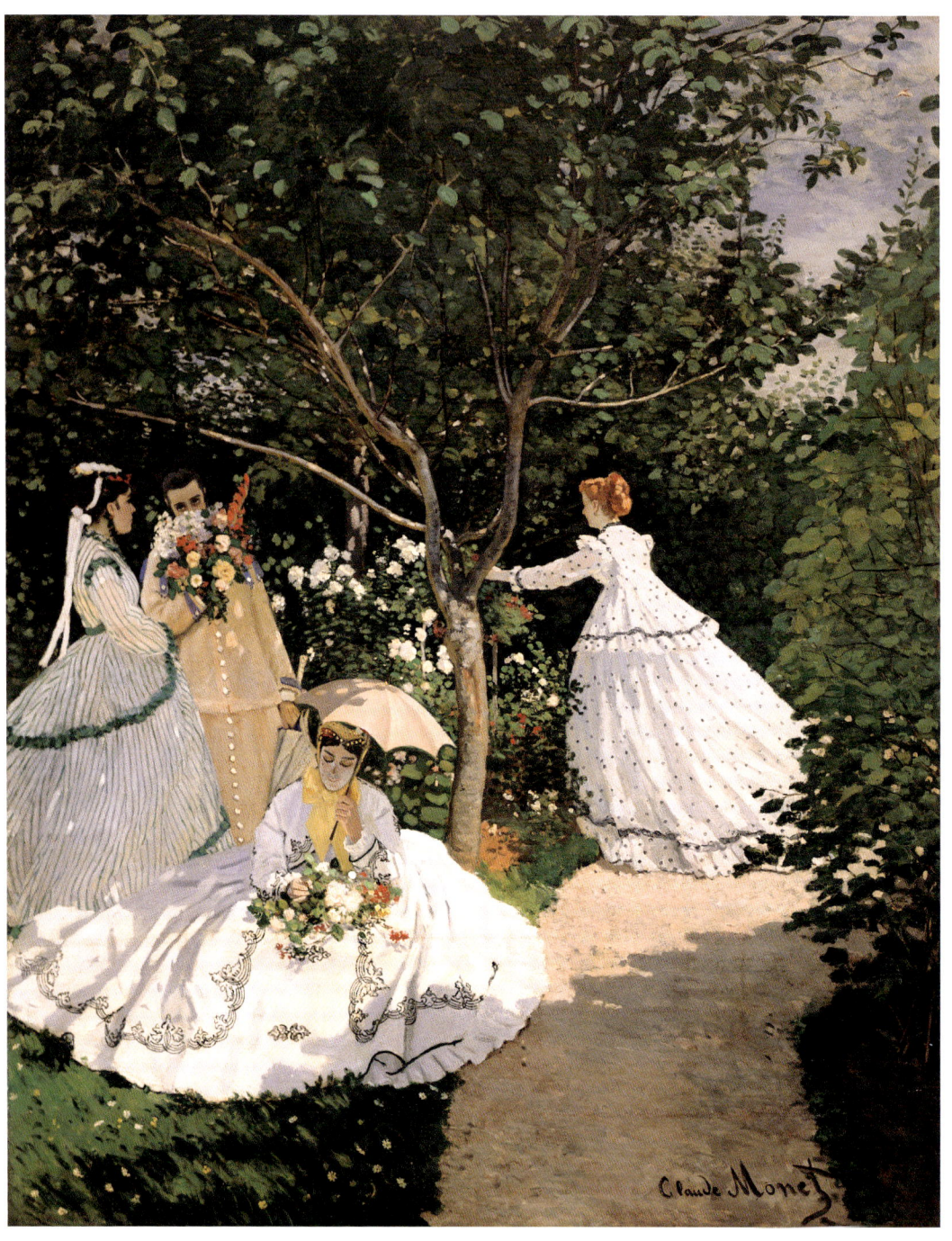

Pictures Created from Light and Colour

On the Banks of the Seine

Shortly before his death in 1926, Claude Monet, one of the best-known Impressionist painters, wrote in a letter: "I always hated theories … My only merit is to have painted directly from nature and to have tried to reproduce my impressions of the most fleeting moods; I am deeply depressed to have been the cause of a name that was applied to a group, most of whose members were not Impressionists." And indeed, there is no general theory of Impressionism and no general agreement as to who was, or was not, an Impressionist. Pierre-Auguste Renoir, too, said of his art: "I have neither rules nor methods. Anyone can come and look at what I use, or watch me painting – they'll see that I have no secrets." (ill. pp. 26 and 14)

The demarcation of Impressionism from other currents in art is no more clear-cut than the waters of the Seine which reflect the light in all directions. This is a motif that the French Impressionist painters at the end of the 19th century depicted time and again. And just as the light is reflected by the surface of the water, no less strong was the effect on their environment of a small group of painters who jointly exhibited their works between 1874 and 1886. They influenced not only other artists worldwide, but showed the bourgeois society of their age a new, modern way of painting and of seeing. In so doing, they excited so much uproar that they were regarded as revolutionaries, and were largely excluded from the traditional art community of the academies. The Impressionist artists formed an opposition to this conservative art world.

The term "Impressionism" was applied to a whole current of art that started in France in the 1860s, although, as Monet said, most of the painters thus labelled were not Impressionists. Monet regretted the fact that it was the title of his picture *Impression – Sunrise,* shown at their first joint exhibition in 1874, that provided the label in the first place. Apropos this title: the French art critic Louis Leroy wrote very disparagingly of an "exhibition by the Impressionists". "Oh, it was a strenuous day when, in the company of the landscape painter Joseph Vincent, a … recipient of medals and awards from various governments, I ventured into the first exhibition on the Boulevard des Capucines … He thought he would find, as one does everywhere, good and bad painting – more bad than good – but not crimes of this nature … against the great masters and against form." The exhibition-going public were incidentally no less dismissive than some of the critics. The artists who had taken part in the exhibition soon adopted the negatively intended description for themselves, for the "impression" was a central aspect of their art, and not just the title of one of the pictures on display at this first exhibition.

Claude Monet
Women in the Garden, *c.* 1866
Oil on canvas,
255 x 205 cm (100½ x 80¾ in.)
Paris, Musée d'Orsay

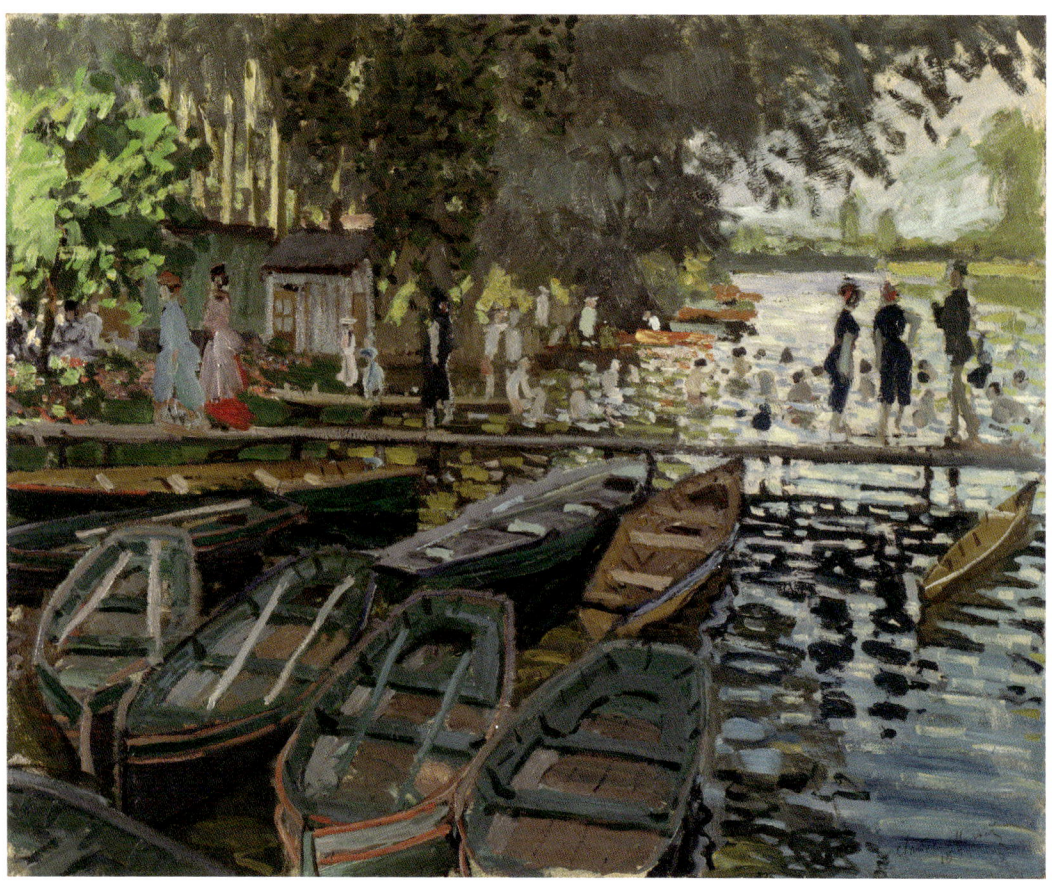

Claude Monet
Bathers at La Grenouillère, 1869
Oil on canvas,
73 x 92 cm (28¾ x 36¼ in.)
London, The National Gallery

OPPOSITE
Mary Cassatt
The Tea, c. 1880
Oil on canvas,
64.8 x 92.1 cm (25½ x 36¼ in.)
Boston, Museum of Fine Arts,
M. Theresa B. Hopkins Fund

"Perfection rests on what they share in common"

… thus the painter Eugène Boudin on the Impressionists as a group. He even thought: "Without the others, none would have achieved the perfection which they did achieve." The individual artists would not have been in any position to resist the power of the Academy, nor their massive rejection by art collectors, art dealers and the public at large. But their solidarity and consistency gave them the strength to survive and eventually overcome the lack of interest shown by the art market. The special thing about the Impressionist movement is that the artists who comprised the group were bound by ties of friendship. Claude Monet, Pierre-Auguste Renoir, Edgar Degas, Alfred Sisley and Camille Pissarro worked and lived together, they suffered jointly during the years that their art was ignored, and joined forces to organize their own exhibitions and thus combat their constant exclusion from the annual exhibitions held by the French Academy of Art. For they were profoundly convinced that their pictures were worth exhibiting.

In 1867 Frédéric Bazille reported to his parents of his friends' plan to organize a special exhibition: "I'm sending nothing to the hanging committee any more. It is just too ridiculous … to be exposed to their moods … Besides me, a dozen talented young people are of this opinion. We have therefore decided to hire a large studio every year in which we can exhibit as many works as we want." They were unable to implement the exhibition plan, as they could not get enough money together. Years later, they had another try. At the end of December 1873, Monet, Renoir, Sisley, Degas, Morisot, Pissarro, Beliard, Lepic, Levert, Rouart and Guillaumin formed the "Société anonyme des artistes, peintres, sculpteures, graveures etc."

This company provided the organizational framework for the eight exhibitions which were held between 1874 and 1886. It was laid down that each of the artists should share in the costs, and that ten percent of the proceeds of any sale would be paid into the joint kitty. The hanging of the pictures was to be decided by lot in order to avoid any dispute. The photographer Nadar placed his studio, which he had cleared out because he was about to move, at their disposal free of charge. The rooms were on the second floor of a building on the Boulevard des Capucines. These Impressionist Exhibitions, as they are known today, did however include the work of many non-Impressionist painters.

On 15 April 1874 they were ready to open their doors to the public with 165 paintings on display. Edmond Renoir, Pierre-Auguste's brother, compiled the catalogue. The exhibition ran for four weeks, and was not exactly overrun with visitors: a total of some 3,500 came to see the unusual works of the young artists. This was an insignificant number compared with the official Salon, which was visited by some 400,000 people. By 1886, a total of 55 artists had taken part in the Impressionists' exhibitions. Thirty were involved in the first show in 1874, but already by the time the second was held in 1876, this number had approximately halved. The founding members of the company had, to start with, successfully persuaded other painters of the advantages of a self-organized exhibition. Later, the friends concentrated on a smaller number of artists.

For all the differences between the individual members of the group, and in spite of the fact that it dissolved in the late 1880s, the Impressionists remained in close touch. In 1899, Monet hurried to see the dying Sisley, in order to perform a final duty of friendship. In the years following 1893, Renoir, as the executor of Caillebotte's will, attempted to ensure that matters were arranged as his

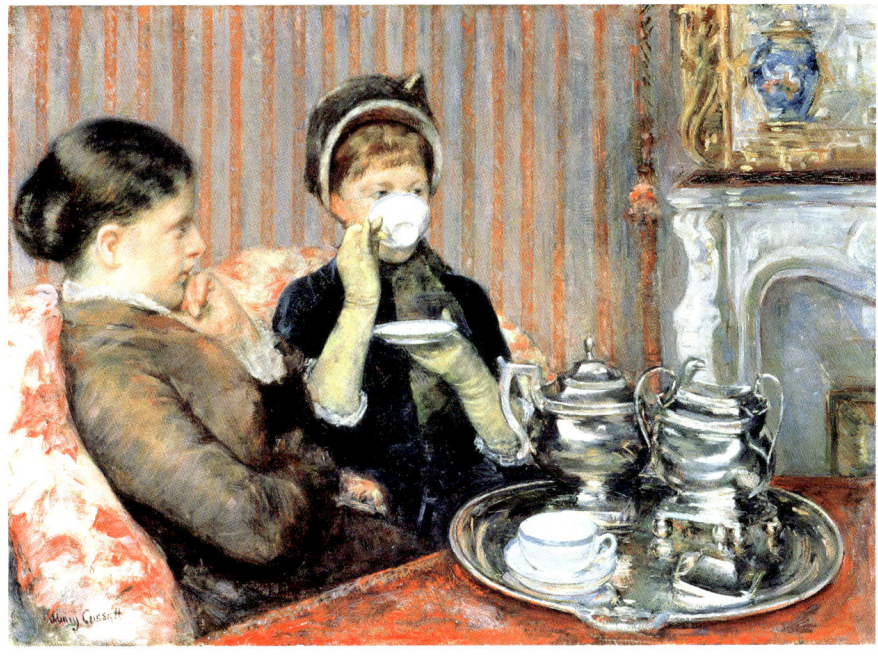

friend had wished. But he failed in the attempt to present Caillebotte's entire art collection as a gift to the French state, and thus to get the many Impressionist paintings into a museum. The cultural officials and responsible politicians were unable to imagine these pictures, which most of them did not recognize as serious art, in any museum. Gauguin had said, and it was meant critically, that the Impressionists were "tomorrow's official painters," but this tomorrow still seemed a very long way off. Gauguin himself had turned away from Impressionism in 1895, but stood by his Impressionist roots: "He [Pissarro] has borrowed something from everyone, it is said! Why not? Everyone else has borrowed from him … He was one of my masters, and I do not deny him."

Camille Pissarro was also known by other artists and critics as the "father of Impressionism". Pissarro's works showed the way for the modern art of the 20th century. He influenced Gauguin and Cézanne no less than they influenced him. Many of the Impressionist pictures reflect the joint work of different artists. We can see this in Monet's and Renoir's pictures of La Grenouillère (ill. p. 14), a bathing lido with restaurant near Chatou, to the west of Paris. The two painters not only chose the same motif, but also a very similar way of painting. Likewise when looking at Cézanne's painting *The House of the Hanged Man* (ill. p. 17) and Pissarro's work *Hillside of the Hermitage* (ill. p. 16) we cannot help noticing how similar their approaches are. In fact with numerous Impressionist pictures, the amazing similarity of painting style, technique and choice of motif is striking. Pissarro himself thought that it was wrong to think that "artists were the sole inventors of their style and they lacked originality when they resembled others".

Impressionism is, to stress the point once more, also the history of a friendship. Some of the friends are famous still, others are well-nigh forgotten. Too little attention has been devoted to artists such as Gustave Caillebotte, Frédéric Bazille, Félix Bracquemond and Armand Guillaumin in the historiography of art hitherto. The same is true of marginalized women artists such as Berthe Morisot, Mary Cassatt, Marie Bracquemond and the Pole Olga Boznańska (ill. p. 30). Many of these names are no longer even names to a broader public, astonishing in view of the popularity enjoyed by the Impressionists today!

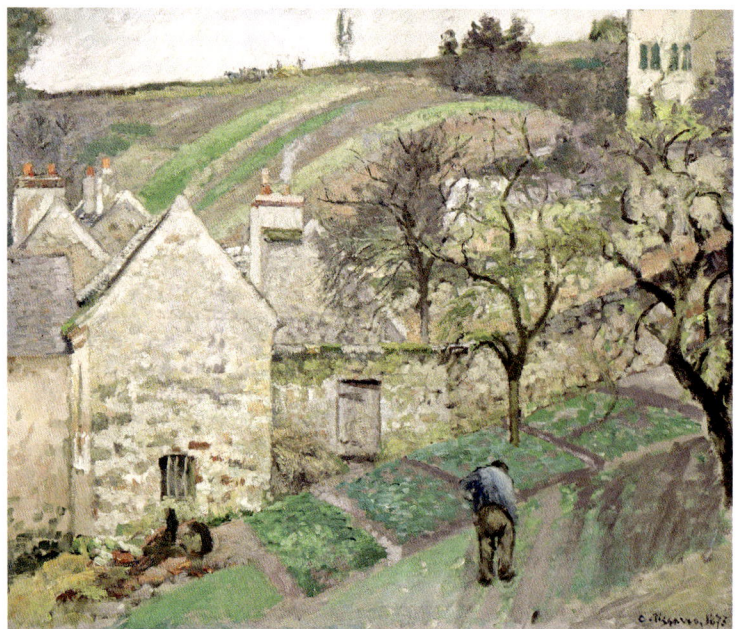

Camille Pissarro
Hillside of the Hermitage, Pontoise, 1873
Oil on canvas,
61 x 73 cm (24 x 28¾ in.)
Paris, Musée d'Orsay

OPPOSITE
Paul Cézanne
The House of the Hanged Man, Auvers-sur-Oise, 1873
Oil on canvas,
55.5 x 66.3 cm (22 x 26 in.)
Paris, Musée d'Orsay

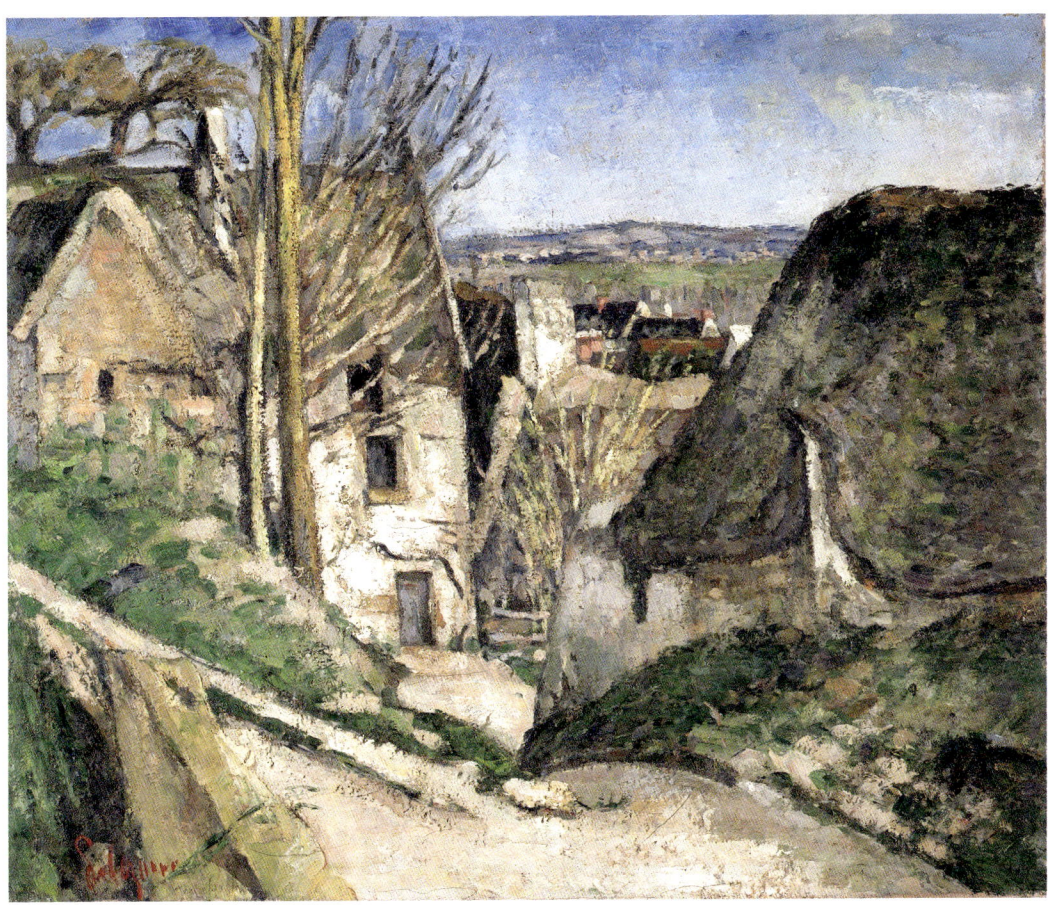

Modern Moments

There is neither a set of rules nor a particular aesthetic programme by which Impressionism can be defined, and this makes the question of what Impressionism actually is all the more exciting. Instead of a precise characterization, which, if we are to believe Monet and Renoir, was not present in the 19th century either, all we can do is name a few criteria of varying importance which distinguish an Impressionist painting.

The Impressionist vocabulary includes without a doubt the direct, living "impression" of a moment, which is often reproduced in what seems a chance detail of the total event. These are scenes and figures of modern everyday life as opposed to the depictions from Classical or mythological stories, such as formed the stock-in-trade of traditional art until the end of the 19th century. Workers and prostitutes, passers-by in the street or guests in the café – the Impressionists were the first to regard such people as artworthy. "I have chosen something from our present age, because I understand it best and it seems to me to be the most alive for the living," wrote Frédéric Bazille.

The locations of modern life were depicted in ways as modern as they were unusual: railways and bridges, streets and parks, stations and cathedrals, opera-house foyers and cafés, the pleasures of bathing, beach life, regattas and horse races (ill. p. 33). Life in the city of Paris, the anonymous, big-city passers-by and their leisure and pleasure became the focus of attention. The innovation of the Impressionists lay not just in their choice of motifs, for depictions of cathedrals or cafés were nothing new. What they added was a specific execution and goal: "The joint intentions of the group, which lend it collective strength in the midst of our disunited age, consist not in striving for a polished execution, but in being content with a particular general aspect. Once the impression has been captured, their activity seems to be at an end. If one wished to characterize their intentions in a single word, one would have to create the new term Impressionist. They are Impressionists in the sense that they do not reproduce a landscape, but the impression that it invokes." (Castagnary)

In contravention of the existing rules of traditional painting, the works of the Impressionists seemed sketchy, spontaneous and "unfinished", as though they had been done in a few minutes and had not progressed beyond the preliminary stage. The rapid brushstrokes and the abandonment of painterly perfection are deliberate metaphors of the fleeting moment and the speed of everyday life.

Speed and dynamism were positively identical with modernity for 19th-century man. Movement was staged and celebrated via the depiction of ships and railways, horses and dancing girls. In addition, the movement of the brush in the hand of the painter remains visible as a brushstroke or spot of paint – spontaneity becomes the hallmark of the painting process. Impressionism unites dynamic movement in the motif and in the execution.

Compared with Jean-Auguste-Dominique Ingres (1780–1867), the chief exponent of 19th-century French Neo-classicism, who took years to perfect a painting and conjured up on his pictures an enamel-smooth surface without a single visible brushstroke, the young artists could indeed be thought of as quick workers. They were not concerned with naturalistic or idealizing depiction, as Ingres had still endeavoured to achieve, but with a spontaneous, present sensation. The Impressionists sought to reproduce as direct as possible an impression that emanated from the subject.

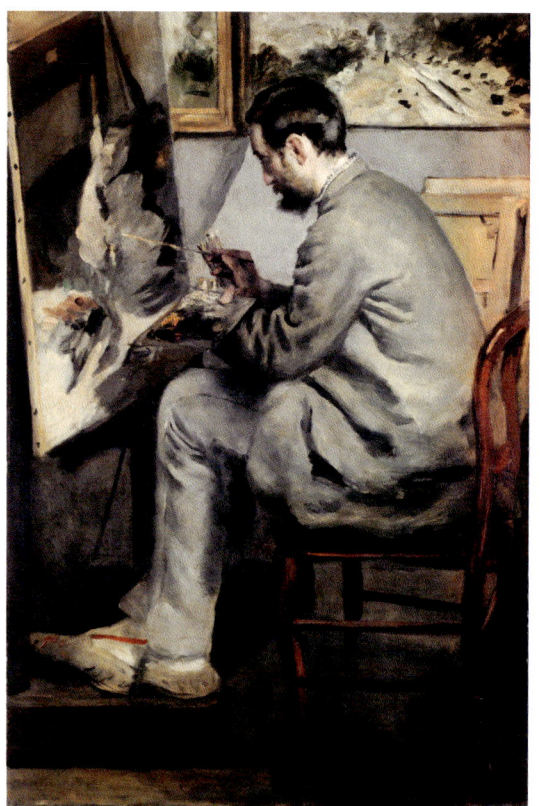

By placing such an "impression" at the focus of their art as a subjective sensation, they emphasized the aspect of individuality, which is quite generally a characteristic of modern societies. Impressionist art thus reflects the process of social change.

Inseparable from the creative concerns of Impressionism is its treatment of colour and light. The fact that shapes, contours and lines played a relatively subordinate role was one of the innovations which many of those who viewed these pictures at the time found incomprehensible, indeed ridiculous. Ingres had given the 20-year-old Edgar Degas, who admired the old classicist, this piece of advice: "Draw lines, young man, many lines, from memory and from nature. Then you'll be a good artist." Unlike his friends, Degas remained largely faithful to this counsel.

For most Impressionist painters, by contrast, colour and light were the preferred means of capturing the brief moment, the speed of passing time. In addition, the desired subjective impression can be reproduced with colour and light far more exactly than with exact contours or internal lines. Frédéric Bazille explained this in a letter to his parents in 1866: "I think, by the way, that if my work is interesting as painting, the motif is not very important."

The motif, whether an isolated object or a scene, receded into the background vis-à-vis the colour, light and painterly execution. For Bazille and Monet, colour and light were more important than the motif itself. What comes across as "normal" for today's beholder – corresponding as it does to today's visual habits – was in the 19th century tantamount to an unheard-of sensation, a revolution in seeing. If Pierre-Auguste Renoir depicted his *Nude in the Sunlight* (c. 1875/76, Paris, Musée d'Orsay) with green, blue, red and white patches on her skin, it was to visualize the play of light and the

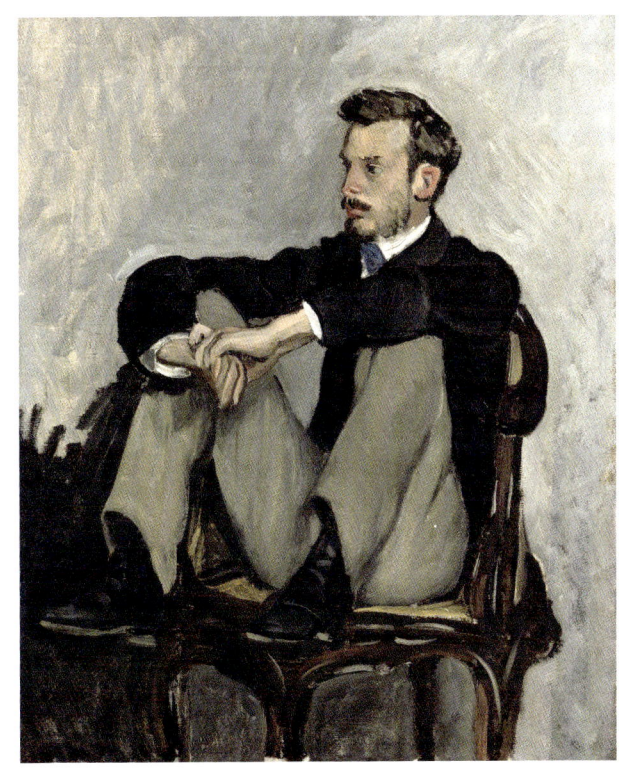

reflections of the colours that characterized the surroundings. "I look at a naked body and see innumerable tiny colour shades. I have to find those that bring the flesh to life and vibrancy on my canvas." Just how unfamiliar and disturbing this manner of seeing was is made clear by the reaction of the art critic Albert Wolff, who, in an article for *Le Figaro* on the second Impressionist exhibition in 1876, interpreted the colourful sun-spots on the skin as "rotten meat".

The great importance of colouration in Impressionist art went hand-in-hand with a growing colourfulness in the world outside of art. From the beginning of the 19th century, various chemical and technical advances had led to an enormous growth in the availability of dyestuffs. The market had been flooded with synthetic dyes like mauve (since 1856) and alizarin red (since 1868) which were more permanent than natural dyes. Textiles and clothing became more colourful, and, thanks to mass production, they also became cheaper and consequently more affordable to a broad public. One visitor to the first Impressionist exhibition in 1874 expressed the view, more or less jokingly, that the artists must have loaded a pistol with a number of tubes of paint and fired them at the canvas, leaving only the signature to be added. There was indeed a serious core at the heart of this remark: namely the visual strain on the public caused by the intensity of the colours and the free colouration, which depended not on the object, but on the light.

Already since the late 1860s, Monet had been using the new green known as viridian, which had been available since 1862. Unlike the traditional "vert émeraude", this chromium oxide was non-toxic and did not trigger chemical reactions when it came

OPPOSITE
Pierre-Auguste Renoir
Frédéric Bazille at his Easel, 1867
Oil on canvas,
105 x 73.5 cm (41¼ x 29 in.)
Paris, Musée d'Orsay

TOP
Frédéric Bazille
Portrait of Pierre-Auguste Renoir, 1867
Oil on canvas,
62.2 x 50.8 cm (24½ x 20 in.)
Paris, Musée d'Orsay

into contact with other pigments. The purple, too, a cobalt phosphate which Monet used for the mauve flowers in his painting *Bathers at La Grenouillère* (ill. p. 14), had only just appeared on the market. The Impressionists very much preferred working in the open air, and a further development in paint technology also encouraged this: in 1841, paints were supplied for the first time in metal tubes with replaceable caps. The laborious fiddling around with powdery pigments that could be blown away by every breath of wind was no longer necessary, nor did the pigment any longer have to be stirred. This does not mean, however, that the Impressionists from then on abandoned the use of traditional pigment paints.

Until well into the 19th century, there had been a maxim that "the painter should never attempt to paint a landscape in the midday sun, as pigments were unable to do justice to this particular light effect, and the sun itself should never be depicted directly" (John Gage, *Colour and Culture*, 1993). Now the young Impressionists took up this gauntlet. For the searing light of the midday sun on the *Pont Neuf* Renoir chose white, grey and yellow shades, in which individual dabs of red stand out in the clothing and on the flag. The pavement, the roadway, the houses, the people, the horses, the carriage on the bridge, everything is bathed in the same glaring noonday brightness.

The availability of paints and appropriate pigments in the second half of the 19th century created the material basis and an important precondition for Impressionist art. In addition, there was the wealth of ideas and the courage of the young generation to use the new opportunities, even if, as a result, it meant contravening the precepts of the old masters.

Apart from the similar motifs and comparable painting technique, the French Impressionists also shared the same paint dealer, namely Julien Tanguy, known as Père Tanguy, who started off as an itinerant trader before opening a shop in Paris in 1871. Tanguy supported the young artists, who were always in financial difficulty, by accepting their pictures, which most contemporaries regarded as worthless, in exchange for paint and canvases. In this way he was not just a supplier of paints, but also an art collector. Without his support, many a picture could never have been painted. One has only to think how Renoir gathered the paint tubes thrown away by other students, and how Monet and Pissarro scraped off the paint from finished pictures in order to use the canvas a second time.

Continuity and Innovation

From today's point of view, Impressionism certainly did not just arise from nowhere. On the contrary, it was part of a continuous development from Realism, Naturalism and Neo-classicism. Alongside the various currents in French art, another major influence was Japanese woodcuts, which were on show in Europe for the first time.

Otherwise, the exponents of Realism, Théodore Rousseau, Camille Corot, Johan Barthold Jongkind, Charles-François Daubigny, to name but a selection, had already helped the landscape genre, which hitherto had not counted for very much, to obtain its just deserts. In the relevant works by these artists, we already see the reflecting light which was to play such an important role in Impressionist art. In the mid 19th century, some of the Realist painters had left the hustle and bustle of the city to withdraw to the countryside. They lived and worked in Barbizon in the forest of Fontainebleau, which is why they are known as the "Barbizon School".

The Barbizon artists worked in the open air, or as the French say "en plein air". The painting of landscapes as realistically as possible "liberated" them from more complicated contents. The landscape was staged purely for painterly effects. This meant a positively absolute freedom from the existing rules and constraints of art as traditionally taught in the academies. These artists made a thoroughgoing break with what till then had been the usual studio painting. The effect of light, in

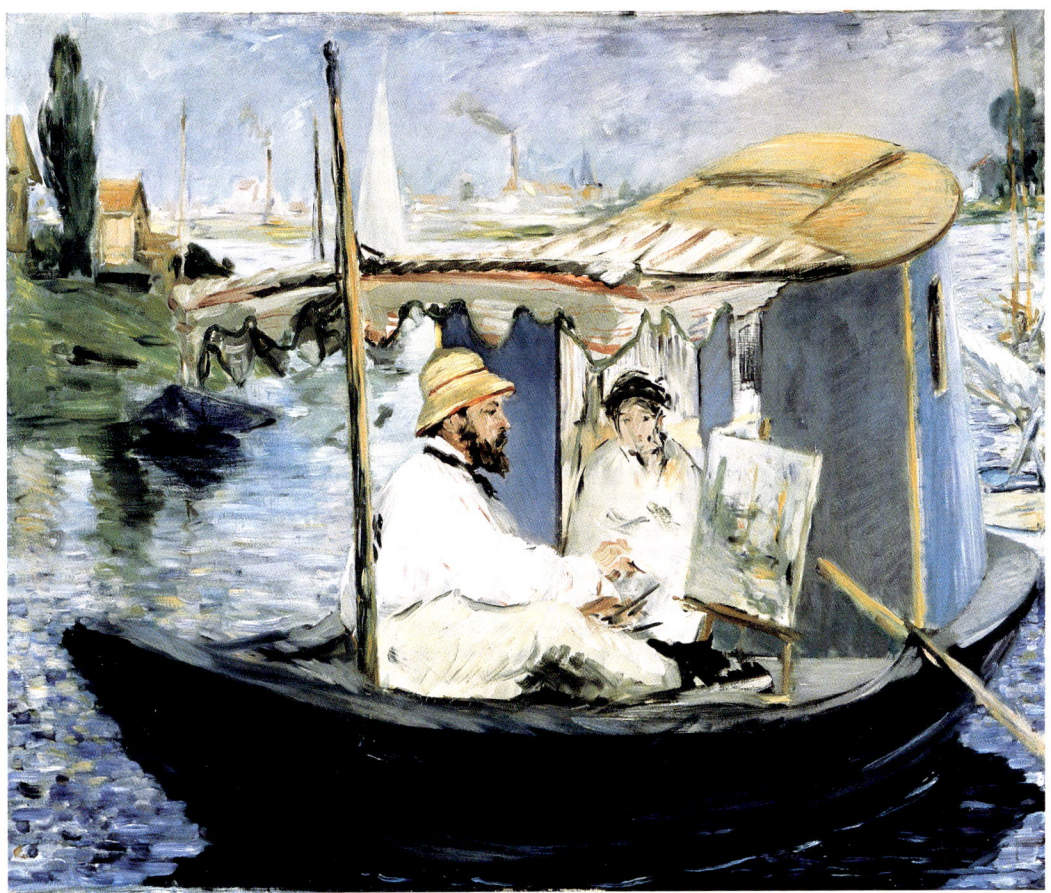

Édouard Manet
Claude Monet Painting in his Studio, 1874
Oil on canvas,
82.7 x 105 cm (32½ x 41¼ in.)
Munich, Bayerische
Staatsgemäldesammlungen,
Neue Pinakothek

the view of the Barbizon school, should be reproduced as realistically as possible. In order to guarantee the authenticity of the painted landscape, it was essential to set up one's easel in the open air. The atmosphere and the colours resulting from this atmosphere were no longer used merely as a means to cast the scenery "in the right light", rather, the light effects took on a certain life of their own, which pointed the way to Impressionism.

Corot's painting *Daubigny at Work on his Boat near Auvers-sur-Oise* depicts, with the boat, a motif which the Impressionists were later often to choose. Corot allows the reflected light to float on the water and sketches the trees in the foreground with rapid brushstrokes. The "master of light", as he was known, was doubtless one of the pioneers of Impressionism. Corot's painting shows a fellow-artist working on the water. Claude Monet, and the Post-impressionist Paul Signac, were later also to paint in boats. Édouard Manet, who can only be assigned to the Impressionist circle for a short time, watched Monet doing so. *Claude Monet Painting in his Studio* (ill. p. 21) is one of Manet's most strongly "Impressionist" paintings. Manet asserted that "the light appeared to him in such unity that a single shade of colour was enough to depict it, and it was better, even if it might come across as coarse, to move abruptly from light to shade than to pile up things that the eye does not see and that not only dulls the power of the eye but also weakens the colouring of the shadows – which are precisely what ought to be emphasized." It was precisely in discussions about

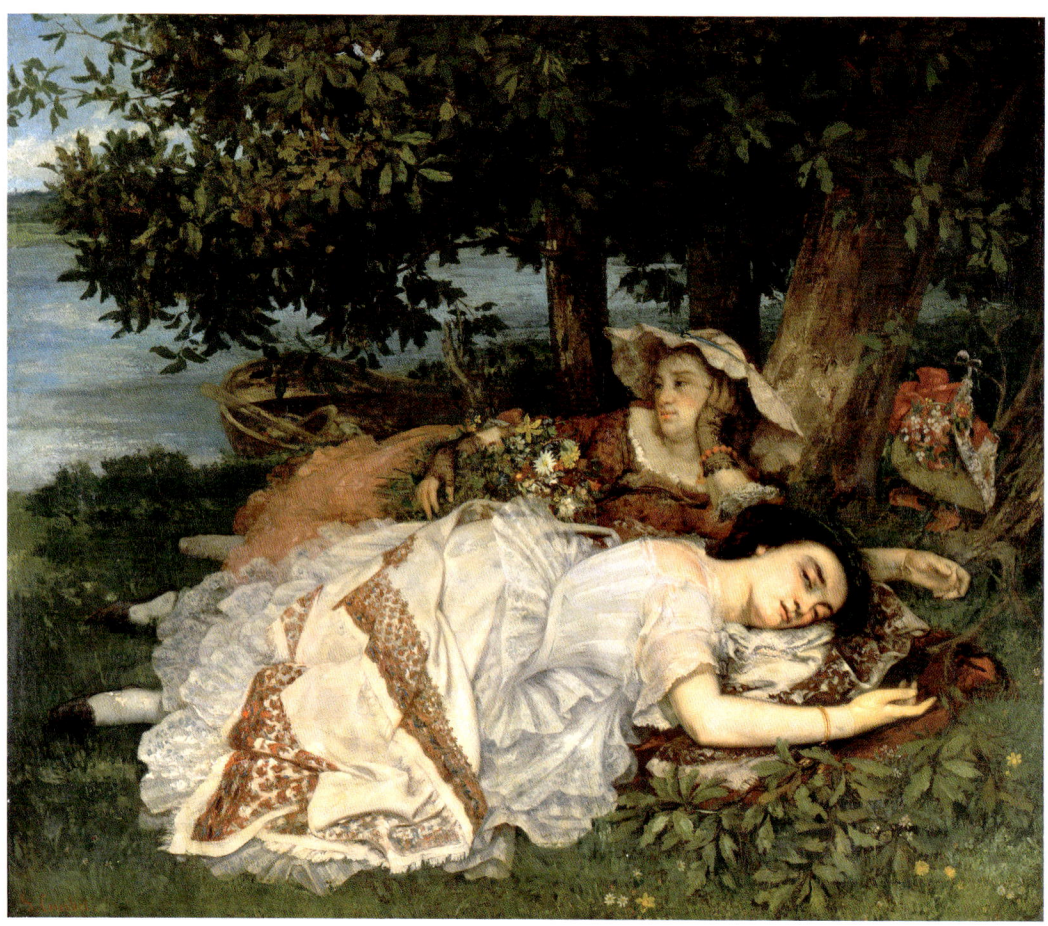

Gustave Courbet
***Young Ladies on the Banks
of the Seine (Summer)***, 1857
Oil on canvas,
174 x 206 cm (68½ x 81 in.)
Paris, Musée du Petit Palais

light and shade that Manet, who stressed the contrast, set himself off clearly from the Impressionists.

Another role model in respect of light and shade was Johan Barthold Jongkind. He was already, in the early 1860s, painting views of Notre-Dame Cathedral in Paris in different lighting conditions. One of his earliest examples in this area is *Notre-Dame in Paris by Moonlight*. The church at night or on a cold, clear winter's day appeared quite differently to its appearance in the atmosphere of a warm sunset. "With him [Jongkind] everything lies in the impression", it was said, before the Impressionist movement had even begun.

Jongkind's initiative was taken up by John Singer Sargent and above all Claude Monet with his sequences of pictures, including those of *Rouen Cathedral,* which were painted thirty years later. The development can be traced from Jongkind's Notre-Dame paintings via Monet's Rouen Cathedral pictures right up to Kandinsky's *St Ludwig's Church in Munich* (ill. p. 157). A comparison shows how much more strongly Monet allows individual forms and details of the building to blur in the light, and how the colours alone determine the impression. This tendency in 19th-century art presupposes that the very personal, subjective impression of an individual is not only worth depicting, but is recognized as the measure of life in society. And so the foundation was laid for the triumphal march of the individual in the modern world.

A picture is determined by individual feeling: that was the demand of Gustave Courbet, who was a decisive influence on Realist painting. Only one's own reality, which also encompasses social and political relationships, can, in his opinion, be the starting point for art and its – ultimately political – function.

Courbet's work thus focused on figural depictions such as the *Young Ladies on the Banks of the Seine* (ill. p. 22). The public of the time would have presumed the girls to be prostitutes. In particular the half-closed eyes of the young woman resting in the foreground, her hands and feet relaxed as she drowses, and the semi-clothed body, allowing more than a glimpse of the sensual shimmer of sweat on her skin, were not perceived in terms of a harmless lunchtime nap beneath the summer sun, but as vulgar and unseemly.

Courbet chose to depict the girls not while they were working, but during their lunch-break, so to speak. It was also their obvious exhaustion that animated Edgar Degas, among others, to depict his tired and enervated ballerinas backstage or after a rehearsal (ill. p. 53). Courbet captures the recumbent girl not from above, but from an angle that puts beholders on the same level, as though they too were lying on the grass. Painter and models, in the work of Courbet and Degas, come across as being on one level, with none of the moral aloofness of bourgeois society. The patches of light, depicted with white paint, and the generally relaxed, lively brushstrokes point the way to the Impressionists, above all to Monet and Renoir. Courbet's work already represented a radical break with the visual habits of the age, ushering in the transformation that was continued by the Impressionists. It became a favourite pastime for city-dwellers on a scorching summer's day to escape the heat of the city and ride on the new railway into the surrounding countryside. The destinations of these excursionists along the banks of the Seine thus in particular provided the Impressionists with many of their motifs.

Among the landscape painters it was Charles Daubigny especially who broke the ground for the Impressionists; Monet in particular was strongly influenced by him. Motifs like haystacks (ill. p. 25) and rows of poplars had been appearing on the canvases of the new style with some regularity since Jean-François Millet and Daubigny. The latter's pictures were already painted exclusively in the open air. He loved riverside views in the changing light; he juxtaposed patches of paint to make it appear improvised and fleeting. This sketchiness underlined the spontaneous and authentic process of painting, and evoked vehement protests from public and critics alike. It was regretted that he should content himself with a mere "impression" instead of producing a "proper" painting, that is to say a finished, smooth-surfaced picture with no visible brushstrokes. Daubigny was even accused by art critics of being the "ringleader of the Impression school".

Realist art therefore had a strong influence on Impressionism, while Neo-classicism à la Ingres also left traces, albeit few, in Impressionist paintings. In particular Edgar Degas and Marie Bracquemond admired Ingres. The importance for Degas, following Ingres' example, of lines and drawings, was reported by Walter Richard Sickert, writing about Degas in 1917: "'I always sought,' he [Degas] said 'to persuade my fellow-artists to look for new combinations by way of draughtsmanship, which, as I think, is a more fertile field than colour. But they would not listen, and took the other path.'"

Unlike other Impressionists, who placed their work almost exclusively in the service of colour, Degas never neglected the aspect of draughtsmanship. As early as 1859, he described the spectrum of his motifs in a notebook: "… to depict all kinds of utilitarian objects in such a way that one can still see what they were used for, in such a way that one can feel in them the life of the man or woman – a corset for example, that has just been taken off, and still bears the shape of the body … Monuments and houses have never been depicted from close up, as one sees them when walking along the street …" His list of the contemporary things that he wanted to study and paint continued:

"Musicians with their various instruments, bakeries from various angles … smoke: cigarette smoke, smoke from railway engines, chimneys, steamers etc … Dancing-girls of whom one sees nothing but the naked legs, observed in full movement, or having their hair done; countless impressions such as all-night cafés with the various graduated shades of light reflections in the mirrors etc."

Degas' predilection for unusual angles, such as had not been shown in art previously, had crystallized at an early stage. His openness towards unusual composition patterns is also revealed in the experimental way in which he handled new techniques such as photography and various print technologies.

The young Marie Bracquemond was encouraged by Ingres in the 1860s, and worked in his studio. The art critic Philippe Burty, a close friend of her husband Félix Bracquemond, called her "one of the most intelligent pupils in Ingres' studio". Probably on account of their shared admiration for Ingres, she was closely more befriended with Degas than with the other painters. The extent to which Marie Bracquemond succeeded in integrating Impressionism with the traditions handed down by Ingres can be seen in exemplary fashion in her painting *Afternoon Tea* (ill. p. 43).

In addition, Ingres, Courbet and, yes, the Impressionists too had in common that they were at first totally rejected by the art world, and had to look out for their own opportunities of displaying their work to a broader public. Ingres only presented his pictures occasionally at small studio exhibitions, even at a time when as a famous painter with an acknowledged reputation, he no longer had to fear the onslaught of the art critics, who had made life very hard for him to start with. In 1855, Courbet, whose pictures had been regularly rejected, decided to hold his own exhibition and even had a pavilion erected at his own expense in which to display his works. Rejection by the Academy exhibition hanging committee was, then, nothing new, and affected others besides the Impressionists.

While Bracquemond underwent a traditional apprenticeship with Ingres, Claude Monet, Pierre-Auguste Renoir, Frédéric Bazille and Alfred Sisley got to know each other in Gleyre's studio in 1862. Marc-Charles Gleyre (1806–1874), like other professors at the Academy, offered private courses alongside the classes which students were obliged to attend. He charged nothing except for each student's share of the model's fee and the cost of hiring the room, and consequently his lessons were always well attended. He taught traditional painting techniques, and was none too happy about Renoir's enthusiastic use of colour. But usually he allowed the students to do what they wanted, said Renoir later, and only occasionally corrected them.

The Impressionists

The appearance of an artistic current like that which is to be found in Impressionism was only possible because there were open-minded young artists looking out for ways of doing something new. This precondition was present only in France. So who were these young men and women who were to form the core of the Impressionist movement?

Unlike the others, Monet was no longer a beginner, but had already painted alongside Jongkind and other fellow-artists. To those young artists who were searching for new forms of expression, his acquaintanceships and wide contacts put across the new ideas of the Realists: open-air painting and the endeavour to depict, in as immediate a fashion as possible, what was there in nature before their eyes.

Monet met Camille Pissarro at the Académie Suisse. In the late 1850s, this academy was a well-known institution in Parisian art circles. It was run by Père Suisse, who had long worked as a model in the studios and now gave artists the opportunity, in a large well-lit room, to paint from life without a teacher, without compulsory attendance, and without instructions.

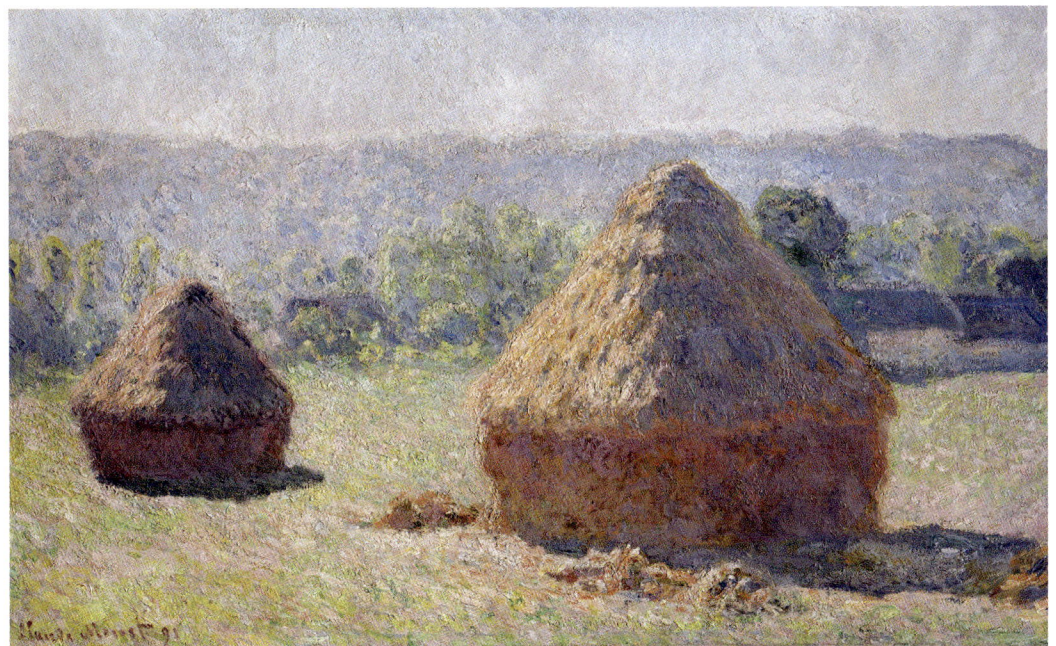

Claude Monet
Haystack, Late Summer, Morning, 1891
Oil on canvas,
60.5 x 100.8 cm (23¾ x 39¾ in.)
Paris, Musée d'Orsay

Here, Monet stood out from the crowd by dint of his unusual talent; he could draw rapidly and accurately, and capture the essentials. Pissarro was technically less mature, even though he was ten years older than Monet and probably no less ambitious. Pissarro and Monet were bound by the common ideal of open-air painting, and they wanted above all to paint landscapes. They wanted to artistically capture all that they saw, irrespective of whether or not it matched society's norms of beauty. Their strong orientation to the Realist school encouraged them to implement nothing but their personal, subjective visual impressions. It was not for nothing that Corot said to Pissarro: "Since you are an artist, you need no advice other than this: you must study the colour values above all. We do not all see identically: you see green, and I see grey and 'blond.' But that is no reason for you not to work out the colour values, for they are the starting-point for everything, however one feels and wishes to express oneself, without them there is no good painting."

To reproduce the mutual relationships of the colour-values on a finely graduated scale from light to dark according to their own perception – that was the method used by most of the young painters in order thus gradually to distance themselves from Realism. It was no longer objective realism that was at the centre of their endeavour, but totally subjective perception.

Pissarro had probably already been in contact with Corot since the late 1850s, as he described himself in the following decade as the latter's pupil. In 1866 Pissarro was mentioned in the press for the first time. The not-yet-famous French writer Émile Zola (1840–1902), then an art critic, wrote with an ironic undertone: "M. Pissarro is an unknown, who will probably not be talked about … Many thanks, Monsieur, on my journey across the great desert of the Salon I was able to rest for half an hour in front of your landscape. I know that your painting was accepted with some difficulty, my hearty congratulations. Otherwise, be aware that no one likes your picture, they say it is too bald and too black. How the devil can you be so blatantly inept as to paint honestly and study nature so frankly? How can you just depict the winter, a simple stretch of road, a hillside in the background

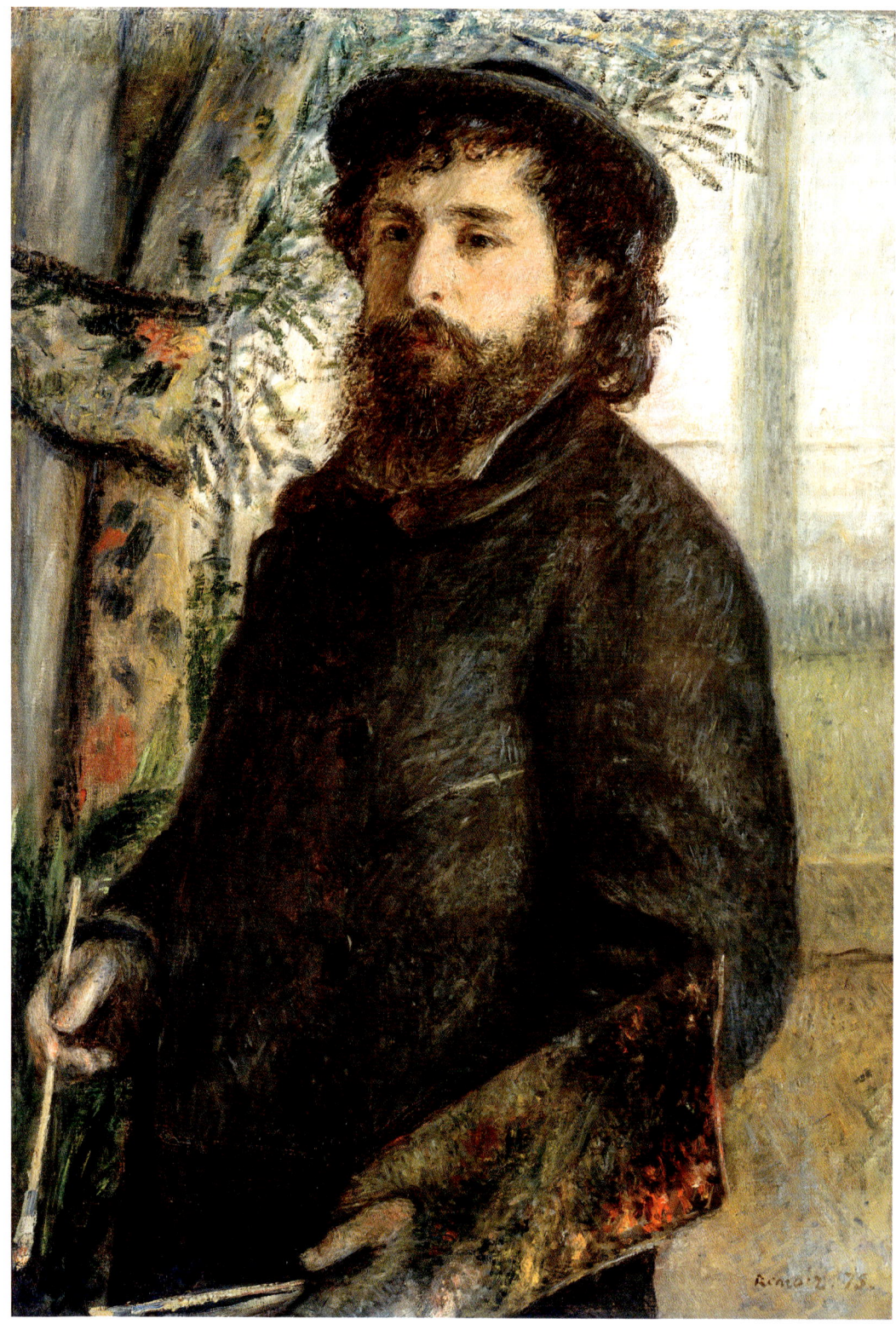

and open fields stretching to the horizon? Nothing for the eye to rest on. An austere, serious style of painting, with an extreme care for truth, an acerbic, strong will. You are very maladroit, Monsieur – you are an artist that I like."

This notice brought Pissarro no customers, who by then was already married and the father of two children, and found himself in great financial distress. He knew from his own experience what social and economic inequality and injustice meant. It was for this reason that the social-critical works of the anarchist writer Pierre-Joseph Proudhon (1809–1865), in particular the passages on the social responsibility of art, aroused his political interest. It was due not least to reading Proudhon that he himself acknowledged his adherence to anarchism as a political creed. Pissarro wrote: "Proudhon says in his work *Of Justice in the Revolution and the Church* that love of the earth is linked to the revolution, and consequently with the artistic ideal." The painter lived for most of the time in the countryside, which is where he found most of his motifs. Pissarro had a fellow-feeling for others that was no less strong than his feeling of solidarity with the group. He became one of the driving forces at the Impressionist exhibitions, and was the only painter to take part in all eight between 1874 and 1886.

Monet, although born in Paris, grew up in Le Havre on the Normandy coast. In his youth he liked to draw caricatures, with which he earned a little money. The landscape artist and picture-frame maker Eugène Boudin (1824–1898) allowed him to display his pictures in his shopwindow. In this way Monet was able to gain access to a public for the first time.

Boudin also put the young Monet in touch with Constant Troyon (1810–1865), in whose Paris studio he continued his artistic training in 1859. Troyon in turn introduced Monet to the Realist landscape painters, Corot and Daubigny. In 1862 Monet met the Dutch painter Jongkind in Le Havre. Monet himself said later: "From then on he [Jongkind] was my real master. I owe the definitive training of my eye to him."

As to the impulses he received from other artists, Monet wrote in a letter to his friend Frédéric Bazille as follows: "You may find a certain reference to Corot, but that has nothing to do with imitation; the motif, and above all the tranquil crepuscular atmosphere are alone to blame for that. I worked on it as conscientiously as possible, without thinking of any particular painter."

Monet, Bazille and Renoir lived together for a time, they painted together and shared their idealistic faith in their modern art.

Renoir's father was a tailor and lived a lower-middle-class life with his family. The son, Pierre-Auguste, had consequently to learn a trade while still quite young, and as he displayed a talent for drawing, he became a porcelain painter. He often copied on to plates and cups the masterworks of French 18th-century art, of which he made an intense study, above all those of Antoine Watteau and François Boucher. Boucher's *Diana Leaving her Bath* (1742, Paris, Musée du Louvre) was for Renoir the first picture "to seize me, and I have never ceased to like it". One of Renoir's early paintings, still in a very realistic style, also depicts a *Diana* (1867, Washington, National Gallery of Art). But then the hand-painting of porcelain was overtaken by technological developments and Renoir abandoned this job. He had saved some money in order to begin a course at the École des Beaux-Arts. The group of friends to which Renoir belonged was the one most strongly oriented towards traditional art. Unlike Pissarro, who absolutely refused to visit museums or to study the old masters, Renoir, Monet, Degas and Bazille were among the many copyists who frequented the halls of the Louvre. To make copies, for them, meant to use the great paintings in the museums to hone one's own composition and colouration skills. This widespread practice was an important part of artistic training at the time.

Pierre-Auguste Renoir
Claude Monet with Palette, 1875
Oil on canvas,
84 x 60.5 cm (33 x 23⅞ in.)
Paris, Musée d'Orsay

The Louvre was of course also an appropriate place to meet like-minded artists. These included Berthe Morisot, who copied paintings in the Louvre together with her sister Edma. The hobby which she pursued as "a well-bred girl" had long since become her profession. That she was also the great-niece of the French Rococo painter Jean-Honoré Fragonard (1732–1806) doubtless encouraged her artistic inclinations. Camille Corot, whom she had met through her teacher in 1861, advised her to go and see Daubigny in Auvers-sur-Oise. In her landscapes and townscapes of the 1860s she did indeed orient herself towards the Barbizon school, as evidenced by *The Harbour at Lorient* (ill. p. 29). She sat a number of times for her close friend Édouard Manet, whose brother Eugène she married, and she also features, together with her daughter Julie, in several works painted by Renoir in the 1880s. In spite of the double burden of being a wife and mother, Berthe Morisot took part in all but one of the Impressionist exhibitions. With her more personal motifs, her pale colours and her daring brush-work, she brought a breath of fresh air into the exhibition rooms. And unlike the other Impressionists, who later went their separate ways, Morisot remained an Impressionist always.

The painting *Harbour at Lorient* is testimony to her concern with questions of figure composition in landscape painting. In this example she placed her sister on the harbour wall. Berthe Morisot said of Frédéric Bazille that he had solved the problem of balance between figure and landscape. Bazille had, a number of times, applied the idea of placing a figure on a wall and thereby achieved an extremely lively and authentic impression.

Unlike Morisot and Bazille, Alfred Sisley attached more importance to the landscape itself. His landscape paintings are either devoid of people or, as in *Autumn: On the Banks of the Seine near Bougival* little figures are present which are perceived more as parts of the surroundings than as beings in their own right. Sisley, born in Paris as the son of an English merchant family, had belonged since the 1860s to the inner circle of friends of Monet, Renoir and Bazille, with whom he often painted together. Renoir has left a loving memorial to him in his *A Couple* (ill. p. 8), which depicts him together with his wife Marie née Lescouezec. Claude Monet also portrayed Sisley in his family circle, where he was a frequent guest. Monet's painting *Dinner at the Sisleys* provides a very private glimpse by a friend into the warmth and intimacy of a family atmosphere.

Sisley's special artistic predilection was for <depictions of water and land together, for example floods, harbours and rivers. In the 1870s he painted more than twenty views of the Seine near Bougival, and displayed his landscapes at a number of Impressionist exhibitions. The scene *Autumn: On the Banks of the Seine near Bougival* is a wonderful example of his typical luminescent colouration, which earned him the epithet of "poet of Impressionism". Sisley's landscape is the depiction of a crossing in a double sense: the passing from one season to the next, and the physical crossing of the river on the ferry.

The great importance of Impressionism for the future development of art was clearly recognized by Vincent van Gogh, who only came to Paris in 1886. "What the Impressionists achieved by way of colour will be further increased; but many forget that they are directly linked with the past …"

When van Gogh visited Paris and his brother Theo, he still had no proper idea of Impressionism and arrived just in time to see the eighth and last Impressionist exhibition, which opened on 15 May 1886. During the next two years in the French capital he was introduced by his art dealer brother to Pissarro and Degas, whom he greatly admired.

For van Gogh, Impressionism was no more than a transitional phase in the search for a style of his own. It was in his relationship to reality that he himself saw one important difference between him and the Impressionists: "For instead of depicting exactly what I see in front of me, I use colour in a more individual way in order to express myself very intensely." In his use of colours, van Gogh

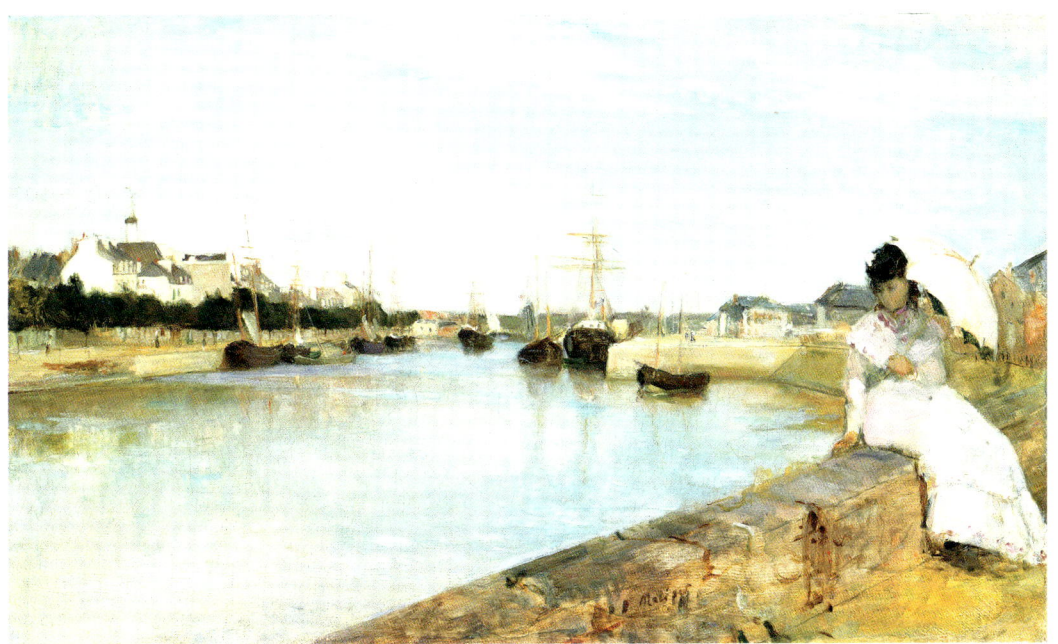

Berthe Morisot
The Harbour at Lorient, 1869
Oil on canvas,
43.5 x 73 cm (17¼ x 28¾ in.)
Washington, D.C., National Gallery
of Art, Ailsa Mellon Bruce Collection

came close in particular to Claude Monet, whom he profoundly admired. "Oh, to paint figures the way Claude Monet paints landscapes! That's something I still have to do, in spite of everything …"

The works which van Gogh painted in Paris, including the *Portrait of Père Tanguy* (ill. p. 57), show his approach to colour under the influence of Impressionism. Monet valued van Gogh's work, telling Theo that he considered his paintings the best in the Indépendants exhibition held in Paris in 1890. Camille Pissarro was the most open to van Gogh's influence, and introduced him to Dr Gachet in Auvers, who hoped to deal with his psychological problems. It was here that Vincent van Gogh took his own life in July 1890. Pissarro said of him, "[I said] this man would either go mad, or leave us all far behind. I had not reckoned on him doing both."

The Last Joint Exhibition

At the last Impressionist exhibition, the only one that van Gogh saw, few of the original artists were represented. Marie Bracquemond, Mary Cassatt and Berthe Morisot were there, as were Degas, Guillaumin, Pissarro and Federico Zandomeneghi (ill. p. 34 and p. 101).

Two new talents in particular, who further developed the Impressionist painting technique, turned up in the list of artists on display in 1886 for the first time: Georges Seurat and Paul Signac. Edgar Degas called the young Seurat "the notary" on account of his invariably correct attire, complete with top hat, the way he always arrived home punctually for dinner with his family, and his world of ideas, which was systematic and scientific.

Seurat occupied himself intensively with optical phenomena and laws, and developed contemporary colour theories to the extent of creating the Pointillist technique. His starting point was the "colour circle" worked out by the chemist Michel Eugène Chevreul (1786–1889), who had influenced all the Impressionists.

Pointillist painting technique involved applying the paint to the canvas in little dots in such a way that a diaphanous, shimmering synthesis arises from the interplay of different colours. This so-called Divisionist style was the basis of the Post- or Neo-impressionist school, to which, alongside Seurat, Signac and for a time Camille Pissarro also belonged. Seurat set up a series of rules, the first of which was: "Art is harmony". The painting *The Bathers at Asnières* was the first work in which he applied the scheme he had developed (ill. p. 85).

Giovanni Segantini, Italian by birth, also adopted Pointillism, combining it with a Realist view of nature. His very individual landscapes of the Swiss and Italian Alps, like the early Impressionist works, lay stress on colour and light. But the scenery for Segantini no longer stands just for itself, but is charged with symbolic meaning. His painting *The Hay Harvest* (ill. p. 83) takes up the "haystack" motif of the early Realists and Impressionists, but the meaning is different. Thus it was that his Symbolism grew out of Impressionist principles.

From France into the World

Impressionism should be seen as an international art movement, not just limited to France. But Impressionist artists who did not live in France have received less than their due share of attention from art-history writers. The art-historical importance of the Italian, American and

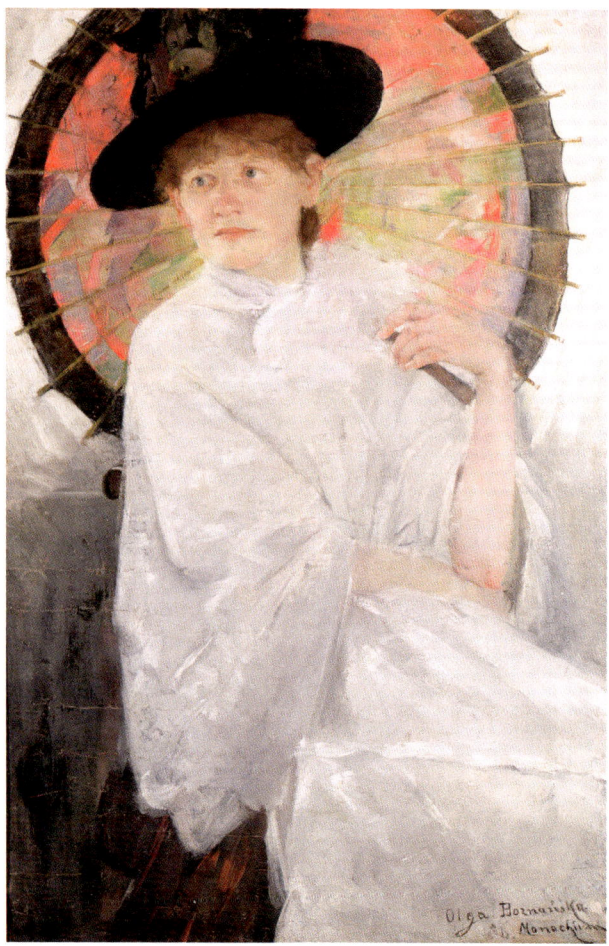

Olga Boznańska
Woman with Japanese Parasol, 1888
Oil on canvas, 88 x 60 cm (34½ x 23½ in.)
Private collection

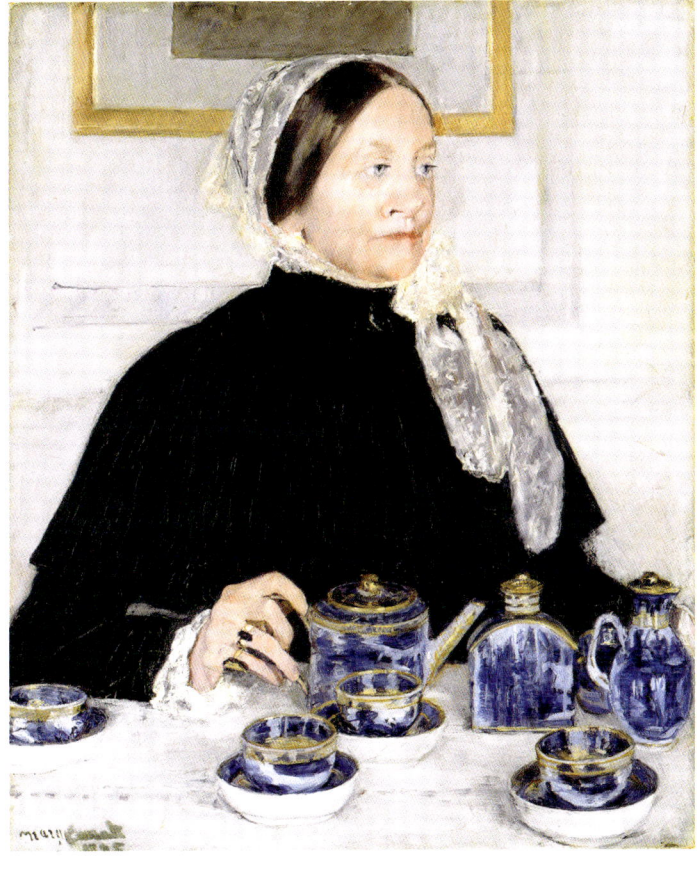

Mary Cassatt
Lady at the Tea Table, 1883–85
Oil on canvas,
73.7 x 61 cm (29 x 24 in.)
New York, The Metropolitan
Museum of Art

German Impressionists, while not on a level with that of the French, should nonetheless not be underestimated.

In the second half of the 19th century Paris exerted an altogether irresistible attraction on would-be artists. Many art students went to live by the Seine, and some remained there for the rest of their lives. A typical example is Giuseppe de Nittis. In 1867, the year he arrived in Paris, he was able to see, at the Exposition Universelle, the latest technical, scientific and artistic developments. The exhibition also included a major retrospective of the works of Ingres, who had died earlier that year.

It was also a special time in the context of Parisian civic history: the whole centre of the city was in the throes of re-planning and redevelopment. As the symbol of modern civilization, the French capital promised innovations not just at the Exposition, but throughout the redesigned streets of the city itself. The new city plan, drawn up by Emperor Napoleon III and his Prefect of the Seine, Baron Haussmann, subjected Paris to radical changes. The narrow medieval streets disappeared, whole neighbourhoods were sacrificed to the broad modern boulevards, and not least to make room for the growing population.

Not just foreign artists such as Giuseppe de Nittis, who concentrated particularly on Parisian city-scapes, but local painters too were fascinated by this gigantic rebuilding project. With logical consistency they made construction sites and prestigious boulevards a theme of their paintings. Even though we can detect perhaps a little nostalgia for the now-lost "old" Paris in the works of Pierre-Auguste Renoir and others, the artists welcomed the modern development.

Since the early 1860s, Paris had been the rendezvous of the international art world. And the elegant and creative life of the city made it a focus for the rest of the world. For artists from elsewhere visiting Paris, the works of the French Impressionists were among their most important sources of inspiration. They brought the Impressionist movement back to their home countries and provided the impulse, there too, to turn away from the prevailing academic artistic ideals. Many non-French artists followed the path mapped out by their French counterparts, but arrived at different solutions of their own by dint of different preconditions in each case.

Some of the Italian and American Impressionists belonged to the Parisian circle of friends of Monet, Pissarro, Renoir and Degas, some of them displaying their works at the Impressionist exhibitions. As a result of family connections, Degas had close links with Italy and the United States, and was extremely receptive to the foreign artists in Paris. Degas' father came from southern Italy, and his mother from New Orleans, so that Degas himself was positively predestined to make contact with Italian and American artists. Giuseppe de Nittis, Federico Zandomeneghi and Medardo Rosso were all closes friends of Degas.

Especially following the end of the American Civil War, Paris welcomed a constant stream of American tourists, students and artists. Travel was becoming easier and more comfortable, and Europe was easier to reach. The writer Henry James noted with amazement: "It sounds like a paradox, but it is a very simple truth, that when today we look for 'American art' we find it mainly in Paris. When we find it out of Paris, we at least find a great deal of Paris in it." About one-third of the American visitors to Paris were women, among them the artist Mary Cassatt, who found more scope for her development here than she did back home.

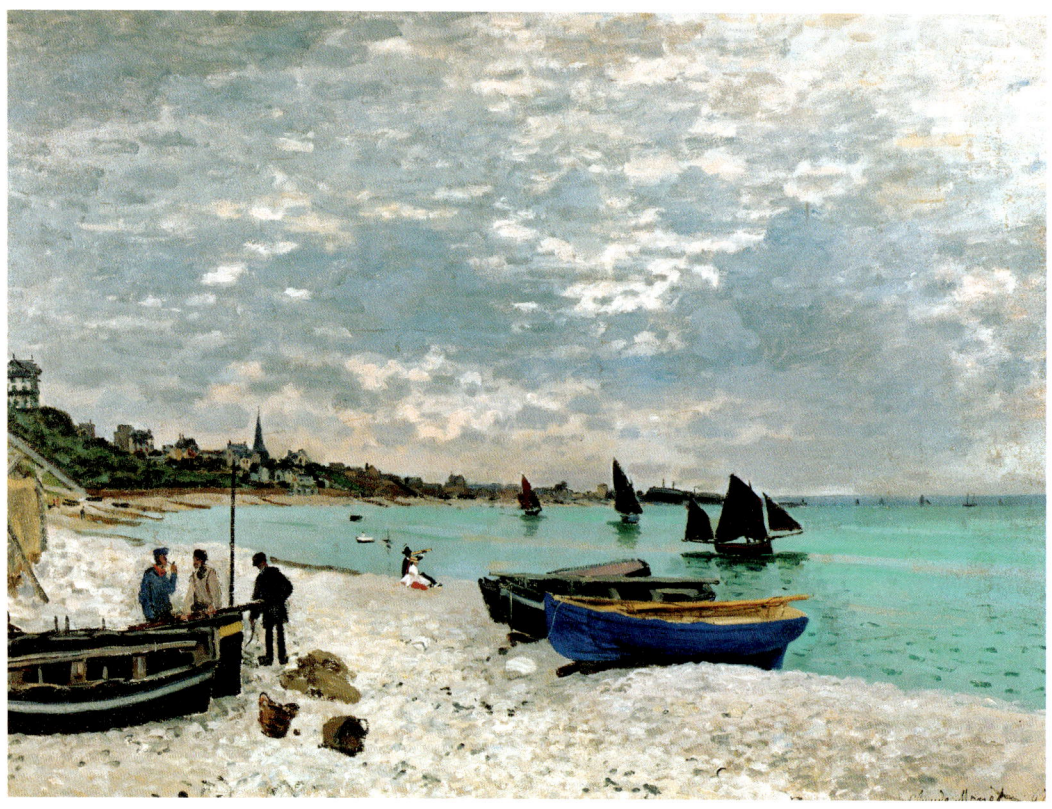

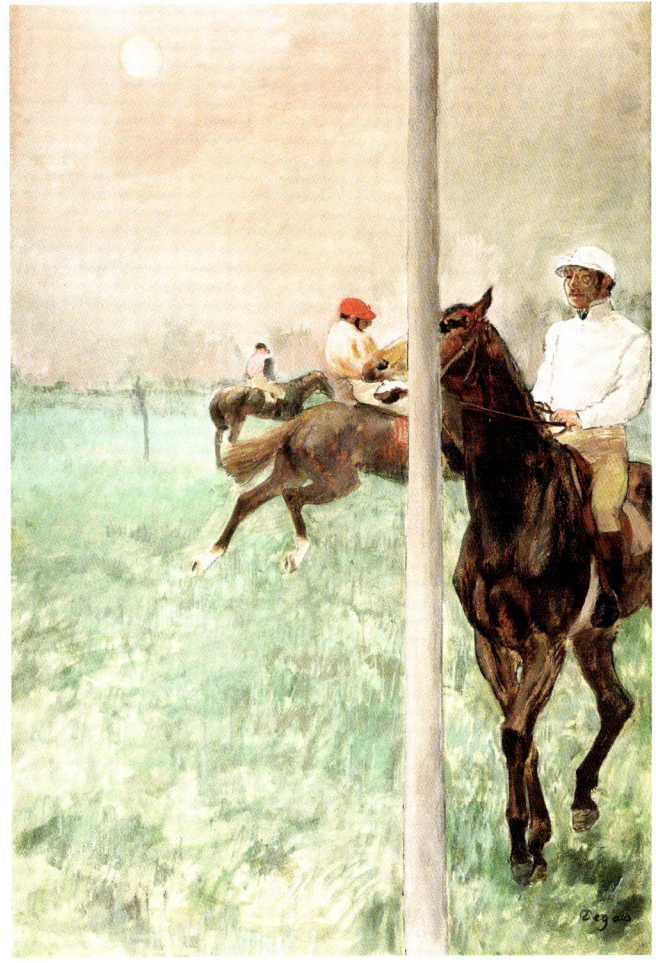

"Monet is the god of the young landscape painters," wrote an American newspaper in 1891. John Singer Sargent and Monet had probably met in Paris as early as 1876 and they remained lifelong friends. In the mid-1880s Sargent experimented with the Impressionist painting technique, and worked alongside Monet in Giverny. The painting *Claude Monet Painting at the Edge of a Wood* (ill. p. 35) dates from a visit by Sargent in the summer of 1885. He acted as agent between Monet and American collectors, and himself bought a number of Monet's paintings. *Claude Monet Painting at the Edge of a Wood* he kept as a memento in his private collection. The painting depicts his friend working near Giverny. Among the trees can be seen a woman dressed in white, either Monet's partner of many years, Alice Hoschedé, or her daughter Suzanne.

Paris, and this went for all the artists, was "the capital of the 19th century", as the German writer and philosopher Walter Benjamin wrote in retrospect. Following the horrors of the Franco-Prussian War of 1870/71, friendly contacts between German and French artists were rare during the 1870s. The newly formed German Empire often looked askance at French influences. Max Liebermann, for example, while he lived for some time in Paris, evidently had no personal contacts with the French Impressionists, and probably visited none of the Impressionist exhibitions. Even so, later, having returned to his home city of Berlin, he was notable for being one of the first German collectors of

French art, including Impressionist works. The heyday of German Impressionism can be dated to the 1890s and the early years of the 20th century, until about the start of the First World War in 1914.

Impressionism in Germany was not concentrated in a single city as it was in France, as Berlin was still very young as a centre of the arts, and faced stiff competition from Munich, Düsseldorf, Weimar and Dresden. And also German Impressionism was not tied up with individual artist personalities, who after all did not remain Impressionists all their lives, but for whom, rather, it was merely a transitional phase. In consequence, German Impressionists have less in common than their French counterparts, and Impressionism in Germany is less homogeneous than in its homeland. Max Liebermann, Fritz von Uhde and Max Slevogt, indeed even Wassily Kandinsky were influenced by Impressionism, albeit not equally profoundly, nor equally long. All these differences from the development in France make it questionable to what extent one can talk about "German Impressionism" as a genuine movement at all. Rather, what we have are German artists who painted Impressionist pictures for a time, albeit as individuals and not as a movement.

The Moscow-born Wassily Kandinsky lived and worked in the French capital from 1904 to 1906. There, he exhibited his works in the Salon des Indépendants and doubtless also saw exhibitions of Impressionist art, which he had encountered at an early stage. Kandinsky continued his experiments with strong colours, an impulse he had received from Impressionist models. As the 20th century progressed, he abandoned figural painting entirely, and described one of Monet's haystack pictures as the decisive factor on his road to abstraction: "I had the vague sensation that this picture lacked an object."

He and many other 20th-century artists fulfilled van Gogh's prophecy: What the Impressionists achieved by way of colour will be increased still further.

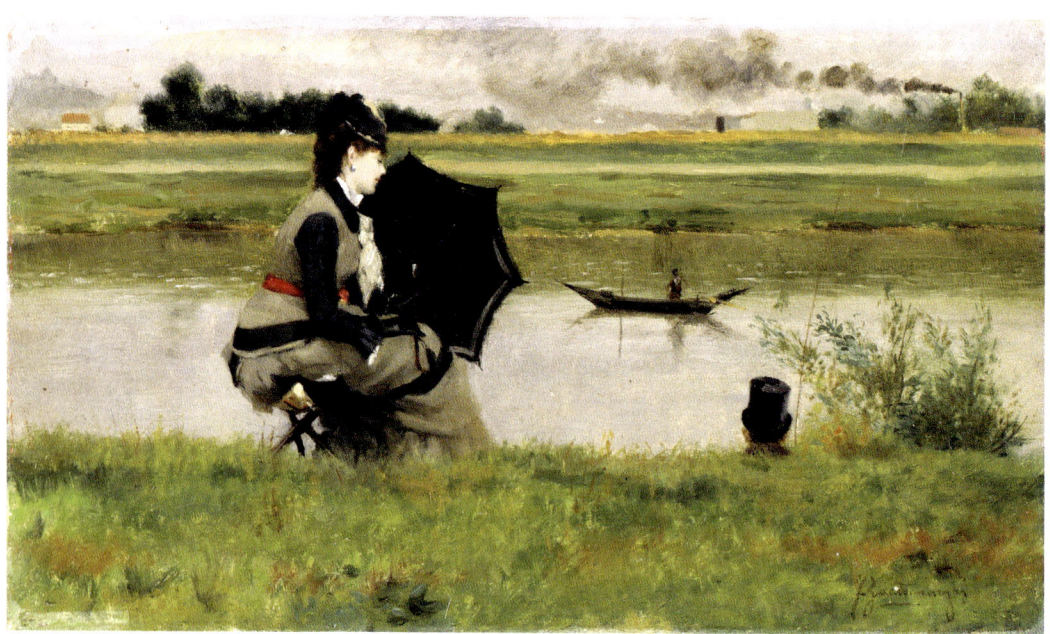

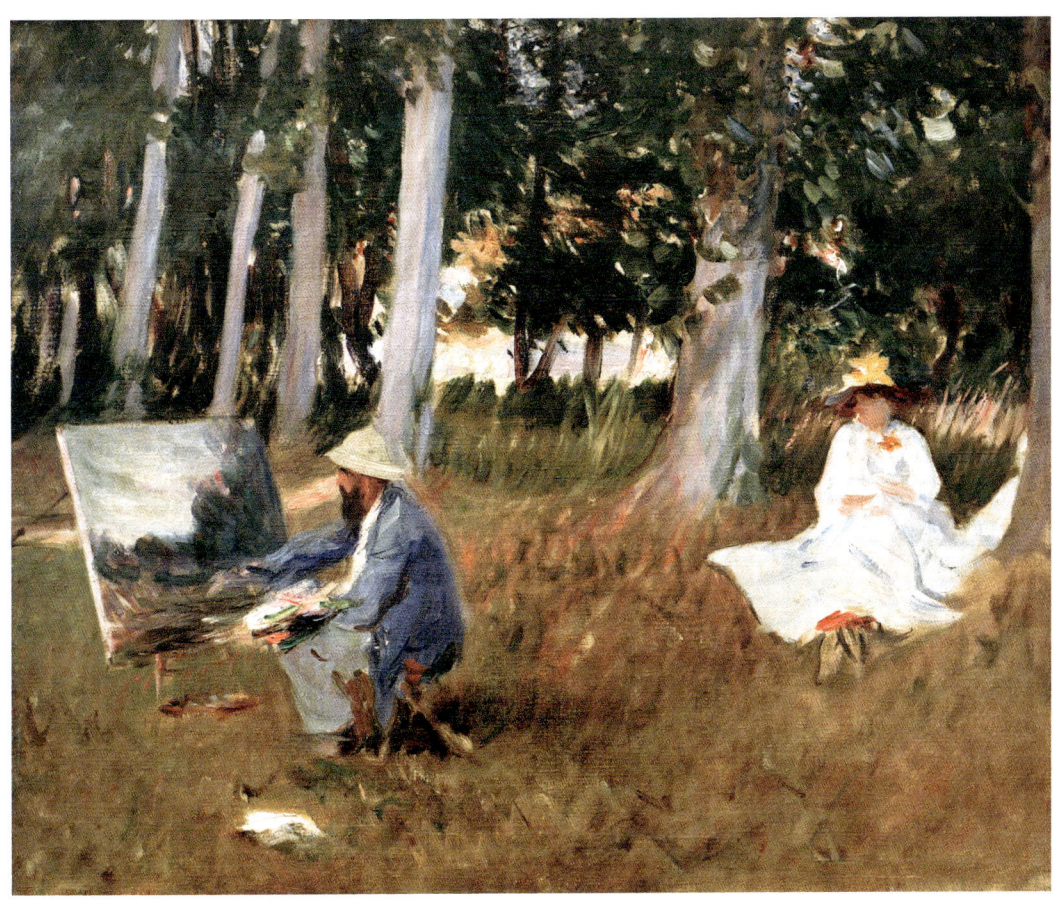

John Singer Sargent
**Claude Monet Painting at the
Edge of a Wood**, 1885
Oil on canvas,
54 x 64.8 cm (21¼ x 25¼ in.)
London, Tate

OPPOSITE
Federico Zandomeneghi
Fishing on the Seine, 1878
Oil on panel,
16 x 29 cm (6¼ x 11½ in.)
Florence, Galleria d'Arte Moderna,
Collezione Diego Martinelli

PAGES 36/37
Claude Monet in his first studio
at Giverny, *c.* 1913, showing
Luncheon on the Grass (1865)
to a visitor
Private collection

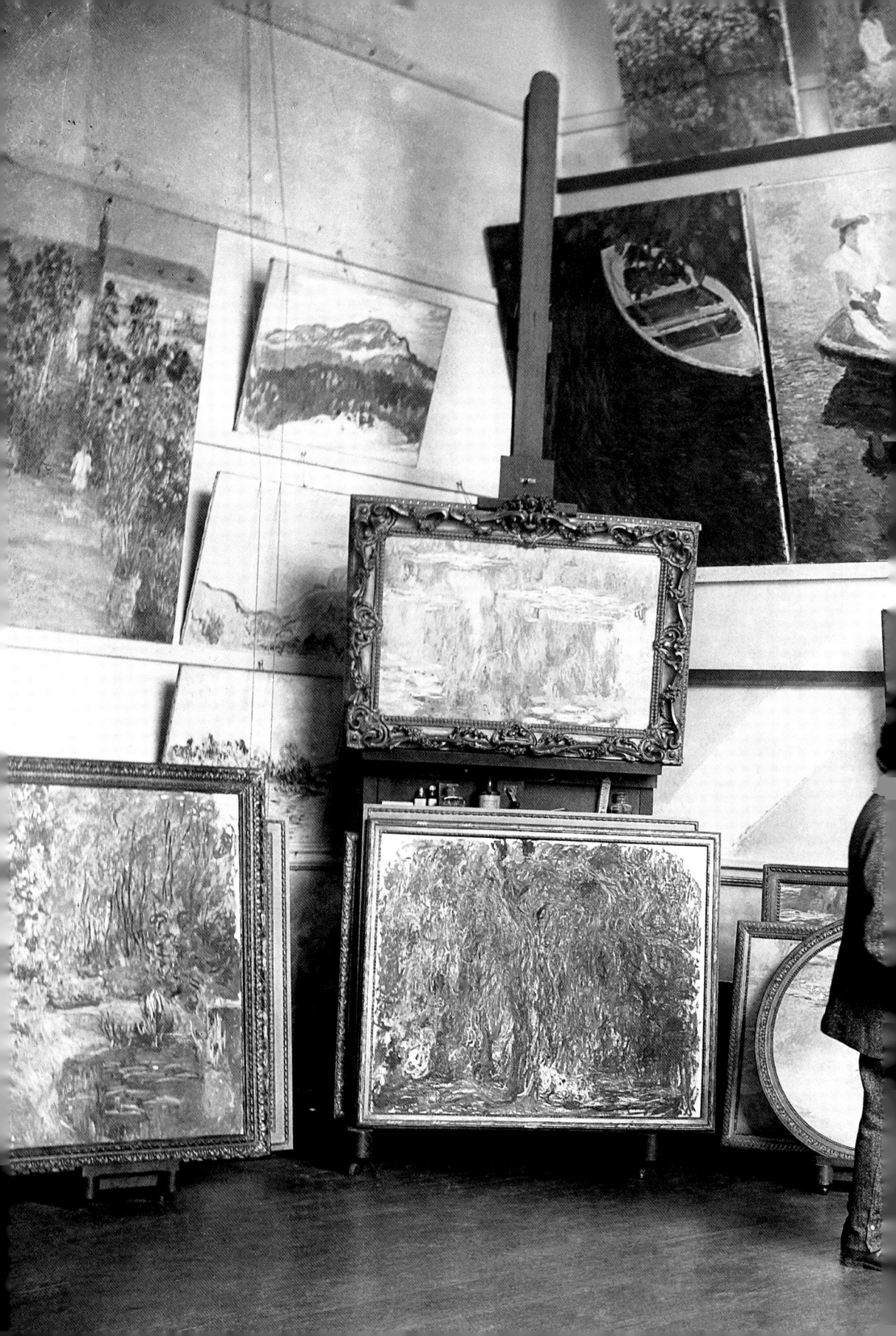

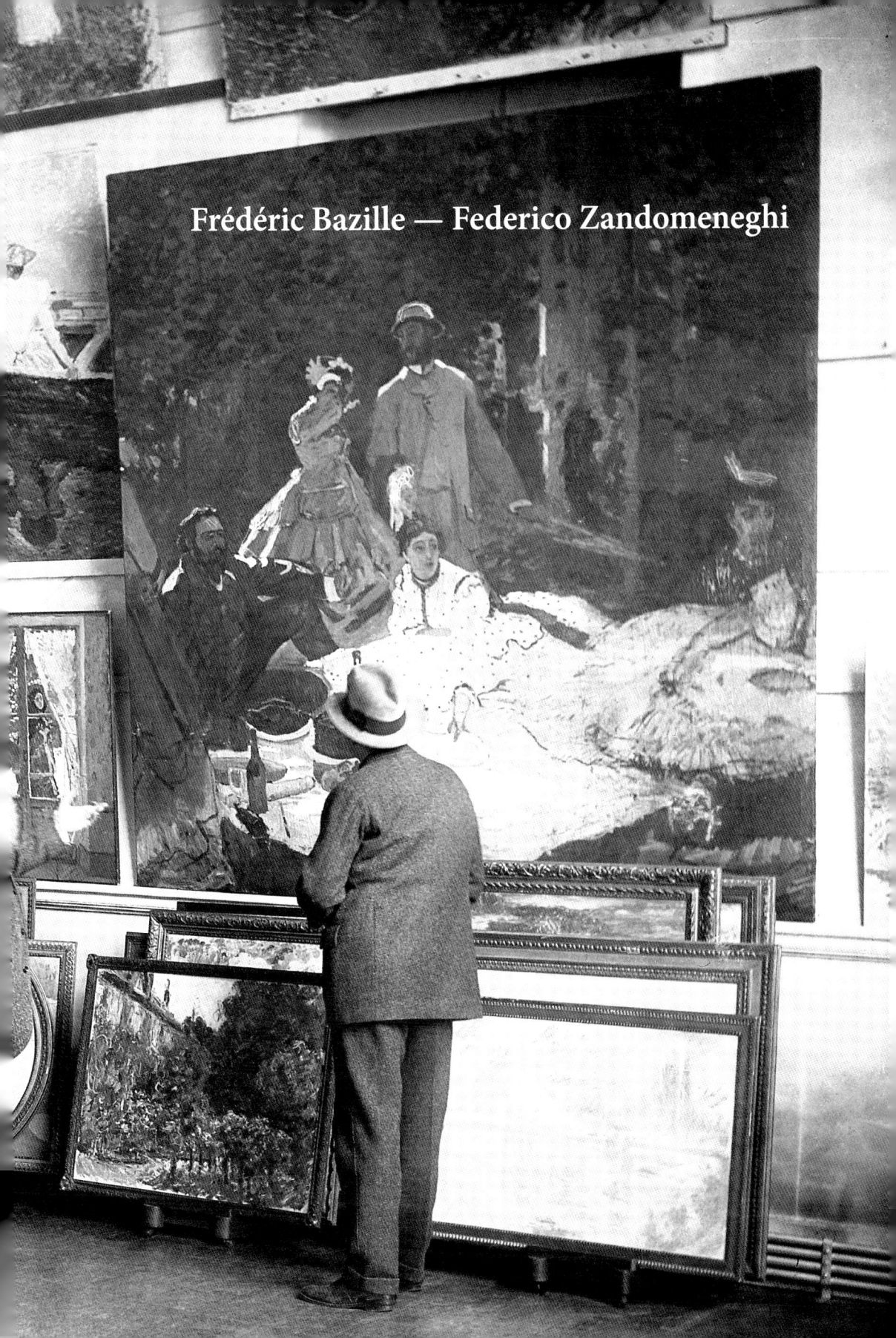

Frédéric Bazille — Federico Zandomeneghi

Frédéric Bazille
Still Life with Fish, 1866

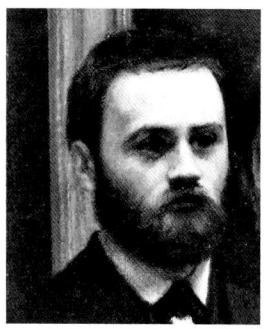

b. 1841 in Montpellier, France
d. 1870 in Beaune-la-Rolande, France

Still-lifes from the early days of Impressionism, in other words from the 1860s, are largely unknown today, even though almost all the Impressionist artists painted such subjects.

When Bazille decided to submit the *Still Life with Fish* for the 1866 Salon, it was because he doubted whether his *Young Woman at the Piano*, the picture originally intended for the exhibition, would be accepted. Now he sought a more moderate motif and format. He was probably inspired by one of Édouard Manet's fish still-lifes, which had been exhibited in 1865: "You cannot imagine how much I have learnt by looking at the pictures! A session there is worth as much as a whole month's work." At the same time he was also being encouraged by his friend Claude Monet to paint still-lifes. Monet recommended him to paint from nature, and above all to paint flowers. The still-lifes Monet himself was painting at this time were likewise oriented to Manet, the motifs consisting of objects arranged on a white table cloth against a dark background.

Flowers, fruit and fish were easier to get hold of than human models, who were rarely good and often too expensive. Occasionally Bazille and Sisley shared the cost by, for example, buying a dead heron which they both painted. Gustave Caillebotte reduced his costs even further by not even buying the objects, but painting them on display in a shop. With his *Still Life: Chickens, Pheasants and Hares* (1882) he brought entirely new aspects to the still-life genre. A piece of modern life is reflected in the choice of a shop-display and in the depiction of a sequence. Caillebotte no longer depicts one or two fish in a domestic setting, with a table and tablecloth in readiness for being prepared for a meal, but nine chickens, three pheasants, two hares and five smaller birds in a shop window. At the same time, Caillebotte renounces any attempt to create spatial depth. His austerely parallel arrangement of the display slab and the metal rod on which the hares and pheasants are hanging against a black background, stress the flatness of the image.

Bazille and many of his friends could not afford in the 1860s to keep buying new canvases. Instead, they would scrape off the paint from ones already used and paint them again. An x-ray examination of the painting *Still Life with Fish* has shown that the canvas had been used for a different still-life depicting apples and pears, and was turned through 180° before being used for this one.

One very important reason for choosing to paint still-lifes was the hope that the conservative-minded members of the hanging committee for the Salon exhibition would react more benevolently towards a genre which was generally accepted and at the same time less closely regimented. And indeed Bazille's *Still Life with Fish* was accepted for the 1866 Salon and put on public display. The few critics who delivered themselves of an opinion stressed the successful depiction of the fishes in the sense of their being true to nature, but criticized the too-dark colouration. The art critic Charles de Sarlat wrote in a short notice on 21 June 1866: "The carp is very realistic: one would like to see it on one's dinner plate, it looks so delicious."

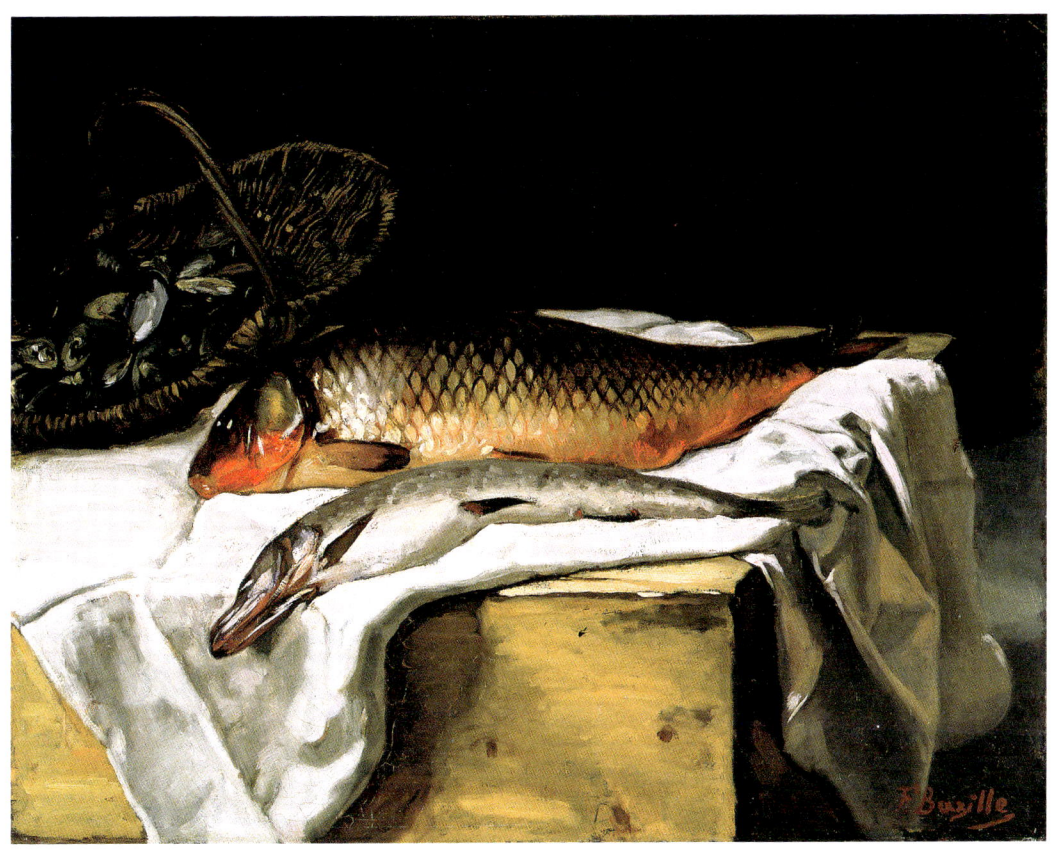

Still Life with Fish, 1866
Oil on canvas, 63.5 x 81.9 cm (25 x 32¼ in.)
Detroit Institute of Arts

Frédéric Bazille
Family Reunion, 1867

Frédéric Bazille came from Montpellier in the south of France. His family had wanted him to study medicine, but from 1864 supported his final decision to pursue a career in art. It was to be a short career, as he was killed in action in the Franco-Prussian War six years later. Consequently his work was not represented at the Impressionist exhibitions. But it was from him that the original idea came of holding exhibitions of one's own, where one was not dependent on the selection processes of a conservative hanging committee.

Family Reunion occupies a central place in Bazille's œuvre, because it was painted at mid-point in his career, and is the largest of his paintings still extant. In the 1860s he formed an intensive friendship with Monet and Renoir, collaborating closely with Monet in particular. Their paintings *The Beach at Sainte-Adresse* (ill. p. 32) and *View of the Coast at Sainte-Adresse* (1865, Atlanta, High Museum of Art) bear witness to this co-operation. These young painters were interested in depicting the human figure in the landscape. Together, they gathered their first impressions with open-air painting; Bazille painted his *Family Reunion* completely in the open air, as had Monet his composition *Women in the Garden* (Paris, Musée d'Orsay); all that he did later in the studio was to make detailed revisions and add himself to the group (on the left-hand edge of the picture).

The occasion for the motif was a reunion of the whole family beneath the great chestnut tree on the terrace at Méric in the summer of 1867. Bazille's parents are seen sitting on a bench on the left of the picture. Uncle, aunt, cousins and his brother Marc with his wife are gathered on the terrace as though they had just returned from a walk together. The white, black-dotted dresses of the ladies, very similar to those to be seen in Monet's *Women in the Garden,* were in fashion in the summer of 1867. In addition, white clothing was seen as an unmistakable sign of the bourgeoisie and bourgeois values in the 19th century.

For the painters, it was the effect of light and shade and the way white reflected the ambient colours that was particularly interesting. Renoir's painting *Lise with Parasol* (ill. p. 75) provides a further example. Bazille placed the turquoise cast of the dress of his cousin Thérèse, the young woman at the table, at the focus of the composition. This is the actual purpose of the picture: it is not the motif which is crucial, but the way it was painted.

Bazille's work *Family Reunion* was shown at the Salon in 1868, unlike Monet's *Women in the Garden,* which was rejected by the conservative hanging committee. The young Émile Zola wrote a critique of Bazille's painting, in which he emphasized three aspects: the sensitivity of his treatment of the natural light on the terrace; the exact portraiture of eleven people, whose poses and gestures characterize their personalities; and the detailed attention paid to the clothing, which Zola regarded as a contribution to modern life.

Eight of the eleven sitters are looking directly at the beholder, but there is no interaction between them. 21st-century beholders link this pose with a photograph, and indeed the painting has often been compared to a group photograph. Painting and photography overlapped in the second half of the 19th century. The parallel with photography highlights Bazille's endeavour to integrate narrative and the passage of time into his painted snapshot.

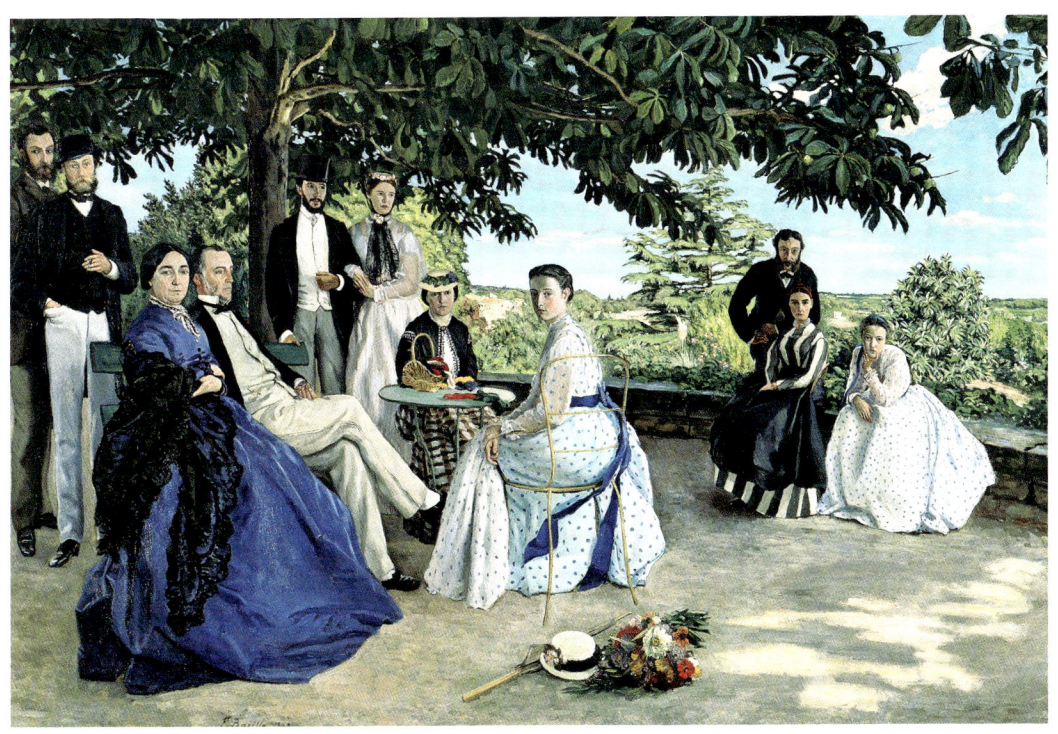

Family Reunion, 1867
Oil on canvas, 152 x 230 cm (60 x 90½ in.)
Paris, Musée d'Orsay

Marie Bracquemond
Afternoon Tea, c. 1880

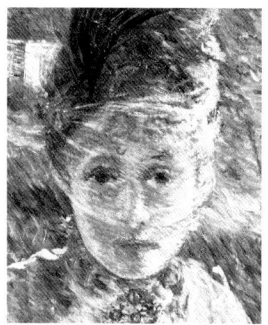

b. 1840 in Argenton-en-
Landunvez, France
d. 1916 in Sèvres, France

Alongside Mary Cassatt and Berthe Morisot, Marie Bracquemond was one of the three great women exponents of the Impressionist style. She took part in three Impressionist exhibitions: in 1879, 1880 and 1886. Today she is largely unknown, since she gave up painting in 1890 and few of her works are in public collections. This reticence was in line with the traditional role of women on the one hand, and also due, on the other, to the dominance of her husband, the graphic artist Félix Bracquemond, who was not supportive of the modernity of her painting. Evidently Marie Bracquemond finally abandoned painting for the sake of marital harmony.

Marie Bracquemond was trained by Jean-Auguste-Dominique Ingres in the Neo-classicist manner. Her second master was Paul Gauguin, whom her husband brought home in 1880, the year that *Afternoon Tea* was painted. It shows Marie Bracquemond's sister Louise sitting at a table in the open air. The open book in her hand seems not to be holding her attention, for her gaze is turned to the lower right. The frontally depicted, symmetrical, motionless face recalls portraits by Ingres, such as that of *Madame Moitissier,* which dates from 1851 (Washington, National Gallery of Art, Samuel H. Kress Collection). The little still-life on the tea table, in particular the silver tray with grapes, is reminiscent of similar elements in Ingres' œuvre, for example the little stool with fruit at the front edge of the painting *The Turkish Bath* (1863, Paris, Musée du Louvre). Bracquemond juxtaposed short, closely spaced strokes with fine gradations of red, green and blue shades in order to represent light and shade. The face and the uncovered hands are in this respect particularly sensitively depicted. The eyes and forehead are shaded by the hat, and there is a fluid transition to the lower, lighter half of the face. Individual patches of light on the clothes and the shrubs in the background are painted in pure, glaring white. The fashionable clothes, which her teacher Ingres had been wont to stage in masterly fashion, were emphasized no less strongly by Bracquemond, Bazille and for example Giuseppe de Nittis. Manet too expressed his admiration for Ingres in this regard: "Oh! Ingres was clever. We are just children. He knew how to paint textures." Ingres however only very rarely painted white clothes, Bracquemond by contrast deliberately sought out this colour.

In *The Tea* (Boston, Museum of Fine Arts) Mary Cassatt's sister Lydia is drinking tea in a room with a visitor, who can be recognized as such by her hat and gloves, which were not removed for – customarily short – tea-time calls. Cassatt has spread a still-life on the table at the front edge of the picture: The silver tea-service, from which the light is reflected, plays the same role as the bright patches of sunlight in Bracquemond's afternoon scene. Cassatt's style is softer, because she used a broader brush; on the armchair cover, the loose brushstrokes slip in places into the abstract. The different shades of red in the wallpaper, the armchair cover and the table harmonize with the greyish-silver hues in the fireplace, in the tea service and, again, in the wallpaper. Red and silver dominate, summarizing into an unusual unity. The brief impression is emphasized by the position of the cup, which is hiding the visitor's face. It is the "impression" of the moment of drinking.

Afternoon Tea, *c.* 1880
Oil on canvas, 81.5 x 61.5 cm (32 x 24¼ in.)
Musée des Beaux-Arts de la Ville de Paris,
Petit Palais

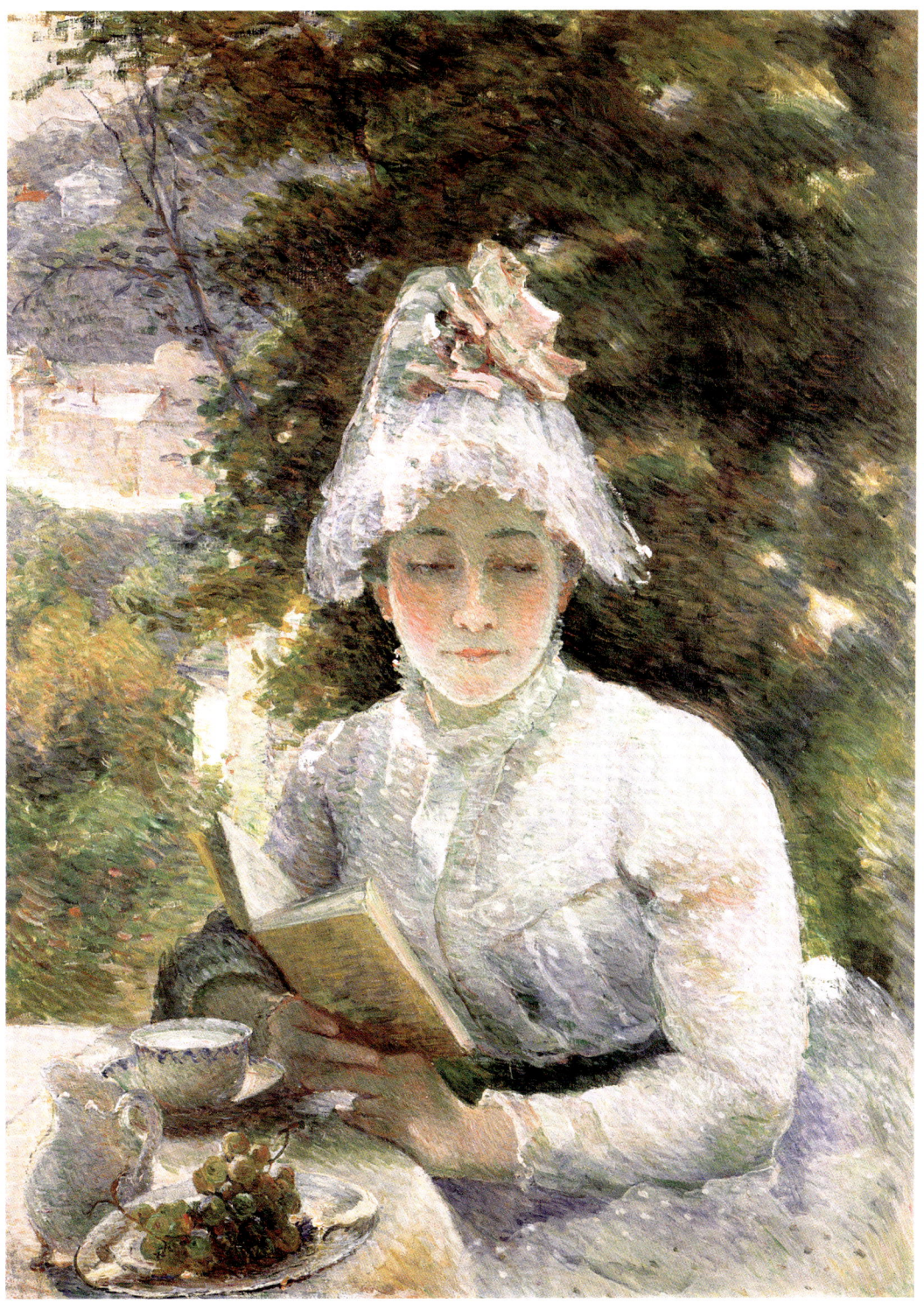

Gustave Caillebotte
The Floor Strippers, 1875

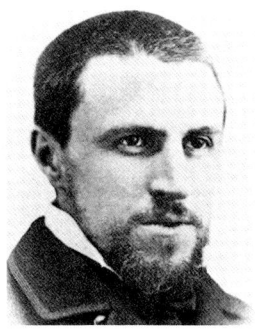

b. 1848 in Paris
d. 1894 in Gennevilliers, France

Gustave Caillebotte joined the Impressionist circle in the early 1870s. He had begun to paint under the influence of Monet and his friends. At first self-taught, he then enrolled at the École des Beaux-Arts. Unlike the rest of the Impressionists, Caillebotte had substantial independent means. He could afford to support his friends by buying their pictures. The collection which he built up in this way he bequeathed to the French state on condition that a large part of it should be publicly exhibited. When he died in 1894, Renoir, his executor, had great difficulty in actually executing the will, because those in charge of cultural policy found it inconceivable to display in a museum the works of an Impressionist which the public still largely rejected. Renoir was able to transfer only parts of the collection to state ownership, including *The Floor Strippers.*

Caillebotte here depicts working men going about their business. *The Floor Strippers* can be seen in the context of similar works such as Degas' *Women Ironing* (*c.* 1884, Paris, Musée d'Orsay), Paul Signac's *The Milliners* (1885/86, Zurich, Foundation E. G. Bührle Collection) and *Young Woman Washing Dishes* by Camille Pissarro (1882, University of Cambridge, Fitzwilliam Museum). The Impressionists depicted urban labour alongside the rural tasks which already featured in the works of the Barbizon school. That Caillebotte, a member of the privileged haute bourgeoisie, who himself led a Bohemian lifestyle, should have chosen to depict such a motif, came as a surprise to his contemporaries. And to consider simple workers like these floor strippers as at all artworthy, especially on a large canvas, was at the time a provocative innovation. *The Floor Strippers* was for this reason rejected by the hanging committee at the Salon, and Caillebotte did not, as planned, take part in the official Academy exhibition, but in the second Impressionist exhibition of 1876.

The light entering the room through the balcony door in the background produces a magnificent contre-jour effect. The light is reflected off the backs and arms of the workmen, which appear shiny as a result. The strips of remaining dark varnish on the floor glisten in the light, while the already stripped floorboards come across by contrast as matt, whether they are illuminated from the door or in the shadow of the workmen's bodies. The rhythm of the workmen seems to accord with the rhythm of the floor. The two at the front perform an identical movement and are further linked to each other by their heads, inclined in mutual conversation. Their workmate, who is further back, is cropped by the edge of the picture, thus emphasizing the snapshot nature of the depiction. His back is aligned with the horizontal line of the wood panelling and seems to be bent beneath some confining surface. These are rhythmic movement studies, comparable to Edgar Degas' ballerinas and racehorses.

Backlight and the rhythm of work are also at the focus of Monet's painting *Men Unloading Coal* (*c.* 1875). Barges are being unloaded on a quayside of the Seine, the dockers balancing on long wooden planks as they ply back and forth. The light is shimmering on the river, which is framed, so to speak, by the bridge spanning it. This is labour in a modern city which sets the rhythm of life. Like Monet, Caillebotte here presents himself as a painter of urban working life, and not just of leisure.

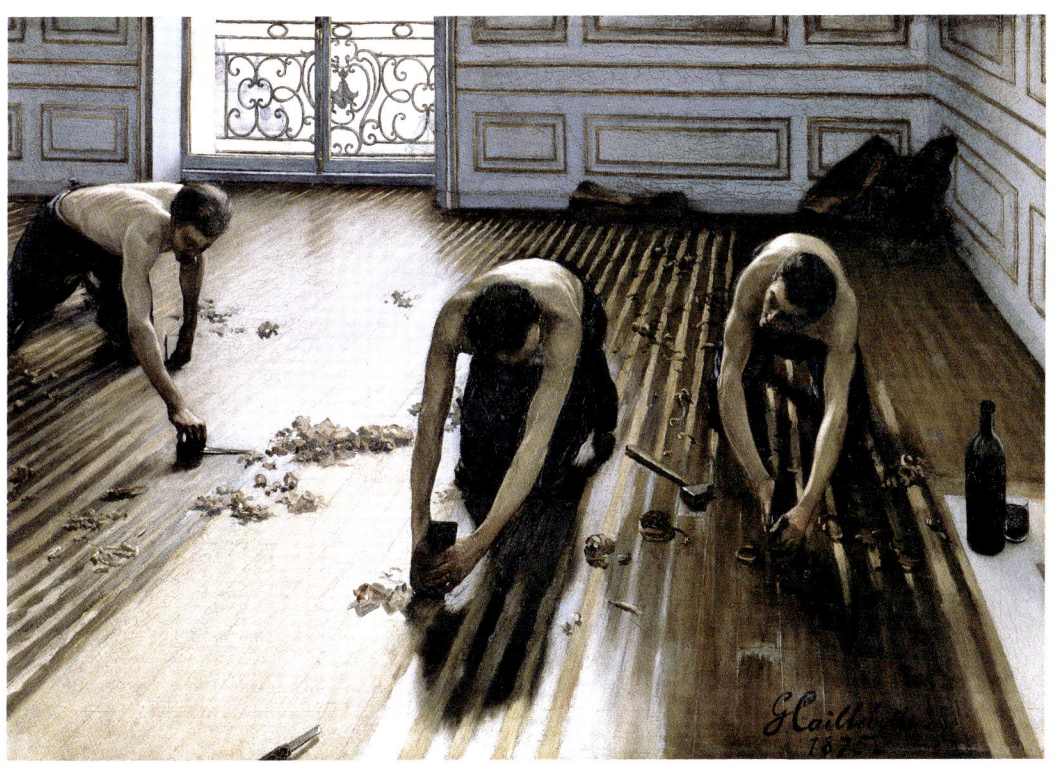

The Floor Strippers, 1875
Oil on canvas, 102 x 146.5 cm (40¼ x 57¾ in.)
Paris, Musée d'Orsay

Gustave Caillebotte
Man Drying his Leg, 1884

A man has just stepped out of the bathtub. Naked as he is, he sits down on a chair to the left of the picture, with one leg stretched out in order to be able to better rub it dry with a towel. The light-flooded room is laid out in that steep perspective which is typical of the majority of Caillebotte's paintings.

The genre motif of a male nude drying himself is a snapshot of what for today's beholder is a very ordinary, everyday action. Incidentally, Caillebotte varies the theme of the man in the bathroom in a number of his works. They all display an almost too physical, perceptibly erotic quality. This is even more astonishing when one considers that Caillebotte conceived such nudes as paraphrases of "classical" studies of the human body: One is tempted to associate a contemporary example from 1884 of a standing, bathing figure with a warrior as perhaps could have been portrayed by the French Neo-classicist painter Jacques-Louis David (1748–1825). In contrast, the athletic sitting figure in its complex posture is distantly reminiscent of the motional repertoire developed from 1504 by Michelangelo for the bathing soldiers of the (lost) *Battle of Cascina* fresco. There are many depictions of the naked male body in the history of art, but among the Greek heroes, fallen warriors, gods and images of Christ, there had been no men in bathrooms. Bathing and indeed the whole routine of body-care, in other words dressing, combing etc., was something that, as far as art was concerned, only women indulged in. Among the Impressionists too, the woman in or at her bath was a frequent motif. Degas alone devoted more than two hundred pictures to it. Caillebotte, who admired Degas, had two of them in his own collection.

The male body is here being shown in a new context, thus casting into question the previously unquestioned role assignment. Until the end of the 19th century, the man was seen as the conqueror, the ruler, and at all levels of society and in private life as the dominant figure. As the modern age dawned, with the women's emancipation movements and the assertion in society of bourgeois values and standards such as cleanliness and personal hygiene, this traditional view of the masculine role began to falter. Caillebotte's men are modern not least because they have bathtubs, in those days an absolute novelty in the private sphere, and only affordable for the upper middle-class.

Maximilien Luce's *Man at his Toilet* (1887) is unable to afford this luxury. He is washing in what was then the usual way in a bowl on a wash-stand, and the other furnishings also point to his being a member of the lower classes. The Neo-impressionist Maximilien Luce took up the motif of the man at his toilet just a few years after Caillebotte, and combined it with the new painting technique developed by Paul Signac and Georges Seurat. The highly intensive colouration stands out by comparison with Caillebotte's subdued palette. Luce enhanced this dominant interplay of colours by having light enter from the side. The shadow of the man bending forward falls on the right-hand wall and forms an unusual, fascinating shape. The frame on the wall behind the man's torso, where we might expect a mirror, is revealed on closer inspection to be not a reflection and extension of the depicted room, but as a "picture within a picture", a further play with light and colours.

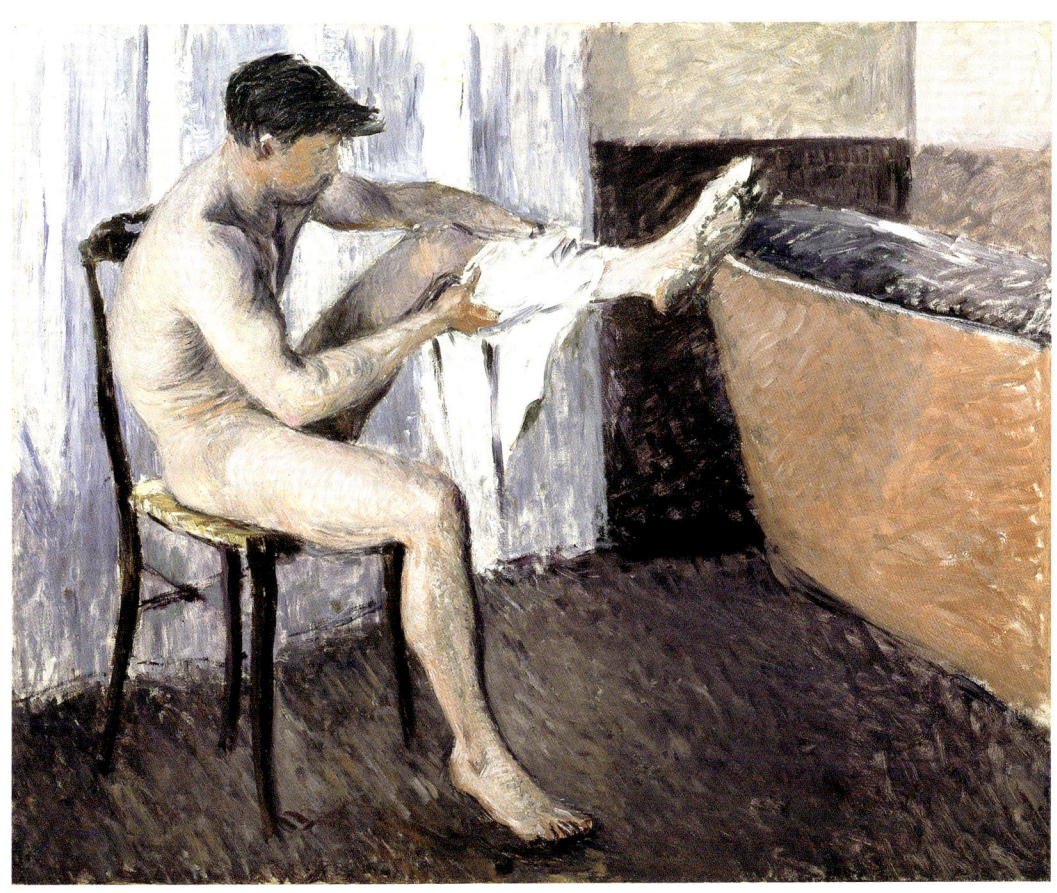

Man Drying his Leg, 1884
Oil on canvas, 100 x 125 cm (39¼ x 49¼ in.)
Private collection

Mary Cassatt
Woman with a Pearl Necklace in a Loge, 1879

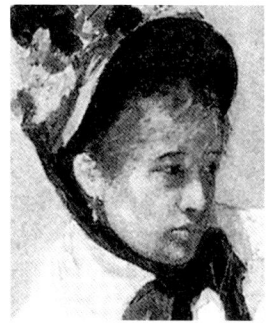

b. 1844 in Allegheny City,
Pennsylvania
d. 1926 in Mesnil-Théribus,
France

Unlike Marie Bracquemond, as a foreigner in Paris Mary Cassatt had relatively good career prospects. Many American women artists reported that Paris offered them more opportunities than they had back home, where bourgeois conventions still held considerable sway.

Mary Cassatt arrived in the French capital to continue her artistic training in 1865. From 1868 she was regularly represented at the exhibitions of the Salon, and was the only American woman represented at a number of the exhibitions of the Impressionists. The painting *Woman with a Pearl Necklace in a Loge* was first shown at the fourth Impressionist exhibition, where a whole room was filled by Mary Cassatt with subjects from the world of the theatre and the opera. This picture was one of the few to find a buyer at the exhibition, being sold to the French collector Alexis Rouart.

Her introduction to the circle of Impressionist painters was largely due to Edgar Degas, who had become her friend and mentor. Like Degas and Renoir, Mary Cassatt painted the major theatres and the Paris Opéra as centres of modern culture and modern life. With their evening glitz and colourful audiences, these places provided numerous motifs.

In her theatre pictures, Cassatt devoted less attention than Degas to what was happening on the stage or in the orchestra pit; she was more interested in the women in the audience. These ladies thus became objects of dual attention: first, from fellow-theatregoers, and then from beholders of the pictures. The theme of the theatre as such receded as a result into the background, forming no more than an appealing setting for the mise-en-scène of the female visitor.

Exhibiting her physical charms, be it on a walk in the park or in the audience at the theatre, was an expected part of a woman's behaviour in the late 19th century. Mary Cassatt's theatregoers seem perfectly aware of this. The fans in their hands, which could if need be provide shelter from prying eyes, remain closed. This is made particularly clear in her 1878 painting *In the Loge* (Boston, Museum of Fine Arts) by a man who is leaning well out of his box to look not at the lady whom he is escorting, but through his opera glass at the opera-goer in the foreground. She in her turn is gazing at the stage through her own opera glass. The woman in the pearl necklace is evidently also being observed by the theatregoers in the background. She though, is looking not at the stage, but at the seats in the box which are reflected in the mirror behind her. By adding a mirror directly behind the red armchair, Cassatt creates a surprising spatial effect. The elegant curve of the boxes only becomes apparent through the reflection, which also generates the strangely two-dimensional spatial effect. The radiance of the chandelier not only illuminates the lady with the pearl necklace from the front, but thanks to the reflection produces a backlight at the same time. It lights up her bare white shoulders and on her glove too, with which she is holding the fan in her right hand. The whole painting comes across as being steeped in a reddish-gold light, and can be seen as one of Mary Cassatt's most harmonious colour compositions.

Woman with a Pearl Necklace in a Loge, 1879
Oil on canvas, 81.3 x 59.7 cm (32 x 23½ in.)
Philadelphia Museum of Art, Bequest of
Charlotte Dorrance Wright, 1978

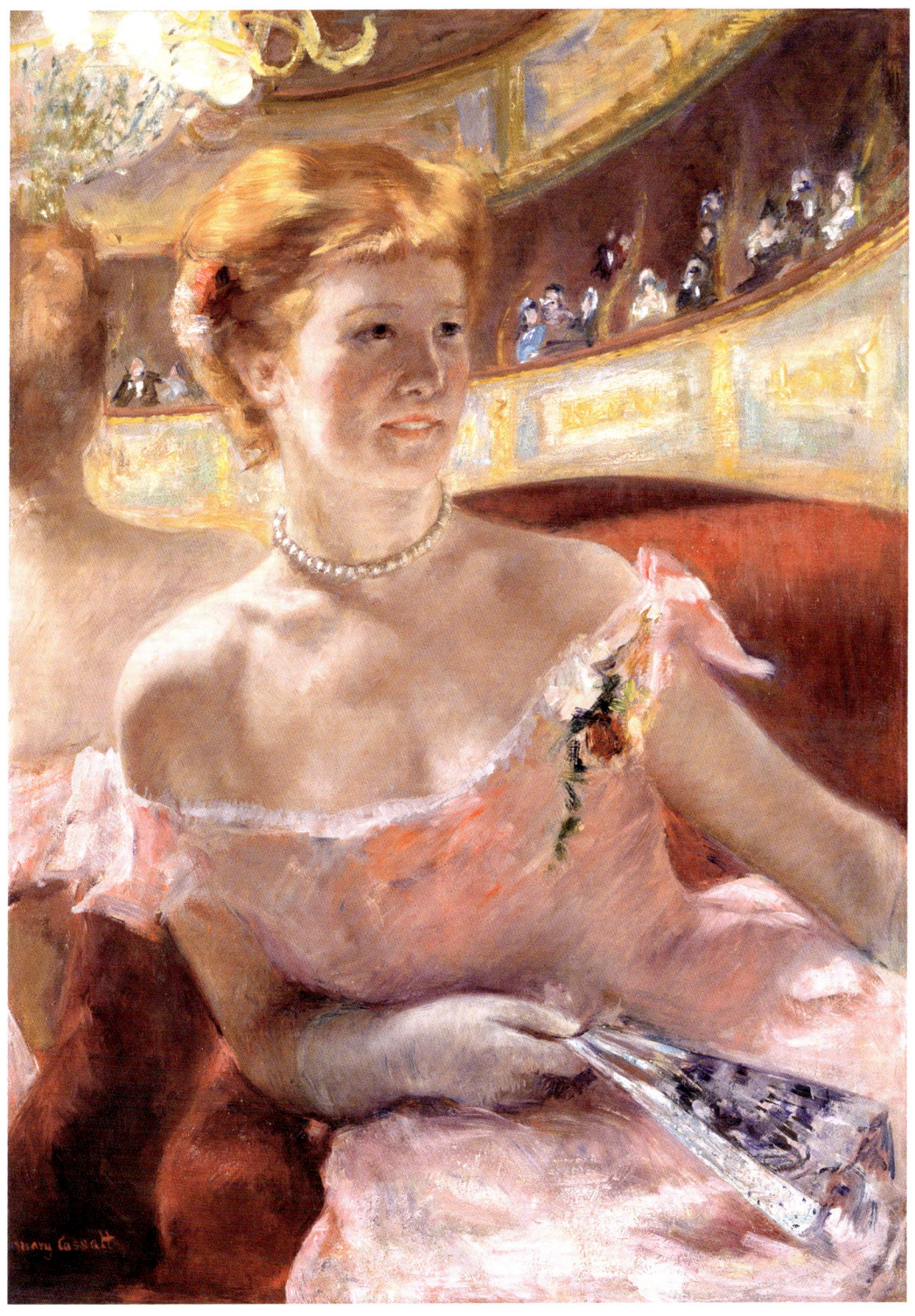

Mary Cassatt
Woman Sitting with a Child in Arms, c. 1890

Mary Cassatt depicted women at home, in the theatre, in the park, or on the bus, but never anywhere where it was inappropriate for a lady of respectable status to be, for example a café. She herself never took part in the evening conversations and discussions held by the Impressionists, for example at the Café Guerbois. Such a place was not decent for a lady of the respectable classes to be seen in. Thus it was an exclusively feminine bourgeois world that we see through Mary Cassatt's eyes. It is their own everyday sphere that she and Berthe Morisot depict with their portrayals of mother and child.

About the Impressionists Mary Cassatt wrote: "I … must as joint initiator of the Independent exhibition stick to my principles, our principles: no hanging committee, no medals, no awards. Our first exhibition was held in 1879 and was a protest against the official exhibitions, and not a union of artists pursuing the same stylistic line. Since then we have been called 'the Impressionists', a description which may apply to Monet, but is meaningless in connexion with the name Degas. Freedom is the greatest good in this world, and the liberation from the tyranny of a hanging committee is a goal worth fighting for, for no profession is so enslaved as ours."

Mary Cassatt focuses on the depiction of the child. The mother, whose back view is further concealed by the back of the chair, is hinted at only by the bun of dark hair and her white dress. The naked infant is looking at the beholder over its mother's shoulder. The washing bowl and jug, along with some other bathroom utensils in Cassatt's œuvre stress the mother's attention to the cleanliness of the child, and in a figurative sense, to its purity and innocence. The infant's pinkly shimmering skin seems to reflect the mother's warmth.

Cassatt's painting technique, which she developed during the 1880s, is worthy of note. The sketchiness of the depiction is underlined by the free, rapid brushstroke and the "unfinished" appearance of the painting. Parts of the canvas are left unpainted. We have the impression that the painter was reproducing a spontaneous, immediate impression and concentrating only on the essentials. In this work too, Mary Cassatt shows herself to be a master of red tones.

The Cradle (1872), Berthe Morisot's best-known work, which was shown at the first Impressionist exhibition in 1874, concentrates on the infant's mother, the artist's sister Edma, who has pushed back the semi-transparent muslin canopy over the cradle. Supporting her head on one hand, she is looking contemplatively at the child. Morisot here harmonizes the gestures of the individual persons: the child too has placed its hand against its head. And the curtain of the cradle finds its parallel in the lace curtain in the background of the room.

In this sensitive painting, Morisot plays with shades of white. There are reddish and yellowish whites in the cradle, and a more bluish white in the window. The limpid composition is marked by the vertical line between the curtain and the wall. It is supported by the diagonal, corresponding arrangement of dark and light. Composition and colouration are thus in a very balanced relationship.

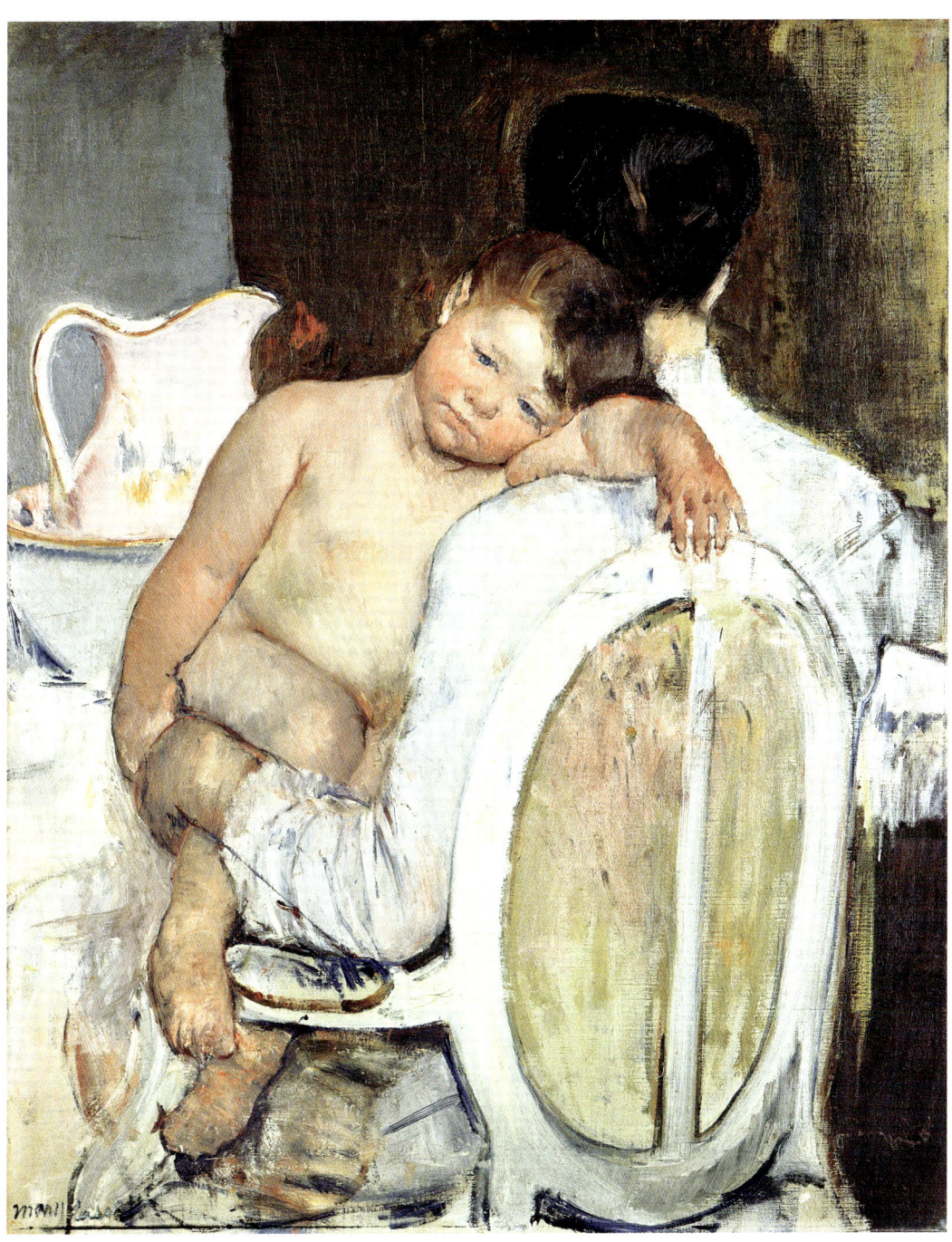

Woman Sitting with a Child in Arms, *c.* 1890
Oil on canvas, 81 x 65.5 cm (32 x 25¾ in.)
Museo de Bellas Artes de Bilbao

Edgar Degas
Dancer at Rest, c. 1879

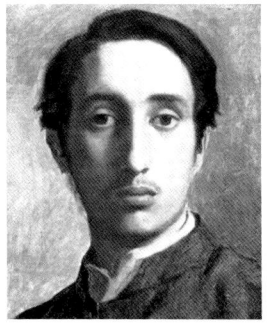

b. 1834 in Paris
d. 1917 in Paris

The name Degas is, for today's art-lovers, closely linked with his numerous depictions of ballerinas. Hundreds of paintings, pastels, prints and – as here – photographs, make ballerinas Degas' most frequently chosen motif. He was fascinated by the movement of dance and the atmosphere of the stage as an expression of contemporary city life. At the same time, the grace and elegance of the ballerinas was the result of constantly repeated training and disciplined instruction. Degas shows them practising and being taught, as well as their evening performances. Their "révérences" at the close, and the subsequent exhaustion, allowed a fascinated insight into their working lives. His ballerinas need to be seen in the context of Caillebotte's *The Floor Strippers* (ill. p. 45) or Monet's *Men Unloading Coal.*

Degas was extremely open to new techniques, which aroused both his curiosity and enthusiasm. Among the Impressionists he was probably the one who experimented the most and was always most receptive to innovations. In the late 1870s he discovered a passion for photography and modern printing technologies. In addition, he executed a number of sculptures of ballerinas and devoted one of his poems to one. Degas pursued an "uninhibited pleasure in experimentation, in the unusual and also in the planned coincidence". Ingres, the Neo-classicist artist of the first half of the 19th century, for whom Degas had a profound admiration, had also used methods derived from printing techniques. He made use of the possibility of reproducing his depictions back to front, as a mirror image. Degas now integrated this into his work too. Of many of his ballerina photographs, he made, alongside a normal positive print, also a negative print and a mirror-image print.

What Degas admired most of all about Ingres was his ability to use the outlines of the body to create an almost ornamental, two-dimensional depiction. The consequence was that Ingres' paintings did not always accord with anatomical realities, but rather with his aesthetic idea. Degas once said that Ingres' importance was that he "used the formal arabesque to escape from a style of drawing which was concerned simply and solely with the correctness of the proportions …" Degas took up where Ingres left off, and, especially towards the end of his life, showed the great importance he attached to the contours of the female body. The result was ornamental, arabesque-like forms, which were continued in the Art Nouveau of the early 20th century.

Degas sought for artistic expression in the various media of his age. Movement, music and dance form an unusual sequence in this context. In his poem *Ballerina* he plays with different levels of meaning. Cythera, the Greek island of Aphrodite, is a reference to Antoine Watteau's famous painting *The Embarkation for Cythera.* Degas makes an ironic comment on the aesthetic ideas of his age when the elegant movement of the dance on points becomes a clumsy jump by a frog and the beautiful dancing girl herself turns into an ugly frog.

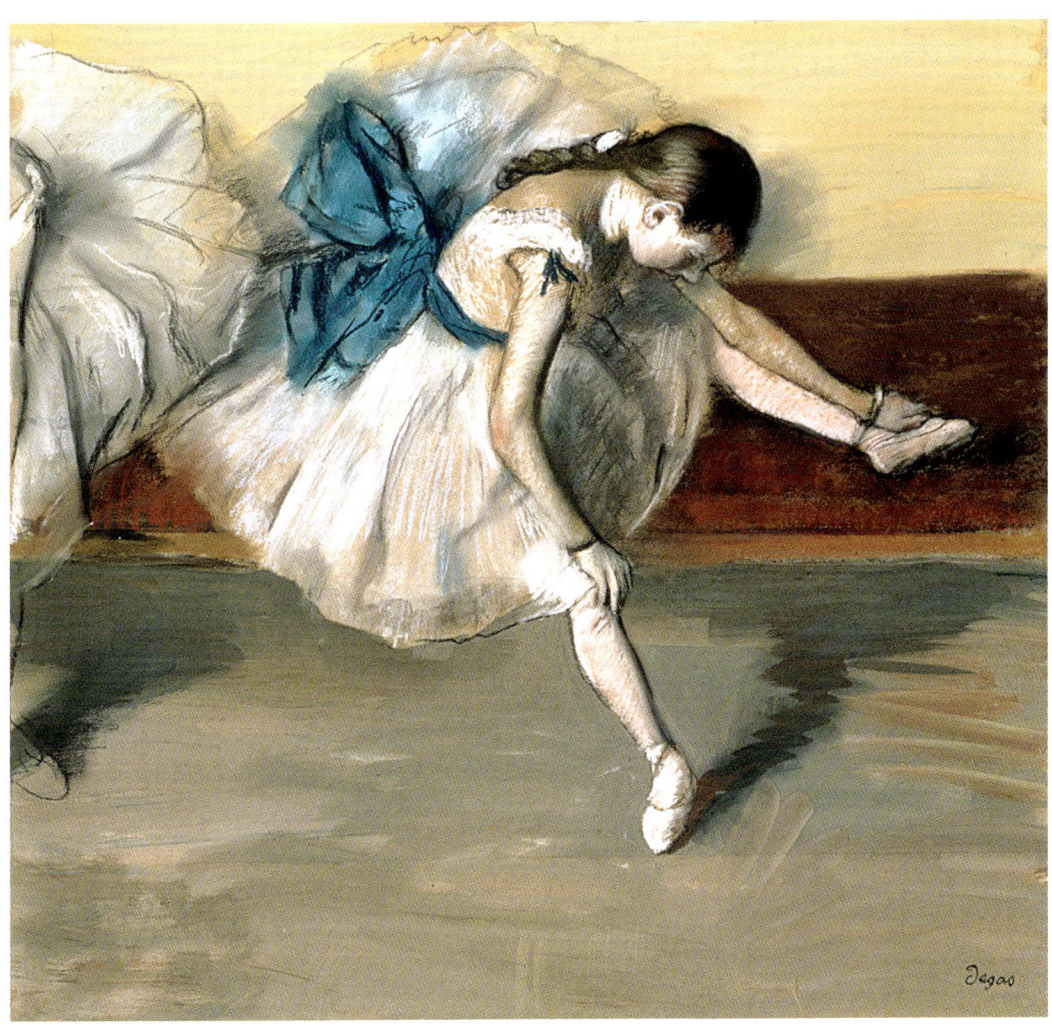

Dancer at Rest, c. 1879
Pastel and gouache on paper,
59 x 64 cm (23¼ x 25¼ in.)
Private collection

Edgar Degas
Absinthe, 1876

In 1876, when it was exhibited at the second Impressionist exhibition in Paris and the following winter in London, this picture bore the more harmless-sounding title *In a Café*. Degas depicts a woman and a man sitting next to each other, the woman with a glass of absinthe in front of her on the table, while the man, dressed in clothes that have seen better days, is holding a pipe. Among contemporary British art critics, the name *Absinthe* for this picture quickly caught on, obviously under the influence of a novel by Émile Zola. A well-known model, Ellen Andrée, who often worked for the Impressionist artists, and the engraver Marcellin Desboutin were the sitters here. They are depicted in the Café de la Nouvelle Athènes, a meeting-place for friends in the Impressionist circle.

Degas also depicted Desboutin as a pipe-smoker in an identical pose in a lithograph. Another painting executed the same year shows him together with their mutual friend Ludovic Lepic. A year earlier, Édouard Manet had completed a portrait of Desboutin. Manet's work *The Artist* (1875, Museu de Arte de São Paulo) shows Desboutin once again with a crushed hat pushed boldly to one side. The open white collar with a cravat loosely tied in a bow is a hallmark of all the pictures. It is only in these details that Degas keeps to Manet's original, but he turns this motif and composition into something quite different, because he does not centre the picture on Desboutin, who is placed right on the right-hand side of the picture, so much so, in fact, that he is cropped by the edge of the painting. The woman too, demoted in the same way to a marginal position, appears in some way to underline the impression of a spontaneous, immediate snapshot. The hurried brushstrokes hinting to a certain extent at clothing create the impression of a sketch.

The composition is determined by the oblique lines of the table edges and the chair back, between which the figures come across as captives. This emphatically asymmetric arrangement was inspired by Japanese woodcuts, which Degas admired. The artist makes bright light fall mercilessly and frontally on the wretchedness of the two figures, the dark shadows of their heads in the mirror seeming only to double their woe. On the table next to the woman Degas has placed a little Impressionist still-life: an empty bottle on a silver tray.

The absinthe-drinking woman has become a metaphor for the dark side of the modern age. She stands for loneliness and helplessness, the anonymity and harshness of modern city life. Shortly after the turn of the century, another modern painter, Pablo Picasso, painted the same symbolic figure a number of times. In his 1901 picture of an absinthe-drinking woman (St Petersburg, The State Hermitage Museum) he comes even closer to the woman, abandoning the detachment and aloofness still palpable in the picture by Degas. Picasso's absinthe-drinker is also sitting in a café, the framed mirror on the wall providing a muted reflection of the lights in the room. On the table stands a glass filled with the green liquor, next to an empty bottle. The reflections, the harsh strong light on the woman's face, and the dominating colours all point to the young Pablo Picasso's confrontation since the 1890s with Impressionism. Already in that decade, Picasso had studied the motifs and technique of the Impressionists.

Absinthe, 1876
Oil on canvas,
92 x 68 cm (36¼ x 26¾ in.)
Paris, Musée d'Orsay

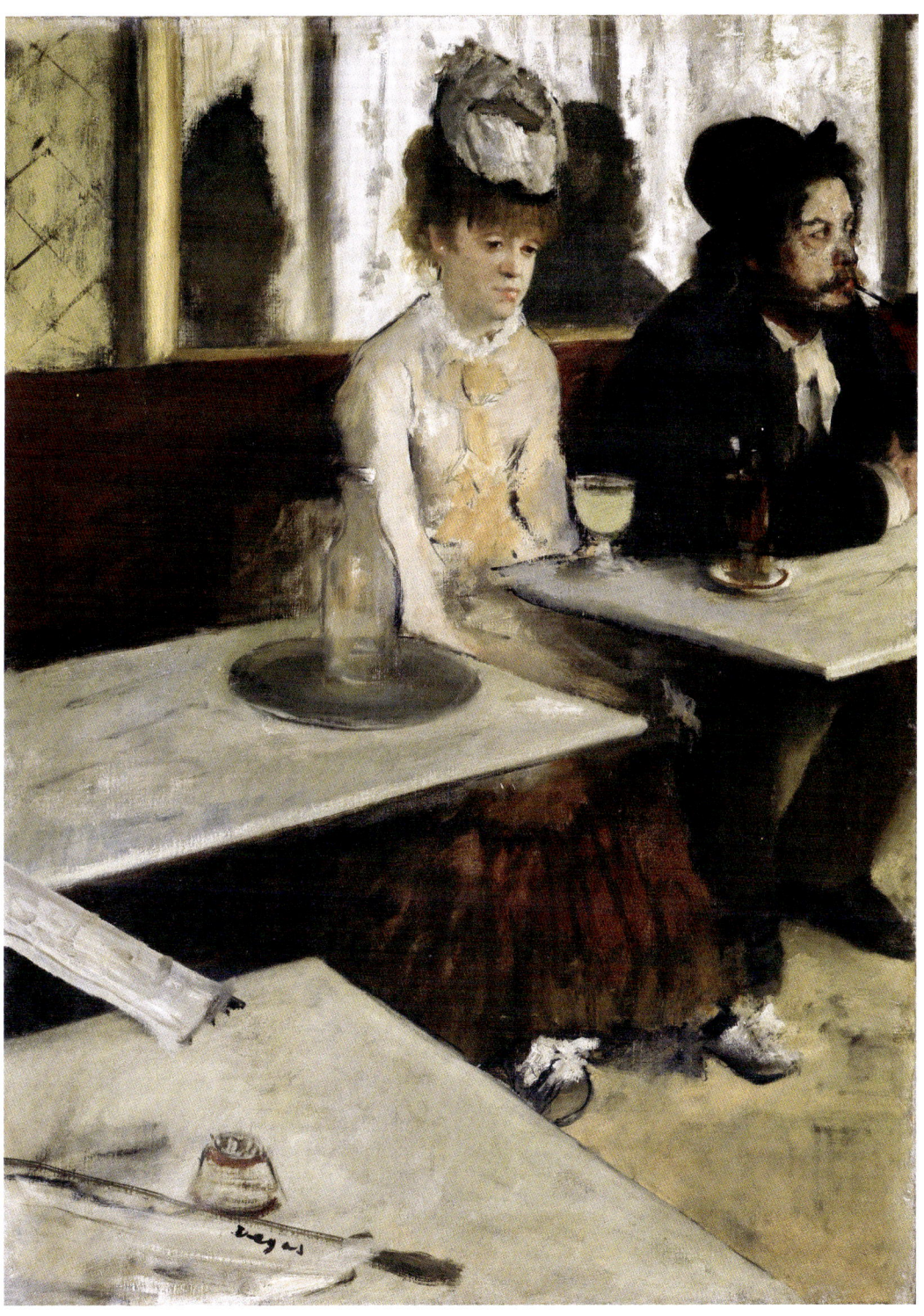

Vincent van Gogh
Portrait of Père Tanguy, 1887

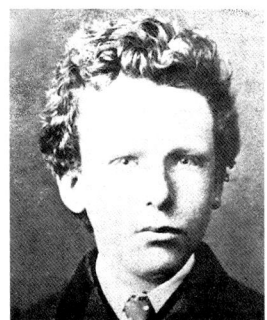

b. 1853 in Groot-Zundert,
The Netherlands
d. 1890 in Auvers-sur-Oise,
France

Van Gogh painted three different portraits of his paint dealer and friend Julien Tanguy, known to all the Impressionist artists who went in and out of his shop as "Père Tanguy". This last version dates from the winter of 1887. Tanguy was an important institution both for the Barbizon artists and for the Impressionists. After all, for impoverished artists he represented the only possibility of obtaining the materials they needed, for he was prepared to take their pictures in payment. In this way he also became the first collector of Cézanne's works. His shop thus became a rendezvous for the painters, and an exhibition room for their pictures, while he himself was a friend and father-figure, hence his nickname. "He's a droll, good-hearted fellow, and I often think of him," wrote van Gogh in a letter from Arles to his brother. "Don't forget to give him my regards … and tell him, if he needs pictures for his shop window, he can have some from here – in fact, the best." Tanguy thus had a considerable number of van Gogh's most magnificent works in his shop to sell on commission.

During the whole of his artistic activity from 1882 until his suicide in 1890, van Gogh worked with a "sensuous love of materials" and an existential urgency that reflected the existential urgency of the Impressionists before him. While Cézanne, Seurat and Pissarro slowed down the painting process in the 1880s, van Gogh accelerated it once more, and produced an incredible body of work in just a few years. "For I only have a lust for life when I work like a wild thing," he had once commented. This fast, spontaneous, immediate way of painting in a certain sense contributes to his work a strongly marked "Impressionist" aspect.

Van Gogh has composed a frontal portrait of the seated Père Tanguy, with his hands folded, a pose that he had seen in portraits by Rembrandt. The wall behind Père Tanguy is covered in Japanese woodcuts, which van Gogh had acquired cheaply from Siegfried Bing, the specialist for Japanese art in Paris. A depiction of the holy mountain, Mount Fuji, can be seen in two of van Gogh's portraits of Père Tanguy directly behind the sitter's head. The mountain comes across as a symbolic image of Tanguy's appearance and personality, above all of his dignity and humanity.

The painter Émile Bernard was close friends with both van Gogh and Gauguin. Van Gogh dreamed of a community of artists in his house in Arles. In their portraits of Père Tanguy, both van Gogh and Bernard used the divisionist method of the Neo-impressionists. They placed dots or lines in close proximity, and broke up the local colour in any one place into its individual colour components. Both artists placed their sitter in front of a wall and chose the two-dimension pictorial space which they so greatly admired in the Japanese woodcuts.

Although Bernard depicts Julien Tanguy from much closer up, van Gogh's portrait is more intensive and penetrating. He really has succeeded in representing reality more "intensely" through the use of colour.

Van Gogh later wrote to his brother Theo: "When I am old enough, I may become like Père Tanguy. Of course I can know nothing of our personal future. We only know that Impressionism will last."

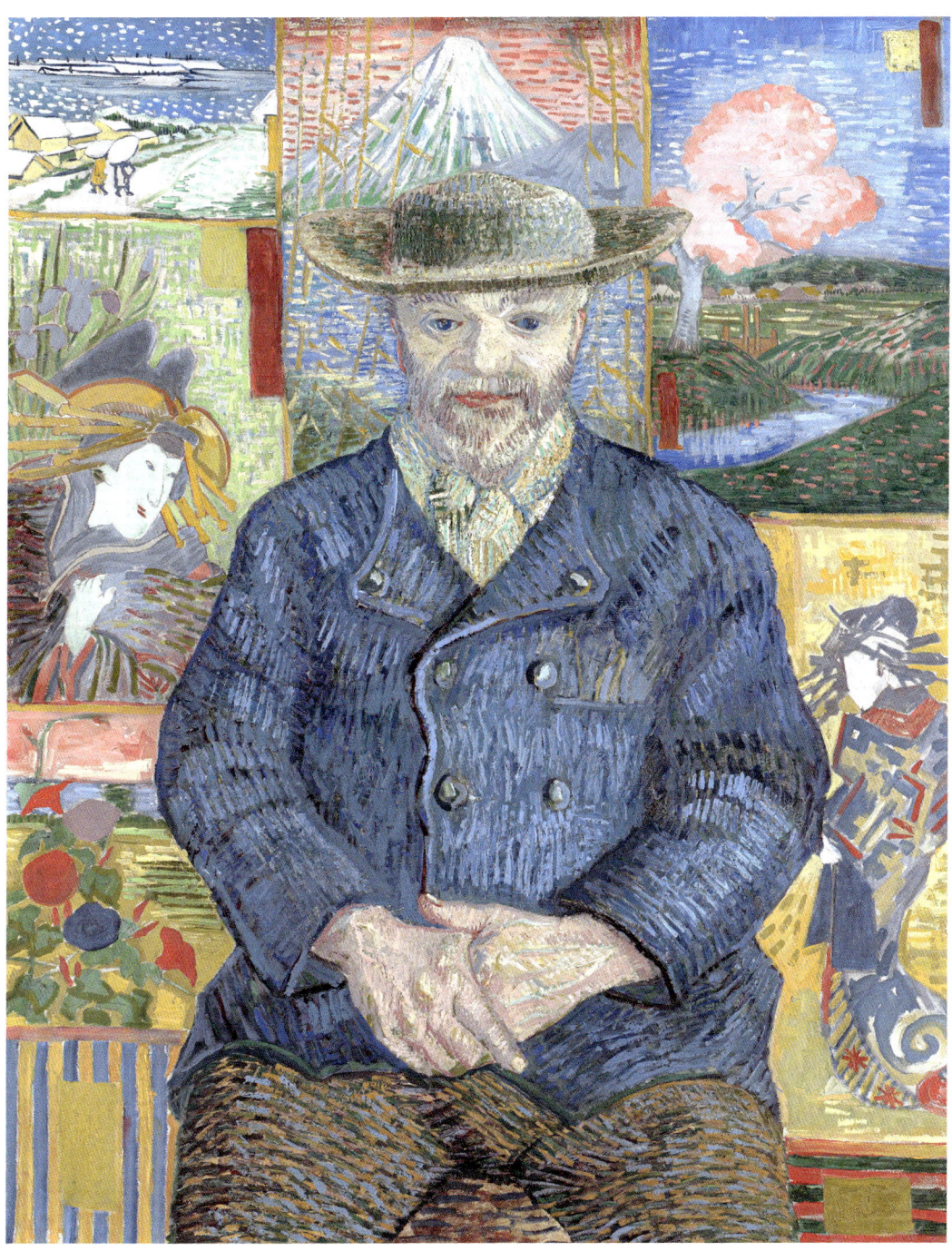

Portrait of Père Tanguy, 1887
Oil on canvas, 92 x 73 cm (36¼ x 28¾ in.)
Paris, Musée Rodin

Armand Guillaumin
Sunset at Ivry, 1873

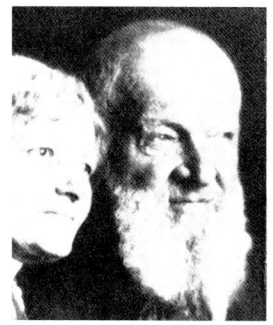

b. 1841 in Paris
d. 1927 in Orly, France

It is a splendid sunset at Ivry that Guillaumin has depicted here. The sky is glowing reddish-orange, which merges via green into blue. The strong colours are reflected in the water too, thus creating a marked contrast with the row of black trees which extends well above the line of the horizon on the right-hand edge of the picture. Daubigny and other painters of the Barbizon school also painted sunsets in the open air, depicting the glowing colours. But while Daubigny remained exclusively concerned with nature, Guillaumin depicts the advance of the modern city in the form of the smoking chimneys on the horizon. The radical changes in the Parisian suburbs brought about by new industrial complexes and the building of workers' estates are often reflected in Guillaumin's paintings.

Neither Armand Guillaumin nor one of his close friends of the 1870s, Paul Cézanne, whom he had met along with Pissarro at the Académie Suisse, were interested in the elegant life of the "grands boulevards".

Guillaumin was represented with this painting, *Sunset at Ivry,* and two more landscapes at the first Impressionist exhibition in 1874. Until 1886, he exhibited alongside the Impressionists several times. In 1873, while his fellow artists Pissarro, Monet and Sisley depicted the creeping industrialization of the towns along the Seine if anything "en passant", Guillaumin displayed a number of unprettified views of the squalid industrial suburbs.

The painting *The Seine by Ivry,* which dates from 1869, depicts the same view of the river with the town and its smoking factory chimneys in the background. This little oil, painted on panel, comes across as a study for the larger painting *Sunset at Ivry.* The sketchy presentation allows glimpses of the wooden panel between the greyish-brown and dirty-white clouds, so that the sky appears to be covered in ochre dabs. We have here a similar technique to that employed by Sisley in *The Watering Place at Marly-le-Roi* (ill. p. 93). This lowering impression has lifted in the paintings *Sunset at Ivry* and *Snow at Ivry.* In the latter paintings, the factories are so far away on the horizon that they are perceived as part of the riverscape.

The 1869 painting *The Seine by Ivry* found its way into the collection of the physician Dr Paul Gachet, who was friends with this artist as with the other Impressionists. He had treated Pissarro's mother in the 1860s, and, being very interested in art, maintained contact with her son. He owned a country house in Auvers, where Daubigny also lived, and used to invite artists to stay, among them Guillaumin, Cézanne and Pissarro.

Snow at Ivry was painted the same year and depicts a greyish-black building on the banks of the Seine, which in the dirty snow – it is hardly white any longer – makes a dreary impression. Only the reddish shimmer on the overcast sky betrays the low position of the sun. Nowhere is there fresh white snow with blue shadows, such as we find so enchanting in Monet's *The Magpie* or Pissarro's *Hoarfrost, Morning (Snow in Eragny)!* In Guillaumin's *Snow at Ivry* we see not a handsome magpie perched on a fence, but a sombrely clad man in a hat, plodding his lonely way through the cold.

In the same spirit as the other Impressionists, Guillaumin seeks to present the effects of the weather and the changing light, the shadows on snow or the fading of colours in the landscape as the sun sets. But he did not choose places of leisure and pleasure in the green countryside, but

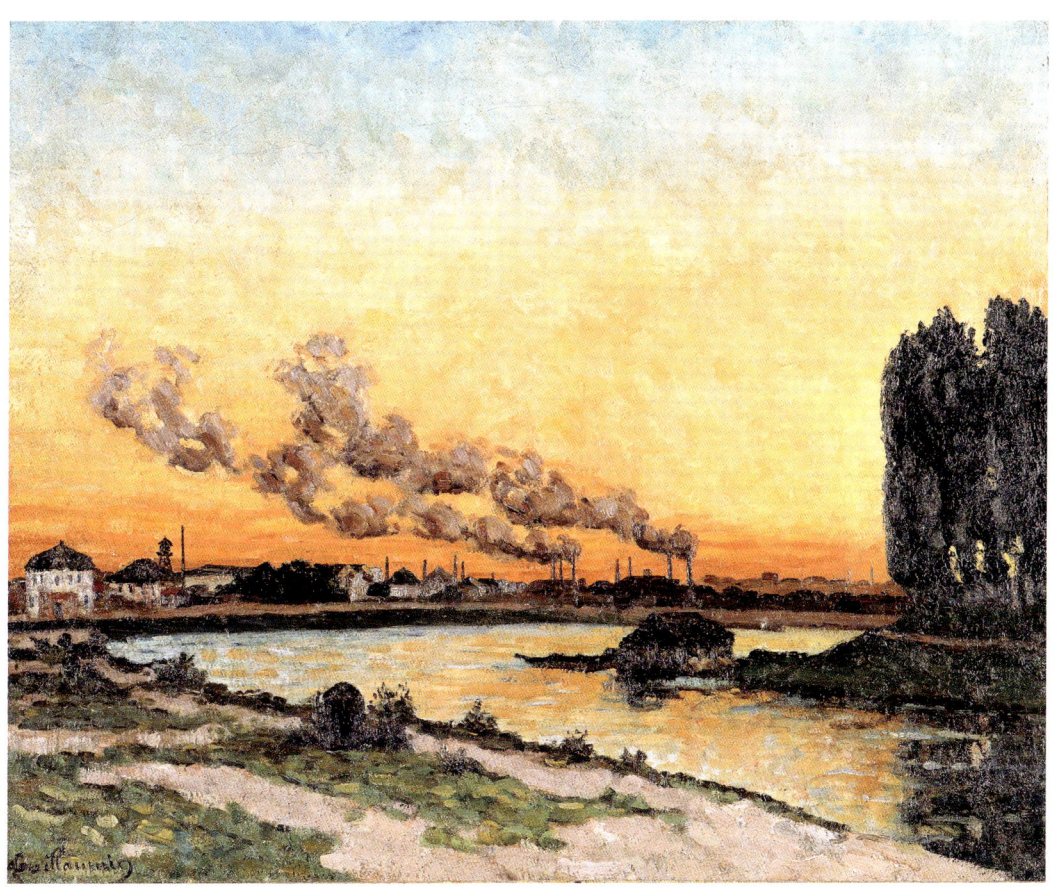

Sunset at Ivry, 1873
Oil on canvas, 65 x 81 cm (25½ x 32 in.)
Paris, Musée d'Orsay

rather industrial sites characterized by manual labour. Such themes were no more popular then than they are now – and it is doubtless not least for this reason that they have remained largely forgotten to this day.

Max Liebermann
The Birch Avenue in the Wannsee Garden, Looking West, 1918

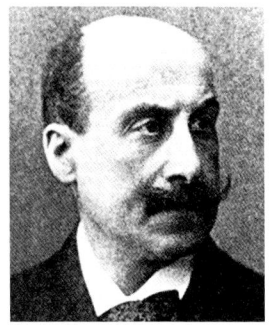

b. 1847 in Berlin
d. 1935 in Berlin

The year this view of the birch avenue in the garden of Liebermann's country house in the Wannsee suburb of Berlin was painted, the art critic Julius Elias published a volume titled *Max Liebermann zu Hause* (Max Liebermann at Home). The book contains a series of drawings and etchings of his family by Max Liebermann himself, and there is also a view of his summer retreat with its garden by the lake. The dedication of the book to 20 July 1917 is a reference to Max Liebermann's 70th birthday. The focus of the author was on Max Liebermann the private individual, for "here, he is a family man, and not just in that socially restricted sense … If his art imagines a power that explains the world – unphilosophically, unsensationally, untendentiously – then this little sketchbook also explains a world, HIS world, a kind of remote island … If he sought in his art intimacy above all, then he was perhaps at his most intimate in these unassuming 'occasional poems,' which paraphrase his view of the poetry of nature and of man so serenely and so purely." In Barbizon in the summer of 1874 Max Liebermann himself had explained his goals as follows: "I sought intimacy in the picture."

In his youth Liebermann had sojourned not just in Barbizon, but also for a time in Paris, but at that stage had not made any contact with the Impressionist artists. Instead, he oriented himself to Dutch painters such as Franz Hals and Rembrandt. Édouard Manet's garden pictures, a few of which Liebermann himself possessed, also probably had an influence on him.

Liebermann's painting of the *Birch Avenue in the Wannsee Garden, Looking West* is one example from a whole series of garden pictures which the artist executed at around this time. "One could paint hundreds of pictures here," he enthused.

Liebermann turned relatively late to Impressionism, long after it had passed its peak. In the *Birch Avenue in the Wannsee Garden* so many Impressionist aspects are addressed that one could justifiably talk of "German Impressionism". The dominance of light and colour in the treatment is articulated most strongly during this particular period of Liebermann's creative life.

Liebermann's garden by the Wannsee lake was laid out in the years after 1909. Monet's and Liebermann's gardens are totally different, Liebermann preferring a more austere layout of beds, which were bordered with box hedges. In Liebermann's garden, in which, unlike Monet, he never worked as a gardener himself, there were none of the meandering streams or luxuriantly blossoming hedges so beloved of Monet.

In his compositions, Liebermann always directed the gaze of the beholder across a number of flower beds in order to take account of the total geometric layout of the garden. The integration of the numerous birches is due to his "veneration of the local and of nature". The wooded Brandenburg landscape is thus integrated into the garden. Trees and hedges give rise to different scenarios, which allow a constant succession of new glimpses. The garden is depicted not just as a place of leisurely enjoyment, as an addition to the modern, urban lifestyle, but as a place of recuperation from the hectic life of the city. Sometimes someone is sitting reading on a bench or going for a walk, while a child is playing under the eye of the governess. In Liebermann's pictures, the yearning for idyll and tranquillity is palpable against the background of city life.

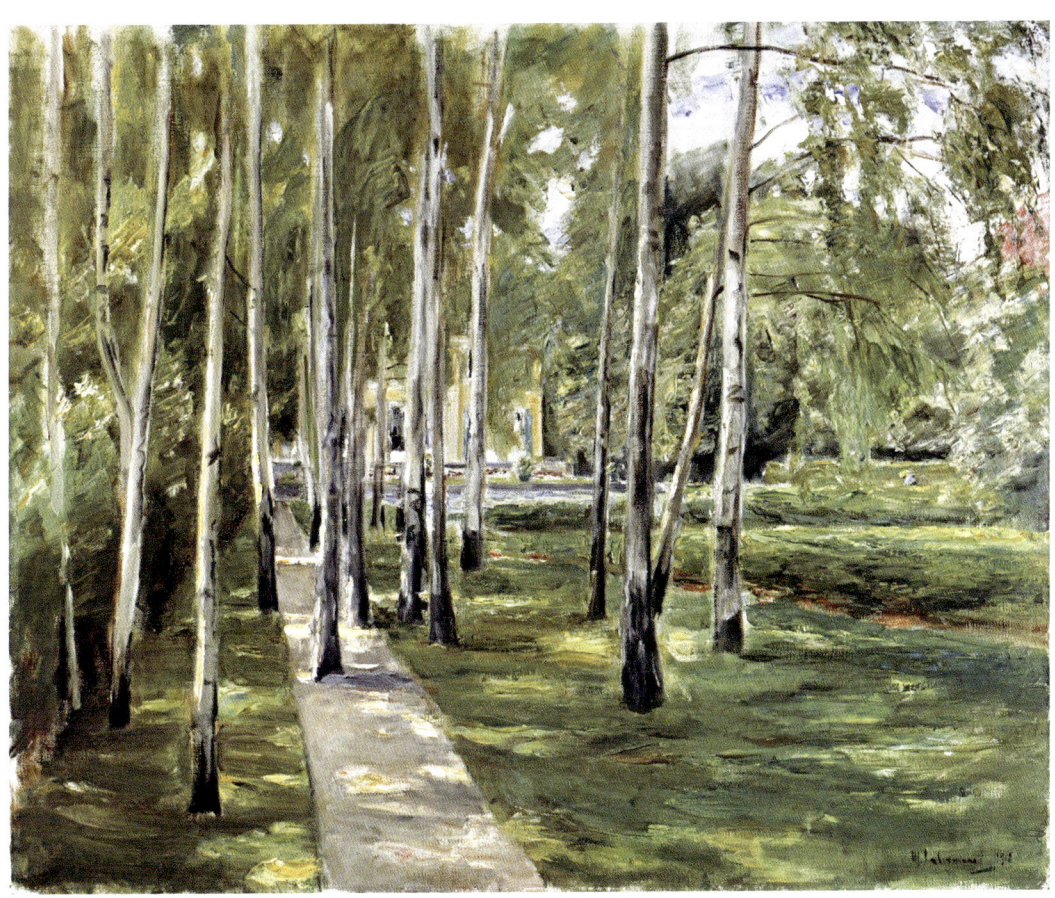

The Birch Avenue in the
Wannsee Garden, Looking West, 1918
Oil on canvas, 85.5 x 106 cm (33¾ x 41¾ in.)
Hanover, Niedersächsisches
Landesmuseum Hannover

Claude Monet
Le pont de l'Europe, Gare Saint-Lazare, 1877

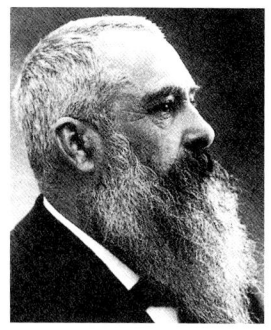

b. 1840 in Paris
d. 1926 in Giverny, France

"This year Monet has exhibited magnificent interior views of stations. In them one can hear the hissing of the arriving trains, one sees the steam pouring out and being stirred up in the spacious train shed. This is painting's place today … Just as their fathers discovered the poetry of the woods and rivers, our artists today must discover the poetry of railway stations."

Émile Zola, the great French writer and friend of the Impressionists, wrote enthusiastically of the seven station motifs that Monet displayed at the third Impressionist exhibition in 1877. Of the total of 250 paintings exhibited, very few were sold. During these decades, the railway station and the railway as such had become the symbol of speed and mobility, indeed of modern life. Édouard Manet, Gustave Caillebotte and many other artists devoted themselves to this motif. In about two months Monet painted twelve views of the Gare Saint-Lazare and the neighbouring bridge, the Pont de l'Europe. He himself lived with his family very close to the bridge and the station in the rue Moncey. The hoped-for artistic recognition was some time in coming, and Monet found himself in financial difficulty. His friend Renoir wrote in relation to this period: "Monet stood above all the changes and chances of life. He put on his best clothes, arranged the lace of his cuffs, and, casually swinging his cane with the gold pommel, handed over his visiting card to the director of the Western Railway line at the Gare Saint-Lazare. The official at the door stiffened, and led him in immediately. The lofty personage asked the visitor to take a seat, whereupon the latter introduced himself with great simplicity: 'I am the painter Claude Monet.'"

Monet was interested above all in the light effects produced by the steam and smoke. That's why he depicted the locomotives going up and down in the train shed and under the Pont de l'Europe. In this way he produced his own poetic image of modernity. The fact that it was a staged picture did not bother him overmuch. Monet's station pictures are neither authentic, spontaneous impressions nor exclusively open-air painting. His works are the result of precise observation and construction, and not at all as snapshot-like as they appear.

Numerous preliminary sketches for the paintings of the Gare Saint-Lazare and the Pont de l'Europe have been preserved, and they show how considered and unspontaneous the paintings were. Monet's painting *Le pont de l'Europe, Gare Saint-Lazare* lives from the tense contrast between the austere geometric form of the stone and iron bridge, and the moving smoke and steam dissolving in the hazy sky. The locomotive pushing into the painting brings a targeted movement from left to right and thus crosses the diagonal formed by the bridge and the ensuing canyon of the street. The crossing area is additionally emphasized by the two pillars of the bridge. Monet's art of composition is particularly apparent here.

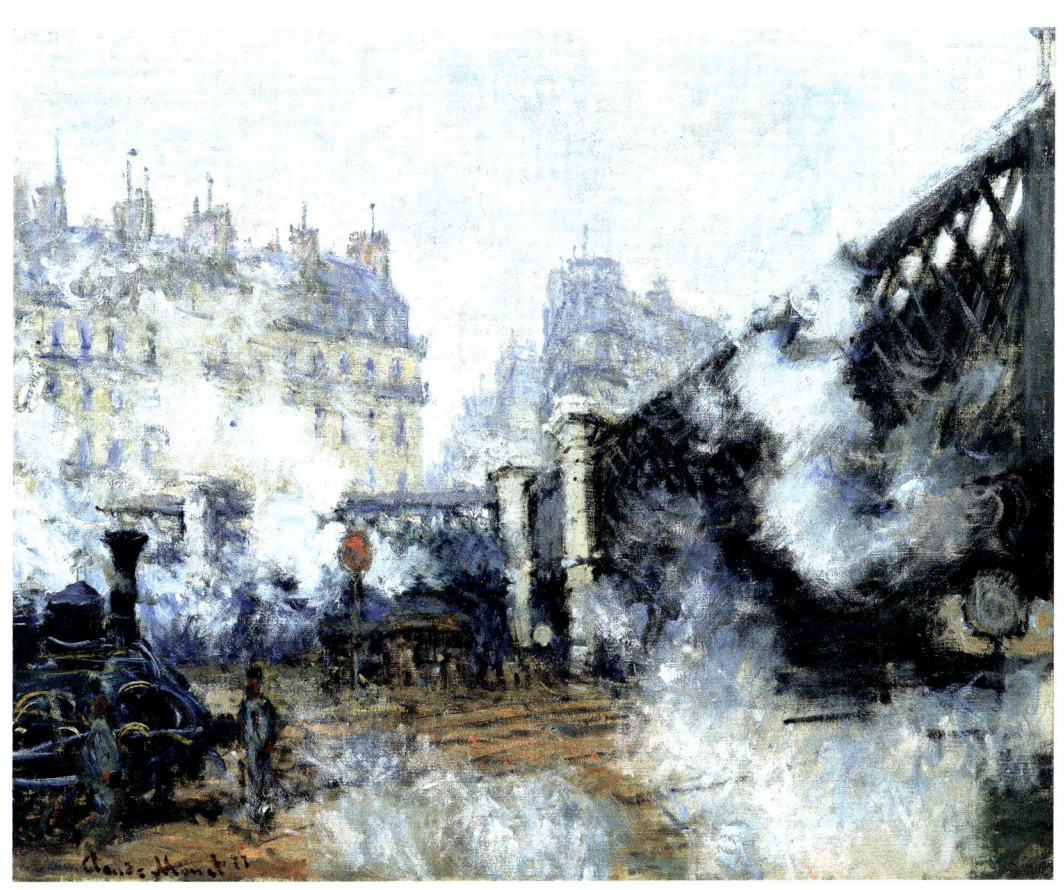

Le pont de l'Europe,
***Gare Saint-Lazare**, 1877
Oil on canvas, 64 x 81 cm (25¼ x 32 in.)
Paris, Musée Marmottan Monet

Claude Monet
Monet's Garden at Vétheuil, 1881

Claude Monet often moved house in the course of his life. But there was only a garden in those houses where he stayed for any length of time: in Argenteuil, Vétheuil and later in Giverny. Monet's famous garden in Giverny often leads us to forget that his concern with gardens and flowers did not begin there. As early as the mid 1860s, when Monet painted his first still-life with flowers, he wrote to his friend Bazille: "There are at the moment some very beautiful flowers … why don't you paint some too, I think it's an excellent thing."

Such "excellent things" sold well in those days – an important aspect in view of Monet's chronic shortage of money. Between 1882 and 1885, the art dealer Durand-Ruel ordered 36 still-lifes from Monet, some of them intended for his private apartment. The Monets had lived since the autumn of 1878 in Vétheuil, a small village on the Seine to the west of Paris. The decidedly rural ambience provided a welcome contrast to the hustle and bustle of the city. Monet reported enthusiastically of the "enchanting surroundings", which he depicted in *Plum Trees in Blossom in Vétheuil* and *Poppy Field near Vétheuil* (1879, Zurich, Foundation E. G. Bührle Collection). Above all his 1881 picture *Field of Wheat* (Cleveland Museum of Art) displays the saturated colours of the broad plain of the Seine in high summer.

Monet's second son and youngest child was six months old when his wife Camille fell seriously ill; she died a year later, in September 1879. Alice Hoschedé, the former wife of Ernest Hoschedé, a friend of Monet's, had moved in as Camille's nurse. She brought the six children from her first marriage into the Monet household, and later became Monet's second wife.

A journalist once asked Monet about his studio in Vétheuil, and Monet answered: "My studio! But I never had one, and I don't understand how someone can shut themselves in a room – maybe to draw, but not to paint." Nonetheless, Monet did not just follow the Impressionist ideal of "plein air", but also sometimes withdrew to his studio to work. In Vétheuil, it is true, his studio was, on account of the large number of people living in the house, confined to a small room in the attic.

The garden lay right next to the Seine, falling away to the river. A flight of steps led from the house to an orchard on the bank. The Seine here was polluted by the sewage of the city of Paris, which was discharged at Asnières, but as a result full of nutrients, which favoured luxuriant vegetation.

In four paintings, Monet chose the perspective from the lower section of lawn with the steps as the central axis of the picture. The view of the steps, with the giant sunflowers in bloom and the red gladioli in blue-and-white flowerpots allowed him to integrate an energetically rising movement into his arrangement. The gaze of the beholder automatically follows the steps upwards and is then led on with the help of the chimney, which is outlined against the sky as a continuation of the same line, ending only just short of the edge of the picture. Precisely on this line, standing at the foot of the steps, is the youngest inhabitant of the house, the four-year-old Jean-Pierre Hoschedé.

This picture also reflects the comment of Émile Zola: "In the fields, Claude Monet prefers an English park to a bit of forest. He likes finding traces of people everywhere. … Like a genuine Parisian, he prefers Paris to the countryside, he is incapable of painting a landscape without introducing a few well-dressed ladies and gentlemen."

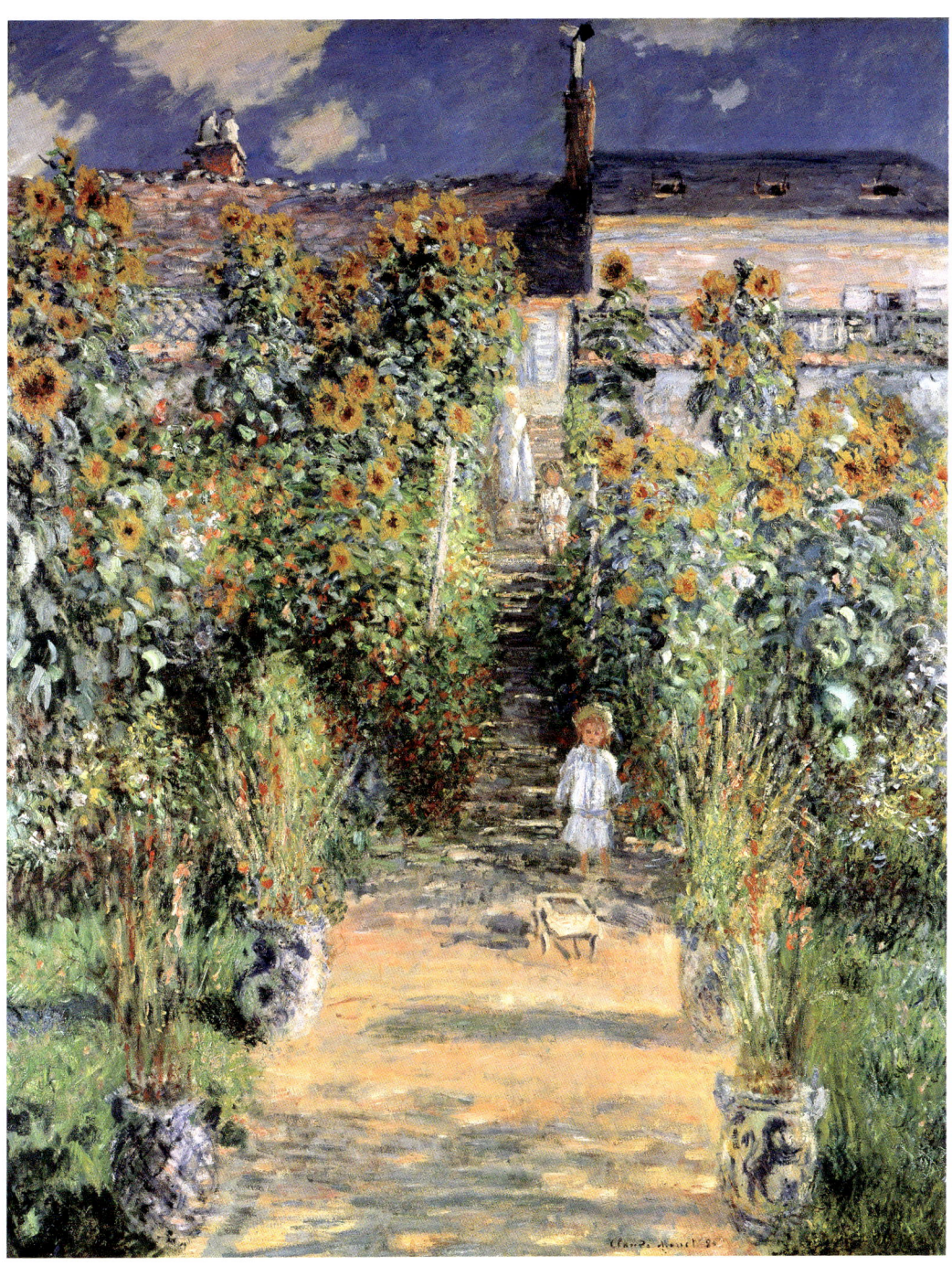

Monet's Garden at Vétheuil, 1881
Oil on canvas, 151.5 x 121 cm (59¾ x 47¾ in.)
Washington, D.C., National Gallery of Art,
Ailsa Mellon Bruce Collection

Berthe Morisot
Psyche, 1876

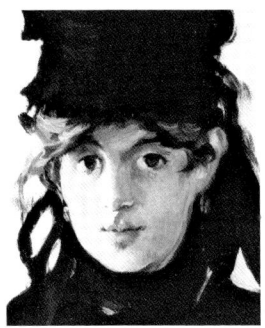

b. 1841 in Bourges, France
d. 1895 in Paris

Édouard Manet
**Berthe Morisot with a Bouquet
of Violets** (detail), 1872
Oil on canvas,
55.5 x 40.5 cm (22 x 16 in.)
Paris, Musée d'Orsay

Of the eight paintings that Berthe Morisot completed in 1876, four of the paintings show a woman at her toilet. Of these, she only gave one a title, namely *Psyche,* a painting that goes beyond a merely objective identification of the motif. Berthe Morisot exhibited the canvases *Psyche* and *Young Woman Powdering her Face* (1877, Paris, Musée d'Orsay) at the 1877 Impressionist exhibition. On this occasion Renoir and Caillebotte expressed their appreciation of the artist by writing: "We count ourselves fortunate in the thought that you wish to participate as usual."

Young Woman Powdering her Face was bought by the collector and patron Ernest Hoschedé and later auctioned together with the rest of his Impressionist collection. Mary Cassatt took the opportunity to purchase the painting, which she doubtless especially liked in view of the closeness of the motif to her own work.

Morisot's *Psyche* shows a young woman looking at herself in a large mirror. As the mirror is evidently placed on a wall between two windows, the scene is fully illuminated, indeed flooded with light. The woman is submerged in her contemplation of herself. She is opening a fastening on the back of her corset, while one sleeve is already slipping over her shoulder. The brushstrokes are very loose. Dabbed and dotted shapes hint at a carpet-pattern, while the sofa in front of the back window, and the mirror itself, are equally lacking in sharpness. The tall frame of the mirror, which is cropped by the top edge of the picture, provides a "picture within a picture", recalling Degas' depictions of ballerinas.

With the title *Psyche* Morisot makes reference to the classical myth of Amor and Psyche, whose episodes were depicted time and again over the centuries. The extensive reception-history of this myth always saw a more profound meaning beneath the surface of this ancient fairy tale. The 19th-century Psyche, whose own symbol was a butterfly, was seen first and foremost as the symbol of the immortal soul. This soul, which underwent metamorphoses just like a butterfly, was often depicted as a young woman with butterfly wings. In Morisot's painting we can see a hint of this in the position of the arms. Morisot's *Psyche* does not, however, come across as a figure from classical mythology. The protagonist is, rather, a contemporary who is questioning her reflection. Nor is there any trace of Amor, her classical lover.

Certainly though, the image of the soul whose fate is closely tied up with the joys and sorrows of love was particularly applicable to Berthe Morisot at this time. In 1874 she had married Eugène Manet, the younger brother of Édouard, and thus embarked on a new phase in her life. Her attempts at combining marriage and, later, motherhood with her career proved difficult. In 1890 she recorded in her diary: "The truth is that our value lies in feeling, in intuition, in our gaze, which is more subtle than that of men. We can achieve something, provided we do not spoil it all through affectedness, pedantry and sentimentality. … I should like to fulfil my duty [to my work] until I die; I wish the others wouldn't make it so difficult for me."

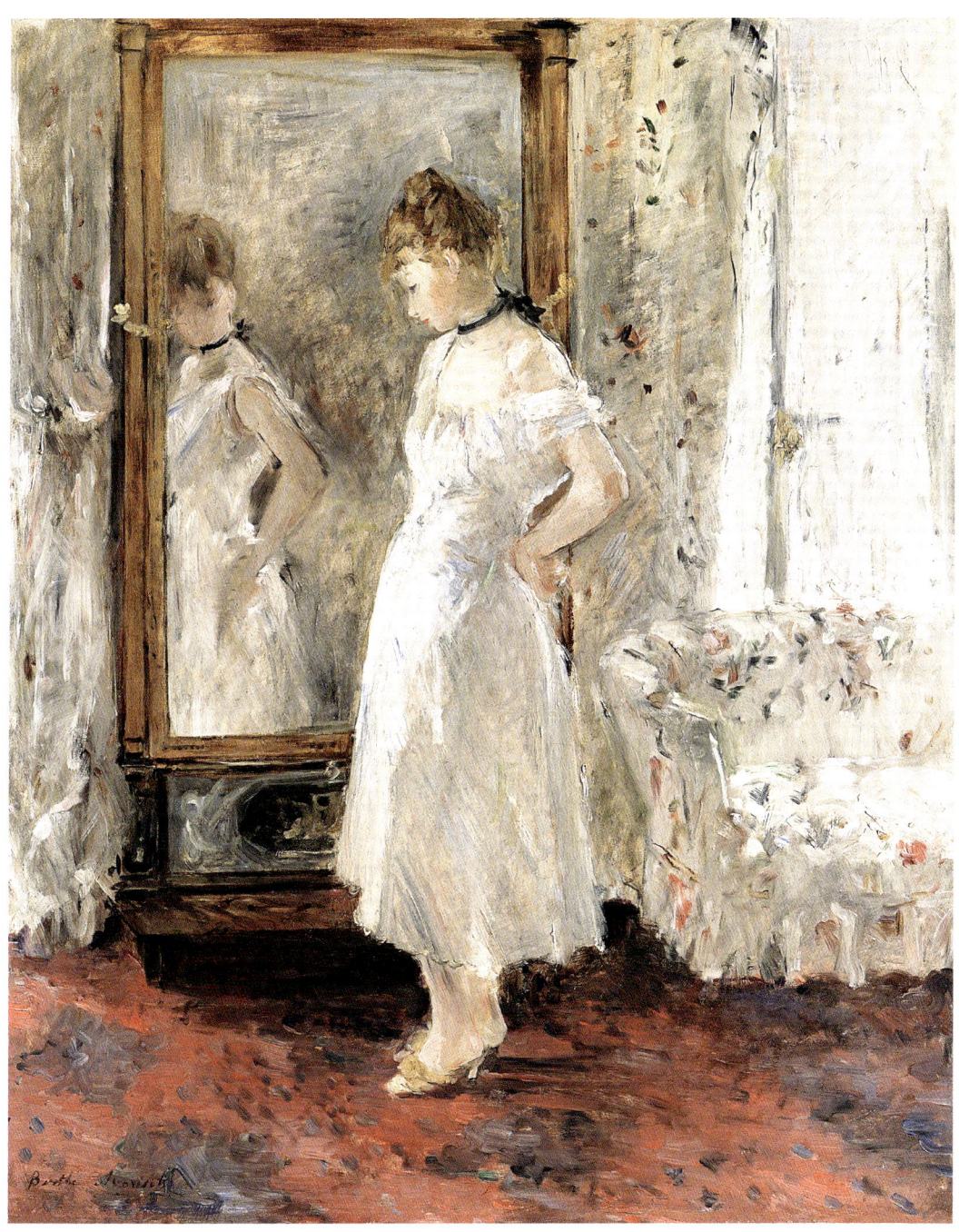

Psyche, 1876
Oil on canvas, 65 x 54 cm (25½ x 21¼ in.)
Madrid, Museo Thyssen-Bornemisza

Giuseppe de Nittis
Flirt, 1874

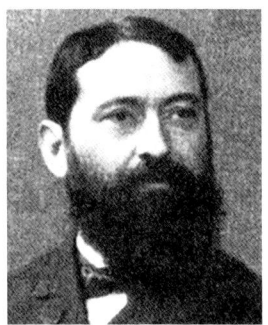

b. 1846 in Barletta, Italy
d. 1884 in St.-Germain-en-Laye,
France

Born in southern Italy, Giuseppe de Nittis came to Paris in 1867. He quickly became a familiar face on the Parisian art scene. He succeeded in interesting two reputable Paris art dealers. Franz Reitlinger was the first to conclude a contract with him, and at first De Nittis had to bow to his will, hence the so-called costume paintings, which were "en vogue" at the time. In 1871 de Nittis changed to the firm of Goupil & Cie.

De Nittis turned to landscape painting, spending several weeks in southern Italy with his friend Gustave Caillebotte. Already there he developed a decidedly spatial approach in his compositional technique. The strong, space-creating lines influenced other artists, not least Caillebotte in his painting *Le Pont de l'Europe* by the Gare Saint-Lazare. Van Gogh, too, found the treatment of space so remarkable that in 1875 he made a drawing of De Nittis' painting of Westminster Bridge in London.

Only once – in 1874 – did De Nittis take part in an Impressionist exhibition, being represented with five paintings. Renoir, who did not think De Nittis should have been admitted, considering him too conservative and his art purely commercial, had hung his works in very unfavourable positions. When the Italian was awarded the order of the "Légion d'honneur" in 1878 for his services to art, he also had to endure harsh criticism from his friend Degas, who denounced him as "bourgeois".

Flirt is one of many paintings by De Nittis that depict the Parisians at the races. Unlike Degas, who was more interested in the movements of the horses and the gesticulations of the jockeys, in all these De Nittis put the focus of his composition squarely on the spectators.

Thus also in *Flirt*. Anecdotally, the picture describes the goings-on on the fringes of the main action. A young couple in the foreground have remained seated while the remaining spectators have left the shady seats. The scene is embedded in the cheerful atmosphere of a Sunday race-meeting, while at the same time the two persons are so isolated from the crowd that the narrative concentrates entirely on them. The broad tree trunk on the left-hand side of the picture marks the foreground, which is cast in the shade of the foliage. The sunny background is marked out by a row of posts. The spatial perspective runs along an energetic diagonal from front left to back right. It corresponds to the gaze of the flirting couple towards the two women who are strolling by on the right-hand edge of the picture.

Typically, De Nittis has not given us a photographically exact reproduction, but rather reinforces the poetic character of a scene. He was working for a balance between authenticity and poetry, which was sometimes called "poetic realism".

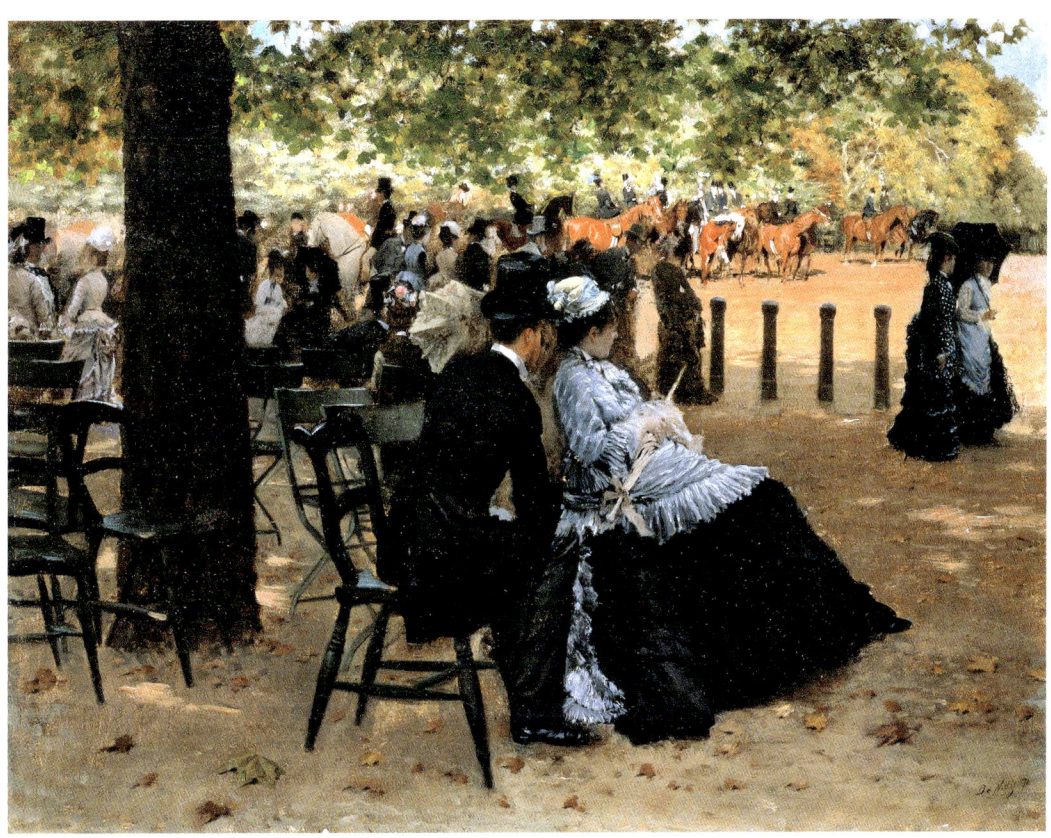

Flirt, 1874
Oil on canvas, 33 x 43 cm (13 x 17 in.)
Private collection

Camille Pissarro
Hoarfrost, 1873

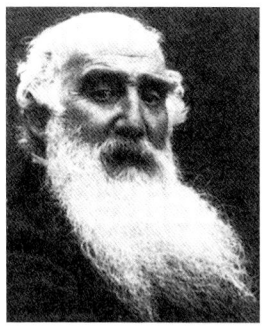

b. 1830 in Charlotte-Amalie,
St Thomas
d. 1903 in Paris

In 1866 Camille Pissarro moved with his family to near Pontoise. Some 30 kilometres to the west of Paris on the banks of the Oise, he found rural scenes and fresh motifs, such as the *Hillside of the Hermitage, Pontoise* (ill. p. 16). Pissarro and his friends painted numerous landscapes in the region. With Cézanne in particular, Pissarro worked together a great deal at this period. In October 1873 the Pissarros moved to the rue de l'Hermitage in Pontoise. Pissarro painted a whole series of works to familiarize himself with the immediate surroundings, one such work being *Hoarfrost*. The painting was shown at the first Impressionist exhibition in 1874, which was violently panned by the art critics. Pissarro reacted by saying: "The critics are tearing us to shreds, accusing us of learning nothing. I'm returning to my work, that's better than reading [reviews] that teach us nothing."

Pissarro understood his artistic work as a learning process. His predilection was for tapering paths in the landscape. His works are not narrative: they depicting not events, but states. The views come across as unspectacular, as though the motif were randomly chosen. *Hoarfrost* shows a broad ascending path lined on either side by fields. A country-dweller with a bundle of brushwood on his back and a stick in his hand is walking up the path. Maybe Pissarro was thinking of Millet's depictions of figures gathering firewood.

Pissarro has placed the line of the horizon very high, so that the hill appears to be relatively steep. The individual bare trees, the haystacks on the horizon and the vanishing path generate a hilly, lonely landscape. Pissarro painted motifs like this time and again, not least in his graphic work *Rain*. What makes *Hoarfrost* and *Rain* particularly interesting are the various lines and diagonals that determine the structure of the picture. *Hoarfrost* works with a path, crossed by long, dark shadows, running into the depth of the pictorial space. The shadow-lines stretch across the whole landscape and in the right foreground of the picture they form a grid with the furrows of the ploughed field. *Hoarfrost* is distinguished in particular by the geometric experiments that Pissarro integrated into his works at this period.

The connoisseur Théodore Duret wrote to Pissarro: "You have … a profound inner feeling for nature and you handle the brush powerfully, so that a picture by you is something absolutely definitive … pursue your own road, that of rural nature. You will travel a new road, just as broad and lofty as any master." Pissarro replied: "I would like you to know that I have been thinking for a long time about what you say to me. What prevented me for so long from directly depicting nature was quite simply the availability of models, not just for painting the picture, but also for studying the subject seriously. As for the rest, I will not hesitate to try it. It will be very hard, because you should know that these pictures cannot always be painted directly in front of nature, but only after it."

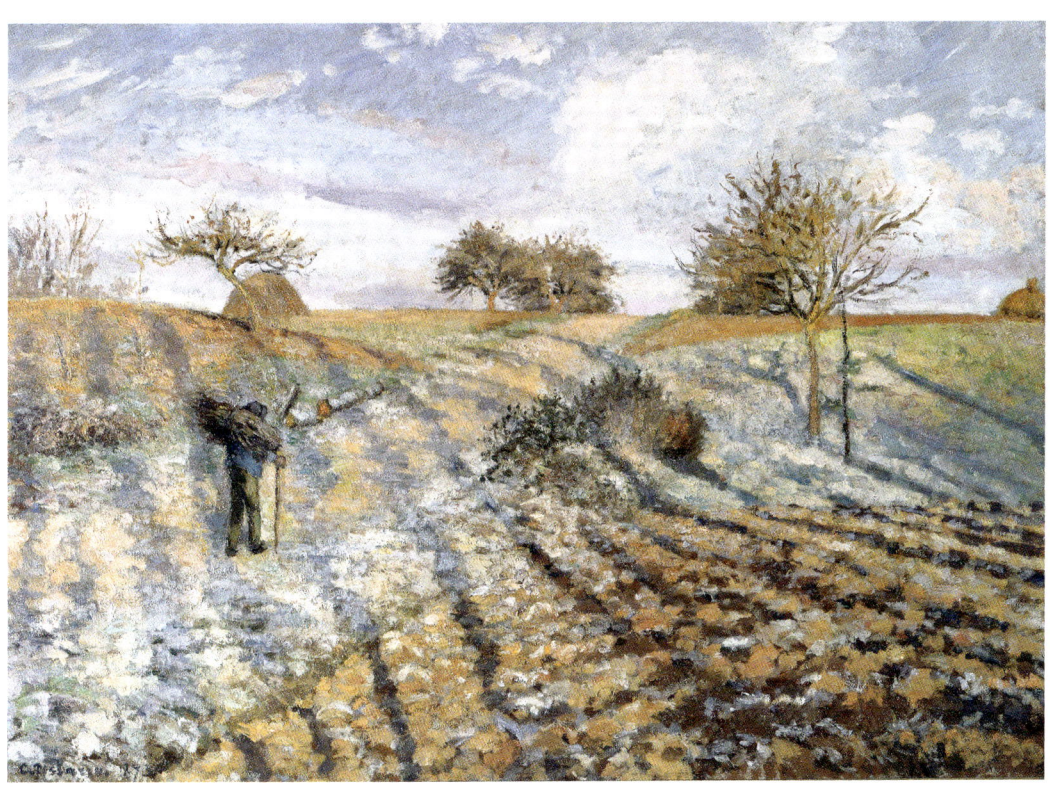

Hoarfrost, 1873
Oil on canvas, 65 x 93 cm (25½ x 36½ in.)
Paris, Musée d'Orsay

Camille Pissarro
The Pork Butcher, 1883

Pissarro had been painting market scenes such as we see in *The Pork Butcher* since 1881. *The Pork Butcher* is accompanied by *Potato Market in Pontoise* (1882), *Poultry Market in Gisors* (1889) and *Grain Market in Pontoise* (1893). All these paintings depict numbers of people trading, chatting, debating, tasting, buying and selling. Pissarro reported on his work in July 1883: "I have not worked much outside this season, the weather was inclement, and I am pursued by the thought of painting particular figure-pictures with whose conception I am struggling. I make a kind of little cartoon, and when I've thought the thing through properly, I set to work. Nini [Pissarro's niece] sat for me as the 'charcutière' in the wind on the Place du Grand Martroy, and I hope it exudes a certain juiciness. The problem is the background. We'll see."

The composition was, then, well thought through, and Pissarro shows himself, in humorous fashion, concerned to express a commonality between the goods and the woman selling them. Both the person and the ham she's selling should exhibit a "certain juiciness". The harmonization of colour in red and white shades, in any case, right down to the butcher's clothes, is successful. With the hustle and bustle of the market scenes Pissarro returned to a theme which had already occupied him at the outset of his artistic career.

Camille Pissarro was born on the island of St Thomas in what was then the Danish Antilles and now forms part of the United States Virgin Islands. The Jewish Pissarro family came from southern France to the capital of the Danish Antilles to engage in the flourishing trade between Europe, South America and the United States. Camille worked in his father's business for some years, and consequently had firsthand experience of commercial life. He had been an enthusiastic draughtsman since his youth, and his first motifs were vibrant markets and the market women calling their wares.

His birthplace, his Jewish ancestry and the experiences of his youth all meant that Pissarro lived in opposition to the spirit of the age, and refused to bow to social or artistic conventions. His capacity for prolonged resistance to social pressure and to organize a group of artists to hold joint exhibitions made him the core of the Impressionist movement. His background also contributed to his political attitude. Pissarro was "an anarchist through and through". His depictions of peasant life have, then, nothing to do with any purported socialist ideals. Pissarro was not a precursor of "Socialist Realism". Maybe it was only logical that in the 1880s, when the Impressionist movement entered a crisis, he should return to the motifs of his youth and thus to the wellspring of his strength. The artistic views of his Impressionist friends were becoming gradually incompatible and the joint exhibitions came to an end in 1886. What Pissarro wrote about this can be understood as his motto: "As far as I'm concerned, I will stick by my right to pursue my path freely."

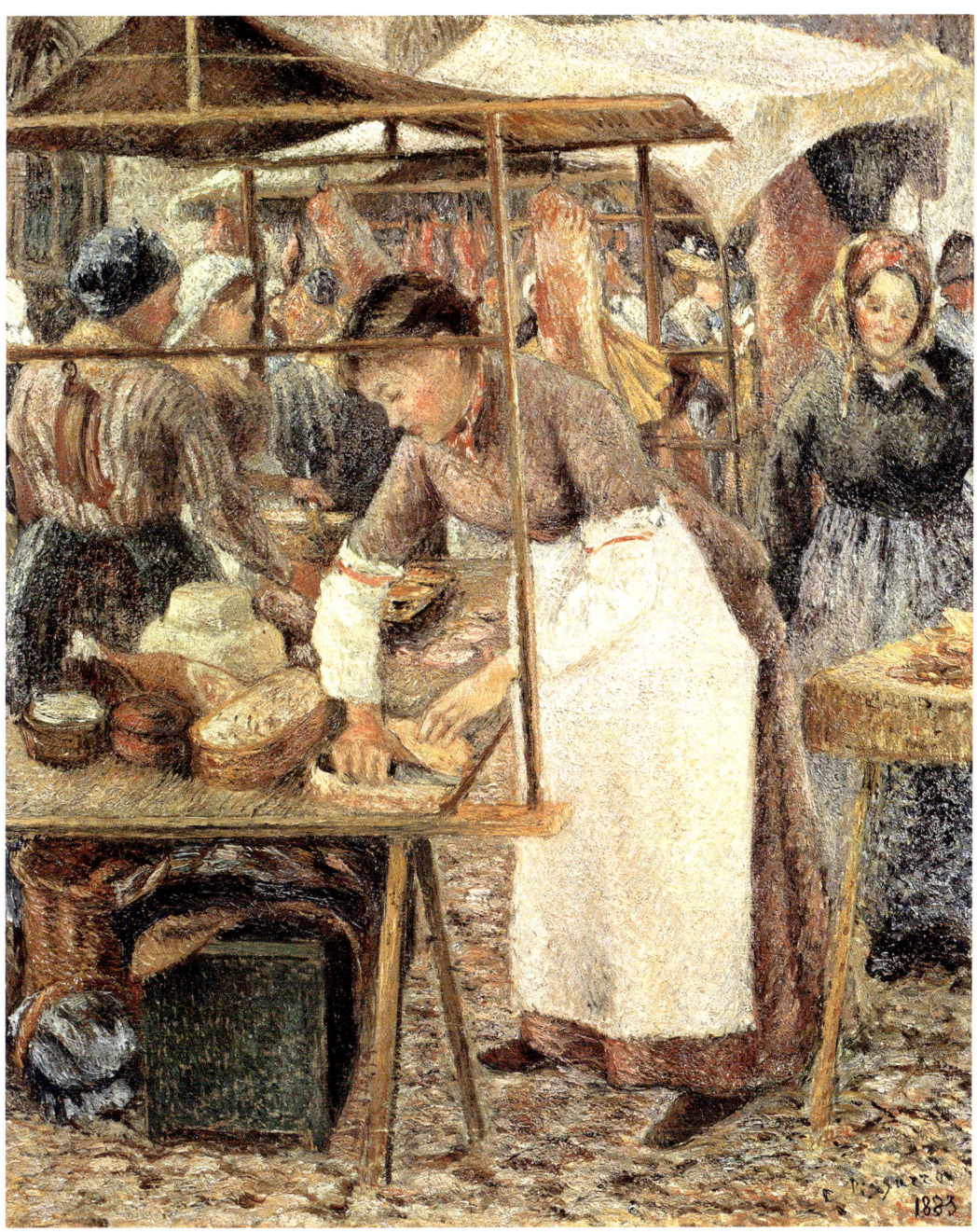

The Pork Butcher, 1883
Oil on canvas, 65.1 x 54.3 cm (25¾ x 21½ in.)
London, Tate

Pierre-Auguste Renoir
Lise with Parasol, 1867

Already at the outset of his career, Pierre-Auguste Renoir was, to a greater extent than Pissarro, Sisley or Monet, a figure painter rather than a landscape painter. The painting *Lise with Parasol* also focuses on a person.

In the 1870s, what was demanded of contemporary modern art was this: "Let us take our leave of the stylized human body that is treated like a vase. What we need is the characteristic, the modern human being in his or her clothes, in the midst of his or her social environment, at home or in the street." (Edmond Duranty)

Statements like these accorded perfectly with the ideas of Renoir and Frédéric Bazille. Renoir had, to start with, sought his motifs in subjects from the world of the Greek and Roman gods, for example in *Diana* (1867, Washington, National Gallery of Art), but in the late 1860s turned increasingly to themes taken from contemporary life. And he sought to capture the effect of light and shade on colours, in particular on black and white. His interest in the art of earlier centuries may have played a role here.

The Impressionists were not the first artists to confront questions like these. Leonardo da Vinci, the great protagonist of the Italian Renaissance, wrote: "If you see a woman dressed in white in the midst of a landscape, that side which sees the sun is so bright that it will dazzle the eyes like the sun; and the side which is towards the air, luminous through being interwoven with the sun's rays and penetrated by them, since the air itself is blue, that side of the woman seen by the air will tend to the blue. If the surface of the ground nearby is a meadow and if she is between the meadow and the sun itself, you will see the parts of those folds which can be seen by the meadow tinged by the reflected rays with the colour of the meadow."

This sounds as if Leonardo were describing an Impressionist picture, for example *Lise with Parasol*. Lise's white dress seems almost unpleasantly dazzling in the sun. In the shade, Renoir added a blue tinge. The same technique was followed by Monet in his snowscape *The Magpie* (Paris, Musée d'Orsay), which was executed only two years later.

Both artists are concerned with the effect of the bright sunlight on white, and with the change that white undergoes in the shade. In order to intensify the radiance of the white even further, Renoir and Monet use strong chiaroscuro contrasts. The oft-repeated assertion that the Impressionist artists used no black, because there is no pure black in nature, is therefore false. Renoir gives Lise's dress a broad black bow and Monet places a mostly black bird, the magpie, on a fence in the middle of a white snowfield.

Renoir, who went as far as to regard black as the "queen of colours", was however one of the few Impressionists – Berthe Morisot was another – to use pure ivory black. Monet and many other artists liked to mix the same pigment with other colours, for example green or blue. Thus the seemingly black railway engines in Monet's painting *Le pont de l'Europe, Gare Saint-Lazare* (ill. p. 63) in a mixture of ivory black and blue.

Lise with Parasol, 1867
Oil on canvas,
184 x 115.5 cm (72½ x 45½ in.)
Essen, Museum Folkwang

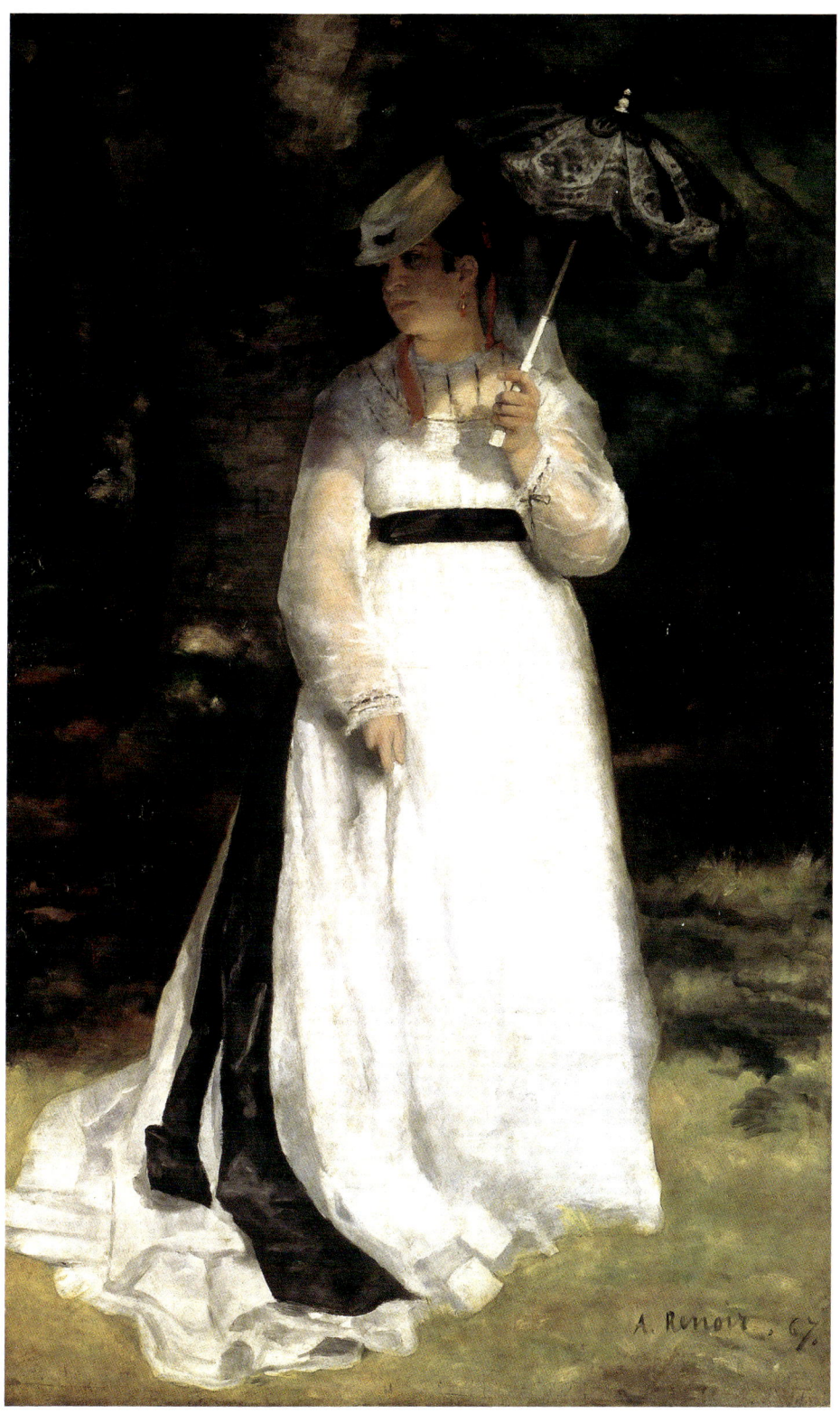

Pierre-Auguste Renoir
The Seine at Asnières, 1875

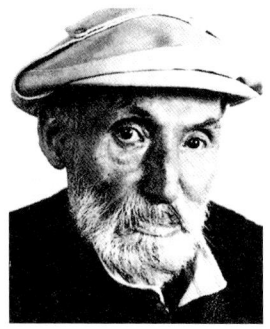

b. 1841 in Limoges, France
d. 1919 in Cagnes-sur-Mer,
France

Renoir had as a young man been apprenticed as a porcelain painter, and was consequently highly familiar with the use of soft round brushes and applications of transparent paint. He then moved on to painting fans, on to which, for example, he copied the early-18th-century motif of *The Embarkation for Cythera* by Antoine Watteau. Then he accepted a number of commissions to decorate Parisian cafés. "I chose as my motif Venus rising from the waters. I can assure you that I was not sparing with my Veronese green or cobalt blue … I decorated some 20 cafés in Paris … Even today I would like to paint decorations like Boucher, transform whole walls into an Olympia …"

And indeed, with the best will in the world, it is impossible to overlook the decorative aspect in Renoir's pictures: sunny, luminous harmonies full of a lust for life, one long "Sunday".

Renoir does not appear to have been sparing with paints in *The Seine at Asnières* either. His palette however consisted of just seven intensive colour pigments: cobalt blue, viridian (a dark green with a large blue component), chrome yellow, lemon yellow, chrome orange, vermilion, and a transparent red gloss. White was also abundantly used for the numerous dabs all over the picture. Black is however absent from this particular painting, as are the earth colours such as brown, sienna, ochre and the like.

The Seine at Asnières is one of a group of related motifs to which Renoir devoted himself in Chatou on the Seine in 1875. Compositionally, the picture is similar to Monet's *The Bridge at Argenteuil,* which had been executed one year earlier. Both artists placed a bridge on the right-hand side of the picture, in both cases with a train passing over it, against the background of a riverbank with a house. But while Monet depicted a specific place, Renoir was concerned with the general depiction of a Sunday atmosphere: two elegant young ladies are having themselves boated down the Seine on a bright Sunday. Renoir structured the brilliant "mosaic" of the water using a number of different painting techniques. The rapid application of liquid paint on a wet surface alternates with more viscous, almost dry paint on a dry surface. At the point where the boat intersects with the surface of the water, we see little white specks of foam. They consist of dabs of thick paint, loosely applied to the canvas. Seemingly random structures like these demonstrate the specific technique of Impressionism.

The contrast of the complementary colours which Renoir chose for *The Seine at Asnières* is what determines the whole picture. The combination of orange and blue follows Eugène Chevreul's colour theory dating from 1839, according to which these colours, when juxtaposed, intensify each other. In Chevreul's colour circle, orange and blue are diametrically opposite, precisely those colours, in other words, which Renoir chose here. By exploiting the contrasting effects and using exclusively pure, unmixed colours, the artist obtained a unique, radiant light.

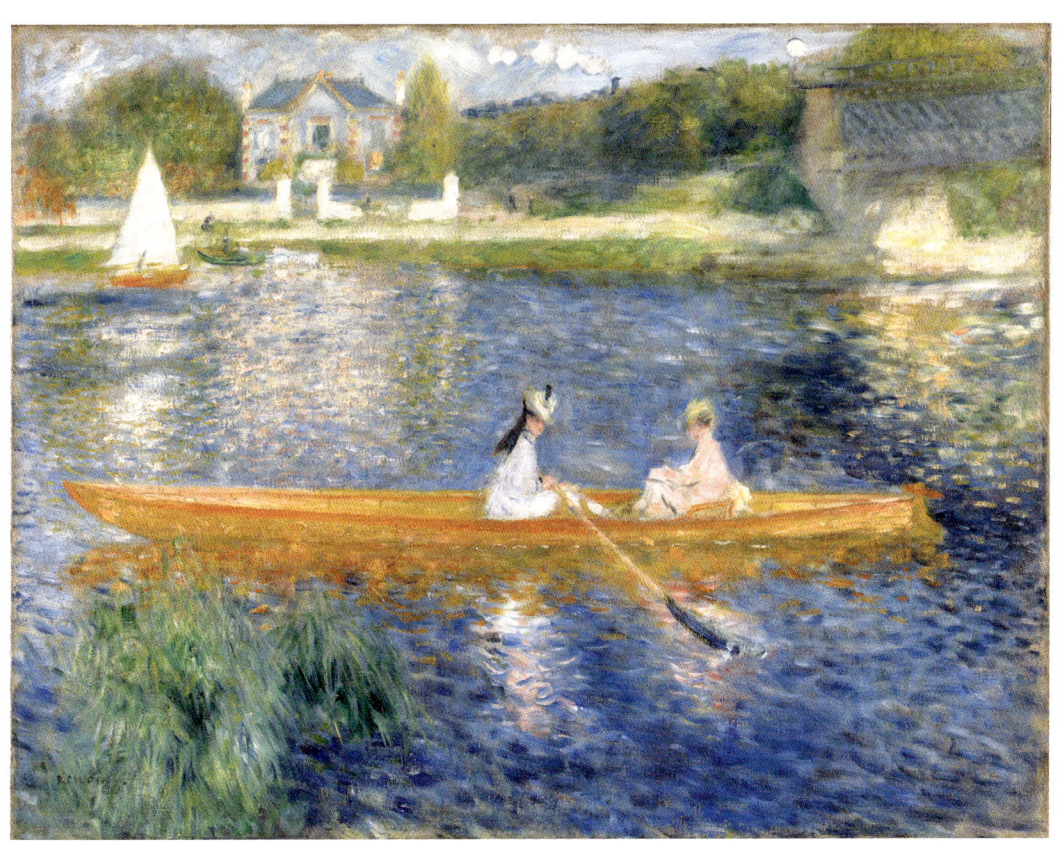

The Seine at Asnières, 1875
Oil on canvas, 71 x 92 cm (28 x 36¼ in.)
London, The National Gallery

Medardo Rosso
Aetas Aurea (The Golden Age), 1886

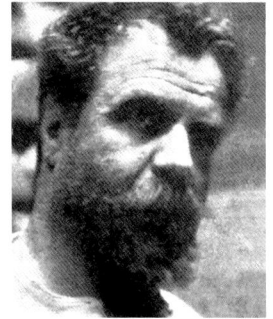

b. 1858 in Turin
d. 1928 in Milan

Among late-19th-century sculptors, Medardo Rosso is one of the least known, but also one of the most interesting. His aesthetic concentrated on light and the dissolution of matter, in contrast to conventional sculptural works, where volume and weight are what count. It is this attempt to integrate light into the way sculpture comes across which create the association between him and Impressionism.

Rosso's works are, in addition, often meant, like a relief, to be seen from only one side. They allow only one view, one aspect. It is said that when Degas saw Rosso's photograph of his [Rosso's] work *Impressione d'omnibus,* he thought he was looking at a photograph not of a sculpture, but of a painting.

The sculpture *Impressione d'omnibus,* which we now know only from the photograph, represented three people on the seat of a bus. Rosso's procedure was similar to that used by Degas in his painting *Absinthe* (ill. p. 55), which predates *Aetas Aurea (The Golden Age)* by ten years. Both artists had models pose at their [the artists'] direction, and in this way reconstructed a detail of their everyday city surroundings.

Rosso chose an experimental treatment of the material. In the 19th century, the production of the finished bronze sculpture from the wax or clay model was traditionally left to specialist craftsmen.

Rosso by contrast intervened in every stage of the process. What hitherto had been seen merely as an intermediate stage on the way to a completed bronze sculpture, Rosso presented as a finished work of art. We can see a comparable process in the work of the Impressionist painters, who saw a finished painting in what for the conservative art world was merely a sketch. In his boundless zest for experimentation, Rosso more than once created a number of versions of the same theme.

The sculpture *Aetas Aurea* is an example of these peculiarities in Medardo Rosso's works, and demonstrates the possibilities of Impressionist sculpture. It is a relief-like work, with the reverse left untreated, executed in wax over plaster. The wax model becomes the final state, not functioning just as a mere intermediate stage on the way to a bronze cast. The fragmentary form, with the seemingly broken-off outer edges and the hollow reverse, is typical of Rosso's intentions.

The sculpture consists of fragments of the human body: the head and arm of a mother and the head of a child. In spite of this fragmentation, any beholder can quickly recognize that the mother is inclining comfortingly over the screaming child and tenderly caressing its face with her hand. Thus she holds the child pressed closely to herself, cheek to cheek. The boundaries between the two figures disappear in the structures that connect them.

Aetas Aurea (The Golden Age), 1886
Wax over plaster, height 52.5 cm (20¾ in.)
Frankfurt am Main, Städel Museum

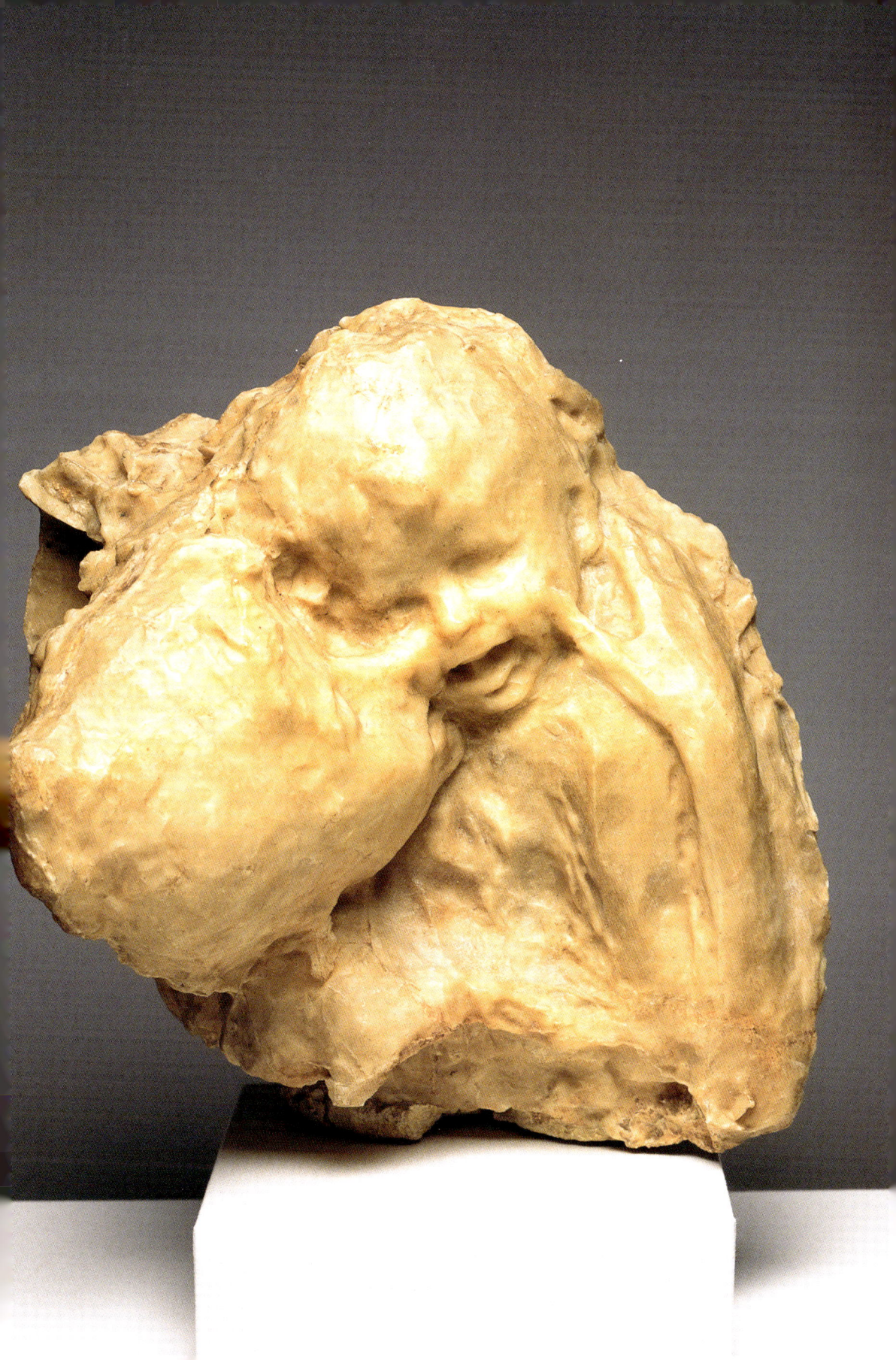

John Singer Sargent
In the Luxembourg Gardens, 1879

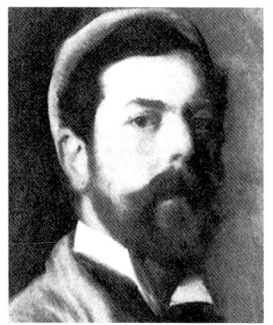

b. 1856 in Florence
d. 1925 in London

The Jardin du Luxembourg in the Quartier Latin was frequented by many artists who, like Sargent, had studios nearby. Sargent chose the large pond in the centre of the park as his central motif. A sketchy depiction, in which the dome of the Panthéon can be seen in the background, he dedicated to a friend. The version illustrated here he exhibited at the National Academy of Design in New York in 1879.

As the largest inner-city open space on the left bank of the Seine, the park fulfilled important social functions. Having a stroll in this classless atmosphere accorded with the Parisian attitude to life at the time.

Sargent had come to Paris in 1874 and enrolled as a student at the École des Beaux-Arts. In the early 1880s he had close contacts with the Impressionist artists, Monet in particular, but did not take part in their exhibitions, showing his works until 1888 at the official Salon instead. Monet for his part had also taken up the "park" theme in 1878. His two pictures painted in the Parc Monceau reflect similar impressions.

In the painting *In the Luxembourg Gardens* the artist focused his attention in particular on the light. Sargent's solution here to the play of light and shade, which occupied the Impressionists so greatly, is to depict the place at dusk, in shimmering moonlight. The whole scene seems bathed in a violet twilight which blurs the differences in light quality. The tender grey-violet tones are broken by individual red dabs of colour: in the woman's fan, in the flower beds, and in the lights on the balustrade. The strong red is all the more striking as these dabs of colour are for the most part placed against their complementary colour, green.

Sargent may have had the famous nocturnal studies by Johan Barthold Jongkind in mind when he painted this twilight scene in the park. Jongkind was seen as a role model by many Impressionists, and Monet, who had been his pupil, said: "From then on Jongkind was my real master. I owe the definitive training of my eye to him." Jongkind's painting *Notre-Dame in Paris by Moonlight* (Reims, Musée des Beaux-Arts) could have provided an important stimulus for Sargent to paint his own moonlight park picture.

Sargent's canvas *In the Luxembourg Gardens* is not a narrative, but depicts a moment seemingly chosen at random: a couple are strolling past, a man by the pond is reading a newspaper, the moon is reflected in the silvery surface of the water. Sargent attached particular importance to the elegant clothing of the couple as they stroll across the empty foreground. "Modernity and fashion were closer to each other, and the modern artists, who included the Impressionists, had a fashionable public, which was not the same as economic success." (Christoph Becker)

The same year Sargent portrayed *Madame Édouard Pailleron* in the garden of her house. Mme. Pailleron is wearing a very elegant black-and-white afternoon dress and gathering the skirt with the same zigzag movement as the young lady in the park. With portraits like this of the social elite, John Singer Sargent became extremely successful.

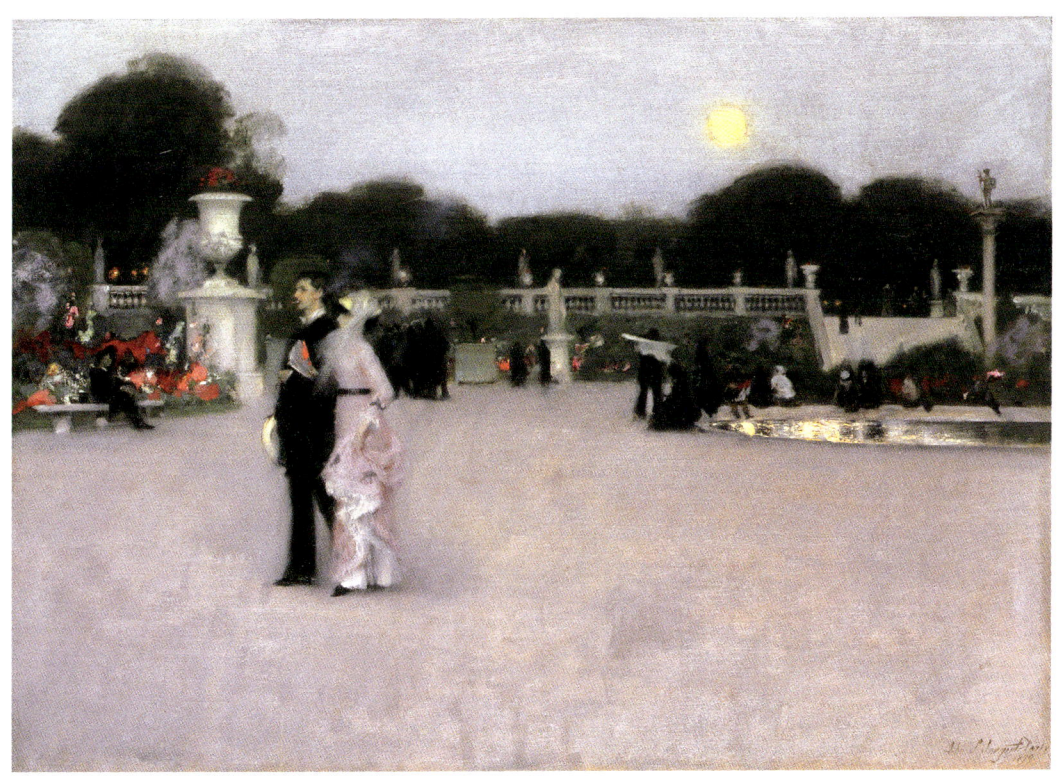

In the Luxembourg Gardens, 1879
Oil on canvas, 65.7 x 92.4 cm (25¾ x 36¼ in.)
Philadelphia Museum of Art

Giovanni Battista Segantini
The Hay Harvest, 1888–98

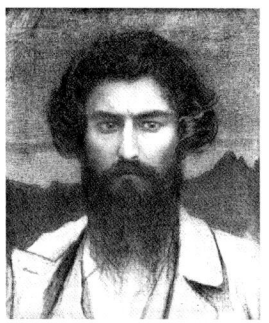

b. 1850 in Arco, Italy
d. 1899 in Pontresina,
Switzerland

"Then I saw how this ray of light got bigger and bigger, until it finally took on human form, the form of a woman. But just as the figure had formed, just as it seemed almost alive, and comprehensible to the eye, it dissolved once more, disintegrating into luminous pink spots. But I continued to gaze fixedly at this place, and she re-appeared, remaining fluid but recognizable in her diaphanous, luminous form … The beautiful divine figure surrounded itself with a silvery pool of light, which spread out and thrust aside the dark shadow of the cloud."

Segantini's arresting description of a vision of divine celestial manifestations points to the semantic content of his motifs. Light and shade, working woman and cloudy sky are no longer a spontaneous expression, a random detail of reality, but become metaphors of divinity and threat, of existence and salvation.

Segantini developed his Symbolist art in the years following 1886 with motifs from the Alps, to which he applied the divisionist painting technique. His early works largely comprise realistic genre scenes, which point to Millet and Daubigny as role models. The painters of the Barbizon School, among them Millet in particular, had become portrayers of the rustic world "par excellence". The hard work of the rural population is shown in Daubigny's *The Haystack* and in Segantini's *The Hay Harvest* to be a constantly repeating, endless process. Erecting the haystack will be followed in the none-too-distant future by taking it down again. Raking the hay together and loading it has, as its sole purpose, distributing it once more to the cattle in winter. Daubigny depicts this as an anonymous process with small figures in the landscape, while Segantini places one figure, and the associated feelings, in the foreground. She arouses pity or else melancholy. Segantini drew on his daily dealings with peasants and shepherds, and generalized their individual experiences into representations of collective destiny. This emotional, "archaic" quality led to the artist being misused by the Fascist blood-and-soil ideology, his work being appropriated for a regressive "homeland" art. Also the later romantic-sentimental exploitation of Segantini's pictures for tourist purposes ignored the complex content of his paintings.

Segantini began *The Hay Harvest* as a narrow landscape format in Savognin in about 1888. In this early version the artist had painted a flat, even horizon, the torso of the peasant woman projecting above it, just as the smaller figures of the peasants and the haystack interrupted the line of the horizon. In 1898 Segantini added a piece of canvas to the top edge, so that an approximately square format resulted. He added the mountain range and the sky in its present form, thus creating the symbolic meaning: the radiant divine light breaks up the dark of the clouds, but in contrast there is human life on earth, which cannot influence fate, but only submit to it, as the peasant woman has to submit to the hay harvest. For Segantini as for the Impressionists, light had top priority, albeit with a quite different interpretation. The painting technique of closely placed short strokes, which constitute a transparent yet powerful colourfulness, is something he adopted from the Neo-impressionist movement.

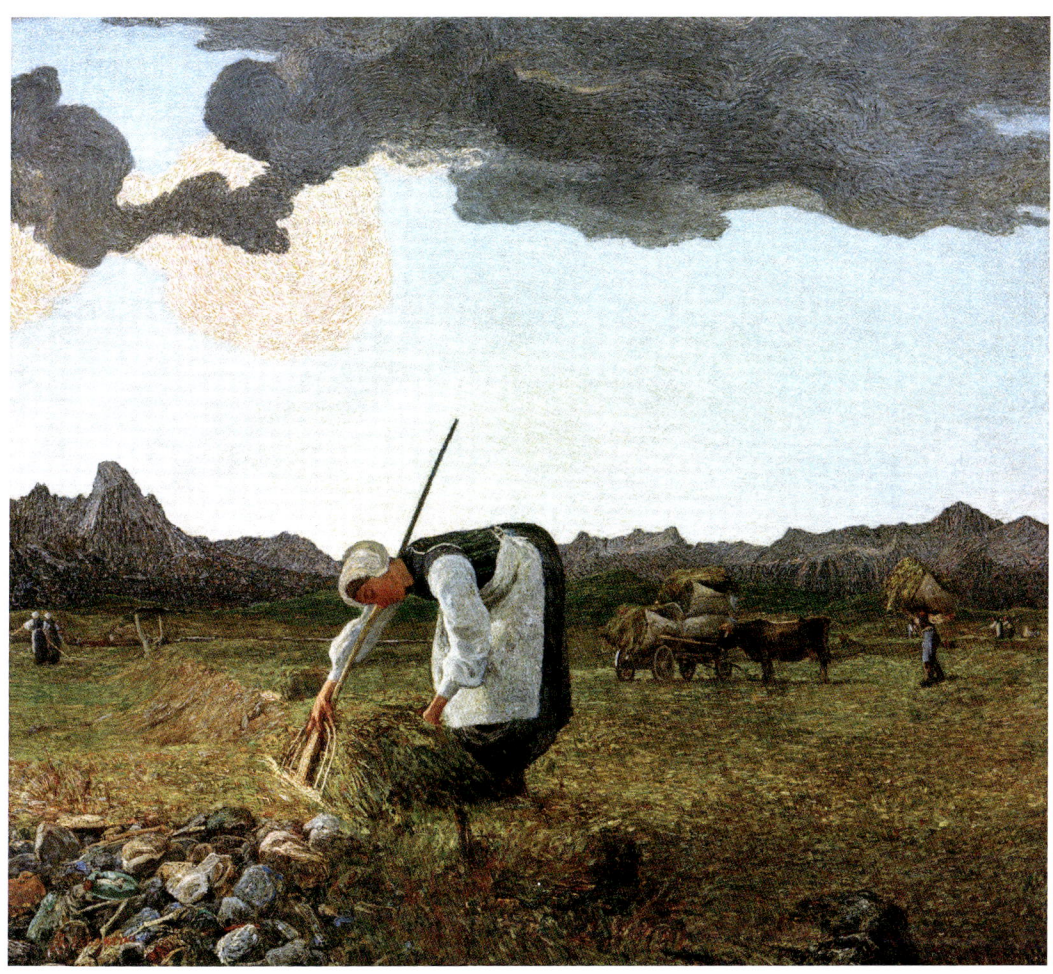

The Hay Harvest, 1888–98
Oil on canvas, 137 x 149 cm (54 x 58¾ in.)
St Moritz, Segantini Museum

OPPOSITE
Self Portrait, 1895
Drawing, charcoal with gold dust
and chalk traces on canvas,
59 x 50 cm (23¼ x 19¾ in.)
St Moritz, Segantini Museum, donation
by the Oskar Bernhard family

Georges Seurat
The Bathers at Asnières, 1884

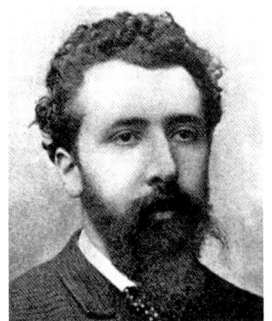

b. 1859 in Paris
d. 1891 in Paris

With *The Bathers at Asnières* Georges Seurat completed his first example of the synthetic style of Neo-impressionism. He displayed this eye-catching painting at the Salon des Indépendants in 1884, after it had been rejected by the official Salon. In 1886 the French art dealer Durand-Ruel, who worked closely with the Impressionist artists, took *The Bathers at Asnières* to an exhibition in New York. It was the most controversial of all the exhibits.

Seurat was also controversial among his fellow artists. His and Paul Signac's participation in the eighth Impressionist exhibition triggered a heated debate. Finally, Pissarro succeeded in achieving a decision in favour of the two young artists. In protest, Monet, Renoir, Sisley and Caillebotte withdrew, and the Impressionist group broke up. A series of articles in the press fêted Seurat and Signac as representatives of a new style which had made Impressionism obsolete. The two were then given the still-current epithet of Neo-impressionists.

Seurat addressed his total energy to the intensity of his artistic work. His œuvre in the space of about twelve years comprised just four large paintings, alongside a number of smaller pictures, draughts and oil-sketches.

His working method differed substantially from that of the Impressionists. He painted a great deal in the studio and not in the open air; and in a fashion not spontaneous and immediate, but systematic and considered.

For *The Bathers at Asnières* a number of individual studies were done on the island of Grande Jatte; these grew together to create the total composition. The study *Horses in the Seine* (private collection) makes it clear how Seurat worked. He followed Corot's maxim of first indicating the strongest colours, and then proceeding systematically to the palest. Accordingly, Seurat first marked the darkest shades, and then the lightest. The brown and white horses, with which he experimented in this way for a long time, ultimately failed to make an appearance on the finished painting *The Bathers at Asnières.*

The execution of the painting then followed exclusively in the studio, which, given the size of the canvas, was virtually inevitable. The work depicts people on the bank of the river opposite the island of the Grande Jatte. In the background can be seen a factory building and a bridge. A ferry is carrying passengers to the island. Although Seurat conceded the highest priority to the Impressionist criteria of colour and light, he came to a completely different result. Seurat's goal was not the fleeting impression, but the configuration of many moments. Addition was what determined the motif. Not the transitory, but the enduring – that was what he wanted to capture on canvas. Accordingly, Seurat's style has been termed "synthetic." His return to the traditional, academic working method was accompanied by a scientific examination of colour. In the following years, Seurat developed, on the basis of physics, optics and geometry, the Pointillist colour theory, which Camille Pissarro also followed for a time.

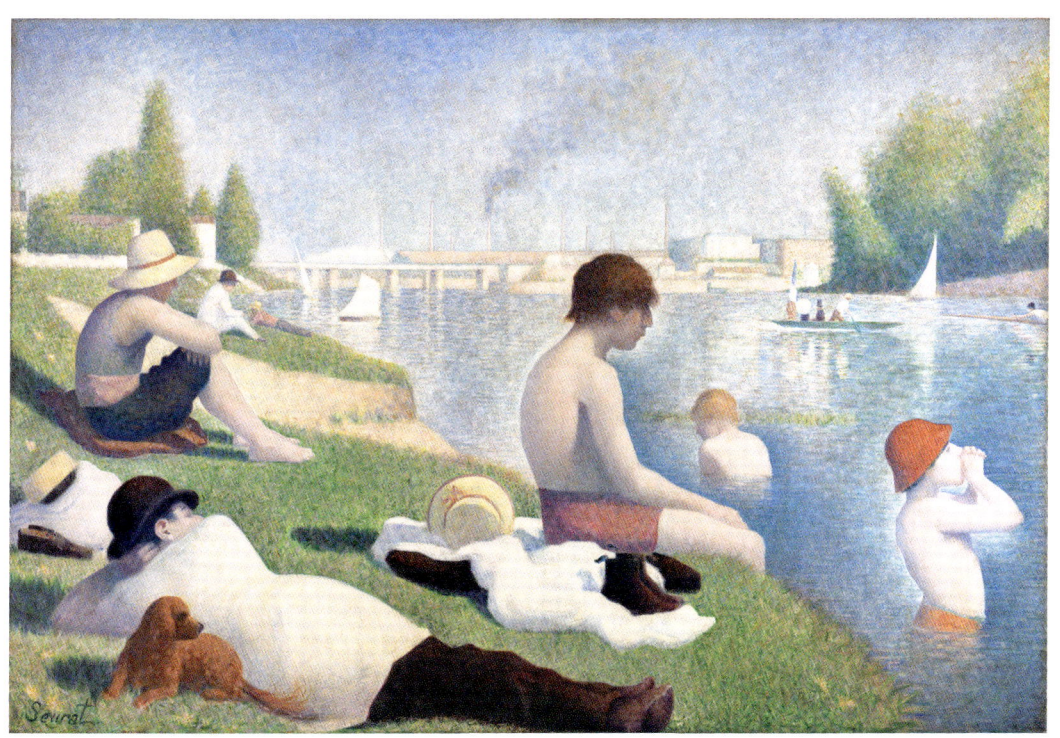

The Bathers at Asnières, 1884
Oil on canvas, 201 x 300 cm (79¼ x 118 in.)
London, The National Gallery

Walter Richard Sickert
The Old Bedford, c. 1895

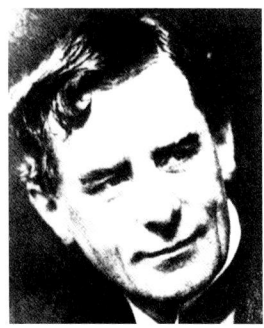

b. 1860 in Munich
d. 1942 in Bathampton,
United Kigndom

Walter Richard Sickert had a particular association with the world of the theatre, having first worked as an actor. Maybe that was why the audience was more important to him than what was happening on stage, as in the painting *The Old Bedford.*

Sickert found his preferred motifs in the world of London's theatres and music halls, in particular the Bedford Theatre in Camden Town provided him with a motif a number of times. In the painting *The Old Bedford* he made the audience the compositional focus of the picture for the first time, a habit which, with few exceptions, was to last into the 1920s. In *The Old Bedford* he also concentrates on the audience in the gallery, rather than the classier types in the stalls.

The painting was probably conceived as a pair to the same artist's *Little Dot Hetherington at the Bedford Music Hall,* in which the little-known singer of that name is depicted on stage. In a performance in November 1888 she sang the well-known song "The boy I love is up in the Gallery", at the same time pointing in the relevant direction, as Sickert depicted. Since this time, Sickert had made drawings of the interior furnishings of this old-fashioned building, and captured various other performances on canvas. *The Old Bedford* is one of a whole series of depictions of the gallery executed in the 1890s, differing principally in colouration and lighting.

Here, we see a pale reddish shimmer on the gallery, reflecting the stage lighting. All the faces of the exclusively male audience are turned towards the stage. In connection with the painting *Little Dot Hetherington at the Bedford Music Hall* it is clear that each of the men is dreaming – in line with the words of the song – that he is "the boy I love". The painting itself is like a dream in red and gold, and is indeed only half "real", the other half being a reflection in the mirror.

During the 1890s Sickert was one of the leading artists of the English avant-garde. He was a member of the New English Art Club, which exhibited and propagated modern art in Britain. As a pupil of James McNeill Whistler and a friend of Edgar Degas, with whom he shared his passion for the theatre, Walter Richard Sickert was a leading exponent of London Impressionism.

Sickert had got to know Degas in 1883, when he took one of Whistler's paintings to the exhibition at the Paris Salon. Whistler, who lived in England, had written letters of introduction for him, including one to Degas. Thus it was that Sickert quickly made contact with the Impressionist painters, being strongly influenced by Degas in particular. In 1885 Sickert, together with Degas and other artists, spent a few weeks in Dieppe and painted under his direction. During their joint sojourn, Degas made a small pastel drawing: one of the *Six Friends of the Artist* (1885, Providence, Rhode Island School of Design Museum) is Walter Richard Sickert. Dieppe was an important place for Sickert, one to which he returned time and again, especially in summer.

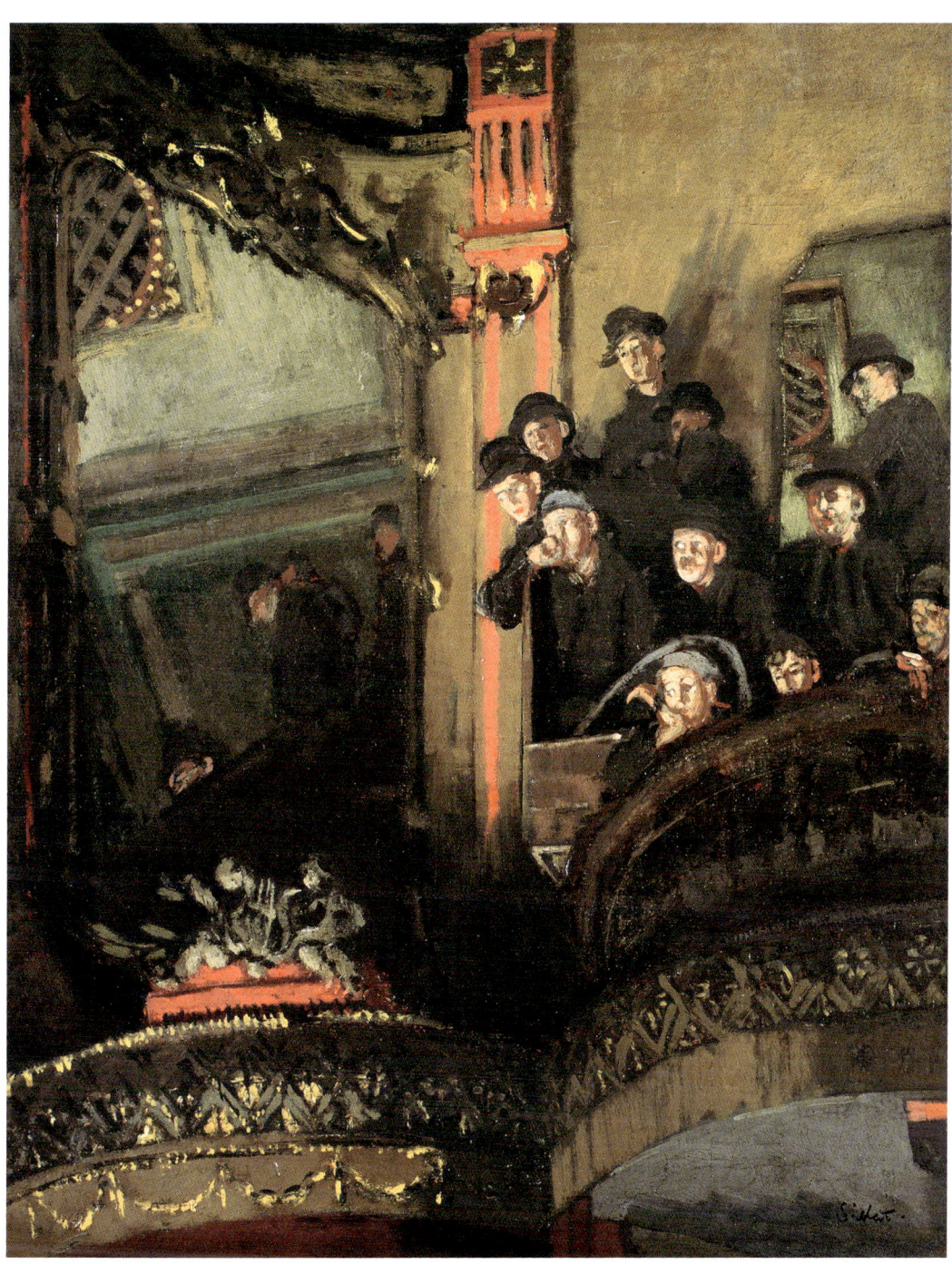

The Old Bedford, *c.* 1895
Oil on canvas, 76.3 x 60.5 cm (30 x 23¾ in.)
Liverpool, Walker Art Gallery

Paul Signac
Capo di Noli, 1898

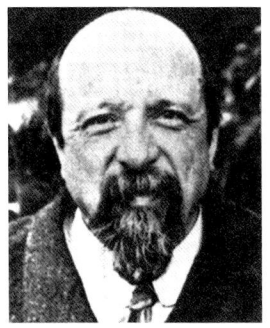

b. 1863 in Paris
d. 1935 in Paris

"I began Capo di Noli, in which I wanted to obtain extreme polychromy. In order to practise, I used my sample of silk dyes, which are so intense and luminous. I shall transfer them one after the other on to my canvas. I do not want one single centimetre of matt colour to remain and I want to transform every bit of the painting to something extreme. If it gets a little garish, it can always be toned down."

As far as we know, Signac did not tone down the colours, but left them as they were. The painting *Capo di Noli* was seen as the climax of Signac's intoxication with colour.

The Mediterranean surroundings doubtless contributed to the use of such strong colours. Capo di Noli is on the Italian Riviera, which Signac liked to visit from his base in Saint-Tropez, where he lived from 1892 to 1900, exploring the surroundings in his yacht "Olympia." He also discovered a new colour dimension in nature, which was reflected in his work of this period. The white and red cliffs, the pale violet horizon, the blue shadows with patches of golden sunlight – all bear witness to Signac's attempt to elevate colour to heights of intensity.

After Seurat's death in 1891, which affected him greatly, Signac increasingly sought artistic paths of his own. His statements at this time constantly centred on concepts such as freedom and harmony. "Let us liberate ourselves! Our goal must be to create beautiful harmonies." By this he meant getting away from the idea of painting from nature, such as he had done until then. It now seemed to him a waste of time to produce an image of nature as precise and faithful as possible. In the years around the turn of the century, he crystallized a personal approach out of Seurat's scientific theory of colours.

In contrast to his earlier works, Signac no longer followed the colour theory determined by the use of two contrasting colours. *Capo di Noli* displays a free and harmonious juxtaposition of a whole variety of colour values, which Signac applied in vertical and horizontal brushstrokes. The cliffs on the left-hand edge of the picture and the vegetation on the right-hand side are reproduced with vertical strokes in accordance with their structure. The path, and the calm, motionless sea have been executed in horizontal brush movements. The sky is painted on the horizon with little dots, and towards the foreground of the picture with diagonal strokes that cross each other. With this structural use of the brush, Signac supports the impressively harmonious composition of the painting. It seems to be an "ideal" view of a timeless, sunny landscape.

In 1894 Signac wrote: "A few years ago, I sought with great effort to prove to others, using scientific experiments, that these blue tones, these yellow colours and these variations on green all existed in nature. Now I am content to say: I paint in this way because this technique seems to me to be the most appropriate way to obtain the most harmonious, the most light-filled and the most colourfully luminous result … and because I like it."

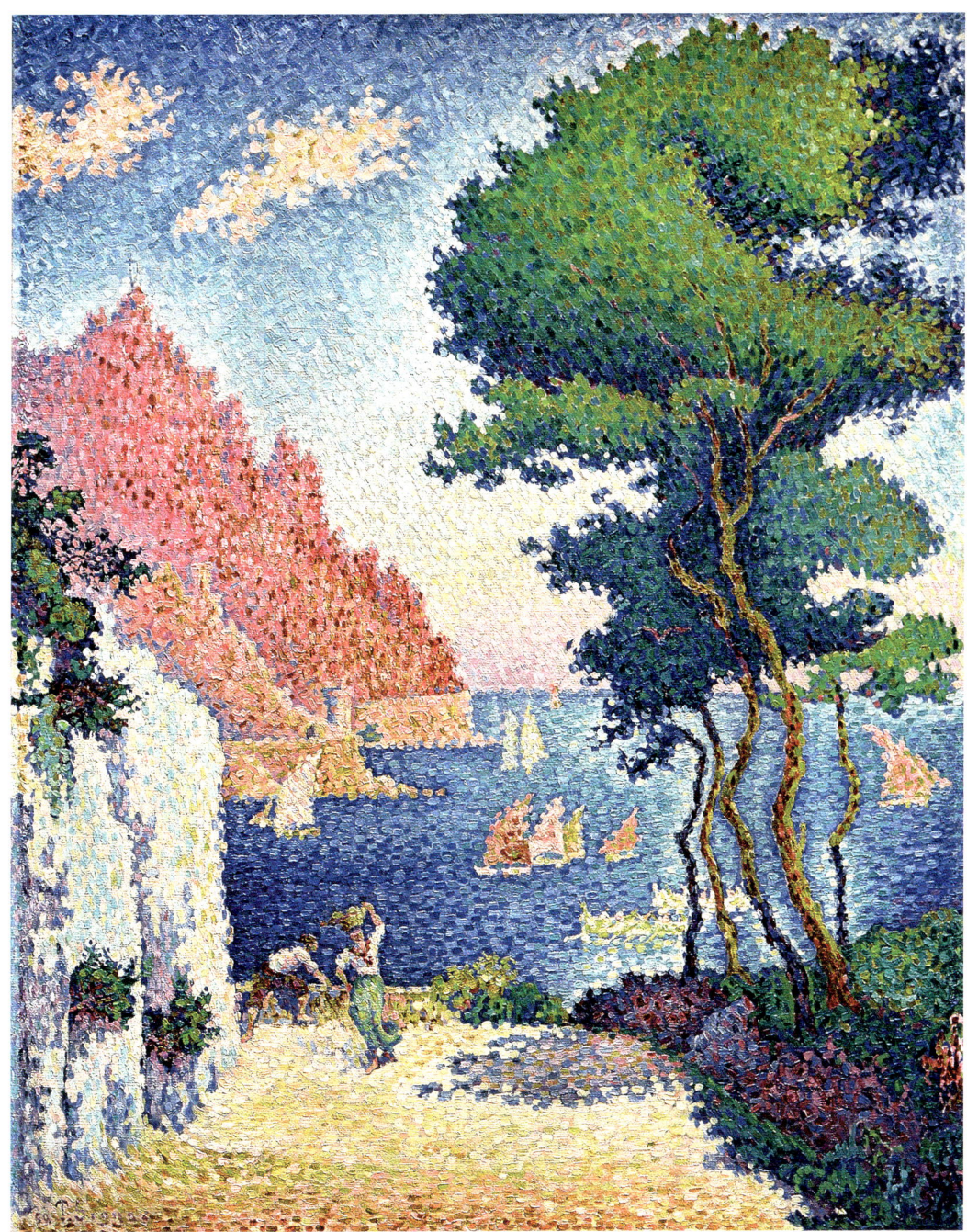

Capo di Noli, 1898
Oil on canvas, 91.5 x 73 cm (36 x 28¾ in.)
Cologne, Wallraf-Richartz-Museum &
Fondation Corboud

Paul Signac
The Papal Palace at Avignon, 1909

In the first years of the 20th century Paul Signac turned time and again to buildings on the water's edge. He produced views of Notre-Dame-de-la-Garde in Marseilles, the church of Santa Maria della Salute on the Grand Canal in Venice, the lighthouse in Biarritz, the town of La Rochelle and the port of St Tropez, all viewed from across the water. Like Daubigny and Monet, he probably used a boat to find the relevant motifs. This also provided him with an opportunity, after all, to depict sophisticated reflections of the colours on the water.

In the 1880s Signac had, along with his friend Armand Guillaumin, painted landscapes and Parisian cityscapes – visibly under the influence of the characteristics of Impressionist art.

Surprisingly, Signac did not undergo the usual training at the École des Beaux-Arts. Especially for the older generation of Impressionists, a formal training at the academy was after all still obligatory. Instead, Signac was self-taught. He adopted Impressionism by looking at its works, and learned chiefly from his close friend Georges Seurat, whose Pointillism had a decisive influence on his style.

At the start of the 20th century, Claude Monet struck out along a similar path to Signac: both worked with simplified forms and fascinating, dominating colours. Monet's *Houses of Parliament, Stormy Sky* even uses the same reddish-violet atmosphere as Signac in his *The Papal Palace at Avignon*.

Paul Signac captured the palace in Avignon in two versions. The painting illustrated here dates from 1909 and depicts the monumental architecture in the morning light. For the second painting, Signac chose the same view at sunset.

The palace was built in the 14th century, when a number of popes resided in Avignon. In order to bestow prestige and dignity on the papal residence, a vast Gothic fortress with a city wall was erected, and the neighbouring cathedral of Notre-Dame-des-Doms extended. The bridge over the Rhône, the Pont d'Avignon made famous by the children's song, was partly destroyed in the 17th century. Signac depicted the still extant surviving arches on the left-hand side of the picture. Like Alfred Sisley in his painting *The Watering Place at Marly-le-Roi* (ill. p. 93) Signac did not portray this impressive architectural ensemble for its historical significance, but used it as a fantastically beautiful motif for the play of colours at sunrise.

Here, Paul Signac was following his maxim: "Simplification of the elements leads you to more colour." He reduced the building to its silhouette and a few features of the internal structure. The edifice, with the adjacent church, the riverbank vegetation and the bridge are still recognizable. Water and sky flow into one another. The palace, radiant in the morning sunlight, rises majestically, like some timeless vision, from the riverbank vegetation still submerged in darkness.

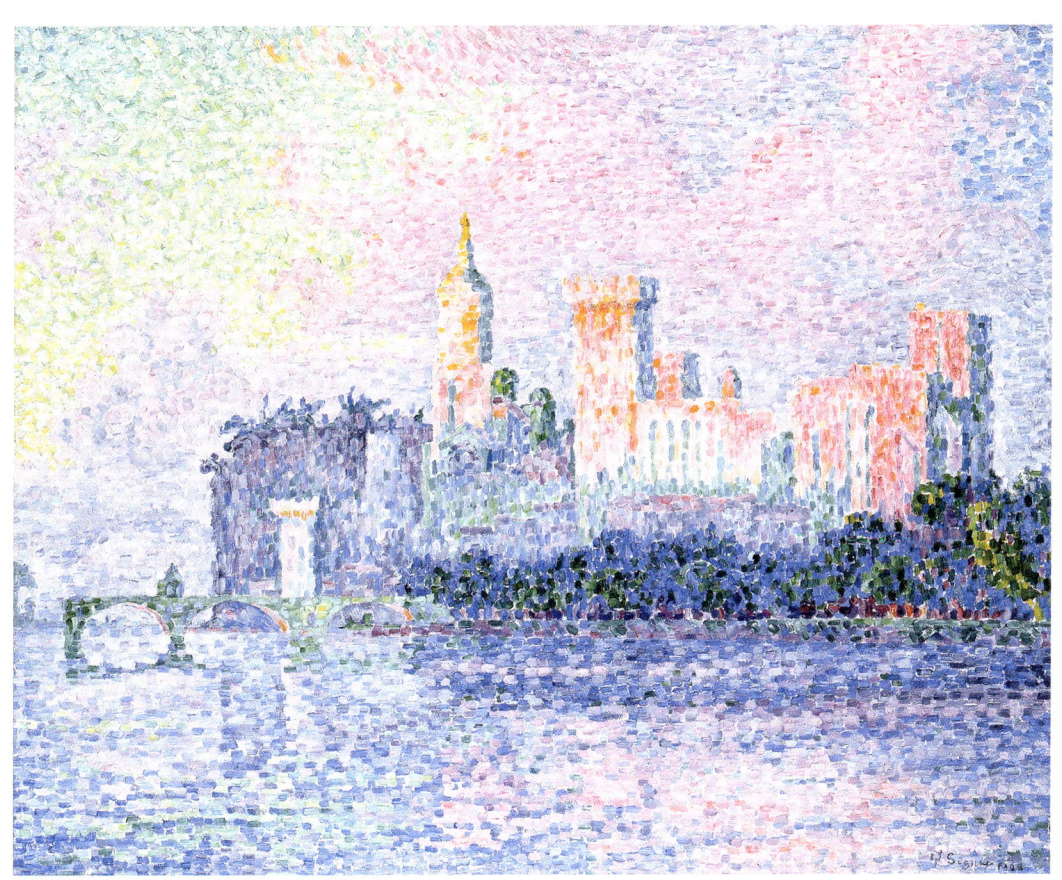

The Papal Palace at Avignon, 1909
Oil on canvas, 73.3 x 91.9 cm (29 x 36¼ in.)
Paris, Musée d'Orsay

Alfred Sisley
The Watering Place at Marly-le-Roi, c. 1875

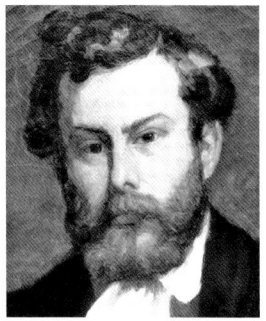

b. 1839 in Paris
d. 1899 in Moret-sur-Loing,
France

"I always begin a picture with the sky," wrote Alfred Sisley, who painted almost nothing but landscapes. "Its planes give depth (for the sky has planes as well as solid ground) and the shapes of the clouds give movement to a picture. What is more beautiful indeed than the summer sky, with its wispy clouds idly floating across the blue? What movement and grace! Don't you agree? They are like waves on the sea; one is uplifted and carried away. But there is another aspect – the evening sky. Clouds grow thin, like furrowed fields, like eddies of water frozen in the air, and then they gradually fade away in the light of the setting sun. Solemnity and melancholy – a sad moment of departure which I find especially moving."

In his painting *The Watering Place at Marly-le-Roi* Alfred Sisley concentrated on the winter sky, in which a milky sun is trying to shine through the layer of cloud. The reddish beige of the canvas primer is visible through the thin layer of paint in many parts of the picture and in large areas of the sky is totally uncovered. The shade of the canvas primer, which was originally lighter, dominates the whole picture. It is very probably a commercial primer, not applied by Sisley himself.

He used the shade of the ready-primed canvas for the leaden light of a winter's afternoon that weighs down on the painting. The thin layer of paint and the narrow range of colours employed are typical of Sisley's work at this period. *The Watering Place at Marly-le-Roi* uses just five colours plus black and white. The hasty brushstrokes point to the picture's having been painted quickly. It was done in one sitting in the open air, only a few dabs of paint being added later when the painting was dry. This picture is, then, one of the few that reproduces an immediate, spontaneous impression in accordance with the Impressionist ideal.

The watering place, which occupies the entire foreground of the picture, is on the edge of the grounds of the former château de Marly, built by Louis XIV in the 17th century and destroyed in the French Revolution. Sisley lived with his family from 1874 to 1877 in Marly-le-Roi, struggling with major financial difficulties.

Sisley painted the motif of the watering place in Marly-le-Roi and other remains of the royal fountains about a dozen times in the winter of 1876/77. At the same time, Gustave Caillebotte painted a view of the Marly Machine.

Sisley used the long Baroque visual axis, which leads across the pool and along the street into the countryside as the composition line of his painting. Like Claude Monet in his painting *Monet's Garden at Vétheuil* (ill. p. 65), Sisley used this central line in order to create depth.

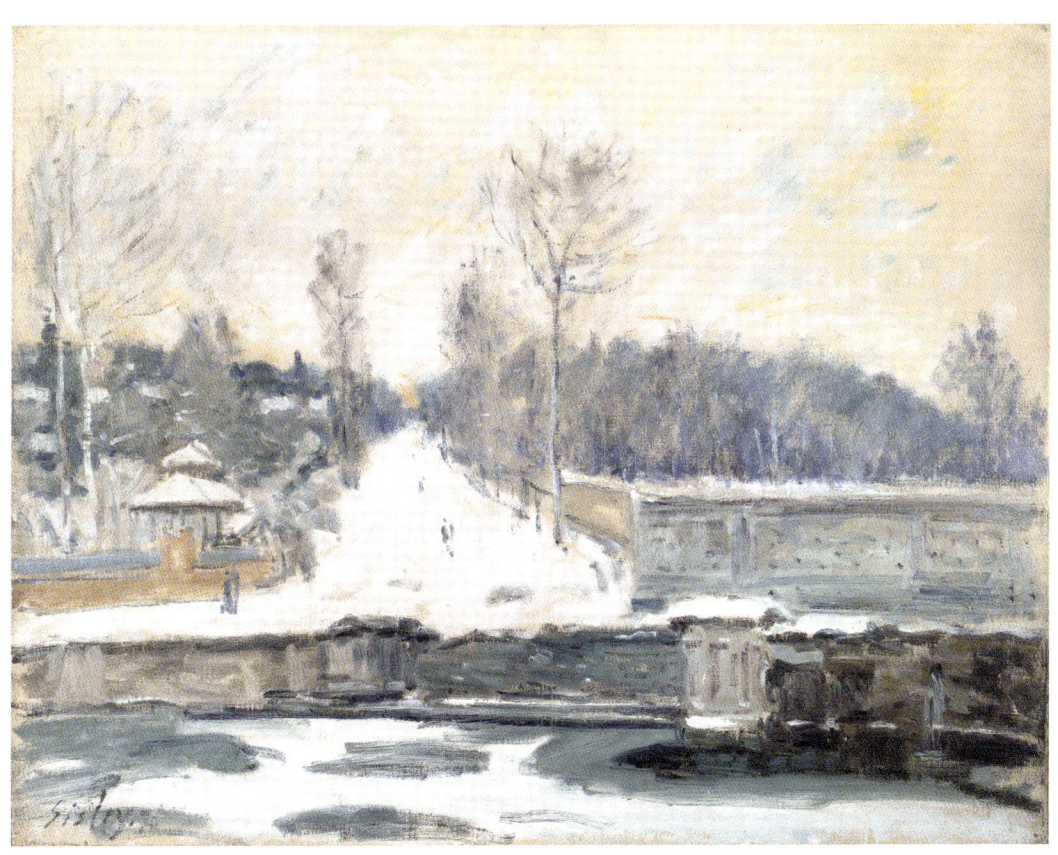

The Watering Place at Marly-le-Roi, *c.* 1875
Oil on canvas, 49.5 x 65.4 cm (19½ x 25¾ in.)
London, The National Gallery

Alfred Sisley
The Path to the Old Ferry, 1880

The Path to the Old Ferry is another of Sisley's landscapes in which the depiction of water is central. As in his early work *Autumn: On the Banks of the Seine near Bougival*, Sisley painted a ferry across the river, a village on the riverbank, a path running down to the bank, and little human figures as accessories.

Not only are the colours stronger, Sisley's brushstrokes too have become more powerful, and the application of paint is no longer quite so transparent as in the 1870s. As his composition line, Sisley once again uses a path, which here runs inwards from the bottom left-hand corner and creates the necessary depth. At the same time, the artist directs the eye of the beholder to the rectangular red patch in the centre of the picture, which is on the opposite riverbank. This red patch in the midst of green surroundings is particularly striking, as Sisley here makes use of the complementary colour pair of red and green. Immediately below this red roof, for that is what it is, we see a group of people standing waiting on the near bank. Thus the beholder anticipates visually the movement that the waiting people still have ahead of them, namely being ferried to the far bank. In this clever fashion, Sisley succeeds in integrating the beholder into the picture, and above all into the movement.

The picture is given, in addition, expected tension by the crossing of two divergent directions of movement: The river, which follows a calm horizontal line from right to left, is painted with horizontal brushstrokes. This is crossed by the ferry and the gaze of the beholder into the depth of the landscape. The resistance of the water to the ferry becomes positively palpable.

Sisley himself wrote of movement in the landscape: "Apart from the motif itself, the chief interest in landscape painting is in life and movement. The animation of the canvas is one of the hardest problems in painting. Everything must contribute: the form, the colour, the execution …The artist's impression is the life-giving factor, and only this impression can free that of the spectator. Though the artist must remain master of his craft, the surface, at times raised to the highest pitch of loveliness, should transmit to the beholder the sensation which possessed the artist."

Sisley thought the artist should leave out superfluous details and that thus "the spectator should be led along the road that the artist indicates to him, and from the first be made to notice what the artist has felt." In the painting *The Path to the Old Ferry* and in many others of his works, the fascinating thing is the crossing of the water, be it on the ferry, over the bridge or with the eye.

"Every picture shows a spot with which the artist has fallen in love …" (Sisley). Sisley felt finding this particular spot to be extremely stimulating when looking at a work of art.

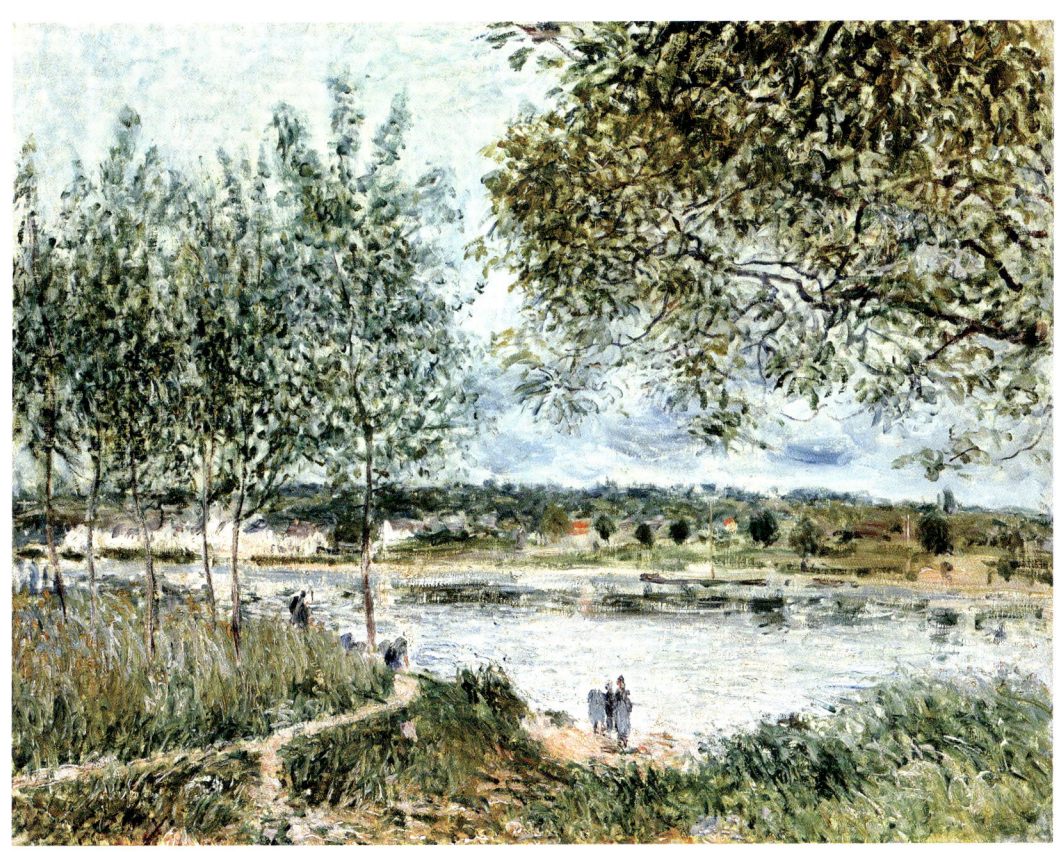

The Path to the Old Ferry, 1880
Oil on canvas, 50 x 65 cm (19¾ x 25½ in.)
London, The National Gallery

Max Slevogt
Parade, 1913

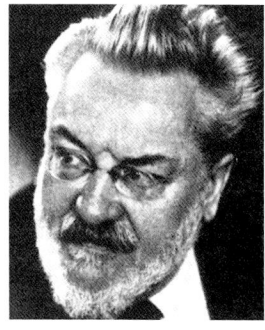

b. 1868 in Landshut, Germany
d. 1932 in Neukastel, Germany

Max Slevogt painted the military parade through the Brandenburg Gate on 17 June 1913, the 25th anniversary of Kaiser Wilhelm II's accession to the Prussian and German thrones. Slevogt watched the parade from the upper storey of a building on the south side of the street.

There are two versions of the event. The painting *Parade* illustrated here depicts the parade in the morning. The second version, with the same format, was painted in the afternoon from a higher balcony. While the morning picture gives us a view of the parade itself, the afternoon painting quickly passes over the crowded street to give us a look at the beflagged roofscape beyond. The large black, white and red tricolour of the German Empire hanging from a crown-topped staff on the neighbouring building finds itself competing for our attention with an advertisement for the Passage Theater situated in the building.

Slevogt's morning impression chooses as its subject the parade itself as it moves from left to right across the picture. The marching soldiers, whose dynamics are underscored by the diagonal course of the street, are merely sketched with rapid brushstrokes. Only the black, white and red of the Prussian flag and the blue coats of the soldiers give us any indication that this is a Prussian military parade. Slevogt concentrates on the staccato of the marching soldiers and the shadows, which lie across the direction of march. These short strokes determine the whole structure of the picture and continue in the background in the slower rhythm of the vertical tree trunks and flagpoles.

It is probably no coincidence that the brushstrokes that characterize the marching soldiers on the right recall musical notes on a score. Slevogt's concurrent work on illustrations to Mozart's *Magic Flute* and his marginal drawings for the score of the opera are clearly reflected here. Slevogt admired Mozart's score: "No visual artist can wield his pen more animatedly, more sensuously, more wittily. One can with the eye alone grasp the sound, the spirit of the work … Just as Mozart forms the heads of the individual notes differently, sensitively stretching the connecting strokes, hastily placing the bar-lines … the thousand ways that he has of crossing something out, the indescribable grace which lies over every page as a whole item, all this can only amaze anyone who has any sense of the line, of its expressive value."

Slevogt in his turn transformed – no less hastily and gracefully – the "expressive value of the line" of marching soldiers into notes. Rhythm and music are permanently integrated into the depiction. Slevogt's method of depiction differs considerably from the parades of the American Impressionist Frederick Childe Hassam. Hassam, who chose as motifs the Bastille Day parade of 14 July 1910 in Paris and the parade down Fifth Avenue in New York on Allies Day, 17 May 1917, drew the flags strongly into the foreground. Slevogt's art collection included Manet's *Rue Mosnier with Flags* (1878, Los Angeles, The J. Paul Getty Museum). Maybe this picture encouraged him to paint his own motif.

It was not Slevogt's intention to glorify the military power of the Reich. A year before the outbreak of the Great War, the Kaiser was notorious in Europe as a sabre-rattler who only too willingly underlined his power with shows of military strength. Slevogt by contrast was concerned, in the spirit of Impressionism, with presenting the cheerful mood and the bright atmosphere. The transience of the moment is expressed in the intoxicating sound of the music as it passes by.

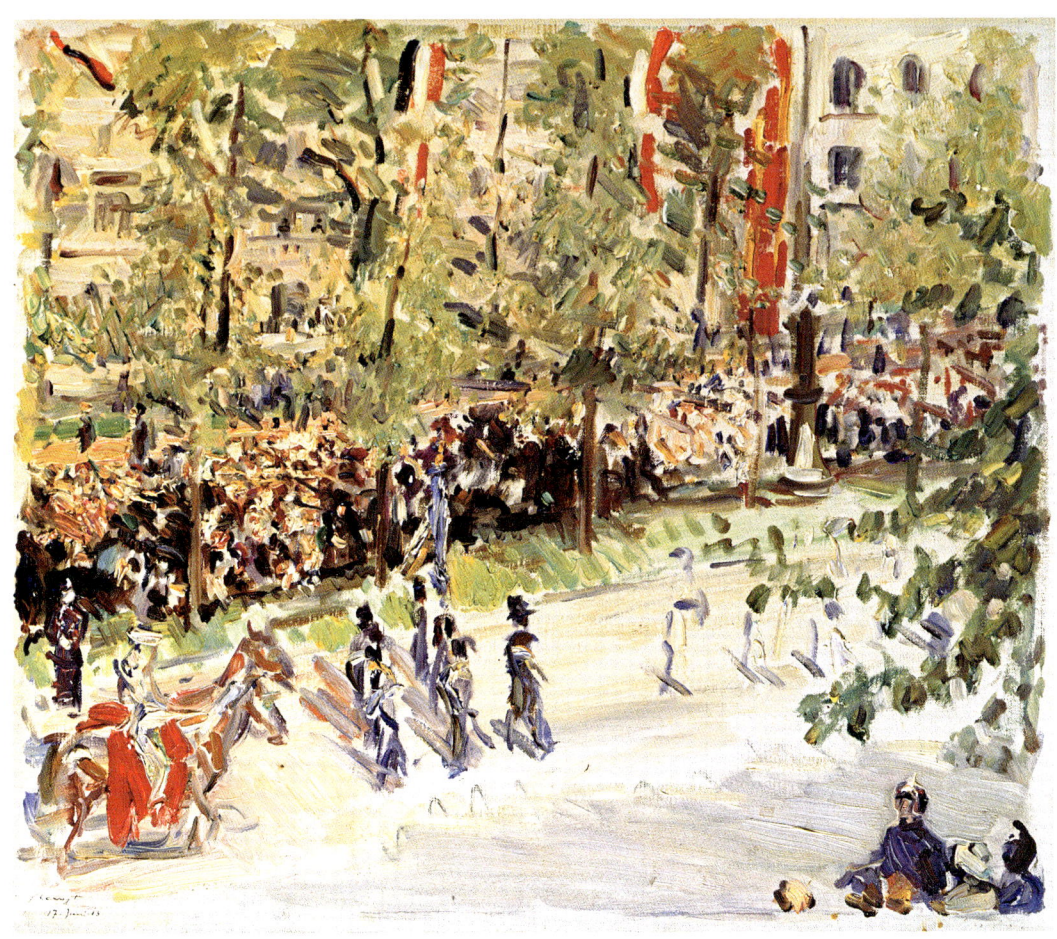

Parade, 1913
Oil on canvas, 48.4 x 57.5 cm (19 x 22¾ in.)
Hanover, Niedersächsisches
Landesmuseum Hannover

Fritz von Uhde
The Garden Path, 1903

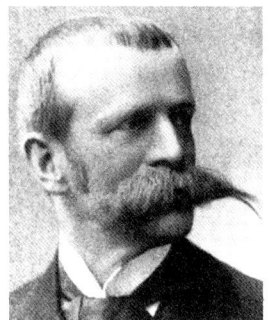

b. 1848 in Wolkenburg, Germany
d. 1911 in Munich

"Today I did something really extraordinary, such as I have perhaps never done before. Working in the open air in fine, airy shades, that seems to be my field. It was also very easy for me, and in addition it is infinitely more interesting to paint from nature like this than in the boring light of the studio," wrote Fritz von Uhde in September 1882, while he was staying in Holland. His time in Paris as a pupil of the Hungarian painter Mihály Munkacsy had come to an end, and he returned to Munich. Already from Paris Uhde had written that he had "got a technique which is simple and perfectly correct, and at the same time colourist to a high degree." Open-air painting led Uhde first and foremost to realistic art, in other words to a depiction of reality which was not only as faithful as possible but included figures like Dutch fishermen's children that had previously not been considered artworthy.

When in 1883 Fritz von Uhde together with Max Liebermann was represented at the International Art Exhibition in Munich, one art critic refused to discuss the two artists in the German section, since "with their latest endeavours they belonged among the French." The young German Reich was occupied with a search for an identity of its own, and this led to a sometimes vehement rejection of everything that had to do with French art and French culture. This tendency delayed the success of Impressionism in Germany.

It was only after the turn of the century that Uhde's Impressionist-like style found any recognition. One picture which did was the painting *The Garden Path,* which was acquired in 1904 by the then director of the Kunsthalle in Bremen, Gustav Pauli. It depicts Uhde's three almost grown-up daughters, to whom he was very close, since their mother had died a few days after the birth of the youngest.

Fritz von Uhde had taken on the then-unusual role of a lone father. This makes it easy to understand why time and again he chose to paint his children, whose world was so familiar to him, be it in the garden, at their lessons or reading. With motifs like these, most of which date from after 1900, he broke increasingly away from Realism and turned to Impressionism. At the same time the garden of his country house in Percha, a favourite place of his daughters, became a refuge, rather like the garden of Liebermann's Wannsee villa.

The Garden Path depicts the corner of a house at the bottom right-hand edge of the picture, where two paths meet and lead to the garden on the left. The three girls are going along the path, followed by their dog, passing the trained fruit trees in the background. The rectangular grid which provides a frame for the fruit trees forms an interesting contrast to the luxuriant greenish-brown wilderness. Bright patches of light play on the girls' clothes and on the path. These shimmering patches are reproduced with filmy bright brushstrokes, loosely distributed on the canvas. The light, filtered through the green canopy of foliage, is Uhde's central concern in this painting.

The garden path was the subject of a total of nine works between 1903 and 1908, seven of them oils and one a watercolour. But unlike Monet's haystack series, Uhde was not concerned with the changing light in the course of a day, but of the changes that occurred over the years. He was to return to the "fine, airy" shades once more at the end of his career.

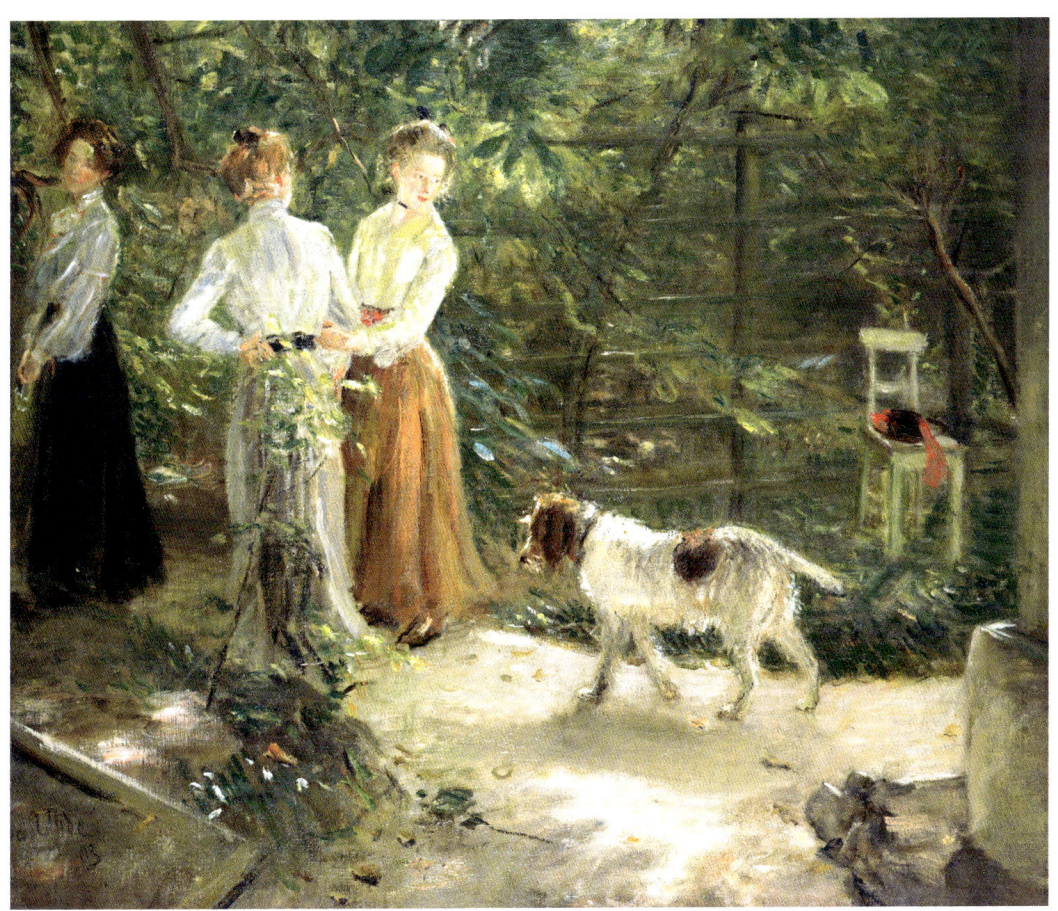

The Garden Path, 1903
Oil on canvas, 61 x 76 cm (24 x 30 in.)
Kunsthalle Bremen

Federico Zandomeneghi
Place d'Anvers, Paris, 1880

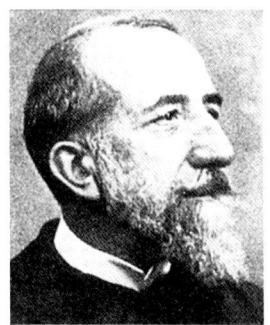

b. 1841 in Venice
d. 1917 in Paris

The Venetian painter Federico Zandomeneghi was, like his compatriots Giuseppe de Nittis and Medardo Rosso, drawn to Paris as if by a magic spell. He settled there in 1874, probably encouraged by the report by his friend the Italian art critic Diego Martelli that year, in which the latter had written enthusiastically about the first Impressionist exhibition. At the fourth exhibition held by the Impressionist artists in 1879, Zandomeneghi displayed, among other works, his portrait of Diego Martelli, who had introduced him to Degas. At the latter's invitation, Zandomeneghi took part in the Impressionist exhibitions of 1879, 1880, 1881 and 1886.

Zandomeneghi had started his artistic training in Venice and Pavia. In 1862 he had got to know the "Macchiaioli" in Florence, the group of artists so called after their predilection for patches (macchia) of colour. Zandomeneghi worked with them in the open air and familiarized himself with their technique.

Zandomeneghi fought with Garibaldi's units in the 1860s for Italian unification, the formation of an Italian national state, and against the country's occupation by Austria and France. In Paris though he devoted himself entirely to art, and was friends in particular with Renoir and Degas. His works were purchased by the Impressionists' gallery owner and dealer Paul Durand-Ruel.

Zandomeneghi followed the example of his role model Degas, devoting himself to the depiction of attractive young women in a variety of everyday situations: washing, combing their hair, powdering themselves or sitting in the garden or café. At the same time, like his fellow Italian de Nittis he developed into a landscape painter of some note. The growing demand for Parisian cityscapes and motifs from the environs was what the dealers had in mind when they got "their" artists to satisfy the needs of the market.

The painting *Place d'Anvers* makes this little square look bigger than it is in reality. Topographical authenticity, as so often with the Impressionist painters, was not guaranteed. Views like this simply do not have the "objective" fidelity of photographs, even if the angle, looking directly on to the back of a figure cut off by the bottom edge of the picture, gives the impression of a snapshot.

The row of trees down the middle of what is in fact not a square but an elongated oblong creates the impression of spatial depth. In the middle of the picture children are playing in the sun, while their mother sits in the shade of the houses. Zandomeneghi has not shied away from depicting the extremely bright sunlight, in which the paving appears almost white. In the shade, the coloured components are dominant: the – in actual fact, grey – cobbles are reproduced in densely packed strokes of blue, red, yellow and white.

This unusually powerful and fresh painting shows Zandomeneghi as a typically Impressionist artist. His relationship to this style was however fragile. Ultimately Zandomeneghi developed an individual style that seems to have little in common with Impressionist principles, but rather with its use of intensive colour comes closer to the Symbolism of artists such as Giovanni Segantini.

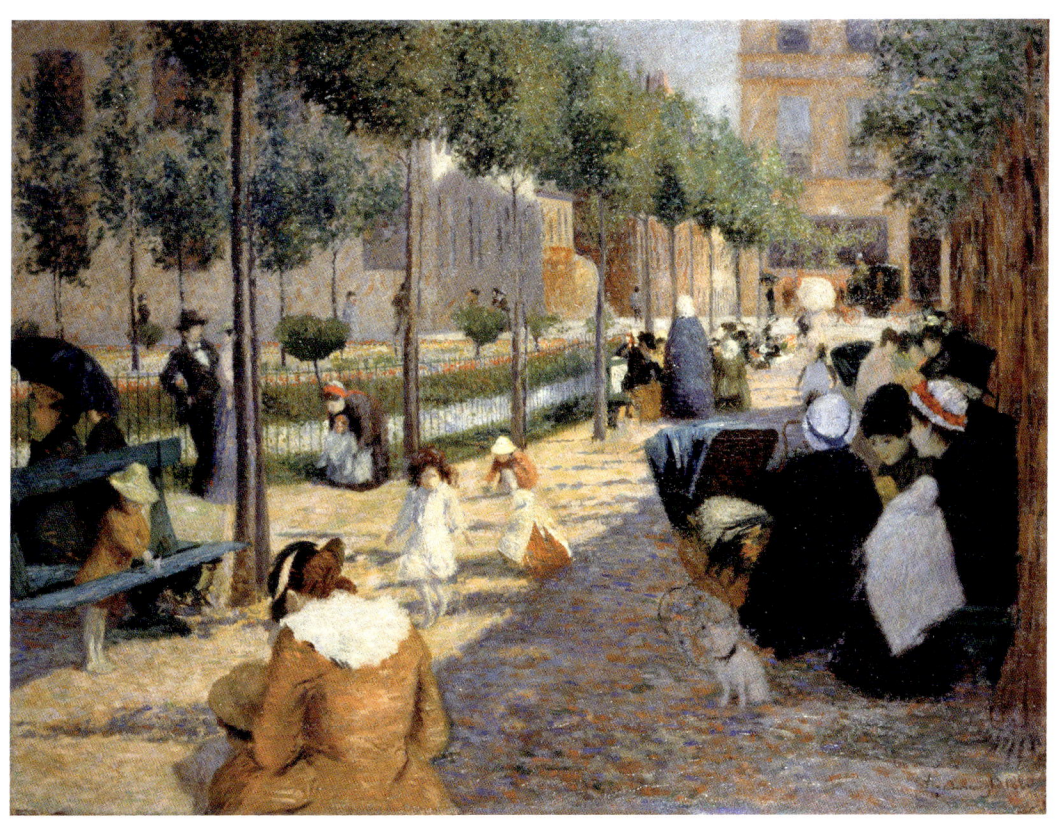

Place d'Anvers, Paris, 1880
Oil on canvas, 100 x 135 cm (39¼ x 53¼ in.)
Piacenza, Galleria d'Arte Moderna
Ricci Oddi

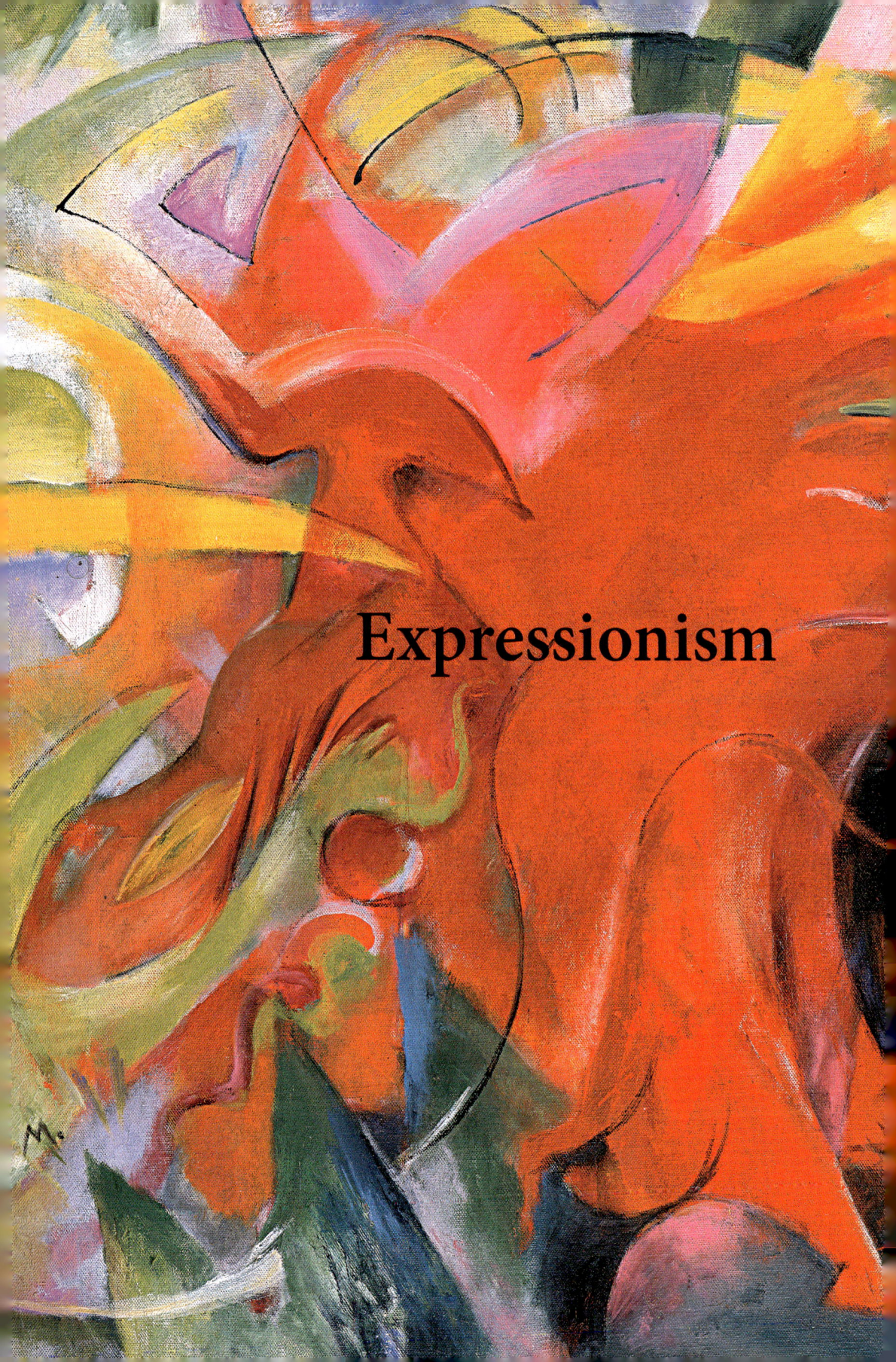

Expressionism

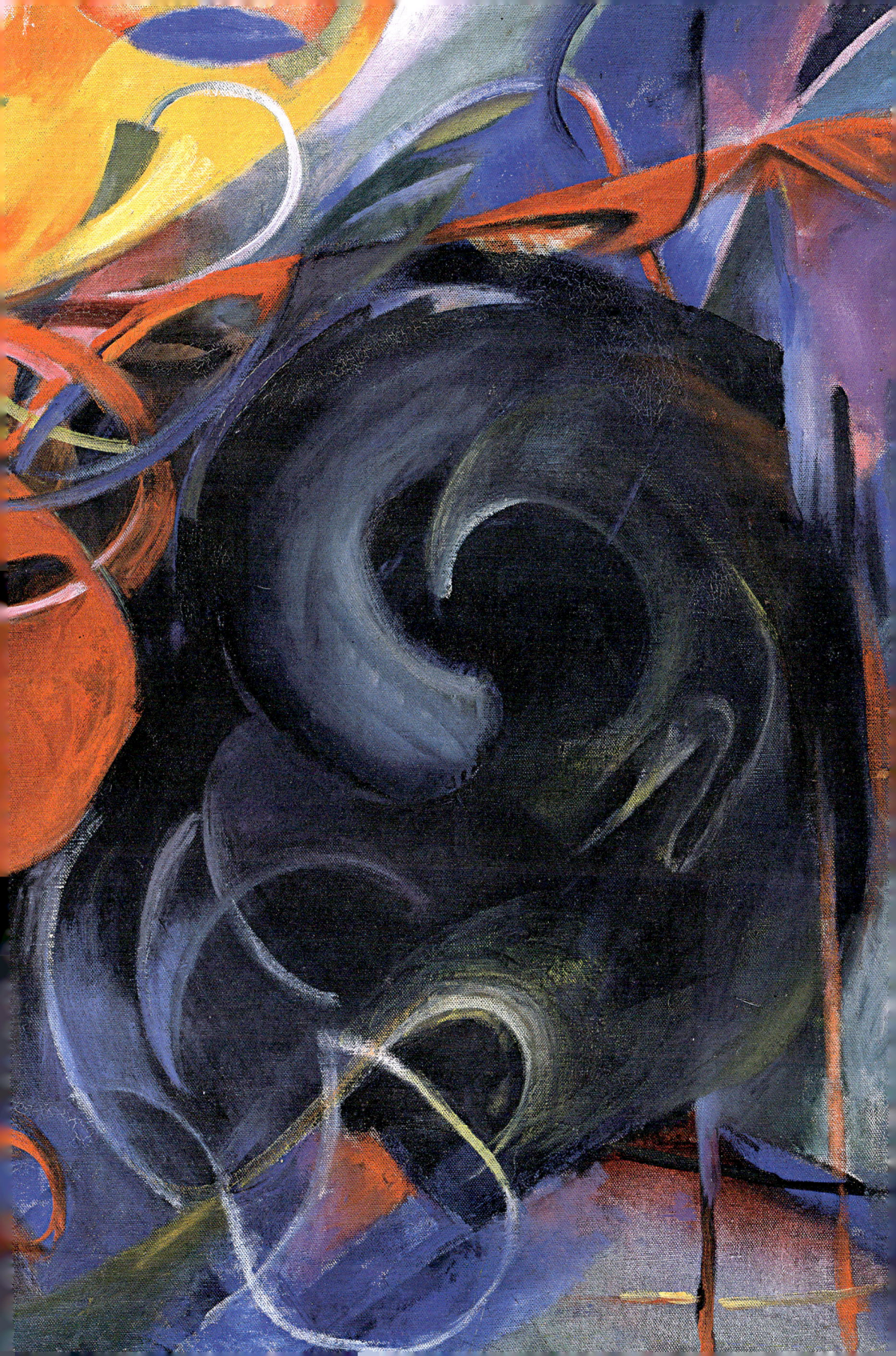

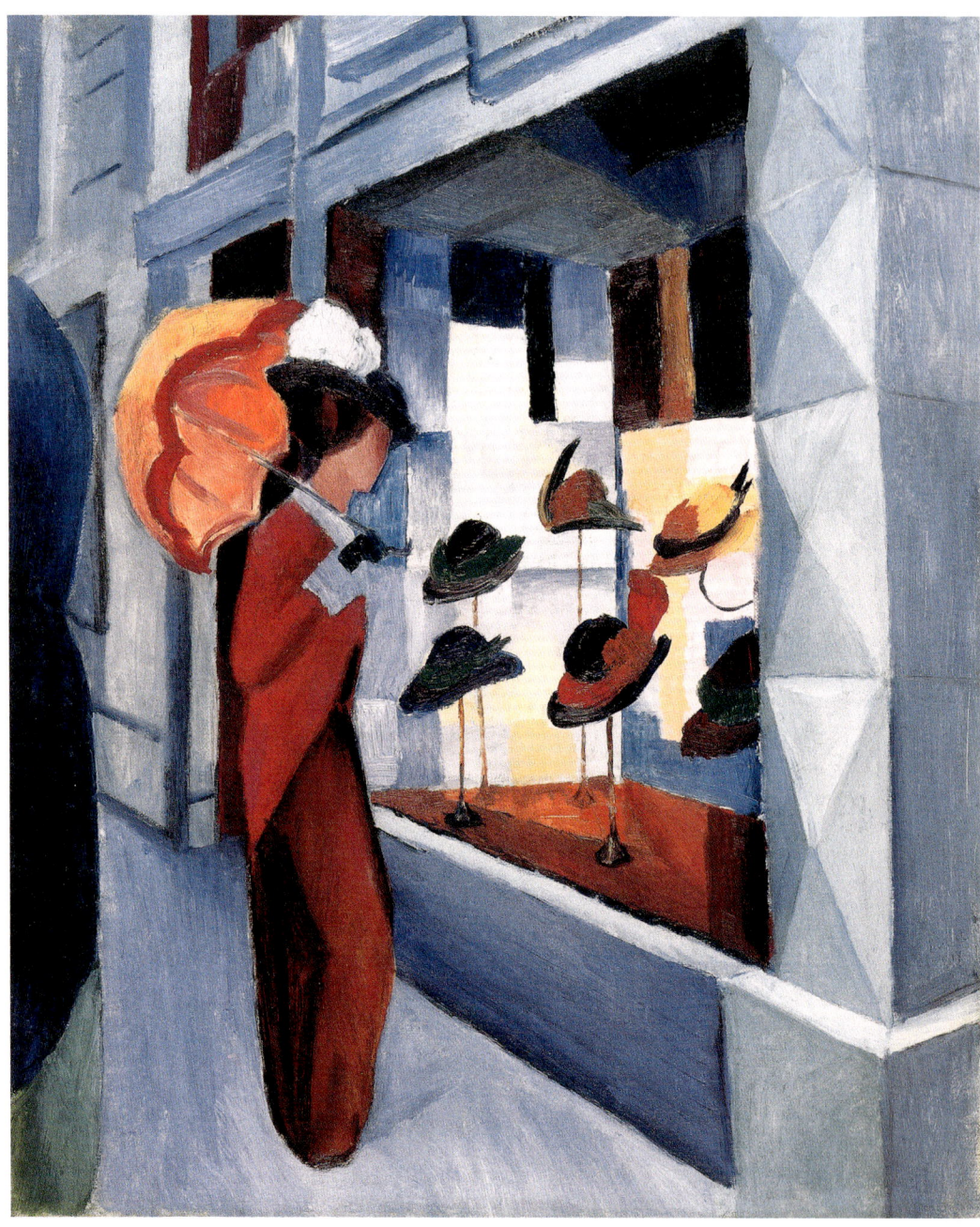

Norbert Wolf
Uta Grosenick (Ed.)

Expressionism

This Visceral Life

*"The deeper the blue becomes, the more strongly
it calls man towards the infinite."*
Wassily Kandinsky

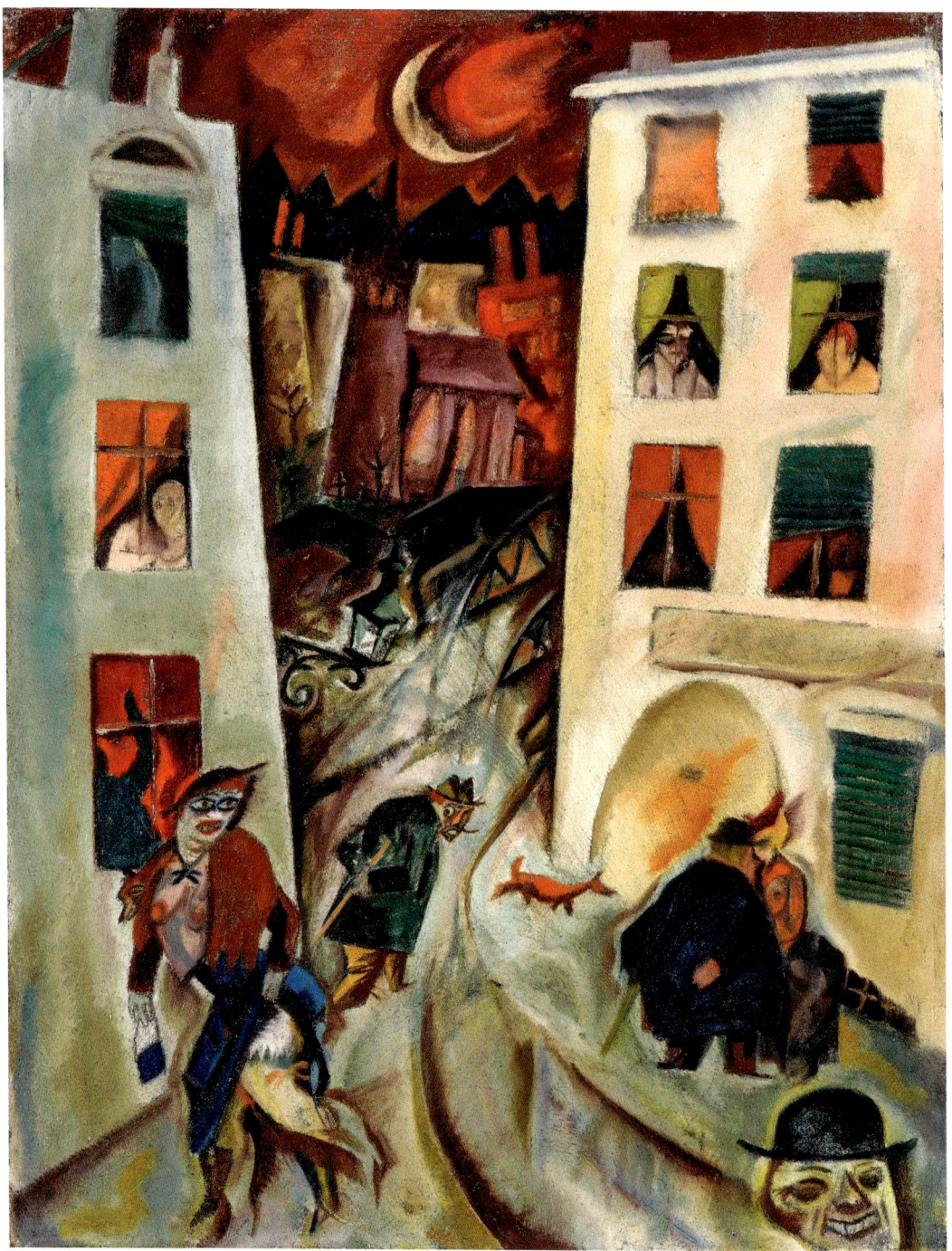

PAGES 102/103: Franz Marc
Fighting Forms (detail), 1914
Oil on canvas, 91 x 131.5 cm (36 x 51¾ in.)
Munich, Bayerische Staatsgemälde-
sammlungen, Pinakothek der Moderne

PAGE 104: August Macke
Milliner: Woman with Parasol
in front of Milliner's Shop, 1914
Oil on canvas, 60.5 x 50.5 cm (23¾ x 20 in.)
Essen, Museum Folkwang

ABOVE: George Grosz
The Street, 1915
Oil on canvas, 45.5 x 35.5 cm (18 x 14 in.)
Staatsgalerie Stuttgart

Contents

Metaphysical German Meatloaf
108

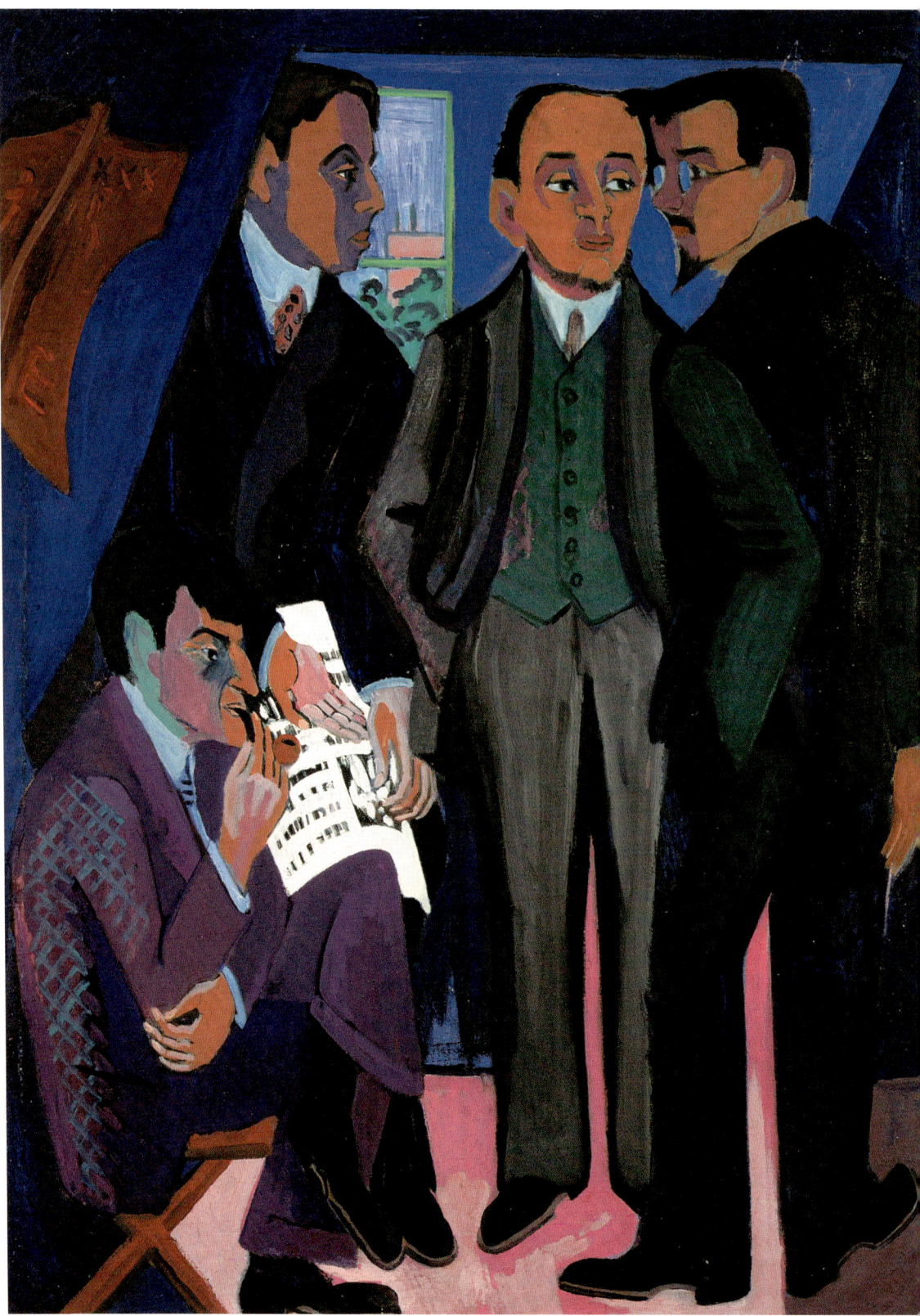

Metaphysical German Meatloaf

"What does my shadow matter? Let it run after me! I – shall outrun it. ..." This proud credo was penned in the 1890s by Friedrich Nietzsche (1844–1900), in *Thus Spake Zarathustra*. Twenty years later, Expressionist artists took the philosopher they idolized at his word and outran the shadow of academic rules, bourgeois taste, and the backward-looking costume plays of Historical Revival art.

The words "expressionism" and "expressionist" first cropped up in the art literature around 1911, initially as blanket terms for avant-garde art in Europe around the turn of the century. Paul Cassirer (1871–1926), the Berlin art dealer, reputedly applied the term to the emotionally charged paintings and prints of Edvard Munch (1863–1944), in order to distinguish the Norwegian's work from Impressionism. The same word was used by art historian Wilhelm Worringer (1881–1965), in the journal *Der Sturm*

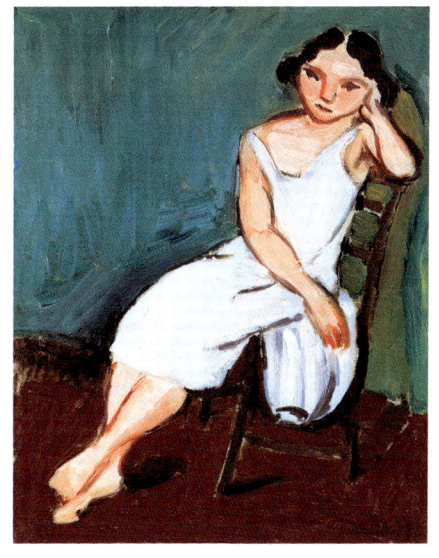

for August 1911, to characterize the art of Paul Cézanne (1839–1906), Vincent van Gogh (1853–1890) and Henri Matisse (1869–1954). In the catalogue to the Berlin Secession exhibition of 1911, Cubist and Fauvist artists fell under this rubric, from Pablo Picasso (1881–1973) to the young French vanguard.

In Herwarth Walden's (1879–1941) book of 1918, *Expressionismus, die Kunstwende (Expressionism, the Turning Point in Art)*, Italian Futurists, French Cubists and the Blauer Reiter in Munich were all subsumed under this term. Yet five years previously, at the "First German Autumn Salon" of 1913, Walden had introduced the Blauer Reiter group as "German Expressionists", and thus limited this stylistic category to the German-speaking countries.

This tendency would soon become the rule. A breakthrough in this regard was Paul Fechter's (1880–1958) 1914 book, *Der Expressionismus*, which focused on the art of Die Brücke and Der Blaue Reiter. In the field of literature, too, the term became current around 1911, and a year later, the first "German Expressionist drama"

OPPOSITE
Ernst Ludwig Kirchner
A Group of Artists, 1926/27
Oil on canvas,
168 x 126 cm (66¼ x 49½ in.)
Cologne, Museum Ludwig

FROM LEFT TO RIGHT
Otto Mueller, Ernst Ludwig Kirchner,
Erich Heckel, Karl Schmidt-Rottluff

TOP
Henri Matisse
Seated Girl, c. 1909
Oil on canvas,
41.5 x 33.5 cm (16¼ x 13¼ in.)
Cologne, Museum Ludwig

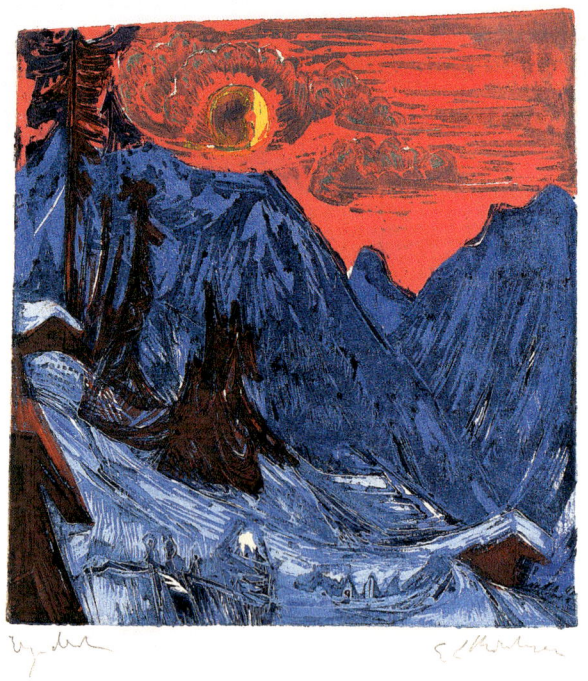

was staged, in the shape of Walter Hasenclever's (1890–1940) play *Der Sohn (The Son)*.

By the outbreak of the First World War, in other words, Expressionism had become almost synonymous with the German contribution to current international developments in art and literature. This national restriction took place despite the great and obvious impulses that German art received from abroad. Although many on the German scene denied such influences, cosmopolitan artists like the Russian El Lissitzky (1890–1941) and the German-French Hans (Jean) Arp (1887–1966) of Alsace saw them very clearly, while scoffing that German artists had only half-digested them. In their book *The Art Isms*, 1925, the two authors declared, "Cubism and Futurism were minced up to create mock hare, that metaphysical German meatloaf known as Expressionism." Nevertheless, the myth had long since been born; or perhaps rather, a myth that had existed since the Sturm und Drang of the late eighteenth century had received fresh fuel: the supposed prerogative of Germans for the expression of extreme emotional states in art.

Now, about 1905, German artists appeared to be bringing what were seen as their Faustian gifts into modern art with revolutionary verve, finally establishing a counterweight to the French avant-garde. And since it was supposedly an outpouring from the national psyche, Expressionism could be explained in language like this: "German man is demonic man per se... Driven, buffeted by such a demonism of Becoming and never Being – this is how the German appears to other peoples." So stated the idealist philosopher Leopold Ziegler (1881–1958), in *Das Heilige Reich der Deutschen (The Holy Empire of the Germans)*, published in 1925. Back in 1920, the creative urge spurred by such mental "buffeting" was evoked by the former Brücke painter Max Pechstein (1881–1955). In a similarly agitated staccato, Pechstein exclaimed: "Work! Intoxication! Brain racking! Chewing, eating, gorging, rooting up! Rapturous birth pangs! Jabbing of the brush, preferably right through the canvas. Trampling on paint tubes..." Shock, provocation, a revolt of the young against the hidebound establishment – these, as not only Pechstein believed, were the driving forces behind Expressionism.

A feverish restlessness, an emphasis on the painting process rather than on the creation of serene, self-contained form, a tendency to mysticism – elements of the "German psyche" that seemed to predestine it for the new style. "The Expressionist does not look; he sees," declared Kasimir Edschmid; that is, Expressionist artists were formative rather than imitative

TOP
Ernst Ludwig Kirchner
Winter Moon Night, 1919
Colour woodcut,
29.5 x 29.5 cm (11½ x 11½ in.)
Kunstmuseum Basel,
Kupferstichkabinett

OPPOSITE
Wassily Kandinsky
Improvisation 9, 1910
Oil on canvas,
110 x 110 cm (43¼ x 43¼ in.)
Staatsgalerie Stuttgart

minds who shaped their view of the world out of their own volition, who in effect "created" reality by dint of their visionary powers.

Judging by such examples, Expressionist diction with its telegram style, its exclamations and explosive, brief phrases not only blasted traditional syntax but apparently conveyed clear and lucid ideas. Yet this impression is deceptive. In reality, it inflated the metaphysical meaning of words, generated arbitrary verbal sequences, and – charged with symbols and metaphors – remained purposely dark and obscure, comprehensible only to initiates. The exalted, harsh character of Expressionist diction was in fact an elixir for those involved in the movement. But it also invited criticism. As August Macke (1887–1914) already told some of his fellow painters, the means of expression they used were perhaps "too big for what they wanted to say".

What would be gained by taking Expressionism at its word and raising the expression of emotions to the main criterion of good art? Wouldn't this be tantamount to exalting a mania into a style? What is implied by describing the effect of art metaphorically, as a slap in the public's face, an attack on

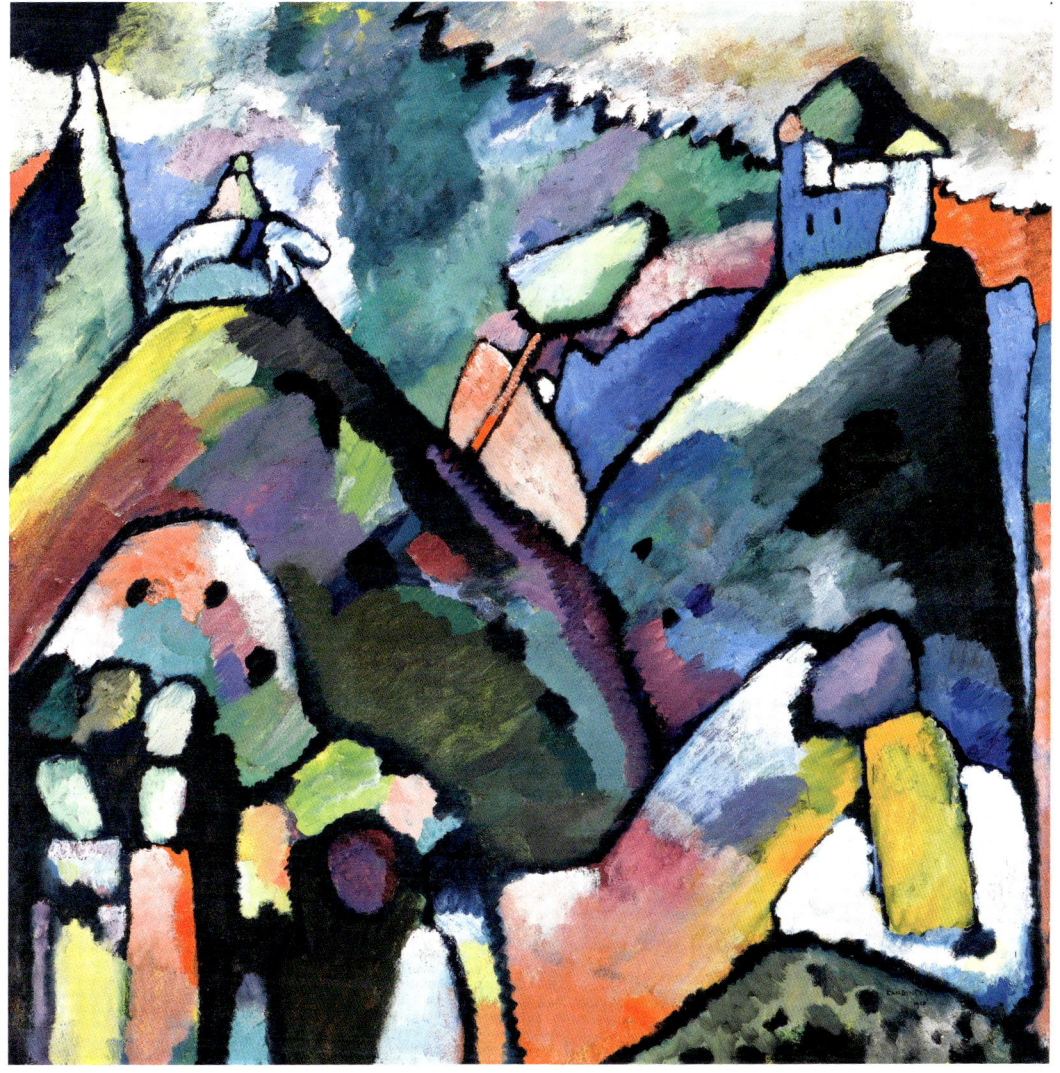

the audience? In 1917 Herwarth Walden gave a terse definition of Expressionist art, saying that it was not an "impression from outside" but an "expression from inside". Yet again, this definition is not so apt as it might seem. When we think about it, it applies just as well to countless past works of art, from the figures of Michelangelo (1475–1564) to the prints of Albrecht Dürer (1471–1528), or from the altar paintings of Matthias Grünewald (c. 1475/80–1528) to the work of El Greco (1541–1614), two artists much admired by the Expressionists. What justifies us in characterizing the expressiveness of early twentieth-century German modernism not simply as a neurotic adventure but as a serious "ism", an established style?

Art historians have always had their difficulties in accepting Expressionism as a style. One need only compare the paintings of Kirchner, Kandinsky, Kokoschka and Dix to see that they have next to no formal common ground. This is why many art historians now prefer to describe Expressionism less as a style than as a "direction" or "tendency", a manifestation of a young generation's feeling for life. This art can just as much be suffused by urban anxiety as reflect nostalgia for a past Golden Age, a paradisal state of innocence. And as frequently as the Expressionists probed new and suggestive forms within the force field of modern art, they just as frequently thought through old and familiar formulas, bringing them up to date, developing them to a radical peak – suggesting that they were not able to outrun that "shadow" invoked by Nietzsche after all.

In fact, Nietzsche himself loomed like a shadow over them. His books were enthusiastically consumed by the younger generation, especially *Zarathustra*. The revolutionary philosopher presented a prime example of self-liberation from authoritarian constrictions, bourgeois narrow-mindedess, materialist thinking. As the poet Gottfried Benn (1886–1956) would later recall, Nietzsche "… was the earthquake of the epoch for my generation". Yet such an overweening "superego" also presented countless problems to Nietzsche's enthusiastic disciples. The two most important artists' groups that appeared in Germany in the years prior to the First World War, Die Brücke and Der Blaue Reiter, attempted nothing less than to realize the ideal of a future existential world order. In their manifesto, the Brücke artists appealed to a "new generation of both creators and lovers of art", to anyone who was capable of expressing "what urges them to create, directly and without adulteration", as welcome adepts of a new and progressive religion of art.

Between Distortion and Abstraction

The dogmas of this art, this religion of art with its projection of a good and true life, were fraught with contradictions. On the one hand stood means of extreme subjectivity; on the other, a desire for individual immersion in and submission to the cosmos. This was reflected in the characters in Expressionist literature, stage plays and art, who acted as if they were marionettes of universal forces. The spontaneous, agitated expression aimed at in both cases led to what Werner Hofmann has called "elementary gestures of sensation and instinct".

At the onset of the development, the crucial thing was to overcome passive depictions of nature à la Impressionism and tap individual emotional powers, by employing brash bright colours and "brutally" reduced forms. The laws of perspective, faithfulness to anatomy, natural appearances and colours counted for little or nothing; distortion and exaggeration became an equivalent for rendering the material world transparent to the psyche. *On the Spiritual in Art* was the revealing title Wassily Kandinsky (1866–1944) gave to the now-famous book he finished in 1910 and published in 1911. The development of an art of the psyche, what Kandinsky termed "spiritualization", opened to painting the realm

Ludwig Meidner
The Corner House (Villa Kochmann, Dresden), 1913
Oil on canvas on cardboard,
97.2 x 78 cm (38¼ x 30¾ in.)
Madrid, Museo Thyssen-Bornemisza

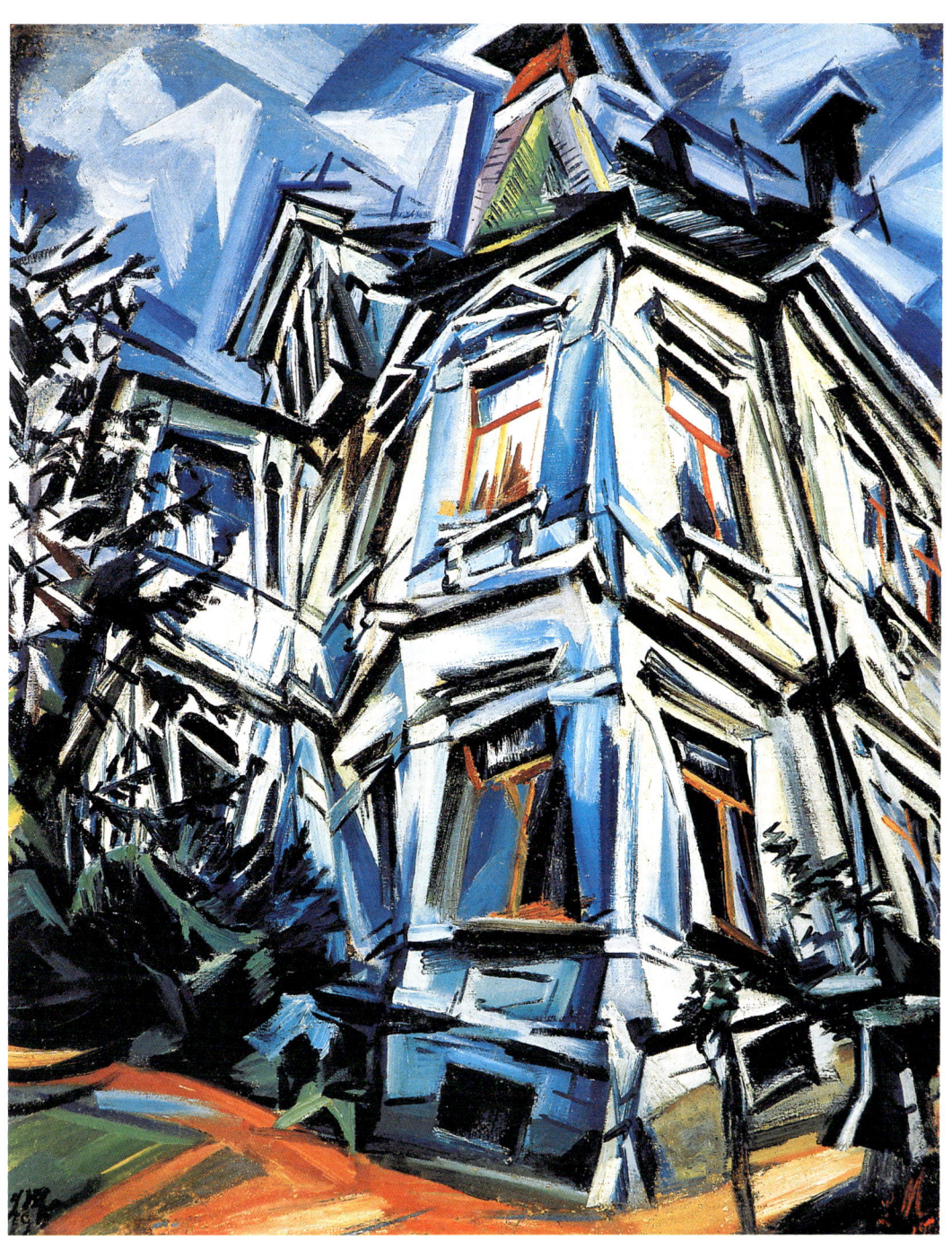

of abstract symbolism, a turning point in art history for which both Kandinsky (ill. p. 111) and the Blauer Reiter in Munich (ill. p. 128) stood. "Nordic man", who yearned for insight into the spiritual and, in that regard, was related to "the Oriental", explained Worringer in his 1908 dissertation *Abstraction and Empathy* "feels a veil between himself and nature", and therefore strives for an abstract art. Accordingly, abstraction and expression would enter a "Faustian" marriage.

Not only with regard to the ecstatically heightened self-consciousness of artists, but also with regard to their symbolic interpretation of the world, their search for metaphysical foundations or cosmological orders, utopian designs and elementary realms beyond history from which they hoped for a rebirth of unadulterated creativity, the Expressionists developed many an idea that originated in German Romanticism. Some of them were quite aware of this. Kandinsky, for instance, was greatly pleased when a critic used the term "Romanticism" in connection with his work. Moreover, Expressionism shared the penchant of one branch of Romanticism for things dark and aberrant.

A case in point is Alfred Kubin (1877–1959), an eccentric artist distantly associated with the movement. Born in Leitmeritz (now Litomerice) in Bohemia, the young Kubin enjoyed torturing small animals, watched flayers and butchers at work, and was fascinated by natural disasters – probably an instinctual reaction to an overly strict father. In 1911 Kubin was among the founding members of Der Blaue Reiter. Years previously he had illustrated ghost and horror tales by the likes of Fyodor Dostoyevsky, E. T. A. Hoffmann, Edgar Allan Poe, and Oskar Panizza, primarily in pen-and-ink drawings, but occasionally in watercolours or oils. Kubin's spidery, scratchy stroke invoked a phantasmagorical and nightmarish realm that seemed to spring straight from the "dark" or "gothic" Romanticism of the early nineteenth century. In twelve weeks of the year 1907, he wrote the novel *The Other Side*, a paraphrase of the Apocalypse in highly expressive diction. Kubin spirits the reader into a dream city by the name of Pearl, in far distant Asia. As the inhabitants search for a hidden meaning in the senselessness of their existence, the devil appears among them in the guise of a "manager" and takes over the helm. The plot turns and the city begins its inexorable demise.

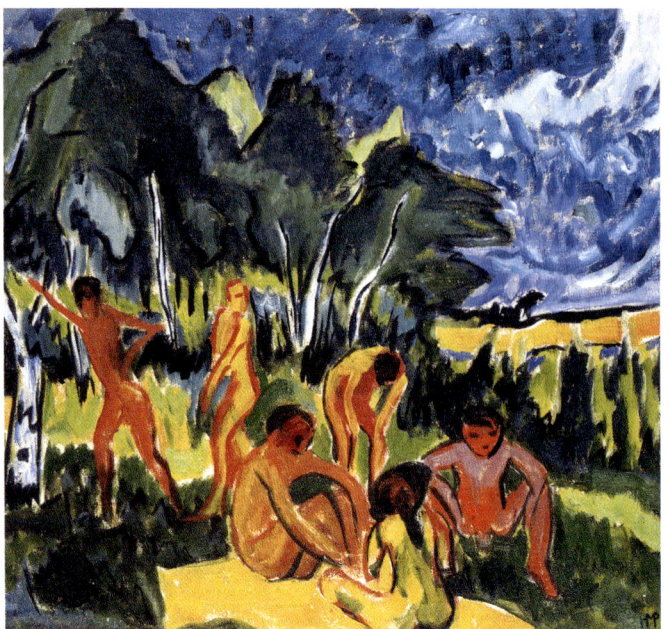

Max Pechstein
Open Air (Bathers in Moritzburg), 1910
Oil on canvas,
70 x 79.5 cm (27½ x 31¼ in.)
Duisburg, Lehmbruck Museum

OPPOSITE
Conrad Felixmüller
Workers on the Way Home, 1921
Oil on canvas,
95 x 95 cm (37½ x 37½ in.)
Private collection

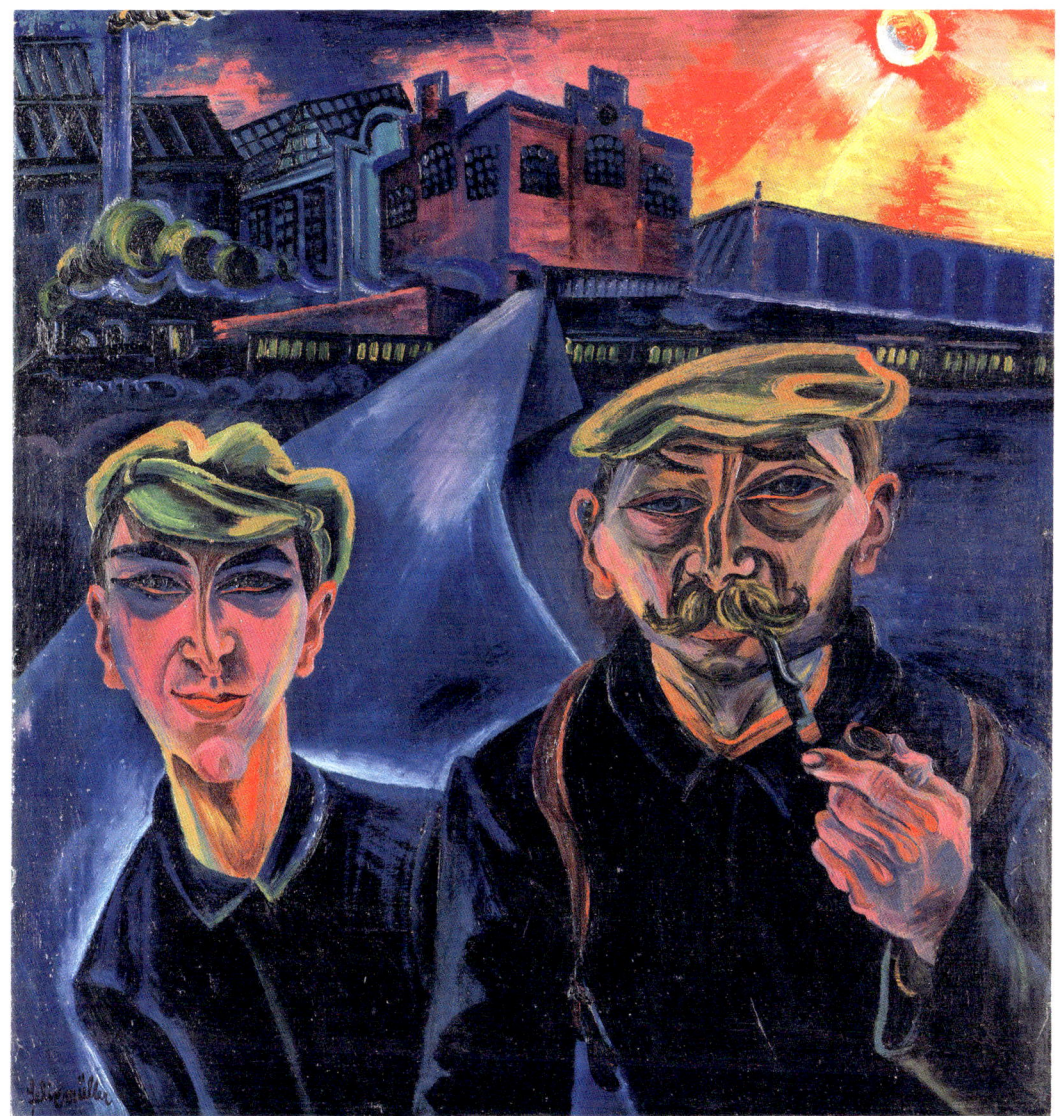

Overexcitedness was characteristic not of all but of many fields of Expressionist activity. Recall the agitated figures in Emil Nolde's (1867–1956) religious compositions (ill. pp. 186/187), the apocalyptic landscapes of Karl Schmidt-Rottluff (1884–1976), Erich Heckel (1883–1970), and especially Ludwig Meidner (1884–1966; ill. p. 179), or the masklike, distorted big-city faces of George Grosz (1893–1959; ill. p 106) or Otto Dix (1891–1969; ill. p. 145). Overexcitedness also marks the highly contrasting planes or nervous, angular forms and hatching in the prints, many of which are among the high points of Expressionist art (ill. p. 110).

An aesthetic of the ugly and brutal came to the fore. This represented an appeal on the artists' part to liberate art from the ghetto of the "beautiful and true", where it had degenerated into pretty, innocuous decoration for home and fireside. This aesthetic went hand in hand with an urge for the "elemental", everything exotic and primitive, which along with free sexuality were celebrated as an

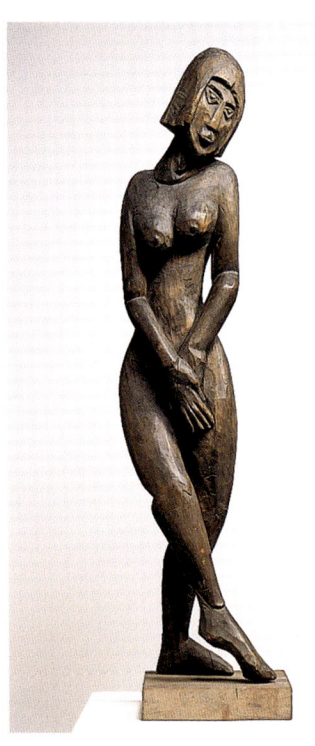

embodiment of "naturalness" and the lust for life of Expressionist creation. As early as 1905, French avant-garde artists had begun to interest themselves in ethnological collections and adorned their studios with African masks and statues from the South Pacific. This desire for supposed primitiveness served two purposes for bohemians: as a way to revolt against the bourgeoisie, and as a source of presumably unspoiled principles of design, embodied in the art of the world's indigenous peoples. Masks, fetishes, ancestor figures – along with folk art, children's drawings and the picturemaking of the mentally ill – advanced to the centre of artists' concerns.

Nolde set off in 1913 on an expedition to New Guinea. Pechstein considered settling in the Palau Islands in 1914. Aesthetically, such interests resulted not least in a number of Expressionist carvings. Schmidt-Rottluff's wood sculptures were probably inspired by Carl Einstein's book *Negerplastik (Negro Sculpture)*, published in 1915. Ernst Ludwig Kirchner (1880–1938), too, created similar works (ill. p. 116). Museums of ethnology became sources of Expressionist inspiration, as did the performances of "exotic artistes" at the circus or cabarets, or magazine photographs of "Negro combos". Primitivistic traits entered depictions of faces especially, with angular noses, full lips and pointed chins, an emphasis on the roughhewn that was complemented by exaggerated gestures and poses.

Yet such excessive tendencies were always paralleled by more domesticated approaches. Kirchner's oeuvre can stand for many in this regard. Kirchner was not the sheer emotionalist for which he his generally taken. Especially after 1920, the intellectual underpinning of his art became increasingly important to him; he began to suppress the impulsive factor in favour of a more considered approach. The resulting decorative, flat structuring and serene, monumental compositions belied the cliché of the Faustian German modernism favoured by many later authors, who accordingly disregarded this phase of his career and excluded it from the panorama of Expressionism.

Purging the World

In 1926, Ernst Jünger (1895–1989) described the mood on the eve of the First World War in retrospect: "War simply had to bring us grandeur, strength, dignity. To us it seemed a masculine act, a merry shootout on blossoming, blood-bedewed meadows. No finer death was there in the world…" Only a few artists, including Pechstein and to some extent Grosz, Meidner and Conrad Felixmüller (1897–1977), were immune to this fascination. Ernst Barlach (1870–1938) and Lovis Corinth (1858–1925), in contrast, added their voices to the patriotic choir. War euphoria swept through Europe from end to end.

The Futurists had long since declared war to be "the only hygiene for the world". Franz Marc (1880–1916) expected the war to bring a worldwide catharsis and a spiritual purging of humankind. Dix and Max Beckmann (1884–1950) volunteered for service; Schmidt-Rottluff looked forward to the chance to "create something as powerful as could be". Yet such exalted visions rapidly gave way to trauma in view of the shell-holed fields, rank trenches, and overflowing field hospitals of France and Flanders – a trauma that the sculptor Wilhelm Lehmbruck (1880–1919) eloquently expressed with his figure of the *Fallen Man* (ill. p. 171). Many young artists – Marc, Macke, Wilhelm Morgner (1891–1917) – were never to return.

Prior to the First World War, Expressionist experiments in form and colour reflected above all individual artists' mental states and moods. Only later did they turn clearly to social issues, depicting victims of war, pillorying social injustice or political repression. Now artists began to advance concrete arguments for improving the world. However, only a few, apart from Grosz and Felixmüller (ill. p. 115), were willing to go beyond the artist's role and engage in actual party politics.

The Expressionist groupings, whether more closely or more loosely knit, all envisaged a community of living and working that partook of Romantic ideals. Naturally they pursued more practical ends as well, especially that of making their work known through group exhibitions and publications. The Brücke painters in particular shared everything, from studios and models to painting materials, partly out of a lack of funds but mainly because fraternal cooperation meant a great deal to them. Living and working in town was interrupted in the summer months by extended country vacations, where they painted from life, swam in the nude, and generally enjoyed themselves with their models and girlfriends. This imitation of an innocent state of nature (ill. p. 114) reflected artists' yearning for that unity of art and life which had been among the demands of the avant-garde ever since the 1890s. This, too, was an attempt to purify a materialistic world by turning back to the utopia of an earthly paradise.

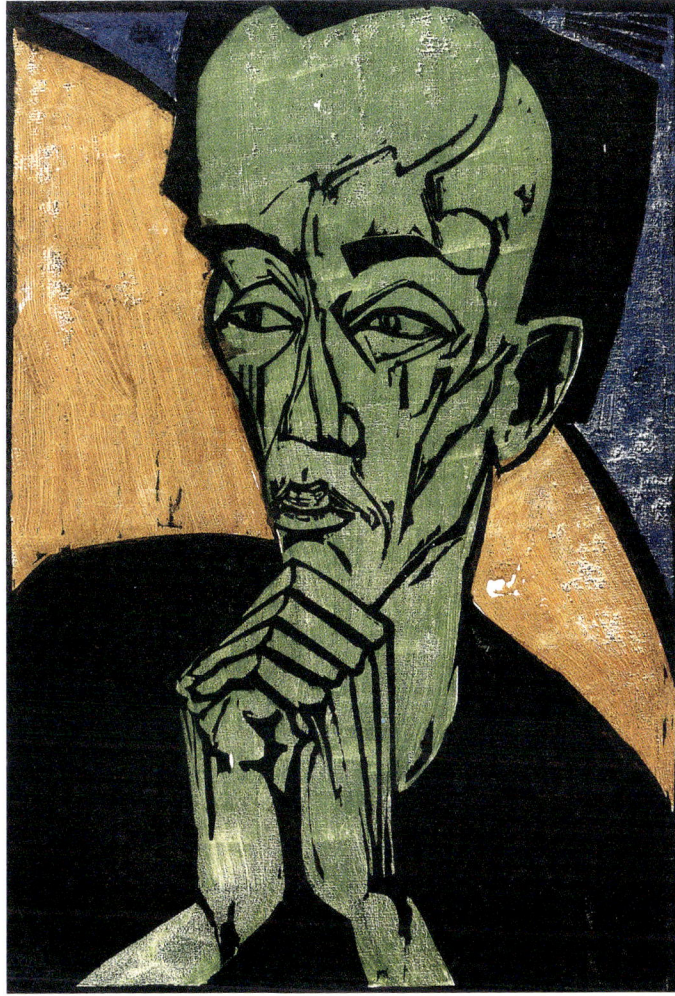

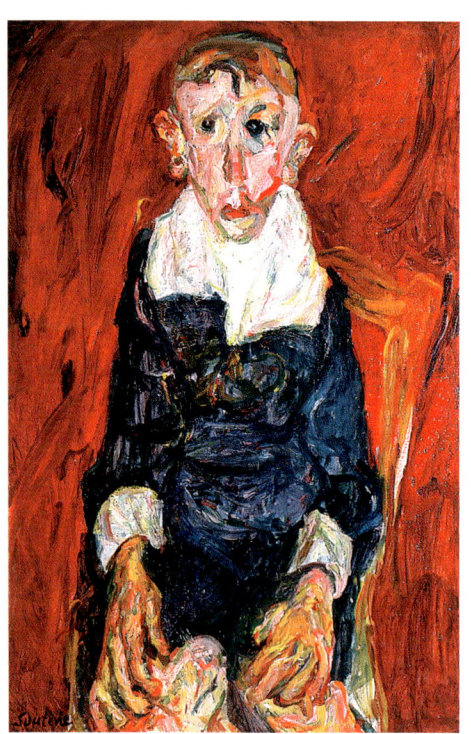

The Topography of Expressionism

Many attempts have been made to divide the map of Expressionism into clear domains. As convincing as it is to focus on Dresden or Berlin (Die Brücke) and Southern Germany or Munich (Der Blaue Reiter), the attempt to define a Northern German group of Expressionists is problematical. The painters concerned barely knew each other, although Nolde had briefly met Paula Modersohn-Becker (1876–1907) in Paris in 1900 and encountered Christian Rohlfs (1849–1938) in Soest in 1907. Otherwise the artists in the north lived at great distances from one another – Modersohn-Becker in Worps-wede, Nolde mostly on the island of Alsen, and Rohlfs in Soest and Hagen. Nolde, in view of his brief, one-and-a-half year membership in Die Brücke, can properly be considered an affiliate of this tendency. Rohlfs, on the other hand, is described in the literature as a representative of "Rhenish Expressionism".

In purely geographical terms, the Rhineland in fact played an important part in the chorus of Expressionist voices. The Museum Folkwang, founded in Hagen in 1902 by Karl Ernst Osthaus (1874–1921), became a key centre of the art scene at that period. August Macke was active in the Rhineland on several occasions, serving in 1912, for instance, as a jury member for the Cologne "Sonderbund" exhibition. Yet the literature tends to put more weight on Macke's contact with Der Blaue Reiter, which he maintained from Bonn and through his friendship with Marc. Actually, Macke's attitude to the Munich group was always ambivalent, and the romantic mysticism they displayed was not to his taste. Classifying Macke as part of Der Blaue Reiter is difficult, and is permissible only when we remain aware of his outsider's role.

Yet it would be even more imprecise to consider Macke a leader in some specifically Rhenish brand of Expressionism. It was not until 1913, on the occasion of a show at the Cohen bookshop near Bonn University, where the key Expressionist ideologist Wilhelm Worringer taught, that Macke tried to marshal an existing group of friends under the title of "Rhenish Expressionists", and establish a third centre alongside Berlin and Munich. Yet there was no commonly held concept to weld together the sixteen candidates, who apart from Macke and Heinrich Campendonk (1889–1957) included the future Surrealist Max Ernst (1891–1976). The latter's characterization of the Bonn show in a newspaper review was indicative. The show revealed, Ernst wrote, "how a series of powers are at work within the great stream of Expressionism who have no outward similarity to one another but only a common 'direction' of thrust, namely the intention to give expression to things of the psyche (Seelisches) through form alone."

The Austrian and Viennese art scene was dominated around 1900 by Jugendstil, or Art Nouveau. Gustav Klimt (1862–1918) was the admired model for Oskar Kokoschka (1886–1980) and Egon Schiele (1890–1918), whose personal Expressionistic idiom developed by way of Klimt's daring form and colour, which the more conservative wing of the Viennese Secession found subversive. Klimt also communicated an existential involvement with subjects such as sexuality, illness and death to the Expressionists. The influence of Sigmund Freud's psychoanalysis on the artistic environment of the day lent Austrian Expressionism its special note.

Countless components made the map of Expressionism into a many-coloured and complex tapestry. Accents were set by a series of lone wolves. For Kandinsky, Feininger, Dix and others, the style represented no more than a brief phase. Nor should we forget that expressionistic tendencies appeared beyond the borders of the German-speaking world as well. In Belgium, for example, the work of Constant Permeke (1886–1952), Gustaaf de Smet (1877–1943), Frits van den Berghe (1883–1939) and Albert Servaes (1883–1966) is spoken of as Flemish Expressionism. Two further painters also deserve mention.

One was Chaim Soutine (1893–1943), a Lithuanian Jew who worked from 1916 onwards in Paris. His friends, including Amedeo Modigliani (1884–1920), had connections with the Berlin journal *Der Sturm* and were familiar with publications on German Expressionism. Soon Soutine (ill. p. 118) began to pursue aims that brought him into close proximity with the prewar work of Ludwig Meidner, a friend of Modigliani's. However, it is uncertain whether Soutine ever saw German Expressionist art in the original. In France and the United States, where he was lauded Soutine was long believed to have influenced Oskar Kokoschka (1886–1980). This is incorrect for chronological reasons alone, and was always vehemently denied by Kokoschka himself. Nor can the occasional reversal of this relationship be proven.

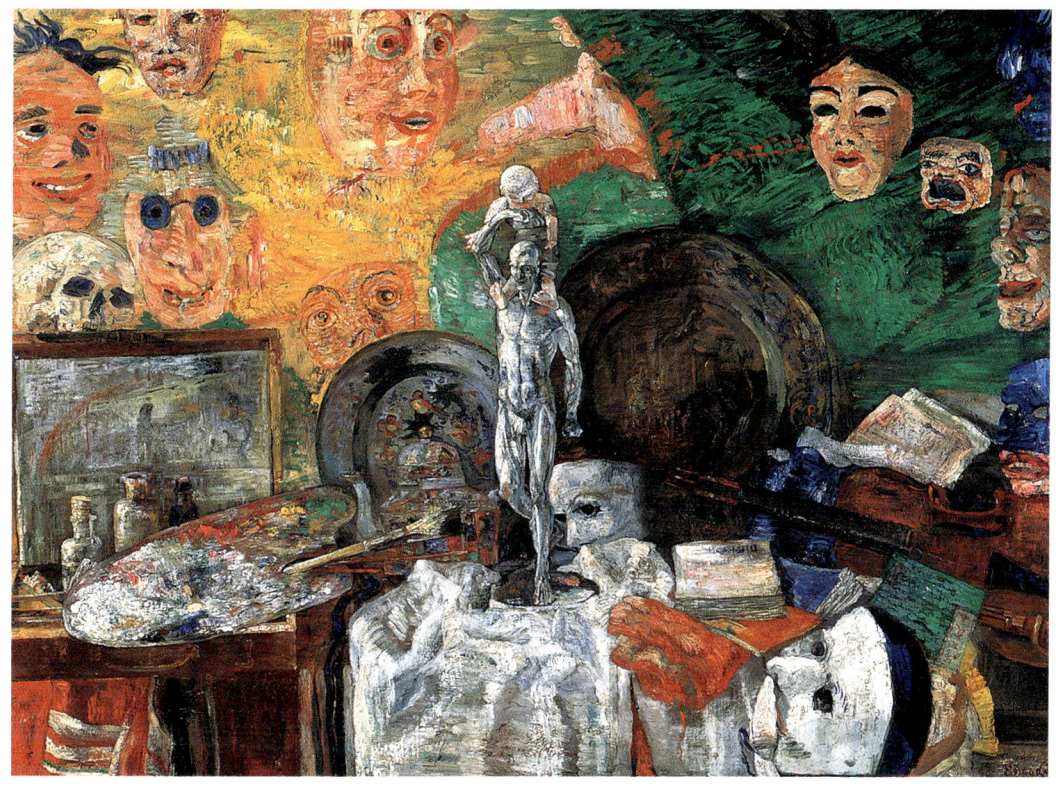

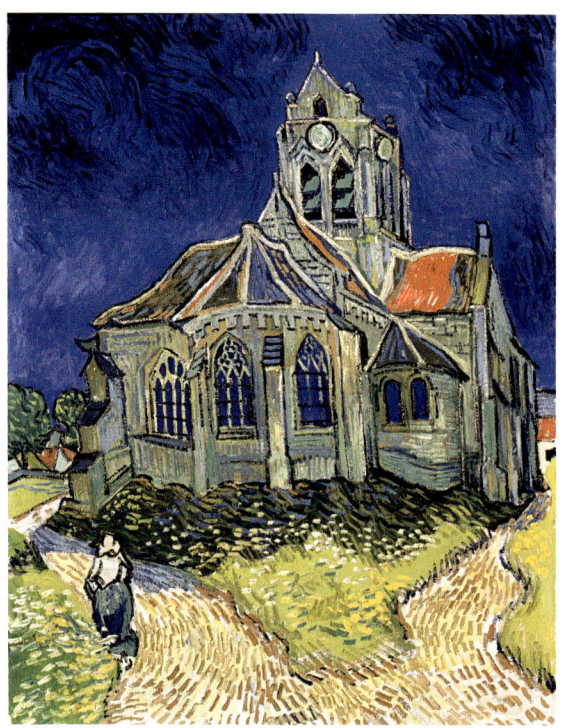

The second artist in question, the Fauvist Georges Rouault (1871–1958), has likewise frequently been compared to Kokoschka in his Dresden period. The French artist outlined his figures with extremely heavy contours and filled the spaces with strong colours. In 1905, he began concentrating increasingly on religious subjects. In these respects Rouault's work came closer than that of any other French artist to German Expressionism, for instance the paintings of Nolde or Beckmann.

Citing names like Soutine, Rouault and others, occasional attempts have been made to define something in the nature of French Expressionism. In 1928, in fact, Galerie Alice Manteau in Paris mounted an exhibition titled "L'Expressionisme Français", at which works by Soutine, Modigliani, Maurice de Vlaminck (1876–1958), Maurice Utrillo (1883–1955) and Marc Chagall (1887–1985) were shown under the premise that they all reflected a heightened awareness of an inner world and employed subjective means of depiction marked by energetic gestures, distortions of form, and orgies of colour – criteria, in other words, that had long been canonized in Germany as those of Expressionism.

From the Reservoir of the European Avant-Garde

What was the art scene like when the Expressionists came on stage? As a point of departure, let us take prewar Berlin, where Die Brücke moved after their first years in Dresden. Wilhelm II, King of Prussia and Kaiser of the German Empire, felt duty-bound to set the tone in artistic matters as well as political, despite the fact that progressive minds thought he had the taste of "a cook or baker's boy". What this dilettante on the throne enjoyed were the pedantic, overloaded pomposities of Anton von Werner (1843–1915), his court artist. Anything that diverged from painstakingly rendered historical costume scenes or innocuous salon paintings was relegated to the category of "gutter art", from the socially committed prints of Käthe Kollwitz (1867–1945) and the earthy Impressionism of Max Liebermann (1847–1935) to the absolutely crazy Expressionists and, of course, every foreign so-called "avant-garde". Most of the revolutionary advances in modern art had long since taken place in Paris, and had been presented to the Berlin public by audacious art dealers, journals and collectors. The Belgian James Ensor (1860–1949) and the Norwegian Edvard Munch, who was long active in Germany, likewise caused a sensation there.

The Expressionists in Berlin and elsewhere welcomed any brand of painting that was based without reserve on subjective experience and its radical translation into expressive forms and colour arrangements,

TOP
Vincent van Gogh
The Church of Auvers, 1890
Oil on canvas,
93 x 74.5 cm (36½ x 29¼ in.)
Paris, Musée d'Orsay

OPPOSITE
Robert Delaunay
Window on the City, 1912
Oil on canvas, painted dead frame,
46 x 40 cm (18 x 15¾ in.)
Hamburger Kunsthalle

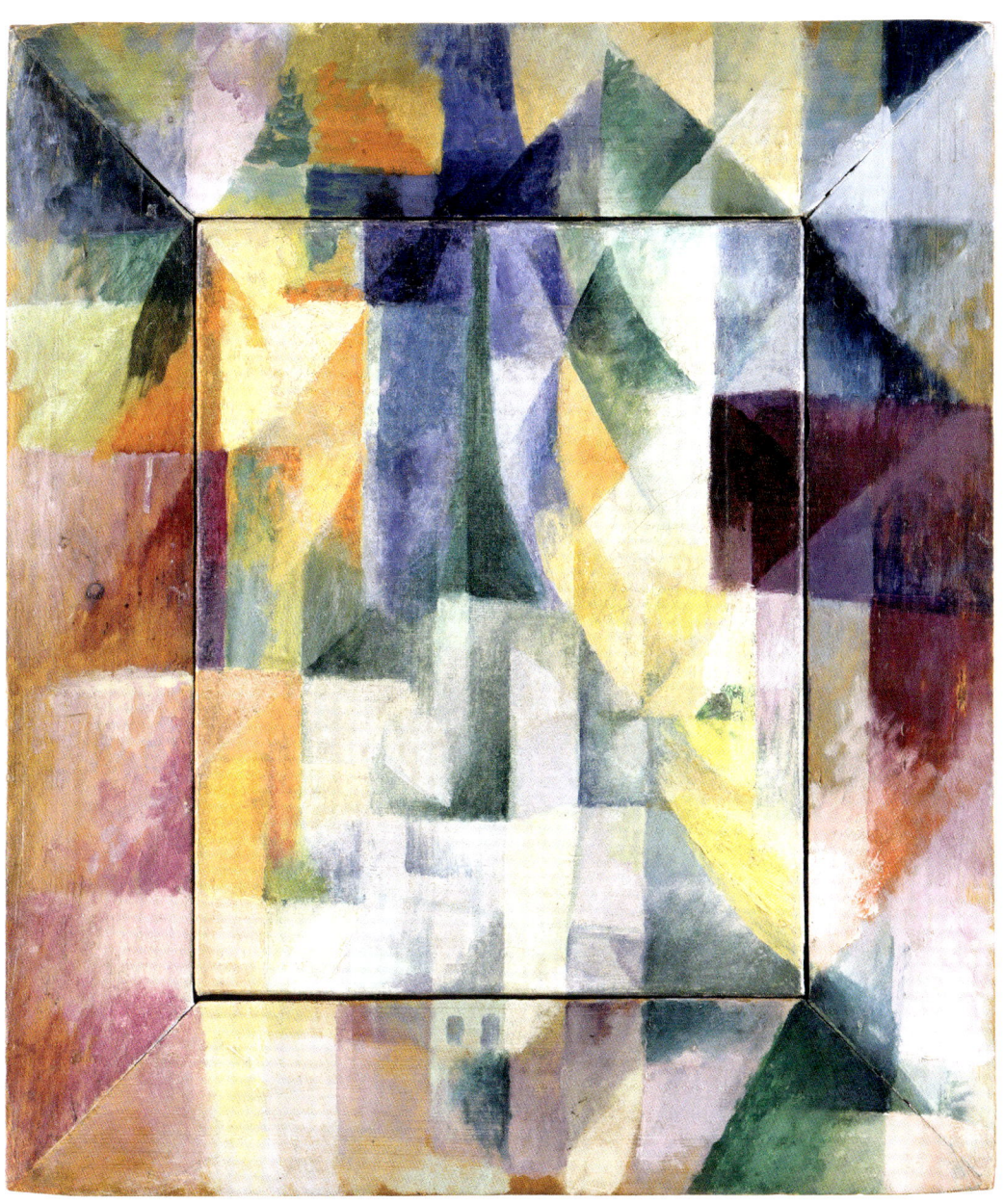

and that accordingly overcame art's conventional function of representing or illustrating appearances. This held for Ensor (ill. p. 119), who revealed the depravity behind the masquerade of modern mass society and by so doing deeply impressed Nolde, for one. And this held even more for the symbolistic art of Munch with its expressive graphic abbreviations, which affected the art of Die Brücke especially. Munch's famous *Scream* of 1893 (ill. p. 125) projected all the torments of life into a face distorted into an emblematic, unforgettable grimace. Munch's inscription in the fiery red sky is indicative: "Could only have been painted by a madman."

And again and again, it was two "fathers of modernism" who cast their spell over the Expressionists: Vincent van Gogh (ill. p. 120) and Paul Gauguin (1848–1903), who shared what Uwe M. Schneede has described as "the 'rough image,' whose distorted perspectives, flatness, deformations… run counter to all well-worn traditions… The 'rough image': made of coarsely rubbed pigment, on ever coarser canvas, in rapidly applied, broad brushstrokes, with parts of the canvas left uncovered… revealing the sequential character of the painting process…"

The first van Gogh exhibition in Germany, whose significance cannot be overstated, was mounted in 1905, the founding year of Die Brücke, at Galerie Arnold in Dresden. However, the same van Gogh touched off a notorious scandal in Germany. In 1911, when a van Gogh work was acquired by the Kunsthalle Bremen, the mediocre painter Carl Vinnen (1863–1922) launched a petition protesting at what he termed "alien domination" of German art. The petition was signed by several renowned artists, strangely including Käthe Kollwitz. Marc and Kandinsky immediately organized a counterprotest, which was supported by museum directors, art historians and artists and appeared in print by the summer of that year by Piper in Munich, under the title *Im Kampf um die Kunst (The Struggle for Art)*.

The exotic, if Europeanized, mythical aura of Gauguin's Tahitian paintings, on the other hand, struck the Expressionists as a perfect synthesis of life and art. They admired Gauguin's emotionally moving figures and were inspired by his generous, sweeping planes and his tendency to the daringly decorative – stylistic means, in other words, of the kind which were later adopted in Gauguin's wake by the Nabis.

In 1905, a band of young artists shocked Paris audiences. One critic called them "les Fauves", or "The Savages", Led by Henri Matisse (1869–1954), Georges Rouault, Maurice de Vlaminck and André Derain (1880–1954), they were joined the following year by Georges Braque (1882–1963) and Raoul Dufy (1877–1953). A movement that was as influential as it was short-lived, Fauvism might be briefly described as painting rich in colours deployed in luminous, flat planes in which figures and objects were abstracted and reduced to essentials. The colours were released from the task of naturalistic description, and were therefore capable of developing an enormous power of expression. At times, tense lines held the colour areas together, yet often these strokes took a loose, approximate course, not always forming definite contours and serving more to accentuate areas than to isolate them.

The fascination exerted on the Fauves by sub-Saharan African and Oceanic art strengthened their resolve to engender decorative effects by means as simple as possible. If the rhythm of a composition made it necessary, they distorted forms or employed "unnatural" spatial relationships. Around 1908, Fauvist painting became widely known in Germany, through the mediation of Die Brücke and the Neue Künstlervereinigung München, or New Artists Association Munich. Fauvism became an inexhaustible reservoir, from which other Expressionists soon began to draw as well.

The representatives of Der Blaue Reiter and Rhenish Expressionism tapped a different source: the Orphism of Robert Delaunay (1885–1941). The highly respected Delaunay began with Cubism,

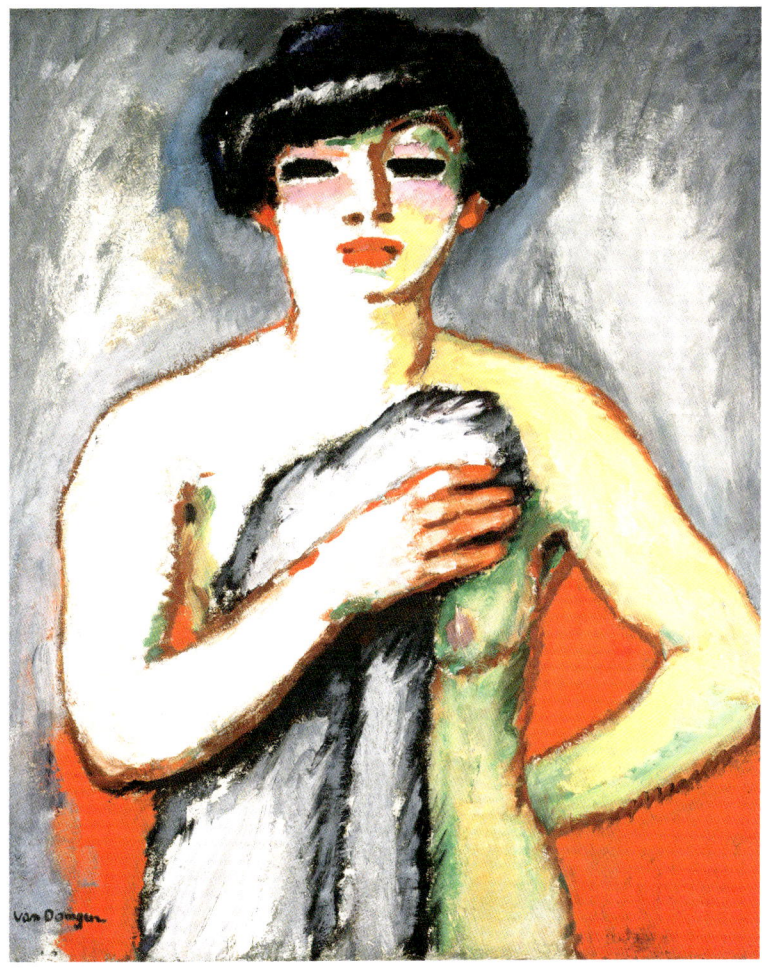

Kees van Dongen
Portrait of Fernande, 1906
Oil on canvas,
100 x 81 cm (39¼ x 32 in.)
Private collection

yet was disturbed by the studio still-life motifs on which Cubist facetting of form was demonstrated. He was intrigued by the vitality and motion of the big city, the simultaneity of its phenomena, its electric lighting, and its new perspectives in time and space, which he transformed into a dynamic, increasingly abstract painting in exquisitely balanced colours (ill. p. 121).

The 1912 "Sonderbund" exhibition in Cologne reflected the rich spectrum of influences that shaped the development of Expressionism. At its centre stood van Gogh, Munch, Cézanne and Gauguin. Picasso, important for the Expressionists working both in Berlin and Munich, was likewise well represented, as were the Cubists, Matisse and the Fauves. Kokoschka and Schiele were on view, and Expressionists from Die Brücke and Der Blaue Reiter. Munch described the exhibition in a letter of May 1912: "The wildest things being painted in Europe are gathered here…"

Die Brücke

On 7 June 1905, the students of architecture Fritz Bleyl (1880–1960) – who, however, was soon to turn his back on art – Ernst Ludwig Kirchner, Erich Heckel and Karl Schmidt-Rottluff formed in Dresden the artists' group Die Brücke (ill. p. 108). The name went back to a passage in Nietzsche's *Thus Spake Zarathustra* (1883–85): "What is great in Man is that he is a bridge and not a goal; what is lovable in Man is that he is a passing over and a passing under…" The four viewed themselves as a chosen elite that set out to make "elbow room and free lives" for themselves "in face of the established, older forces", as stated in their founding manifesto. In 1906 Max Pechstein joined the group, as did Nolde, who, however, left it again only a year and a half later. Otto Mueller (1874–1930) became a member in 1910.

The Brücke programme, published in 1906, was an appeal to all progressive makers of art to join forces and bring into being a revolutionary artistic existence. The appeal was too passionate to be satisfied with local effects, and was accordingly directed to artists outside Germany as well. It reached, for instance, Cuno Amiet (1868–1961) of Switzerland, who was very knowledgeable about the Parisian scene, and Axel Gallén-Kallela (1865–1931) of Finland. In 1908, the Dutchman Kees van Dongen (1877–1968), a Fauvist (ill. p. 123), joined as an honorary member for a good year. The ardently wooed Edvard Munch at least became a passive member, one of the friends and supporters of the group who wasted no time in becoming active – mounting seventy group exhibitions from 1905 to 1913, in Germany and abroad.

Break up encrusted structures – that was the warcry. When Kirchner and his friends painted from the model in group studio sessions they used to change places frequently. This spontaneous change of viewpoint and their rapid working speed facilitated an almost automatic approach to drawing and a summary painting style, and schooled their eye for simplified, reduced form. Summers were spent at the Moritzburg Lakes outside Dresden, where the group envisaged a harmony of man and nature, a life free of the compulsions of civilization, or, as it were, a Gauguinesque Tahiti at their doorstep (ill. p. 114). Yet the Expressionist revolutionaries who tried to leave tradition behind still looked back in awe to the greats of art history, were susceptible as much to Post-Impressionist and Fauvist influences as to medieval woodcuts. It is surely no coincidence that the styles of the individual group members at this time are hardly distinguishable from one another. They were all fascinated by the art of the South Pacific and sub-Saharan African peoples, which they studied at the Dresden Museum of Ethnology. The black contours, angular figure types, masklike faces and vital poses of the figures in their paintings derived in part from this experience. Kirchner discovered in an English illustrated volume examples of ancient Indian painting and rapidly adapted them to his needs. The Gauguin exhibition at Galerie Arnold, Dresden, in 1910 provided a further impetus for the group's concern with the modes of perception and depiction of non-European cultures.

In 1911 the Brücke artists moved to Berlin. There Herwarth Walden had just opened his gallery, Der Sturm, and begun publishing the revolutionary journal of that name, one of whose editors was Oskar Kokoschka. Through *Der Sturm* the Brücke artists made contacts with literary Expressionism, and also with the radical anti-bourgeois circle around Franz Pfemfert and his journal *Die Aktion*, established in March 1911. These contacts resulted in a stronger orientation on the painters' part toward issues of content. A link between Kirchner and *Der Sturm* was forged by Alfred Döblin (1878–1957), a psychiatrist and writer whose big-city novel, *Berlin Alexanderplatz*, would make him famous in 1928. Such contacts facilitated the urge of Expressionist artists to transcend the limitations of art genres and become active in every field of creative work. An example was the forty-seven woodcut illustrations, endpapers, frontispiece and two-coloured woodcut Kirchner created for Georg Heym's (1887–1912) volume of poetry, *Umbra vitae*, of 1924, one of the most cogent and significant works of Expressionist book illustration.

Although the Brücke initially remained together in Berlin, divergences in their previous collective style soon became apparent. Each artist began to react in a different way to the moloch of the big city, from which they occasionally,

Edvard Munch
The Scream, 1893
Oil on canvas,
91 x 74 cm (36 x 29¼ in.)
Oslo, Nasjonalgalleriet

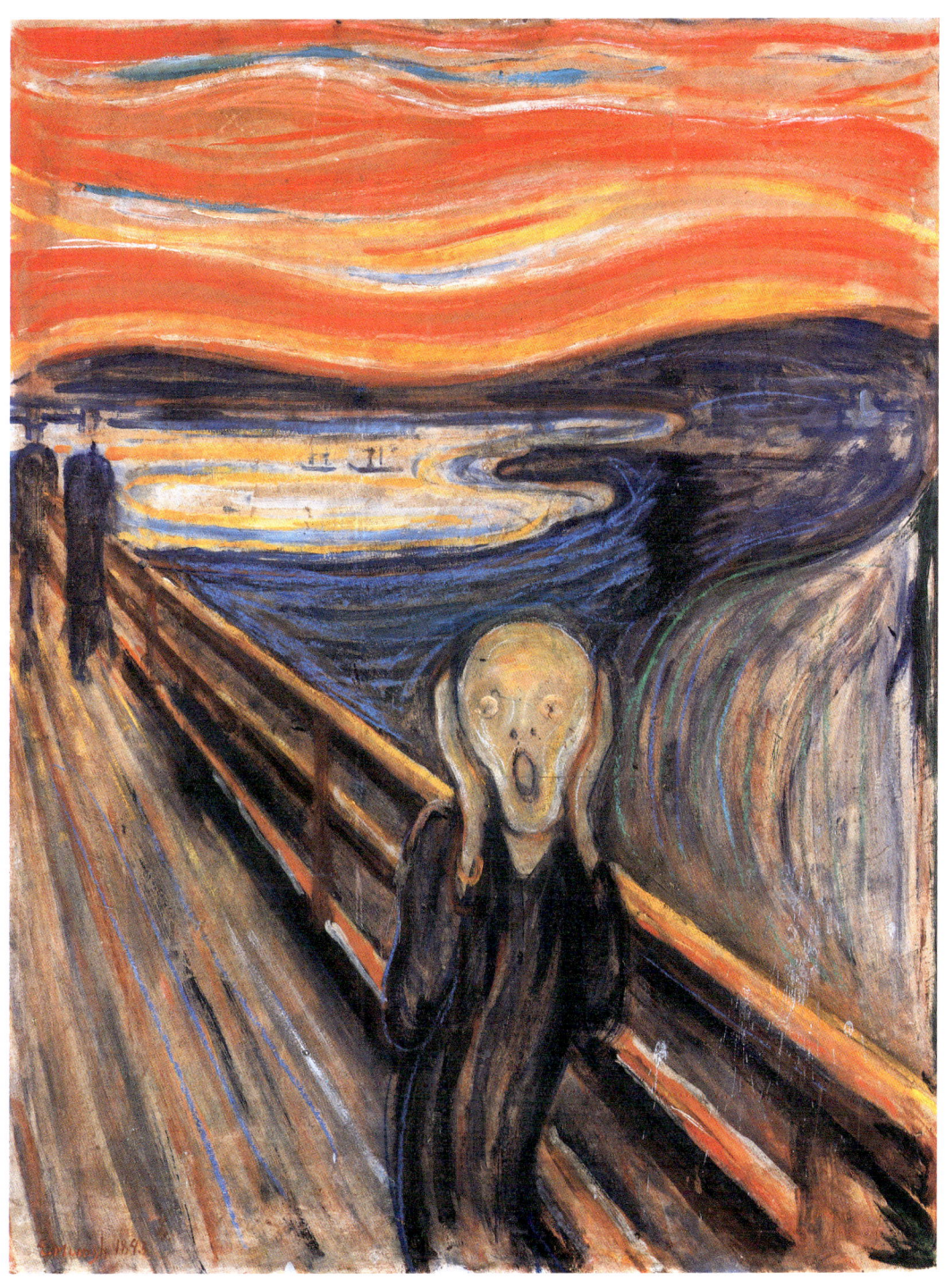

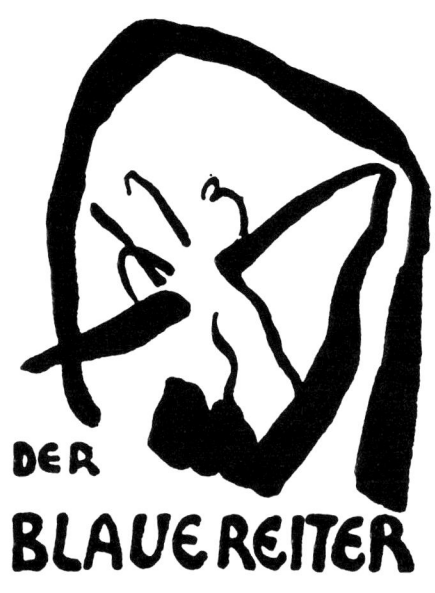

DER BLAUE REITER

if no longer as a group, fled to various idyllic places: the Moritzburg Lakes, the village of Dangast on the North Sea, Nidden in East Prussia, or the Baltic island of Fehmarn. The differences within the group grew, until its final breakup was provoked by Kirchner, as Die Brücke informed its friends and supporters on 27 May 1913.

Der Blaue Reiter

"Munich was resplendent," declared Thomas Mann (1875–1955) in his 1902 story *Gladius Dei*. He probably meant this ironically, for around the turn of the century the Bavarian metropolis hosted not only relatively progressive, Art Nouveau-inspired tendencies but thoroughly commercialized conservative styles. Still, the art centre was resplendent enough to attract the genius of Kandinsky as the century got underway. Initially an adherent of Jugendstil, the German version of Art Nouveau, Kandinsky returned to his new home in 1906 from the Gauguin memorial exhibition in Paris with many new ideas. These he proceeded to combine with elements of Russian folk art, in which he naturally felt at home. Two years later Kandinsky and his pupil and long-time consort, Gabriele Münter, were working in Murnau, Upper Bavaria, studying the folk art of the Alpine foothill region, copying verre églomisé, and adapting this technique based on flat stylized forms, brilliant colours and strong black contours.

And another year later, in 1909, the two artists established the Neue Künstlerver-einigung München (NKVM, or New Artists Association of Munich). The other founding members were Alexej von Jawlensky (ill. p. 127), Marianne von Werefkin (1860–1938), Vladimir von Bechteyeff (1878–1971), the two future Neue Sachlichkeit artists Adolf Erbslöh (1881–1947) and Alexander Kanoldt (1881–1939), the significant Karl Hofer (1878–1955) – who would later, over his own protests, continually be reckoned an Expressionist – and finally, Alfred Kubin. Soon the group was joined by others, including art historians, dancers (Alexander Sacharoff – see ill. p. 155), musicians and literary people. The NKVM, by the way, was the first artists' association to include large numbers of women, as members or guests, a circumstance that was largely the result of Werefkin's strong personality.

Kandinsky, the association's chairman, envisaged overcoming the self-satisfied art of the salons by aiming at a synthesis of all artistic ideals in the sublimating melting pot of the spiritual. Impulses from diverse quarters were welcome. This was illustrated particularly by the second association show at Galerie Thannhauser, Munich, in 1910, which included works by Picasso, Braque, Derain, van Dongen (ill. p. 123), Rouault, and the brothers David (1882–1967) and Vladimir Burlyuk (1886–1917).

Erbslöh exemplified the international networking of the NKVM at the time, in the way in which he proceeded from Art Nouveau, Post-Impressionist and early Cubist influences to a reduced and concentrated imagery in highly luminous colours which could stand beside that of Fauvism. Yet Kandinsky, for his part, had already taken the next step. That same year he painted what he programmatically titled his "first abstract watercolour".

The press was shocked by the association's show. Franz Marc reacted with a positive review, and at the beginning of 1911 joined the NKVM. Yet that December, plans for a third exhibition led to

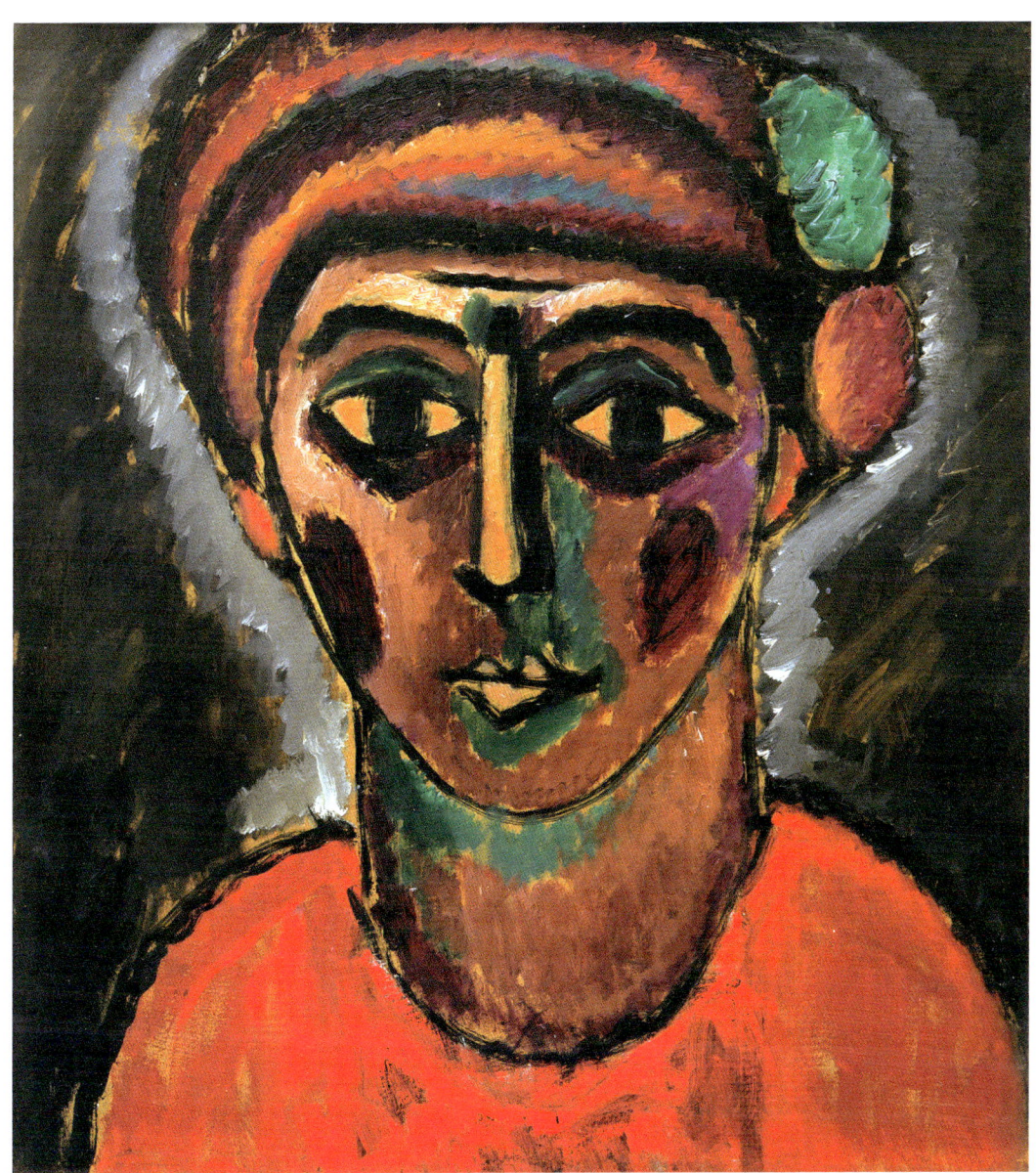

Alexej von Jawlensky
**Head of an Adolescent Boy
(Known as Heracles)**, 1912
Oil on cardboard,
59 x 53.5 cm (23¼ x 21 in.)
Dortmund, Museum Ostwall
im Dortmunder U

OPPOSITE
Wassily Kandinsky
**Cover for the catalogue of the first
Blauer Reiter exhibition, based
on an Indian-ink drawing**, 1911

controversy and a rupture. For spurious reasons the "moderate" faction rejected a largely abstract painting by Kandinsky. In reaction, he and Münter, Marc and Kubin resigned from the NKVM and rapidly arranged a sort of rival exhibition, likewise held at Galerie Thannhauser: "Der Blaue Reiter", 1911–12, at which Macke, Campendonk, Delaunay, and the Austrian composer Arnold Schoenberg were also represented with pictures. Thereafter the works were on view in several other German cities, including Berlin, at the Sturm gallery. Walden additionally showed works by Paul Klee and the Russians Jawlensky and Werefkin (both of whom would leave the NKVM in 1912).

During these eventful years Kandinsky and Marc planned an almanach: *Der Blaue Reiter,* published in May 1912 by Reinhard Piper, which would not go beyond one edition. Kandinsky made ten different cover designs, most of them in watercolour (ill. p. 128). "Both of us loved blue, Marc horses, I riders. Hence the name," as Kandinsky would explain years later. Conceivably associations with the mysterious "blue flower" which the poet Novalis (1772–1801) had placed in the cradle of Romanticism also played some role here.

Revealing for the interdisciplinary conception of the almanach were essays that represent some of the most crucial artists' statements of modernism. There was one by Marc, on "The 'Fauves' of Germany", and one by Burlyuk, on "The 'Fauves' of Russia". Macke wrote about "Masks", Kubin about "Free Music". Kandinsky contributed an essay "Concerning Stage Composition". Schoenberg wrote an article about music and its relationship to words, and two of his paintings were reproduced in the almanach as well. Kandinsky in particular was deeply moved by Schoenberg's compositions and paintings, and saw his dual gift as confirming his, Kandinsky's, theory of the analogy between music and art. The "latest painterly movement", postulated Marc in the almanach, displayed "its fine connecting filaments with the Gothic and the primitives, with Africa and the great Orient, with that so strongly expressive, primal folk art and children's art."

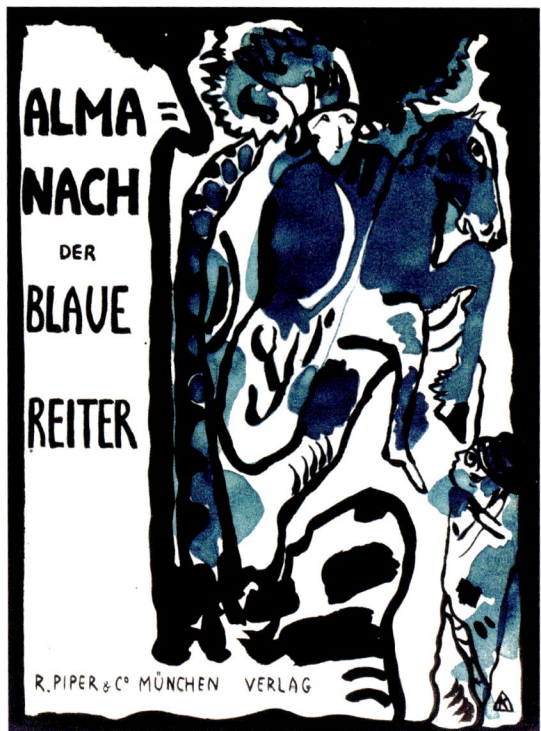

Despite the unity displayed in their yearbook, the artists involved formed no coherent group along Brücke lines. The now-legendary "First Comprehensive Exhibition" of the Blauer Reiter at Galerie Hans Goltz, in February 1912, was not intended to manifest any common style, but to show, "through the diversity of the forms represented, how the inmost desire of artists takes manifold shape". And this was to be demonstrated on an international level, by the inclusion of pictures by Gauguin, van Gogh, Cézanne, Matisse, the "naive" painter Henri Rousseau (1844–1910), by Delaunay, Derain, Vlaminck, Picasso, Braque, by various Brücke artists (despite Kandinsky's serious misgivings), and furthermore, by the Russian avant-gardists Mikhail Larionov (1881–1964), Kasimir Malevich (1878–1935) and Natalia Goncharova (1881–1962).

In his essay "The New Painting", published in the journal *Pan* in March 1912, Marc

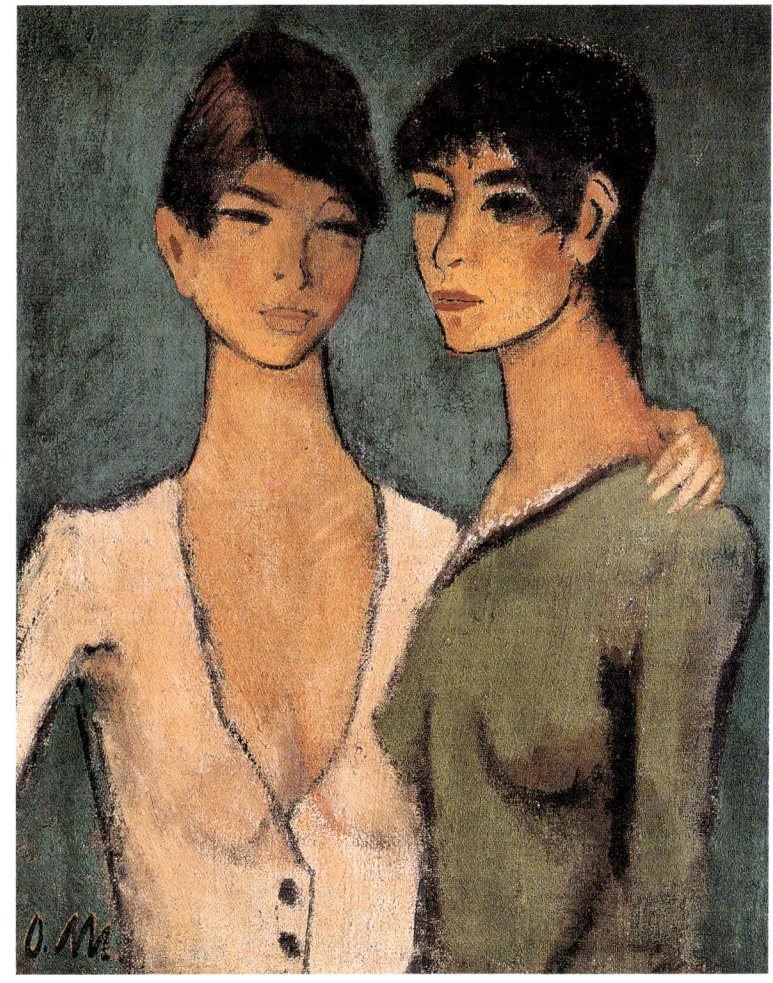

demanded that the profound spiritual aspect of nature be liberated from the fetters of the visible in painting. Max Beckmann replied, in the next issue of *Pan,* that the crucial thing was "artistic perception, combined with artistic objectivity and truthfulness to the things to be depicted", and then went on to rail at "framed Gauguin wallpaper, Matisse-print cloth, little Picasso chessboards, and Siberian-Bavarian martyr posters." This controversy was symptomatic of the polarization of art between abstraction and figuration that now began and would flare up throughout the twentieth century.

Blauer Reiter exhibitions were on view from 1912 to 1914 in twelve cities, not only in Germany but also in Hungary, Norway, Finland and Sweden. The outbreak of the First World War put an abrupt end to these activities, which were such a crucial breakthrough for modernism. New hope followed the debacle when the German-American Lyonel Feininger, who had been affiliated with the Blauer Reiter since 1913, joined with Kandinsky, Klee and Jawlensky in 1924 to form Die Blaue Vier, or The Blue Four, a group that passed on ideas from the Munich period to the Bauhaus.

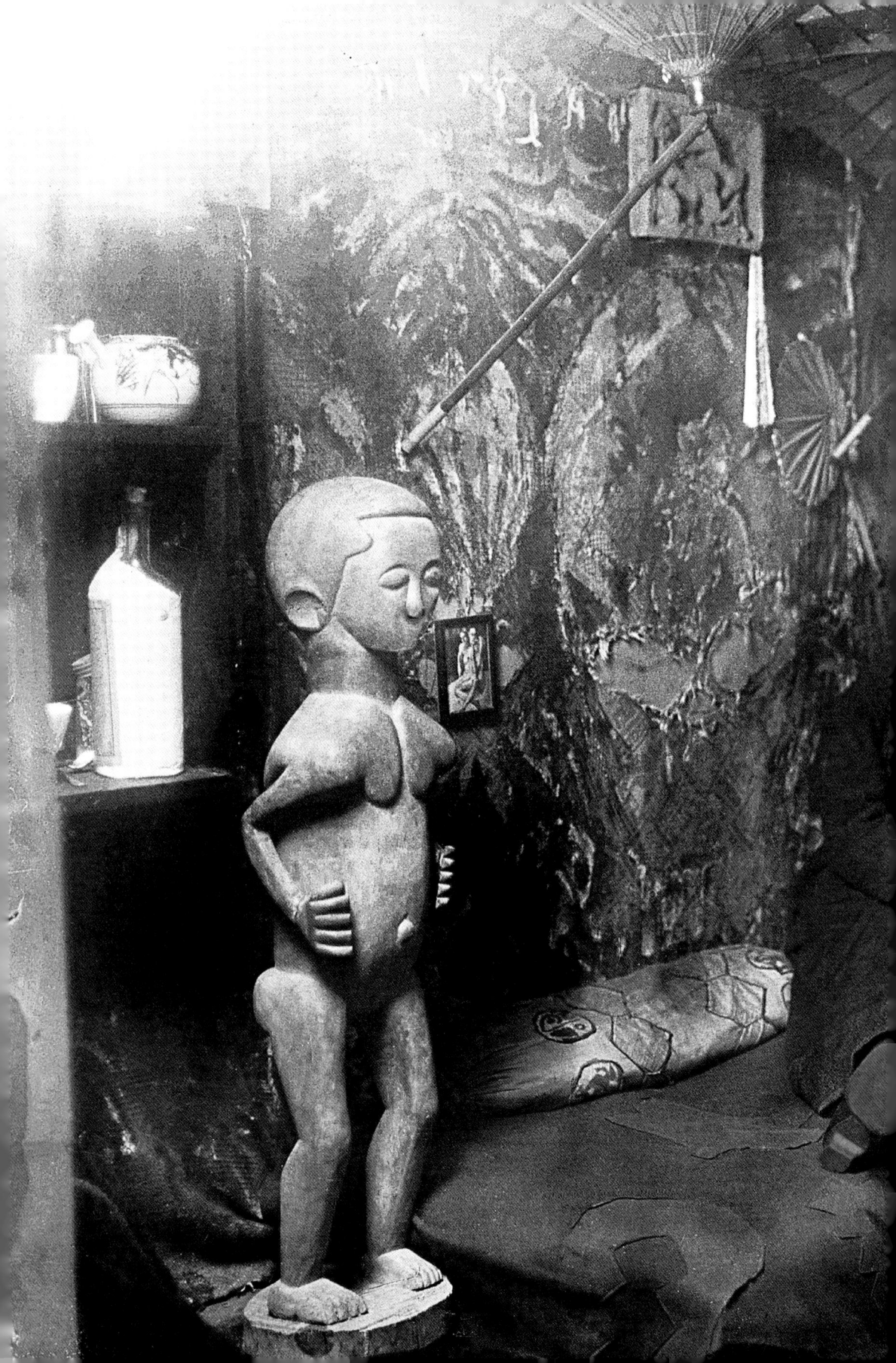

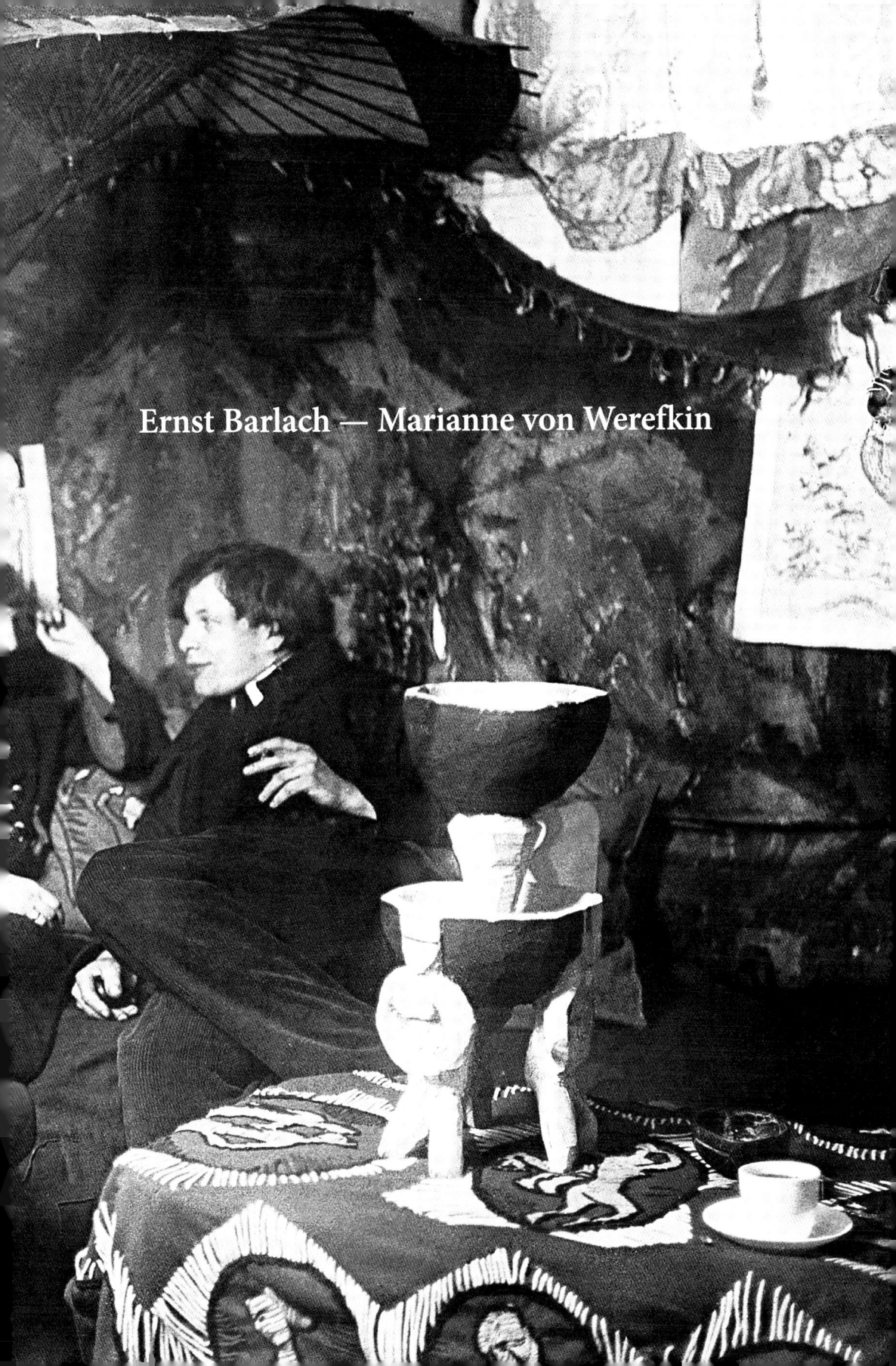

Ernst Barlach — Marianne von Werefkin

Ernst Barlach
The Refugee, 1920

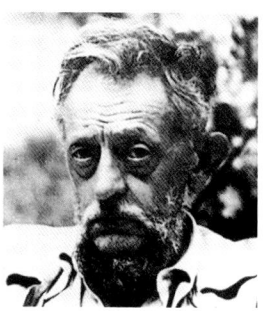

b. 1870 in Wedel, Germany
d. 1938 in Rostock, Germany

More than those Brücke painters who occasionally created plastic works oriented to exotic and primitive art (ill. p. 116), Barlach can be considered an exponent of truly Expressionist sculpture. His central concern rapidly crystallized: to infuse figures composed of heavy, blocky forms with heightened psychological expression. This is perfectly evident in *The Refugee,* which seamlessly links up with Barlach's prewar work.

Here the human figure has been reduced to essentials, the contours and interior detailing being well-nigh abstract. And although conceived to be viewed from a certain vantage point, an ideal plane of relation, the plastic character of the volumes and the incredible way they take possession of the surrounding space are retained. The slight rising of the base to the right leads to the feature that ultimately lends the figure the appearance of a single sweeping movement: a diagonal cut into the wood, running from the bare foot on the left through the folds of the cloak which the refugee draws protectively around himself, then continuing abruptly to the upper right, where the cloak opens into an oval to reveal his hands and face. The striking head is not beautiful in the sense of earlier or academic ideals in art, but has coarse, ugly features that vaguely recall the appearance of Käthe Kollwitz. The gaze, suffering and anticipating worse things to come, is directed into the distance. The painfully visionary nature of this gaze and the face protruding beyond the contours of the wooden block anticipates the uncertain future, while the gently curving contour of the back seems to turn away from everything the anonymous refugee has left behind. The human figure reduced to essentials, as always with Barlach, becomes a symbol of a state, a supraindividual, archetypal situation.

The limited range of well-nigh crude formal means with which Barlach achieved an unprecedented expressiveness and suffused inert matter with spirit resulted not least from an encounter with late-Gothic graphic art and sculpture. Barlach, who was also a significant printmaker and one of the most important playwrights of Expressionism, settled in 1910 in the medieval town of Güstrow on the Baltic coast. At the cathedral there he was continually confronted with statues of the apostles created by Claus Berg (died between 1532 and 1535) – highly dramatic, plastically modelled and yet drawn out into the plane, their coarse-grained, greyish-yellow oak contributing to the both expressive and ascetic impression of the figures. These works etched themselves in Barlach's mind, and his affinity with them is manifested in only a slightly more modern, somewhat abstracted form in *The Refugee.*

After the First World War, Barlach declined offers to teach at the academies in Dresden and Berlin. Long before his success reached its apex in the 1930s, Nazi art critics had set their sights on him. On 30 January 1933, in protest at the forced resignation of Käthe Kollwitz and Heinrich Mann from the Prussian Academy of Arts, Barlach gave a radio talk titled "Artists of the Time". His monuments and public sculptures were destroyed.

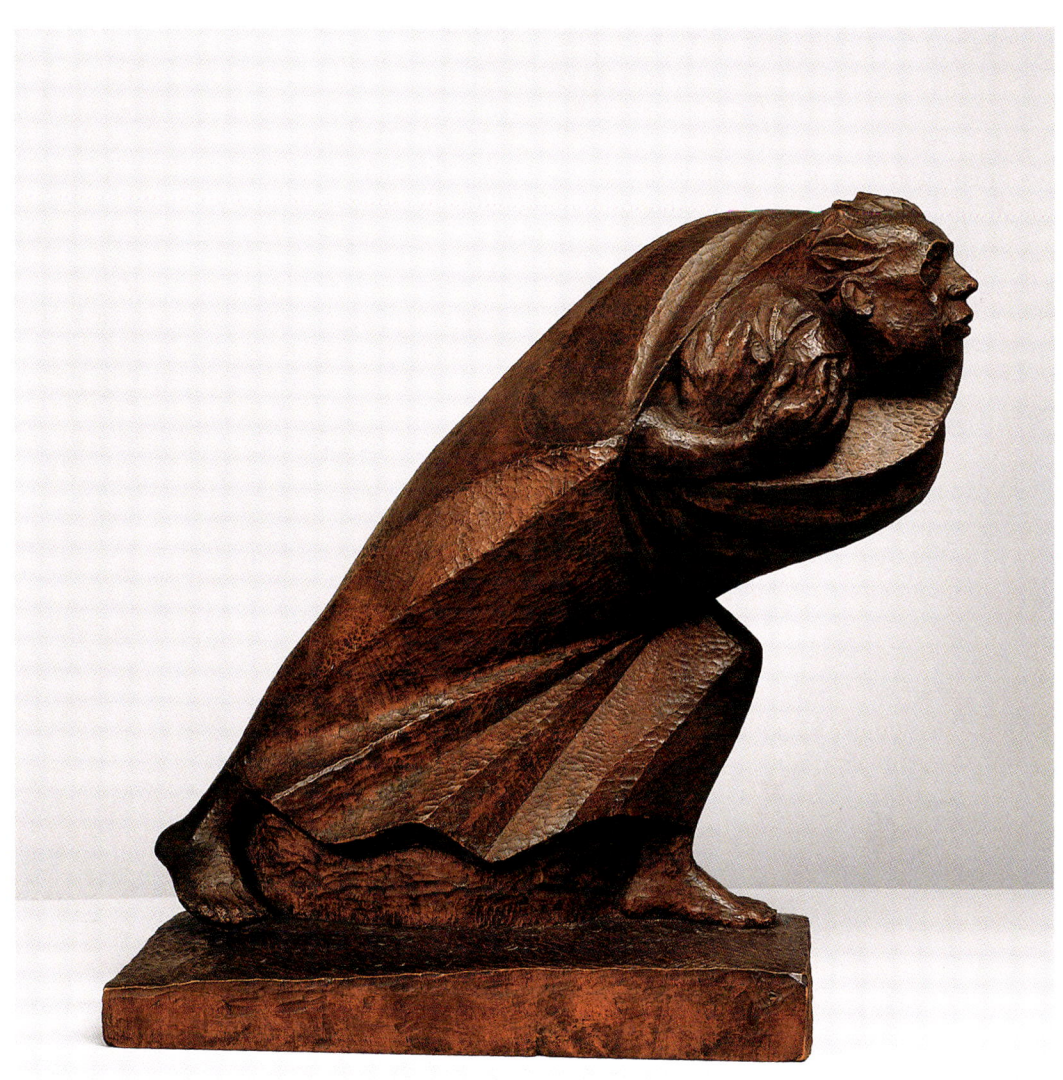

The Refugee, 1920
Oak sculpture, 54 x 57 x 20.5 cm (21¼ x 22½ x 8 in.)
Zurich, Kunsthaus Zürich

Max Beckmann
Scene from the "Earthquake in Messina", 1909

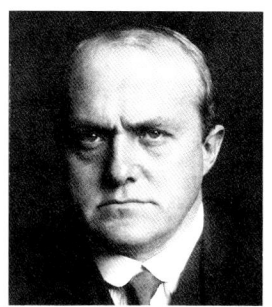

b. 1884 in Leipzig, Germany
d. 1950 in New York City

Max Beckmann played a role in twentieth-century art that overshadowed many others. His œuvre rises like an erratic boulder in the landscape of German art. Yet certain points of contact with Expressionism can be discerned. After finishing his art studies in Weimar in 1903, he made trips to Paris – where he was impressed by the cruel medieval Pietà by the Master of Avignon, by Eugène Delacroix (1798–1863) and Paul Cézanne – and to Florence. From 1907 onwards his enormous canvases, alongside Lovis Corinth's paintings, were among the annual sensations at the Secession exhibitions in Berlin. These included a *Crucifixion*, a vision of the Resurrection, scenes of rapine and slaughter, and even *The Sinking of the Titanic* (1912). The age feverishly doted on just such sensations.

Beckmann began this *Scene from the "Earthquake in Messina"* on 31 December 1908, after reading a news report on the earthquake in southern Italy in which about 80,000 of the 120,000 inhabitants of Messina died. In his diary he noted: "Then I read more in the newspapers about the terrible disaster in Messina, and the passage where half-naked released prison inmates attack other people during the frightful confusion… gave me the idea for a new picture." The painting, in which Beckmann attempted to capture "all pulsating fleshly life", was likely finished in April 1909. The critics of the day found fault with its caricatural exaggeration and sensationalism, only one praising its pathos, which can be traced back to Delacroix.

The varied treatment of the figures gathered into small groups forms the underlying chord of the composition in dull earth colours. The eye is led into the picture by the half-undressed, crouching man in the right foreground, who, seriously wounded in the forehead, bears the pain with waning powers. The naked woman next to him rises up as if trying to avert her fate. The kneeling man behind her likewise seems struggling to maintain his composure. Placed in parallel to this trio of figures, on a rising diagonal, are groups of two figures each – beginning on the left with a rape scene – who are involved in a struggle to the death. Man, the artist seems to say, is simultaneously perpetrator and victim. The relatively intact buildings at the upper edge have the effect of an impenetrable barricade in front of which the battle for survival is taking place.

The young Beckmann was impressed by the vitalism of Nietzsche. This may explain why, apart from the themes of threat, fear and violence that can be seen as a metaphor for the brutality of the modern age, such paintings contain an undertone of fascination with crime, with an unleashing of archetypal instincts of cruelty.

Though artistically not entirely mature, the painting clearly indicates the way in which Beckmann's early work developed out of a sombre, Old Masterly naturalism with scattered Post-Impressionist accents towards an Expressionism whose fundamental feeling and harsh dissonances of content lent it a sense of violence. As the artist confessed, "I would pick my way through all the sewers of the world, through all its debasements and desecrations, in order to paint. I simply have to. Everything in me in the way of formal imagination must come out, down to the last drop…" This was the radical impulse behind Beckmann's decision to volunteer for the medical corps and go to the front. There, in summer 1915, he suffered a physical and mental breakdown.

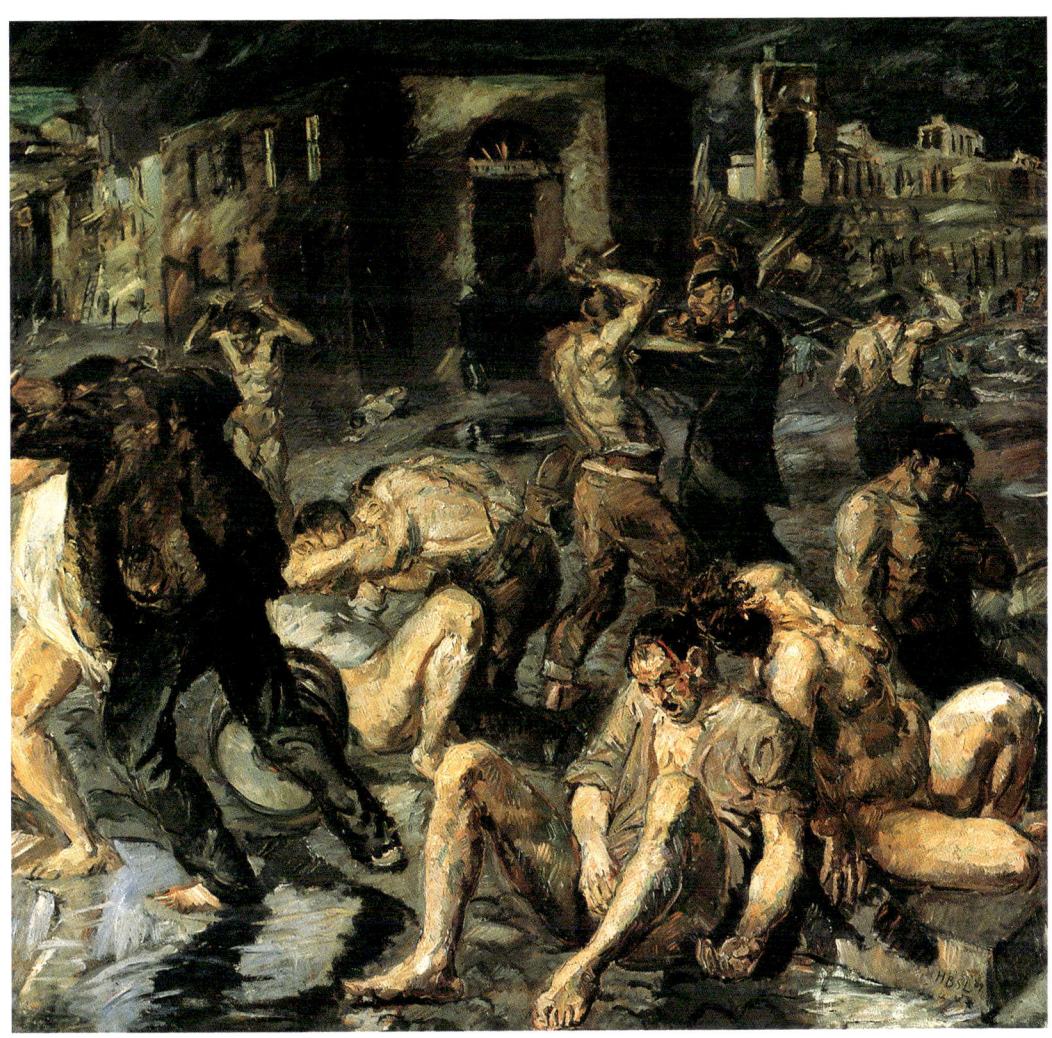

Scene from the "Earthquake in Messina", 1909
Oil on canvas, 254.6 x 267.7 cm (100¼ x 105½ in.)
Saint Louis Art Museum,
Bequest of Morton D. May

Max Beckmann
The Night, 1918/19

His experiences in the First World War, which, as he euphorically wrote to his wife in April 1915, provided "fodder" for his art, soon brought Beckmann to the brink of mental collapse. They also altered his art fundamentally, in both formal and iconographic terms. The paint application grew thinner and more fluid, figures and faces became more "linear" and took on ecstatically distorted poses and features. It was no coincidence that Beckmann created the greater part of his graphic œuvre between 1915 and 1922. Yet everything done in those years was outshone by this large-format oil finished in 1919, *The Night*, in which the world has gone out of joint.

After the outbreak of the November Revolution in 1918, violence and chaos reigned in Germany, and political assassination was the order of the day. Beckmann's painting, too, rips the thin veneer off the aspect of bourgeois civilization. We look into a small, Gothically angled attic room, the perspective lines of whose floorboards turn it into a narrow stage teeming with actors. Three thugs have broken in and are routinely and sadistically raping and murdering the inhabitants, one grabbing a girl as if about to throw her out of the skewed open window. The torso and leg position of the strangled man, whose arm is being twisted by a pipe-smoking "technocrat of violence", recalls the figure of Christ in a Deposition, his cruelly twisted foot perhaps stemming from Grünewald's *Christ Crucified* in his late-Gothic *Isenheim Altarpiece*. The thug at the right in the peaked cap is a paraphrase on a beggar from the fresco *The Triumph of Death* at the Campo Santo in Pisa, from the first half of the fourteenth century. The legs of the female figure who is the true centre of the drama, violently forced apart, serve in formal terms to link the two halves of the composition.

Despite its implicit story, the painting runs counter to every law of logic, a strange, crystalline petrifaction having taken possession of the events and figures. The howling dog remains just as silent as the gramophone; the toppled candle signifies death. Though it would seem plausible to detect references to current events here, for example to the crushing of the Spartacus revolt and the assassination of Karl Liebknecht and Rosa Luxemburg in January 1919, the ambiguous and enigmatic nature of the image remain predominant. In Beckmann's own words, "In my *Night,* too, one should not overlook the metaphysical in the objective." Metaphysics, to again cite the artist, meant "giving human beings an image of their destiny".

In artistic terms, metaphysics implied transforming figures into prototypes and stylizing the pictorial space, making it into a conglomerate or complex network of "Cubo-Futurist" faceted planes and sharp-angled contrasts (which bore parallels with Expressionist film sets), and it implied replacing naturalistic depiction by an alienating distortion.

This key work and masterpiece of German painting between the wars already contains the most important elements with whose aid Beckmann would later find his genuine style, in exile in Amsterdam until 1947, then as an emigré in the United States. The linear, faceted forms would be increasingly abandoned in favour of brilliant expanses of colour and broad, black contours. This amounted to Beckmann's farewell to Expressionism, which he now rejected as being "sentimental morbid mysticism".

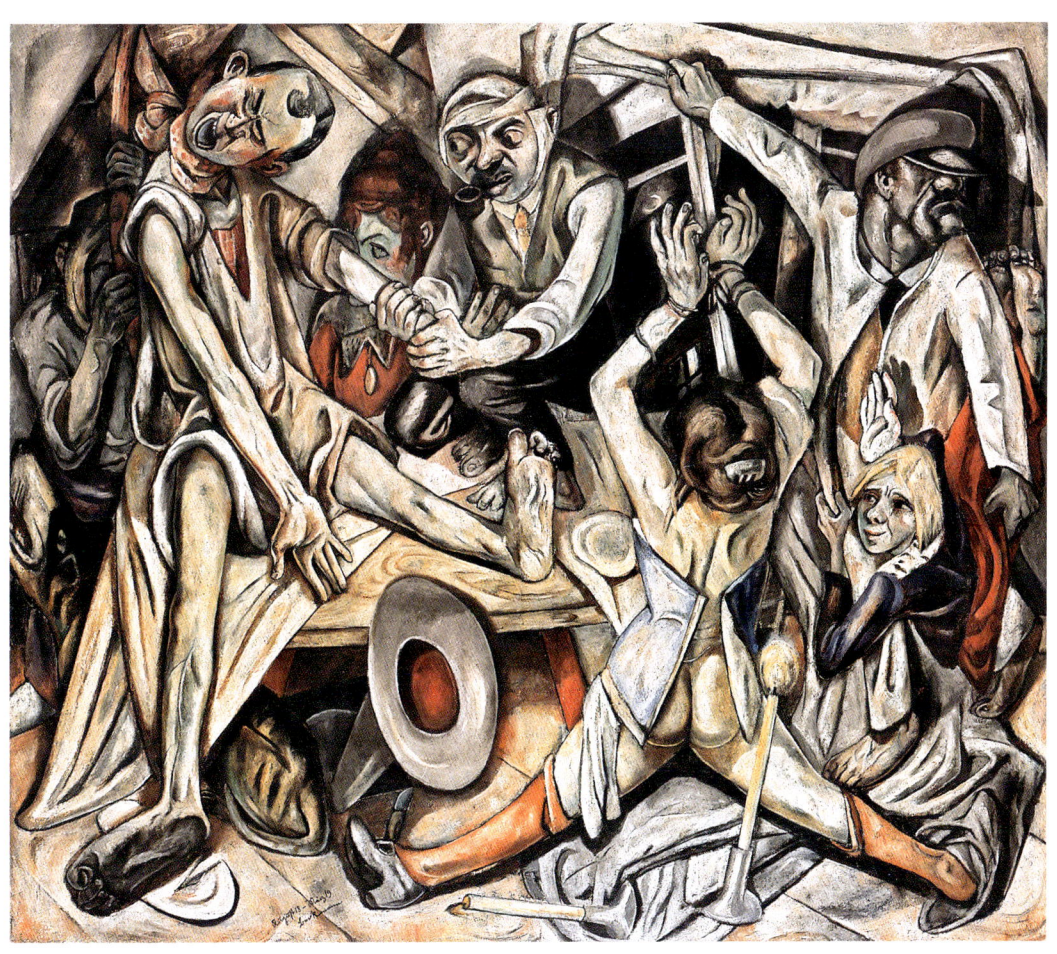

The Night, 1918/19
Oil on canvas, 133 x 155 cm (52¼ x 61 in.)
Düsseldorf, Kunstsammlung
Nordrhein-Westfalen

Heinrich Campendonk
Bucolic Landscape, 1913

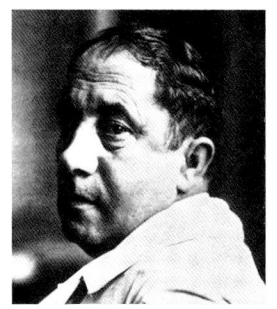

b. 1889 in Krefeld, Germany
d. 1957 in Amsterdam

Campendonk's *Bucolic Landscape*, whose title suggests a kind of earthly paradise out of Antique mythology, is recognizable as such only on closer scrutiny. On first sight the vertical format has the effect of a stage, filled to bursting with forms, as if in reaction to a horror vacui. Yet the geometrically reduced, splintered, occasionally nearly abstract shapes of plants, human beings, animals overlapping one another ultimately produce not an effect of chaos but of a solidly built pictorial structure. The many and various tense oppositions and complementary colour contrasts are brought into an order that is calculated down to the last detail. Partially modelled elements with suggestions of spatial depth are always integrated in the dominant flat pattern. Features of the colouration and the important role played by animals in the scene may bring Franz Marc to mind; other features recall the lyrical, fairy-tale mood of Upper Bavarian verre églomisé. The facetted interpenetration of figures, animals and landscape, the constructive employment of form, colour and light, clearly echo Delaunay's principles of design.

Like his close friend Macke, Campendonk – born in Krefeld and active mainly there and, later, in Düsseldorf – is often associated with the theoretical construct of Rhenish Expressionism. Yet the years that were decisive to his artistic development in terms of style and thematic reorientation were those he spent under the influence of the Blauer Reiter artists in Munich, 1911 to 1914.

From 1905 to 1909 Campendonk was a student at the Krefeld School of Decorative Arts. His teacher there, the Dutchman Jan Thorn-Prikker (1868–1932), introduced him not only to the stylization of Art Nouveau but to the art of Cézanne and van Gogh, and their reliance on the autonomous expressiveness of line and strongly contrasting colours. From 1911, when Campendonk moved to Sindelsdorf in Upper Bavaria and got to know Macke and Marc, he came increasingly under the latter's influence. So avidly did he adopt Marc's Cubist, crystalline compositions shot through with Futurist vectors and Delaunay's Orphist colouration that critical voices complained of Campendonk's lack of originality.

Yet gradually the differences between his more lyrically tuned temperament and Marc's mystical pantheism came to the fore. Though Marc's animal realm continued to fascinate him, Campendonk began to integrate glimpses of the everyday farm life around him into the fairy-tale, almost Romantic atmosphere of his compositions with their free-floating motifs. This approach, which would mature into his personal style, did not find its culmination until the last Munich years of 1913 and 1914, and finally after the dissolution of the Blauer Reiter. In the meantime Campendonk had further reduced his visual idiom to complex and solid geometric terms, a development manifested in *Bucolic Landscape*.

During the First World War, Campendonk was soon discharged from the military and retired to Seeshaupt on Lake Starnberg. In 1926, living in Krefeld, he accepted the offer of a teaching post at the Düsseldorf Academy. His later oeuvre included significant glass paintings. In 1933, Campendonk emigrated to Belgium, later going on to Amsterdam.

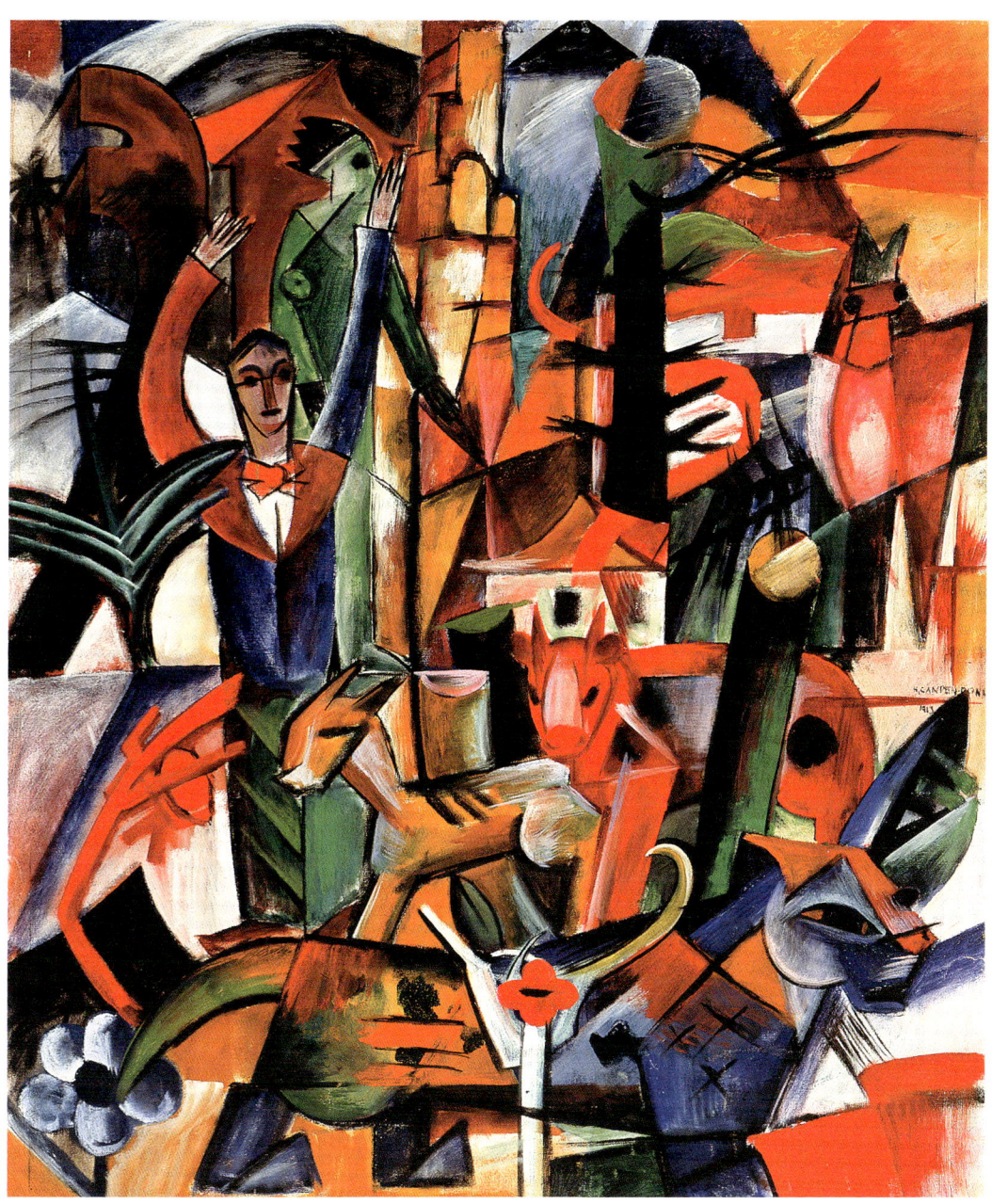

Bucolic Landscape, 1913
Oil on canvas, 100.6 x 85.7 cm (39½ x 33¾ in.)
Saint Louis Art Museum,
Bequest of Morton D. May

Lovis Corinth
The Red Christ, 1922

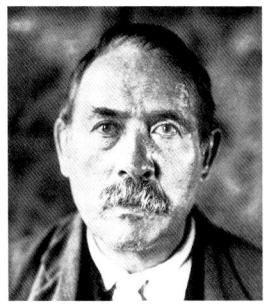

b. 1858 in Tapiau, Russia
d. 1925 in Zandvoort,
The Netherlands

Lovis Corinth's depiction of the Crucifixion is doubtless one of the most moving in all modern art. In accordance with the predominant colour and its symbolism of blood, it bears the indicative title *The Red Christ*. Finished in 1922, the painting immediately caused a scandal when it was exhibited. One critic stated, "But this is not Christ at all, this is more like an apeman with a black woolly beard, protruding crude mouth area (or put less technically, snout), flattened pug nose, huge orbital bulges and devious black eyes. The body lacerated, tortured, blood and more blood wherever the eye turns. The sun, too, is bloody, and its rays look bloody. The picture is one single orgy of bloodlust."

The composition, which brings the motif up to the viewer's eyes like a cinematic close-up, is a combination of various elements from Cornith's earlier Crucifixion scenes. Yet it alienates, abstracts and distorts the details and divorces colour partially from objective representation, such that its impasto substance seems to take on a life of its own and cover the picture field as if with blood spatters. The heavenly cosmos sheds garish accents on the brutality of the nearly faceless henchmen in the foreground and the helplessness of Mary and St John the Evangelist in the background. The paint surface is ploughed by vehement brushstrokes and swaths of the palette-knife. The figure of Christ, victim of murderous bestiality and reduced to a slaughtered creature, takes on exemplary meaning for the increasing loss of human dignity. The Crucifixion serves as a paradigm for the statement that man has become a wolf to man.

To this day art historians continue to have their difficulties with Corinth, especially with his work after 1911. He is very difficult to categorize. During an extremely long training period, at the academies in Königsberg, Munich and Paris, he was impressed primarily by various realistic styles – and even more by the art of Rembrandt (1606–1669). From 1891, when he resided in Munich, and after 1900, when he moved to Berlin, Corinth pulled out virtually all the stops of a theatrical, illusionistic painting located midway between naturalism and Impressionism. His aptitudes seemed anything but avant-garde.

At the apex of his career, in 1911, Corinth suffered a stroke. From then on he had to cope with extreme pressures, was tormented by deep bouts of depression, but also went through happy phases of a creative intoxication, as his famous Walchensee landscapes, among other works, attest. His approach turned radical, broke with academic conventions, unsettled visual habits. As Corinth himself once wrote, "Bad drawing and missing the mark are excused as soon as appearances are captured in their character." Most justice can be done to the artist's late style by considering it a sort of parallel phenomenon to Expressionism, even though Corinth never maintained contacts either with members of the Brücke or the Blauer Reiter. Yet at any rate, on the occasion of the 22nd Berlin Secession Exhibition in 1911, he did describe paintings by French Cubists and Fauvists as expressionistic, and recommended them to the public as highly interesting, precisely on account of their "wildness".

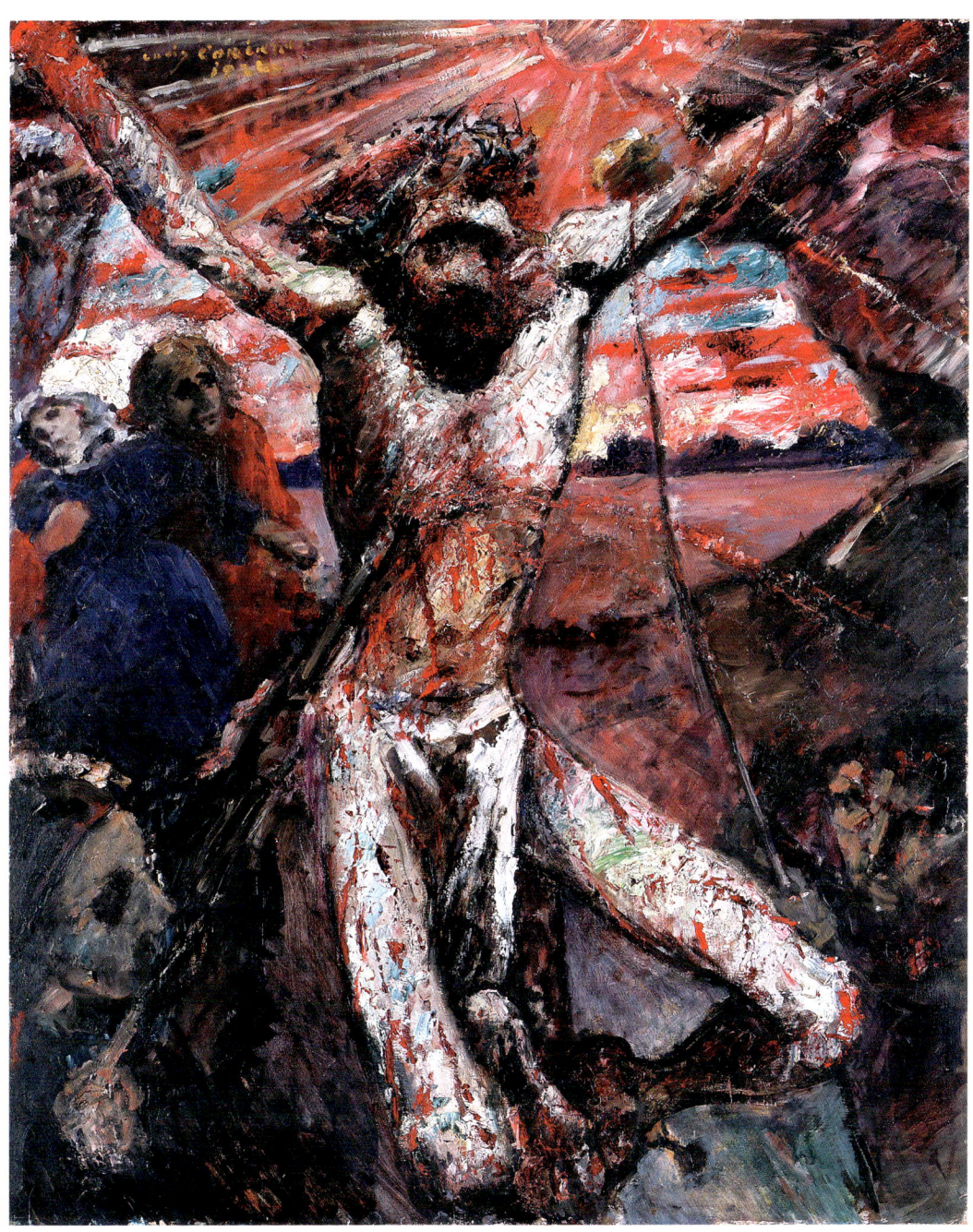

The Red Christ, 1922
Oil on wood, 129 x 108 cm (50¾ x 42½ in.)
Munich, Bayerische Staatsgemälde-
sammlungen, Neue Pinakothek

Otto Dix
Self-Portrait as a Soldier, 1914/15

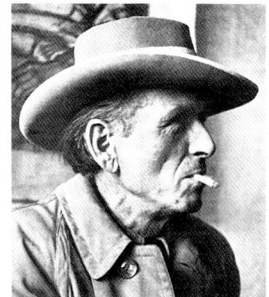

b. 1891 in Untermhaus, Germany
d. 1969 in Singen, Germany

War was the first dominant theme in the work of Otto Dix after his training at the Dresden School of Decorative Arts. In 1915 he was sent to the Western Front in Champagne, France, went through the terrible autumn battle and the trench warfare that succeeded it that winter, in which nearly 600,000 men lost their lives. In November he was promoted to non-commissioned officer, received the Iron Cross 2nd Class, fought in the battles on the Somme, which cost 470,000 lives, then participated in trench warfare in northern France. In November 1917 Dix lay in the Russian trenches and in February 1918 was stationed in Flanders. In August of that year he was wounded in the neck, yet shortly thereafter took pilot training. Dix was discharged in December. He had survived.

"The war was a horrible thing," he later wrote, "but something enormous nevertheless. I wouldn't have missed it at any cost. You have to have seen men in this unleashed state to know something about human beings… I had to experience the worst aspects of life myself – that's why I went into the war, and also why I volunteered."

There is hardly another work that illustrates this existential premise better than Dix's *Self-Portrait as a Soldier*. The artist depicts himself in close-up, presents his physique with an immediacy that almost seems to explode the small format. From the diagonally rotated torso the head, in aggressive red, protrudes like a battering ram and turns to fix the viewer with a provoking stare – and the viewer was of course originally the artist himself, looking at himself in the mirror to study his own physiognomy. The brutal, bald soldier with bony skull, bull neck and fleshy mouth recalls a wounded wild animal at bay. Energetic brushstrokes in blue, red and yellow-orange plough the surface around the face, a formal equivalent for mental torment yet also for a keen expectation of the "enormous" things awaiting the soldier. Human life is first and foremost a struggle for life, and death is an inevitable part of its fascination – this Dix could have read in Nietzsche. Like Beckmann, he took the Bible and Nietzsche's *Gay Science* along with him to the front.

During intervals in the fighting, Dix amazingly executed almost 600 drawings and gouaches between 1915 and 1918. These comprise his actual Expressionist oeuvre. Nearly all of them are covered with a network of intersecting, agitated lines interlocking at sharp angles, vectors of force that combine into an ecstatic rhythm. The colours often strangely recall the hovering notes of the Blauer Reiter, oddly ethereal in view of the dissonant overall structures out of which Cubo-Futuristic, expressively delineated and distorted objects and landscapes emerge. Simultaneity congeals into a "creative chaos" that is a far cry from a depiction of visible reality. Only long after the war's end did Dix begin to capture his experiences in a more realistic manner. In 1923–24 he produced a cycle of fifty etchings entitled *The War*, a twentieth-century counterpart to Goya's (1746–1828) *Disasters of War* (1810–1820) and almost certainly inspired by them.

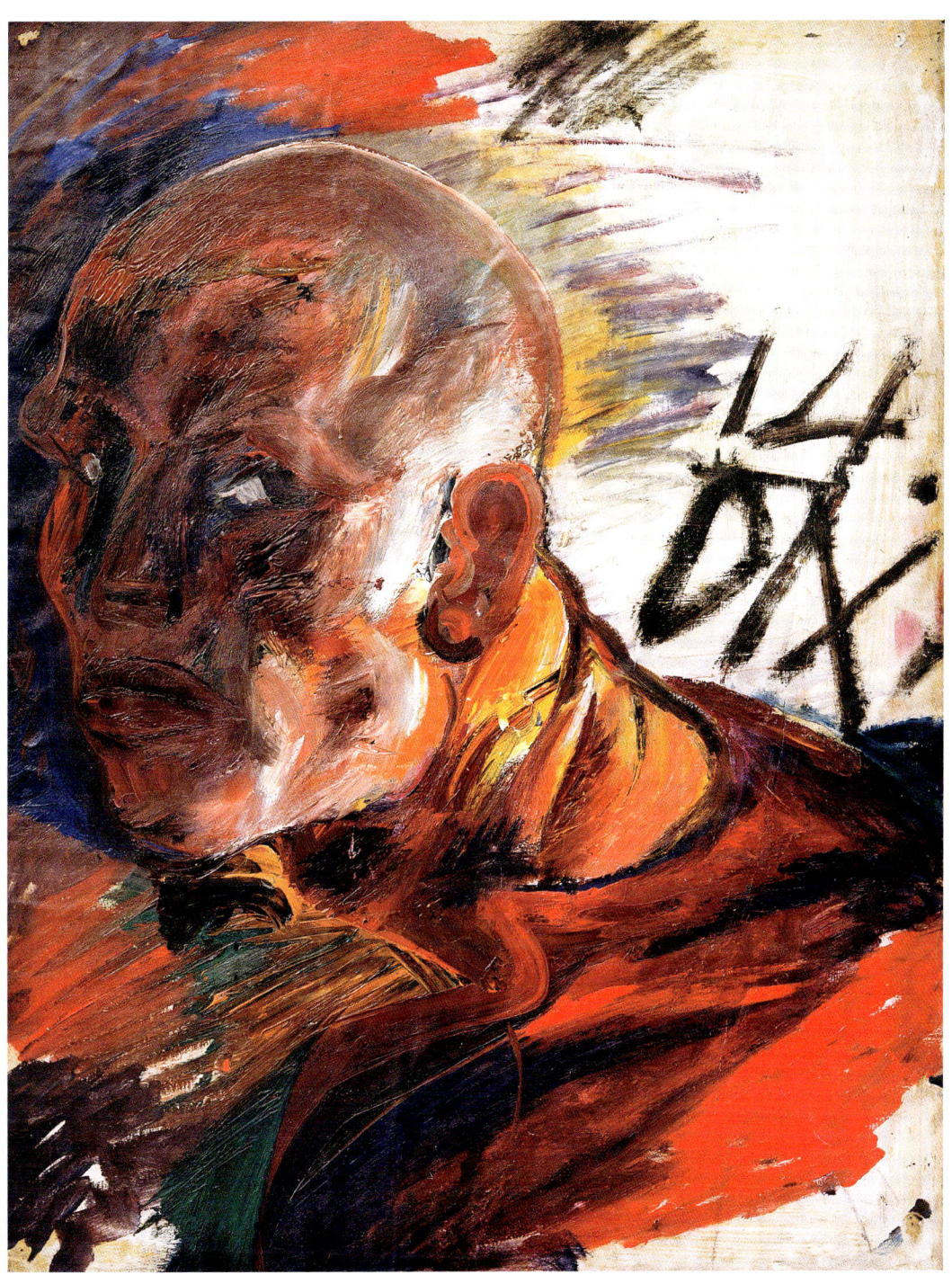

Self-Portrait as a Soldier, 1914/15
Oil on paper, 68 x 53.5 cm (26¾ x 21 in.)
Kunstmuseum Stuttgart

Otto Dix
Prager Strasse, 1920

The Dix who returned to Dresden in 1919 – now as a master student at the Art Academy – probed new ways to react to a society whose brutality and hypocrisy had become evident in the trenches of the First World War. His Expressionist vocabulary was first supplemented by the montage principle of Dada and its method of sarcastic, shocking provocation, before Verism with its hyperreal attention to detail completely replaced the revolutionary formal pathos of Expressionism in Dix's art.

Yet even after the war, life manifested itself in terms of extremes in the artist's eye. He was intrigued by outsiders, including intellectuals and artist colleagues, but above all it was working people, prostitutes and disabled war veterans who now populated Dix's paintings and prints. He focused mercilessly on the transitory nature of the human body, and created icons of sexual ugliness. The factors of exaggeration, distortion and grotesqueness so important to Expressionism were retained, in one form or another, in Dix's postwar work. His earlier main themes – war and the big city – likewise played a key role in the artist's continuing mergers of disparate elements into a "creative chaos".

Prager Strasse, from which this oil painting with collage takes its title, was Dresden's most opulent street. In Dix's starkly Dadaist scene, it metamorphoses into a boulevard of disillusionment. The canvas with its inscription "Dedicated to my contemporaries" centres on bizarrely alienated war veterans, two of the many at that time whose disablement left them no alternative but begging to survive. The wheels of the cart on which the legless man pushes his torso along the pavement are formed of tinfoil. The photos, paper, hair and tickets in the upper part of the macabre shop window displaying disjointed stereotype body parts – torsos, limbs – are likewise pasted on. Between the light-coloured prostheses in the right-hand window Dix has inserted a photo of his own face. The newspaper clipping in the lower left corner – the compositional extension of a barking dachshund's mouth – is another authentic piece of reality that reflects the growing anti-Semitism of the postwar years: "Jews Out!" screams the headline.

Unlike the Zurich Dadaists who had come together in Swiss exile in 1916, the Berlin Dadaists had a clear and definitely left-leaning political attitude, whose message they focused in imagery composed of actual slices of the reality around them. This collage device was supplemented by unreal, overlapping perspectives, disintegrated formal structures, garish colours, and an aesthetic of the ugly – formal principles, that is, of typically Expressionist origin. With the aid of this art of combinations Dix shed a glaring light in *Prager Strasse* on the social injustices that characterized the young Weimar Republic, and he drew attention to the political perversions that would soon become embodied in tyranny.

When Hitler saw paintings by Dix in Dresden in 1937, he declared, "It's a shame one cannot put these people behind bars." By this time Dix had long turned away from Expressionism, having in the 1920s adopted the sharp-focus objectivity of Neue Sachlichkeit and especially Verism.

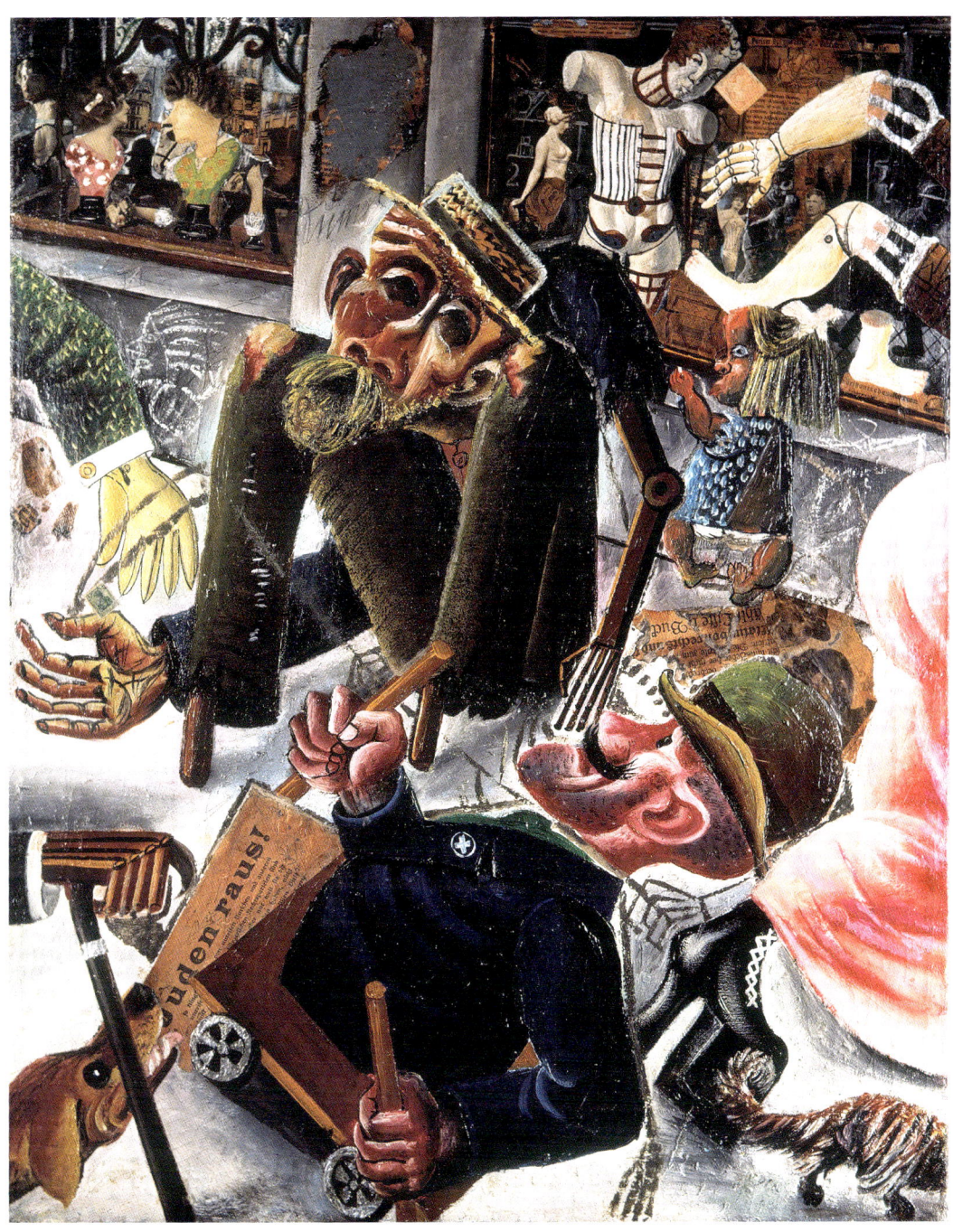

Prager Strasse, 1920
Oil on canvas with collage elements,
101 x 81 cm (39¾ x 32 in.)
Kunstmuseum Stuttgart

Lyonel Feininger
Market Church in Halle, 1930

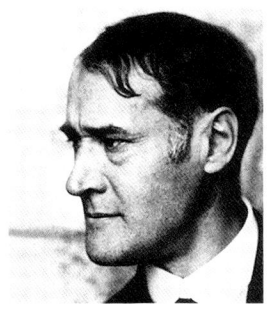

b. 1871 in New York City
d. 1956 in New York City

Feininger's work is almost more difficult to categorize than Klee's. The American-born graphic artist and painter, who was also a talented musician and composer, was associated with various of the German Expressionist groups without truly belonging to them. In 1912 he maintained friendly relations with the Brücke, especially Heckel and Schmidt-Rottluff, in Berlin, and the following year exhibited with the Blauer Reiter in the "First German Autumn Salon". He arrived at his typical style in 1911, in Paris, by way of a confrontation with Cubism. With its aid Feininger translated his favourite motifs – Gothic church spires, cityscapes, seascapes, sailing ships – into compositions of crystalline purity and timelessness that anticipated the Expressionist architectural fantasies of the architects' society Die Gläserne Kette (The Glass Chain) founded by Bruno Taut (1880–1938) in 1919. This is the context in which his woodcut for the founding manifesto of the Bauhaus, *Cathedral of Socialism*, belongs.

Until 1913 many of his pictures were populated by marionette-like, elongated human figures which were subsequently abandoned. Feininger employed an exaggerated perspective to engender a pictorial tectonics consisting of a synthesis of cubic, prismatically refracted, energy-charged units. His early Promenades were probably known to Kirchner, who may well have adapted them in his *Potsdamer Platz* (ill. p. 163). On the other hand, Feininger paid homage to Kirchner's paintings of Berlin cocottes in his *Birds of the Night*, 1921.

As *Market Church in Halle* shows, by this time Feininger's facetting had achieved a rigorous tectonics and intrinsic monumentality. Between 1929 and 1931, on the invitation of museum director Alois W. Schardt, the artist spent several periods of months at a time in Halle to paint a series of city views. Like other examples from this series, the Munich painting has a subtle transparency of colour that reflects not only an adoption of the Orphist colour system of Delaunay but an affinity with international Constructivism, which paralleled Feininger's teaching activity at the Bauhaus, first in Weimar from 1919 to 1925, later in Dessau to 1932. At the Bauhaus, the rational, constructive principle was allied with Expressionist ideals à la Blauer Reiter. As a result, Feininger joined with Jawlensky, Kandinsky and Klee in 1924 to form a successor to the Munich group, The Blue Four.

Feininger has depicted the *Market Church in Halle* from a vantage point that relegates its characteristic spired facade and flying buttresses to the background, and brings the massive late-Gothic nave diagonally into the foreground and to the left edge, like a conglomerate of vectors and dynamic prisms. The complex is rendered in subdued translucent colours of luminous clarity, forming a Cubistically reduced structure shot through with lines, rays and facets. In the refractions and vibrations, interpenetrations, overlappings and mirrorings of forms, the synaesthesia of painting, architecture and music has achieved an overwhelming polyphonic effect, as of light-pervaded space. "Where I used to strive for movement and restlessness," said the artist, who emigrated to the U.S. in 1936, of such pictures, "I now attempt to sense and express the complete total calm of objects, and even the surrounding air. 'The world' that has moved farthest from reality."

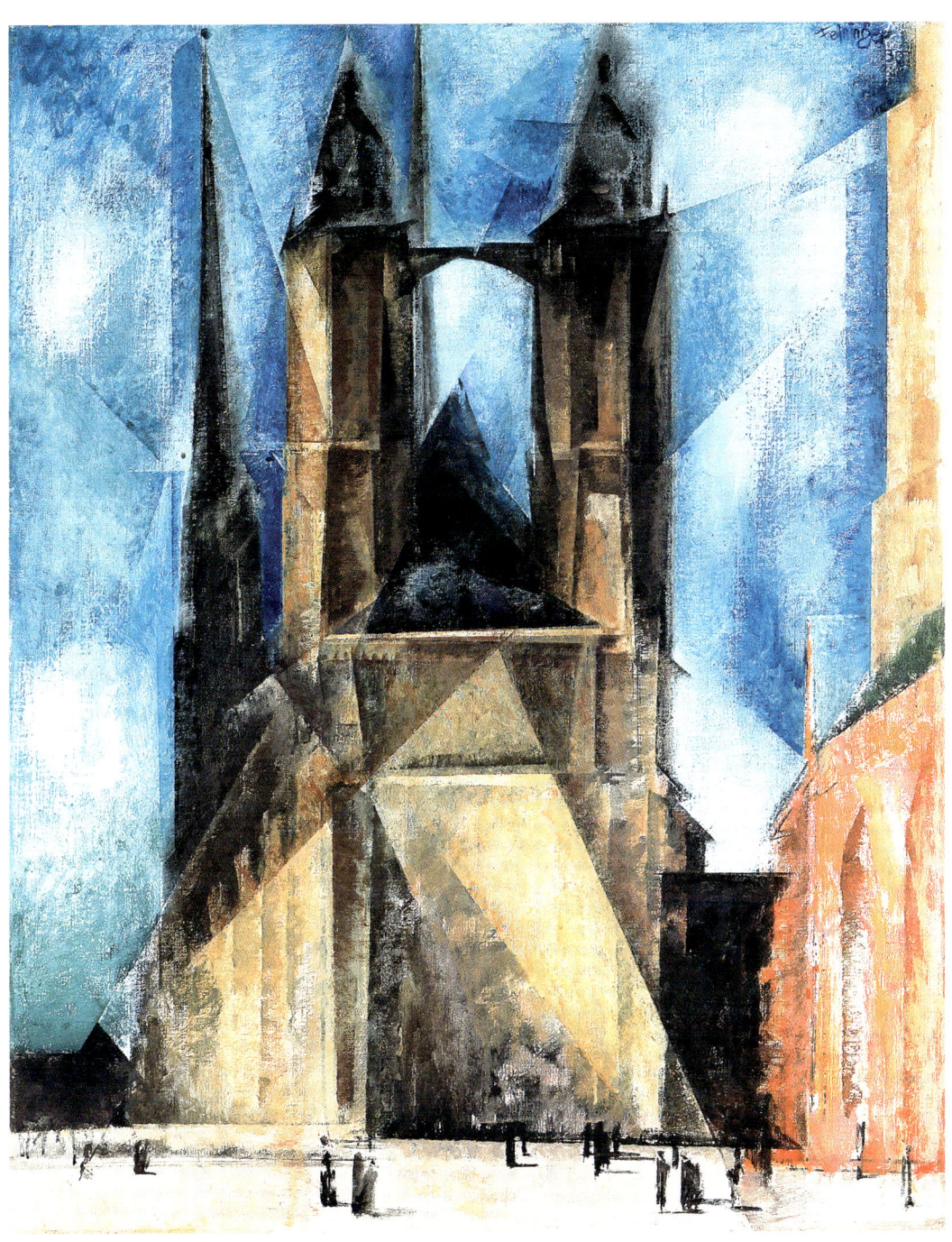

Market Church in Halle, 1930
Oil on canvas, 102 x 80.4 cm (40¼ x 31¾ in.)
Munich, Bayerische Staatsgemälde-
sammlungen, Pinakothek der Moderne

George Grosz
Dedicated to Oskar Panizza, 1917/18

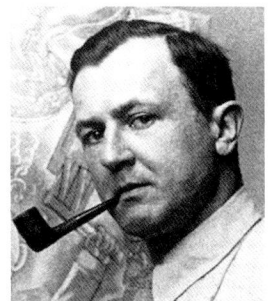

b. 1893 in Berlin
d. 1959 in Berlin

Even more than his future friend, Otto Dix, George Grosz turned his art to political ends – although not in the sense of support for any party line, including that of the Communists, whom he joined in 1918. During his studies at the Dresden Academy from 1909 onwards, he followed the activities of the Brücke with interest, and soon those of the Blauer Reiter as well. Like every young artist in Germany who allied himself with the avant-garde, Grosz was familiar with progressive international developments in art. In November 1914 he hesistantly registered for war service, but by the time six months had passed, he had become unfit for duty. These six months fuelled Grosz's hatred of war and the military, to which a disgust with war profiteers was soon added. In January 1917 he was reinducted, but only a day later he had to be sent to an infirmary, and a few weeks afterwards was admitted to a mental hospital. During the war years Grosz concerned himself with the subjects of circus and variety shows, crime and murder, war and the big city. The last-named would become a synonym for a world gone out of joint for him.

One of Grosz's most striking works on this theme is *Dedicated to Oskar Panizza*. The aggressiveness of the painting inheres not only in the motifs but in the incandescent reds of the palette and the violent energies that stream through the composition. Even the solid architecture is infused with a compelling dynamism. It recalls the vertiginous spaces and toppling housefronts in the sets of Expressionist films. The seemingly endless street is filled with a milling crowd of cubistically simplified figures who intersect and overlap one another. In the tumult of pushing, jostling people with mask-like faces, everyone seems to have lost all sense of direction.

Grosz mixes Futurism and Cubism with a shot of James Ensor to form an overwrought boiling human mass that occupies the borderline between Dadaism and Expressionism. This big-city scene was intended as a homage to Oskar Panizza (1853–1921), an Expressionist writer and physician whose satirical attacks on Church and State appealed to Grosz. A short time earlier, the Italian Futurist Carlo Carrà (1881–1966) had depicted a similarly "political" funeral which ended in a bloody fight. But Grosz's wildly gesticulating mob milling around the coffin on which a schnapps-drinking Death is perched, not only served him as an excuse to evoke urban chaos. He also pointed out its source, in an urban jungle where a tiny church is completely engulfed by nightclubs and bars and office buildings. A highly decorated old army officer brandishes his sword as a moon-faced clergyman pathetically holds the cross on high and a sheep-faced office employee, on the left, demonstrates the herd instinct. The neon sign over the building entrance next to the coffin, "DANCING TONIGHT", says it all – this is a modern Dance of Death. As Grosz himself explained, "In a strange street by night, a hellish procession of dehumanized figures mills, their faces reflecting alcohol, syphilis, plague… I painted this protest against a humanity that had gone insane."

Later Grosz moved from Dadaism to the sober realism of Neue Sachlichkeit and a sociocritical Verism, jettisoning Expressionist formulae but retaining their satirical, critical impact. It was no accident that a "humanity gone insane" soon caught up with him – in 1933 Grosz became one of the first victims of Nazi persecution in the arts. He emigrated to the U.S., where he received American citizenship in 1938. After the war Grosz planned to return to Berlin, and died there during a visit in 1959.

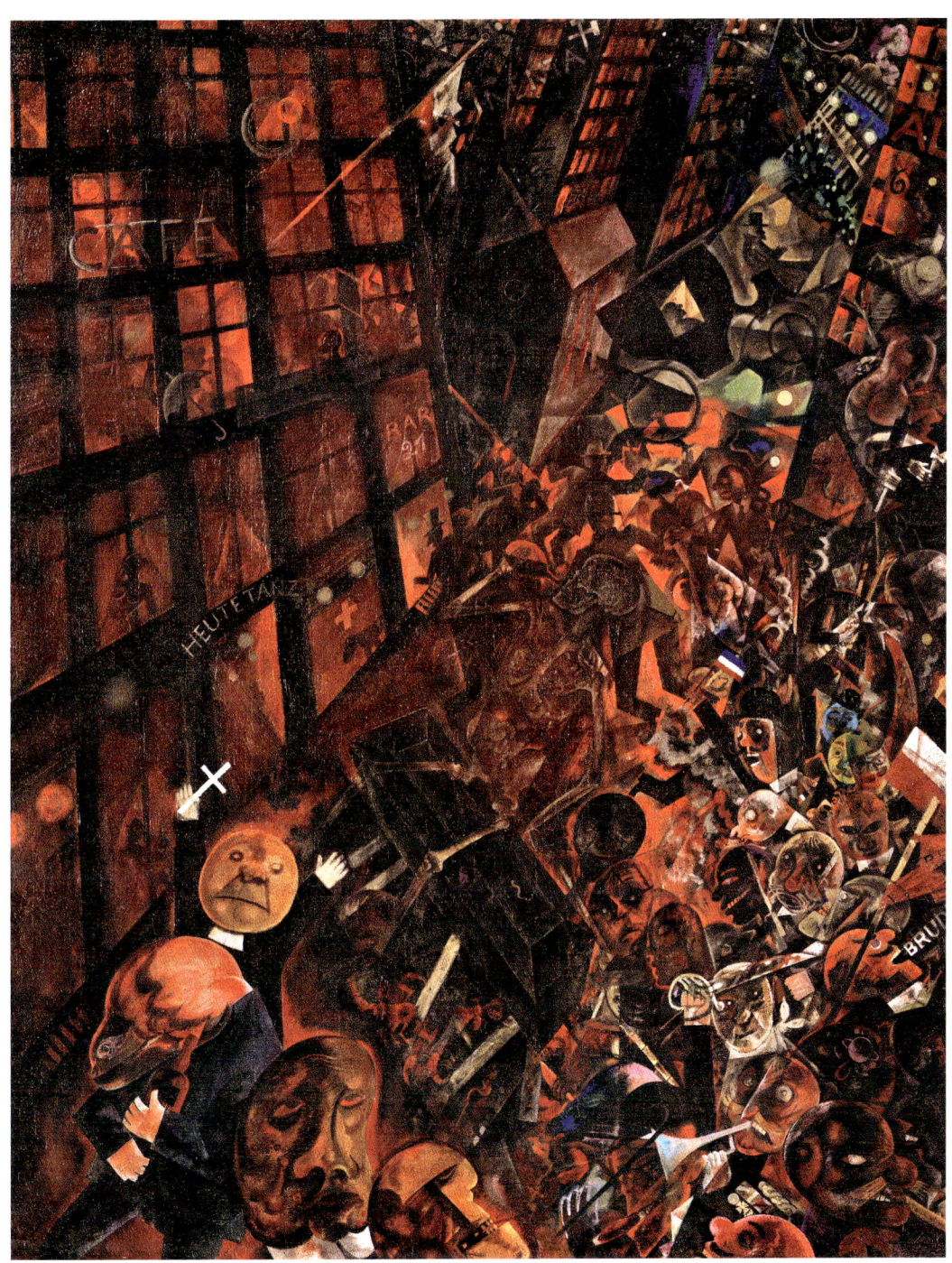

Dedicated to Oskar Panizza, 1917/18
Oil on canvas, 140 x 110 cm (55 x 43¼ in.)
Staatsgalerie Stuttgart

Erich Heckel
Pechstein Asleep, 1910

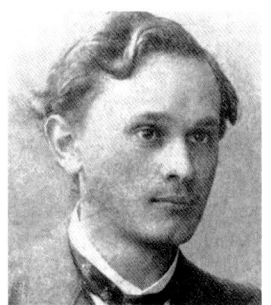

b. 1883 in Döbeln, Germany
d. 1970 in Hemmenhofen,
Germany

Erich Heckel tended more strongly to sentimentality and melancholy than any other Brücke artist. In view of the idyllic landscapes and human images that dominated his work, the group's move in 1911 from Dresden to the hectic big-city pavements of Berlin must have come as a shock. And as if girding himself against the rush of new impressions, he held fast to his previous motifs after that date. Yet the tenor of Heckel's paintings and prints – his woodcuts are among the best that Expressionism ever produced – nonetheless altered. The brushstrokes grew heavier, the contours harsher, and the palette shifted from powerful complementary colours to subtle, earthy tones. Tragic figures full of melancholy supplanted carefree people depicted in unsullied natural surroundings.

A short time before the move, Heckel produced one of the most beautiful works of his early period, the present painting of Max Pechstein asleep. The history of this canvas is associated with the name of a modern connoisseur.

Lothar-Günther Buchheim began to collect Expressionist paintings, drawings and prints at an early date. In 1951 he founded a publishing house dedicated principally to promoting German Expressionism, which after 1945, when the art business concerned itself solely with abstraction, again threatened to fall into discredit. In 1956 Buchheim published a standard work on the Brücke, followed two years later by a book on the Blauer Reiter. It was also he who rediscovered Heckel's portrait of Pechstein.

At an auction Buchheim acquired a not particularly exciting Heckel painting of 1920–21 that depicted rather wooden-looking nudes on a beach. Thanks to earlier research, he knew the back of the canvas must contain a masterpiece of Expressionism, concealed under a thick layer of white paint – Heckel's portrait of his artist friend, fallen asleep in a long chair, which he had finished in 1910 in Dangast and which the experts had long considered lost. They knew only the small woodcut based on this composition, which was reproduced in 1910 in the catalogue of the Brücke show held at Galerie Arnold, Dresden. Now the sensational picture finally came back to light.

The brushwork is no longer as furious as immediately after the founding year of the Brücke, 1905, and in the following storm-and-stress period, to 1909. Instead, the frontal figure is rendered in expansive flat planes suffused with intrinsic power and grandeur. On an Italian journey in 1909 Heckel had been confronted with the monumental rigour of Giotto (c. 1267–1337) and the Trecento, as well as with the iconic dignity of Etruscan sculpture, and these left their mark on his work. In his Pechstein portrait Heckel also avoided the wild, untamed orgies of colour that had previously dominated much of Brücke art, despite the intense red that determines the overall effect. A general disciplining of painterly means, a tectonic composition, and striking figurative formulae now became Heckel's prime aims. Emotional expression continued to play a key role, but combined with well-considered, rationally controlled form. Heckel also addressed the problem of spatial depth in this period, and attempted to solve it by means of geometric reduction and overlapping pictorial planes.

Pechstein Asleep, 1910
Oil on canvas,
110 x 74 cm (43¼ x 29¼ in.)
Bernried, Buchheim Museum

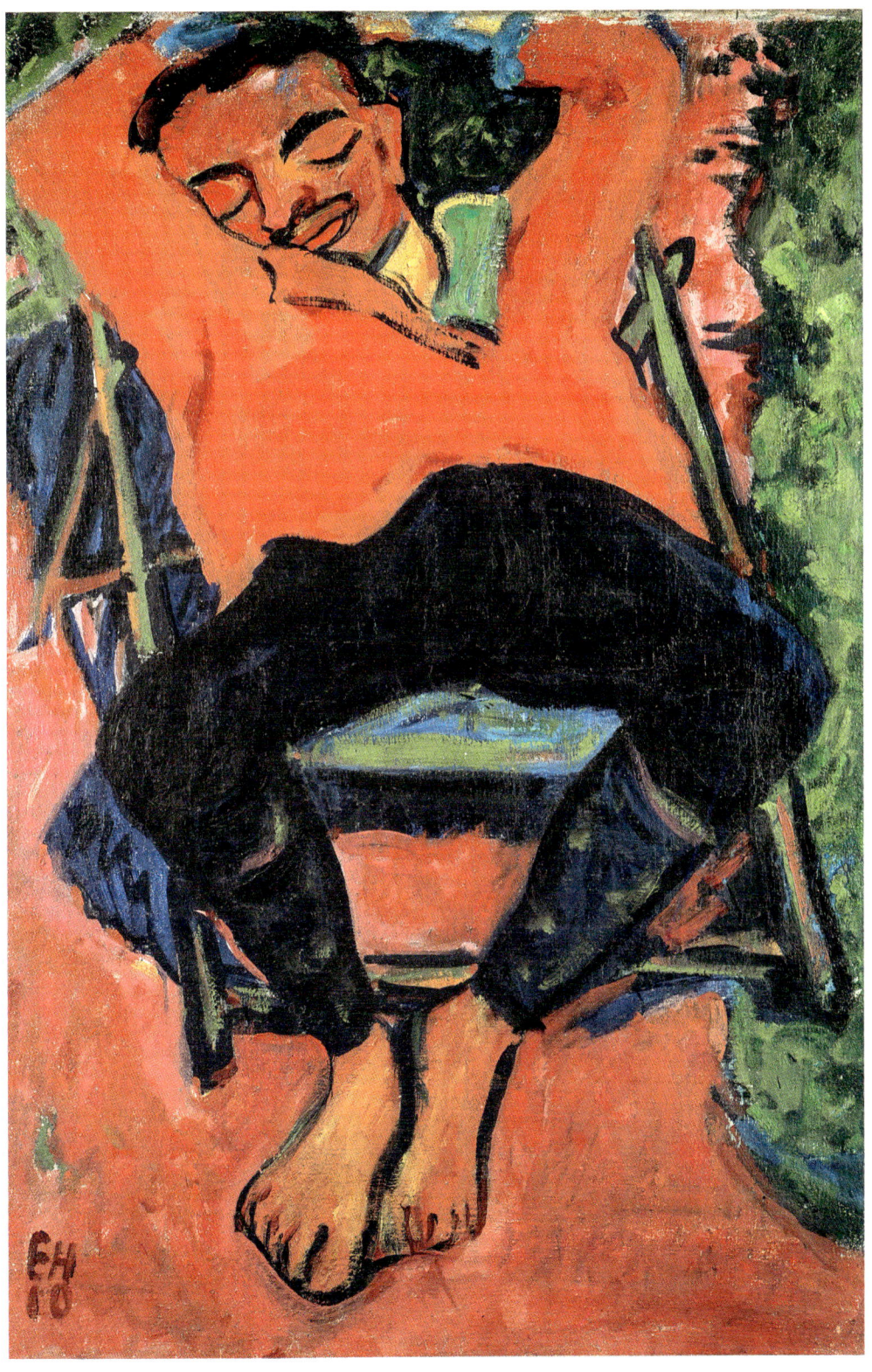

Erich Heckel
Glass Day, 1913

In 1910 and 1911, when Heckel spent relaxing and productive summer months with Kirchner and Pechstein at the Moritzburg Lakes outside Dresden, pictures of bathers, usually female nudes done on the spot, were a predominant subject for him as for the other Brücke artists. The fields of saturated colour were bounded by black contours, the figures simplified and cursorily reduced, the prevailing mood carefree and reflecting that Romantic yearning for a harmonious unity of man and nature, art and life, that characterized Brücke art at that period. Not so much in terms of formal approach as in terms of this fundamental mood, such Expressionist compositions can be compared to Paul Cézanne's *Bathers*, since these, too, aimed at giving form to a vision of an earthly paradise of balance and harmony. The great Cézanne exhibition held in November 1909 at Galerie Paul Cassirer in Berlin gave the Brücke painters an opportunity to thoroughly study his painting.

For Heckel, the year 1911 brought new insights. Although the female nude in the studio or outdoors remained his central theme, his approach in the subsequent works changed decisively under the influence of Cubism and Futurism, but especially after a confrontation with the art of Robert Delaunay. Heckel's theoretical involvement with the Frenchman's work was prompted by Macke, Marc and Feininger, all of whom visited Heckel in Berlin in 1912. *The Glass Day* was his masterful summing-up of this innovative experience.

The painting is no longer executed in the earlier heavy impasto but in thinned oils. Heckel's formerly decorative curving line is supplanted by angular strokes and facetting which transform the motif of a nude figure bathing in a bay into a play of interlocking crystalline figurations. The all-pervading lucid blue of water and sky seems to penetrate even the woman's body in the foreground and the steep coastline in the background. The pictorial space, suffused with brilliant light, robs things of material mass; the colour range conveys an icy, frozen, glassy, quasi spiritualized effect – as already indicated by the title, which, by the way, like the composition itself, anticipated the crystalline fantasies of an Expressionist architects' group that would form a few years later, Die Gläserne Kette (The Glass Chain). Perhaps it is no coincidence that this major work of Heckel's was executed in 1913, after the Brücke had dissolved.

When war broke out in 1914, Heckel volunteered for the medical corps and was stationed in Ostend, where he met Max Beckmann. With the aid of art historian Walter Kaesbach he was able to continue painting despite his duties. In view of the ensuing self-destruction of old Europe, Heckel placed his hopes in a league of like-minded intellectuals and artists, and grew increasingly intrigued by the circle around the poet Stefan George (1868–1933) – who however despised Heckel's Expressionism. This did not prevent the painter from making George the key figure in murals executed in 1922–23 at the Angermuseum, Erfurt, where Kaesbach had become director after the war and built up a collection of contemporary art – Feininger, Heckel, other Expressionists, and Bauhaus artists. In Heckel's fresco with its predominantly male nudes, the earthly paradise of earlier summers shimmers through. In the elongated figures against a background of forbidding Alpine glaciers, despite the new classicism which has shed its erstwhile Expressionist formal vocabulary, a spiritualization reminiscent of *Glass Day* remains much in evidence.

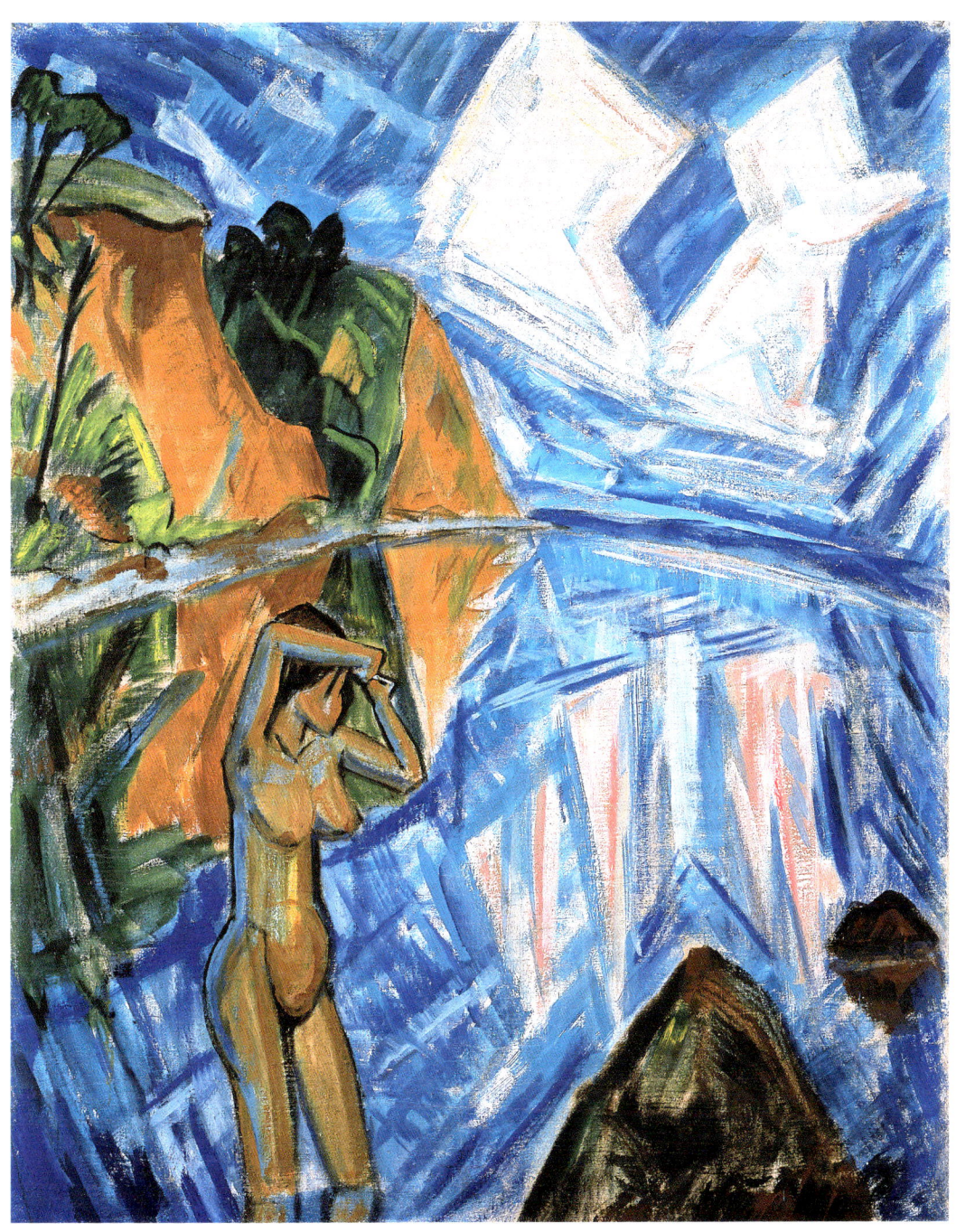

Glass Day, 1913
Oil on canvas, 117 x 92 cm (46 x 36¼ in.)
Munich, Bayerische Staatsgemälde-
sammlungen, Pinakothek der Moderne

Alexej von Jawlensky
Portrait of the Dancer Alexander Sacharoff, 1909

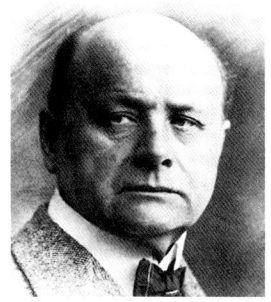

b. 1864 in Torzhok, Russia
d. 1941 in Wiesbaden, Germany

In 1896 Jawlensky came with Marianne von Werefkin to Munich, where they met and befriended Kandinsky. At first the already accomplished artist retained the earthy palette he had learned at the St Petersburg Academy under Ilya Repin (1844–1930), who was then the dominating personality in Russian painting. Yet he soon shook off this naturalistic approach. The catalyst was a confrontation with van Gogh, modern French art – initially the Nabis, later the Fauves – and subsequently with the Dutch artist Kees van Dongen. In 1905 Jawlensky self-confidently announced that after a stay on the Breton coast near Carantec, he had finally managed "to translate nature into colours in conformance with my radiant soul". Ecstatic emotion conveyed through colour, and the ordering force of planar composition, remained the key concerns of this artist, who, like Kandinsky, was esoterically interested and continually pursued the intrinsic essence and harmony of things.

The following years brought numerous international contacts, and above all collaborative work with Werefkin, Münter and Kandinsky in Murnau, followed by participation in the New Artists Association in Munich and – from 1912 – in the Blauer Reiter. Apart from landscapes, representations of heads began to play a prime role in Jawlensky's oeuvre.

In 1907 he began to concentrate in a very original way on the effects of colours on a plane surface. The resulting paintings convey the impression that the colours have been veritably stretched across the surface. They are contoured in heavy black lines that both define the figures and set them in vibrant motion, as in the superb *Portrait of the Dancer Alexander Sacharoff*. Sacharoff (1886–1963), a close friend of Werefkin and Jawlensky's, was a pupil at the Académie des Beaux-Arts in Paris from 1903 to 1904. A theatre performance by Sarah Bernhardt impressed him so deeply that he decided to become a dancer. In 1904 Sacharoff moved to Munich, where he would later contribute to the development of eurhythmic dancing. Above all in the 1920s and 1930s, tours through all five continents brought him world fame.

Reputedly Jawlensky painted the portrait (from the collection of Clotilde von Derp-Sacharoff) at a single sitting, when the dancer, in make-up and costume, visited him shortly before a performance. And Sacharoff is said to have taken the still-wet picture with him, fearing that the artist might paint it over. The sweepingly rendered area of the figure and the made-up face, lasciviously androgynous – possibly Sacharoff was playing a female role – are dominated by the aggressive red of the costume and mouth, and the black contours of figure and coiffure (probably a wig). The greenish shadows in the face are echoed in the brushstrokes that set the background in an enigmatic staccato that seems to reflect the physical energy of the sitter.

Jawlensky would later employ the synthesis of formal sensibility and expressive mysticism achieved here to create increasingly abstracted faces, in a sort of stenography of the soul. The colours became less and less naturalistic, the pictorial structure ever more geometric. The transcendental presence of Byzantine icons seemed to have been reborn in a configuration derived from Cubism. After the outbreak of the First World War, Werefkin and Jawlensky had to leave Germany. They went to Switzerland. Cuno Amiet, a former member of the Brücke, went back to the couple's abandoned apartment and saved the most valuable objects of art there, including a van Gogh painting.

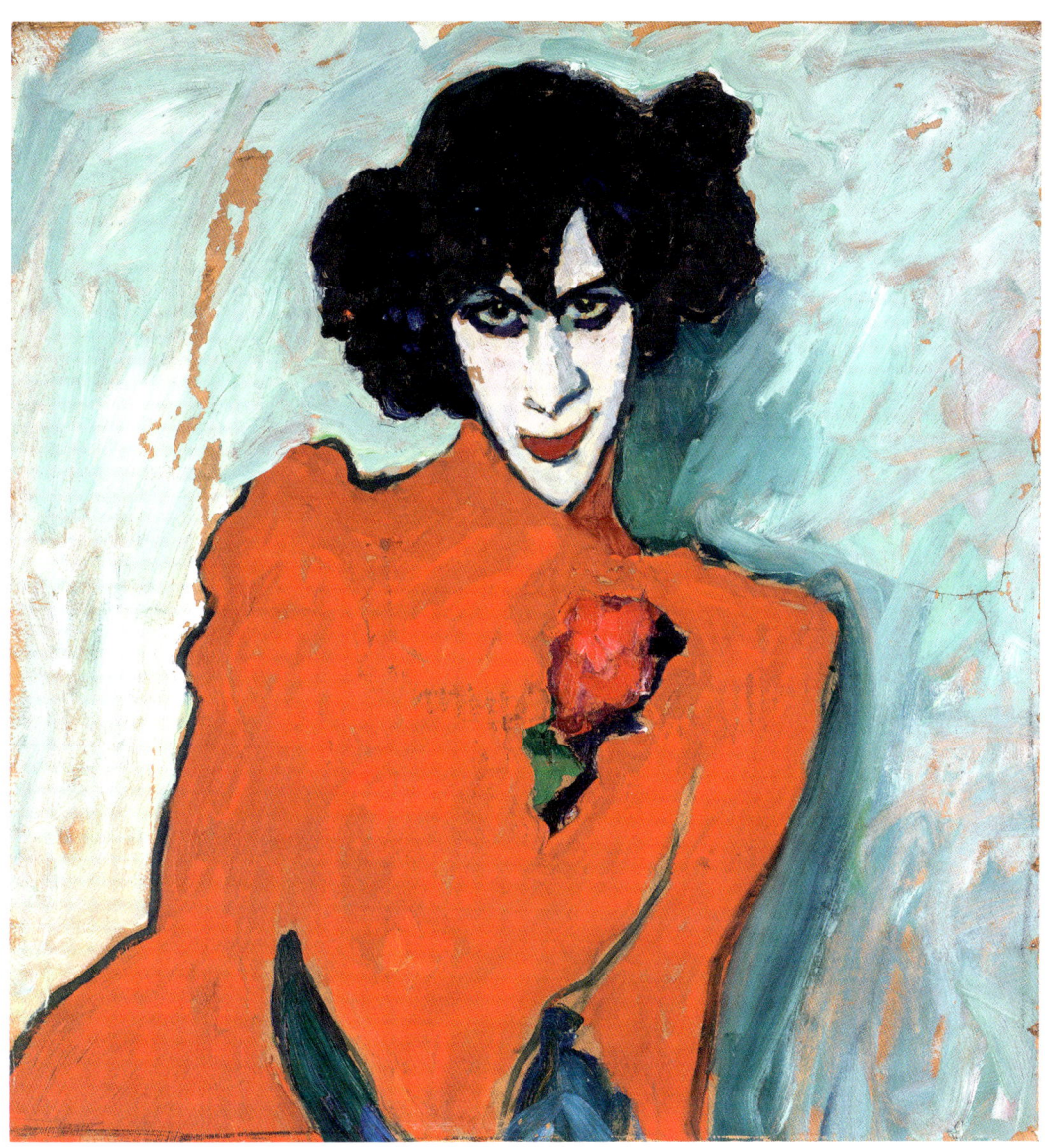

Portrait of the Dancer
Alexander Sacharoff, 1909
Oil on cardboard, 69.5 x 66.5 cm (27¼ x 26¼ in.)
Munich, Städtische Galerie im
Lenbachhaus und Kunstbau München

Wassily Kandinsky
St Ludwig's Church in Munich, 1908

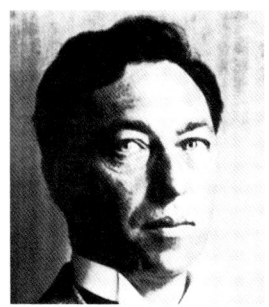

b. 1866 in Moscow
d. 1944 in Neuilly-sur-Seine,
France

The artist focuses on the streetside arcades in the lower façade of St Ludwig's, the Munich University church, which dates from the early nineteenth century. St Ludwig's is located near Ainmillerstrasse in the erstwhile "artists' neighbourhood" of Schwabing, where Kandinsky rented a studio apartment in September 1908. Outside the church portal a crowd of people mills, probably the congregation or participants in a procession, abstracted to glowing dots of colour. The brilliant banner under the middle arch and the group of priests in yellow copes suggests that a Catholic celebration of some kind is going on.

The way Kandinsky brings the short strokes and tiny configurations of glittering, gemlike colour into a dazzling texture, composed in an interplay of light and dark, recalls the folkloristic motifs of the "fairy-tale pictures" in which he depicted his Russian homeland under the influence of French Post-Impressionism and Pointillism in 1906 and 1907. It was no coincidence that in his 1911 book, *On the Spiritual in Art*, Kandinsky referred to Paul Signac's (1863–1935) essay, "D'Eugène Delacroix au néo-impressionisme", the most important theoretical statement of that group, whose works Kandinsky had already given a place of prominence in the tenth exhibition, in 1904, of the Phalanx group, to which he belonged from 1901 to 1905. The brilliant light contrasted with deep shadows underneath the arches lends the picture of St Ludwig's both a flickering atmosphere and a highly abstract decorativeness. This, with the saturated colour tones, reflects the deep and lasting inspiration Kandinsky derived from the Fauves, especially Matisse, during a study trip to Paris in 1906–07.

Pictures like *St Ludwig's Church in Munich* represent the midpoint of Kandinsky's first and decisive phase of development. It began with a literally eye-opening experience. As Kandinsky later recalled, he was standing in front of one of Monet's (1840–1926) paintings of haystacks, Impressionist renderings dissolved into strokes of pure colour, when he realized, "Suddenly I saw a painting for the first time." He admitted to not being able to visually identify the motif, which he found embarrassing. A painter had no right, Kandinsky believed at the time, "to paint so unclearly". He had the sense that "the object was missing in this picture." Yet still he was struck by the "unsuspected force of the palette, which had previously been hidden to me and surpassed all my dreams. Painting took on a fabulous power and glory."

Years later, in 1908, when Kandinsky and his partner Gabriele Münter settled again in Munich and began exploring the Upper Bavarian landscape around Murnau with Jawlensky and Marianne von Werefkin, and when they all joined forces in 1909 to found the New Artists Association of Munich, Kandinsky arrived at an approach his friends called "a synthesis" – a reduction of subject matter to flat, coloured forms, rhythmically arranged and anchored by solid contours, which enabled great detachment from natural appearances and their subjective distortion. From this point of departure, Kandinsky then took his next, revolutionary step to abstraction, in the context of the Blauer Reiter group, which separated from the New Artists Association in 1911.

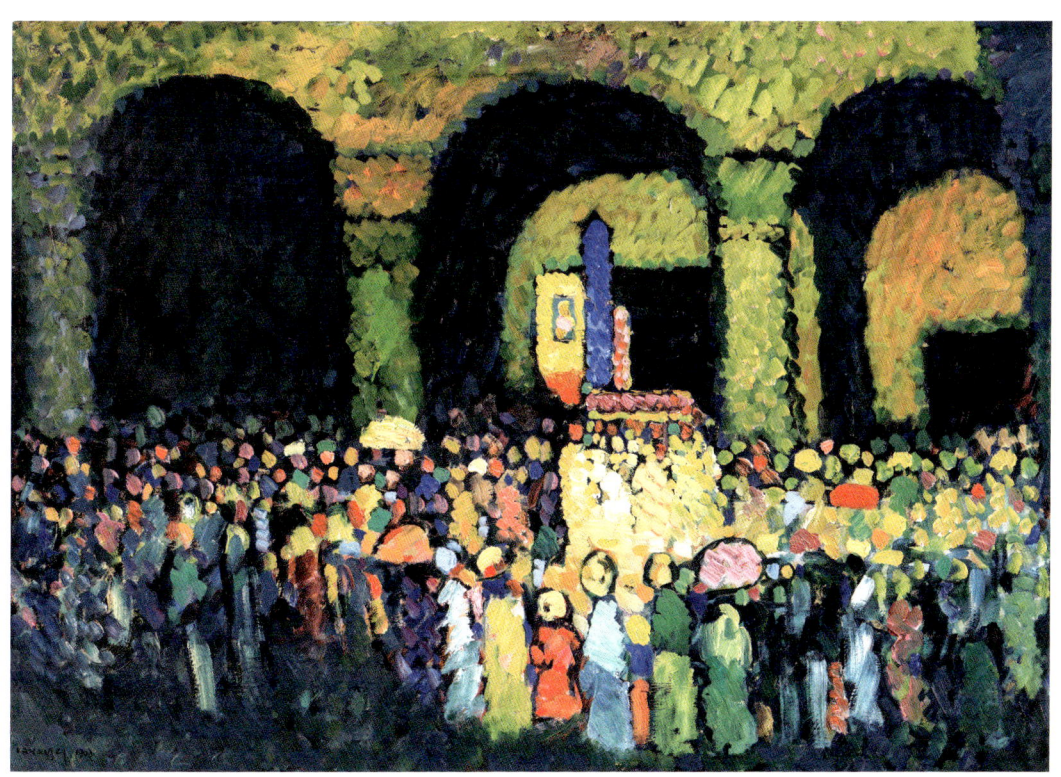

St Ludwig's Church in Munich, 1908
Oil on cardboard, 67.3 x 96 cm (26½ x 37¾ in.)
Madrid, Museo Thyssen-Bornemisza,
on loan from the Collection of Carmen
Thyssen-Bornemisza

Wassily Kandinsky
Improvisation Klamm, 1914

In the Blauer Reiter years, from 1911 to 1914, Kandinsky unerringly pursued the path to abstraction. This was perhaps the artistically most exciting phase of his career, when in his *Impressions* (which, he said, conveyed an impression of "external nature"), *Improvisations* (impressions of "inner nature") and *Compositions,* he retained a modicum of figuration while charging forms and colours with intrinsic effect. As Kandinsky himself explained in 1914, "In the same picture, in other words, I more or less dissolved the objects, so that not all of them could be recognized at once, and so that these spiritual overtones could be gradually experienced by the viewer, one after the other. And here and there even purely abstract forms came in of their own accord, forms, in other words, that had to have a purely painterly effect."

In *Improvisation Klamm*, too, the meanings of objects still reverberate like an undertone in the largely abstract structure. The painting was inspired by an excursion with Gabriele Münter to a valley known as Höllentalklamm, near Garmisch-Partenkirchen, on 3 July 1914. In the upper area one can detect ladders and ropes, at the lower left, a rowboat, and at the lower right, a waterfall. Between these runs a footbridge with a couple standing on it, apparently in Bavarian costume. And yet one by no means has the impression that Kandinsky has simply depicted a country excursion here, let alone invoked an earthly paradise, as August Macke did. It has justifiably been pointed out that the ambience here makes anything but an idyllic impression. Instead, moods of the most diverse kind jar against one another, lending the whole a turbulent, conflicting character – as if the maelstroms of paint were in the process of swallowing up the last remnants of objectivity and figuration.

In keeping with the symbolic language that dominated Kandinsky's work of these years, the suggestion of an "apocalyptic horseman" appears in the left-hand section of the picture. A frequent feature of his compositions, this figure stood for the battle against the dragon of worldliness, the avant-garde's battle against hidebound convention, of the spiritual against the superficiality of modern society. On this point Kandinsky was greatly influenced by the anthroposophy of Rudolf Steiner (1861–1925) and the theosophy of Madame Blatavsky (1831–1891), which augmented his already strong tendency to mysticism. A new age had dawned, he was convinced, an age in which positivism and materialism would be overcome, to be replaced by the new ideal of spirituality – actually an old ideal which had already been pursued by German Romantics such as Caspar David Friedrich (1774–1840) and Philipp Otto Runge (1777–1810) Kandinsky now set out to convey symbolic meanings not only through motifs but through pure lines and colours, their contrasts and harmonies, their "musicality" and synaesthetic effects.

Seen against this background, *Improvisation Klamm* looks less like a paradise lost than an attempt to continue those aesthetic battles and incursions into uncharted territory that characterized Kandinsky's Munich period, despite the dangers that loomed in the real world. For just four weeks after completing this work Kandinsky left Germany and returned by devious paths to Russia, where he assumed a key role in the development not only of an avant-garde but a veritably revolutionary art.

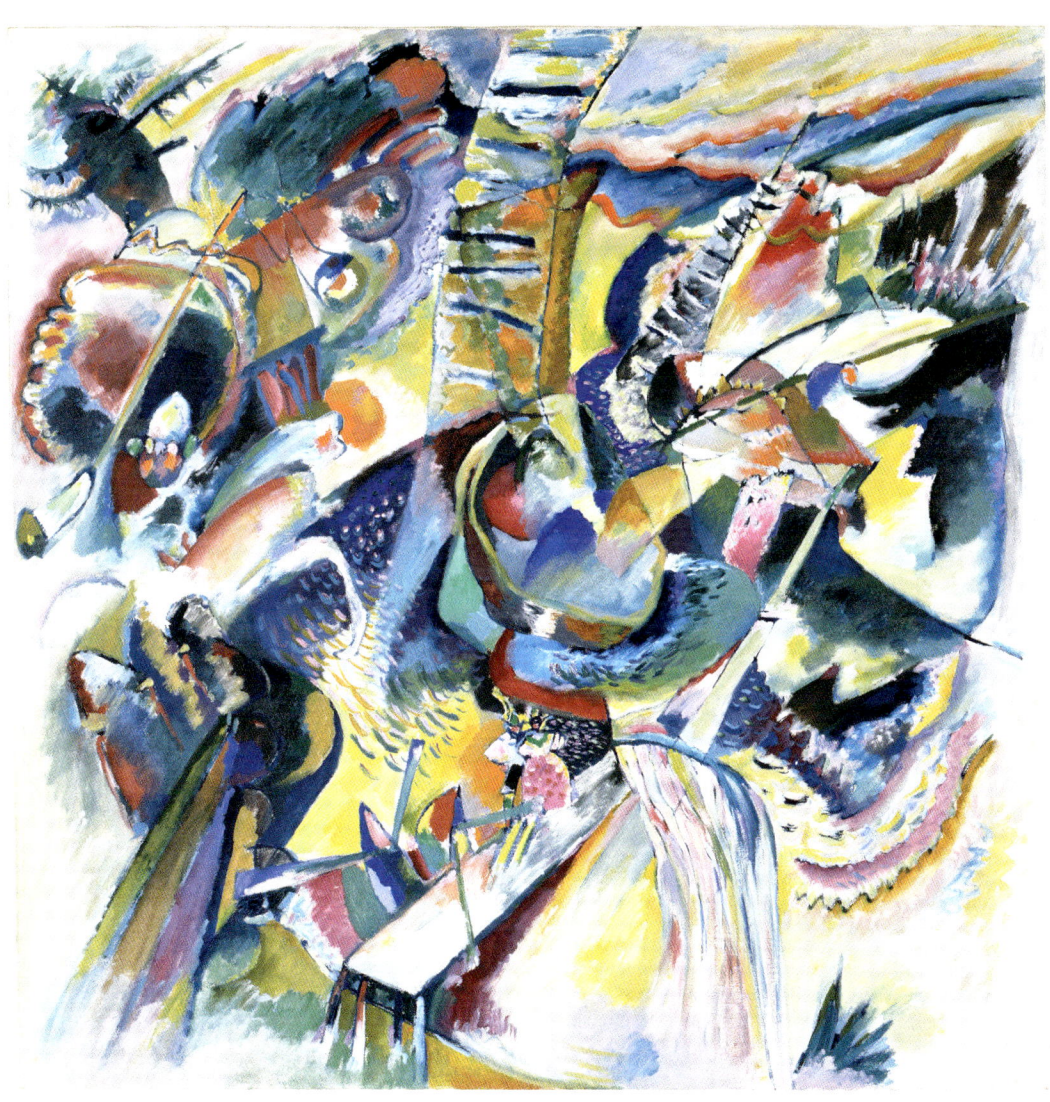

Improvisation Klamm, 1914
Oil on canvas, 110 x 110 cm (43¼ x 43¼ in.)
Munich, Städtische Galerie im
Lenbachhaus und Kunstbau München

Ernst Ludwig Kirchner
Artiste (Marcella), 1910

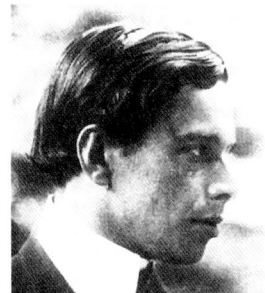

b. 1880 in Aschaffenburg,
Germany
d. 1938 in Frauenkirch,
Switzerland

Kirchner, criticized Max Beckmann, was never able to escape the influence of French art, something Kirchner himself loudly denied throughout his lifetime. Yet he was already intrigued with Post-Impressionism while still a student of architecture in Dresden, and briefly in Munich. After taking his engineering degree, he became a convert to painting and, on 7 June 1905, joined Bleyl, Schmidt-Rottluff and Heckel to form Die Brücke in Dresden. Now it was the agitated brushwork of van Gogh that left a deep impression on the four. In 1908–09 the Fauves, or "savages", electrified the young German artists, above all Henri Matisse, to whom Galerie Cassirer in Berlin devoted an exciting retrospective. Kirchner marvelled at Matisse's brilliant, flat colour-fields and began to adapt them to his own approach in untiring experiments. They taught him never to entirely lose conscious formal control under the pressure of spontaneous expression. As a result, Kirchner's art developed into one of the most tension-charged of any twentieth-century European painter.

In view of this involvement, it becomes clear why Kirchner should have been primarily interested in the aesthetic, decorative aspects of Matisse's art. In the midst of the formal turbulence and agitation of the Brücke repertoire, of which he was a pioneer, Kirchner nevertheless continually concentrated on a stylization of the planar composition, a rational reduction and clarification of visual vocabulary beyond all sheer expressiveness, as seen in *Artiste (Marcella).*

From early 1910, two adolescent sisters, Marcella and Fränzi, reportedly the daughters of an artiste's widow who lived in Kirchner's neighbourhood, began to play an important part in the lives of the Brücke artists. Thanks to their willingness to pose in the nude outdoors, the two girls became the painters' favourite models, and like others before them, likely had a more than platonic relationship with them. The present portrait, which probably represents the fifteen-year-old Marcella, is one of Kirchner's most impressive paintings. It is characterized by intrinsic monumentality and ludicity. The girl has assumed a relaxed pose, one leg drawn up, her head resting on her right hand. The setting is pervaded by a relaxed, introverted mood that is underscored by the cat asleep in the foreground. The apparently so simple effect of the painting should not deceive us as to the refinement of the composition and its skilled disposition of planes. The motifs are arranged on a diagonal, leading from the lower left to the upper right. Smooth, homogeneously opaque colour areas, limited to a few intense hues including a dominant green, and closed contours lend a graceful rhythm to the composition. The unusual, high vantage point, from which the figure is seen diagonally from above, was a brilliant idea on Kirchner's part. It brings the girl close to the viewer, yet at the same time, it shows her turning away as if to escape from any voyeuristic gaze, puts visual and existential distance between model and viewer.

In 1925 in Switzerland – where the mentally and physically shaken Kirchner had retired to a farm near Davos in the last year of the war – he was confronted by original works by Picasso. Their masterful exercises in Cubist facetting tempted Kirchner for a time to make his own attempts at rational pictorial composition. As a result, Kirchner's oeuvre as a whole came to represent both poles of the Expressionist potential: an emotionally-charged, gestural art in heightened colourism and a taming of the expressive through conscious control over pictorial means.

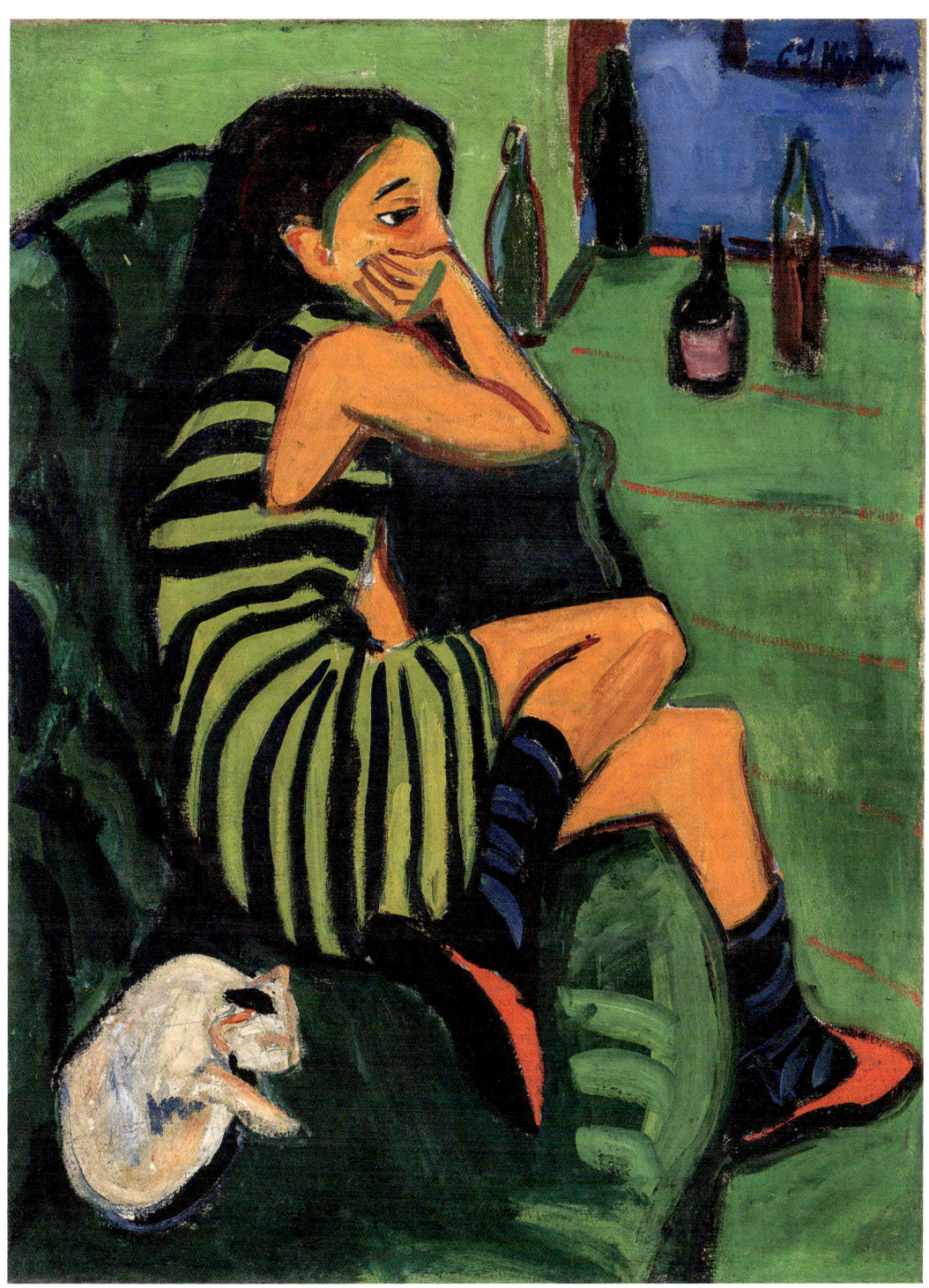

Artiste (Marcella), 1910
Oil on canvas, 100 x 76 cm (39¼ x 30 in.)
Berlin, Brücke-Museum

Ernst Ludwig Kirchner
Potsdamer Platz, 1914

In 1911 the Brücke painters moved from Dresden to Berlin, the only true metropolis that Germany had to offer at that period. Now the moloch of the big city became one of their cardinal themes. Kirchner, too, plunged into the symphony – or rather, cacophony – of urban life, with an unprecedented creative furore in which he came to terms, among other influences, with that of Italian Futurism, which had first appeared on the scene in 1909. The Futurists, too, loved the city streets, their garish electric lights and rushing traffic, translating them into a dynamic staccato of lines, a simultaneity of various impressions and events, and interpenetrating visual levels. Kirchner populated his street scenes with prostitutes, decked out as if in the ruffled feathers of birds of prey, bizarre hats, bright feather boas, and tight corsets. Such cocottes prowled in bevies along Friedrichstrasse (whose Café National was the city's best-known streetwalkers' haunt) and around Potsdamer Platz, to which Kirchner made regular excursions from his nearby studio.

The monumental canvas *Potsdamer Platz* is justly celebrated in art history as an illustrious icon of German big-city Expressionism. Gleaming in the background are the red brick walls of Potsdam Station. In the foreground stand two streetwalkers of different ages, both "ladylike", as police regulations demanded. Behind them hover black-suited men, anonymous, faceless. The triangle of the pavement, its shape echoed by the striding legs of the male figures, is thrust like a lance between the converging streets towards the round traffic island, where the female figures present themselves as if on a revolving stage. The combination of forms, round and pointed, possesses clear sexual connotations. The street is suffused by a noxious green, which, as Roland März has said, "fans out in a cold light on wet asphalt, overflowing the banks between pavement and traffic island, inundating it."

An earlier opinion of this picture was less favourable. On 16 February 1916, Franz Servaes wrote in the *Vossische Zeitung* that Kirchner "presents true monstrosities of human figures with distorted limbs, doing ridiculous hopping movements in a surrounding space that totters as if drunk." The fact that one of the women in Potsdamer Platz wears a widow's veil indicates that the picture was not finished until after 1 August 1914. That day marked the outbreak of the First World War, and from then on, prostitutes were officially required to dress as soldiers' widows on Berlin's streets – strangely patriotic sex workers!

In 1915 Kirchner volunteered for military service. After only two months he was temporarily discharged, on condition that he enter psychiatric treatment. By this time Kirchner had begun to view war as a "bloody carnival", and wrote, "Now one is just like the cocottes I used to paint. Blurred, then gone the next moment…" In 1917, after attempting to quell attacks of panic with alcohol, morphine and tablets, Kirchner tried to escape them by going to a series of sanatoriums before settling in a farmhouse near Davos. In Switzerland, his art developed from renderings of the forbidding Alpine realm in a monumental Expressionist idiom to experiments in Cubist form inspired by Picasso. In 1937, thirty-two Kirchner works hung in the Nazi exhibition "Entartete Kunst", or Degenerate Art. He felt himself completely misunderstood, as he had always looked upon himself as a quintessentially German artist. Kirchner relapsed into profound depression. On 15 June 1938, he put a pistol to his chest and pulled the trigger.

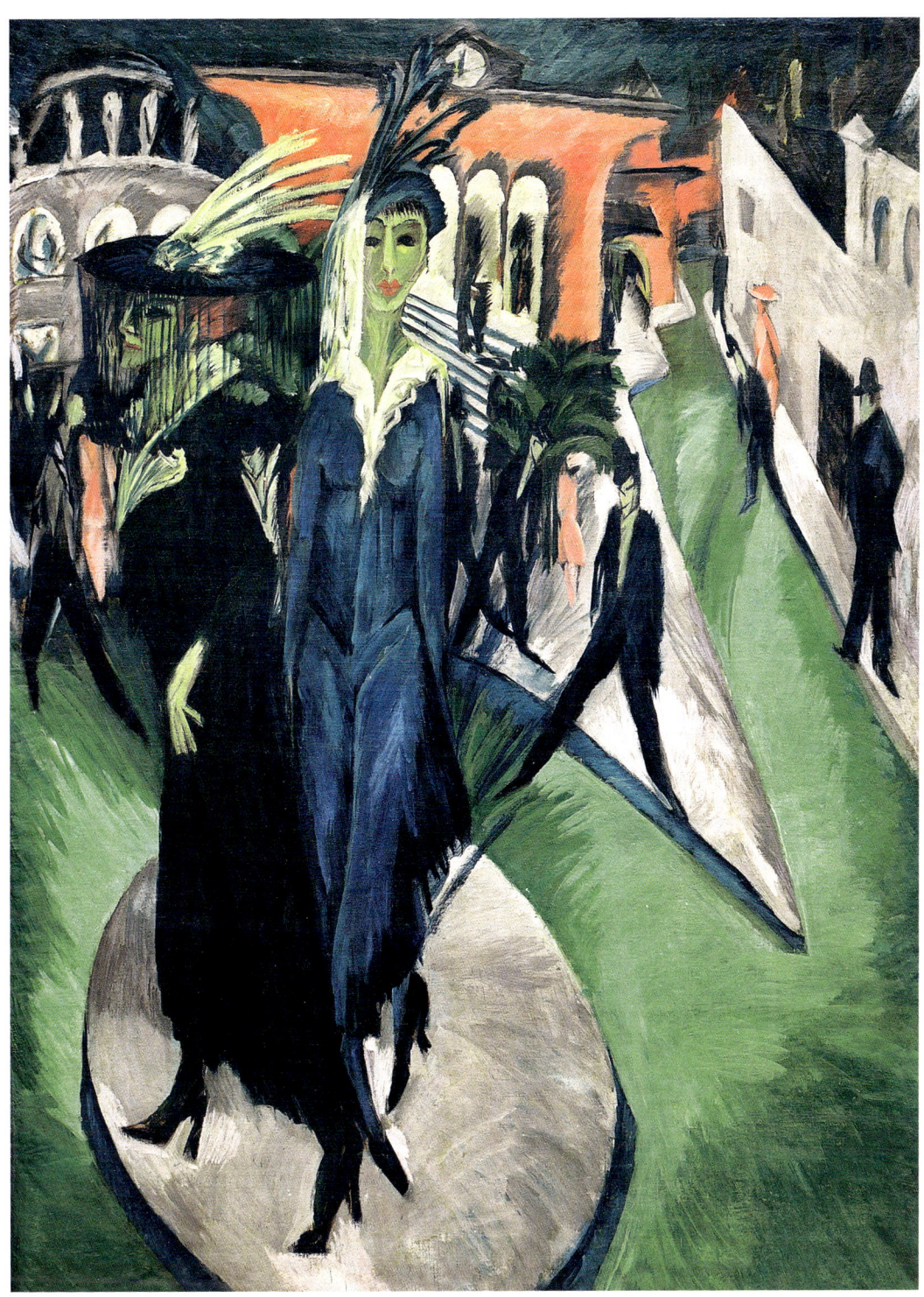

Potsdamer Platz, 1914
Oil on canvas, 200 x 150 cm (78¾ x 59 in.)
Staatliche Museen zu Berlin,
Neue Nationalgalerie

Paul Klee
Föhn Wind, in Franz Marc's Garden, 1915

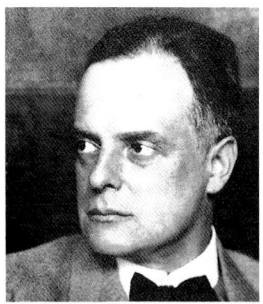

b. 1879 in Münchenbuchsee, Switzerland
d. 1940 in Muralto, Switzerland

The Swiss artist Paul Klee is one of the most outstanding personalities in modern art and also one of its greatest individualists. His oeuvre does not conform to any of the many directions in twentieth-century art. His watercolours, prints and (comparatively few) oil paintings bear little relation in form and content to the common motifs of the period. Klee's stylistic independence goes hand in hand with a brilliant assurance that lends his world-renowned art an enigmatic but irresistible charm. Due to this creative autonomy he is one of the many lone figures who briefly added their voices to the choir of Expressionism without being a member of the ensemble or, indeed, even adhering to the score of the performance.

Nevertheless, Klee was lastingly influenced by his brief connection with the Blauer Reiter. It was his acquaintance with Kandinsky and other artists of the Expressionist vanguard in Munich that brought his breakthrough. His invitation to the Blauer Reiter exhibition of May 1912, to which he submitted seventeen drawings, actually marked the beginning of Klee's international career. Prior to that point, between 1903 and 1905, still living in Bern, he had been active as a draughtsman and etcher of allegorical, grotesque subjects in the wake of Symbolism, formally and substantially related to the Austrian Alfred Kubin (1877–1959), with whom he became friends in 1911. Klee, too, developed a unique linear style and oriented himself to the ambiguity and bizarreness of Romantic literature, such as that of E. T. A. Hoffmann. In early 1912 Klee – like the majority of the Expressionists – confessed his leaning to primitivism: "Because there are still primal beginnings of art, of the kind we tend rather to find in the ethnographic museum or at home, in the nursery (don't laugh, reader)." After a reference to the drawings of the mentally ill, he adds, "All of this must in truth be taken much more seriously than all art museums put together when it is a matter of reforming contemporary art."

Klee's final breakthrough to the "magic of colour" and stylistic maturity resulted from impressions gleaned on a trip to Tunis, undertaken in 1914 with August Macke and the sculptor Louis Moilliet (1880–1962). This journey and its artistic yield became legendary, an absolute apex in the history of modern art. Over the following years the light-flooded watercolours of this period were paralleled by increasingly strict, crystalline abstractions, encouraged by Klee's friend Franz Marc.

This is the context in which *Föhn Wind, in Franz Marc's Garden* belongs, one of the most beautiful watercolours from Klee's Blauer Reiter period. It was done on the occasion of a visit to Marc in Ried, near Benediktbeuren, in July 1915, when Marc was on a brief leave from the front. The motif, rendered in an interplay of colours so subtle that "musical" is the only word for it, is abstracted yet still recognizable. We see the wall of a freestanding house, the red roof of a garden house in the midst of dark firs, and a mountain silhouette in the background. Yet ultimately the landscape is reduced to a pattern of Cubistic geometrical shapes that interlock and partially overlap each other.

The watercolour also represents Klee's reaction to his reading, in 1912, of Wilhelm Worringer's book *Abstraction and Empathy*, published in 1908. From that point on Klee strove to take an "elevated vantage point" from which he would be able to integrate the "horror-filled world" in a universal context – as here, where Marc's garden is transformed into a universal image. Although this reflects points of contact with the visions of Expressionism, soon, in his Bauhaus period, Klee's art would burgeon into a universe in its own right.

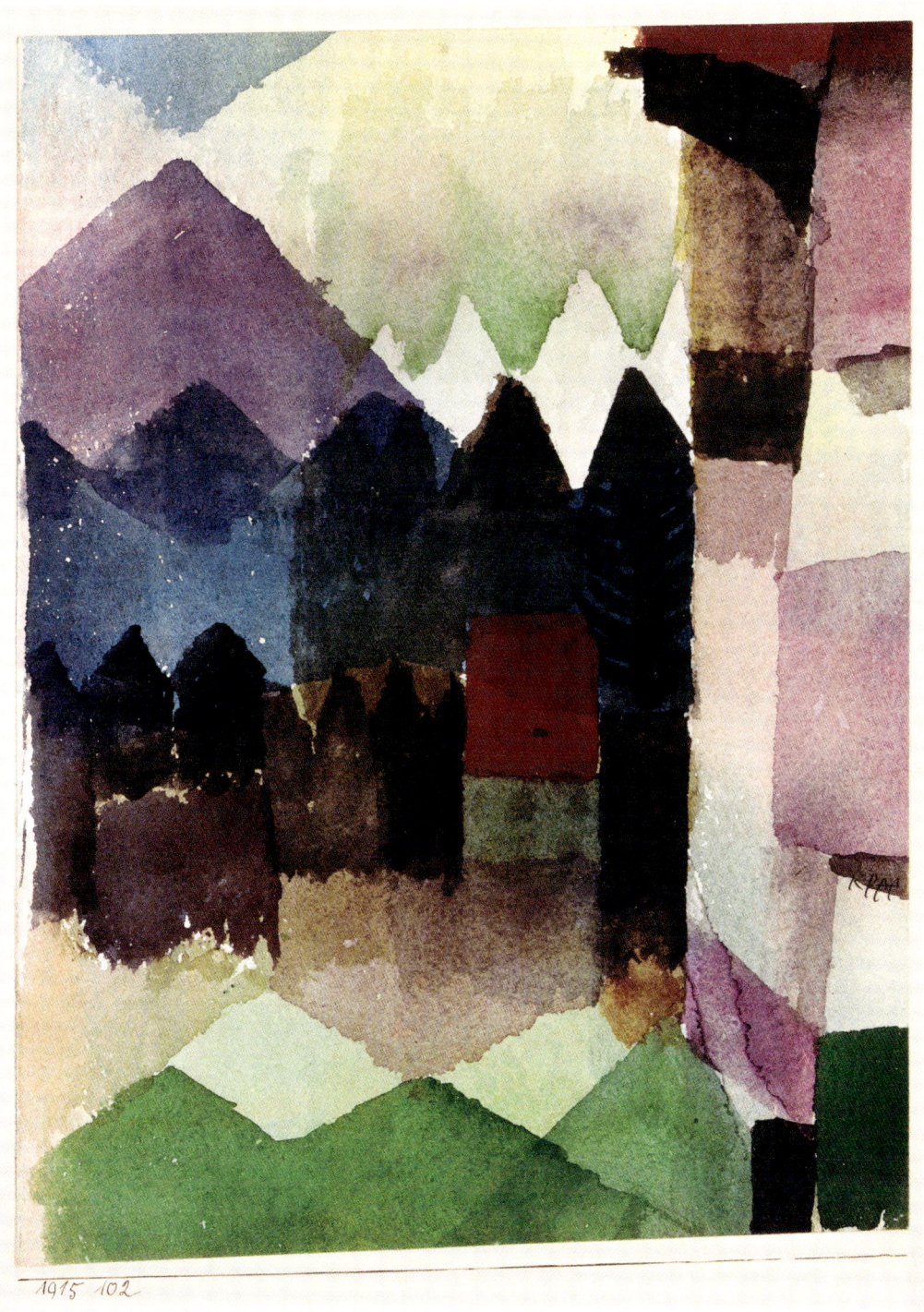

Föhn Wind, in Franz Marc's Garden, 1915
Watercolour on paper on cardboard, 20 x 15 cm (8 x 6 in.)
Munich, Städtische Galerie im Lenbachhaus und
Kunstbau München

Oskar Kokoschka
Portrait of Herwarth Walden, 1910

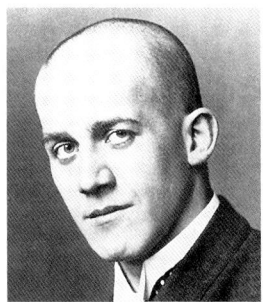

b. 1886 in Pöchlarn, Austria
d. 1980 in Villeneuve,
Switzerland

Oskar Kokoschka began his career as a commercial artist for the Wiener Werkstätte, the renowned crafts workshop in Vienna, while he was still a student at the Vienna School of Decorative Arts. His painting style, dominated by Art Nouveau influence, soon began to show features of Expressionism, such as bizarre idiosyncrasies and distortions, as well as a tendency to psychological penetration. The following year, at the Vienna "Kunstschau", the young artist's tapestry designs were accompanied by drawings and gouaches of young nude girls that touched off a scandal and immediately made Kokoschka the enfant terrible of the Vienna scene. Yet there were others, like Gustav Klimt, who recognized his genius.

Between 1908 and 1912 there emerged a series of portraits in thin oils, applied almost like watercolour washes, and agitated lines scratched with the brush handle into the wet paint, which established his early reputation. In these portraits Kokoschka stripped the mask of centuries of convention from the human image. The facial features appear furrowed, the complexion flecked with various hues and incised or scratched off with a brush handle or fine needle. These portraits, accompanied by similarly structured illustrations and lithographs full of nervous lineatures and physical distortions, amount to a laying bare of the sitter's soul. Their intense Expressionist attack is combined with a refinement of brushwork that also makes them masterpieces of a highly cultivated aesthetic.

Kokoschka's Expressionism, as was later often noted, bears "covert Baroque traits". Something ecstatic and visionary indeed suffuses his art, and distinguishes it from that of most of his Viennese contemporaries. This is why his portraits, in particular, are among the most compelling examples of Expressionist art. The nervous blurring of contours, the violent traces scratched into the paint surface, as if in an attempt to plumb the sitter's subconscious mind – some have credited Kokoschka with having "X-ray eyes" and psychoanalytical acumen – combined with a certain morbidity that lies over the faces of the people depicted, amount to a compelling analysis of the intellectual atmosphere of the fin de siècle.

Especially in the early portraits, Kokoschka's analytic eye focused on neurotic or even pathological traits. Even the half-figure portrayal of his patron Herwarth Walden, whom he met in Berlin in 1910 and in whose journal, *Der Sturm,* he immediately published his drama *Murderer, Hope of Women*, appears to reflect an overstrung mind, hypersensitivity, or perhaps merely restlessness. Although the reality of the sitter's appearance, one of the main aims of portraiture, is retained, a veil of irrationality seems to lie over the features, as if actual appearances had been abandoned in favour of a spontaneous evocation of inward forces. As in his portrait of Walden, Kokoschka preferred the half-figure portrait type, since it permitted him to underscore the nervous tension of the facial expressions with gestures of the hands, which are usually disproportionately large. The space in the picture, diffuse despite its uniform tone, can be seen as an equivalent to the sitter's state of mind.

Portrait of Herwarth Walden, 1910
Oil on canvas, 100 x 69.3 cm (39¼ x 27¼ in.)
Staatsgalerie Stuttgart

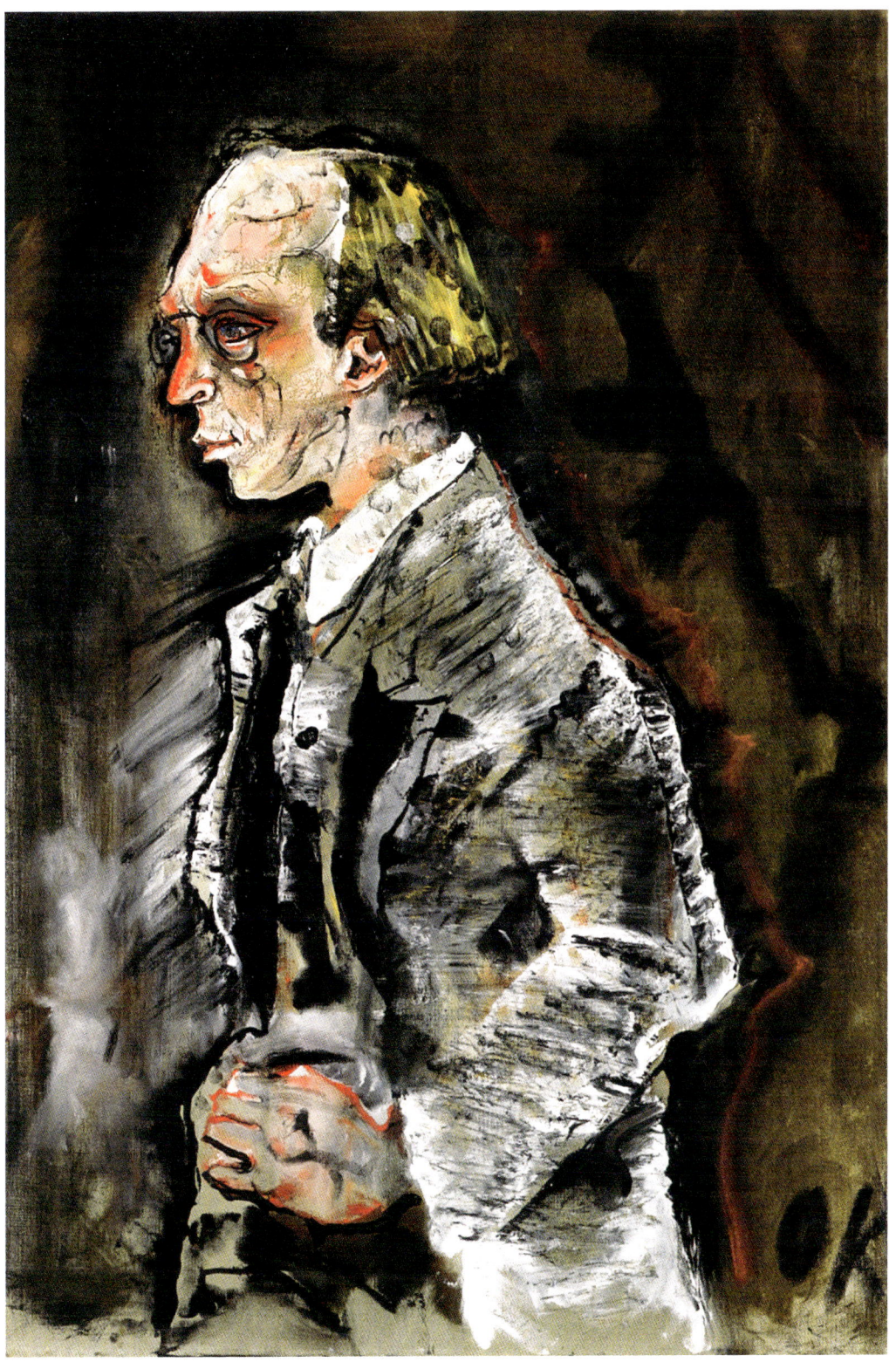

Oskar Kokoschka
The Wind's Bride (The Tempest), 1913

After his move to Berlin in 1909 and his activity for Herwarth Walden's journal, *Der Sturm,* Kokoschka gradually abandoned the thin paint application seen in his portrait of Walden. He began to employ thicker colours, an impasto applied in energetic brushstrokes that built the painting surface up into low relief. This manner grew ever more marked after 1912, when Kokoschka, back in Vienna, met Alma Mahler, widow of the composer Gustav Mahler. The ensuing passionate relationship with this lovely woman precipitated in a series of portraits and numerous other paintings, drawings and prints.

The present painting, now in the Basel Kunstmuseum, is a key work in Kokoschka's oeuvre. Finished in 1914, it is also the most famous witness to his great and stormy love. Kokoschka used to tell the following anecdote about the picture. Georg Trakl (1887–1914), an Austrian poet with Expressionist leanings, had come to visit him in his studio. When Trakl saw the yet-unfinished composition, it inspired him to compose a poem on the spot: "The Night". It included the following lines: "Over blackish cliffs / Plunges death-drunken / The incandescent bride of the wind." Trakl pointed at the picture with a pale hand, Kokoschka went on to relate, and titled it *Die Windsbraut* (literally "Windsbride", but generally known in English as *The Tempest*).

In German folklore the term Windsbraut connoted the Wild Hunt, a stormy whirlwind that abducted young girls and put them at the mercy of the Wild Hunter. An interpretation of this kind accords well with Kokoschka's painting, which shows him and his lover Alma Mahler drifting on a shell-like wreck through a "universal ocean" – confession of a love that was already threatening to descend into a battle between the sexes and founder on it. This message is conveyed by the contradictory attitudes of the two figures. Next to Alma, who has fallen into a deep and trusting sleep, lies a restless, brooding Oskar, staring into empty space – a complicated relationship put in terms of a universal human parable. The restless traces that plow through the paint congeal – as if in anticipation of Action Painting – into signs and abbreviations for intense emotions. The forms – or better, deformations – flung out into an unreal space are just as "overwrought" as the spotlighted passages in an otherwise subdued colouration. All of this works together to do justice to a typical Expressionist aim, to confront what Karl Kraus termed bourgeois "sexual hypocrisy" with the ideal of a liberated sexuality that would not hesitate to go to extremes even if it meant self-annihilation.

The break-up with Alma Mahler, from which Kokoschka never recovered, occurred in 1914. On the outbreak of war he volunteered for the cavalry. The expressive impasto brushwork in his paintings grew ever more agitated. A despairing attempt to find a surrogate muse in a lifelike doll shed light on the overwrought nervous state Kokoschka was in at the time. This obsession was to pursue him for years. In 1919 he received a professorship at the Dresden Art Academy. Two years later he launched into his superb series of cityscapes. These brought relief from his personal problems – and from Expressionism, which was now replaced by visual impressions conveyed in impressionistic terms.

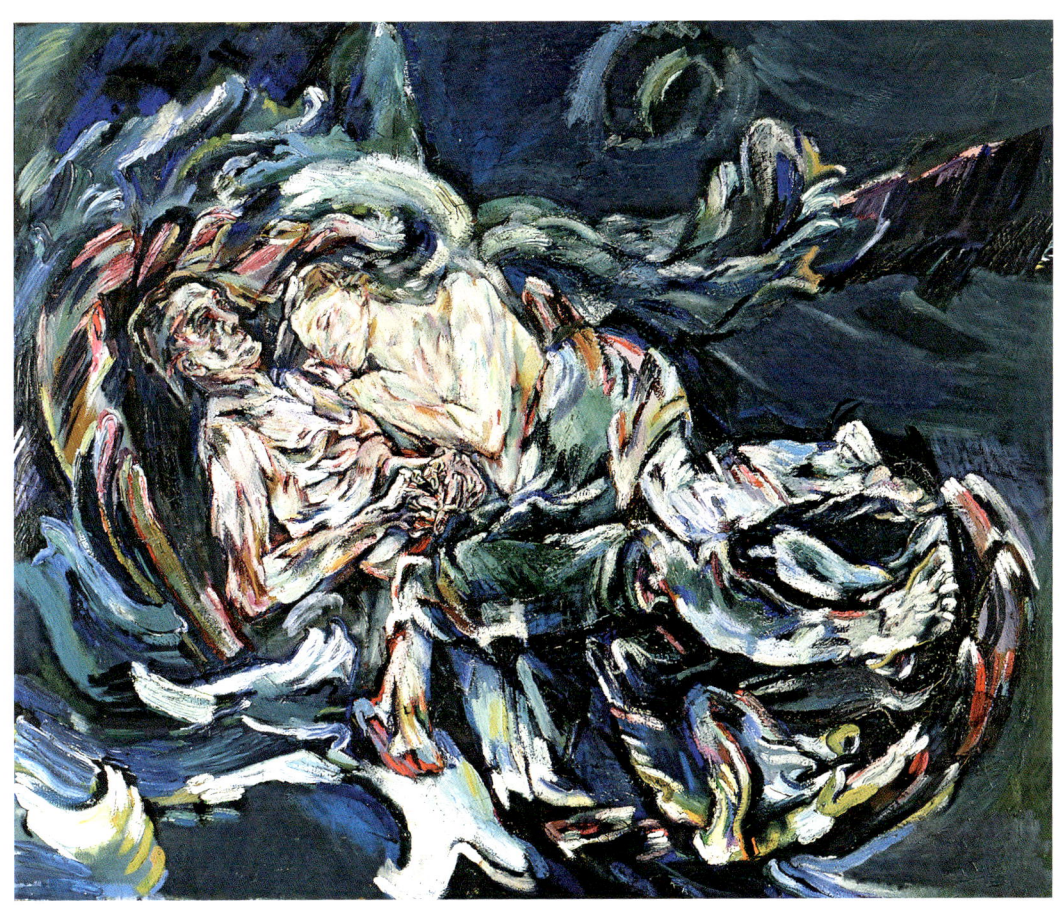

The Wind's Bride (The Tempest), 1913
Oil on canvas, 180.4 x 220.2 cm (71 x 86¾ in.)
Kunstmuseum Basel

Wilhelm Lehmbruck
The Fallen Man, 1915/16

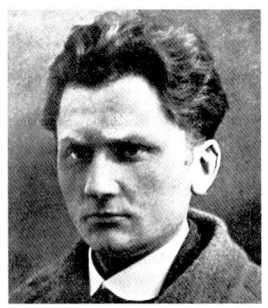

b. 1880 in Meiderich, Germany
d. 1919 in Berlin

When we stand before wood sculptures carved by Ernst Ludwig Kirchner (ill. p. 116) or Karl Schmidt-Rottluff, or view the sculptures of Käthe Kollwitz or Ernst Barlach (ill. p. 133), we have no trouble in seeing a fundamentally Expressionistic approach in their blocky angularity of configuration, regardless whether it was inspired by exotic or medieval European models. Yet when many authors call Wilhelm Lehmbruck the most significant sculptor of German Expressionism, this faces the viewer of his so different and finely articulated figures with certain difficulties.

Lehmbruck was born near Duisburg, one of eight children of a miner and his wife. Despite difficult circumstances, he was able to attend the Düsseldorf School of Decorative Art from 1895 to 1899. In 1901 he became a master student at the Düsseldorf Academy, where he studied for five years, punctuated by trips to Italy, Holland and England. In 1910 he moved with his wife and child to Paris, where he lived until the outbreak of war in 1914, remaining largely uninfluenced by the formal breakthroughs of the Cubists, some of whom were his friends. In 1915 Lehmbruck was conscripted into medical service in a Berlin hospital. During the war years he produced only a few sculptures, including *The Fallen Man*, 1916, which might be considered a symbol of the generation who fell at Langemarck in 1914. Between 18 October and 30 November of that year, 45,000 volunteers lost their lives, a slaughter that put an abrupt end to the war euphoria felt by so many Expressionists.

The elongated figure with its almost Gothic silhouette has very little surface texture, and the facial features are not pronounced. What remains is drama of expression. Due to the existential experiences of the Great War, many artists, and most of the Expressionists, lost their faith in the "exalted man" of the type Nietzsche had described and Wilhelm Worringer had advocated in his 1908 dissertation *Abstraction and Empathy*. Lehmbruck, who counted Henri Matisse, Amedeo Modigliani, the sculptors Aristide Maillol (1861–1944), Alexander Archipenko (1887–1964) and Constantin Brâncuşi (1876–1957) among his acquaintances and inspirers, formulated his protest against the disastrous period in terms of a symbolic, melancholy, introverted formal language.

The man, fallen, despairing, crawls on all fours. Yet he is not finished yet. He still supports himself on knees, lower arms and head, and still grips his sword. In view of the original title, *Dying Warrior,* the weakened figure with torso extended horizontally over the long base recalls a bridge between life and death – a moving reply to all conventionally heroic war memorials. The figure's elongated slender limbs enclose an interior space, and embody Lehmbruck's credo, "Sculpture is the essence of things, the essence of nature, that which is perpetually human."

Kirchner and Lehmbruck knew each other from 1912 at the latest and lived not far from each other in Berlin. Though their contacts were apparently not close, there is evidence that the Brücke painter knew and appreciated originals by Lehmbruck. So beyond a general Expressionist philosophy, the two probably shared interests, such as dance, which played an eminently important role in both artists' stylization process. Such similarities led to parallels in their intentions and approaches for a brief period.

Lehmbruck was discharged from the army in 1916 because of a hearing impairment. In 1917 he began to suffer from bouts of deep depression, and in 1919 he put an end to his life.

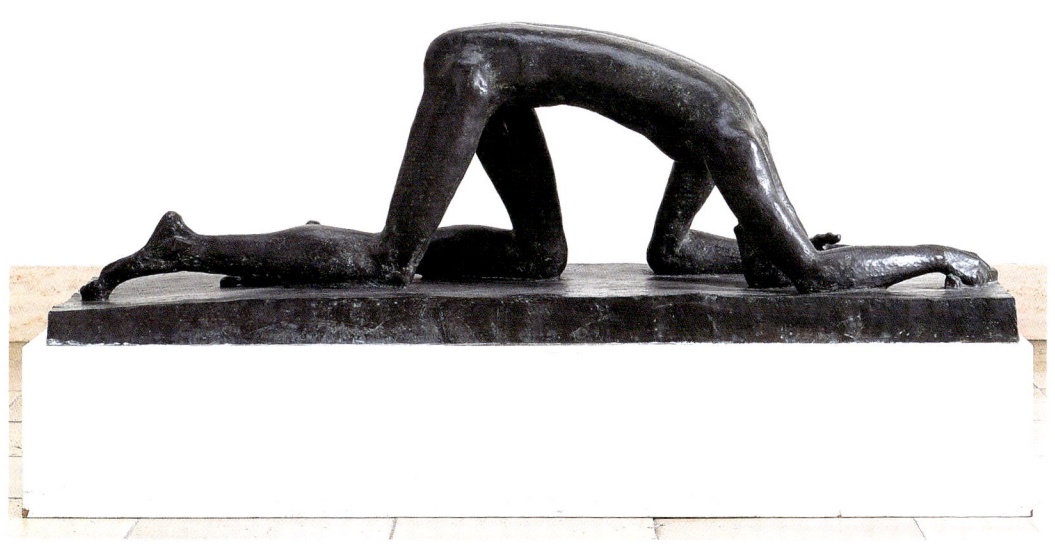

The Fallen Man, 1915/16
Bronze, 78 x 239 x 83 cm (30¾ x 94 x 32¾ in.)
Munich, Bayerische Staatsgemälde-
sammlungen, Pinakothek der Moderne

August Macke
Lady in a Green Jacket, 1913

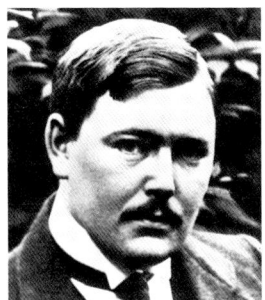

b. 1887 in Meschede, Germany
d. 1914 in Perthes-les-Hurlus,
France

August Macke, one of the most highly regarded German artists of classical modernism, was a wanderer between two worlds. Although his name is inevitably mentioned whenever the topic of Expressionism comes up, emotional excess was not his thing. His art evinces neither the explosive forms, garish colours or primitivism of the kind the Brücke painters loved, nor the sociocritical subjects of Dix, Felixmüller or Grosz, nor the brutal ugliness with which the Expressionists enjoyed provoking the philistines. Quite the contrary. Macke preferred to depict civilized urban scenes, well-kept streets and parks, cafés and shop windows, people on an evening stroll – and above all, colourful women's fashions.

In terms of palette and lyrical approach to nature, Macke's works resemble those of Marc, whom he befriended from 1910. Yet he did not share Marc's pantheism despite the fact that he, too, was impelled by the vision of an earthly paradise. And although Macke maintained close contacts with the New Artists Association of Munich and contributed to the *Blauer Reiter* Almanach in 1911, he was sceptical of the mysticism indulged in by Kandinsky, or even by Schoenberg. This may explain why after moving to Bonn in 1911, he never trod the path to abstraction, apart from a few experiments in watercolour and drawing.

Yet there was another new frontier he explored with great success, the frontier that ran between French and German painting. Like no other Expressionist, Macke translated the language of French art into German. And he began to do so at an early date. Already between his studies at the Düsseldorf Academy and a brief stint at the painting school run by Corinth in Berlin (1907–08), Macke immersed himself in French Impressionism and Cubism, which were later supplemented by impulses from Fauvism. But what shaped him above all was his contact, beginning in 1912, with Delaunay, which soon led to oils and watercolours of an expressive yet wonderfully harmonious character, always based on impressions of nature, and always taking the effects of light as their point of departure.

This is confirmed by one of Macke's major works, one of the first done after he and his family moved to Hilterfingen on Lake Thun. *Lady in a Green Jacket*, painted on a well-nigh square format, exudes compositional balance. The lady of the title is not only slightly shifted out of the central vertical axis, she is faceless – i. e., exemplary, like all of Macke's figures of that period. Her gracefully elongated figure is flanked by four smaller figures, farther in the background; a couple each to her left and right, walking towards a wall, and behind them a panorama with river valley and houses simplified in the early-Cubist manner of George Braque. The light-flooded foliage of the trees grows together at the top to form a roof accented in greenish-yellow, their limbs regularly branching in a compositional device perhaps taken from the writings of Leonardo da Vinci, in which Macke immersed himself at that period. The whole is suffused by an enchantment that recalls Romantic paintings by Caspar David Friedrich, with whom Macke shared a penchant for figures seen from the back. Spatial values are coordinated with principles of planar order and brought into a fine-tuned equilibrium. Compositional rhythm is established by prismatically broken hues, transparent, vibrating colour contrasts which themselves seem to be the source of light. When Macke set out in 1914 with Klee and Louis Moilliet (1880–1962) on their now-legendary Tunis journey, he had already long developed that sense of colour which Klee hoped he would find in North Africa.

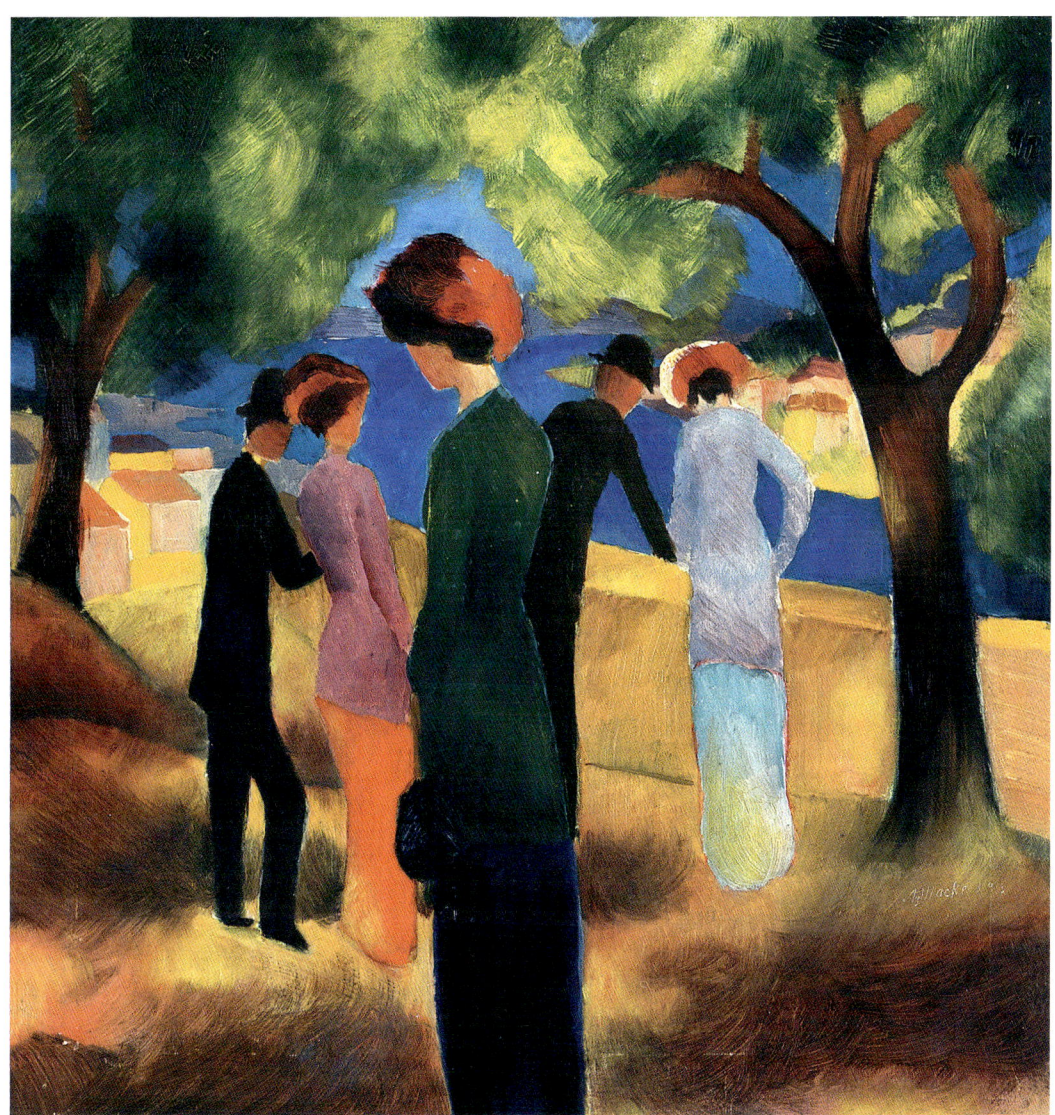

Lady in a Green Jacket, 1913
Oil on canvas, 44 x 43.5 cm (17¼ x 17¼ in.)
Cologne, Museum Ludwig

When the First World War broke out Macke donned a uniform, and was killed only a few weeks later. In his touching obituary his friend Marc says: "Of us all, he gave colour the brightest and purest ring, as clear and bright as his entire character."

Franz Marc
The Small Yellow Horses, 1912

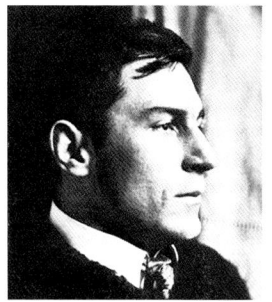

b. 1880 in Munich
d. 1916 near Verdun, France

Franz Marc, co-editor of the *Blauer Reiter* almanach, is probably the best-known animal painter in modern art. Of course this label does little justice to Marc's qualities, which Kandinsky later described as follows: "Everything in nature attracted him, but above all animals… But he never lost himself in details, and for him the animal was always only one element in the whole… What attracted him was the organic whole, in other words, nature in general." Marc himself, who originally wanted to become a pastor, described his vision of a religion of art thus: "Art is metaphysical, will become so… Art will liberate itself from human ends and human desires. We will no longer paint forests or horses in the way they appeal or appear to us, but how they really are, how a forest or a horse themselves feel, their absolute being…" A new religion would be born, as Marc repeatedly stated in a correpondence full of references to the anthroposophy of Rudolf Steiner and echoes of German Romanticism. On its altars would grow a new art whose spiritualized lyricism would mirror the "animal soul". Accordingly Marc attempted to capture the spiritual purity of animals by increasingly stylizing their forms, a process that by the end of his brief artistic life had led him to abstraction (ill. p. 102/103).

The Small Yellow Horses gives a good sense of the sacred utopia Marc envisaged. He takes up the idea of paradisal harmony by basing his animal depiction on a pattern traditionally employed for depictions of human figures. His preference for groups of three may go back to the convention commonly used since Antiquity to depict the *Three Graces*. Marc sets the three powerful horses' bodies circulating in a cosmic landscape panorama and at the same time within their own force field, their gracefully rounded forms in complex interaction. There is not one line too many, and, to the artist's mind, every colour field possesses symbolic meaning: the blue representing the "male principle, severe and intellectual," contrasted to a yellow representing the female, gentle, joyful, sensual principle. The red, in turn, embodies matter, "brutal and heavy", and is being fought by the two other colours in an attempt to overcome it.

Marc, studying first philosophy at the university then art at the academy, took two study trips to Paris that confronted him with the key stylistic directions of the French avant-garde. After summering in Lenggries in 1908, he began increasingly to concentrate on depictions of animals, to the point that the human image almost entirely disappeared from his art. In 1909 Marc moved from Munich to the country idyll of Sindelsdorf in Upper Bavaria. Yet he did not lose contact with happenings in the art centre, developing, for instance, a deep friendship with August Macke.

Artistic exchange within the Blauer Reiter and above all an involvement with Robert Delaunay, whom he met in 1912 on a visit to Paris with Macke, increased the degree of abstraction of Marc's painting and the evocativeness of his palette. In September 1912, in the Berlin journal *Der Sturm*, he published a woodcut to a poem by the Expressionist poet Else Lasker-Schüler (1869–1945). This marked the beginning of a long friendship between two like-minded artists. It precipitated in a series of wonderful watercolour postcards by Marc and Lasker-Schüler, first published as "Letters to the Blue Rider Franz Marc" in the journal *Die Aktion*.

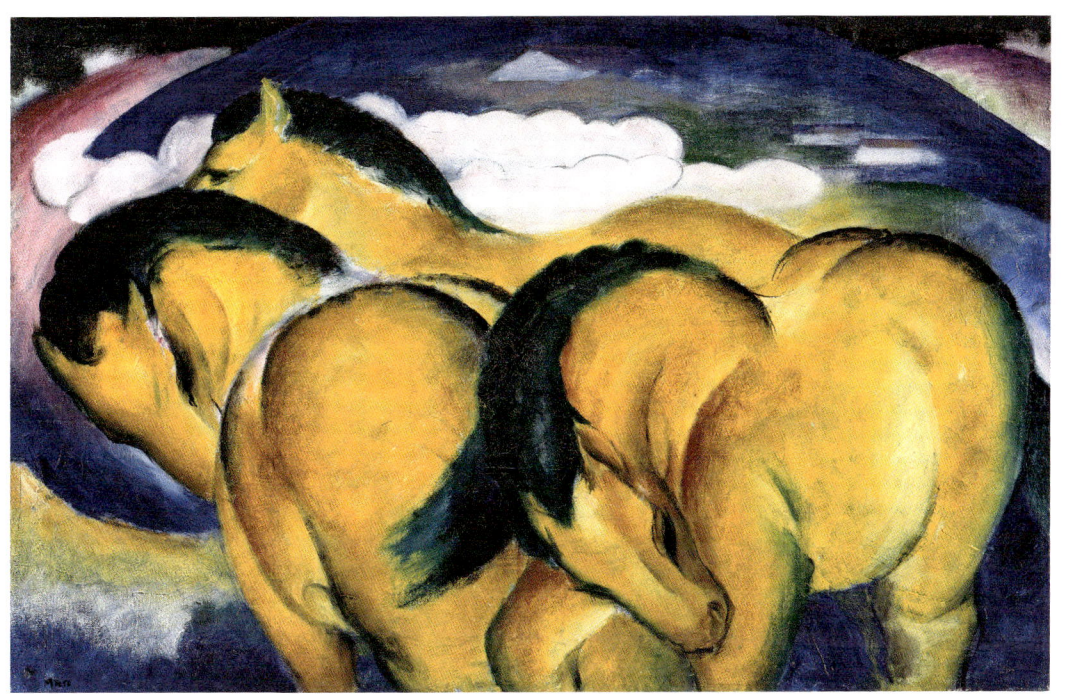

The Small Yellow Horses, 1912
Oil on canvas, 66 x 104 cm (26 x 41 in.)
Staatsgalerie Stuttgart

Franz Marc
Tyrol, 1914

In 1912 the events in Marc's life came to a head. While in Berlin he met the Brücke painters, and immediately made a selection of their prints which would subsequently be shown at the second and final Blauer Reiter exhibition in Munich. And conversely, the Munich artists were present that year in Berlin, where Herwarth Walden introduced them to the public as "German Expressionists". That autumn Marc went to Bonn with his friend Macke. From there they continued on to Paris, to visit Robert Delaunay, who impressed them both, though Macke far more than Marc. The latter, for his part, was enthusiastic about the Futurists, whose pictures he hung and intensively studied in a large Bonn exhibition mounted after his return from France. Their influence is apparent in one of his masterpieces, the oil *Tyrol*.

In 1913 Marc was involved in a great undertaking. He played a material role in organizing, at Herwarth Walden's Berlin gallery Der Sturm, the "First German Autumn Salon". Represented were ninety artists from France, Germany, Russia, Holland, Italy, Austria, Switzerland and the United States. A great deal of room at this, the most important overview of modern art prior to the First World War, was accorded to Delaunay, Marc, Macke, Kandinsky, Campendonk, Münter, Klee, Kubin and the Futurists. Marc showed seven paintings, including his renowned *Tower of Blue Horses* (lost; based on a composition on a New Year's postcard of 1913 to the poet Else Lasker-Schüler), *The Unfortunate Land of Tyrol*, and *Tyrol*. Marc had travelled to Tyrol with his wife Maria in March 1913. In the first painting done thereafter (New York, The Solomon R. Guggenheim Museum) he arranged houses, gloomy cemetery crucifixes and a few animals in a landscape seemingly pervaded by profound resignation. The next picture, *Tyrol,* was more strongly marked by the traditional interpretation of the Alps as a scene of the "sublime", the potentiated locale of man's insignificance in face of the vastness of nature. After being briefly on view in the Autumn Salon, the painting was removed by Marc and reworked in 1914, shortly before he was sent to the front lines, when he added the madonna on a crescent moon. Every element of this forbidding landscape with farmhouses cowering at the base of a mighty mountainside seems absorbed into the diagonal facets pulsating with Futuristic energy. Luminous crystalline shapes are penetrated by black passages. A huge charred tree trunk in the foreground recalls an apocalyptic scythe. No living creatures are to be seen; Marc's beloved animals have fled. At the top right a blood-red sun shines behind threatening peaks, while a second sun, the black sun of the Apocalypse, appears in the midst of the turbulence and steep mountains. The suns are counterbalanced by several crescent moons at the upper left. The madonna on a crescent moon, focus of the cosmic turbulence, is simultaneously a symbol of divine grace and an apocalyptic motif – the pyramid of her garment spreads over the farmhouses like a protective cloak. From the figure emerge rays that perpendicularly intersect the mountains. No other work of Marc's, with the exception of a few planned Bible illustrations, conveys such a clearly religious statement. In addition, the painting seems to announce an abandonment of the theme of animals, which the artist began to consider in 1913 and increasingly put into practice as he set out on the path to abstraction.

In 1914, halfway down this path, Marc volunteered for military service. In 1916, aged thirty-six, he fell near Verdun. Marc's *Tower of Blue Horses* was included in the "Degenerate Art" exhibition of 1937. The Nazis sold many of his works out of the country. Yet after the Second World War, his art experienced a second, true triumph. In 1989, one of his temperas brought DM 2,600,000 (approx. $1,300,000), the highest price ever paid for a work of art at a German auction to that date.

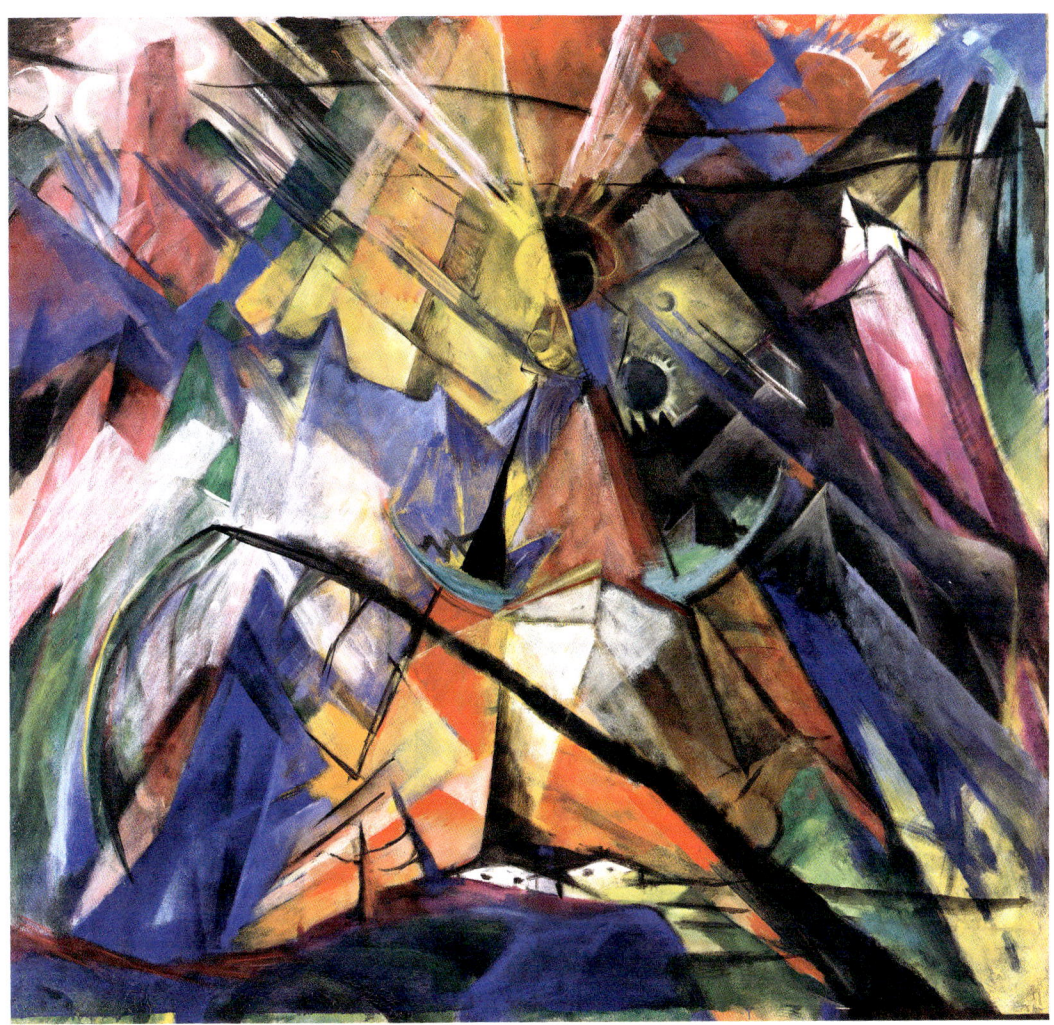

Tyrol, 1914
Oil on canvas, 135.7 x 144.7 cm (53½ x 57 in.)
Munich, Bayerische Staatsgemälde-
sammlungen, Pinakothek der Moderne

Ludwig Meidner
Apocalyptic City, 1913

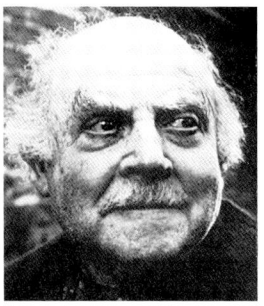

b. 1884 in Bernstadt, Germany
d. 1966 in Darmstadt, Germany

Meidner has been called the most Expressionist of the Expressionists, but this is true only of a limited part of his total oeuvre, which is characterized by numerous caesuras. After studying from 1906 to 1907 in Paris, where he met Amedeo Modigliani, he moved definitively to Berlin in 1908, the city which he described as "the intellectual and moral capital of the world". In 1912, together with two other Jewish artists, he founded the group known as the "Pathetiker", whose breakthrough was assisted by Herwarth Walden's gallery Der Sturm. At that time, Meidner, whom George Grosz had described as a restless little man, "like a figure out of one of E. T. A. Hoffmann's short stories", and who, in his youth, had devoured Nietzsche's *Thus Spake Zarathustra*, had begun creating not only his portraits in oils, Indian ink, and other graphic media, but also his analytical self-portraits, which, in his own words, were "consciously demonic". All the energy was concentrated in rhythmic lines, zigzag folds, an almost caricature-like exaggeration, and in gestures of great pathos.

In Berlin, encouraged by Max Beckmann, an extra component was added in the form of an emergent big-city euphoria, the fascination with a tumultuous and effervescent urban world, which was responsible for, among other pictures, the series of *Apocalyptic Landscapes* up to 1916, on which Meidner's fame was based. These were panoramic fantastical cityscapes, depicted from a bird's-eye perspective, bursting open as if under bombardment from the cosmos. The city in the present painting is the victim of such an infernal catastrophe; ant-like, a few people are fleeing from the exploding stars and the terrestrial conflagration. The tectonic interplay of verticals and horizontals is dissolved in distorted and disparate perspectives and shifted proportions. The whole structure is torn apart by extreme colour contrasts and by diagonals reminiscent of comets' tails. In this and related compositions can be seen the extent to which Meidner was influenced by the flickering colourfulness and splintered picture backgrounds of the Mannerist El Greco, by the Italian Futurists (whose work could be seen in Berlin in 1912), and by Robert Delaunay's prismatically fanned out views of the Eiffel Tower. In addition, he was familiar with the photographic double-exposure technique. For the film *Strasse* (Street), directed by Karl Grune (1890–1962) in 1923, Meidner created the sets, staging a big-city street once more, with collapsing façades, houses seemingly transfixed by deep shadows, and the atmosphere heightened yet further by cones of light.

The *Apocalyptic Landscapes* resulted, it is thought, from a premonition of the First World War. This may well be true in part, but above all they were triggered by Meidner's intense involvement with ancient Jewish prophecies of doom and with the New Testament Book of Revelation. In 1918, after the war, he was active in the revolutionary Arbeitsrat für Kunst, a kind of artists' council, and by 1923 at the latest he had turned his back on Expressionism and the "modern spirit" and rediscovered the faith of his fathers, orthodox Judaism, to which he gave expression in naturalistic symbolic depictions. Meidner, previously also at home in proto-Expressionist literary circles, and himself – like Barlach, Kokoschka and Kubin – a superb writer, was in 1937 branded a "degenerate Jew". From 1939 to 1952 he lived – reluctantly – as an exile in England, before returning to Germany, where in 1964 he received the Bundesverdienstkreuz, the Federal Republic's award for merit.

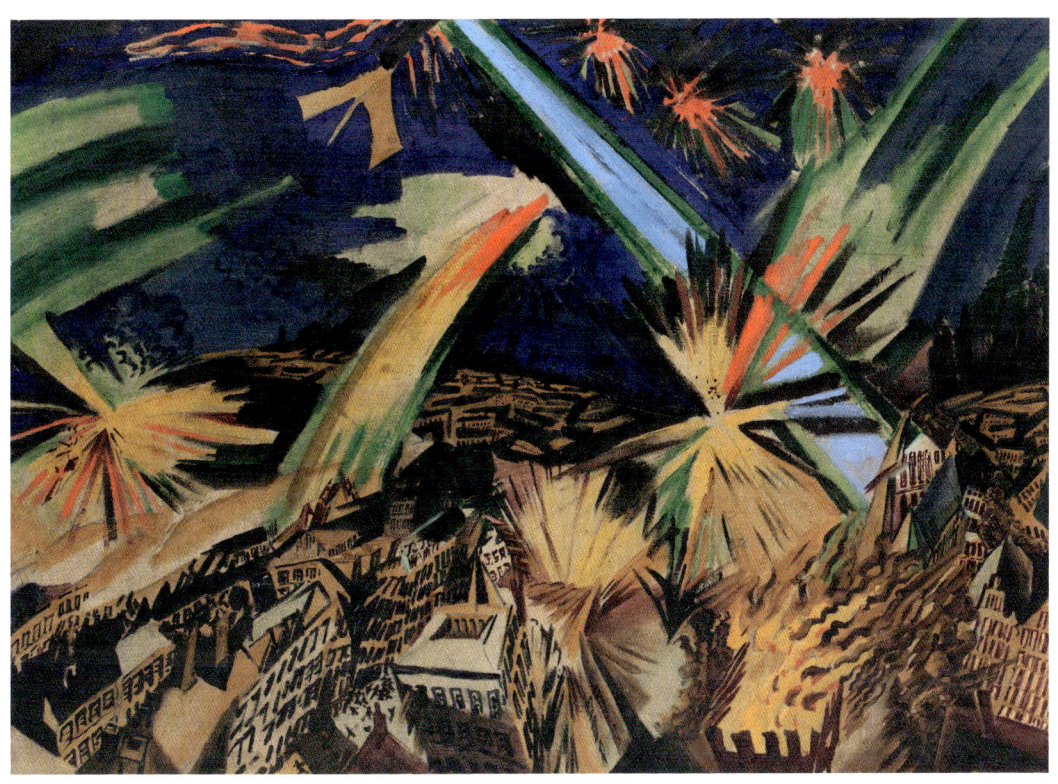

Apocalyptic City, 1913
Oil on canvas, 79 x 119 cm (31 x 47 in.)
Münster, LWL-Museum für Kunst und Kultur

Paula Modersohn-Becker
Self-Portrait with Camellia Branch, 1906/07

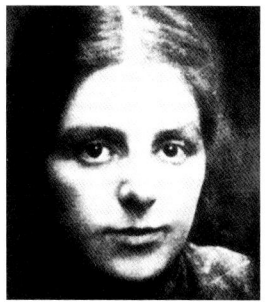

b. 1876 in Dresden, Germany
d. 1907 in Worpswede, Germany

The year 1905 was relevant not only as the founding year of Die Brücke. It also marked an important transition for three northern German artists, Nolde, Rohlfs and Modersohn-Becker, all of whose art then began to take an emotional, expressive direction. Paula Modersohn-Becker had gone in 1899 to Worpswede, a village outside Bremen where Fritz Mackensen had established a colony of landscape painters in 1889. One of them, Otto Modersohn, married the young Paula, who soon met the poet Rainer Maria Rilke in Worpswede. Everyone in the group back then dreamed of a new unity of man and nature. The small community, which promised an escape from the anxiety and loneliness of modern city life, as well as freedom from the constrictions of the academy, seemed a perfect setting to realize this utopian vision.

Modersohn-Becker had become familiar with a suitable lyrical approach to nature in the works of Cézanne and, even more, of Gauguin, during her brief studies in Paris. Back in Worpswede, she spontaneously began to depict ordinary rural people, using earth colours and heavy contours. Her concentration on broad expanses of colour and rigorous outlines owed much to Gauguin.

Her *Self-Portrait with Camellia Branch* is one of the finest examples of self-searching in art, something by which Modersohn-Becker always set great store. At the same time, the small painting reveals a knowledge of reproductions of Egyptian mummy portraits of the second to fourth centuries B.C., striking coffin depictions with overlarge eyes, clearly delineated faces, reduced, flat forms, and expressions of great mystery. Beyond this, Modersohn-Becker accentuates the colour contrast between the sonorous browns of the shadowed, strictly frontal bust and the light-flooded blue of the background, which surrounds her head like an aureole. The camellia branch, demonstratively placed on the central vertical axis, is a traditional symbol of growth and fertility.

Finally, as the pervading melancholy of this portrait reveals, a stranger ultimately remains a stranger, even in an apparently idyllic, unsullied rural setting. Modersohn-Becker was in fact the only Worpswede artist to sense the danger of provinciality that goes hand in hand with an idealization of country and peasant life. As she complained in a letter of 29 February 1900, to Otto Modersohn, "We cling to the past too much in Germany. All of our German art is too bogged down in the conventional… At any rate, I think more highly of a free person who consciously puts convention aside…"

In 1905 Modersohn-Becker found her way to just such an unconventional art, emotionally powerful and far from the idealization of genre scenes. During a second Paris sojourn she again studied Cézanne and Gauguin, as well as the Nabis. Back in Paris the following year, she saw the first paintings by the Fauves. In 1907, shortly after the birth of her first child, she died in Worpswede.

Although she avoided all Expressionist exaggeration, especially in terms of bright palette, Modersohn-Becker's art has an emotional depth and power that gives it a definite, if reserved, affinity with Expressionism.

Self-Portrait with Camellia Branch, 1906/07
Oil on wood, 61.5 x 30.5 cm (24¼ x 12 in.)
Essen, Museum Folkwang

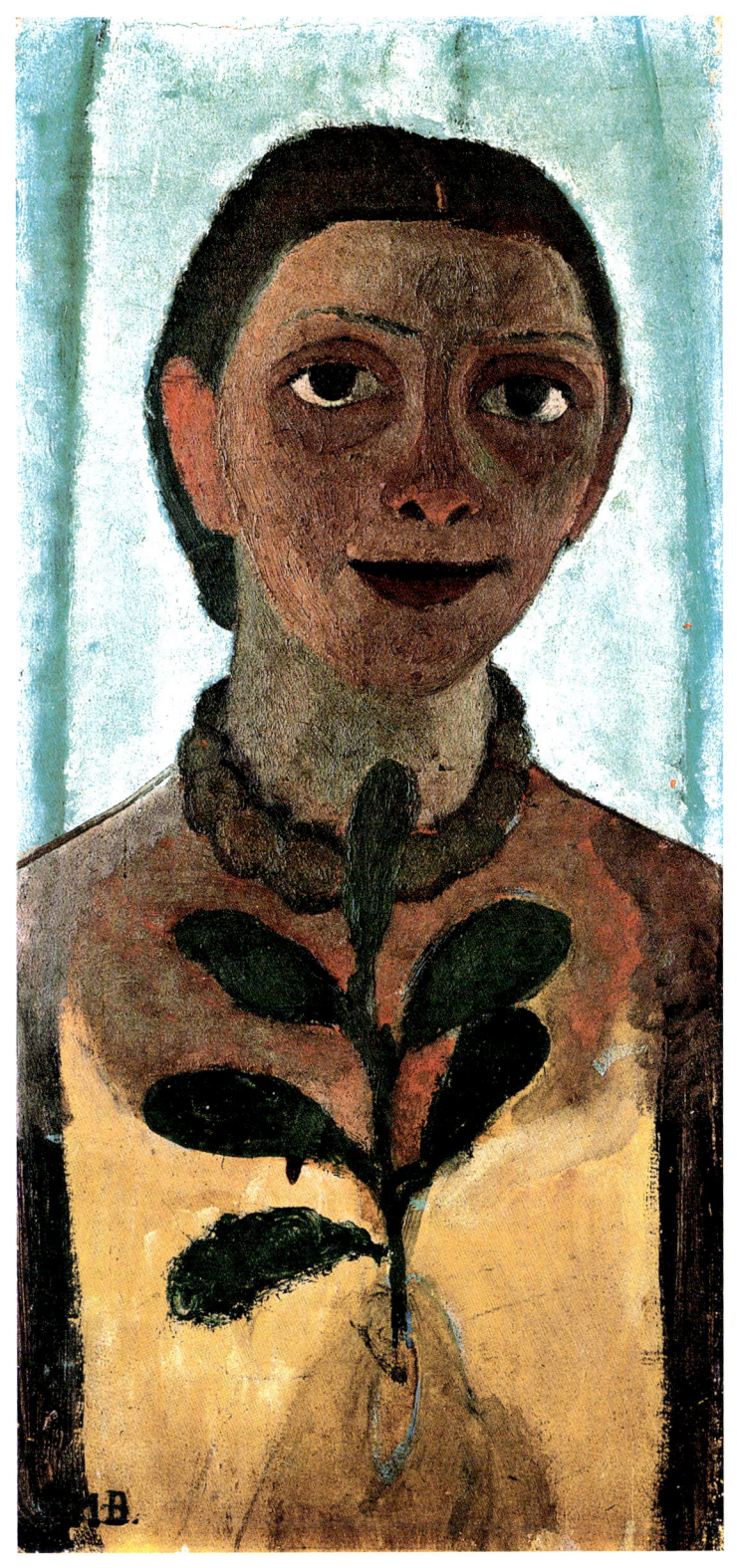

Otto Mueller
Gypsies with Sunflowers, 1927

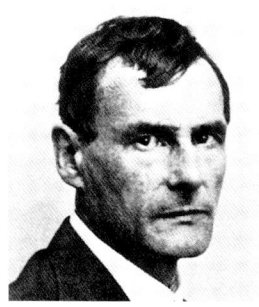

b. 1874 in Liebau (now Lubawka)
d. 1930 in Breslau (now Wroclaw)

"Gypsy Mueller" was the nickname of the painter who became the last member of the Brücke in 1911. Reputedly his mother was a gypsy. At any rate, Mueller felt attracted from boyhood to the carefree life of these vagabonds on the margins of society, as he did to those slender young nude girls lost in thought among the reeds or bathing in woodland lakes who embodied the Expressionist ideal of a reconciliation between art and life.

After training as a lithographer in Görlitz, Silesia, Mueller studied in 1894–96 at the art academies in Dresden and Munich, where he felt out of place. He received encouragement from the author Gerhart Hauptmann (1862–1946), a distant relative. He met Paula Modersohn-Becker and, more importantly, the sculptor Wilhelm Lehmbruck, whose spiritualized figures apparently made a lasting impression on him. Among the Brücke artists Mueller, with his quiet, introverted personality and lack of interest in provocation and posing, was an outsider. Technically, too, he set a personal accent by adopting distemper instead of oil in 1911. Distemper colours dry in nuances that differ from those with which they are applied. Their handling entails an exact, careful consideration of the drying process. Mueller was a master of distemper, lending his pictures an inimitable charm, a friable airiness and poetic immateriality. This technique fairly demanded the use of large formats and simplified forms. Mueller's burlap painting surfaces (often from unstitched sugar sacks) occasionally recall the rough-textured surface of frescoes.

Gypsies with Sunflowers, finished in 1927 during a period of emotional conflict arising from a difficult personal relationship, indicates Mueller's fidelity to his established style and favourite subject matter even in the face of official postwar recognition of a kind accorded to no other member of the Brücke. In spring 1919 the artist was offered a professorship at the Breslau Academy (which admittedly could not prevent 357 of his works being confiscated and largely destroyed in 1937). The same prototype adolescent girl, with identical features in narrow faces, dark, medium-long hair, and "Gothically" slender figures, appeared over and over again in his work. Even the nursing mother in the present picture takes on the standardized youthfulness of the girl who is compared to the open sunflower beside her. The actual world of gypsies, their village surroundings, are suggested, but without a trace of sociocritical interpretation. Even the melancholy undertone that now makes itself felt points in a different direction. The outsiders of modern industrial society seem embedded in an idyllic, Romantic context, reflecting a yearning for a paradise lost much like that projected by Gauguin in his paintings of Tahitian islanders.

Between 1924 and 1929 Mueller found material for his gypsy paintings on travels to Hungary, Dalmatia, Rumania and Yugoslavia. For a time he even lived in a gypsy camp outside Budapest. Such experiences also inspired his famous *Gypsy Portfolio*, nine partly hand-tinted colour lithographs, among his most outstanding works of graphic art. Apart from early experiments, Mueller's oeuvre remained stylistically and thematically quite limited. In 1926, four years before the artist died of tuberculosis, art critic and playwright Carl Einstein noted in his book, *Art of the 20th Century*, "With an easy laxness Mueller sweetens nudes or German landscapes… Charm may occasionally be achieved, but most [of his art] sinks into a shallow saccharinity of blue and green and monotonous quiet lineature." Today voices of this kind may have become rarer, but they have not grown entirely silent.

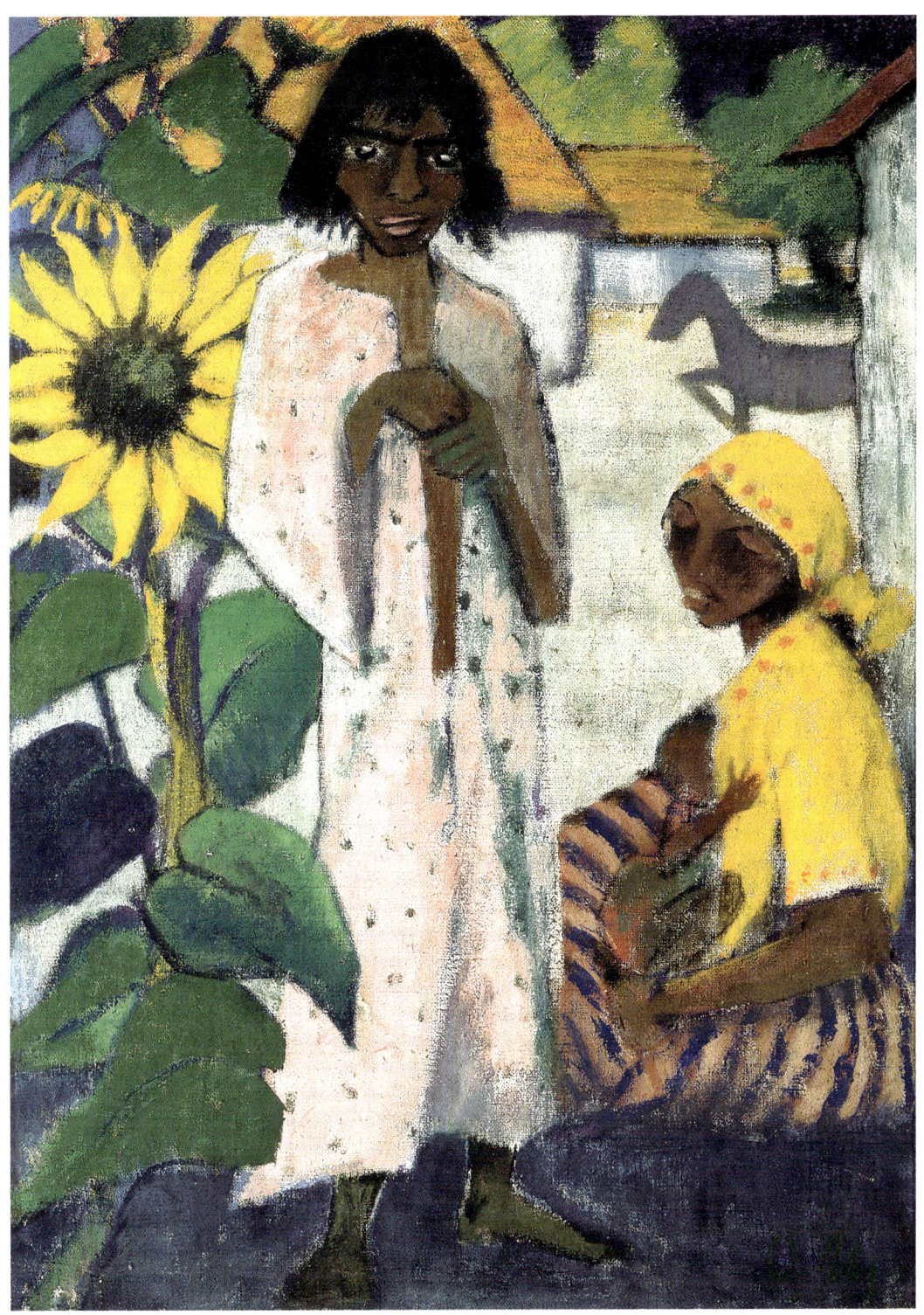

Gypsies with Sunflowers, 1927
Distemper on burlap, 145 x 105 cm (57 x 41¼ in.)
Saarbrücken, Saarlandmuseum, Moderne Galerie

Gabriele Münter
Schoolhouse, Murnau, 1908

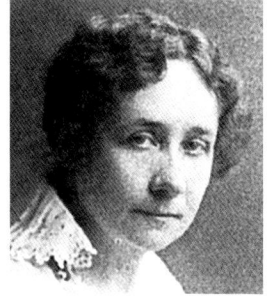

b. 1877 in Berlin
d. 1962 in Murnau, Germany

At first glance it seems quite unassuming, this small view of the schoolhouse in Murnau. And yet this picture stands at the beginning of a decisive turning point in Münter's development.

At the age of twenty Gabriele Münter enrolled in the School of Art for Ladies in Düsseldorf, with the intention of becoming a drawing teacher, the only art career then socially acceptable for women. After an inheritance brought financial independence, she risked the leap into freelance art. In 1901 she settled in Munich, where she became acquainted with Kandinsky. In 1904 the two set off on journeys that took them to Venice, Tunisia, Holland, France, and, on more than one occasion, to Russia. As a member of the New Artists Assocation of Munich and a short time later of the Blauer Reiter, Münter advanced to become one of the most significant southern German Expressionists of the first hour.

In summer 1908 Münter, her partner Kandinsky, Jawlensky and Marianne von Werefkin explored the foothills of the Bavarian Alps from their base in the provincial town of Murnau on the Staffelsee. "It was a lovely, interesting, enjoyable period of work with many conversations about art," recalled the artist in her diary.

A document of this fruitful collaboration was the present view of the schoolhouse, the fourth done on that 27 August, as indicated by the precise dating in the lower centre. It depicts one of Murnau's largest and plainest buildings, in a radically simplified composition of a total of eight flat elements separated by heavy contours. The colour fields enclosed in these contours have hardly any internal nuances, modelling or shading, being enlivened solely by short, colourful brushstrokes. This reduction to a nearly geometric planar order nevertheless contributes to the equilibrium and harmony of the detail depicted. In contrast to this calculated balance, the thinly brushed areas, sketchy details and unpainted cardboard ground suggest an incredibly rapid painting process charged with intuitive expression.

With this and comparable paintings began a transition from Münter's earlier Impressionist-oriented style to an Expressionism that was developed jointly by her, Kandinsky and Jawlensky that summer in Murnau. In this regard Münter relied on various sources, apparently suggested above all by Jawlensky: Gauguin and van Gogh for the contoured colour fields, Munch and Matisse's Fauvism for the range of hues. Also, similar formal approaches were found in examples of the folk art of verre églomisé. "After a brief period of torment," she wrote, "I made a great leap – from copying nature – more or less impressionistically – to feeling a content – to abstracting – to giving an extract." However, Münter never took the final step to abstraction, as Kandinsky did. When war broke out she followed him to Switzerland, yet soon their paths diverged. Münter went through years of personal and artistic crisis before finally returning to painting at the end of the 1920s.

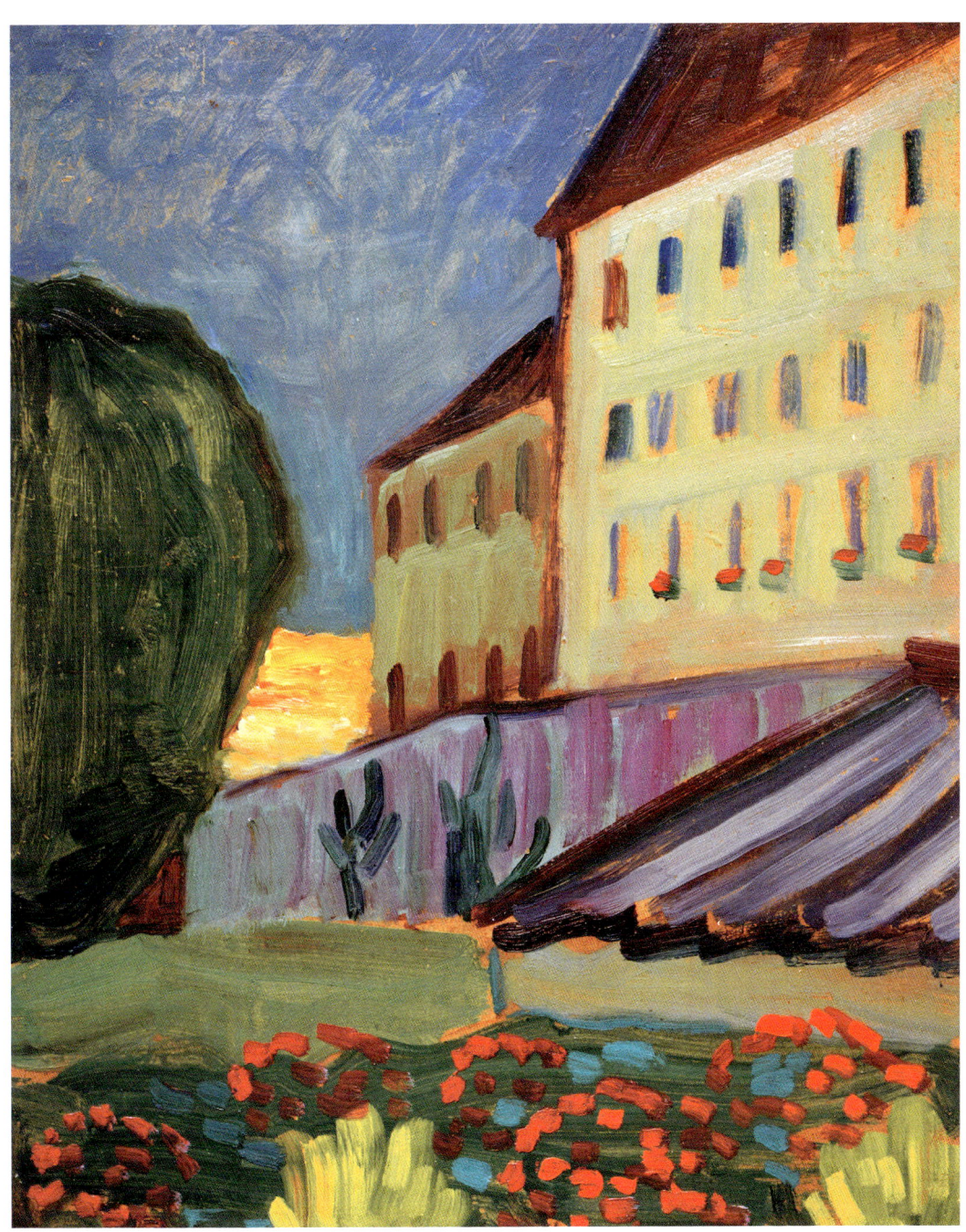

Schoolhouse, Murnau, 1908
Oil on cardboard, 40.6 x 32.7 cm (16 x 13 in.)
Madrid, Museo Thyssen-Bornemisza,
on loan from the Collection of Carmen
Thyssen-Bornemisza

Emil Nolde
The Legend of St Maria Aegyptiaca, 1912

Emil Hansen, born in Nolde near Tondern, Schleswig (now Tønder in Denmark), adopted his birthplace as a pseudonym in 1902. After training as a furniture draughtsman and studying at the Karlsruhe School of Arts and Crafts, Nolde became a teacher at the St Gallen School of Arts and Crafts in 1892. Numerous study trips followed – milestones on his to becoming one of the most out-standing graphic artists, watercolourists and oil painters of Expressionism. When he settled in 1903 on the island of Alsen and began to concentrate on garden and floral motifs, his palette gradually developed to become a vehicle of ecstatic emotion. In 1906, in the circle around Karl Ernst Osthaus, Nolde studied works by van Gogh, Gauguin, Ensor, and met Edvard Munch.

The suggestiveness of his colour and the intuitive passion of his painting attack brought Nolde into proximity with the aims of the Brücke, to which he belonged from February 1906 to the end of 1907 and with whose members he later remained on friendly terms. To cite George Grosz's descrip-tion of Nolde's working procedure during those years, he "no longer painted with brushes. He later said that, when the inspiration took him, he threw away his brushes, dipped his old paint rag into the paint, and smeared around on the canvas in blissful intoxication." Nolde's pictures looked as if they had been produced by liquid colours that had bled into each other, unconstricted by contours, which led to the frequent impression of misdrawing.

His group of religious paintings, commenced in 1909, was one of Nolde's major contributions to modern art. The compositions are entirely focused on the transcendental, spiritual meaning of the scene depicted. The figures are brought up very close to the viewer; their masklike faces often have a distorted expression verging on caricature; the eyes stare, the features are primitivistically coarse,

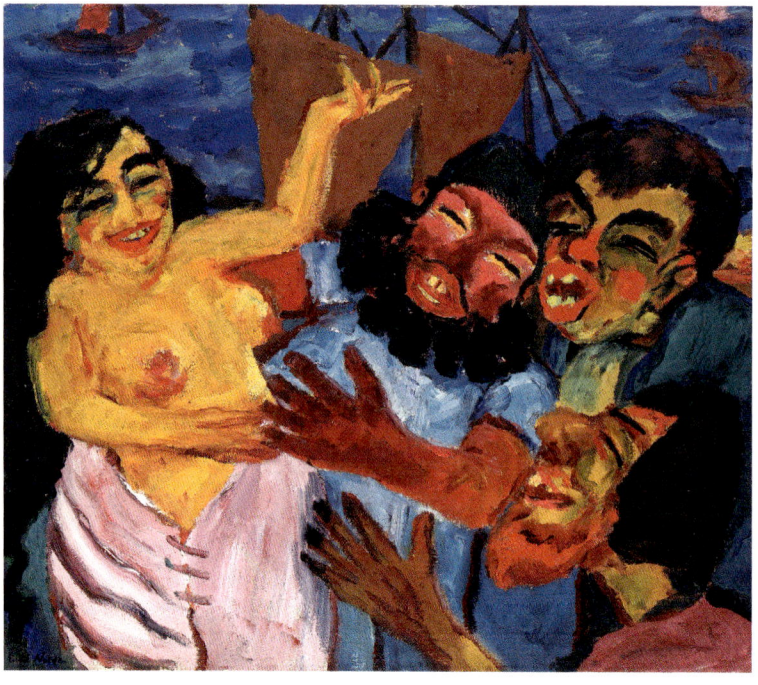
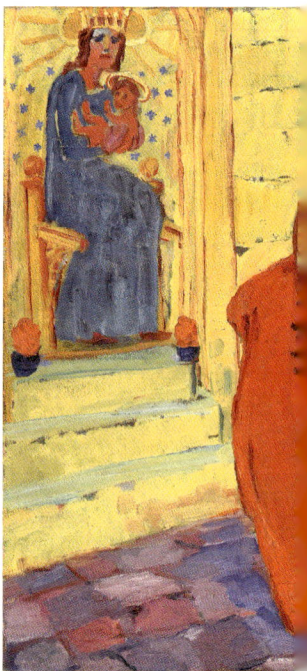

and the whole of the canvas is suffused by saturated, luminous colours which, in Nolde's own words, reflected "the mystical depths of human-divine being".

In the middle panel of the present great triptych of 1912 devoted to the legend of *Maria Aegyptiaca*, the saint, clad in a bright red cloak, is shown in prayer with arms raised ecstatically towards heaven. A blue-clad Madonna statue stands in a niche in the golden yellow wall. Nolde, a Protestant, lends the impassioned worship of Mary an inspirational force of the very kind which earlier church reformers and opponents of Mariolatry denied it. Yet the former prostitute from Egypt does not turn to the idol, but addresses her ecstatic prayer straight to God. The left-hand panel depicts her earlier licentiousness in a range of glaring colours. Mary's figure is suffused with golden yellow, and the nipples of her heavy breasts shimmer purple. Grinning with lust, she extends her arms towards three greedy, grotesque male figures clad in blue, green and purple. On the right panel, the converted sinner and penitent lies in the throes of death. An ascetic says a prayer over her prostrate body, as a lion awaits his chance to spring and play his part in the miraculous event. The background of the "waste land" is formed by a jungle in gradations of green and blue – perhaps a sultry, exotic counterpart to the Christian Garden of Eden.

Like his other religious compositions, this triptych was not meant to be viewed as an altar painting. All of them, as Nolde stated, were "artistic evocations, intended to serve art".

The Legend of St Maria Aegyptiaca, 1912
Oil on canvas, triptych: central painting
105 x 120 cm (41¼ x 47¼ in.),
wings 86 x 100 cm (34 x 39¼ in.) each
Hamburger Kunsthalle

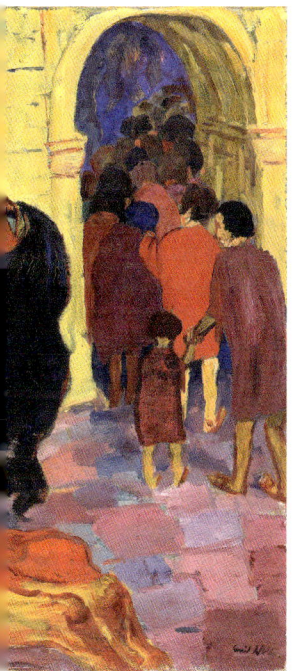
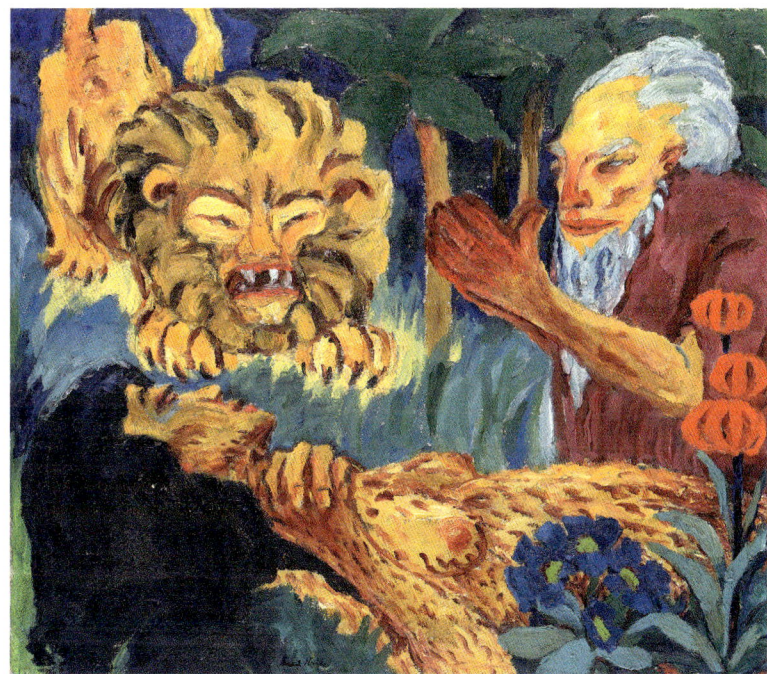

Emil Nolde
Tropical Sun, 1914

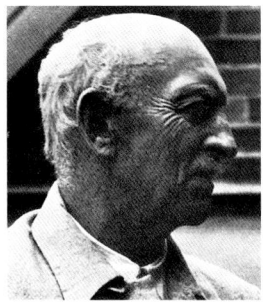

b. 1867 in Nolde, Kingdom of Prussia (now Germany)
d. 1956 in Seebüll, Germany

When in July 1905 Nolde returned from Switzerland to northern Germany and the island of Alsen, he stopped over in Weimar and visited a Gauguin exhibition, noting, "I have never before seen such glorious colours in modern art." The exotic realm to which the French artist escaped became a destination for which Nolde also yearned. Not that he was a Romantic escapist. Rather, he pursued a well-defined artistic goal – to recover the "primal", the source of all creativity that had been buried under the flotsam of civilization. In 1911 Nolde planned a book on "Artistic Manifestations of the Natural Peoples", in which he intended to confront the ritual objects of the "savages", as he noted in his autobiography, with the "saccharine tasteless forms" exhibited in the "glass cases of the salons". The book was never published. But while preparing it Nolde studied objects by the Egyptians, Assyrians, the indigenous peoples of Africa, Southeast Asia and the South Pacific, with which the Berlin Museum of Ethnology overflowed.

Two years later the forty-six-year-old artist took an opportunity offered to him and his wife to accompany a scientific expedition to New Guinea. Their trip took them to the South Pacific by way of Russia, China, Korea and Japan. In addition to numerous sketches and watercolours, Nolde executed nineteen oils in the provincial town of Kaewieng, on the northwest point of present-day New Ireland, an island the German colonial administration of the day called New Mecklenburg. One of this group of works is *Tropical Sun*, which was preceded by a small preparatory drawing.

Having gone down to the beach, Nolde looked from sea level towards the horizon, where the sun is either rising or setting. The horizon line divides the horizontal format just below its central axis. Visible there is the dark green, forested silhouette of Nusa Lik island. This undulating form penetrating the composition from the left finds a correspondence in the white cumulus cloud above the horizon and in the foaming breakers in the foreground. The sun stands over the treetops like an incandescent red disc in the midst of a radiant aureole that is surrounded by darker cloud formations. The range of colours, applied for the most part in broad, impasto strokes, rises to a frenzy of vermilion red, cadmium orange and cobalt violet. The individual tones are no longer applied wet in wet as in Nolde's earlier landscapes but spread into expansive areas. Their intensity or brilliance is not to be confused with garishness, as the artist repeatedly emphasized in view of his impressions of the South Pacific. Far from requiring any expressive exaggeration, he said, these colours conformed with actual phenomena in the tropics.

Nolde did not address the First World War in his art. He painted no visions of destruction or apocalyptic landscapes like, say, Meidner. Instead, to his tropical paintings Nolde added northern German lowland landscapes, coastlines and gardens, replying to the vicissitudes of the age by charging nature and religious subjects with an optimistic mysticism. Kirchner described Nolde's art in his diaries as "often morbid and too primitive". He thought Nolde's mysticism diverted his colleague too far from the formal issues of modernism. That same tendency led Nolde to make a grave error in 1933, when he stated that his Expressionist painting was a genuine expression of the "German soul". He was rudely awakened from this dream by the Nazis, who the following year delivered Nolde's paintings over to the derision of the philistines.

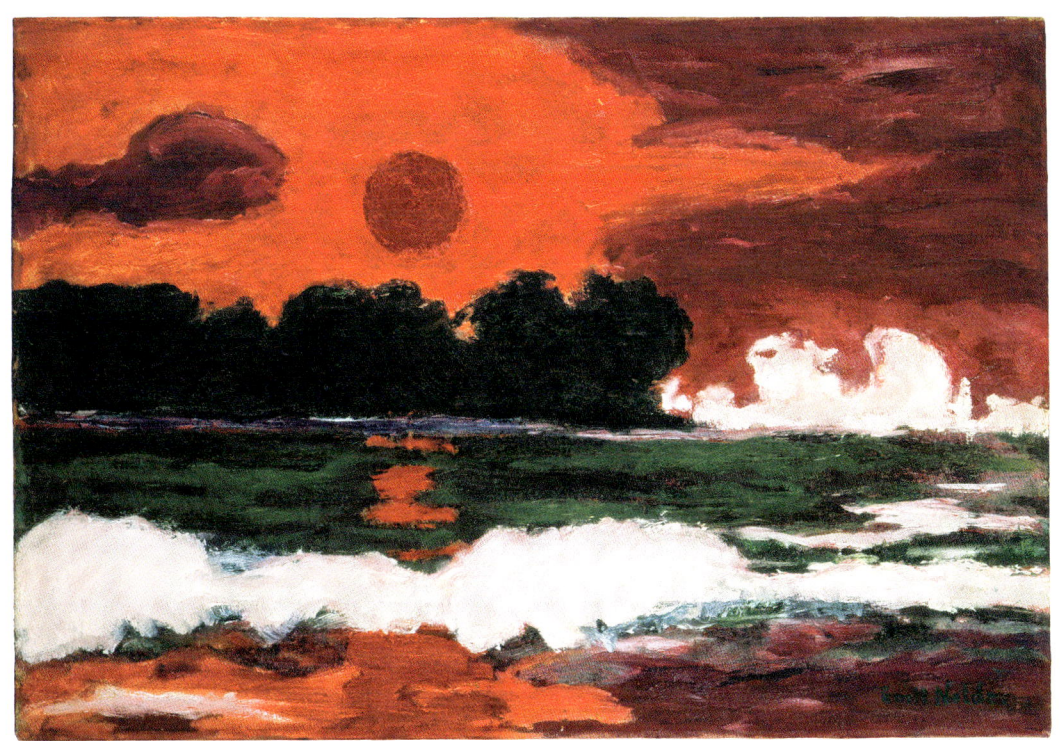

Tropical Sun, 1914
Oil on canvas, 71 x 104.5 cm (28 x 41¼ in.)
Nolde Stiftung Seebüll

Max Pechstein
Palau Triptych, 1917

The Expressionists enthusiastically adopted the modern aesthetic of individual creativity, which implied that artists view the world solely from the standpoint of their own ego or self. One of the leading protagonists of this aesthetic, Paul Gauguin, shifted the scene of nature suffused by the artist's ego into an exotic realm: here, life seemed to run its course unaffected by the conflicts of civilization.

Max Pechstein, too, took this road. In his eyes the carved and painted roofbeams from the South Pacific island of Palau, which he and other Brücke artists studied at the Dresden Museum of Ethnology, embodied an archetypal unity of art and life. They seemed to reflect, in a different way, just what the group had pursued during their carefree months on the Moritzburg Lakes: a utopian alternative to the perverted industrial world. And perhaps these indigenous carvings affected Pechstein all the more because he was the first Brücke artist to forsake quiet Dresden for the big city of Berlin. Coloured by his idealistic attitude, he could say of them: "I see the carved idol images, into which trembling piety and awe of the incomprehensible forces of nature have impressed [their makers'] hope and terror, their fear and their submission to an unavoidable fate."

Pechstein was only acting consistently when in April 1914, like Nolde the previous year, he set off for the South Seas to spend a few years in the Palau Islands. But he was surprised there by the war, was taken prisoner by the Japanese, managed a daredevil escape, and returned as a coal trimmer on freighters by way of Hawaii, New York and the Netherlands to Germany – where he was immediately inducted into the army.

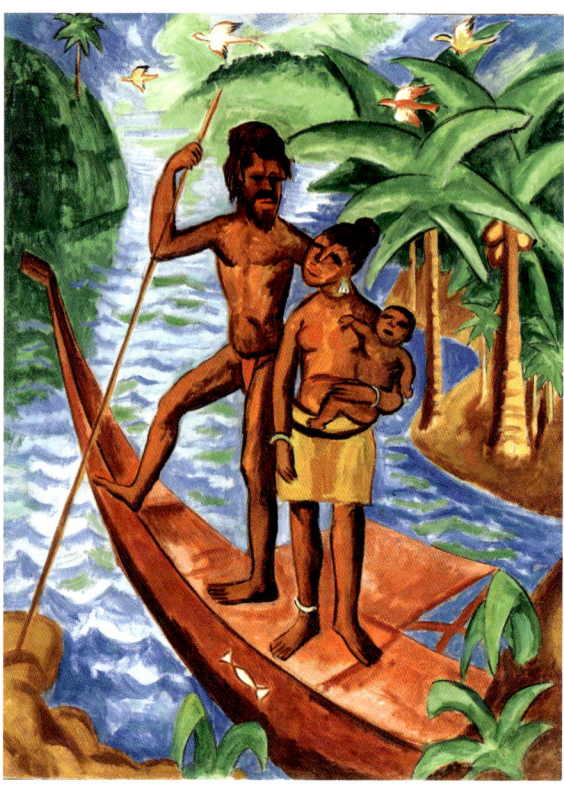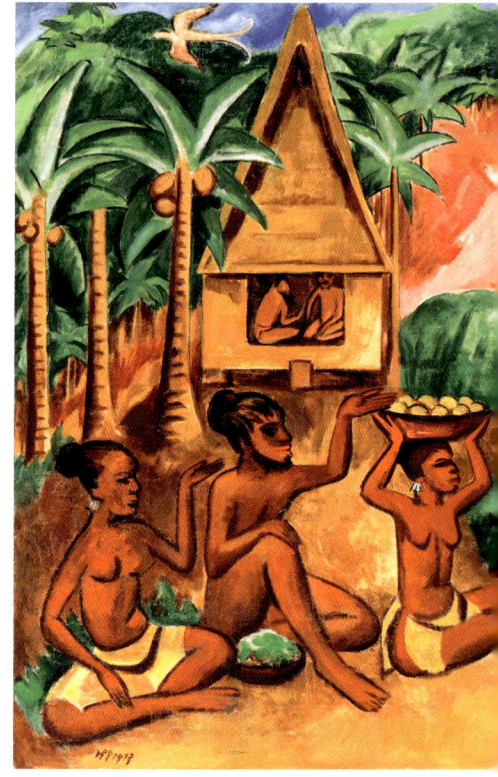

The horrors of the front lines proved too much, and he returned to Berlin after suffering a nervous breakdown. Now Pechstein began to distil his travel memories into the composition of his *Palau Triptych*, unfolding a peaceful world in face of a murderous civilization, suppressing the Brücke period's "savage" manner in favour of tranquil harmony.

Within the landscape panorama, various decoratively stylized, not so much expressive as neo-classical scenes spread across the central panel and two flanking wings. On the left is a family of islanders in a boat. The central panel is likewise dominated by a trio of seated figures, who together with a fourth, standing person turn to the three male figures in a boat opposite. The motifs of water, earth and air, and correspondingly, fish, human beings and birds, form a symbolic triad. Mirroring Gauguin, Pechstein interpreted Palau in terms of his own Romantic expectations, as a counterimage to "materialistic" Europe, an ideal paradise, rather than an island within a colonial empire.

After the war, Pechstein was a founding member in 1918 of the revolutionary yet short-lived Arbeitsrat für Kunst (Working Council for Art), and after it disbanded he remained politically engaged. He joined the League for Human Rights, helping produce propaganda for the young Soviet Union. Thus it was no surprise that when the Nazis clamped down on modern art in 1933, Pechstein was one of their first Expressionist victims.

Palau Triptych, 1917
Oil on canvas, 119 x 353 cm (47 x 139 in.)
(central panel 119 x 171 cm (47 x 67¼ in.),
wings 119 x 91 cm (47 x 36 in.) each)
Ludwigshafen, Wilhelm-Hack-Museum

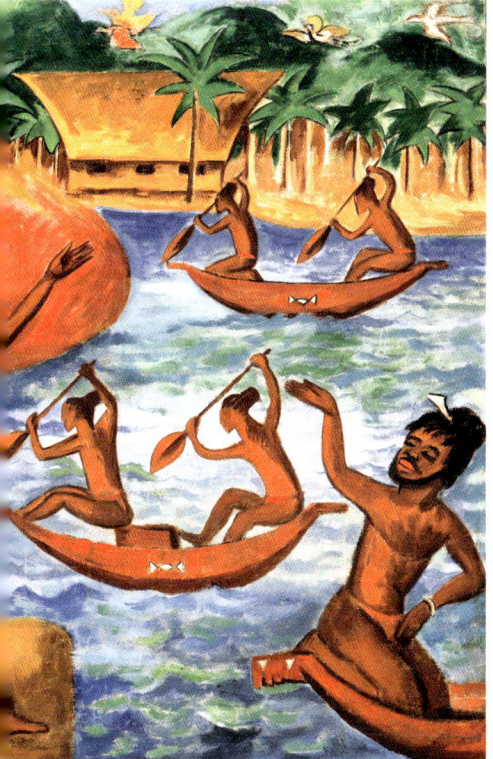
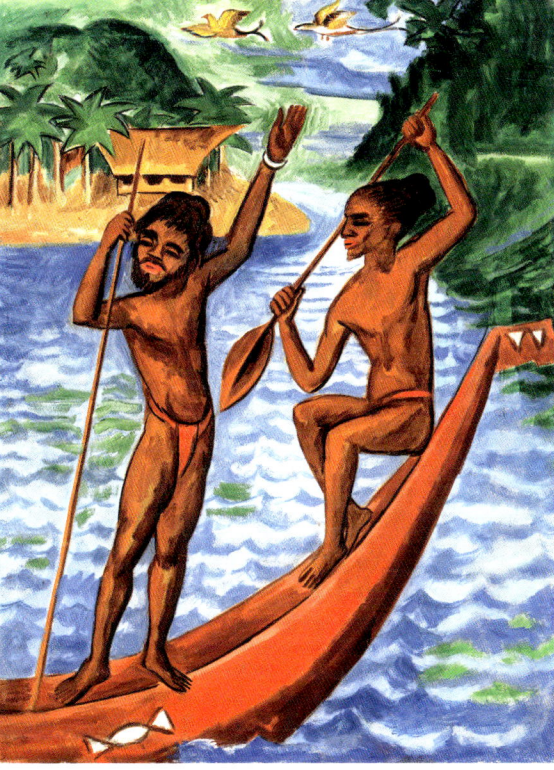

Christian Rohlfs
Acrobats, 1916

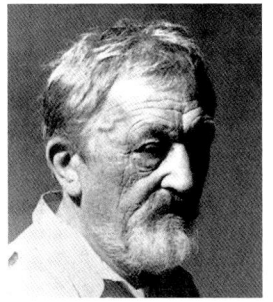

b. 1849 in Niendorf, Germany
d. 1938 in Hagen, Germany

As in the preceding French art of the nineteenth century, subjects from the circus, dance and vaudeville enjoyed great popularity among the Expressionists. Such performers were viewed as embodying marginal groups in society, as underdogs who, like artists themselves, sold their souls on the marketplace, not respectable yet dependent for their livelihood on the money of respectable middle-class citizens. The exaltation of dancers, the daring of artistes, seemed the perfect symbol for the "tight-wire act" of the Expressionist artist who pushed himself to the limits.

Christian Rohlfs, too, treated this motif, transforming it in a subtle way very typical of him. This is seen in his vital *Acrobats* picture of 1916, based on contrasts and tensions, and evincing a refined, parallel composition. Against the bright red background, the pair are depicted in complementary poses that form, as it were, a single, rotating comprehensive figure. The motif employs every possibility of equilibrated, graceful movement – upright and head down – to convey an impression of great vitality. The figures are elongated almost to the point of mannerism, with the main accent on heavy contour lines and overlapping picture planes, whose transparency is achieved through the tempera technique Rohlfs began to develop about 1913. This gives the figures an airiness that belies their physical massiveness, convincing us that it was not acrobats as individuals with whom the artist was concerned but abbreviations or ciphers for movement per se, archetypal forms in motion such as those seen in ancient Mycenean vase paintings. The graphically textured paint surface of the background reveals the influence of Fauvist colour field painting, which Rohlfs had intensively studied, as well as inspiration from Emil Nolde, whom he befriended in 1905 and 1906 in Soest.

Rohlfs was what is known as a late developer. Due to a serious injury that eventually necessitated a leg amputation, the son of a Holstein farmer was confined to his bed for two years. A fellow Holsteiner, the author Theodor Storm (1817–1888), suggested he go into painting. Rohlfs had almost turned fifty before he saw Impressionist art for the first time, in 1897 in Weimar. Henry van de Velde (1863–1957), the Belgian architect and then-director of the Weimar School of Decorative Arts, introduced him to the art patron Karl Ernst Osthaus, who in 1901 offered Rohlfs a post at the Folkwang Museum then being built in Hagen. There he became acquainted with French Post-Impressionism and Pointillism as well as with van Gogh. Yet the decisive impulse to strike out into uncharted territory came from Edvard Munch, whom Rohlfs met in 1904.

A highly productive artist, Rohlfs began increasingly to sympathize with the avant-garde currents in Germany, and from 1912 at the latest, he could be called an Expressionist – a representative of that version of the style that drew its expressive force primarily from colour values, in his case initially brilliant, then increasingly subdued, as it were washed out. In 1906 the Brücke artists saw Rohlfs's work in the "Third German Arts and Crafts Exhibition" in Dresden. They considered inviting him to become a member, but Nolde, for obscure reasons, objected.

Acrobats, 1916
Tempera on canvas,
110 x 75.5 cm (43¼ x 29¾ in.)
Essen, Museum Folkwang

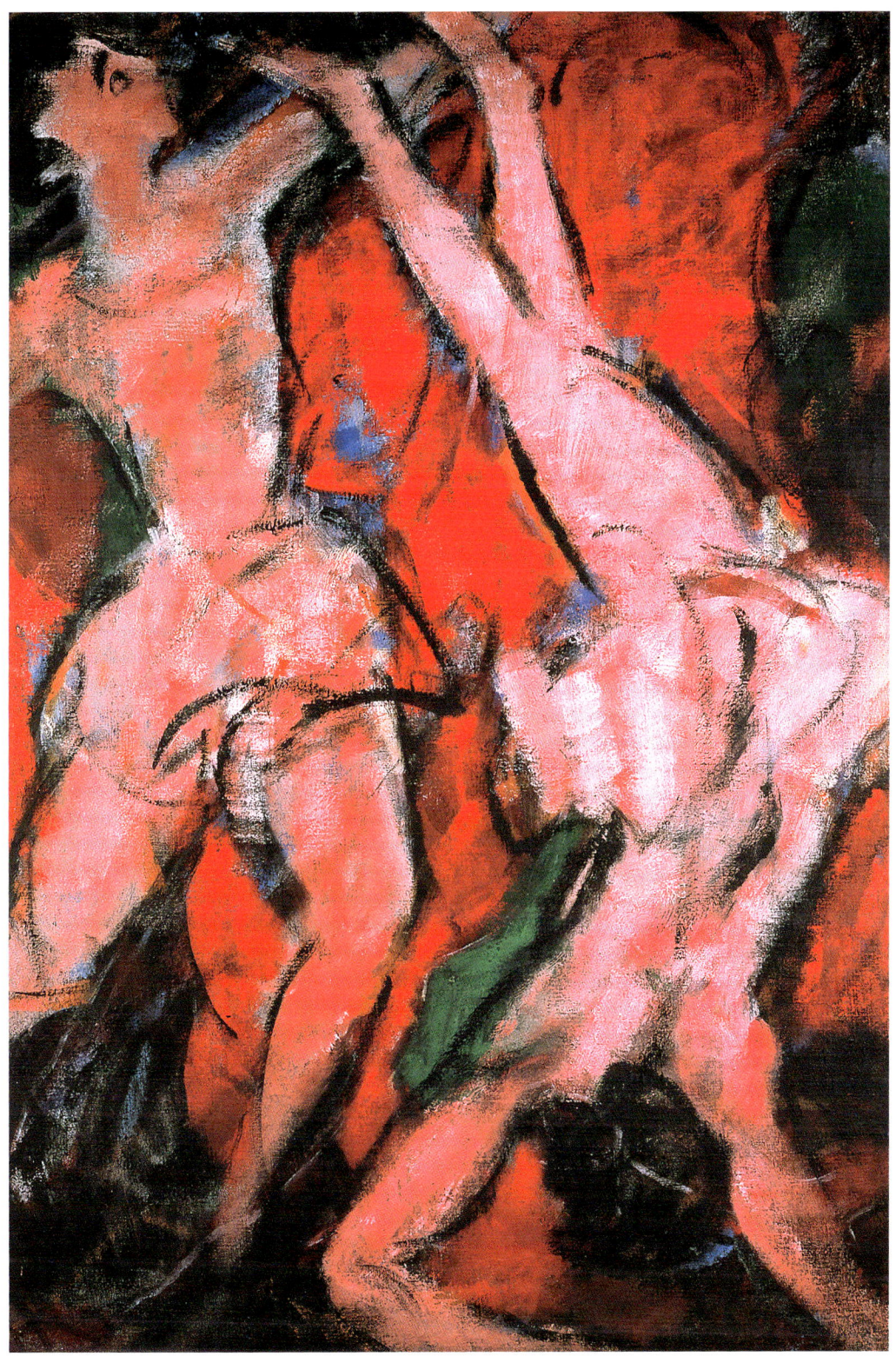

Egon Schiele
Nude Self-Portrait, Grimacing, 1910

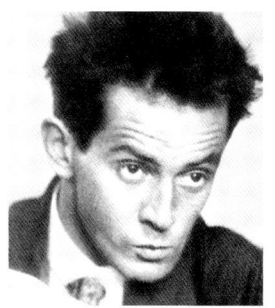

b. 1890 in Tulln, Lower Austria
d. 1918 in Vienna

Alongside Oskar Kokoschka, Schiele was the most prominent personality in Austrian Expressionism. He was repeatedly supported by the famous Gustav Klimt (1862–1918), who recognized Schiele's talent early on. In the short period from 1906 to 1909, while still a student at the Vienna Academy, Schiele passed rapidly through various creative phases, from a dry, nondescript academic style through an adaptation of decorative Art Nouveau à la Klimt to a radical formal vocabulary of great expressive force, including figurative distortion and a vehement gestural paint application.

By 1910 Schiele had arrived at his inimitable style. His work was dominated by only a few motifs, centring on the portrait and the nude. Yet, to cite Dietmar Elger, "unlike the other Expressionists, [Schiele] did not attempt to read physiognomic content from the face of his models alone. With Kokoschka, the play of the hands was itself often a more eloquent testimony than the face of the person portrayed. Schiele now made the entire body and every limb into equal bearers of artistic expression." Generally Schiele did without any indication of interior space or landscape surroundings, concentrating solely on the hypersensitive lineaments of the human body.

On 25 August 1913, the artist noted in a letter: "Mainly I now observe the physical motion of mountains, water, trees and flowers. Everywhere one is put in mind of similar motions in the human body, similar stirrings of pleasure and pain as in plants…" In many of his portraits and self-portraits this observation appears reversed, in that the human figure takes on a plantlike character – not, of course, rendered in the elegant, sinuous lines of Art Nouveau but with a nervous, evocative, hesitant, as it were splintered contouring that lends the figure an association with frozenness, desiccation, crippling.

In the present large-format portrait, the artist's naked torso rises like a leaning tree stump though the vertical format, the right arm, in contrast, extended stiffly into the horizontal, only to abruptly turn down at the joint like some tree branch struck by lightning. On this bizarre physical framework sits a masklike skull with a face distended into a scream. With unprecedented expressive radicality, the potential of experiencing one's own mirror image is transformed into an artifice that verges on hallucinatory self-insight. The shaping of form becomes an extreme experience, the line becomes a thin, sharp, often cutting edge that dissects and, avoiding no dissonance, penetrates into the no-man's land of the empty plane.

Despite this verve, economy of means is maintained. There is not one line too many or one too few. The creaturely aspect of the human image is worked out to the full, an existentialism reminiscent of late-Gothic images of mercy, recalling the tortured body of the suffering Christ.

In 1912 Schiele was accused of "disseminating pornographic drawings" and given a prison sentence. His art triggered hostilities from many quarters, yet a small, committed group of supporters made possible exhibitions and sales – if more in Germany than in Austria – of the short-lived artist's work.

Nude Self-Portrait, Grimacing, 1910
Gouache, watercolour and pencil
with white heightening,
55.8 x 36.9 cm (22 x 14½ in.)
Vienna, Albertina, Grafische Sammlung

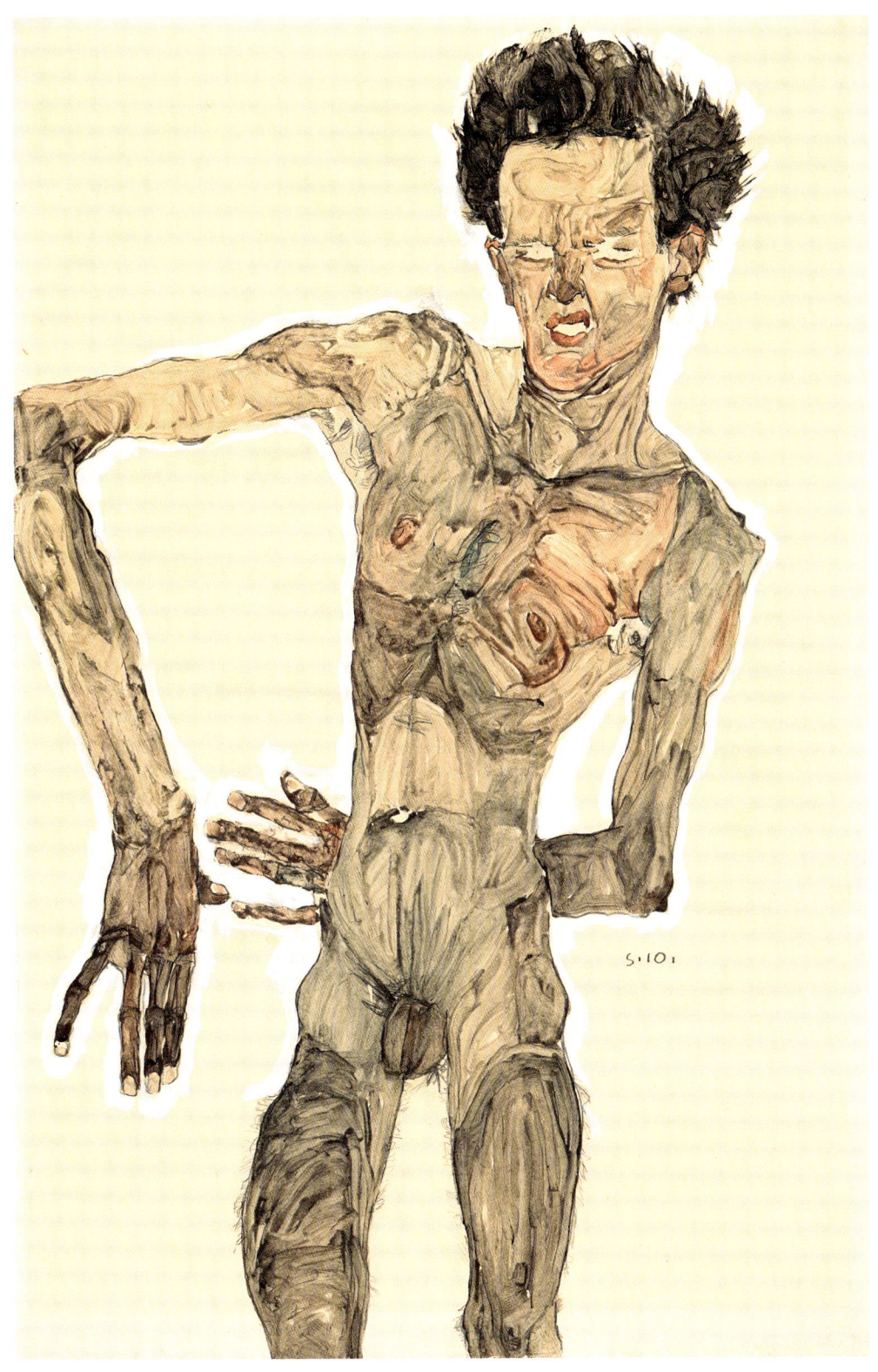

S 10

Karl Schmidt-Rottluff
Portrait of Rosa Schapire, 1911

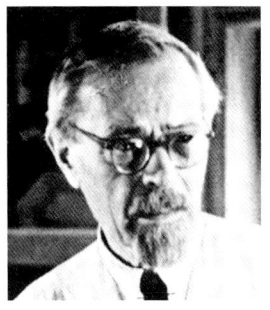

b. 1884 in Rottluff, Germany
d. 1976 in Berlin

Karl Schmidt (who in 1905 added the name of his birthplace, Rottluff, to his own) was not only the youngest Brücke artist but the one who retained the most autonomy during his membership in the group. Even in 1910, when a decidedly collective Brücke style developed, the character of his works remained unique. Schmidt-Rottluff went his own way whenever possible, for instance not taking part in the group's excursions to the Moritzburg Lakes outside Dresden but remaining faithful to the village of Dangast in Oldenburg province. "There are almost no theoretical statements by him," notes Lothar-Günther Buchheim. "In contrast to Kirchner he never subjected his style to written analysis. The few letters and notes… were destroyed in the last war, when his Berlin apartment with about 2000 drawings and many watercolours and paintings went up in flames."

Schmidt-Rottluff's beginnings around 1905 were marked by a monumental Impressionism, rapidly executed in heavy impasto with an excited, expressive touch inspired by van Gogh and often making use of the palette knife. After a visit to Nolde on Alsen island in 1906, that artist's influence also made itself felt. From about 1909, Schmidt-Rottluff's Dangast landscapes began to show a change in style. Expansive, daringly juxtaposed areas of thinned, unmixed colour now spread across the canvas, whose white showed through in places and whose grainy texture determined the surface character of the image. The forms increasingly grew in size, and compositional lines resulted from the intersection of separate colour fields. A short time later came a framework of black contour lines, as seen in the *Portrait of Rosa Schapire*.

Schmidt-Rottluff had met Rosa Schapire (1874–1954), a Hamburg art historian and passionate supporter of the Brücke, in 1907. She furthered him unreservedly, propagating his art in numerous articles, cataloguing his prints, purchasing many works. Schapire commissioned the young painter to furnish a room in her apartment (which was later destroyed), for which he designed virtually everything, from murals to furniture, carpets and utilitarian objects. Schmidt-Rottluff portrayed his patron a total of four times between 1911 and 1919. The first of these portraits, now in the Brücke-Museum, has become the most famous, and was one of the earliest Schmidt-Rottluff ever executed. The composition is a half-length, format-filling depiction of the artist's friend, seated in an armchair. Her head under the broad-brimmed hat rests musingly on her left arm. In contrast to this calm pose, the colour veritably explodes, accented by energetic brushstrokes and broad expanses. The predominant brown gradations and the green of the dress set a complementary contrast to and amplify the light red. The raised arm in front of this red ground leads the eye to the reddish-violet face with its brilliant blue eyes.

Schmidt-Rottluff's brief involvement with French Cubism in 1912 lent his subsequent paintings a greater succinctness that, it must be said, occasionally slipped into the merely iconic. In about 1914 he began to supplement this style with impulses from exotic, blocky wood sculptures, lending his portaits an African look. After the First World War Schmidt-Rottluff reverted seamlessly to the themes of the Brücke period, and in spite of many variations, he continued to cultivate the Expressionist gesture to a ripe old age.

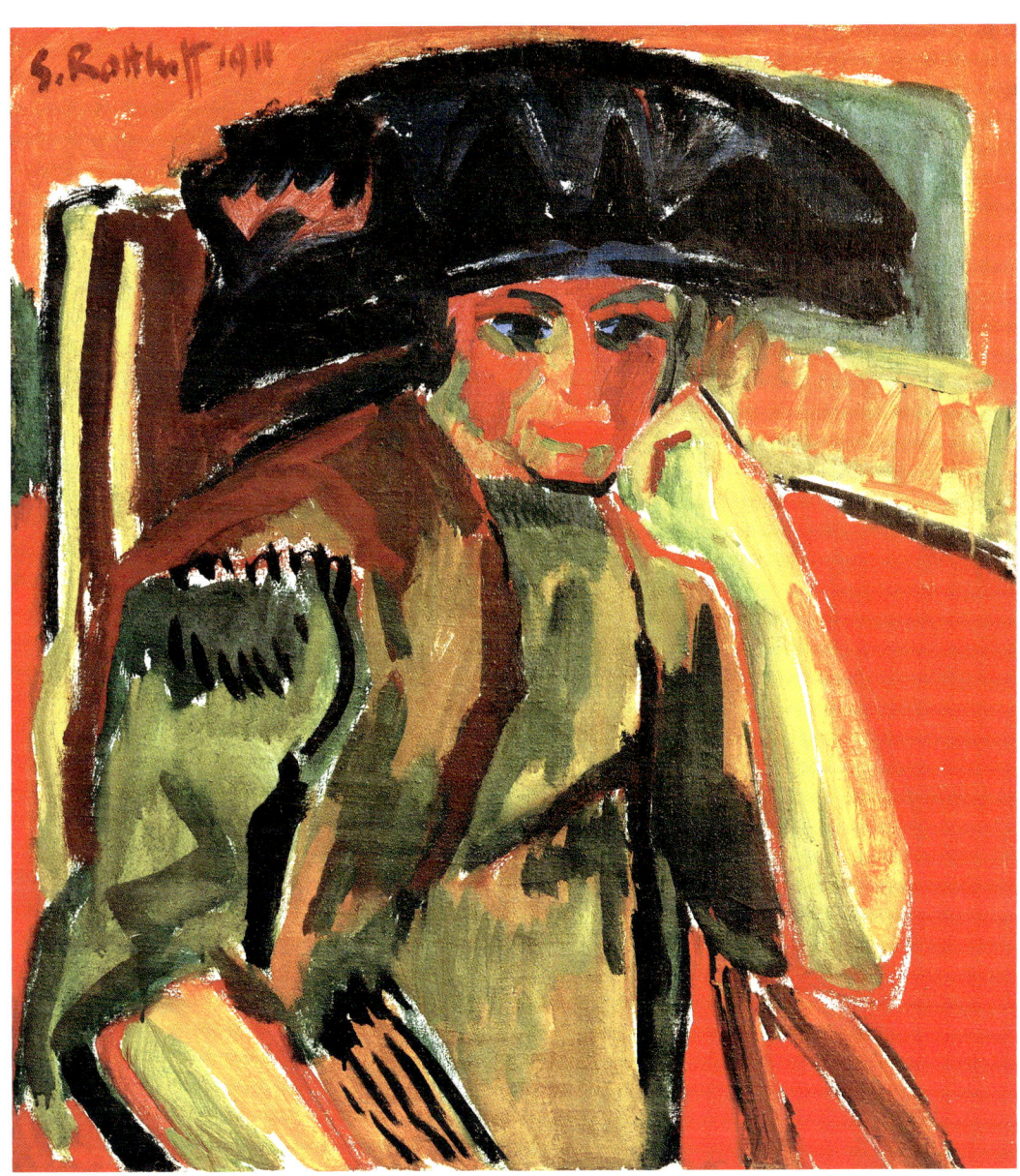

Portrait of Rosa Schapire, 1911
Oil on canvas, 84 x 76 cm (33 x 30 in.)
Berlin, Brücke-Museum

Arnold Schoenberg
The Red Gaze, 1910

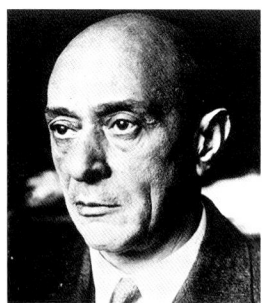

b. 1874 in Vienna
d. 1951 in Los Angeles

The composer Arnold Schoenberg, who had been in at the beginnings of the Blauer Reiter group, began painting in 1907 in the hope of making his mark in this metier as well. He received brief instruction from Richard Gerstl (1883–1908). Launching at that period into atonal music, in art Schoenberg abandoned all of the superficial illustrative tasks of painting, including that of depicting the face. "I have never seen faces, but, because I have looked people in the eye, only their gazes," stated Schoenberg.

This tendency was also reflected in his painting titles, such as *The Red Gaze*. Here the human visage is dissolved into schematic, diffuse colour structures from which the eyes "are directed like mirrors of disturbed souls at the affected viewer…" The heads seem to drown "in the surrounding colour field" and yet emerge from this maelstrom "like visions of horror", as Peter-Klaus Schuster put it, or like mental precipitations from the depths of a dream. These fantasies rely to some extent on the palette of a Robert Delaunay or the Fauves; there are a few points of contact with Gerstl and Kokoschka's painting of the day; and there is surely an inner affinity with the visions of Munch (ill. p. 125).

The immediate catalyst for these ghostly faces may well have been Gerstl's suicide. Living in the same house as Schoenberg, Gerstl hung himself in November 1908 after breaking off his relationship with Mathilde Schoenberg. But it would be mistaken to interpret such depictions as *The Red Gaze* solely in biographical terms. There was a larger, Symbolist conception behind them. From about 1908 onwards, Schoenberg devoted himself to the idea of an interdisciplinary work of art on stage, a true synthesis of the arts rather than a mere addition of their means. From these considerations he derived a definition of colour, gesture, movement, light and music as vehicles of meaning in their own right, which conveyed not "alien" content but their own intrinsic autonomy, their suggestive force, their expressiveness, and not least, their dissonances. Human beings and their image appeared in this context as de-individualized prototypes, embodying universal forces and energies.

Schoenberg's friendship with Kandinsky dated to early 1911. Their respective notions about the essence of art revealed many points in common. Their interest in then-emergent theosophy out of cultural pessimism and an opposition to materialism resulted in a parallel search for the ineffable, metaphysical, purely spiritual. In Schoenberg's oils and watercolours Kandinsky detected the presence of a kindred spirit. Franz Marc and especially August Macke, in contrast, were sceptical. The latter described Schoenberg's faces as "green-eyed waterlogged breakfast rolls with an astral gaze". Yet it cannot be gainsaid that Schoenberg's *Harmonielehre*, published in 1911, had a considerable influence on the Munich circle of the Blauer Reiter.

To cite Kandinsky's opinion: "We see that in every picture by Schoenberg the inner desire of the artist speaks in the form suited to it. Just as in his music… Schoenberg does without the superficial (i. e. the harmful) in painting and goes by a direct path to the essential (i. e. the necessary)… I would very much like to call Schoenberg's painting sheer painting."

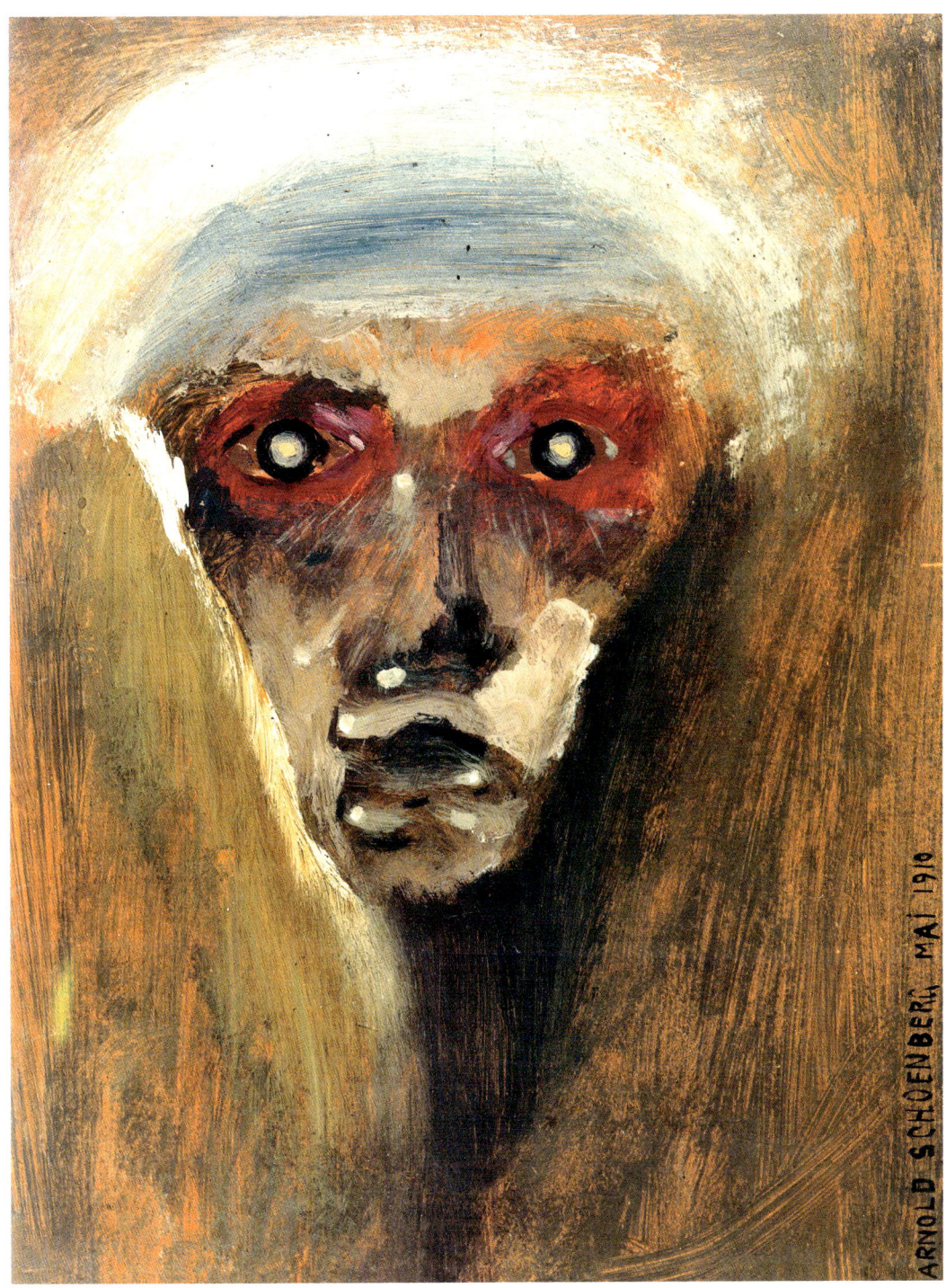

The Red Gaze, 1910
Oil on cardboard, 32.2 x 24.6 cm (12¾ x 9¾ in.)
Munich, Städtische Galerie im Lenbachhaus
und Kunstbau München

Marianne von Werefkin
Self-Portrait, 1910

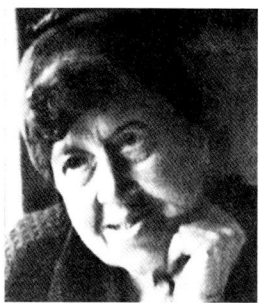

b. 1860 in Tula, Russia
d. 1938 in Ascona, Switzerland

Marianne von Werefkin came from a prosperous Russian aristocratic family who had close ties with the czar's court. Her mother, herself a painter, approved of her idea of becoming an artist from the beginning. After receiving private instruction, von Werefkin attended art school in Moscow and, from 1886, spent ten years as a private pupil of the renowned history painter Ilya Repin (1844–1930) in St Petersburg. In 1888, apparently in connection with a tragic affair with a young doctor, she received a gunshot wound that crippled her right hand. Yet thanks to enormous will-power and arduous training she learned to handle brush and pencil again, and with great success – in academy circles she was celebrated as the "Russian Rembrandt".

The year 1891 brought an encounter that would have great consequences for her life. She fell in love with a young, penniless officer by the name of Alexej Jawlensky. Since marriage was precluded for reasons of status, the pair moved abroad, arriving in Munich in 1896. There, on Giselastrasse, von Werefkin brought into being a salon that soon became a gathering point for intellectuals and artists, especially Russians.

Around 1900, inspired by the early-nineteenth-century Romantic group known as the Nazarenes, she formed a community of artists which was soon joined by Kandinsky. She worshiped Romanticism and revered French Symbolist literature. The symbolistically tinged painting of the Nabis also impressed her. In 1907, after a ten-year break in which she concerned herself primarily with her partner's career, she returned to painting. In 1909 she became a founding member of the New Artists Association of Munich, but did not go along with the Blauer Reiter when they split off in 1911, and thus stood between the two camps.

Her *Self-Portrait* at the Lenbachhaus in Munich was done during the happy years of her close artistic contacts with Kandinsky and Gabriele Münter. The energetic pose, striking facial features, and extravagant headgear reveal much about the worldly and shrewd personality of the sitter. The strong colours applied in broad brushstrokes and the continuous contour holding together the elongated forms reflect the influences that held most importance for von Werefkin: the Nabis, and the "soul painting" of Edvard Munch. Beginning from such points of departure, the artist augmented her colour range to include those brilliant contrasts typical of Expressionism. Yet the configurations were not yet abstracted to the point that they became subordinate to the colour, as in the case of many Brücke paintings. Line continued to play the key role in defining the composition. This is why the pictorial field does not take on the extremely flat effect seen, for instance, in Jawlensky's portraits.

Her evident traditionalism, infused with a mystical, Symbolist undertone, seemingly kept her from fully embracing the abstraction she championed in theory – viewing women's role chiefly as communicative. She likely played a key role in introducing Kandinsky to the anthroposophical ideas of Rudolf Steiner and the early theosophy of Madame Blavatsky, which influenced his shift toward spiritual abstraction.

In 1920, von Werefkin and Jawlensky separated in Switzerland, where they had gone to escape the war. She died impoverished in Ascona in 1938.

Self-Portrait, 1910
Tempera on paper on cardboard,
51 x 34 cm (20 x 13½ in.)
Munich, Städtische Galerie im
Lenbachhaus und Kunstbau München

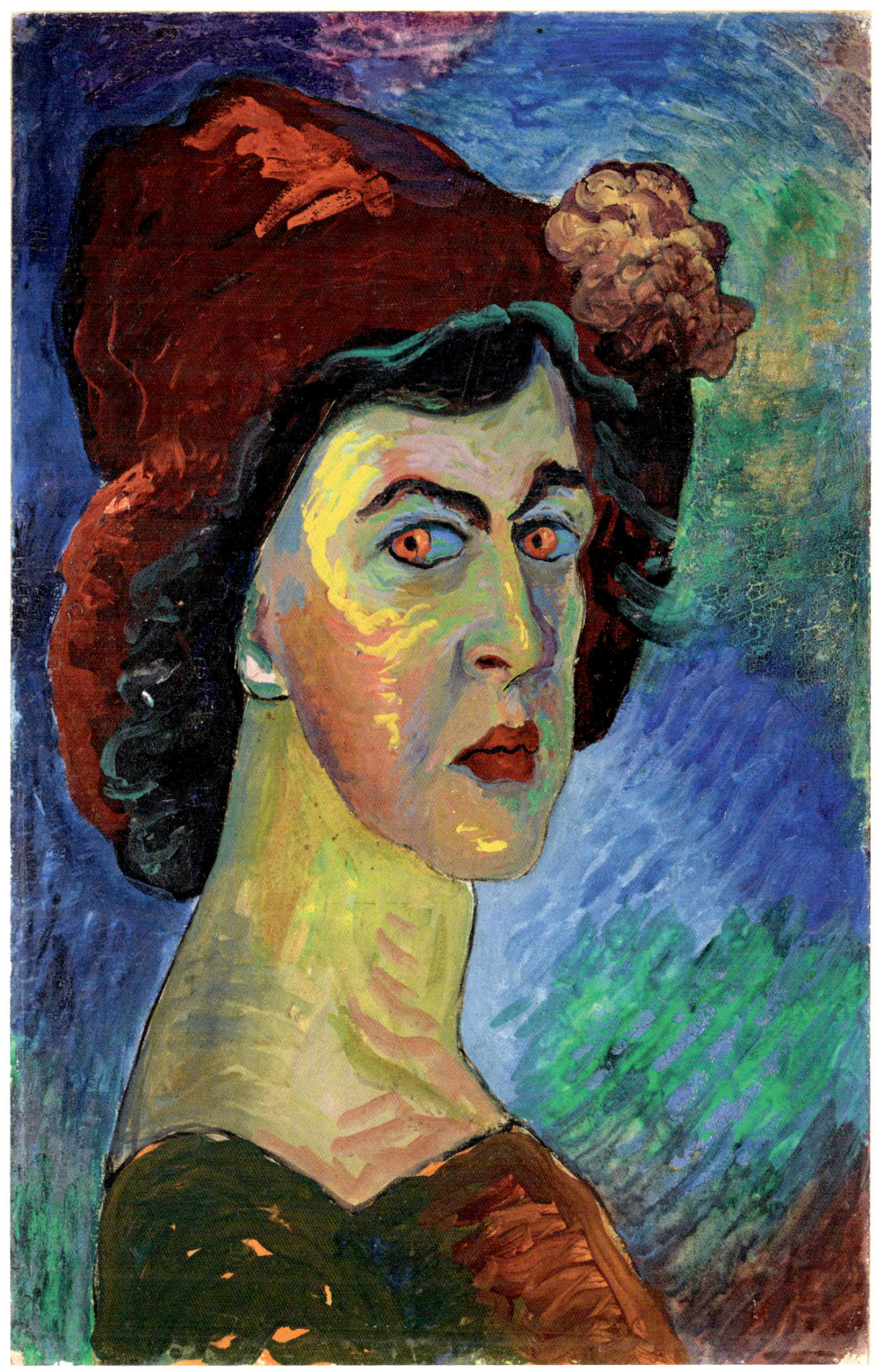

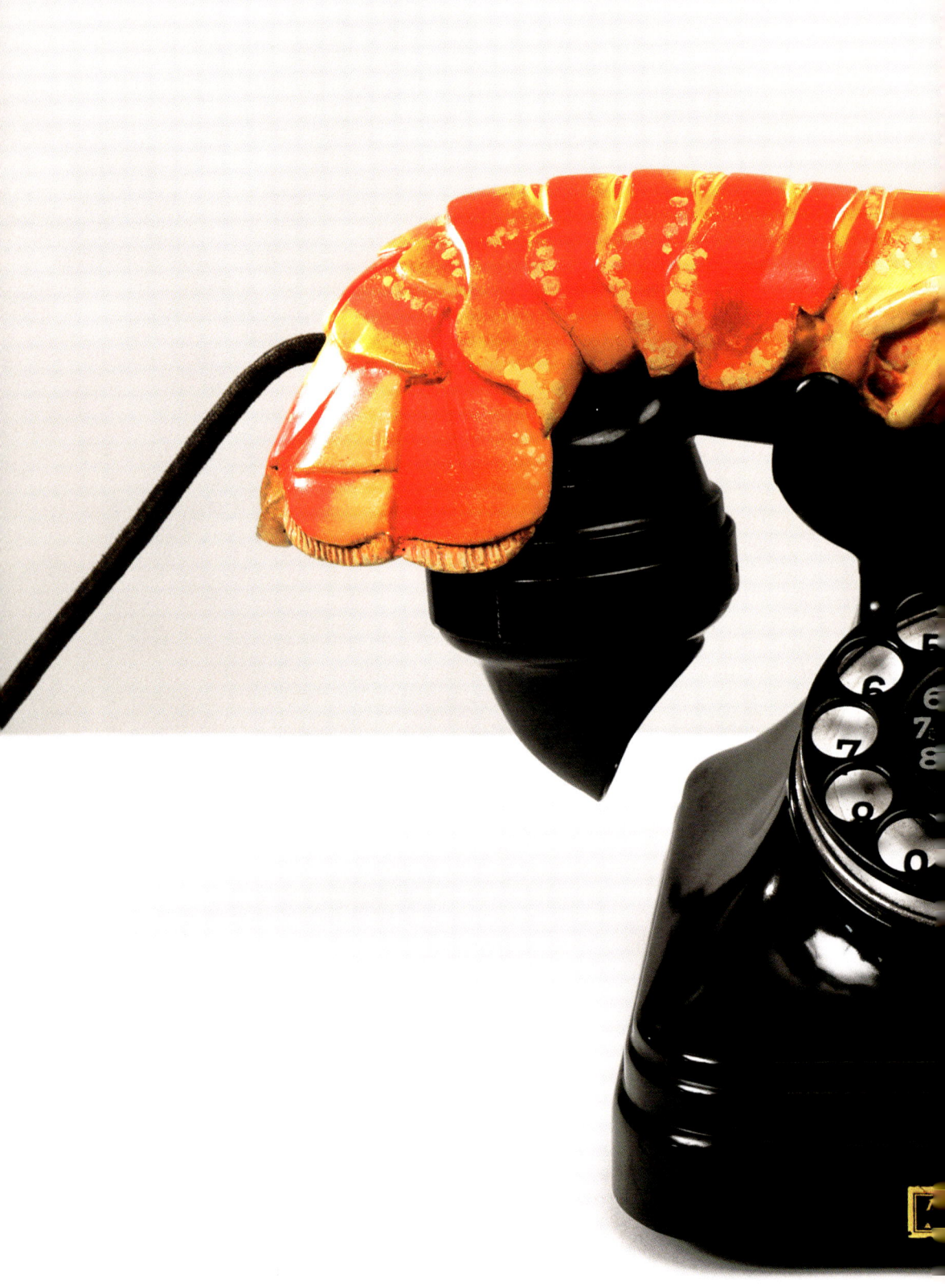

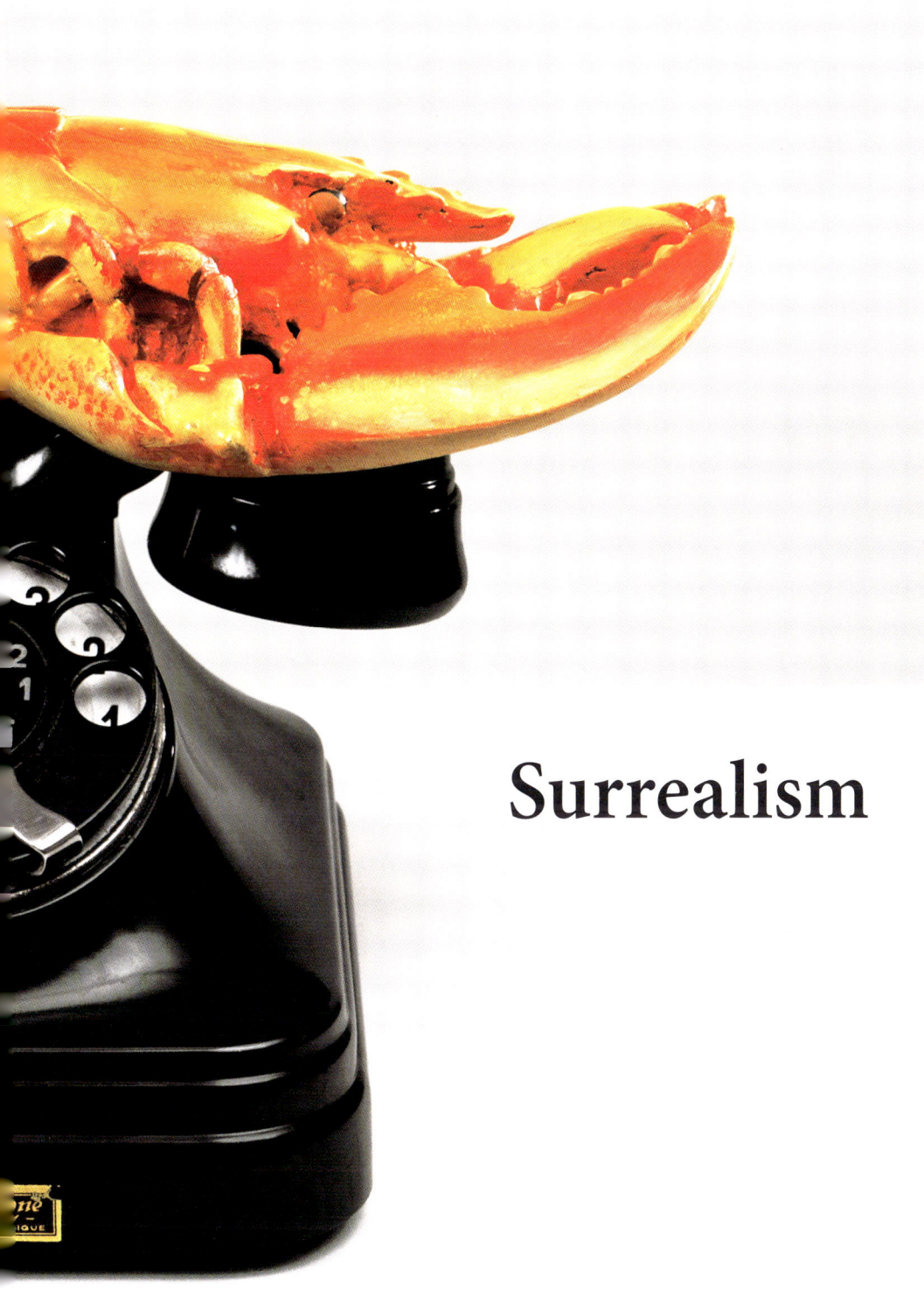

Surrealism

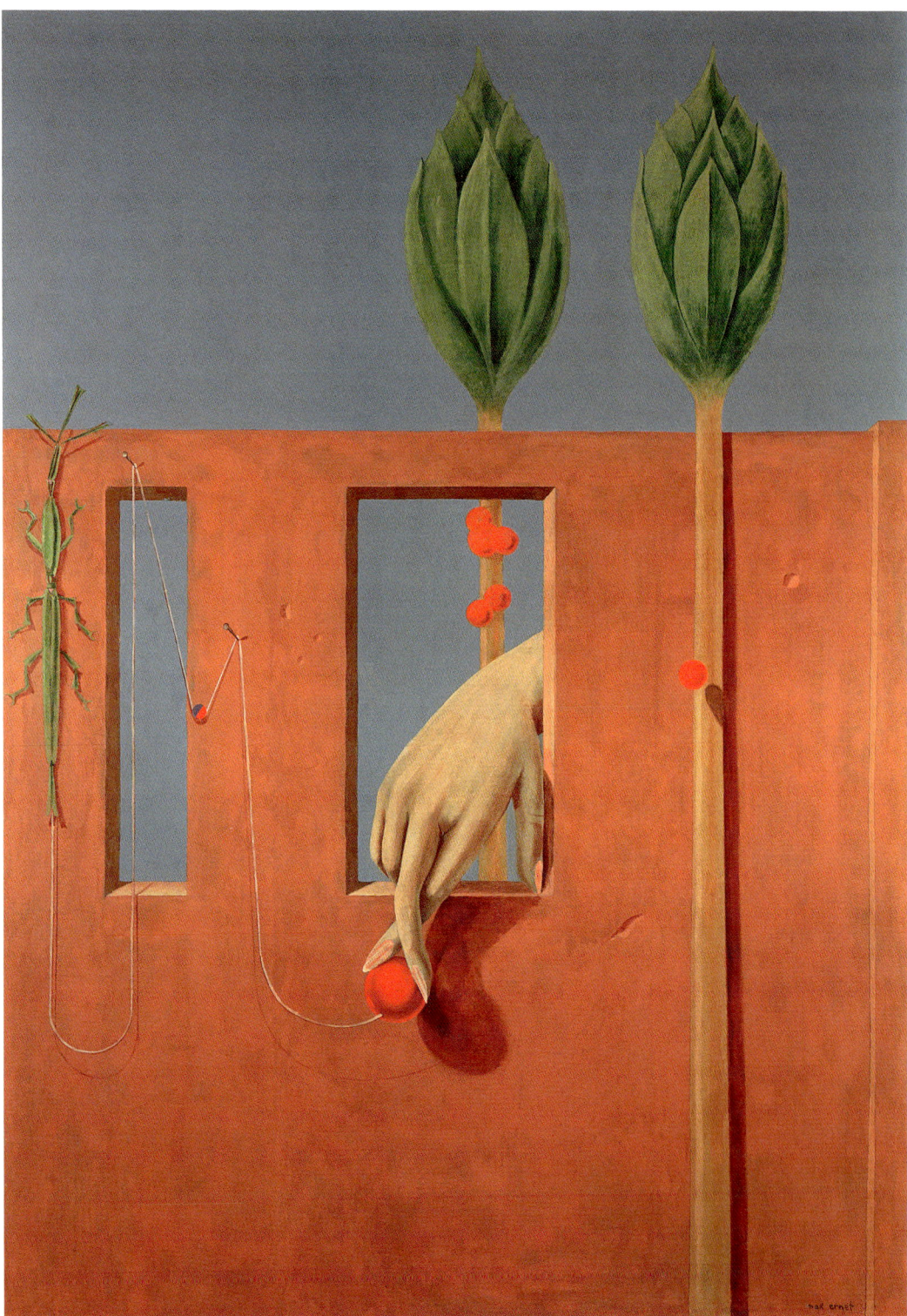

Cathrin Klingsöhr-Leroy
Uta Grosenick (Ed.)

Surrealism

Unleashing the Unconscious

"I believe in the future resolution of these two states,
dream and reality, which are seemingly so contradictory, into
a kind of absolute reality, a surreality, if one may so speak."
André Breton

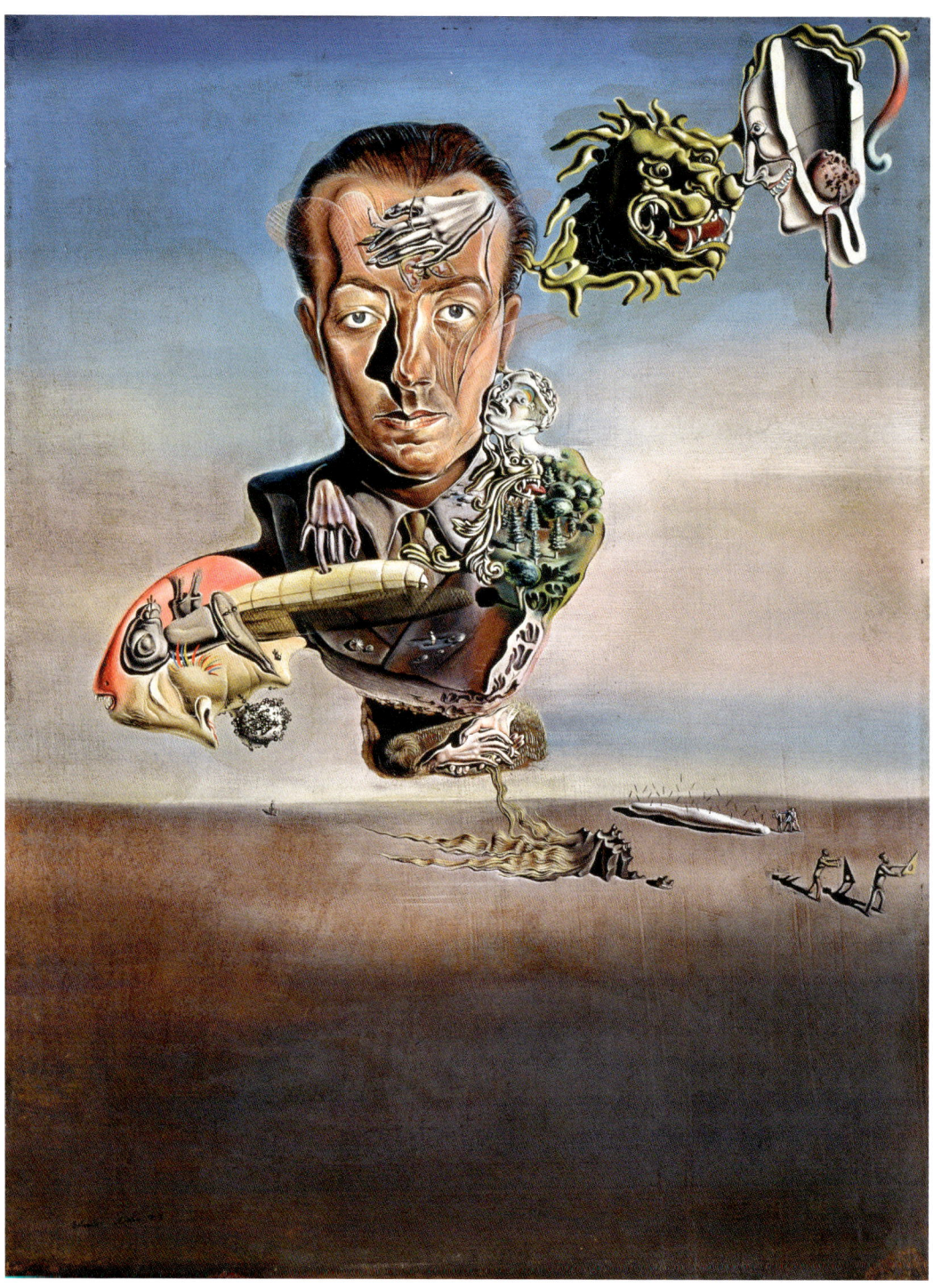

Contents

PAGES 202/203: Salvador Dalí
Aphrodisiac Telephone, 1938
Mixed media, including steel, plaster,
rubber, resin, and paper,
17.8 x 33 x 17.8 cm (7 x 13 x 7 in.)
London, Tate

PAGE 204: Max Ernst
At the First Clear Word, 1923
Oil on plaster transferred to canvas,
mounted from a mural in Paul Éluard's
house, 232 x 167 cm (91¼ x 65¾ in.)
Düsseldorf, Kunstsammlung
Nordrhein-Westfalen

OPPOSITE: Salvador Dalí
Portrait of Paul Éluard, 1929
Oil on cardboard,
33 x 25 cm (13 x 9¾ in.)
Private collection

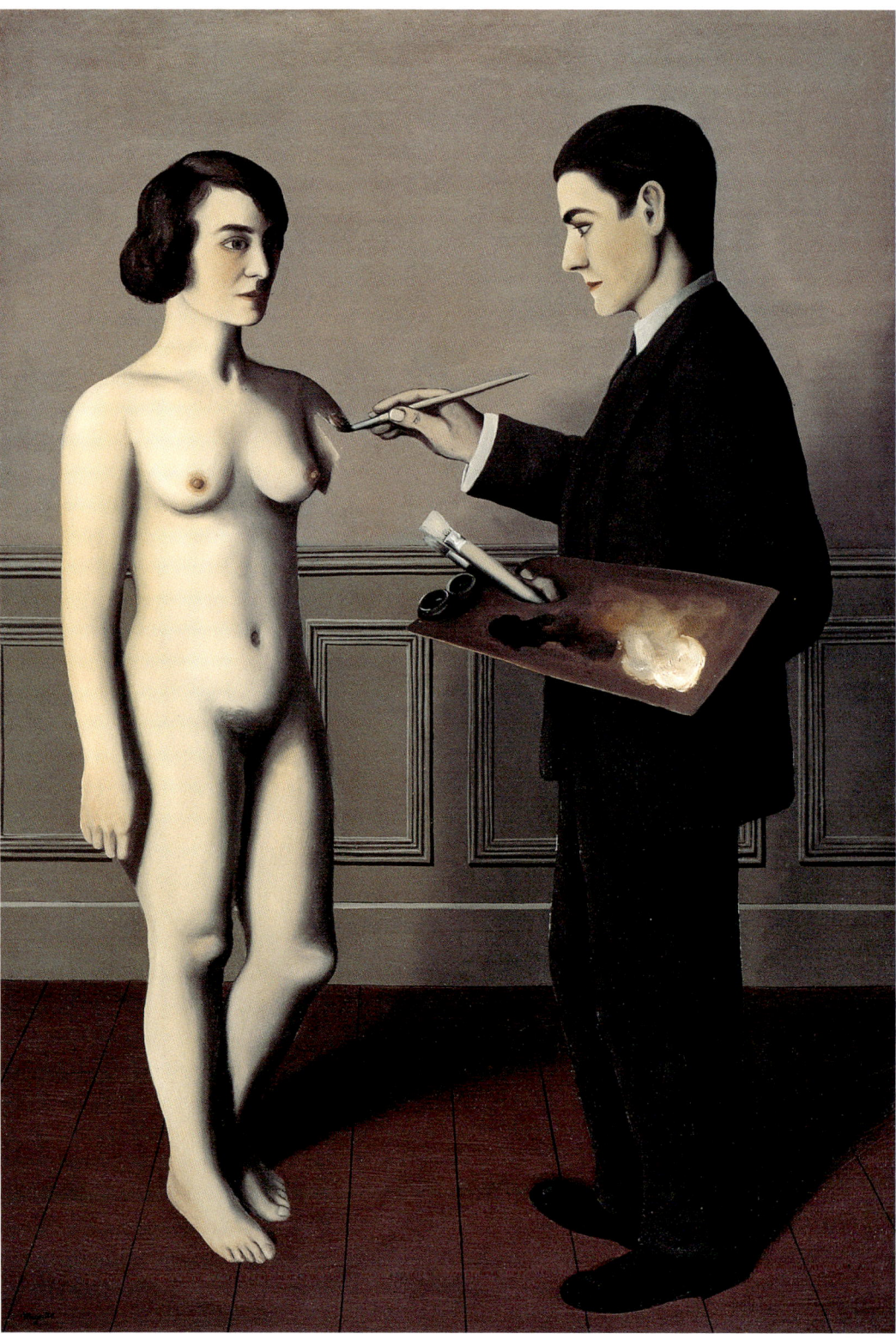

A New Declaration of the Rights of Man

What is Surrealism? Searching for a definition in his first *Manifesto of Surrealism*, published in 1924, André Breton resorted to the phraseology of dictionaries and encyclopaedias:

"SURREALISM, noun. Pure psychic automatism by which it is intended to express, either verbally or in writing, or otherwise, the true function of thought. Thought dictated in the absence of all control exerted by reason, and outside all aesthetic or moral preoccupations.

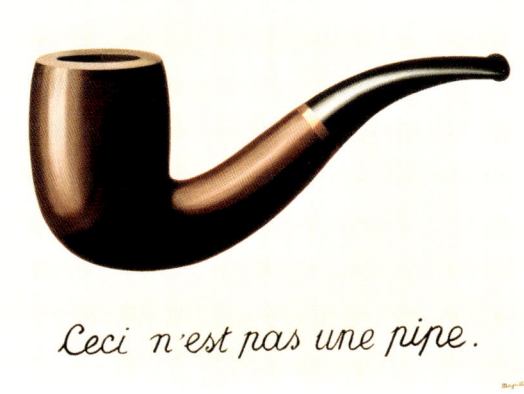

ENCYCLOPAEDIA. Philosophy. Surrealism is based on the belief in the superior reality of certain forms of association heretofore neglected, in the omnipotence of the dream, and in the disinterested play of thought. It leads to the permanent destruction of all other psychic mechanisms and to its substitution of them in the solution of the principal problems of life. Have professed absolute surrealism: Messrs. Aragon, Baron, Boiffard, Breton, Carrive, Crevel, Delteil, Desnos, Éluard, Gérard, Limbour, Malkine, Morise, Naville, Noll, Péret, Picon, Soupault, Vitrac."

This pseudo-scientific explanation, intended to throw more light on the art movement that Breton dubs "Surrealism", introduces yet another stylistic change to this rambling, disjointed manifesto, whose structure defies all logic.

On reading the names of those who, in Breton's estimation, represent "absolute Surrealism", we might imagine that this is a purely literary movement. However, in a footnote, Breton opens up this new domain to practitioners of the fine arts. He lists Uccello, Seurat, Moreau, Matisse, Derain, Picasso, Braque, Duchamp, Picabia, de Chirico, Klee, Man Ray, Ernst and Masson as members of a group who, without having heard the "Surrealist voice" are nonetheless sympathetic to the cause.

Astonishingly, Breton names not only contemporaries but also previous generations, represented by Uccello, Seurat and Moreau – and

OPPOSITE
René Magritte
Attempting the Impossible, 1928
Oil on canvas,
105.6 x 81 cm (41½ x 32 in.)
Toyota Municipal Museum of Art

TOP
René Magritte
The Treachery of Pictures, 1928/29
Oil on canvas,
62.2 x 81 cm (24½ x 32 in.)
Los Angeles County Museum of Art

Dante, Hugo and Chateaubriand in the field of literature – as if Surrealism were a fundamental intellectual position dating back centuries.

However, a look at history will clearly show that, while there were always artists whose works were inspired by dreams, the supernatural, the irrational and the absurd, we can only understand the precise significance of Surrealism as an artistic movement if we see it in the context of a particular period, the years between the two World Wars.

It was Guillaume Apollinaire who coined the term "surrealism" in 1917. He first used it in the programme for Erik Satie's ballet "Parade", also describing his own play "Les mamelles de Tirésias" (The Breasts of Tiresias) as a "surrealistic drama".

Critique of a Saturated Society

Apart from tracing the origin of the name, we also discover that two historic events were crucial to the birth of the Surrealist movement.

The artists who came together in Paris in the early 1920s shared a deep mistrust of materialistic, bourgeois society, which, they believed, was responsible for the First World War and its terrible aftermath. Not only that, but with its smug, superficial way of life and its belief in the omnipotence of technological and scientific achievement, society had succumbed to a process of degeneration to which the only answer was a revolutionary new anti-art. Already the Dadaists' anarchistic manifestations had attacked outdated ideas and those who clung relentlessly to them. The Surrealists shared some Dadaist ideas, but they set out to be better organised and more relevant to the real world. André Breton, the unifying figure and charismatic leader, who over the next two decades would co-ordinate activities and rally the troops, envisaged a movement that could really make a difference. Surrealism would not only embrace art and literature but would also play a part, as the first *Manifesto* put it, in "solving all the principal problems of life". It would affect every aspect of existence and bring about social and psychological change.

Central to this concept were the ideas of Sigmund Freud, which André Breton adapted to suit his own purposes. He regarded Freud's findings as the fortuitous rediscovery of the power of dreams and imagination that had long lain hidden behind the purely rational outlook that predominated at the time. Now, Breton predicted, the psyche would come into its own. A new intellectual tendency would evolve and artists could develop a perspective enabling them to free themselves from the control of reason. Sigmund Freud's contribution had been to define and describe the subconscious mind as a genuine phenomenon that governed human thought and behaviour. Breton translated this understanding into an artistic and literary methodology, based on the subconscious and the imagination which, he believed, had been repressed by rationalism, civilisation and progress. Breton used Freud's theories to inspire those willing to fight against a culture that he saw as threatened by the censoriousness of the superego.

In 1916, while working as a junior doctor in the neurology department of a hospital in Nantes, Breton met Jacques Vaché, whose anti-bourgeois attitudes were expressed through his profound admiration of the playwright Alfred Jarry and his nonsensical Dadaist antics. Breton, meanwhile, took a special interest in and kept records of the dreams and thought processes of mental patients. After Vaché's suicide in 1919, Breton and Philippe Soupault began work on a series of texts based on the technique of "free association", which was published later the same year under the title *Les champs magnétiques* (Magnetic Fields). This is now regarded as the first-ever manifestation of *écriture automatique*, described by Breton

OPPOSITE
Max Ernst
The Fugitive, Natural History, sheet 30, 1925
Frottage, pencil on paper,
26 x 43 cm (10¼ x 17 in.)
Stockholm, Moderna Museet

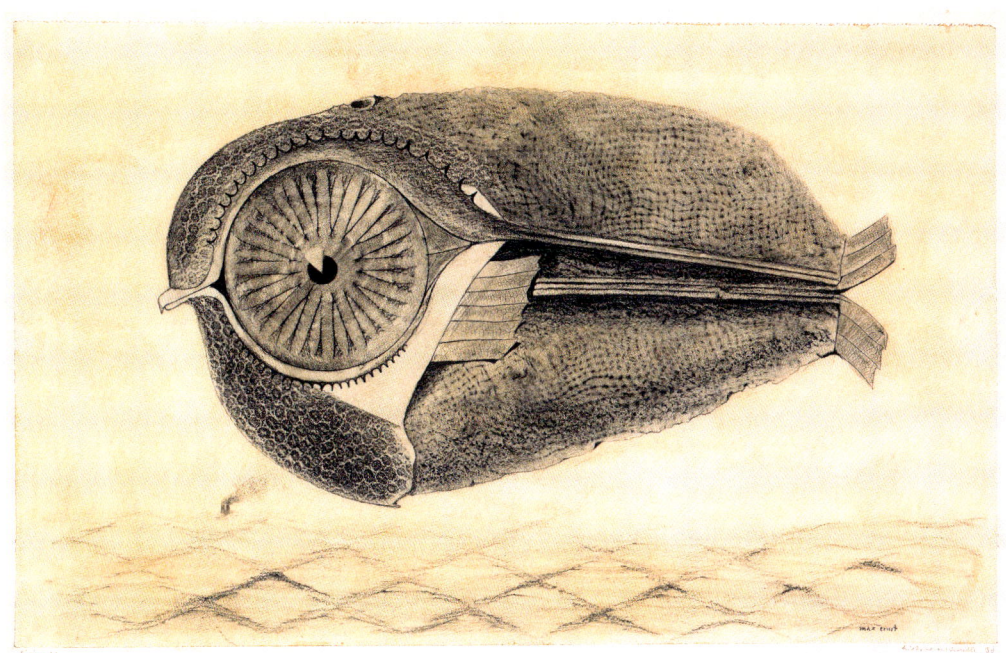

in the first *Manifesto*: "Completely occupied as I still was with Freud at that time, and familiar as I was with his methods of examination which I had some slight occasion to use on some patients during the war, I resolved to obtain from myself what we were trying to obtain from them, namely, a monologue spoken as rapidly as possible without any intervention on the part of the critical faculties, a monologue consequently unencumbered by the slightest inhibition and which was, as closely as possible, akin to *spoken thought*."

The Chance Meeting of a Sewing Machine and an Umbrella on an Operating Table

The significance of the method of "automatic writing", so often mentioned in the same breath as Surrealism, is far more symbolic than practical. To the writer, *écriture automatique* stands for the need to allow creativity to feed on the deepest levels of the unconscious, on dreams and hallucinations, and at the same time to exclude rational thought as far as possible. Those engaged in the fine arts introduced practices, which, according to the medium used, plumbed new, non-rational sources of inspiration for creativity. In his 1934 treatise "What is Surrealism?" Max Ernst recalled how hard it was in the beginning for painters and sculptors to find ways of working that corresponded to *écriture automatique* and to use the techniques at their disposal to achieve poetic objectivity, namely to banish reason, taste and conscious will from the creative process. Theoretical investigations were of no help; only practical experiments would do. Ernst described Lautréamont's "chance meeting of a sewing machine and an umbrella on an operating table" as a well-known, almost classic example of the phenomenon discovered by the Surrealists, which involved bringing together two or more seemingly incompatible objects on an incompatible surface. This could provoke "the most powerful poetic detonations". Countless individual and collective experiments had proved the usefulness of this procedure. It had also become clear, said Ernst, that the

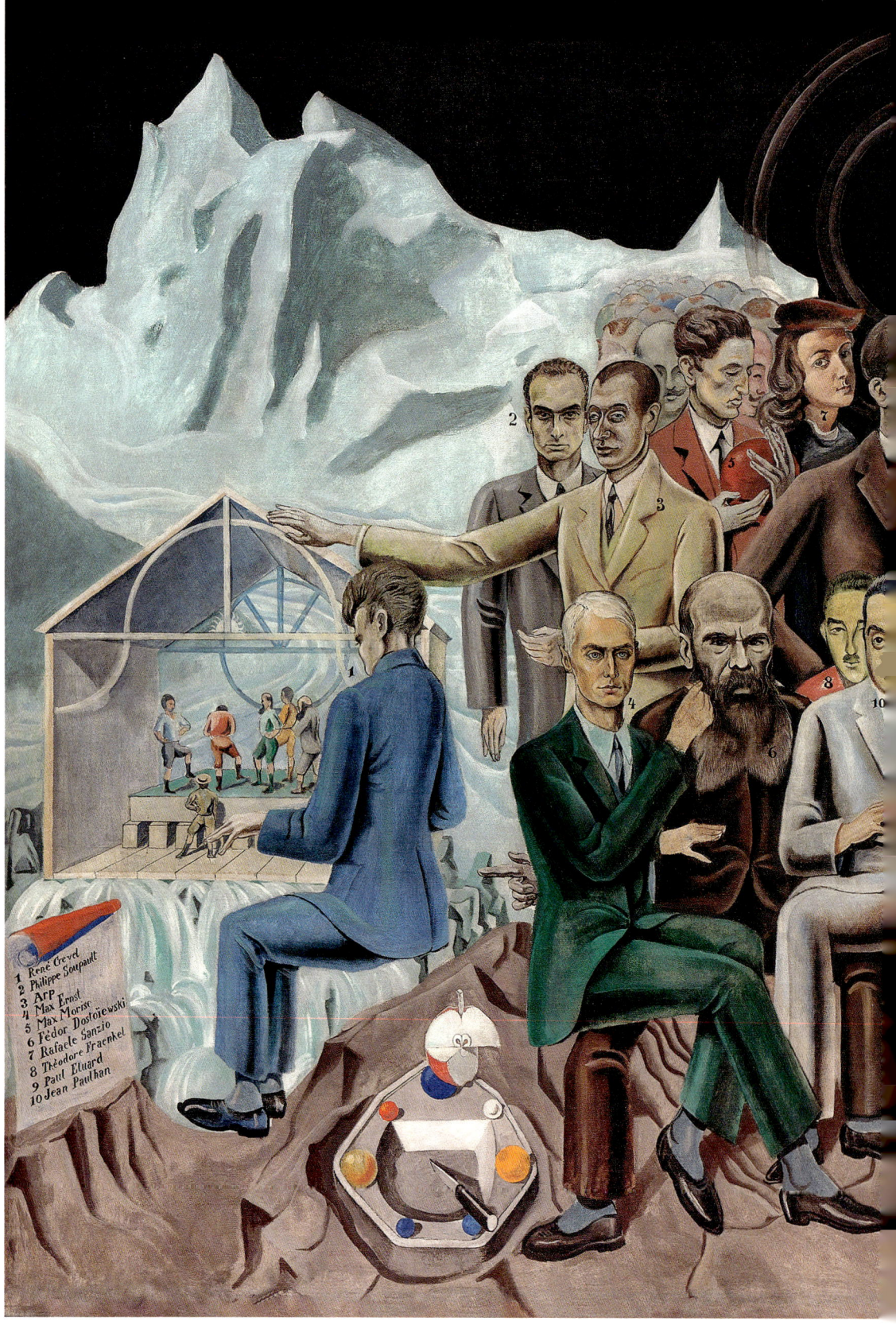

1 René Crevel
2 Philippe Soupault
3 Arp
4 Max Ernst
5 Fédor Dostoïewski
6 Rafaele Sanzio
7 Théodore Fraenkel
8 Paul Eluard
9 Jean Paulhan
10 Jean Paulhan

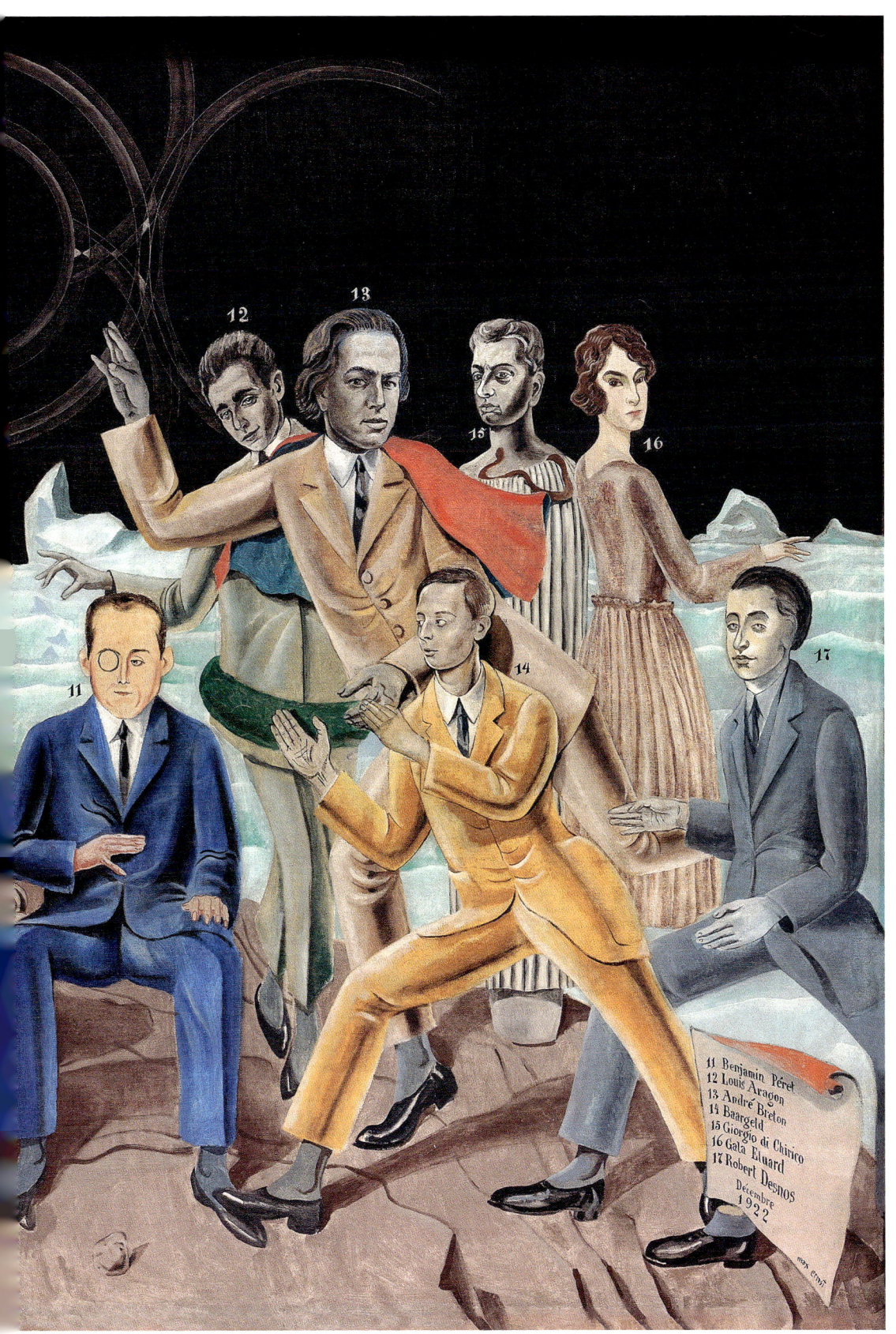

11 Benjamin Péret
12 Louis Aragon
13 André Breton
14 Baargeld
15 Giorgio di Chirico
16 Gala Eluard
17 Robert Desnos
Décembre
1922

PAGES 212/213
Max Ernst
Rendezvous of the Friends, 1922
Oil on canvas,
130 x 195 cm (51¼ x 76¾ in.)
Cologne, Museum Ludwig

PERSONS DEPICTED:
1. René Crevel 2. Philippe Soupault
3. Hans Arp 4. Max Ernst 5. Max Morise
6. Fyodor Dostoevsky 7. Rafael Sanzio
8. Théodore Fraenkel 9. Paul Éluard
10. Jean Paulhan 11. Benjamin Péret
12. Louis Aragon 13. André Breton
14. Johannes Theodor Baargeld
15. Giorgio de Chirico 16. Gala Éluard
17. Robert Desnos

more arbitrarily the elements were brought together, the more dramatic and poetic the results.

A typical example of this process is collage, of which Max Ernst was the principal exponent. As early as 1919, when the artist was still a leading light among the Cologne Dadaists, he discovered the hallucinatory effects of combining graphic elements from different contexts. Clippings from department-store catalogues, anatomical diagrams and old etchings provided the raw materials for his collages. He cut them up, re-mixed them and presented surprising combinations against a new background. Replying to demands for a purely technical definition of collage, Ernst wrote in "What is Surrealism?" "While feathers make plumage, glue does not make collage."

For him, the process went far beyond the realm of the visual. It was a paradigm of the Surrealist mindset. "A ready-made reality, whose naïve purpose seems to have been fixed once and for all (an umbrella), finding itself suddenly in the presence of another very distant and no less absurd reality (a sewing machine) in a place where both must feel out of their element (on an operating table), will, by this very fact, escape its naïve purpose and lose its identity; because of the detour through what is relative, it will pass from absolute falseness to a new absolute that is true and poetic: the umbrella and the sewing machine will make love. The way this procedure works seems to me to be revealed in this very simple example. A complete transmutation followed by a pure act such as love will necessarily be produced every time that the given facts – the coupling of two realities which apparently cannot be coupled on a plane which apparently is not appropriate to them – render conditions favourable."

In 1936, when Max Ernst expressed these thoughts on collage in his essay "Beyond Painting", he also recognised in retrospect how important the technique of mixing objects and ideas had been to the artistic and intellectual development of Surrealism. Collage had succeeded in making irrationality part of every branch of art, poetry and even science and fashion. With the help of collage, he said, the irrational had found its way into our private and public life. Without collage, the Surrealist film would have been unimaginable. Moreover, its influence on the further development of Surrealist painting, especially the works of Magritte and Dalí, should not be underestimated.

In 1925, Max Ernst discovered frottage, an activity popular with children which, like collage, allowed plenty of room for the unexpected in the creative work of the artist. It involved rubbing a pencil or almost-dry paintbrush on paper or textile placed over an object with an uneven surface, revealing the texture of the underlying object. The use of this technique is referred to in the creation of *Histoire Naturelle* (ill. p. 211). Writing over a decade later in "Beyond Painting" (1936), Ernst was as enthusiastic as he had been about collage. Frottage was a semi-automatic process that intensified the painter's visionary capabilities and had a more marked effect on the image produced than the conscious, active intervention of the artist, he said. "My curiosity being aroused and struck with amazement, I came to use the same method to question all sorts of materials that happened to enter my visual field: leaves and their veins, the ravelled edges of a piece of sacking, the knife-strokes of a 'modern' painting, a thread unwound from a spool of thread, etc." These in turn revealed "human heads, animals, a battle that ended with a kiss". The rubbing process intensified the artist's mental capacity while blocking off all conscious controls such as reason, taste or morality and restricting to the minimum the active role of the person who would once have been called "creator".

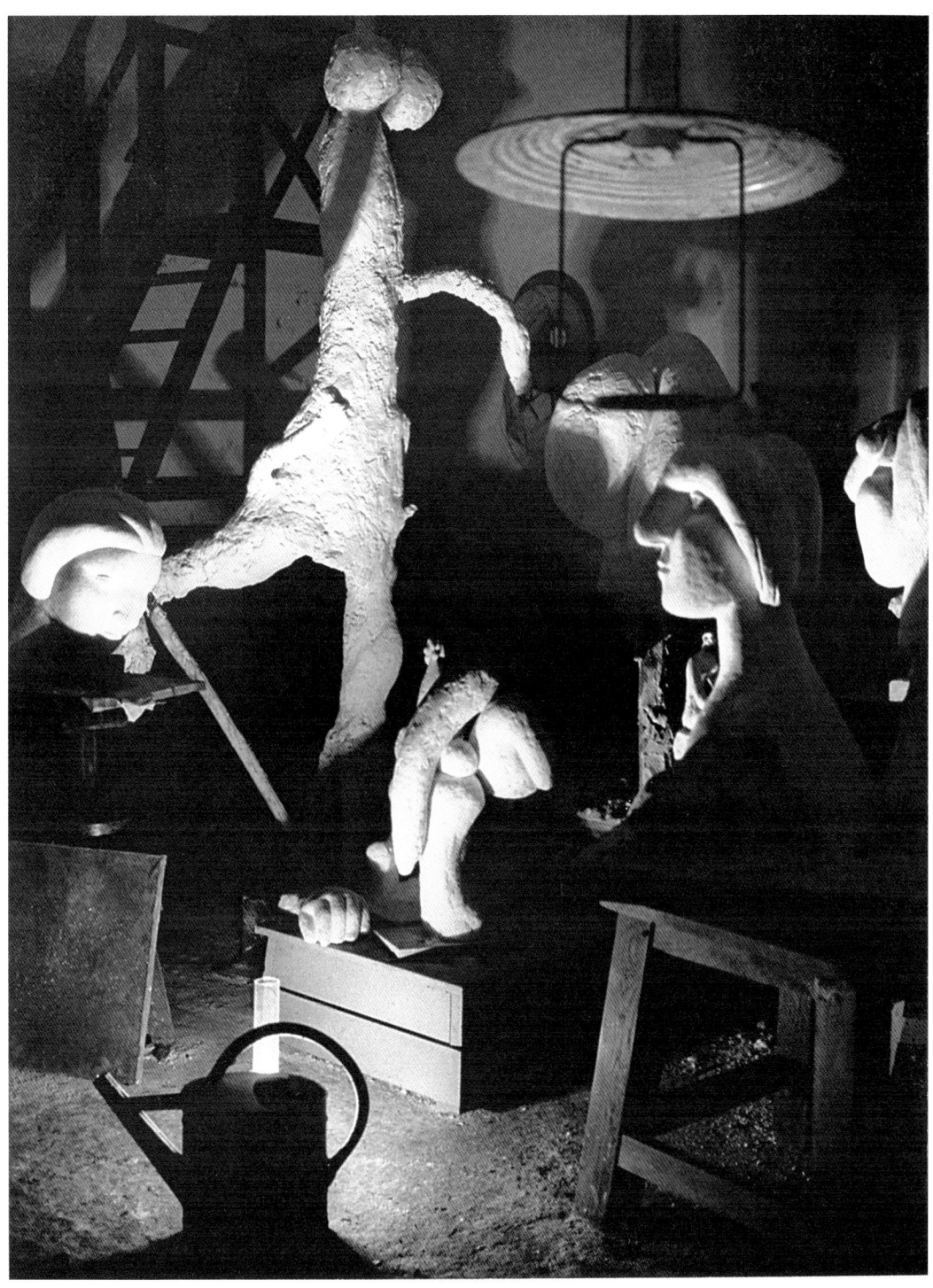

Brassaï
*Pablo Picasso's Studio at
Boisgeloup by Night*, 1932

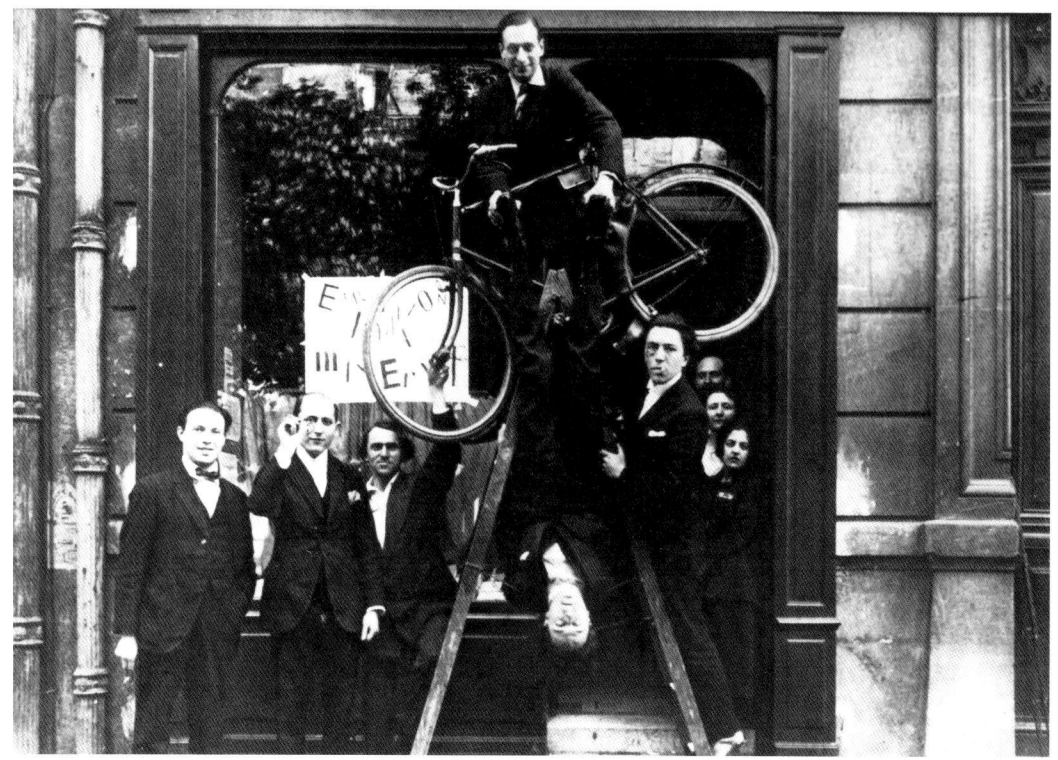

"Dada Max Ernst"
Opening of the exhibition in the
Galerie Au Sans Pareil, Paris, 2 May 1921

FROM LEFT TO RIGHT
René Hilsum, Benjamin Péret, Serge
Charchoune, Philippe Soupault, Jacques
Rigaut (head down), André Breton

A "Bureau for Surrealist Research"

The Surrealists' activities were not confined to literature, poetry and the fine arts. Shortly before the publication of the first *Manifesto of Surrealism* in 1924, the Bureau for Surrealist Research opened in the rue de Grenelle in Paris and later placed the following revealing advertisement in the *La Révolution surréaliste*, the Surrealist journal that also began publication in 1924. "The Bureau for Surrealist Research using all appropriate means aims to gather all the information possible related to forms that might express the unconscious activity of the mind." The description in Louis Aragon's essay "Une vague de rêves" underlines the fact that this was an initiative aimed at putting Surrealism to practical use: "We've hung a sculpture of a woman from the ceiling of an empty room, where every day worried men, bearers of heavy secrets, happen by … The visitors, whether born in faraway climes or on our doorstep, contribute to the elaboration of this formidable war machine designed to kill and help decide what can and cannot be achieved. At 15 rue de Grenelle, we have opened a romantic refuge for unclassifiable ideas and single-minded revolts. Whatever hope lives on in this desperate world will turn its last delirious gaze toward our pathetic little shop. Somehow we must put together a new Declaration of the Rights of Man."

The people who formulated the idea of comprehensive social renewal appear in a group photograph taken by Man Ray in December 1924 (ill. p. 230/231). We see the Surrealists under the sculpture mentioned by Aragon, in front of a painting by de Chirico.

Surrealism and Painting

Giorgio de Chirico, whom Breton described in the 1924 manifesto somewhat ambiguously as "so admirable for so long", was one of the first painters to attract Breton's attention when the Surrealists broadened their initial focus on literature and poetry to include the fine arts.

In 1925 Breton began publishing, in serialised form, a history of modern painting in *La Révolution surréaliste*. He had come across de Chirico while researching the connections between modern art and Surrealism, and single examples of the painter's early works had appeared in the magazine. Breton's attitude to de Chirico turned to disapproval after the artist moved away from *Pittura metafisica*. Nonetheless, at least before he "fell from grace" by returning to a naturalistic style of painting, Breton was eager to get him on board with the Surrealists. He saw de Chirico's work as fulfilling his main criteria for "Surrealism in painting", a deliberate turning away from reality.

Writing of de Chirico, Breton said that the artist's greatest folly was to have strayed over to the side of an army laying siege to a city, which he himself had built and made impregnable. It would forever resist him as it has so many others with its terrible forces, for that is how he meant it to be. What happened there could not happen elsewhere. How often, Breton continued, had he himself tried in his imagination to find his way around those buildings and to picture the eternal sunrise and sunset of the spirit, the mysterious chronology of the colonnades, the ghosts, the lay figures and the inner spaces.

Mysteriousness and unreality were terms that could not necessarily be applied to Picasso, many of whose works appeared in *La Révolution surréaliste*. Breton was careful not to call Picasso a Surrealist in so many words. But could not Picasso's work be seen as going beyond painting, thereby proving that there was such a thing as Surrealist painting? If Breton acknowledged that painting had the same powers of expression as language, if he recognised that a new direction had been forged from the moment the painter ceased to reproduce the external world and concentrate instead on his inner visions, was he not defining a wider framework for painting as a Surrealist statement?

Obviously Breton was aware how significant Picasso's admittance to the Surrealist camp would be for the popularity of the movement. In his book "Surrealism and Painting", published in 1925, he commented in some detail on Picasso, writing with admiration of the artist's "rebelliousness" and of the studio in which "divinely unusual" figures were fashioned. While some had claimed that there

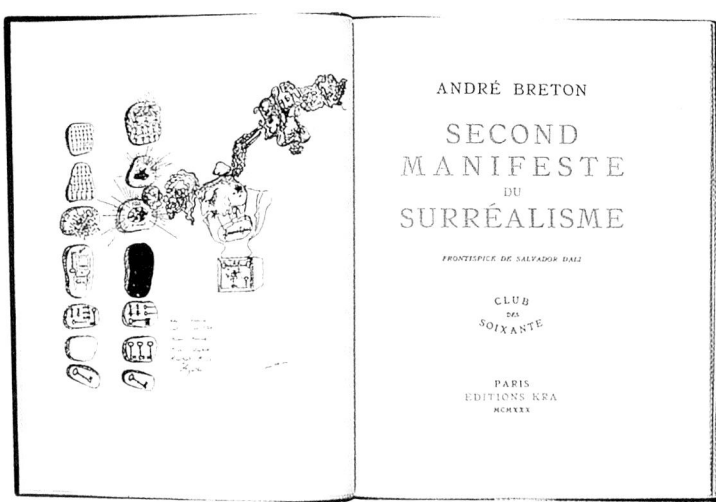

André Breton
Second Manifesto of Surrealism, 1930
Original edition
Paris, Bibliothèque Paul Destribats

could be no such thing as Surrealist painting, Picasso had lifted the spirit to its highest level, said Breton, going far beyond mere protest.

The Surrealists and the Artists Around Them

From 1920 an array of artists began to congregate around the Surrealists in Paris. Max Ernst, who had initiated or taken part in numerous Dadaist activities in Cologne, showed his first collages 1921 at Galerie Au Sans Pareil (ill. p. 216). In his 1936 treatise "Beyond Painting" he described these works as "the miracle of the complete transformation of living beings and objects, with or without change to their physical or anatomical form" – words that capture the surprising and, in the Surrealist sense, the mysterious nature of Ernst's creations. In the same year Max Ernst renewed contact with Paul Éluard, whom he had first met in Cologne, marking the beginning of a lasting friendship. Éluard acquired a series of early works from Max Ernst, who also painted important murals for Éluard's house in Eaubonne. Not only did the friendship between poet and painter survive a number of crises – Max Ernst travelled to Paris in 1922 on Éluard's passport and it was also thanks to Éluard that he was released from an internment camp in southern France at the beginning of the German occupation – but it also led to their collaboration on several Surrealist books, which sympathetically combined text and illustrations. The first of these, *Les malheurs des immortels* (Misfortunes of the Immortals), appeared in 1922. Further publications, like

Alberto Giacometti
Moving and Dumb Objects
In *Le Surrealisme au Service de la Révolution*, December 1931

Une semaine de bonté (A Week of Kindness), followed in the 1930s, testifying to the deep mutual understanding between Max Ernst and Paul Éluard and the close connection between literature and painting in Surrealism.

OBJETS MOBILES ET MUETS

Toutes choses... près, loin, toutes celles qui sont passées et les autres, par devant,

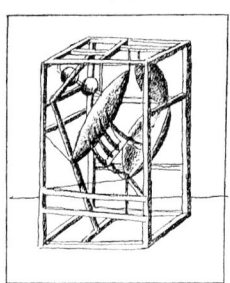 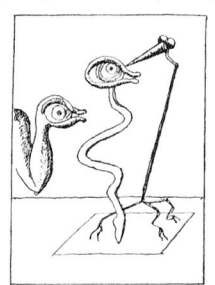

qui bougent et mes amies — elles changent (on passe tout près, elles sont loin), d'autres approchent, montent, descendent, des canards sur l'eau, là et là, dans l'espace, montent,

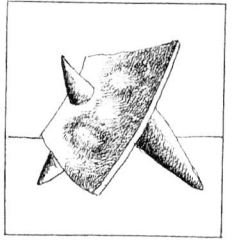 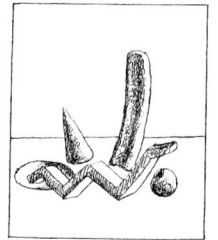

descendent — je dors ici, les fleurs de la tapisserie, l'eau du robinet mal fermé, les dessins du rideau, mon pantalon sur une chaise, on parle dans une chambre plus loin : deux ou

18

trois personnes, de quelle gare? Les locomotives qui sifflent, il n'y a pas de gare par ici,

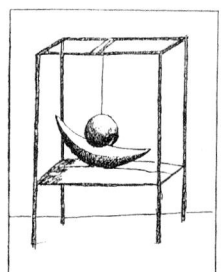 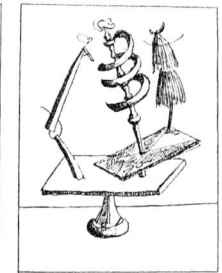

on jetait des pelures d'orange du haut de la terrasse, dans la rue très étroite et profonde — la nuit, les mulets brillaient désespérément, vers le matin, on les abattait — demain je sors —

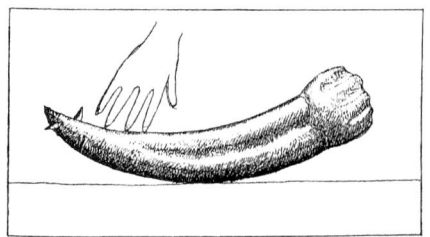

elle approche sa tête de mon oreille — sa jambe, la grande — ils parlent, ils bougent, là et là, mais tout est passé.

ALBERTO GIACOMETTI.

19

There were also other notable friendships, like that of the painter Yves Tanguy and Marcel Duhamel, publisher of the "Fantômas" novels that were held in high esteem by the Surrealists. For some time Tanguy and Duhamel shared a small house on the rue du Château in Paris. With Duhamel's financial support, Tanguy was able to devote himself to his artistic career. In 1927, the works of this self-taught painter were exhibited at the Galerie surréaliste in Paris. André Breton wrote the foreword for the exhibition catalogue.

In 1922 Tristan Tzara, who in 1916 was one of the co-founders of the Dada movement in Zurich, was enthusiastically taken up by the Surrealists. Tzara collaborated with Man Ray on *Champs délicieux* (Delicious Fields), a book that brought together Tzara's text and Man Ray's "Rayographs". In 1921, Man Ray invented the process he called Rayography. This was a photographic method whereby the object to be photographed was placed directly on light-sensitive paper to create a kind of shadow picture.

André Masson met Breton in 1924 following the artist's first solo exhibition at the Kahnweiler gallery. Masson's *dessins automatiques* – a designation based on Breton and Soupault's *écriture automatique* – had already appeared in early numbers of *La Révolution surréaliste*. Since the beginning of the 1920s, Masson had been one of a circle of friends which included Antonin Artaud, Robert Desnos and Michel Leiris, who met at his home on the rue Blomet. Next door to Masson's studio at 45, rue Blomet, was Joan Miró's apartment, as the two artists discovered quite by chance when they met at a party in 1923. "Masson was always a great reader and was full of ideas," said Miró recalling their friendship. "He was friendly with nearly all the young writers of the day. I came to know them through Masson … I found them more interesting than the painters I met in Paris. I was spellbound by the new ideas they advocated and above all by the literature they talked about. I spent nights devouring their ideas."

Some of the Surrealist painters and photographers were represented at an exhibition held from 14 to 25 November 1923 at the Galerie Pierre in Paris under the title "La Peinture surréaliste" (Surrealist Painting). They included Miró, Klee and Arp, as well as Picasso and de Chirico. It was the first group event to focus on painting and bring together the work of the leading Surrealists. They represented the first phase of Surrealism in painting as it took shape during its "heroic" period between the first *Manifesto* of 1924 and the second, published in 1929.

The most important intellectual concept was automatism, the graphic counterpart of free association with words, which led to the "abstract surrealism" of Masson, Miró and Arp, in which biomorphic, soft forms predominated along with sometimes extraordinary textural qualities. By contrast, the Surrealism of Magritte, Tanguy and Dalí, painters who only joined the movement later, was characterised by dream paintings.

However, the common denominator between them was their visionary, poetic and metaphorical treatment of their subjects. The Surrealists did not paint non-representational pictures. All Miró's, Masson's and Arp's works, however abstract they may appear, always relate to or at least suggest a subject. These artists continually tried to work towards an internal image which was either improvised through automatism or represented an inner vision.

Rendezvous of the Friends

A group portrait of the Surrealists entitled *Rendezvous of the Friends*, painted by Max Ernst in 1922 (ill. p. 212/213), shows the close contact between writers and painters, although the latter are less strongly represented in the picture. Along with Max Ernst himself, we see Hans Arp and de Chirico, as well as a self-portrait of Raphael inserted like a piece of collage. Surrealist writers and poets are joined by Fyodor Dostoevsky, mentioned by Breton in the first *Manifesto*, who appears as Raphael's literary counterpart. The subjects appear alienated, all of them looking in different directions with no contact between them. Johannes Baargeld appears to be taking long strides and making meaningless gestures, while Breton is behind him, staring straight at the spectator, his right hand raised as if bestowing a benediction on the group. Not least, this group portrait by Max Ernst, a snapshot of the year 1922, leads us to question how much cohesion there was between the various members and what it was that held them together.

Part of the answer to this question can be found in the Surrealists' many collective activities and their shared fascination with the same phenomena. They did things that always broke the usual bounds of existence, opening up areas of thought beyond rationality and reason, which were new, unknown and often funny. In 1926, they invented the game of *Cadavre exquis*, or "exquisite corpse", rather like "consequences" in which several people are involved in creating a sentence or a drawing on one sheet of paper. As it passes from hand to hand it is folded over so that no player can see what his predecessor has done. The prototype gave the now classic game its name: the first sentence that came about in this way contained the words: "Le – cadavre – exquis – boira – le vin – nouveau" (The exquisite corpse will drink the new wine).

Parisian Coffee Houses: Venues of the First Surrealist Scandals

Although membership of the group continually changed and the Surrealists' fields of interest expanded from purely artistic or literary issues to politics and social problems, a constant feature of the movement was the very specific group feeling of the Surrealists. Matta, who only joined the Surrealists in the 1930s, described this in a later interview. "We used to meet in the Flore," he recalled, "apart from us there was no one there – so it was always the same people. At that time we recognised that we were adopting a certain position. It wasn't that anyone demanded that one should behave in a certain way, like a guy who was out to destroy the whole structure of the bourgeois intelligentsia. It wasn't like that at all. It was much more that we were striving to achieve another kind of intellectual approach – a collective intellectual approach. The Surrealists had a strong group feeling – we worked out problems together. That was what was new."

The history of Surrealism gives the impression that certain subjects and issues always concerned the whole community. Whether it was about the case of Violette Nozière who murdered her father and whose cause was taken up by the Surrealists, or questions of sexuality or political commitment, or such phenomena as dreams, hallucinations and free associations, artists from every field always contributed ideas and works.

For its adherents, Surrealism was a way of life, a kind of existence that left room for playfulness and creativity. It was about living for the moment, with spontaneity and internal intellectual freedom and a lack of materialism, all of which were completely opposed to the values of the bourgeoisie. The Surrealists' preferred meeting place was the café. Their experiments in collective individuality took place in one of the typical big-city institutions that were the hallmark of the vibrant life of the French capital, anonymous and noisy, accessible to anyone at any time. The Surrealists met at the Café Certâ, at Le Petit Grillon in the Passage de l'Opéra or at Cyrano on the Place Blanche near Breton's apartment. The Cyrano had nothing in common with the artists' cafés in Montmartre and on the Left Bank, associated with Toulouse-Lautrec or Picasso's Blue Period. It was a favourite haunt of pimps, prostitutes, money-changers and drug dealers who, like the Surrealists themselves, went there after seeing a show at the Grand Guignol on the other side of the street. The Cyrano attracted the Surrealists as a place on the margins of society where they could mingle with outsiders and eccentrics.

Marcel Duchamp
Bottle Rack, 1914/1964
Readymade, galvanized iron, height
64 cm, Ø 42 cm (25¼, Ø 16½ in.)
Jerusalem, The Israel Museum

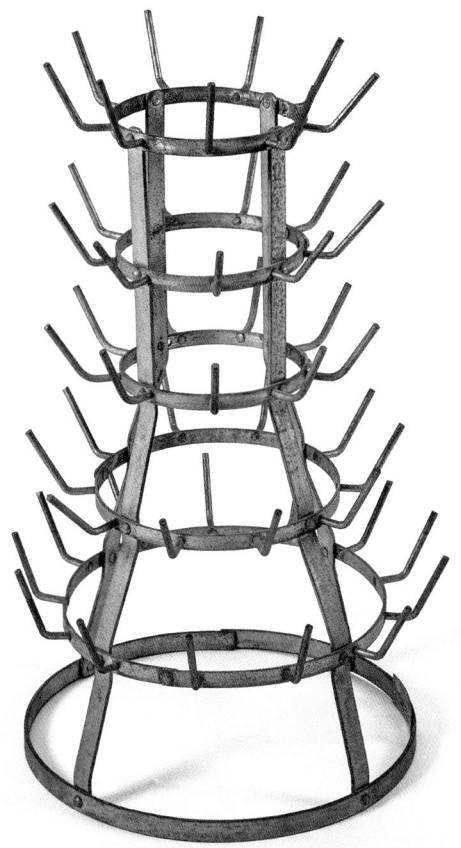

A café, the Closerie des Lilas on the Boulevard Montparnasse, was also the scene of one of the first scandals created by the Surrealists at the literary banquet of the "Mercure de France" in honour of the poet Saint-Pol-Roux on 2 July 1925. Tables were overturned, crockery trampled, the Surrealists screeched rousing slogans, blows were exchanged and windows smashed. A number of arrests were made.

On the day following these incidents, the committee of the *Société des gens de lettres* denounced the "scandalous behaviour of the Surrealists". They were also condemned by the committee of the *Association des écrivains combattants*, which declared they should be "held in contempt by the public" and critics vowed neither to mention their names nor to write the name of any movement ending in "ism".

The incident itself is characteristic of the Surrealists' anarchistic and anti-bourgeois attitudes. Their actions were an attack on established bourgeois order, designed to undermine all that was generally accepted and revered by respectable society.

Parents, Tell Your Children Your Dreams

By 1925 these largely Dada-inspired activities were abandoned in favour of a new agenda which was more political and more closely attuned to reality. The first step along the road was the foundation of the Bureau for Surrealist Research, although at first the bureau was mostly concerned with intellectual and literary matters. It was from here that the famous Surrealist *papillons* were distributed. These "butterflies" were small, brightly coloured handbills with headlines such as "Parents, tell your children your dreams" and "If you love love, you'll love Surrealism" which quickly became famous all over Paris.

To the bourgeoisie whose value system was being called ironically into question, these imaginative and entertaining activities did not represent any real affront. This was the view expressed by the Surrealist writer Pierre Naville in his reflections on the socio-political relevance of Surrealism.

Precisely because the Surrealist campaigns operated on the level of "morality" the social classes under attack could be sure that the manifestations of Surrealism would never be enough to destroy social or even moral values. There were only two alternatives – to persist with a negative, anarchistic attitude or steer decisively towards a revolutionary path, the path of Marxism. *La Révolution surréaliste* contemplated collaboration with the Communist periodical *Clarté* and in the late 1920s there were those among the Surrealists who had a definite involvement with Marxism.

All the members of the movement either approved of Marxism or at least stood on the political left. The word "revolution" in the title of the magazine *La Révolution surréaliste* had nothing to do with the Russian Revolution. The meaning was quite different and in many respects completely the opposite, for individuality was much more important to the Surrealists than communality. The new, political orientation naturally led to tensions within the group, predictably causing a crisis because of the contradictory tendencies within the movement, whose aim, according to Breton, was to give spontaneous

Salvador Dalí
Advertisement for the publication of the screenplay "Babaouo", 1932
Written by Salvador Dalí
Gouache and collage,
27 x 37 cm (10¾ x 14½ in.)
Private collection

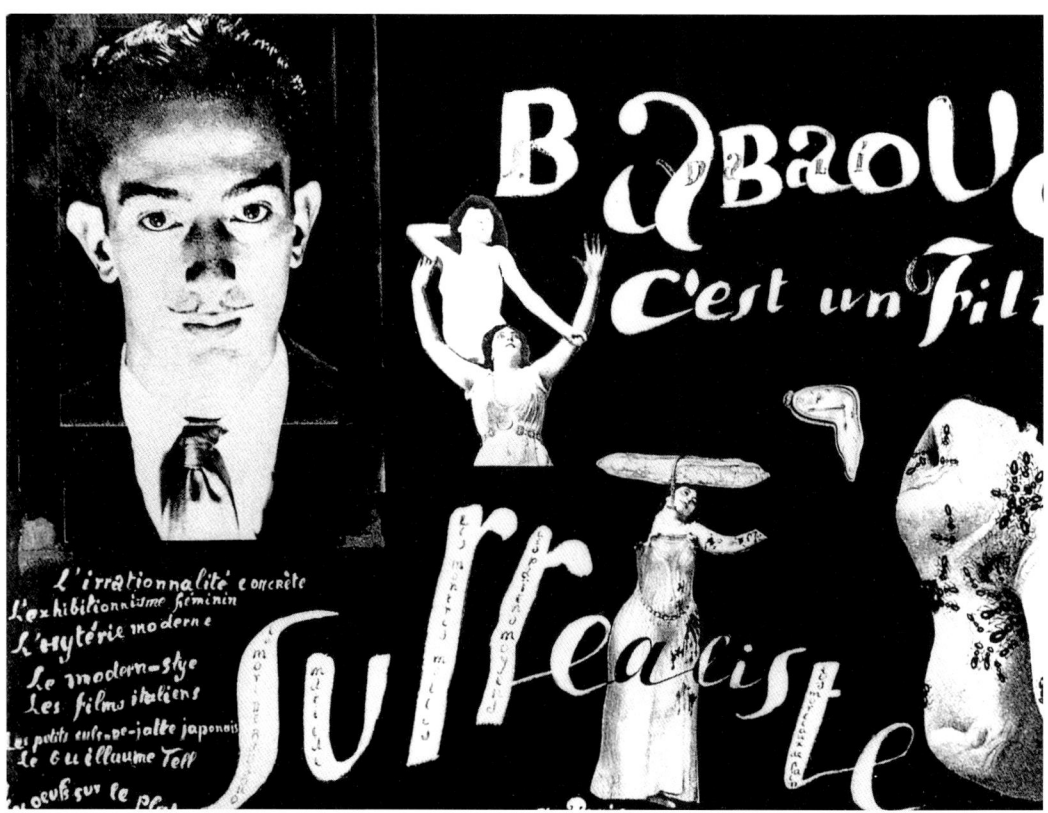

expression to the intellectual relationship between artists working independently. However, a group that carried out psychological and literary experiments, that published manifestos on current issues, that produced books and magazines, that organised rallies and staged art exhibitions could not really be said to work spontaneously. It needed a central organisation and must ultimately insist on an official intellectual stance.

"Leaving aside matters of detail, personal problems and incompatibility of opinions and capabilities which are bound to occur between individuals and which become even more acute between groups, it appears that at the moment it is possible to define a general intellectual position from which many of our activities derive, and also to see the danger that it might quickly and fundamentally change." So said Naville in his 1927 essay "Mieux et moins bien" (Better and Worse), which advocated co-operation with the Communist Party. Breton responded, claiming that Communism failed psychologically because it sought to persuade people to act, spurred on by the hope of a better life in the future. "There is not one of us who would not be happy to see power taken out of the hands of the bourgeoisie and handed over to the proletariat," he wrote in "Légitime défense" in 1926. "Meanwhile, however, it is just as necessary that our experiments relating to the interior life should continue, without any control from outside, including from the Marxist side."

Given the divergent individual points of view within the group, Breton's attacks on a number of Surrealist figures in his *Second Manifesto* of 1929 could not have been unexpected. Breton rejected poets and authors of the past, such as Baudelaire, Poe, Rimbaud and de Sade, previously seen as role models by the Surrealists. He also carried out a kind of purge and expelled, among others, Picabia, Tzara, Artaud, Soupault, Masson and Desnos from the movement. A meeting that Breton called at the Bar du Château in the rue du Château on 11 March 1929 to debate the fate of the exiled Trotsky was transformed into a courtroom drama in which the convictions of individual Surrealists were put on trial. Not only had Breton circulated a list of relevant questions to all those who sympathised with the group, but during the meeting he also read out in a condescending or offensive manner some of the answers given by absentees. The gathering degenerated into a discussion of the internal troubles of the Surrealist group, leaving unsolved the political question it had been called to debate.

Mysticism of the Inanimate

The tone of Breton's *Second Manifesto*, published in 1929, is so mystical and speculative it comes as no surprise that parts of the text are concerned with alchemy. Breton regarded himself as the heir to a tradition going back to Nicolas Flamel and the fourteenth-century alchemists. Now Surrealism was seeking the "philosopher's stone" that would enable the human imagination to "take brilliant revenge on the inanimate".

This change of direction launched the concept of the mystical qualities of inanimate objects that typified the later phases of Surrealism, so clearly expressed in Magritte's paintings. From the "revelation of the remarkable symbolic life of quite ordinary, mundane objects" which Breton demanded in the *Second Manifesto* – it was only a small step to the creation by the Surrealists of their own objects.

In 1936 an "Exposition surréaliste d'objets" (Surrealist Exhibition of Objects) took place at the Galerie Charles Ratton in Paris. The exhibition focused on the mystification of everyday things that the Surrealists constantly promoted, and presented extraordinarily complex configurations of unrelated objects. In a photograph of an installation at the exhibition we see a showcase containing a series of disparate artefacts, bewilderingly arranged side by side. In the middle is Marcel Duchamp's *Bottle Rack* (ill. p. 221), an everyday object declared a work of art, created in 1914. To its left is a 1934

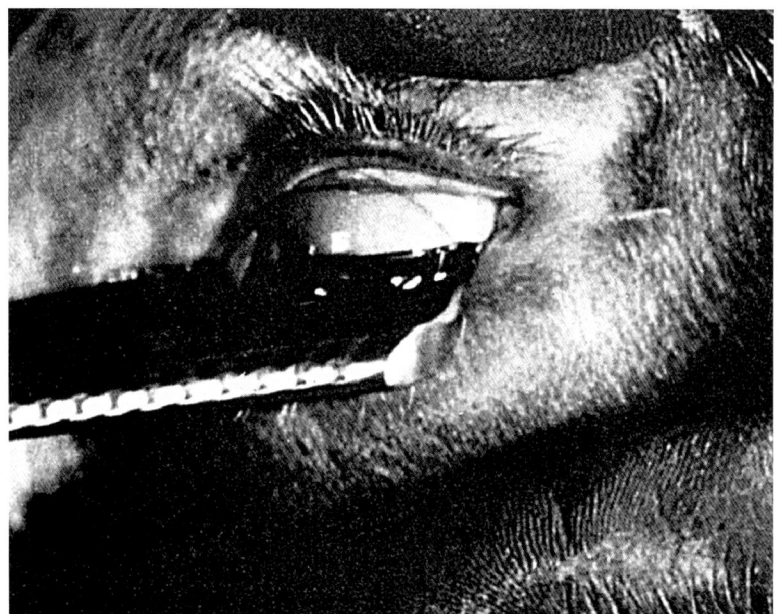

sculpture by Max Ernst and nearby Meret Oppenheim's *Fur Breakfast*, made in the same year as the exhibition, alongside African sculptures, *objets trouvés* and complicated wire constructions.

If we read Salvador Dalí's thoughts on single examples of these inventions and the Surrealist object in general, it becomes clear that in the 1930s the awakening interest in the object was closely bound up with a perplexing and convoluted Surrealist method – largely influenced by Dalí himself – of exploring the subconscious. In the December 1931 issue of the magazine *Le Surréalisme au service de la révolution* Dalí published a series of drawings introduced by an absurd but poetic classification system. For example, Dalí distinguished between the "symbolically functioning object" (of automatic origin), the "transubstantiated object" (affective origin) and "objects to project" (oneiric origin). The first of these he described as "an object which lends itself to a minimum of mechanical functions and is based on phantasms and representations liable to be provoked by the realisation of unconscious acts. The realisation of acts, the pleasure of which is inexplicable, or which tell us about the false theories hatched by censorship and repression. In all cases analysed, these acts respond to clearly manifested fantasies and desires." Dalí's decidedly objective description of complex, puzzling and even absurd-looking objects finds its counterpart in a series of drawings of objects by Giacometti (ill. p. 218) which also appeared in the December issue of *Le Surréalisme au service de la révolution* accompanied by the artist's own dreamlike and poetic text. Here, too, the text and the visual images stood in strong contrast to each other, although in this case the text was the more bizarre.

Salvador Dalí's "Paranoid-Critical Method"
Along with Alberto Giacometti and René Magritte, Salvador Dalí was one of the artists who shaped the Surrealist movement in the 1930s. His "paranoid-critical method" led to new departures in art, producing astonishing results, especially in the realm of the Surrealist object.

Dalí's concept of critical paranoia made an important contribution to the mystification of the mundane. As André Breton put it: "The uninterrupted transformation of the object under the paranoiac's scrutiny permits him to regard the very images of the external world as unstable and transitory, if not as suspect, and it is, disturbingly, in his power to impose the reality of his impression on others." In Dalí's art, this power is expressed in what has been described as "three-dimensional colour photography of the superfine images of concrete irrationality entirely made by hand". Dalí had a unique way of observing and distorting the world around him that, as the photographer Brassaï recalled in a 1964 memoir, permeated reality with mysterious and previously undiscovered dimensions. Brassaï recounts how he and Dalí worked together on *The Phenomenon of Ecstasy* and "involuntary sculptures" – bus tickets, screwed-up metro tickets, bits of soap and cotton wool, shaped by automatism.

Breton, too, had an innocent, unbiased and even distorted view of the real world. One of his greatest and most profitable pleasures seems to have been rummaging around flea markets. He recalled one such expedition when he and his companion were impressed by a metal half mask – something they had never seen before. It occurred to Breton that this rigid object that seemed to serve no particular purpose might be a thing of noble lineage, the result of a romantic encounter between the helmet of a medieval knight and a velvet half-mask.

In his astounding and at times almost unfathomable paintings René Magritte also explored the enigmatic world of everyday things and the magical effect of placing familiar objects in new contexts, an effect that is not always obvious at first sight. His specific contribution lies in the realm of language, or rather the visual representation of his musings on the links between words and images. In the magazine *La Révolution surréaliste* in 1929, Magritte published a sequence of pictures to illustrate the particular problems arising from this relationship. The pictures were accompanied by captions such as "Some objects can do without a name" above a picture of a rowing boat, or "Sometimes a word serves only to designate itself" above the word "ciel" (sky) with a ring drawn around it, all of which engenders a feeling of unease that goes beyond pure intellectual uncertainty. What is called into question is the assumption that calling an object by its name is tantamount to taking possession of it. Magritte questions how we can grasp, understand, order and control the world when we can no longer be sure what things are called. In his word-picture paintings he uses the

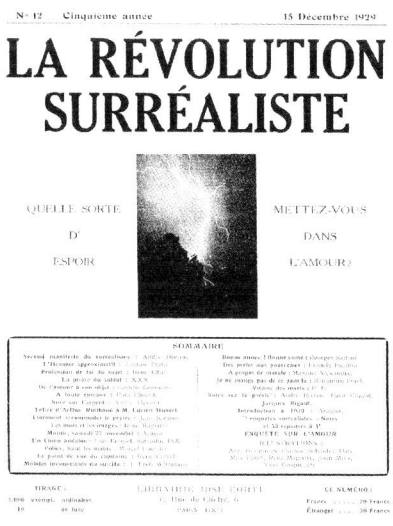

sense of insecurity triggered by the incorrect, unaccustomed naming of objects to alert the spectator to the complexity and absurdity of normality.

Minotaure

"One afternoon when I went to see Picasso, I caught him composing the first cover for *Minotaure* (ill. p. 227)," says Brassaï in *Conversations with Picasso*. "He had made an unusually felicitous montage. With thumbtacks, he attached to a block a piece of corrugated cardboard, similar to the pieces he was also using for his sculptures. On top of it, he placed one of his prints depicting the monster, and around it he arranged ribbons, lace made from silver paper, and slightly faded artificial leaves, which, he confided, came from an out-of-fashion hat Olga had thrown away. When this montage was to be reproduced, he was very insistent that the thumbtacks appear on it. It was under this splendid cover that, on 25 May 1933, the first issue of *Minotaure* appeared."

"At that time," Brassaï continues, "the Surrealist group was at a turning point. The first *Manifesto of Surrealism* was already nine years old. The scandals, the excesses and the quarrels were things of the past. Gone were the hopeless despair, the anger and the regular sabotage. They no longer talked of memorable meetings to discuss *écriture automatique*, the hypnotic trances, the accounts of dreams which, as Breton hoped, would inspire all future poetry. In a matter of a few years the mysterious source they believed to be infinite and 'accessible to all' was exhausted. In 1933 Surrealism was no longer a wild rebellion but a successful revolution whose activists had achieved power. With a new sense of responsibility, André Breton and Paul Éluard were trying to consolidate the foundations of the movement. Brassaï felt that even if the Surrealist spirit could be kept going through *Minotaure*, it must nevertheless cast off the aggressive attitudes which had previously been the hallmark of Surrealism. This glossy magazine whose print run was limited to 3,000 copies – 1,500 for further editions – was beyond the reach of proletarian purses and could only serve a milieu of rich, titled snobs, the first patrons and collectors of Surrealist works."

Brassaï's views about *Minotaure*'s arrival in 1933 were borne out by the fact that *Le Surréalisme au service de la révolution* had been founded in 1929 superseding *La Révolution surréaliste*, while the same year saw the publication of the first issue of Georges Bataille's *Documents*. The 1930s witnessed an upheaval in the movement, epitomised by the contradictory nature of its two official organs. The one supported confrontational Surrealism while the other placed emphasis on Surrealism as an art movement engaged in ongoing research.

Documents provided a platform for an international debate that covered all artistic genres. Georges Bataille's numerous contributions appeared alongside articles by Carl Einstein and Georges Babelon. Leading specialists wrote on ethnography and medieval art, and there were articles on Paul Klee, Pablo Picasso and Karl Blossfeldt. It was not simply a Surrealist journal but a publication whose style and range of topics would have been unimaginable without Surrealism. But the magazine also represented a new Surrealist tendency. There were striking differences between *Documents* and *La Révolution surréaliste*. The former's clearer page layout was a sharp contrast to the style of a purely informative scholarly journal, which *La Révolution surréaliste* consciously aspired to be. Also noticeable was the predominance of visuals, leaving poetry and literature fighting for space.

As well as the new-style Surrealist magazines, a new genre – Surrealist film – appeared on the scene in 1929 with the screening of Salvador Dalí and Luis Buñuel's *L'Âge d'or* and *Un chien andalou*. *Un chien andalou* contains the famous scene in which a razor blade slices through an eyeball (ill. p. 224), an image that inspired Georges Bataille to write reflectively in *Documents* in 1929, "The eye, which Stevenson so exquisitely calls a 'cannibal dainty', is for us an object so disturbing that

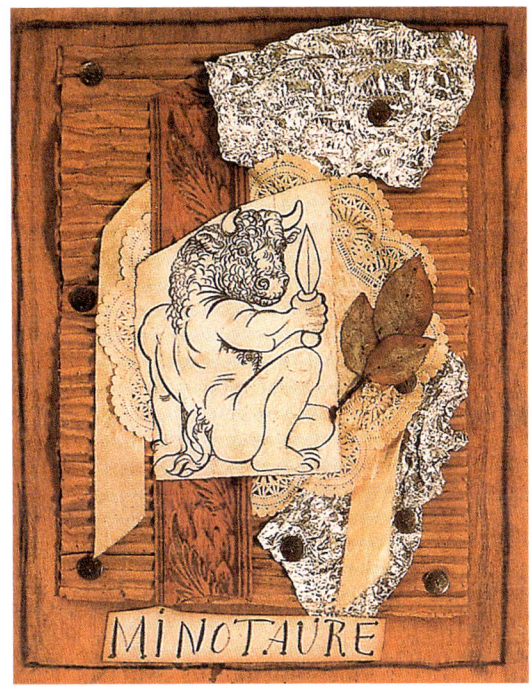

Pablo Picasso
Minotaure
Title page of the first edition,
15 February 1933

we will never bite it. The eye also occupies an elevated position in horror, being among other things the eye of the conscience. We are also well acquainted with Victor Hugo's poem, the obsessed and lugubrious eye, the living eye so terrifyingly dreamt by Grandville in the course of a nightmare shortly before his death …"

Surrealism – Thought Dictated in the Absence of All Control?

With Surrealism well into its second decade, Bataille here sums up the important aspects of Surrealism and the visual arts. Compared with other avant-garde movements of the first half of the twentieth century Surrealism was attempting to move beyond the definition of the visual image and its function. Physiological sight and the normal functioning of the eye are meaningless. Imagination and the ability to look inwards are crucial. In this sense the eye can be personified and behave like a nightmarish apparition. The act of seeing is subject to new conditions and so too is Surrealist art, which is the product of the inner voice, visual hallucination and dreams.

Decalcomania was one of the last manifestations of the Surrealist myth. This was a kind of printing technique that involved spreading paint onto a flat surface, pressing a piece of paper or canvas onto the coated area, and then separating the two. The resulting pattern could be altered, transformed into a new composition, or left as it was as a work of art in its own right.

Whether the artist used paper for this new technique, as its inventor Óscar Domínguez did or, like Max Ernst, preferred canvas, the process raised serious questions about the role of chance and the unconscious. For in most cases the result of this process, related to collage and frottage, was not, as Max Ernst claimed in 1936 in "Beyond Painting", achieved without the artist's conscious intervention. As *écriture automatique* was to the realm of literature so collage, frottage and decalcomania were to the plastic arts. They represented a concept that could not be translated into reality, or at least not in the sense that Breton preached in the first *Manifesto*, namely "thought dictated in the absence of all control exerted by reason, and outside all aesthetic or moral preoccupations". The methods the Surrealists chose to adopt in order to exclude rationality and reason from the creative process could only play an intermediary role. They could trigger associations, fantasies, and instinctive behaviour and could also include chance. However, the artist always translated these phenomena into a work of his own invention.

The concept of opening up the subconscious made it possible to think differently and to analyse and undermine the "advanced civilisation" of which the Surrealists were so critical. In this sense, what Surrealism, and in particular Surrealist painting, achieved had less to do with technical innovation than with a new understanding of art. What mattered to the Surrealists was not the perfect, self-contained work of art, but the procedure through which it was created and the ideas it conveyed. This focus on the subject of a painting, the thinking behind it and not least its title, without which the work would be incomprehensible – we only have to think of Magritte – explains why the Surrealists attached such importance to the relationship between painting and literature.

Surrealism saw itself as a movement embracing many artistic genres, a "thought factory" whose products were based on the attempt to address social, artistic or literary problems. It was a collective experience, which came to an abrupt end with the rise of Fascism and the outbreak of the Second World War, when many Surrealists were forced into exile.

After France capitulated, a number of them fled to the unoccupied zone, hoping to find their way to America. Supporters from the US got together to form the American Committee for Aid to Intellectuals. The organisation found accommodation for the refugees at a château near Marseilles and arranged their passage to the United States. Breton, Wifredo Lam, Masson and Claude Lévi-Strauss left for Martinique in Spring 1941. From there, Lam travelled onwards to Santo Domingo. The rest went to New York. In July 1941, Max Ernst also managed to leave for New York. By August 1941 Man Ray had already returned to the United States and soon afterwards settled in California.

By 1942 New York and its surrounding area had become the centre of Surrealist activity. It was a historically unique situation in which the Surrealists found themselves rubbing shoulders with other émigré artists like Chagall, Léger, Lipchitz and Mondrian. But it was impossible to recreate the atmosphere of Paris. They found it hard to keep in touch with one another. "We missed café life," Max Ernst later wrote. "We had artists in New York, but no art. One person alone cannot make art. It very much depends on being able to exchange ideas with others."

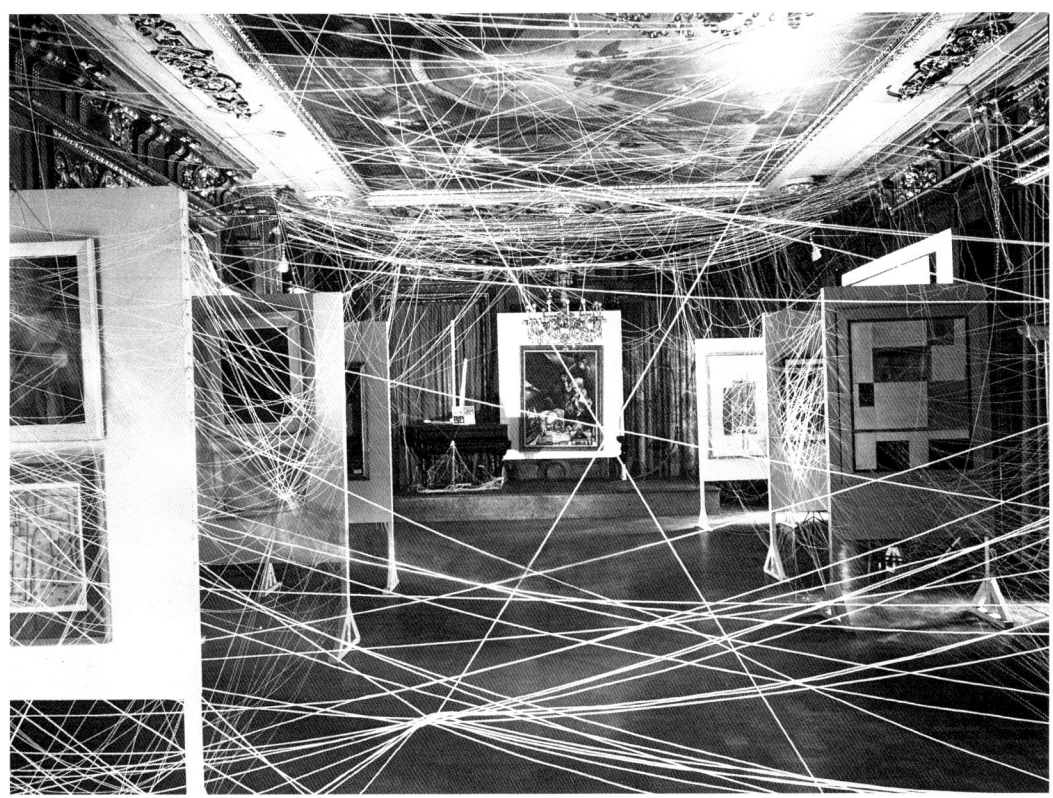

"First Papers of Surrealism",
October 1942
Installation in the exhibition,
451 Madison Avenue, New York
Philadelphia Museum of Art, Marcel
Duchamp Archive, Gift of Jacqueline,
Peter and Paul Matisse

PAGES 230/231
Man Ray
"Bureau for Surrealist Research"
At the premises of the Surrealist Centre,
rue de Grenelle, Paris, December 1924

FROM LEFT TO RIGHT, STANDING:
Charles Baron, Raymond Queneau, Pierre
Naville, André Breton, Jacques-André
Boiffard, Giorgio de Chirico, Roger
Vitrac, Paul Éluard, Philippe Soupault,
Robert Desnos, Louis Aragon
SEATED: Simone Breton, Max Morise,
Marie-Louise Soupault

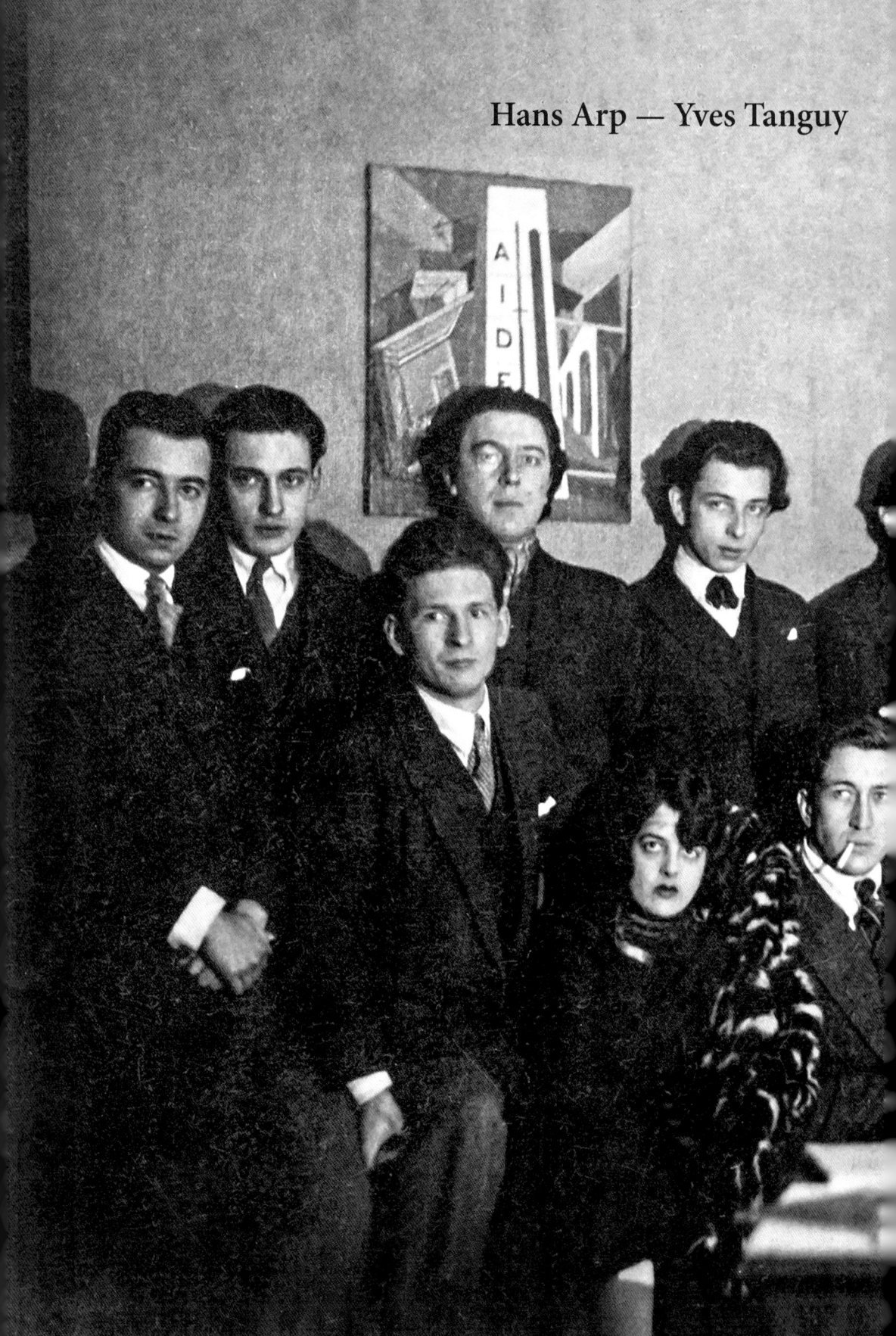

Hans Arp — Yves Tanguy

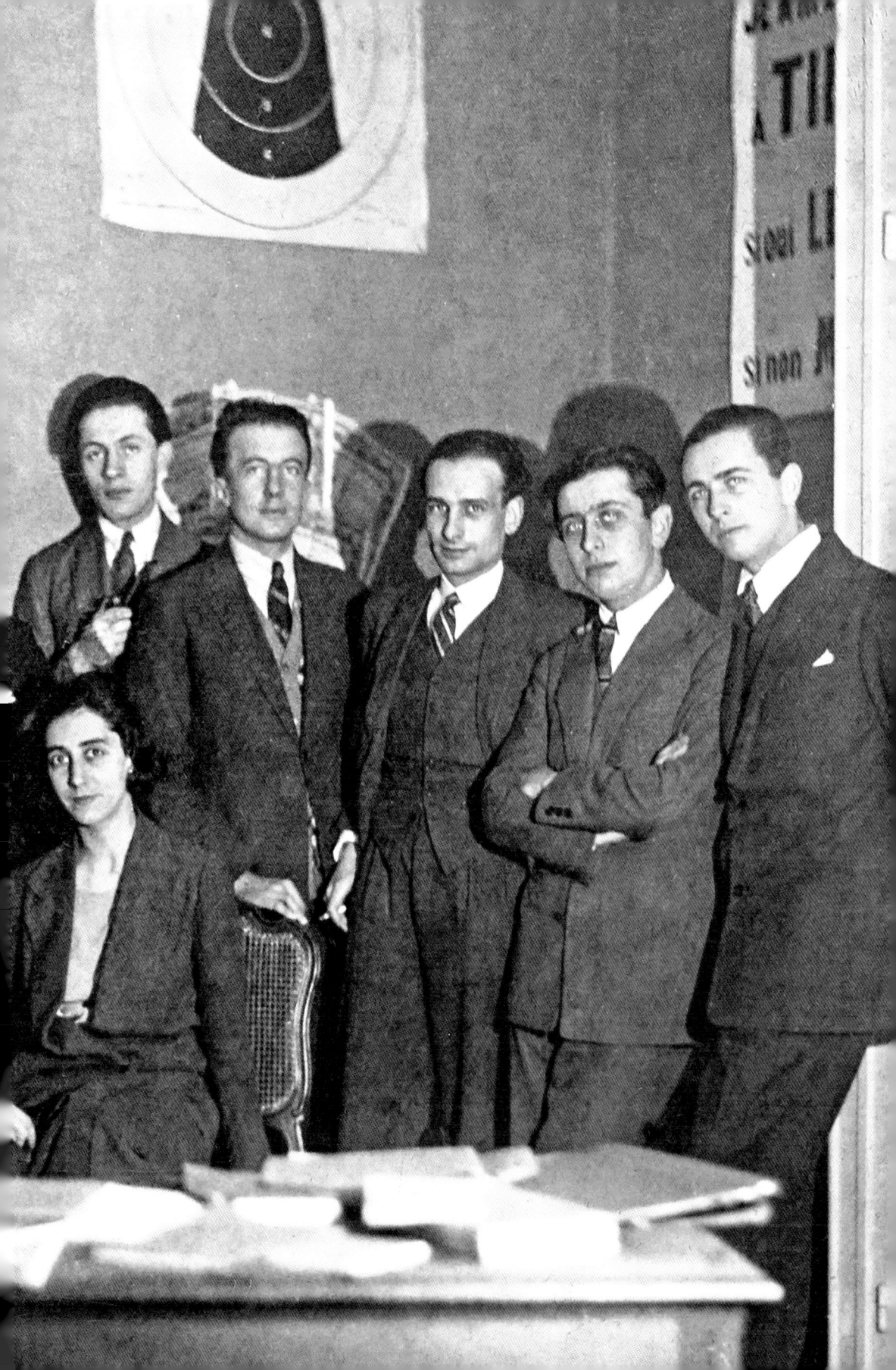

Hans Arp
Concrete Sculpture, 1934

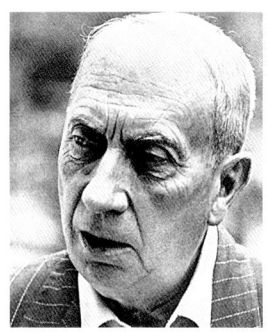

b. 1887 in Strasbourg, France
d. 1966 in Basel, Switzerland

For several years Hans Arp developed his art against the backdrop of the Surrealist movement in Paris. In 1916, he was one of the group, which included Hugo Ball, Richard Huelsenbeck and Tristan Tzara, who founded the Cabaret Voltaire in Zurich. In 1919/20 he was in Cologne where he was closely involved with the Dadaists based in the city, especially Max Ernst. In 1924, the year in which André Breton's first *Manifesto of Surrealism* was published, Arp finally joined the Surrealist movement, taking part in the first Surrealist exhibition in 1925. On this occasion he showed only pictorial works, since he only began sculpting in 1931, shortly before the creation in 1932 of the Abstraction-Création group of which he was co-founder.

Arp's work could be described as standing between two poles – Surrealism and Abstraction. His early collages are simple and austere and mainly concerned with the exploration of form. Meanwhile, the playfully poetic titles of his work owe more to the traditions of Dada and Surrealism. Arp's working methods allowed room for the "law of chance" and intuition, and his spontaneous, constantly innovative, creative processes were very much in line with Surrealist thinking.

Another aspect of his Surrealist-inspired work was his interest in the metamorphosis of the female body, which led to the creation of sculptures recalling Picasso's and Miró's soft and infinitely changeable forms of the early 1930s. A typical example is *Concrete Sculpture (Sculpture concrète)* from 1934 in which a trunk, head and the rounded stumps of legs, which appear to have evolved naturally but in condensed form, capture the sensuous shapes of a female torso. Designed to be free-standing, it can be viewed from several different perspectives.

It has no obvious top or bottom, front or back, as if to underline the idea that it is still in the process of taking shape. Arp saw this process that he called "concretion" as a natural occurrence, as opposed to the creation of a form chosen by the artist, which is a human as distinct from a natural act.

Concrete Sculpture is part of Arp's continuing exploration of this theme. One of the earliest examples from a series of "configurations" in relief dating from 1927/28 reduces the female body to parts of the shoulders, waist, hips and tops of the legs. A key element in the composition is the strategically placed navel. For Arp this was a symbol of life and fertility, but it does not feature in his 1929 relief of *Amphora Woman,* which shows a small feminine figure in front of a streak of red.

As it draws level with the little female shape, the streak broadens into a wide bowl shape, a recurring motif in Arp's work. This can be interpreted either as a peaceful, feminine refuge from the turmoil of life, or as the belly of a pregnant woman sheltering the embryo.

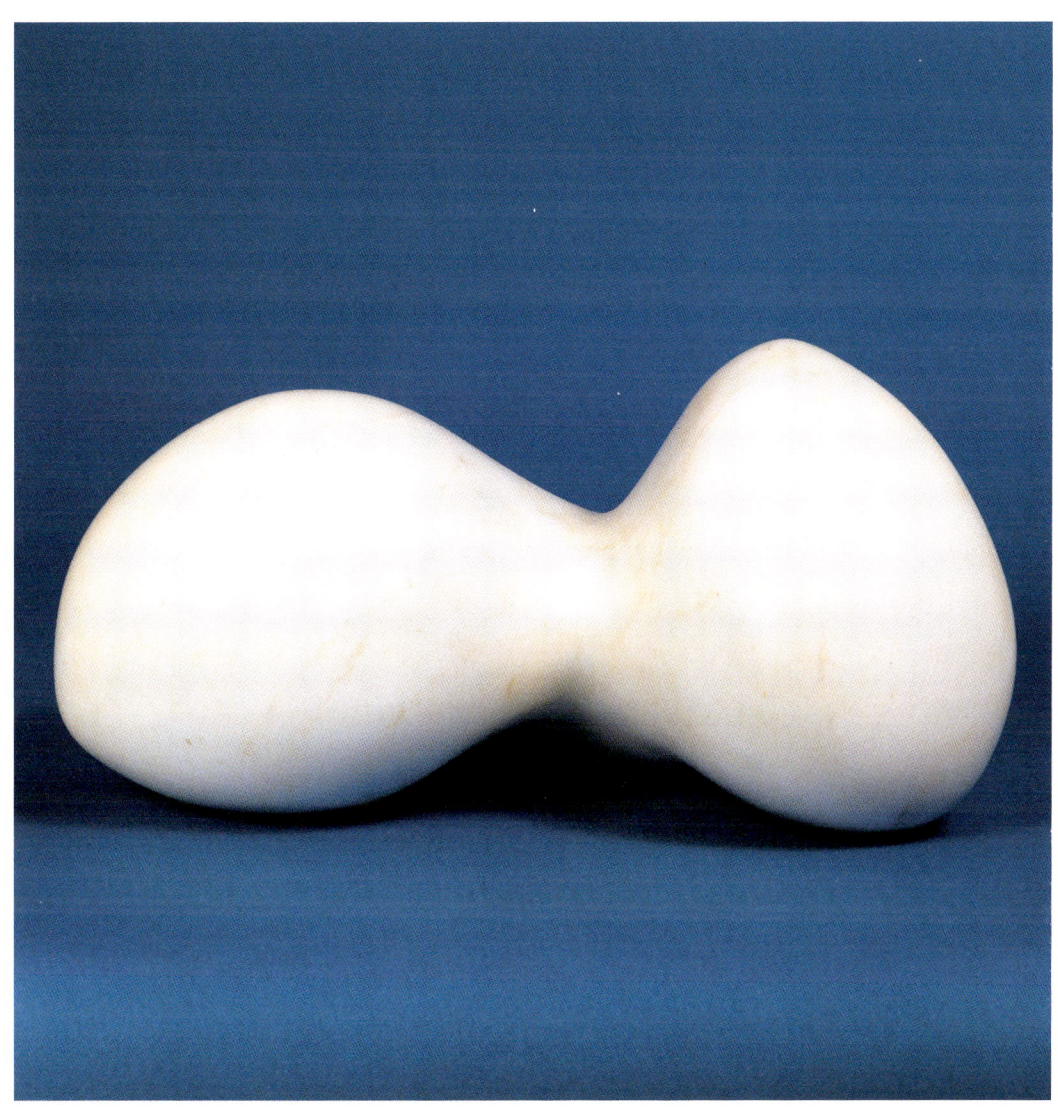

Concrete Sculpture, 1934
Marble, 37 x 75 x 32 cm (14½ x 29½ x 12½ in.)
Private collection

Hans Bellmer
The Doll, 1932/1945

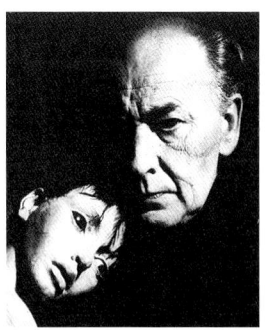

b. 1902 in Katowice, Poland
d. 1975 in Paris

Hans Bellmer created his first *Doll (Die Puppe)* in 1933. In the context of his artistic activities at the time, it was a unique and independent work, inspired by a variety of influences. With the rise of Fascism in Germany, Bellmer, who was then working as a graphic designer, decided to cease producing anything that could be of even indirect benefit to the state and to concentrate on his art. The doll was the result not only of that decision but also of Bellmer's meeting with his 15-year-old cousin Ursula. The artist was forced to resist the teenager's powerful erotic attraction and sublimated his desires in the creation of the doll.

In 1934, after the publication, at his own expense, of his essay "Die Puppe" (The Doll), Bellmer made contact with the Surrealists in Paris, prompted by an issue of the Surrealist magazine *Minotaure*. Over the next few years he studied the works of Baudelaire, Lautréamont and Jarry, the Surrealists' great literary role models. Then, in 1938, following the death of his wife Margarete, he finally left Berlin to settle in Paris.

Bellmer's first doll was brought to life mainly in the form of photographs taken by the artist. It was the only way in which he could present his creation in the many different poses into which it could be manipulated. However, on a visit to Berlin's Kaiser-Friedrich-Museum, Bellmer saw an articulated doll from the age of Albrecht Dürer, which inspired him to equip his own dolls with joints. The versatility achieved in this way is crucial to the example at the Pompidou Centre. In the words of German art critic Wieland Schmied, the doll appears "as a mirror image with the ball-and-socket joint situated at the navel – a monster with two pelvises, two pairs of legs, two pairs of feet in small, black, patent-leather children's shoes and a superfluous head, at once the stuff of fantasy and frighteningly real, capable of change yet always the same, innocent and knowing, childlike and depraved, vampire and succubus, an articulated construction of enormous intensity and at the same time one of the most convincing sculptures of our age".

Bellmer's central idea was the eroticization of the body, a body which – according to characteristic Surrealist thought processes – even in its absurd distortions, always reflects the same basic sexual pattern. "I think that the different categories of expression – posture, movement, gesture, action, sound, word, visual imagery, arrangement of objects – are all born of the same mechanism, and that their origin displays a similar structure. The basic expression, insofar as it is not from the outset intended as communication, is a reflex. To what need, what bodily urge might it respond? … The genitals project onto the shoulders, the leg naturally projects onto the arm, the foot onto the hand, the toes onto the fingers. And so a strange hybrid is created, of the real and the virtual, of what is permitted and forbidden to each of the two elements, of which the one acquires such reality as the other has forfeited."

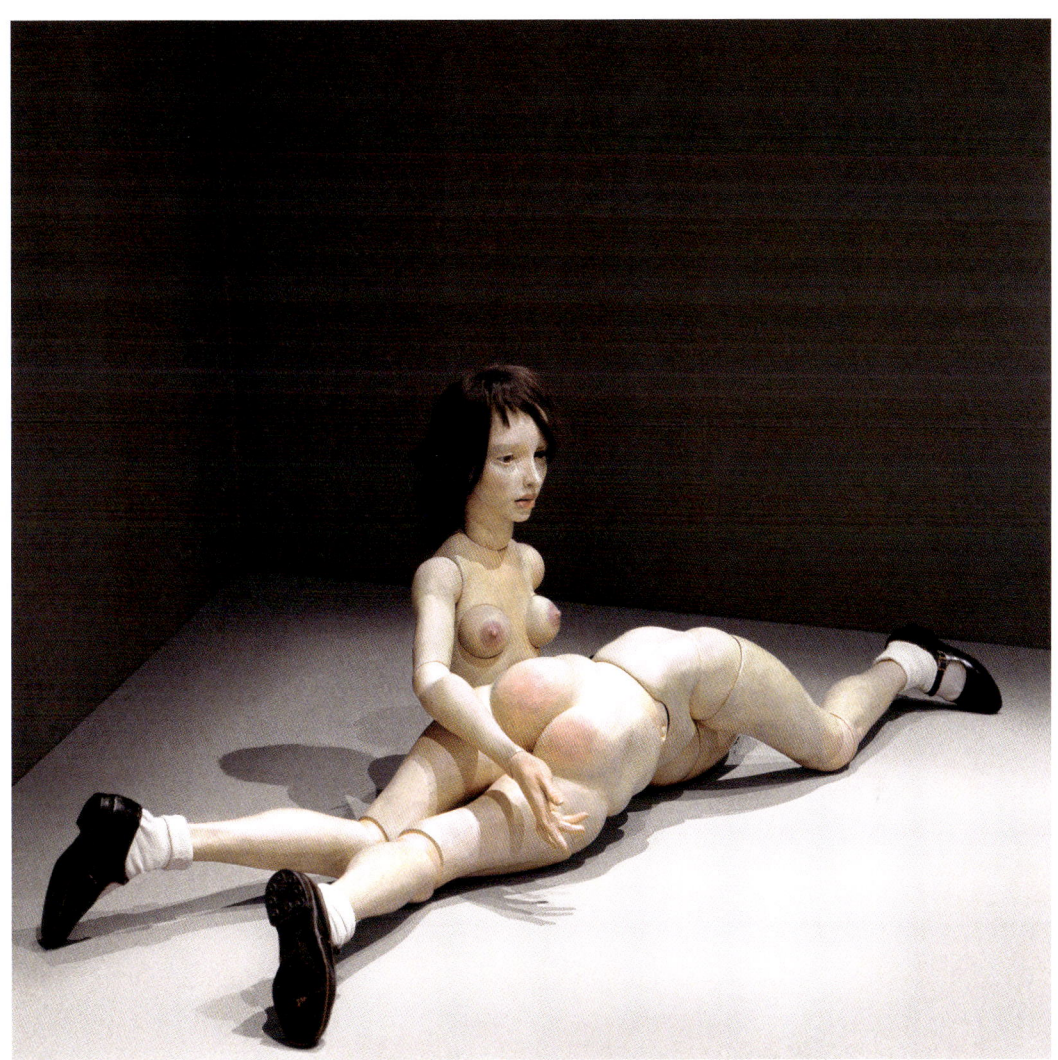

The Doll, 1932/1945
Painted wood, hair, socks and shoes,
61 x 170 x 51 cm (24 x 67 x 20 in.)
Paris, Musée national d'art moderne,
Centre Pompidou

Brassaï
The Image as Produced by Automatic Writing, 1934

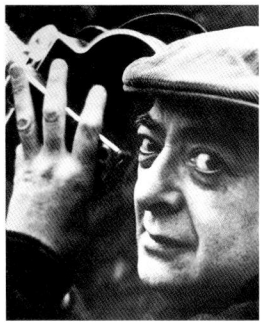

b. 1899 in Brassó, Hungary (now Brasov, Romania)
d. 1984 in Beaulieu-sur-Mer, France

Gilberte Brassaï
Brassaï with camera, 1955
Private collection

The series of photographs by Brassaï (Gyula Halasz) *Paris by Night* and *Secret Paris* show that, as far as themes and atmosphere were concerned, his work already had much in common with Surrealism. However, it was only later, at the beginning of the 1930s, that he began working directly with the Surrealists. On several occasions Brassaï's photographs were used to illustrate Breton's essays in the magazine *Minotaure*. One such was the abstract *Image as Produced by Automatic Writing (L'image, telle qu'elle se produit dans l'écriture automatique)*. The photo, whose title was intended as an allegory or symbol of "automatic writing", shows what looks like a feathery spider's web against a deep, dark background, which might be interpreted as electrically charged lightning against the night sky, or a plant floating in water. The fine fibres of the figure branch out in every direction and the image appears too complex, but at the same time too orderly, to be the work of a human hand – even when free of all rational control, which is the assumption behind automatic writing. Thus, a natural phenomenon is transformed into an image encapsulating notions of the irrational, the fortuitous and the uncontrolled, which were central to Surrealist thinking.

Similar ideas inspired a series of photographs entitled *Sculptures involontaires* on which Brassaï and Dalí worked together. The subjects are everyday bits and pieces that have been subjected to involuntary manipulation – torn bus tickets, rolled-up Metro tickets, carelessly screwed-up bits of paper, pieces of soap or squashed cotton wool. Photographed in extreme close-up and lit to magical effect, these mundane objects acquire an air of mystery. The unconscious process they have undergone seems to imbue them with a life of their own.

Light plays a crucial role in making Brassaï's photos so effective. The semi-darkness that dominates his shots engenders the same mysterious atmosphere and feeling of uncertainty that Surrealist artists deliberately set out to create. At first, any similarities with the Surrealist vision in Brassaï's photographs were purely unintentional, as he made clear in an anecdote recounted in conversation with Picasso. André Breton asked the photographer for some night-time shots of Les Halles, the Paris flower market, and the Tour St Jacques to illustrate his poem "La nuit de tournesol" (Night of the Sunflower). Breton's poem and Brassaï's illustrations appeared first in *Minotaure* and then in Breton's book *L'Amour fou* (Mad Love). But these photos were not, as Breton assumed, taken especially for him. Brassaï revealed that they had been in his possession for some time. They included an image of the Tour St Jacques exactly as Breton described it "sous son voile pâle d'échafaudages" – "beneath its pale veil of scaffolding".

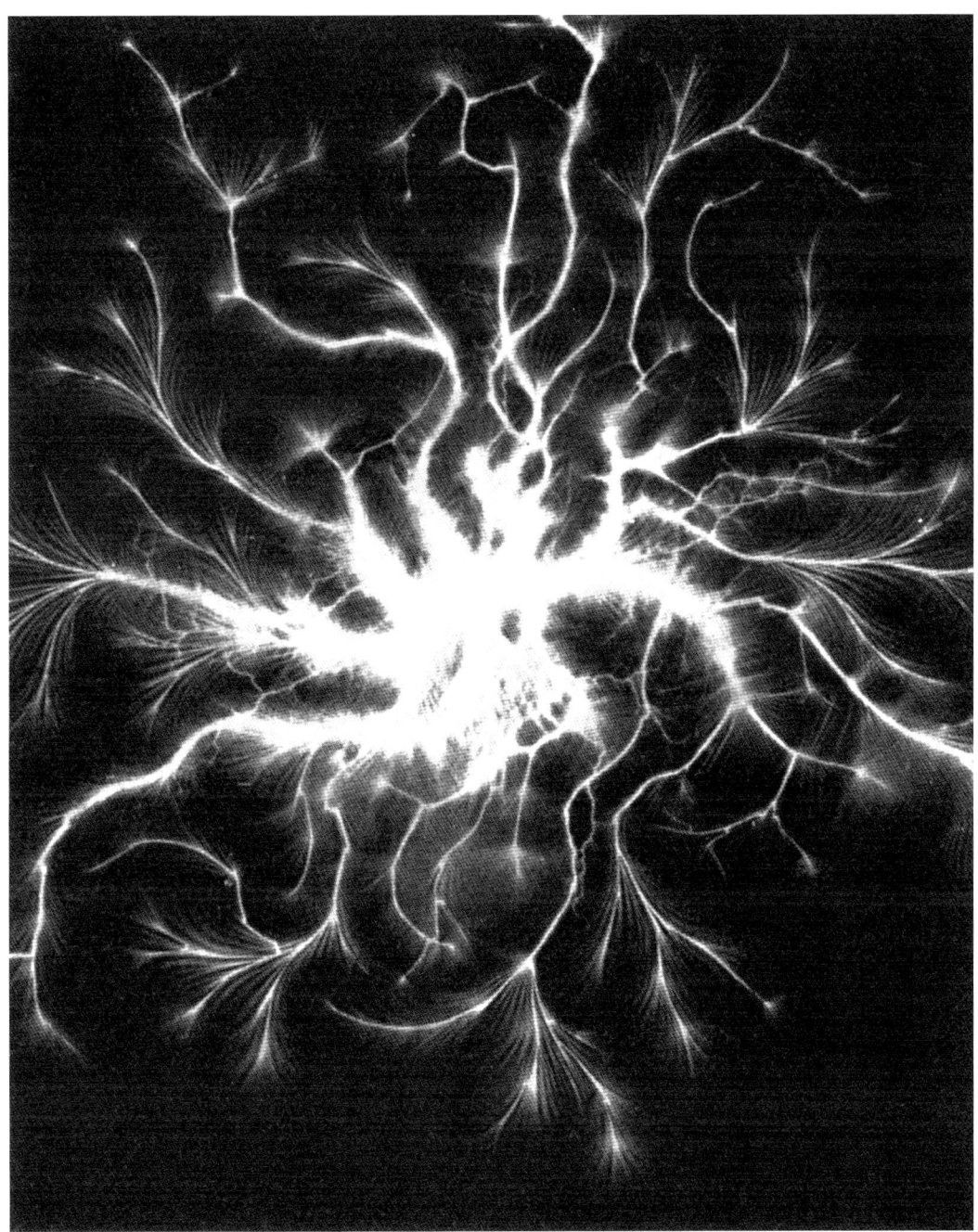

The Image as Produced
by Automatic Writing, 1934
Photograph
From *Minotaure*, no. 5, May 1934

Giorgio de Chirico
Mystery and Melancholy of a Street, 1914

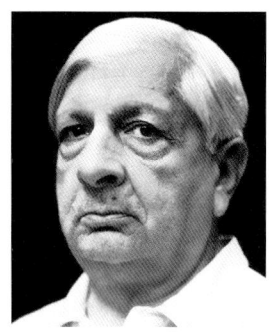

b. 1888 in Volos, Greece
d. 1978 in Rome

Deep silence reigns over the scene that Giorgio de Chirico opens up before us. We can almost hear the little girl's soft footsteps as she makes her way through the arcades and into the square, bowling her hoop along in front of her. Absorbed in her play, she seems oblivious to the heavy atmosphere and the ominous signs that surround her. What is the meaning of the circus wagon standing open like a trap? Whose is the shadow cast across the square? Who is hiding in the darkness of the long arcade?

"In the years from 1913 to 1917 Giorgio de Chirico disdainfully refused to be enslaved by outward appearances as most of his contemporaries were, including innovators such as Matisse and Picasso. His mind schooled in the ways of the Presocratics and Nietzsche, he was only willing to respond to the secret life of things … Such painting, which only records those external aspects that evoke an air of mystery or that radiate some premonition, will inextricably unite the art of fortune-telling and actual art. It inspires foreboding and works by means of shock." André Breton's description of de Chirico's painting during the period from which *Mystery and Melancholy of a Street* dates, which appears in *L'Art magique* (Magic Art), published in 1957, not only explains de Chirico's style (idiosyncratic, concise, devoid of detail or illusionism); it also casts light on his recurring use of the same forms, objects and buildings.

De Chirico paints emotions, enigmatic, all-pervasive moods, largely inspired by his intensive study of Nietzsche in 1910 and 1911. Both the titles of his paintings, always revolving around words like "melancholy", "mystery", "dream" or "meditation", and his repertoire of forms appear to be interchangeable, since they do not refer to a real situation but serve the painter as theatrical props as he constructs an imaginary space in which we the spectators come face to face with ourselves.

If we accept Breton's interpretation, we encounter here long-hidden thoughts, experience the shock of recognition of images and dreams that lie buried in the unconscious. The image of the little girl running through the empty streets of an abandoned city is a particularly apt one in relation to recollections of childhood experiences. However, in most works from this period, de Chirico uses symbols with more general meaning than this particular figure.

His many melancholy, mysterious squares and streets are constructed from deep, harsh shadows and surrounded by arcades. Although deserted, they are eerily "inhabited" by statues, most frequently by classical-style female sculptures that allude to a sleeping figure of Ariadne in Rome. In 1912, the artist portrayed *Melancholy* in a painting of the same name. Built of marble, an echo of a bygone age, the sculpture nevertheless appears more human and intimate than the endlessly repetitive rows of cold, shadowy arcades surrounding it.

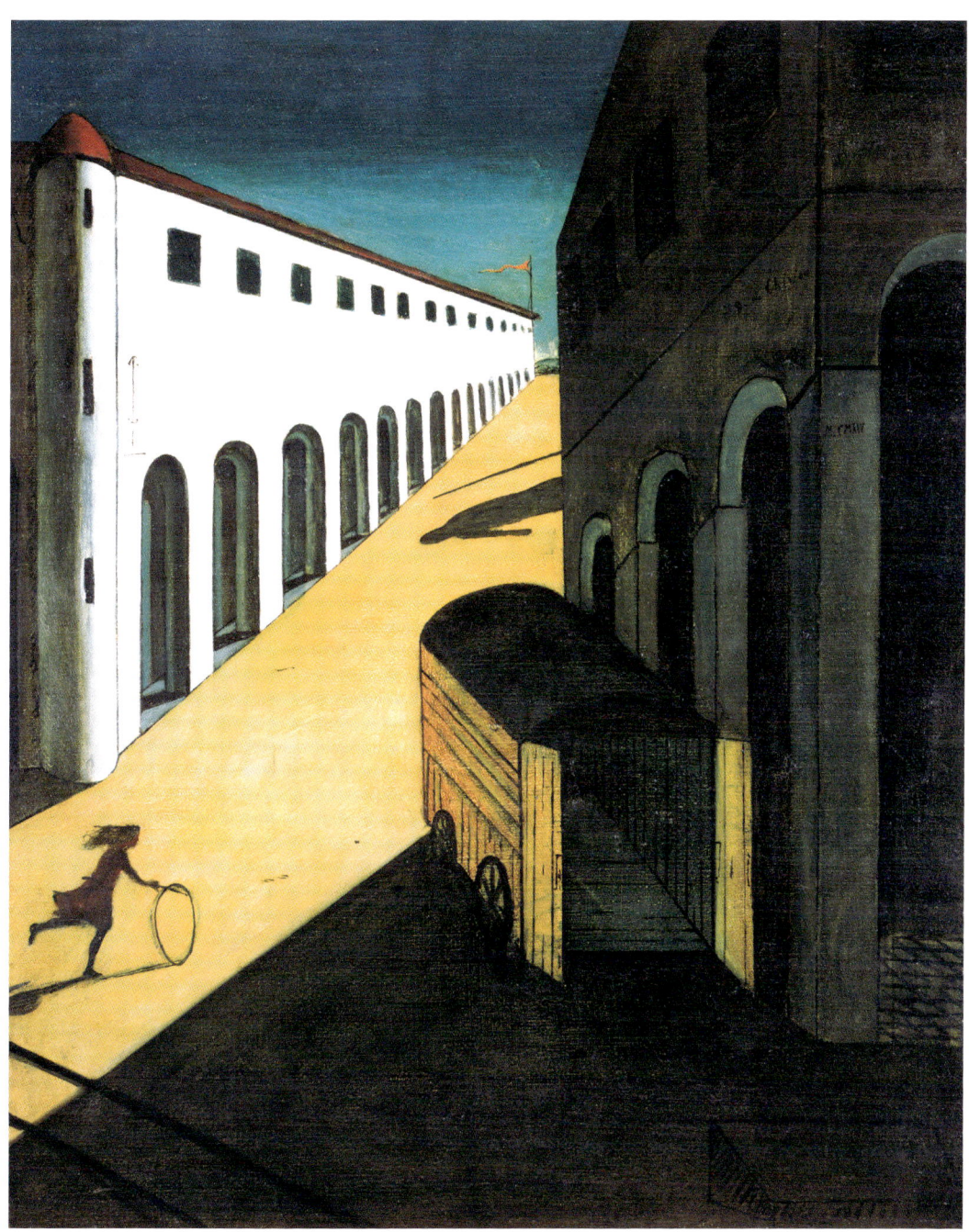

Mystery and Melancholy of a Street, 1914
Oil on canvas, 87 x 71.5 cm (34¼ x 28¼ in.)
Private collection

Giorgio de Chirico
The Disquieting Muses, 1917

By 1912, along with statues and monuments Giorgio de Chirico had begun to introduce other figures into the lifeless atmosphere of his paintings. These were huge marionettes, whose anonymity and physical shape recalled both shop window dummies and the lay figures used by artists for anatomical studies. These beings, without arms and sometimes with hinges, nails and strings, sometimes supported by complicated devices, are completely without identity and function merely to convey a mood. We are reminded not only of the mechanised people in Francis Picabia's Dada works, but also of the Cubist deconstruction of the human figure, with which de Chirico became intensely involved in Paris, largely through his close association with Guillaume Apollinaire and Pablo Picasso.

The concept of the world as a stage on which an absurd and meaningless puppet show was played out, an idea that drove de Chirico's "metaphysical" paintings from the very beginning, becomes even more meaningful with the introduction of these fragile jointed figures. In de Chirico's own words: "In the face of the increasingly materialist and pragmatic orientation of our age … it would not be eccentric in the future to contemplate a society in which those who live for the pleasures of the mind will no longer have the right to demand their place in the sun. The writer, the thinker, the dreamer, the poet, the metaphysician, the observer … he who tries to solve a riddle or to pass judgement will become an anachronistic figure, destined to disappear from the face of the earth like the ichthyosaur and the mammoth." From this, we can conclude that de Chirico thought the world had become meaningless and that people no longer felt entitled to try to make sense of it.

His representation of *The Disquieting Muses* makes this abundantly clear. They are pictured in the city of Ferrara in front of the former residence of the Este family, whose members were great patrons of the arts. Significantly, this urban palace near which de Chirico lived during the First World War, is forced to hold its own behind a rising stage alongside industrial buildings, factory chimneys and a silo. The rust-red, fortified building looms up against the backdrop of a turquoise-blue sky. At the front of a stage broken up by areas of deep shadow are the two muses – featureless lay figures in classical garb. One standing, the other seated, they are placed among a series of props. These include a red mask and a staff, allusions to the traditional attributes of Melpomene and Thalia, the muses of tragedy and comedy. Meanwhile, Apollo, leader of the muses, is represented as a statue on a pedestal in the background. He looks as subdued and lifeless as the muses. The spectator has to wonder where he will lead them, given the deeply melancholic state of his headless companions.

The Disquieting Muses, 1917
Oil on canvas, 97 x 66 cm (38¼ x 26 in.)
Private collection

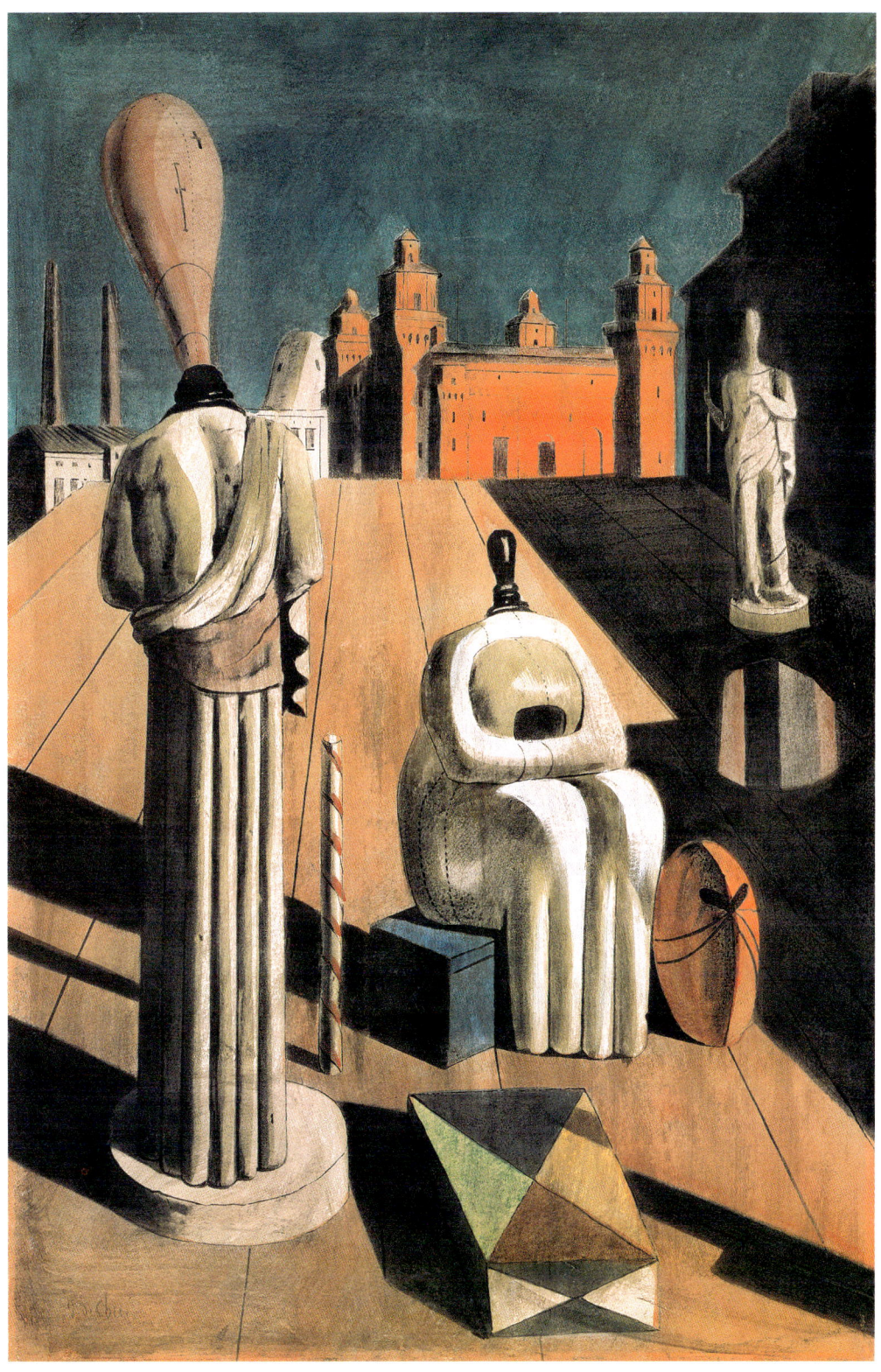

Salvador Dalí

The Enigma of Desire or
Ma mère, ma mère, ma mère, 1929

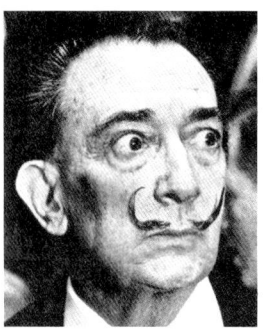

b. 1904 in Figueras, Spain
d. 1989 in Figueras

One way to approach Salvador Dalí's works is to understand that the stuff of which they were made was the product of the artist's own psyche. From it he deliberately fashioned paintings that appear irrational, enigmatic and complex. It therefore comes as no surprise that Dalí himself features in many of his compositions either as a hidden figure or a distorted face.

We spot one such self-portrait in *The Enigma of Desire or Ma mère, ma mère, ma mère*. Dalí's head lies on the ground with eyes closed, seemingly asleep or half-dead – the ants streaming out of his ear suggest decomposition and decay – while the monstrous body, which takes up virtually the whole picture, seems to oppress and paralyse the painter. It is a strange object, whose indeterminate shape resembles that of an embryo capable of further development, but which also recalls a rigid geological formation. The painter is the prisoner of this body covered with oval cavities in each of which appear the same two words – "ma mère" (my mother). They are the key to the meaning of the painting and are complemented by a further seminal element, the little lion's head, its face twisted into a grimace. It seems to represent the father who clings, as if in triumph, to the highest point of the mountainous body, apparently pressing his son's face to the ground.

The lion's head reappears above Dalí's self-portrait as part of a complex group of figures. We also see the dejected, grizzled head of an old man in the sentimental embrace of a youth with his back turned to us. Nearby is a fish head on which sits a grasshopper holding in its hand a knife, threateningly raised, and the head of a woman – perhaps the mother – her face a picture of despair as she observes a scene she cannot comprehend. The aggressive lion and the white-haired old man seem to be the two faces of the father. He runs away from his son, who clings to him in fear, oblivious to the dagger the father clutches behind his back. Perhaps he wants to protect his son and defend him from the monsters, fish and spiders that surround him. Whichever way we put together and interpret the details of the picture, the deeper meaning of the work always seems to lead back to the suffering, seemingly paralysed face of the central figure, the artist himself. "How can he escape?" we want to ask. At which point, through one of the holes in the body in the centre of the painting, we catch sight of the naked, blood-covered upper body of a young woman, half-hidden in a grotto-like space. Almost like something out of a fairy tale, this female figure seems to hold out the prospect of release, enabling the enslaved creature lying on the ground to free himself from the shackles of fear and obsession.

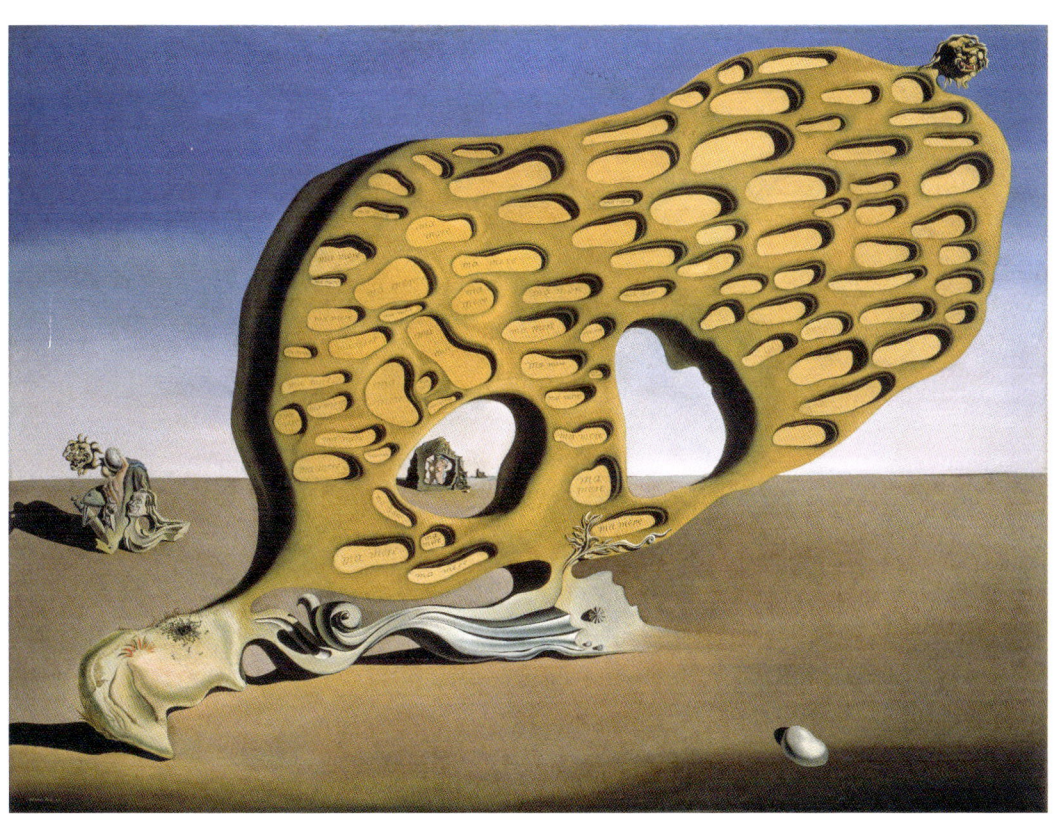

The Enigma of Desire or
Ma mère, ma mère, ma mère, 1929
Oil on canvas, 110.5 x 150.5 cm (43½ x 59¼ in.)
Munich, Pinakothek der Moderne

Salvador Dalí
The Persistence of Memory, 1931

The Persistence of Memory is a work in which many characteristics of Salvador Dalí's painting come together. In the distance is the rocky coastline of Port Lligat. Against a multi-level background several motifs are juxtaposed, amazing the spectator because of their total incongruity and bizarre appearance.

The painter's portrait in the foreground resembles a snail creeping along the ground, its body like a trail of colour vanishing into the dark sand. In the foreground are three soft watches, one gold, two silver; they appear soft, one snuggling close to the snail-like body, one draped over the branch of a leafless tree and the third hanging over the edge of the projecting section of a wall. The only clock that seems to have retained its normal consistency is painted a meaty red and is being devoured by the ants that have collected on its surface.

Not only the physical characteristics of the composition, but also its colours and coherence are subverted in Dalí's painting. The indicators of time – which form the real subject of the painting – undergo a far-reaching transformation almost impossible to grasp through the use of logic. It is not the forward movement of the watch hands but the melting of the watches themselves that shows that time is slipping away. The ravages of time are also symbolised by the dissolving snail, the painter's self-portrait. Meanwhile, the red watch besieged by ants and the skeletal tree on the far left of the picture are premonitions of approaching death. Do these intimations of mortality refer to the lifeless head and liquefying body of the painter lying on the ground? Is the picture about his unconscious fear of death or the *Persistence of Memory* that paralyses him?

In his memoirs, in which Dalí tells at some length how the painting came into being, he does not go into its symbolic content. He goes so far as to claim that its enigmatic meaning and unconscious content were hidden even from him. In *The Secret Life of Salvador Dalí* he describes how, after a dinner concluded with a very soft Camembert, he remained alone at the table contemplating the cheese and pondering the philosophical problem of "supersoftness". As was his habit, he then went to his studio to take a final look at the painting on which he was working at the time. It was a landscape near Port Lligat. The cliffs lay in a transparent, melancholic twilight and in the foreground stood an olive tree, with branches chopped off and no leaves. He knew that the atmospheric landscape he had managed to create would serve as background for an amazing picture, but he had not the slightest idea what it would be. As he went to turn off the light he suddenly "saw" the solution – three soft watches, one of them hanging pitifully from the branch of the olive tree. Although suffering from a splitting headache, he eagerly prepared his palette and set to work.

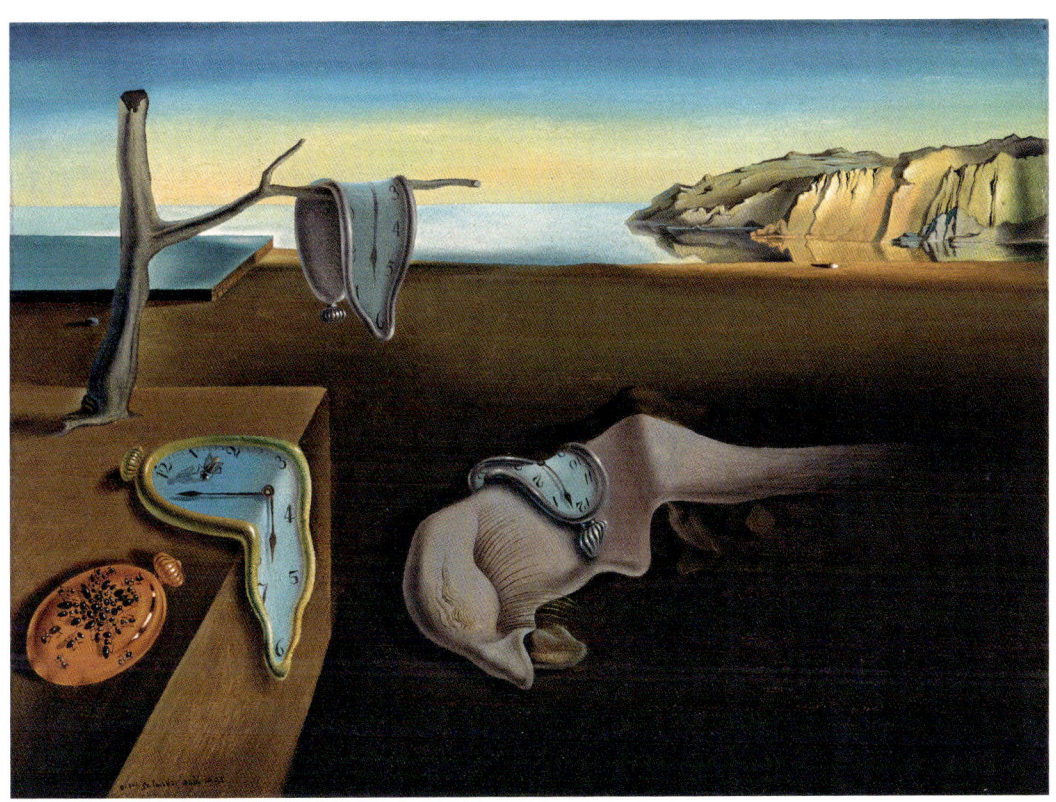

The Persistence of Memory, 1931
Oil on canvas, 24.1 x 33 cm (9½ x 13 in.)
New York, The Museum of Modern Art

Salvador Dalí

Soft Construction with Boiled Beans (Premonition of Civil War), 1936

Around the mid 1930s some of the titles of Salvador Dalí's paintings had obvious political connotations. One such example was *Soft Construction with Boiled Beans (Premonition of Civil War)*. Describing himself as "a painter of internal paroxysms", Dalí told how he painted his "premonition" six months before the outbreak of the Spanish Civil War. The picture featured "a vast human body breaking out into monstrous excrescences of arms and legs tearing at one another in a delirium of autostrangulation," which he then "embellished with a few boiled beans".

How is it possible to appreciate the political dimension of a painting that displays the same characteristics as many other "apolitical" works of the same period? The picture itself – a construction of human limbs, supported by a fossilized foot and a gnarled hand resting on a small chest of drawers – provides no information. Occupying the entire canvas, the structure stands in the bay of Port Lligat. In the background, banks of clouds move across an ominous sky. A man's face, riddled with pain, tops the construction, whose unbearable internal tension contrasts with the apparent lack of connection between the individual elements. This painfully irreconcilable, and at the same time completely inorganic relationship between the various body parts can in fact be interpreted as a metaphor for the Civil War, which the artist sees as a fateful catastrophe rather than a historic event. This point of view corresponds with the apolitical attitude that Dalí displayed throughout his life. His anarchism, dressed up as snobbery, led him to analyze social and political situations so as to exploit them in his own painting. For example, the glorification of Adolf Hitler, for which the Surrealists condemned Dalí, sprang not from admiration of the dictator and his political propaganda, but from what the artist saw as the Hitler's aesthetic and erotic appeal. Dalí often used political allusions to heighten the scandalous effect of his paintings. Speaking of references to Hitler and Fascism in his work he said: "I was fascinated by Hitler's soft and fleshy back, always so firmly laced up in his uniform …" Dalí's apparent exaltation of Fascism led to a clash with André Breton and finally to Dalí's exclusion from Surrealist circles. In alluding to contemporary events, Dalí sought the wonderful and bizarre and the neurotic, in the widest sense of the word, choosing to tackle clearly political themes for purely aesthetic reasons. This was at a time when the Surrealists as a group were debating whether to take a direct political stand on the side of the Communists, or to continue to limit themselves to isolated, purely artistic activities.

It was an attitude that Dalí in no way shared. Ultimately his works, with their virtuoso painting and inexhaustible wealth of imagination and subject matter, were always a glimpse into his inner world. In his own words: "My whole ambition where painting is concerned consists in materializing mental images of concrete irrationality with the power-craziest precision …"

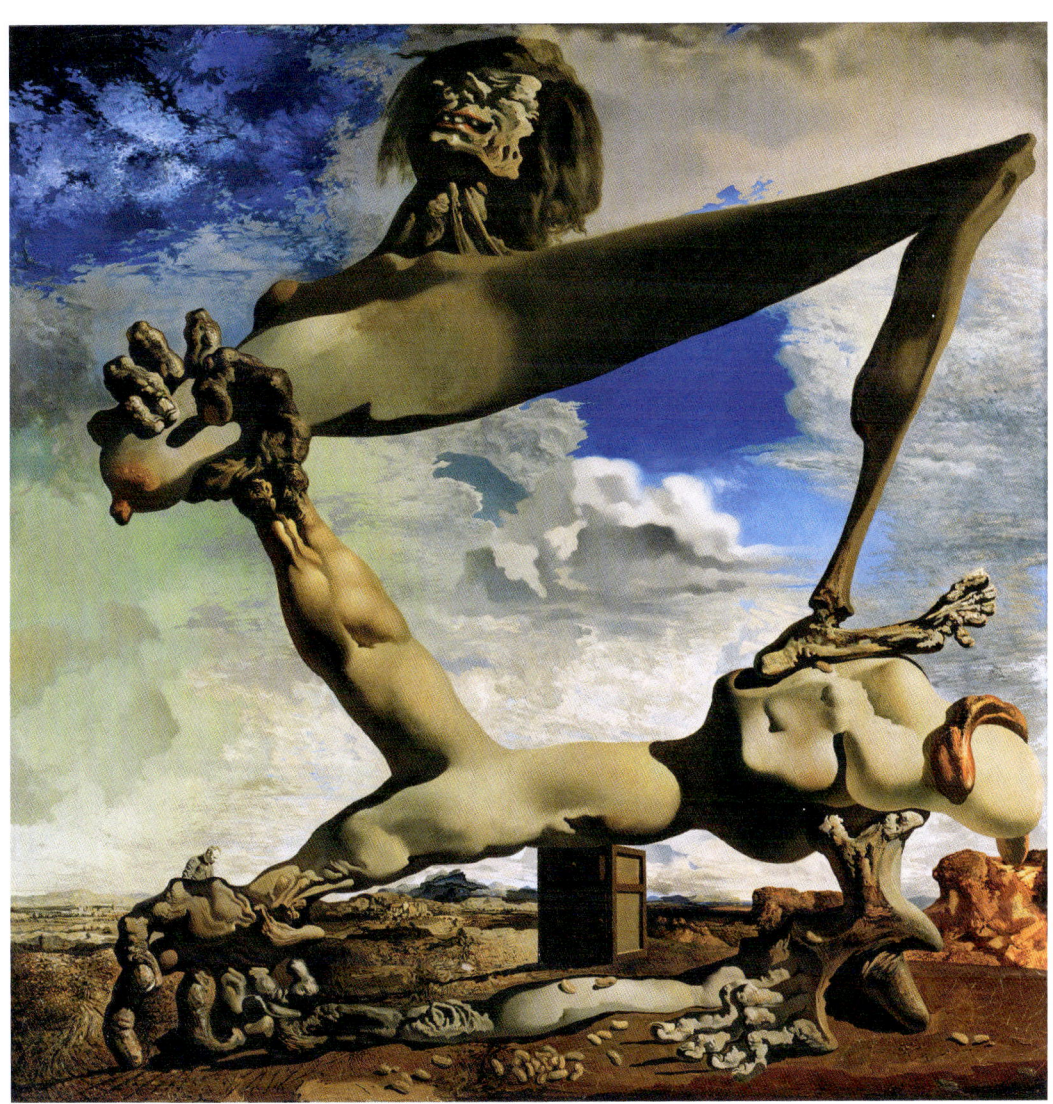

Soft Construction with Boiled Beans
(Premonition of Civil War), 1936
Oil on canvas, 99.9 x 100 cm (39¼ x 39¼ in.)
Philadelphia Museum of Art,
The Louise and Walter Arensberg Collection

Salvador Dalí
Burning Giraffe, c. 1937

The famous motif of a human body fitted with drawers crops up several times in Salvador Dalí's 1936 paintings. The most provocative example is a copy of the Venus de Milo, which Dalí equipped with drawers at belly, breast, head and knee level, with coquettish fur pom-poms for handles. By manipulating the ancient statue, the epitome of classical beauty, admired and alluded to in European art from the Middle Ages to modern times, Dalí not only downgrades it to an object but questions its very nature. What is at issue here is not so much the concept of beauty embodied by the *Venus de Milo* as the Surrealists' theory that the idealistic, balanced and harmonious version of beauty represented by the statues of Antiquity was no longer valid.

Behind the beautiful surface lurked unsuspected, confusing and terrifying things. This line of thought continues with the image of the drawers, suggesting that what lies beneath in the human psyche can be made accessible and visible.

The traumatic nature of such an idea is clear to see in *Burning Giraffe*, dating from the same year as *Venus de Milo with Drawers*. The classic white of the statue has changed to an intense dreamy blue, the colour of night, covering not only the sky but also the two female figures, moving slowly along with eyes closed, as if sleepwalking. Their thin, bony bodies are hampered by drawers, unnatural protuberances and crutches, and only with difficulty can they grope their way forward. The balanced contrapposto of the *Venus de Milo* has made way for a unwieldy figure engaged in a balancing act, struggling to maintain equilibrium in the knowledge that she is loaded down by the mysterious contents of the drawers.

Only with the aid of crutches can the figures stay upright, struggling blindly at the mercy of the night which, we assume, is intended as an allegory. It stands for the "other" side of human beings, for the unconscious and inaccessible regions of the self which cannot be controlled by reason but which nevertheless dictate our lives.

We cannot see where we are going, or what drives us. We live in a world that has become alien to us. Perhaps we may interpret the burning giraffe as a symbol of the absurdity of human existence in the modern world. As Wieland Schmied writes in *Salvador Dalí. Das Rätsel der Begierde* (Salvador Dalí. The Enigma of Desire): "Unlike man, in animals nature is still as it should be. Their animal being appears indestructible. The giraffe that simply bursts into flames is at one with the elements. Without thought and without passion it can surrender to the flames and be destroyed by them. The realm of nature, minerals and the elements will endure, as will animals. By contrast, man is subject to time, age and impermanence whose ravages can be seen in the faces, hands and movements of the sleepwalkers in the painting."

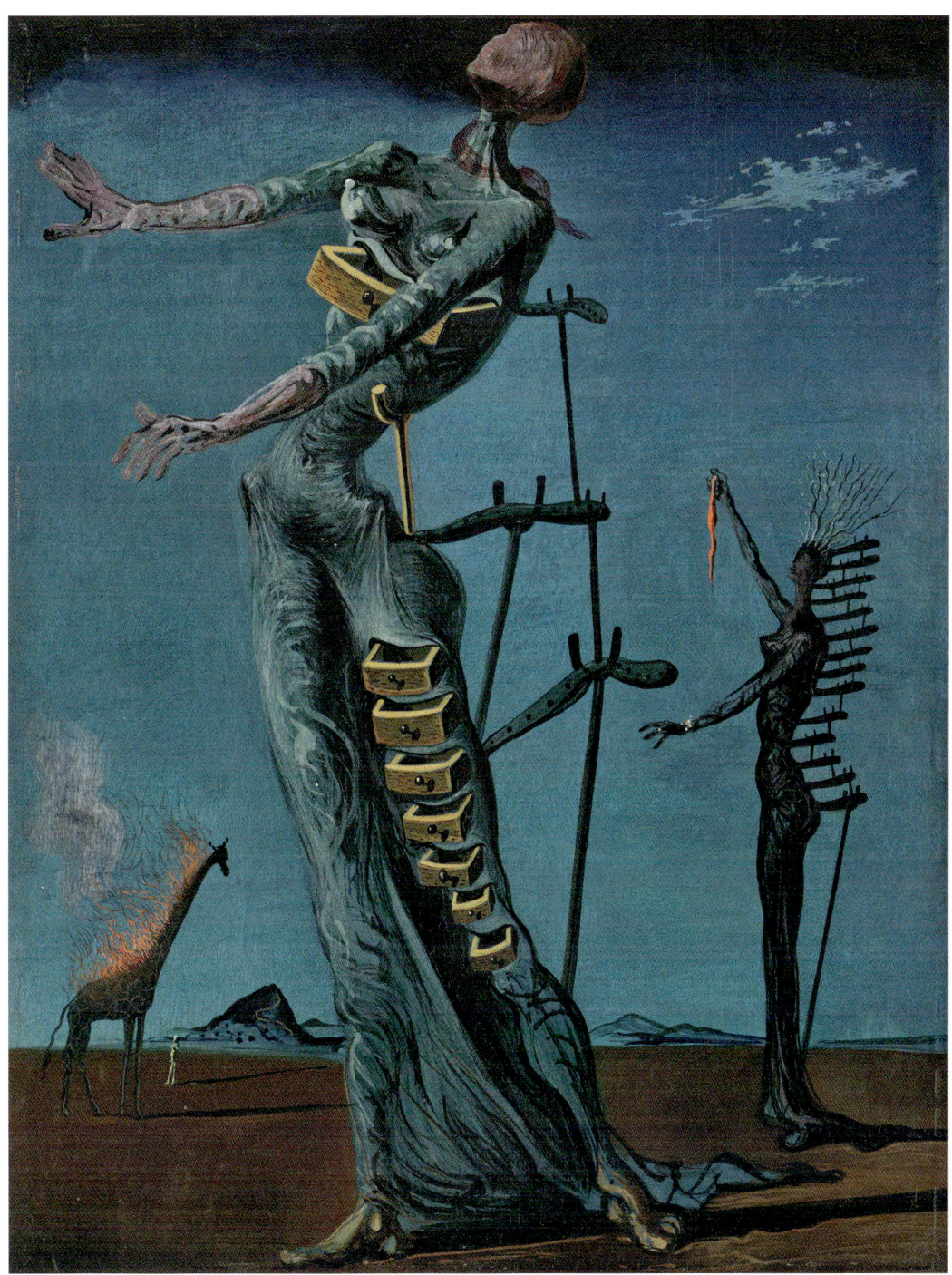

Burning Giraffe, c. 1937
Oil on wood panel, 35 x 27 cm (13¾ x 10¾ in.)
Basel, Emanuel Hoffmann Foundation,
on permanent loan to the Kunstsammlung Basle

Salvador Dalí

Dream Caused by the Flight of a Bee Around a Pomegranate a Second Before Awakening, c. 1944

At the centre of this complex and brilliantly executed dream painting *Dream Caused by the Flight of a Bee Around a Pomegranate a Second Before Awakening* is Dalí's wife Gala. Is she the dreamer or is she part of the painter's – or the spectator's – vision? Both the spatial construction of the picture and its complicated chronology make it hard to find a meaningful answer to the fundamental question the work poses.

The stretched-out, naked body of the sleeping Gala hovers above a rocky promontory. The glistening blue surface of the water in the background looks supernaturally still, as if to reinforce the magical silence of the dramatic happenings in the sky. A fish leaps out of a pomegranate and from its gaping mouth emerge the head and forepaws of a tiger. From the maw of the beast a second tiger springs. The line of its body, ready to attack and aimed straight at the sleeping woman, is extended to form a rifle armed with a bayonet, the point of which is about to stab Gala in the upper arm. In her dream, the genuinely threatening bee sting of the title becomes a symbolic stab wound, which the mind can connect with many other ideas and images.

In his painting Dalí not only captures the unreality of the dream but also encapsulates its complexity. The painter enables us to experience the multifaceted event in a single moment. The sleeping woman awakens from a dream lasting only seconds imagining she has seen a long, multi-layered and complicated film. Likewise the spectator is aware of the painting's peculiar chronology. In the space of a moment a series of monsters too complicated to describe in words appears above Gala's head. At the same time an elephant with extraordinarily long, insect-like legs strides across the horizon bearing an obelisk. It is a distorted image of a real work of art, Bernini's famous elephant statue in Rome, which somehow fits into the strange logic of the dream. At the same time, we see in the foreground an echo of the main event in the shape of a pomegranate encircled by a bee.

To some extent, this is the painter's own interpretation of the picture which he disguises as part of the dream, in the same way that medieval painters hid the meaning of their works behind allegorical references. Extraordinarily well-versed in the history and tradition of European painting, Dalí shows the pomegranate floating between two dewdrops, an allusion to the pearls of Venus, and casting a shadow in the shape of a heart – a fertility symbol. The connection between the pomegranate and the phallic symbolism of the series of aggressors striking out against the sleeping woman seems to be a reference to the relationship between Dalí and Gala, whose importance as the artist's muse, lover and adviser is well known. Dalí extends the spatial and chronological structure of the work so as to make it clear that it is he who has created both the dream and the masterly painting.

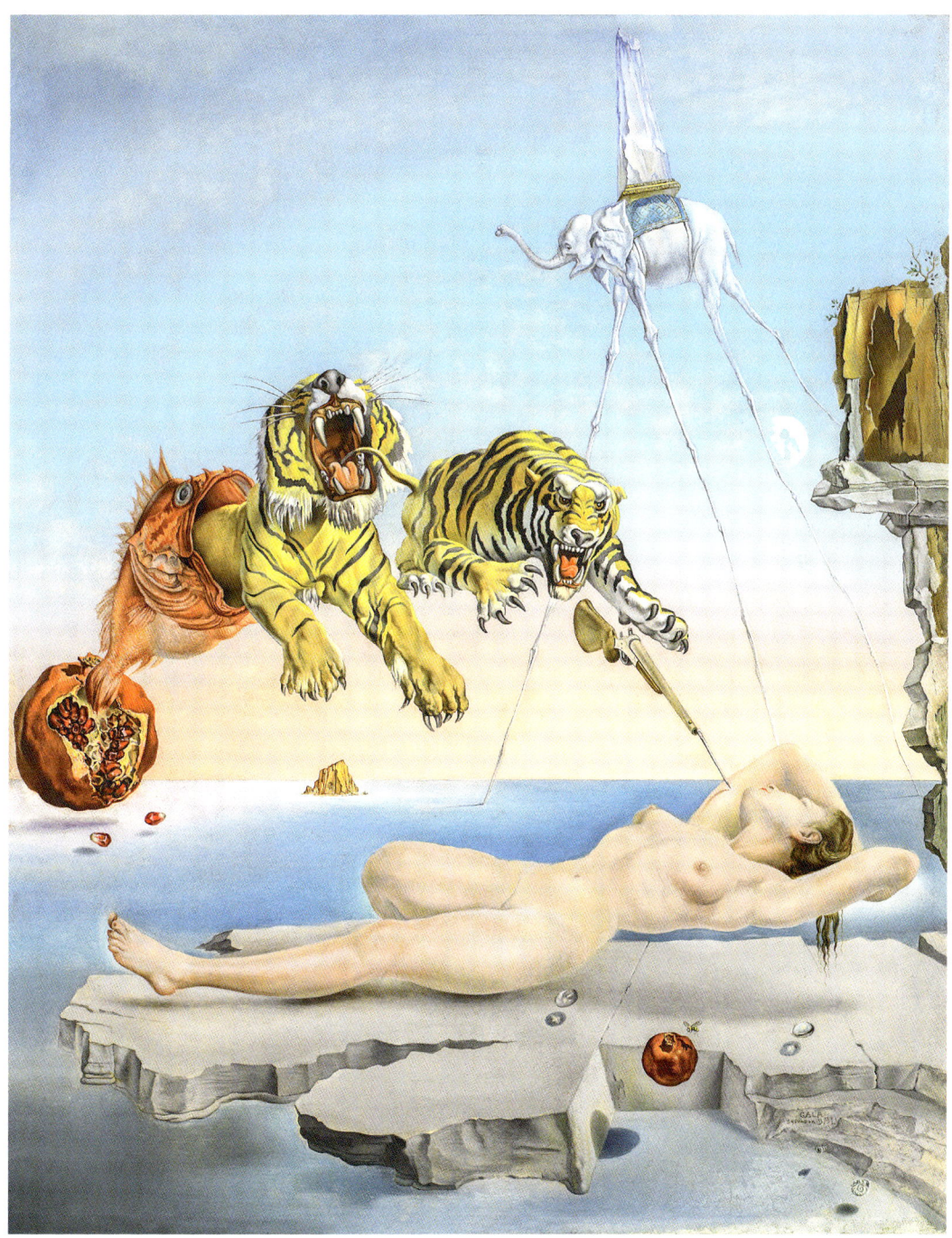

*Dream Caused by the Flight of a Bee Around a
Pomegranate a Second Before Awakening*, c. 1944
Oil on wood panel, 51 x 41 cm (20 x 16 in.)
Madrid, Museo Thyssen-Bornemisza

Paul Delvaux
Dawn Over the City, 1940

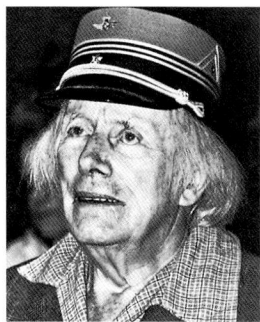

b. 1897 in Antheit, Belgium
d. 1994 in Furnes, Belgium

Among the most important influences on Paul Delvaux's artistic development were the paintings of Giorgio de Chirico and the works of René Magritte. Delvaux first came across the two artists in the late 1920s, when he visited an exhibition that included works by de Chirico and, shortly afterwards, made Magritte's acquaintance.

Like Magritte, Delvaux worked in seclusion. What linked Delvaux to the Surrealists was not the feeling – so important to many artists – of belonging to a group, but the fact that the painter also sought to create in his art an atmosphere evoking dreams and unreality. "Surrealism! What is Surrealism? In my opinion, it is above all a reawakening of the poetic idea in art, the reintroduction of the subject but in a very particular sense, that of the strange and illogical." This was the definition Delvaux offered during a 1966 lecture.

The strangeness of his paintings dates from the mid 1930s with the introduction of nude figures in a world in which the intimacy of nakedness is portrayed in a very public setting. In *Dawn Over the City*, a central, male figure – a self-portrait of the artist – is surrounded by naked women slowly approaching him as if sleepwalking. They seem to represent a kind of existence impossible to reconcile with the normality of everyday life. As in de Chirico's paintings the "classical" architecture, with its closely converging vanishing lines, is no more than lifeless decoration. It is part of a completely unreal space and provides a backdrop for encounters without sense or coherence.

"No one here thinks of eating, they are nourished by time, which passes and passes again; they drink the hours. Now I am in the presence of Claude Lorrain, but is not the heat, broken by sea breezes, too strong for this light?" These lines by the French author Michel Butor on *Dawn Over the City* describe another important feature of Delvaux's painting – the inspiration of the Old Masters. Following the principles of collage devised by the Surrealists, Delvaux combines dream and painting. Thus he creates an imagined reality in which the protagonists, like the painter himself in *Dawn Over the City*, seem like intruders set on causing trouble in the dream world.

However, Paul Delvaux's paintings not only reflect dreams, which he depicts using a seemingly naïve vocabulary. His art could also be termed mythological, since his paintings possess an encoded message only accessible to those who are familiar with the meaning of the place and its inhabitants, in other words, those who understand the language of the subconscious.

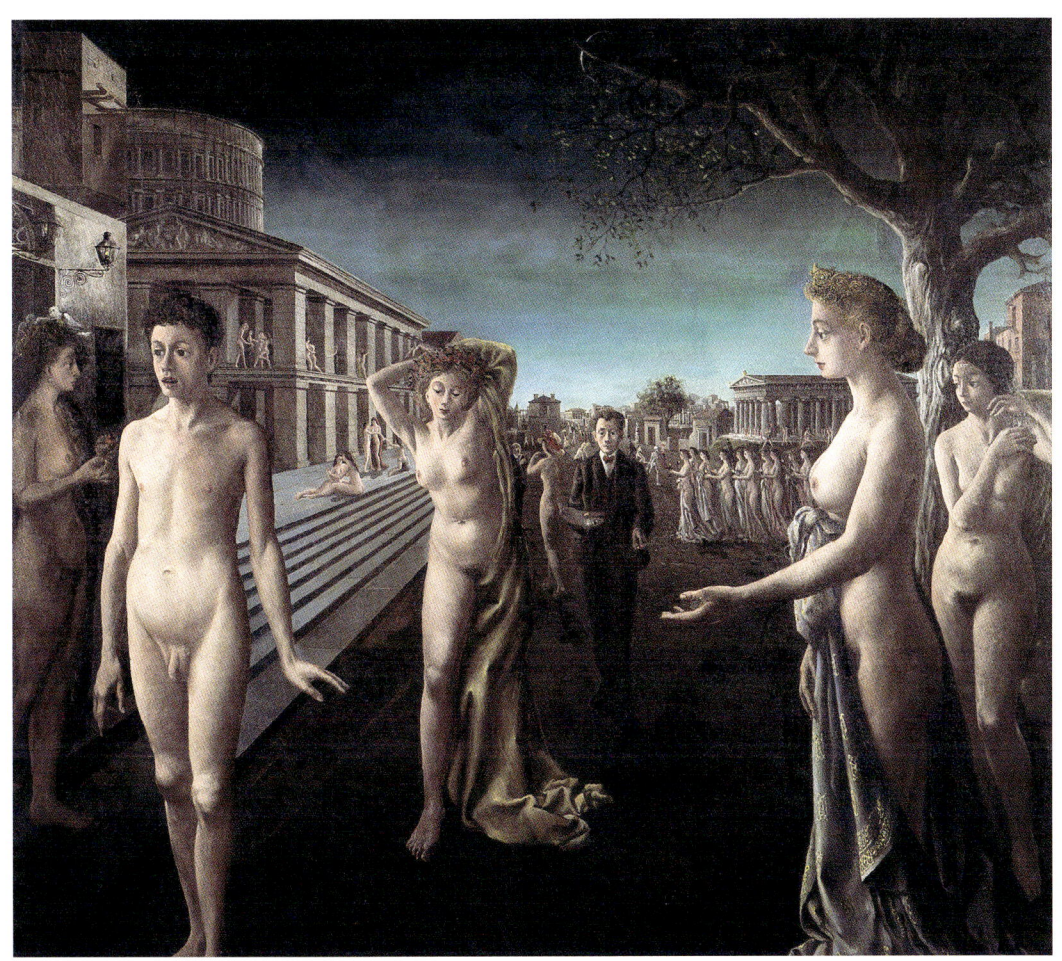

Dawn Over the City, 1940
Oil on canvas, 175 x 215 cm (69 x 84¾ in.)
Private collection

Max Ernst
Approaching Puberty or
The Pleiades, 1921

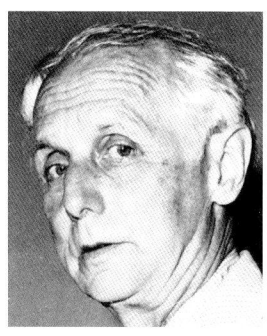

b. 1891 in Brühl, Germany
d. 1976 in Paris

In 1921, the year in which *Approaching Puberty* or *The Pleiades* was created, Max Ernst was closely involved with the French Dadaists. His friendship with André Breton and Paul Éluard led to some joint projects and Ernst's active participation in the early stages of Surrealism.

Approaching Puberty or *The Pleiades* juxtaposes image and script. The detailed commentary underneath the picture harmonises with the image in terms of colour and composition. The text reads: "Approaching puberty has not yet removed the fragile grace of our Pleiades/Our shadowy gaze is directed at the paving stone which is about to fall/ The gravitation of the waves does not yet exist." It determines our approach to a picture whose odd assortment of images defies spontaneous understanding.

In Max Ernst's "Biographical notes" the artist draws attention to the different levels of the work. We instinctively associate the grace of the Pleiades with the naked, headless female figure cut out from a photograph and positioned in the centre of the picture. With certain trepidation we focus on the tumbling paving stone as it falls to the bottom of the picture, leaving a black trail behind it. Finally, gravitation can be linked to the blue background, which is in turn associated both with the female form hovering in mid-air and with the movement of the waves referred to in the text.

Of course, these connotations make no sense if we do not also take account of the meaning of the Pleiades in Greek mythology. Thus, the nude female figure can be seen to represent one of the seven daughters of Atlas, who was pursued by Orion. In order to protect them, Zeus turned them into a heavenly constellation. She might be Electra, who hid her face at the fall of Troy, which would explain why she appears headless in Max Ernst's collage. The word "Pleiades" may originally derive from "peleiades", meaning a flock of doves, so that the blurred outlines at the top of the collage could be interpreted as soaring birds.

This analysis of the contents of the collage leaves us with feelings of vagueness and the possibility of multiple meanings. There are various ways of understanding the work that may overlap or be mutually exclusive. Nor are interpretations based on reason likely to be satisfactory. We are looking at a universe ruled by the laws of dreams and the subconscious, a primitive world where neither gravity nor clear boundaries exist. Things of totally different consistencies stand side by side. Perhaps it is only now, as we view the composition so many years later, that we are able to witness the development of a new aesthetic, embracing suggestivity and the notions of decay and disintegration.

Approaching Puberty or ***The Pleiades***, 1921
Collage of partly retouched photographs, gouache and oil on paper, mounted on cardboard, 24.5 x 16.5 cm (9¾ x 6½ in.)
Private collection

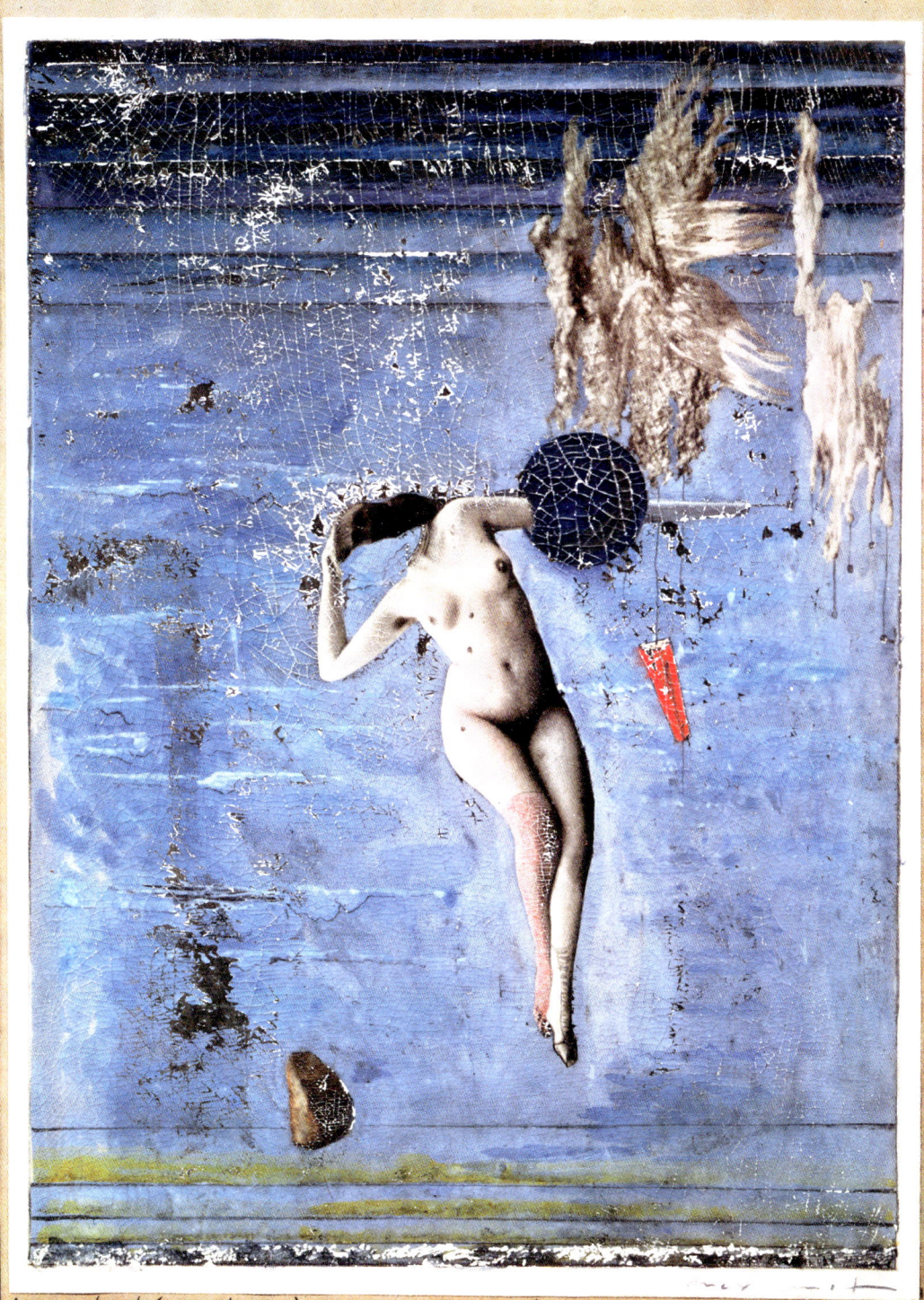

La puberté proche n'a pas encore enlevé la grâce tenue de nos pléiades/ Le regard de nos yeux pleins d'ombre est dirigé vers le pavé qui va tomber/ La gravitation des ondulations n'existe pas encore

Max Ernst
Celebes, 1921

In 1921 Paul Éluard bought *Celebes* from Max Ernst, whom he had recently met and subsequently visited in Cologne. It was the first of several of his friend's works that Éluard was to purchase. In addition, Ernst painted murals for Éluard's house in Eaubonne.

Celebes, painted while Ernst was still in Cologne, applied the principle of paper collage to painting. The individual elements of this composition are not cuttings from different books, encyclopaedias or catalogues. Instead, Ernst translates the concept of collage, namely the bringing together of an assortment of incongruous and contradictory elements, into a *trompe l'œil* style of painting that simulates different materials. It is precisely the "realism" of the images that produces the "hallucinatory" effect the painter tried to achieve, an effect that Max Ernst associated with collage, as a passage in his autobiographic notes reveal: "One rainy day, in Cologne on the Rhine, my attention was attracted by the catalogue of an institution supplying teaching materials. I saw models of all sorts, mathematical, geometric, anthropological, zoological, botanical, anatomical, mineralogical, palaeontological and so on. Elements of such a different nature that the absurdity of collecting them confused the eye and the senses, provoking hallucinations and giving the objects represented new, rapidly changing meaning. I felt my visionary faculties suddenly so intensified that I seemed to see newly created objects in a new setting. In order to capture this it required only a little colour or a few lines, a horizon, a desert, a wooden floor and suchlike. So I obtained a fixed image of my hallucination." (1919)

In the case of *Celebes*, the "new setting" is the first sign of another, different reality. The monstrous figure stands in a space that it takes us a few moments to realise is an underwater landscape. In what is supposedly the sky, two fish frolic against a background which, puzzlingly, is punched with holes through which cables protrude. But these are only minor causes of confusion. The beast with its round body and sturdy hosepipe-like protuberance looks like an elephant. It is, in fact, a machine based on a picture of a corn bin that Max Ernst came across in an anthropological journal. He adopted its simple, rounded shape and then added a trunk, which he adorned with a frilly cuff, a horned head and tusks.

The monster's name is taken from a line in a smutty schoolboy poem with sexual connotations, which Ernst remembered from his youth. In this context the de Chirico-style tower on the right of the picture can be interpreted as a phallic symbol. There is also a possible mythological explanation for the presence of the graceful nude figure. Max Ernst could be alluding to the abduction of Europa by Zeus, father of the gods, disguised as a bull. The horned head at the end of the elephant's trunk could refer to the same myth.

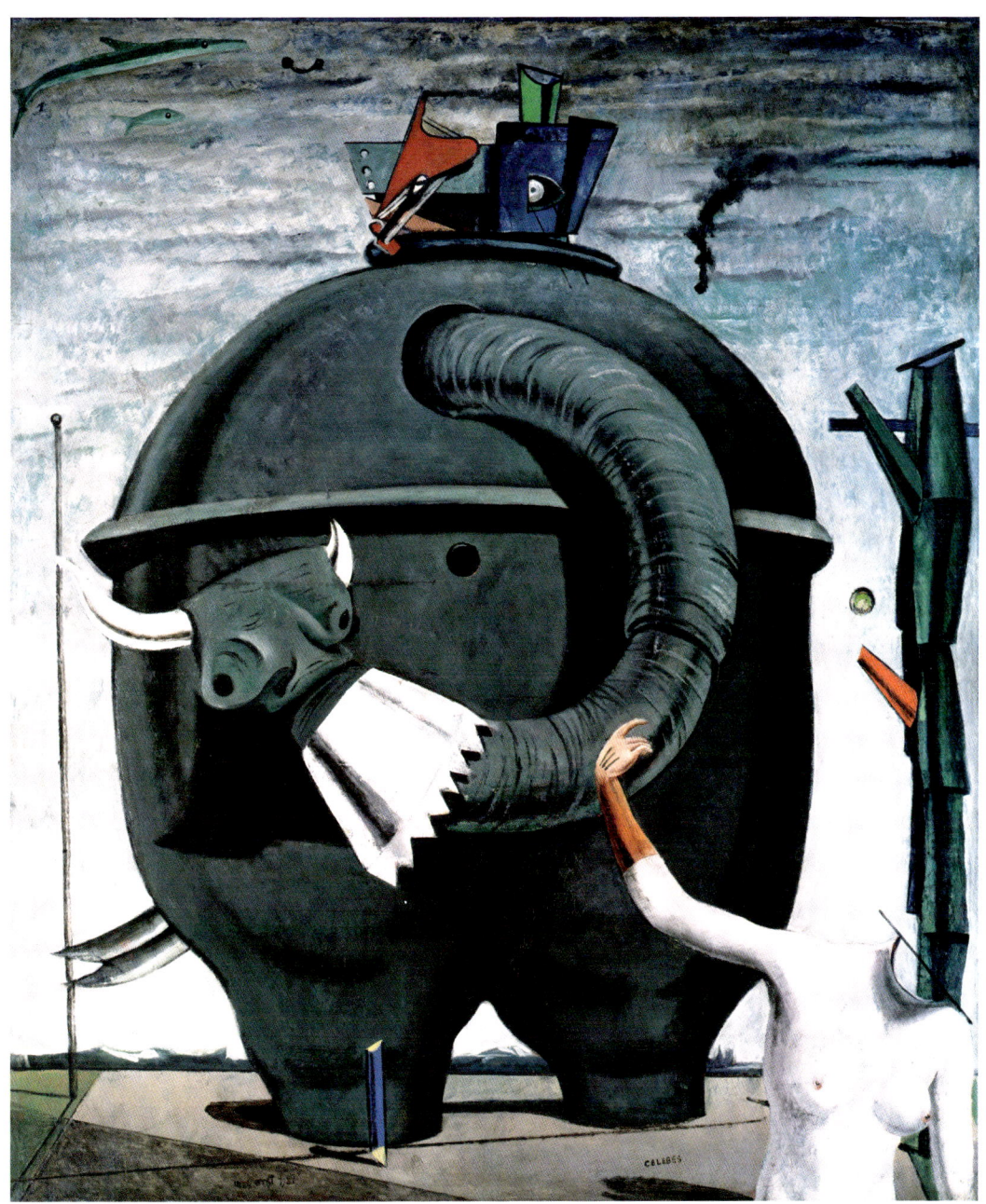

Celebes, 1921
Oil on canvas, 125 x 108 cm (49¼ x 42½ in.)
London, Tate

Max Ernst
Loplop Presents a Flower or *Anthropomorphic Figure with Shell Flower*, 1930

In his "Biographical notes", Max Ernst described Loplop, his alter ego, as a protagonist in the novel of the same name. The catalogue to a 1930 Max Ernst exhibition at the Galerie Vignon in Paris contained the words: "Loplop presents Loplop (private phantom related to Max Ernst, sometimes with wings, but always masculine)." This quotation is especially revealing – at least for spectators of the series of Loplop pictures created in the 1930s – for it confirms firstly Loplop's function as master of ceremonies and secondly his close connection with Max Ernst.

Loplop appears in the picture *Loplop Presents a Flower* or *Anthropomorphic Figure with Shell Flower* as commentator and instructor, without the gestures and facial expressions that characterised history paintings of earlier eras. Instead, his body serves as an easel on which works are placed. Loplop, presenting a flower, is a typical representative of his genre. On top of the flat, right-angled body resting on a rostrum-like base, sits a small naïve-looking chicken's head, the only living creature in the painting. To some extent this provides a point of contact for the spectator, who is confronted with not one but several images. However, anyone hoping for an illuminating commentary will be disappointed. Loplop does not create a connection or suggest any unifying theme between the visual elements, each of which has been produced by a different technique.

Loplop, whose impudent face presides over the whole scene, wraps us in visual confusion. He ironically combines quotes from other pictures, artistic set pieces, allusions to reality and deceptive illusionism. Art presented in this way, like a blackboard on an easel, is not to be taken seriously, he seems to be saying. Pathos is out of place – a message that becomes particularly pithy when applied to another Loplop picture, *Loplop Presents the Marseillaise*. Here, Loplop's head is replaced by the capital of a column, lending him a certain dignity, which does not prevent the spectator from seeing the painting he is presenting as completely ludicrous and ironic.

Loplop presents the picture in the usual way – as an easel on wide feet – and also pops up in the picture itself, appearing as an opulent female figure with a bird's head, sitting on a throne, gesticulating expansively, apparently singing or conducting "La Marseillaise". But this rendering of the French national anthem is not the only charade. Nothing in the picture is to be taken at face value. The composition itself is a sham. With the aid of frottage, Max Ernst creates a picture comprised of structures so dramatically different from each other that they undermine the whole concept of classic artistic unity.

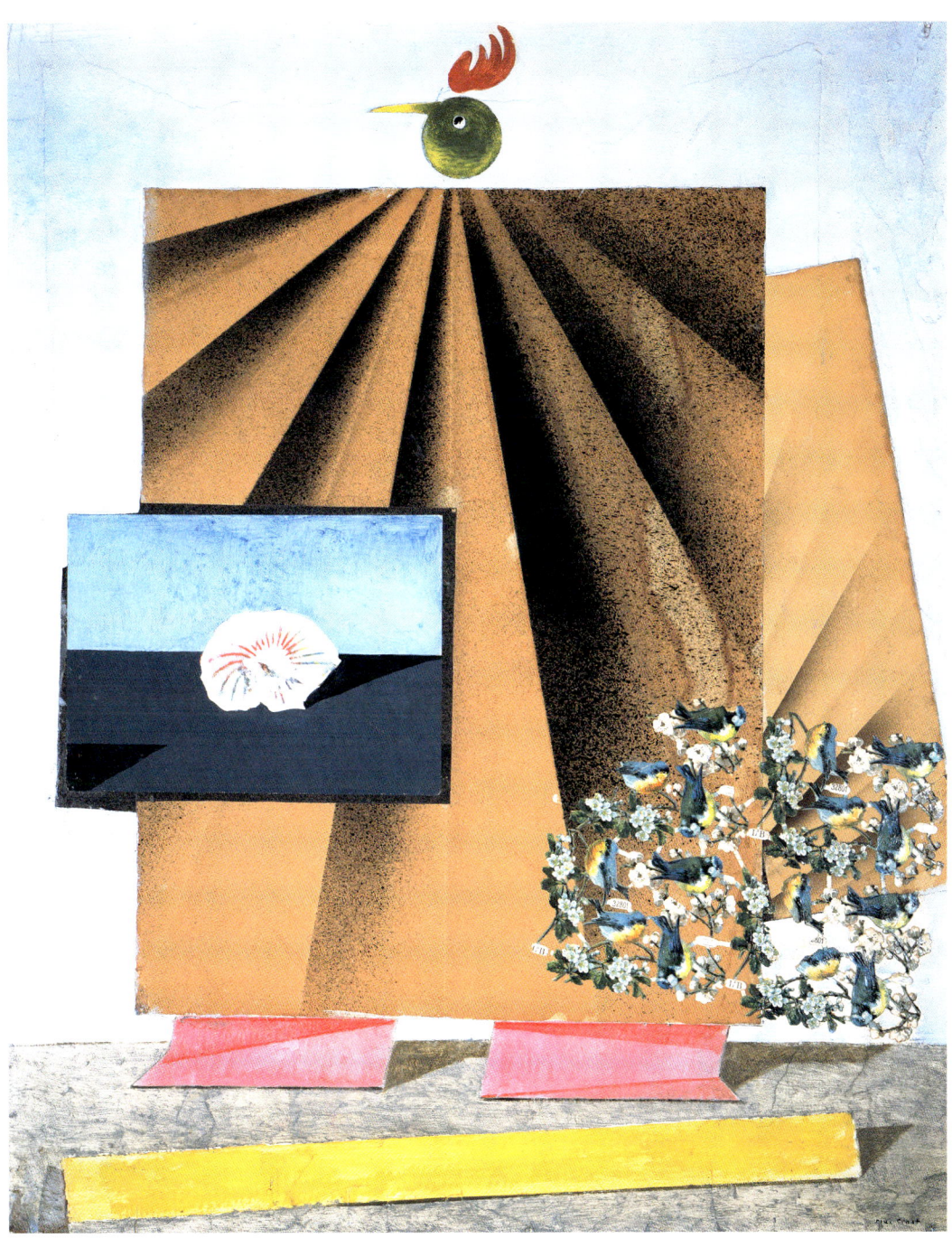

Loplop Presents a Flower or *Anthropomorphic Figure with Shell Flower*, 1930
Oil and collage on plywood, 99 x 81 cm (39 x 32 in.)
Geneva, Galerie Jan Krugier, Ditesheim & Cie

Max Ernst
The King Playing with the Queen, 1944

Max Ernst and Dorothea Tanning spent the summer of 1944 as guests of the gallery owner Julien Levy on Long Island. There, Ernst embarked on a thorough investigation into the intricacies of chess. Having modelled chess pieces and turned them into sculptures in 1929, he once again used chess-men as the basis for works whose meaning and effect went far beyond the technical problems of the game. Unlike Marcel Duchamp, who in 1923 started playing chess impassionately and by 1932 was even writing about chess problems for a specialist magazine, Max Ernst was more concerned with the game's magical and literary qualities. The world opened up to the spectator by his chess pieces could be compared to the kingdom created by Lewis Carroll, a favourite author of Ernst's. In *Through the Looking-Glass*, Carroll leads his young heroine Alice into a different reality, a world inhabited by chess pieces on the other side of the mirror.

The scene set by Max Ernst is played out on a flat surface over which looms the half-length figure of the king. The king is both a chess piece and a player. His two long arms seem to move, preparing to shift the other pieces. His right arm shields the relatively large queen, while the remaining, smaller pieces are lined up on his left. It is obvious from the position of his left hand, which looks as though it might be about to produce a pawn from up his sleeve, that he is less interested in the other pieces than he is in protecting the queen.

The special relationship between king and queen is clear from the title of the sculpture – *The King Playing with the Queen.* As well as romantic, fairy-tale associations, this also has erotic connotations, intensified by the horns on the head of the king who possessively and protectively surrounds the queen. He reminds us of the sensual and violent Minotaur that terrorises beautiful naked women in the works of Picasso, although Max Ernst's sculpture is characterised by strong, abstract forms. Observing the king's demonic appearance, his authoritarian manner towards the smaller pieces and the line of his arm as it encircles the queen, we think of an omnipotent ruler, a despot or prehistoric deity directing and manipulating the drama being played out on the world stage.

The King Playing with the Queen could be interpreted as an image of the power struggle taking place in the great arena of history, the tragic armed conflict that was at its height in 1944, the year in which the work was created. The war also cast its shadow over Ernst's own life as he was forced to escape from France and into exile in America. But his sculpture seems to possess even more layers of meaning. In the context of the artist's Surrealist connections, *The King Playing with the Queen* can be read as a symbolic representation of "the other side" of each of our lives. It can be seen as the image of a superior force whose hidden manipulations control and decide our action without our realising it.

The King Playing with the Queen, 1944
Plaster (original version),
97.8 x 46.4 x 52.3 cm (38½ x 18¼ x 20½ in.)
Riehen/Basle, Fondation Beyeler

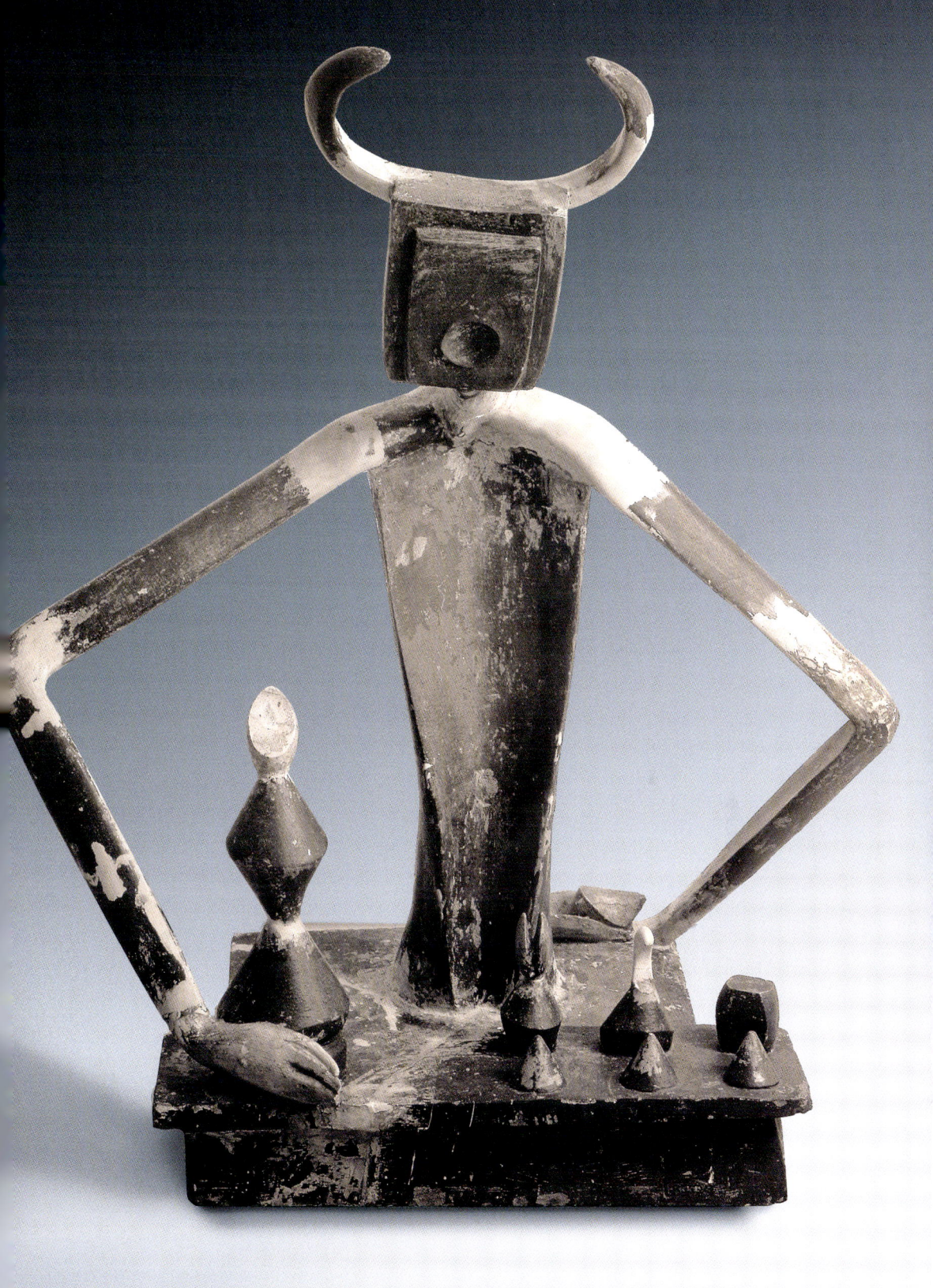

Alberto Giacometti
Man and Woman, 1928/29

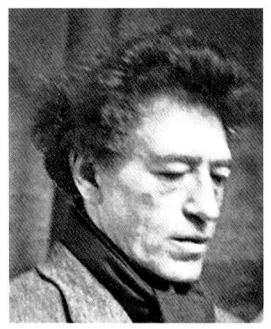

b. 1901 in Borgonovo,
Switzerland
d. 1966 in Chur, Switzerland

In 1922 Alberto Giacometti moved from Geneva, where he had studied for a year at the city's École des Arts et Metiers, to Paris, where he was a pupil of the French sculptor Antoine Bourdelle. His work was shown in public for the first time when he took part in an exhibition at the Salon des Tuileries in 1925. In 1930, Giacometti met the Surrealists Louis Aragon, André Breton and Salvador Dalí. The photographer Brassaï visited Giacometti's Paris studio around this time, describing it as a "plaster grotto", filled with sculptures, which he compared to "stalactites and stalagmites". Brassaï saw them as objects that would become part of dreamlike configurations, as symbols of unconscious feelings and suppressed desires.

Brassaï's point of view captures the essence of Giacometti's sculptures dating from that particular creative period. *Man and Woman* seems to use the language of forms to reduce the relationship between man and woman to physical desire, which according to Freud is the motivating force behind all human behaviour. Giacometti develops his sculpture from two elements. These are clearly identifiable as male and female, in the sense that the two are presented as the personification of their respective sexual organs.

The male part of the sculpture is reminiscent of a bow and arrow, while the female element is shaped like a goblet ready to receive the spike pointing towards it. With *Man and Woman*, Giacometti sculpted a highly abstract and austere piece of symbolism, which the spectator can instinctively understand and interpret in different ways. On the one hand it is a very dynamic composition, in which the soft vitality of the female figure and the zigzag lines of her upper body respond to the tension of the bow which provides the propulsive force that drives the masculine arrow. On the other, the figures representing man and woman also form a static, immovable structure which seems to confirm that fate has bound them together for all eternity.

This bond finds violent expression in *Woman with Her Throat Cut*. Like a giant insect, the woman lies dead on the ground. The inordinately long, thin arms and legs are spider-like, the large vertebra and ribcage are reminiscent of a beetle's shell and the small head could belong to a worm. Only the breasts curving above a narrow waist belong to a human body. In creating this complex structure in which the victim appears as the aggressor, could Giacometti be playing with the biological phenomenon that the Surrealists elevated to mythical status – the female praying mantis that eats the male after mating?

Man and Woman, 1928/29
Bronze, 40 x 40 x 16.5 cm (15¾ x 15¾ x 6½ in.)
Paris, Musée national d'art moderne,
Centre Pompidou

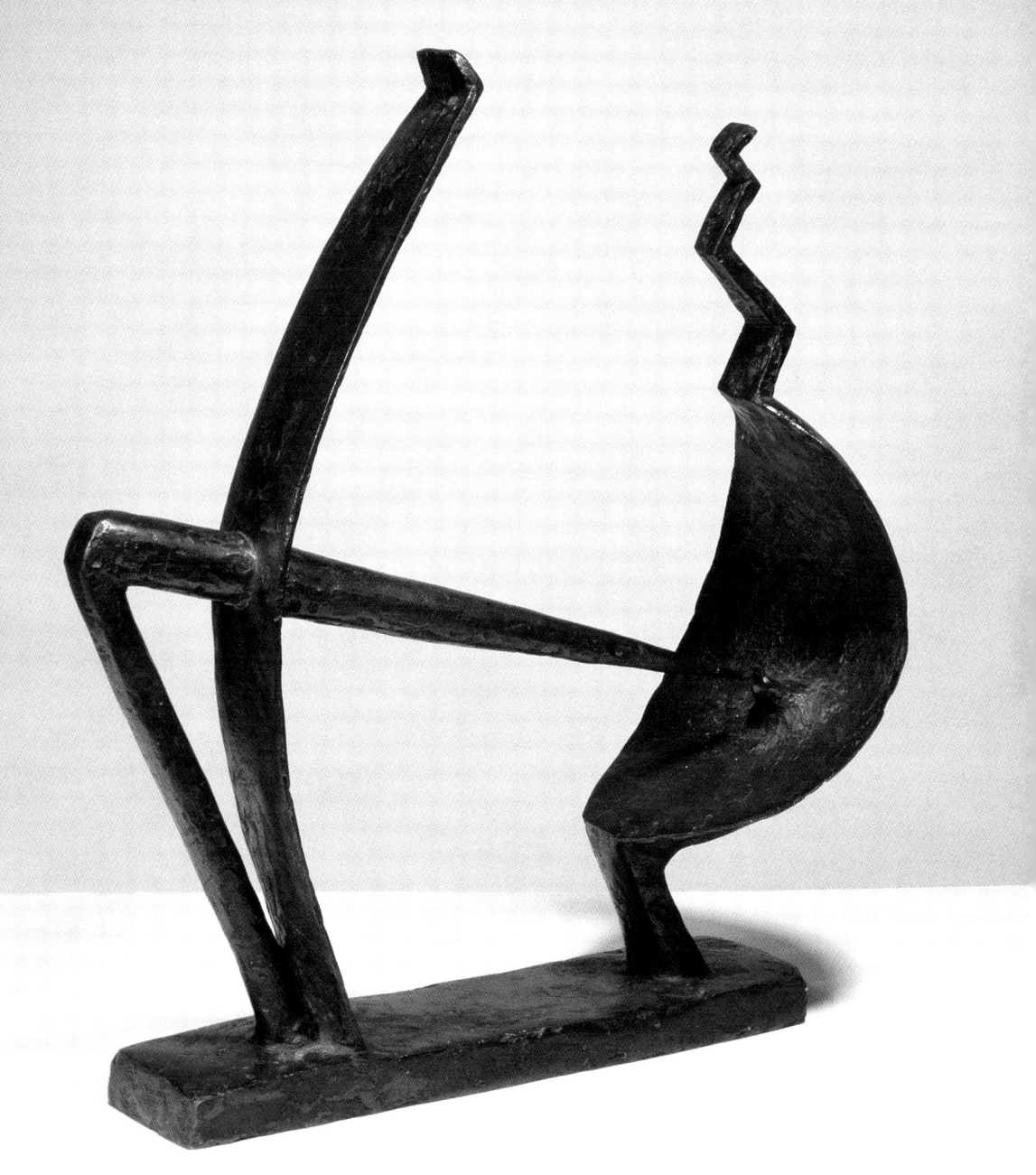

Paul Klee
Room Perspective with Inhabitants, 1921

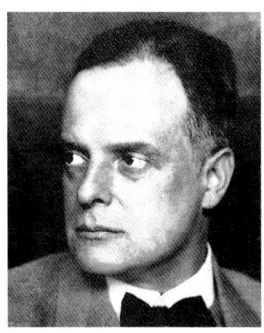

b. 1879 in Münchenbuchsee, Switzerland
d. 1940 in Muralto, Switzerland

In the first *Manifesto of Surrealism* of 1924, André Breton lists a number of poets and writers who, in his view, were sympathetic to Surrealism. Only once does he mention visual artists present and past, among them Paul Klee. In fact, in 1925, Klee exhibited alongside the Surrealists, Hans Arp, Pablo Picasso, Man Ray and Pierre Roy at the Galerie Pierre in Paris. Klee did not select any of his current works for the show, turning instead to two watercolours painted in 1920 as a response to seeing works by de Chirico. The first of these, *Room Perspective with Inhabitants*, was pictured in the exhibition catalogue and significantly renamed *Spirit Room*. The new title was not only more in tune with the Surrealist world of the imagination than Klee's laconic title; *Spirit Room* accords perfectly with the shadowy and dramatically foreshortened perspective of a space in whose vanishing lines several figures are helplessly entwined. The introduction to the catalogue, written by André Breton and Robert Desnos, suggested a quite different approach to the work, more poetic and rich in associations. They saw the unsettling tunnel-like image as an opening in a mountain: "Très loin un homme s'apprête à gravir la montagne entr'ouverte" (In the far distance a man prepares to climb the half-open mountain). It is difficult to gauge now how far Klee agreed with such an interpretation. Even so, at that time he was striving to make artistic connections with ideas other than the Constructivist and Functionalist tendencies that predominated at the Bauhaus in Dessau, where he was a teacher. Klee sought to give his art a broader framework and to liberate the spectator from a banal reality that was no more than a surface beneath which other worlds lay hidden. His objective of revealing the "true" ideas behind visible things – a deeply Romantic way of thinking – brought him very close to the Surrealist position.

In a whole series of prints dating from the early 1920s in which Klee played with variations on the theme of perspective, we the spectators are admitted to some bewildering spaces. We look, as though through a tunnel entrance, into a room that extends endlessly into the distance with walls, ceilings and floors covered with vanishing lines. People, pieces of furniture and objects are caught up, as if in a spider's web, in this structure, which began life as a framework to guide the artist but has now turned into a net – or prison bars. In 1919 Max Ernst had visited Klee in Munich and introduced him to works by de Chirico published in the periodical *Valori Plastici*. These must certainly have been an important source of inspiration for Klee's experiments with perspective.

Room Perspective with Inhabitants, 1921
Watercolour over oil transfer drawing on French Ingres paper mounted on cardboard, 48.5 x 31.7 cm (19 x 12½ in.)
Berne, Zentrum Paul Klee

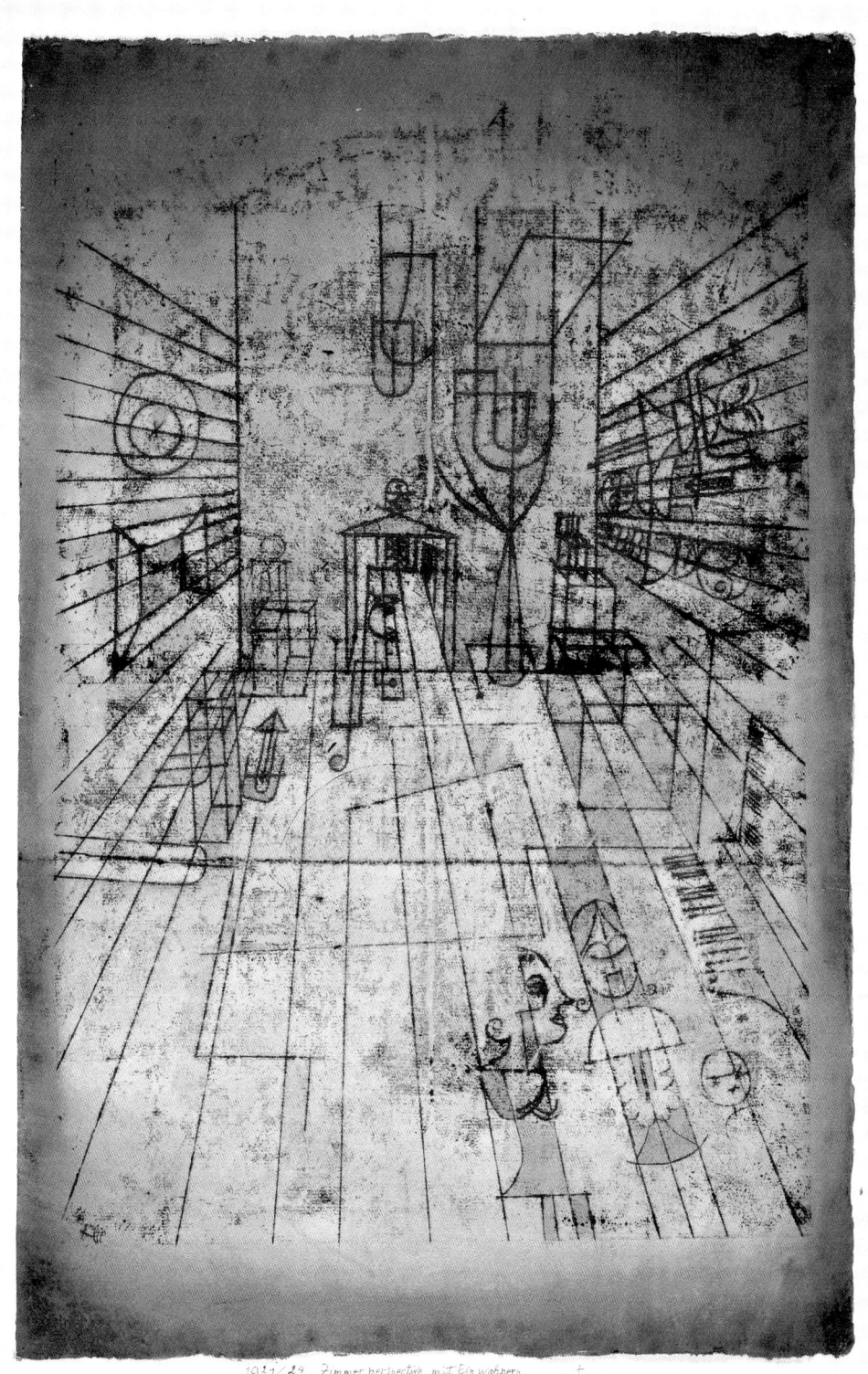

1927/24 Zimmer perspective mit Einwohnern †

Wifredo Lam
The Jungle, 1943

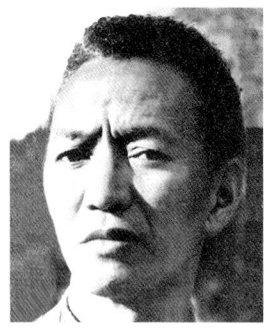

b. 1902 in Sagua la Grande, Cuba
d. 1982 in Paris

Wifredo Lam's mature work, created in the 1940s, reflects both the painter's roots in the culture of his native Cuba and his relationship with artists of the European avant-garde. It was under their influence that he rediscovered, and mirrored in his art, the primitivism he had known during a childhood spent in close contact with the natural world.

After training at the Escuela de Bellas Artes in Havana, in 1923 Lam began attending free painting classes in Madrid and continued his artistic education by studying the Old Masters in the Prado. But it was the four years spent in Paris, from 1938 to 1941, that were to be the most decisive for Lam's development as a painter. There, he formed a close relationship with Pablo Picasso, and together they exhibited their work at the Perls Galleries, New York in 1939.

Of course, while he was in Paris, Lam also came under the influence of the Surrealists, whose interest in the supernatural, the irrational and magic was fertile soil for the Cuban painter. "When I was small, I was frightened of the power of my own imagination. At the end of the town of Sagua la Grande, near our house … the forest began … I never saw any ghosts but I invented them. When I went for walks at night I was scared of the moon, the eye of the shadows. I felt I was an outsider, different from the rest. I don't know where it comes from. I have been like that since childhood."

The forest of his childhood crops up again in Lam's jungle pictures, which date from the early 1940s, before he fled Fascism and returned to his homeland. In his greatest composition, *The Jungle* (1943), now in New York's Museum of Modern Art, he intersperses monstrous beings, close relatives of Picasso's surreal creatures of the period, among the Cuban sugar cane. Unlike Picasso, Lam does not create monumental versions of these creatures inspired by African sculpture and primitive art. Instead he stresses their diversity and their omnipresence amid the dense vegetation, through which their constantly murmuring voices seem to penetrate.

"When I painted it (*The Jungle*), the doors and windows of my studio were open so that passers-by could see in. They cried: 'Don't look, it's the Devil!' And they were right. One of my friends correctly found in the picture a spirit close to that of some representations of Hell done in the Middle Ages. In any case, the title does not correspond with the reality of nature in Cuba, where one does not find jungle, but *bosque, monte, manigua* – woods, mountains, open country – and the background of the composition is a sugar-cane plantation. My painting had to communicate a psychological condition."

Both creatures and plants in the jungle display the same metallic materiality. They are bathed in a subdued light that makes them seem like figures in a fantasy, a fantasy that has much in common with the Surrealists' interest in sexuality and violence. Lam's stylization of plant and organic forms is a long way from the old-masterly illusionism of Salvador Dalí, and it doesn't bear much relationship to Max Ernst's forest pictures. On the contrary, it is much closer to the painting of Matta. Despite all the figurative elements in their work, both Lam and Matta appear, in their rhythmic repetition of non-representational forms, to point the way towards Abstract Expressionism.

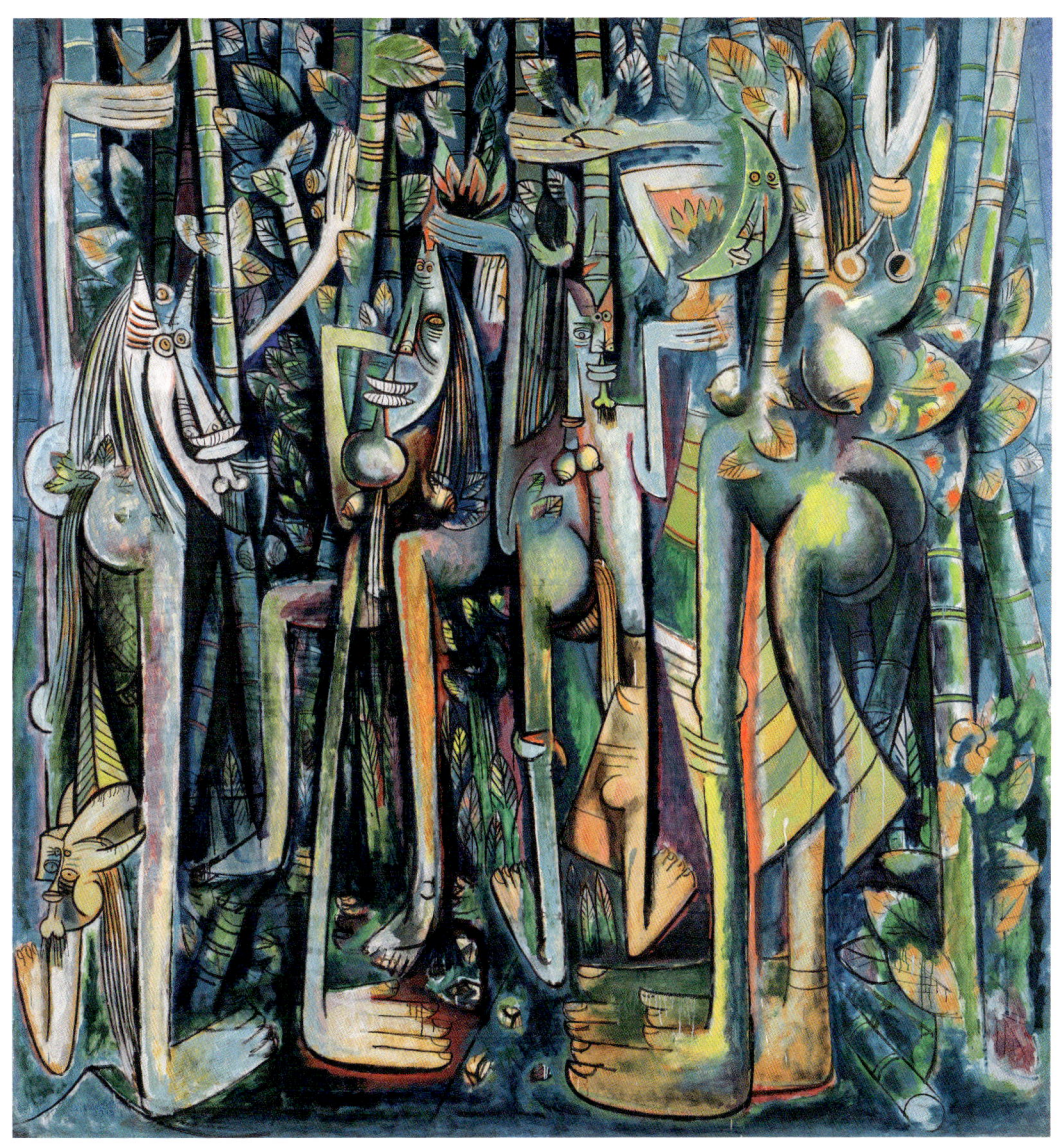

The Jungle, 1943
Gouache on paper on canvas,
239.4 x 229.9 cm (94¼ x 90½ in.)
New York, The Museum of Modern Art,
Inter-American Fund

René Magritte
The Key to Dreams, 1927

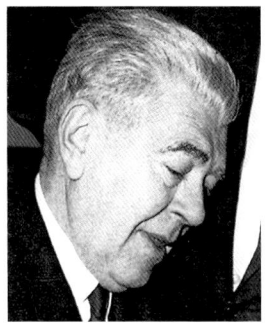

b. 1898 in Lessines, Belgium
d. 1967 in Brussels

The series entitled *The Key to Dreams*, which plays such a special and central role in René Magritte's work, was painted between 1927 and 1930. Magritte's "word-pictures" tackle the notions that characterise his landscapes – mystery, the unsayable and the unnameable – on many different intellectual levels. At first, however, they seem simplistic and banal.

The Key to Dreams is a composition divided into four equal sections and seen as if through a painted-on window frame. In each of the quarters, which look like small blackboards, Magritte has painted highly realistic objects, labelled underneath in a schoolboyish hand. Only one – "L'éponge" (sponge) – has the correct caption. The three other objects are wrongly labelled. A handbag is entitled "Le ciel" (The sky), an open pocket knife is "L'oiseau" (The bird) and a leaf is identified as "La table" (The table). To the spectator standing in front of the picture, which calls up associations of carefully formed handwriting on a school blackboard, or the accurate illustrations in an encyclopaedia, the incorrect labelling would at first seem to be a mistake, were it not for the correctly named sponge, where name and image correspond. Because this system of classification is not totally incorrect, we instinctively look for a different way of ordering things. The fracture in the system, the thin crack in what we see as normal and customary, provokes the thought process the painter intended.

During his time in Paris, Magritte was already becoming interested in the relationship between word, image and object as a theme in the visual arts. His concern was reflected in the many variants of the word-picture he produced at that period. As for the theory, Magritte's first contribution to the journal *La Révolution surréaliste*, in the same edition that carried the *Second Manifesto of Surrealism*, reported on the results of his explorations. He outlined eighteen rules, each illustrated by a sketch, governing the relationship between word and image. These highlight the difference between the written and spoken word and visual language, which, as Magritte wrote in a letter to Camille Goemans, is a condition of the mind. When we examine the differences between words and objects and between mind, body and ideas, they become even greater.

Magritte's eighteen rules show that, in reality, an object's image (i. e. the one assigned to it by convention) and its name (i. e. the one assigned to it by another convention) have different functions. In view of those differences – which at the same time imply independence and equality – a word or an image can take the place of a real object or can designate an object. This occurs through the conscious evocation of a "mental image". Words and images may, however, designate nothing but themselves. Their meaning only becomes clear when they are used and mixed together.

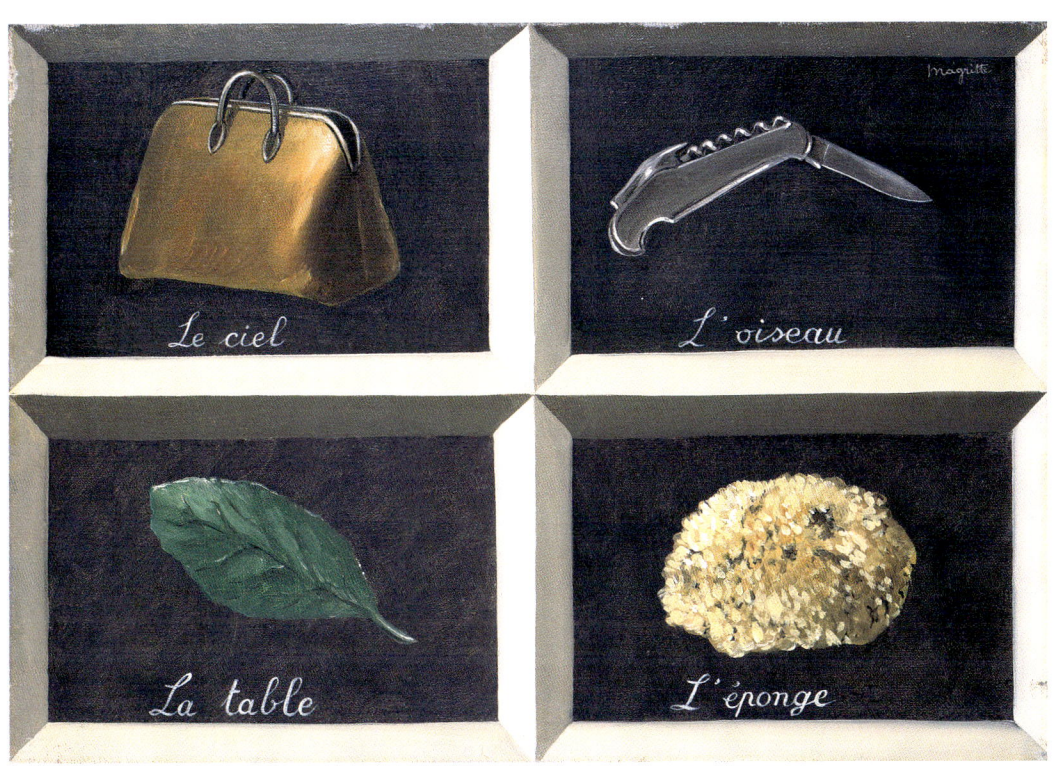

The Key to Dreams, 1927
Oil on canvas, 38 x 53 cm (15 x 21 in.)
Munich, Pinakothek der Moderne

René Magritte
The Door to Freedom, 1933

After studying at the Académie Royale des Beaux-Arts in Brussels and working briefly as a commercial artist, René Magritte, impressed by the paintings of Giorgio de Chirico, painted his own first Surrealist picture in 1925. In Paris, Magritte joined the group of Surrealists led by André Breton and from 1927 to 1930 made his home at Perreux-sur-Marne close to the French capital. However, after this relatively short stay, he returned to Brussels where he remained until his death, living a quiet, unspectacular and outwardly normal middle-class life.

The life of the painter, whose public demeanour diverted attention from a real existence devoted entirely to his art, is mirrored in his paintings of seemingly ordinary subjects whose real intention is to point to something hidden, to provoke feelings of insecurity and create an air of mystery. Magritte's landscapes, which constitute a major part of his output, set out to explore these issues, although at first they appear much easier to understand than traditional landscape paintings. The "realistic", eye-catching style of Magritte's painting, his simple clear compositions and his concentration on essentials, are like plain language without any deeper meaning. Only close analysis reveals the ambiguity of his works.

The Door to Freedom is a particularly striking example of the hidden presence of something mysterious. Through a window we see a gentle, hilly landscape. At the end of a broad meadow extending uphill stand several leafy trees, above them a dome of delicate blue sky. This would be a perfectly cheerful image, if it were not clearly breaking up before our eyes. As we look though the window pane, it shatters into a thousand fragments. Pieces of broken glass remain in place like transparent film in front of the vista. The shards that have fallen to the floor are like pieces of a jigsaw reproducing the scene observed through the window.

Was the landscape only painted on the window pane? Is this not a transparent pane at all, but a painting? No clear explanation is possible and so we conclude that the pieces of glass on the painting are a contradiction. The landscape beyond the broken window is still unscathed and visible. At the same time, the broken glass that has fallen to the floor is not transparent but shows pieces cut out from the landscape, while we can still see through the glass that remains stuck in the window frame. We as spectators feel called upon to carry out a visual reconstruction but, try as we may, we cannot achieve any complete certainty.

The relationship between reality and painting is permanently destroyed; despite Magritte's talent for creating an illusion, we can no longer sustain any real belief in either image or reflection. The certainty guaranteed by paintings of centuries past, recalled by the *trompe-l'œil* curtain drawn to the sides of the window, is no longer there.

The Door to Freedom, 1933
Oil on canvas, 80 x 60 cm (31½ x 23½ in.)
Madrid, Museo Thyssen-Bornemisza

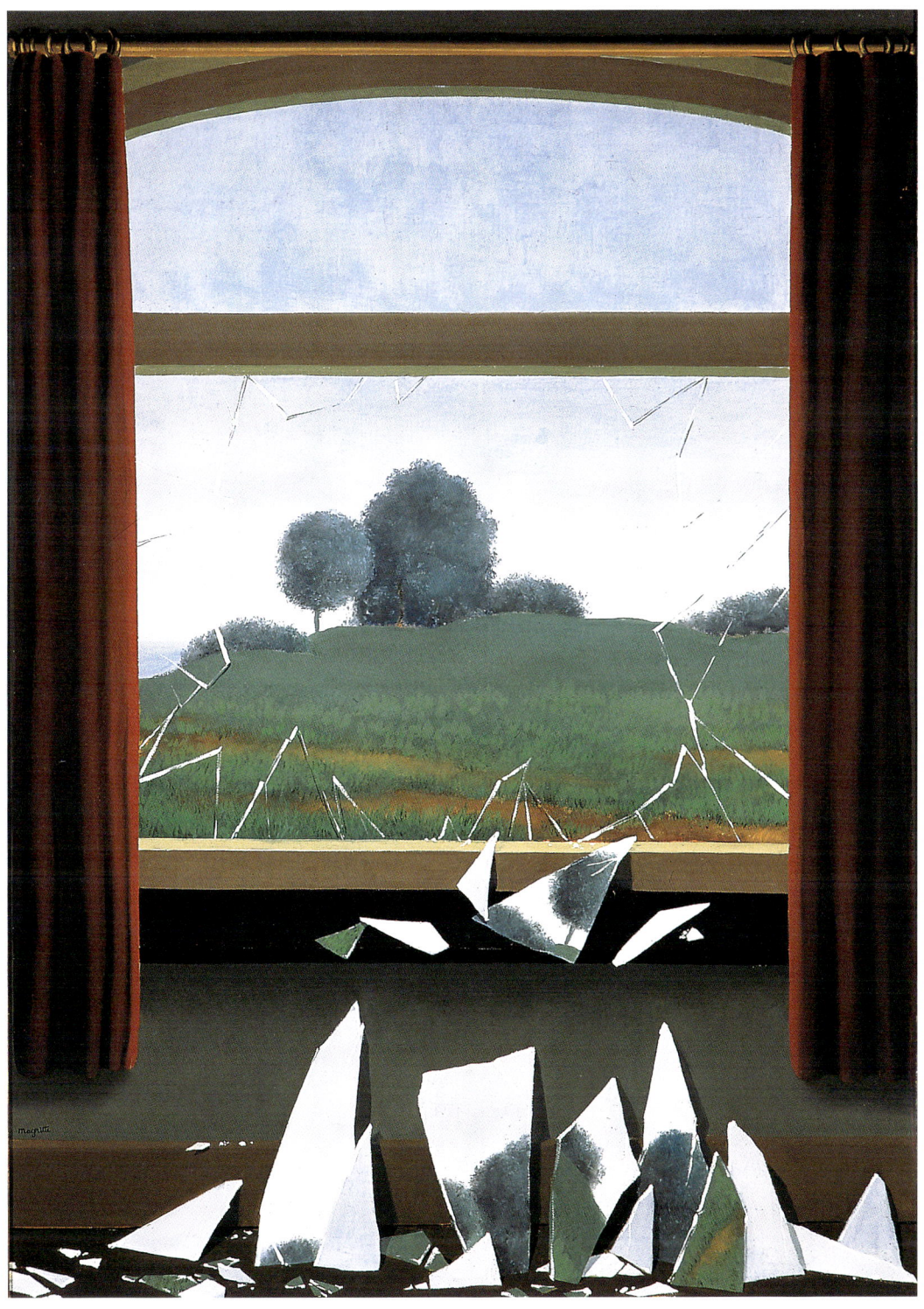

René Magritte
Time Transfixed, 1938

In the painting *Time Transfixed* René Magritte seems to capture all the feelings associated with time standing still. Every detail of his museum-like setting reflects the slow passage of the minutes shown on the clock on the mantelpiece. Nothing ever seems to happen, nor, one suspects, will anything ever happen in this room, a section of which Magritte reproduces in meticulous detail. Only the monotonous ticking of the clock between the two candlesticks breaks the silence, adding even more to the boredom. What are we waiting for? What has happened here? What is going to happen?

In this atmosphere fraught with tension, the locomotive penetrating the fireplace, absurd as it may seem, comes almost as a relief. Only an event on this scale, unstoppable and ear-splitting, could shatter the forbidding silence of this strange, hostile space. Moreover, we have the odd impression that this undersized engine with its smoke billowing up the chimney actually belongs with the room. Drawn with draughtsman-like precision, it shares a certain kinship with the other objects and structures in the room – the black clock, the classical fireplace, the simple frame of the mirror and the uncomplicated candlesticks. All of which makes the scene even more puzzling.

In an essay written in 1928 and entitled "Theatre in the Midst of Life", Magritte portrayed his art as a stage on which the natural laws of time and space cease to apply. Scenes are played out in which a princess strides through a wall, pieces of fruit on a table represent birds, there are unexplained shadows and open doors with nothing behind them.

A similarly surreal atmosphere pervades Magritte's 1928 painting *The Voice of Silence*. It is a picture of two halves. On the right, we see a cosy middle-class living room with a sofa, a picture on the wall, shelves and house plants. The left side of the picture, however, is plunged into impenetrable darkness, opening up a way into the void. We are given a glimpse into the murky world of imaginary dangers and fears, as vague feelings of menace and entrapment increase. Suddenly the familiar room on the right seems no more than a façade behind which lurk unknown horrors, a mask behind which we hide in dread.

How is it possible to live with this sense of bewilderment that Magritte chose as the theme of his art? How can we deal with the sudden disorientation that can shatter the most banal existence? As Magritte understood it, the artist first and foremost directs his consciousness to life, not to ideas, like the philosopher, or to art, like those artists content merely to achieve success in the art world. To the Surrealist painter, nothing apart from life itself can be an end in itself. Art (a vehicle for ideas) is a by-product of life, and works of art do not impinge on real life.

Time Transfixed, 1938
Oil on canvas, 147 x 99 cm (58 x 39 in.)
The Art Institute of Chicago,
Joseph Winterbotham Collection

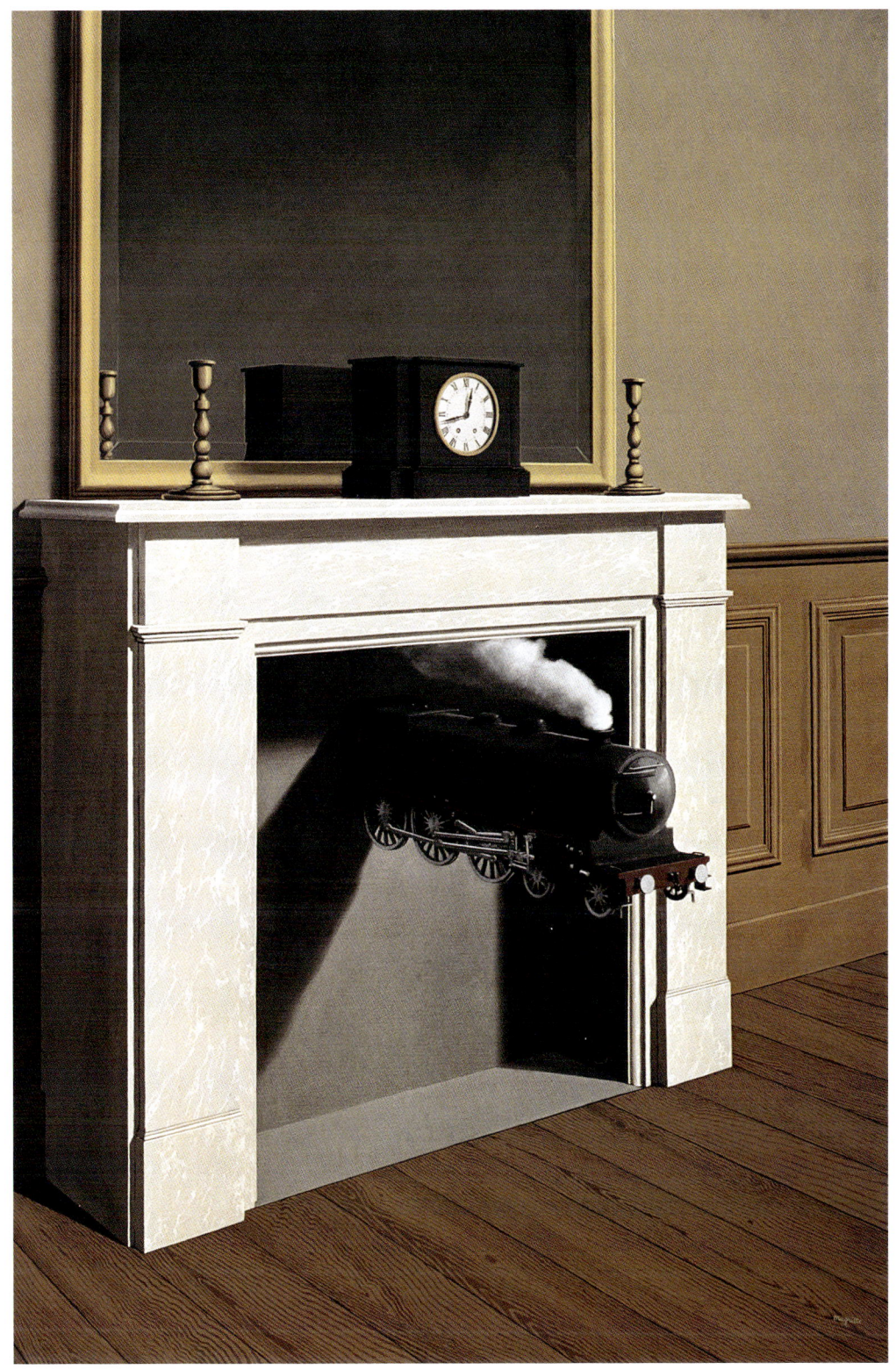

René Magritte
The Empire of Light, 1954

The Empire of Light, a theme that René Magritte revisited several times in the 1950s, shows a peaceful scene. A house with a street lamp outside stands in a quiet square in front of a tall tree. The shutters are closed, apart from those at two upstairs windows, where the lights are on. Everything is silent. The dark trees surrounding the house seem to watch over it as it sleeps. Only slowly do we grasp the fact that there is a fracture running through the entire composition. Above house and trees we see a bright, daytime sky, scattered with fleecy white clouds. It is part of the picture but nevertheless alien and otherworldly, since the light from the sky has no effect on the scene in the foreground. Day and night collide but do not connect. They are part of the same world and yet are estranged. They are as different from one another as the states of wakefulness and sleep.

Magritte was fascinated by this association of opposites. As he explained in an essay on *The Empire of Light*, the idea behind a particular painting is not visible in the painting, in the same way an idea is not visible to the eye. The eye can see what the picture represents, but what it represents are the things that result from the process of thinking. *The Empire of Light* also represents these things or, to be more precise, it shows a nocturnal landscape and a daytime sky. The landscape recalls night, the sky, day. Magritte writes that the evocation of night and day appears to have the power to surprise and delight us. His name for this power is poetry and the reason he believes in its existence is because he has always been interested in night and day, without preferring one to the other. Both fill him with astonishment and wonder. This insoluble puzzle not only fascinated Magritte. It was also at the very centre of Surrealist thought.

André Breton, who also wrote about *The Empire of Light* in 1964, characteristically emphasised the close and confusing relationship between light and shadow in Magritte's painting. The work, he said, defied generally accepted ideas and conventions to such a degree that anyone passing quickly by the painting might imagine seeing stars in the daytime sky. Since the publication of Breton's first *Manifesto of Surrealism*, the Surrealists had proposed new ways of seeing as an alternative to "generally accepted ideas and conventions". Their ideas were much more relevant to the realm of creativity than actions guided by reason. The language and imagery of dreams were crucial factors in the creation of Surrealist art, and individual artists each had quite different ways of exploiting these rich sources of inspiration.

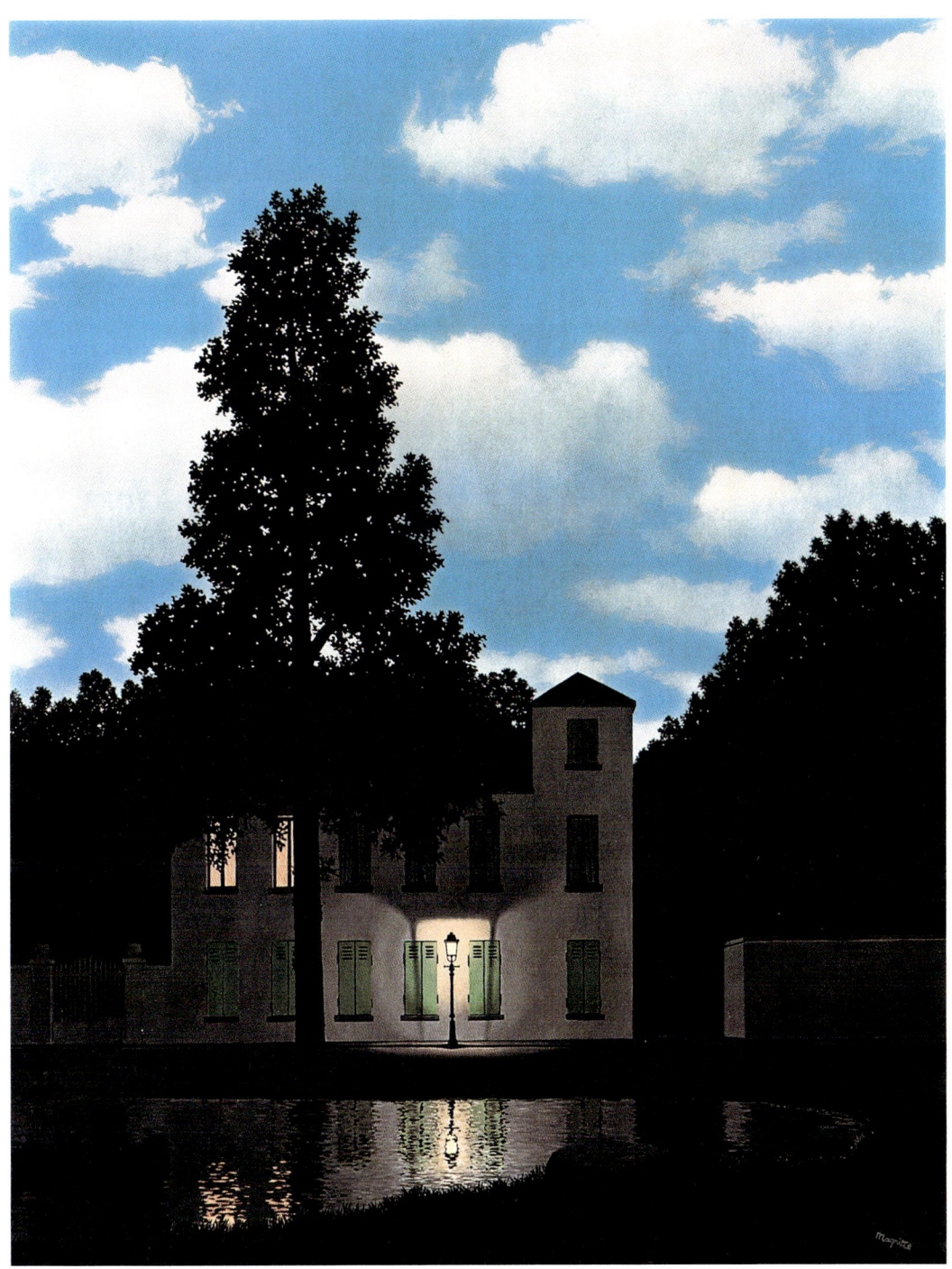

The Empire of Light, 1954
Oil on canvas, 146 x 114 cm (57½ x 45 in.)
Brussels, Musées royaux des Beaux-Arts de Belgique

André Masson
The Villagers, 1927

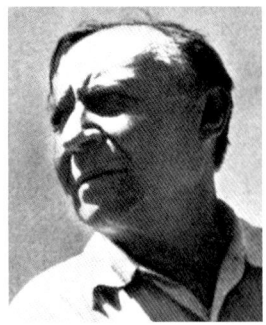

b. 1896 in Balagny-sur-Thérain, France
d. 1987 in Paris

The group of friends who in the early 1920s used to meet regularly at André Masson's studio on the rue Blomet in Paris – among them Antonin Artaud, Robert Desnos and Michel Leiris – appreciated Masson's clear awareness of human ambiguity. But what relevance does this have to Masson's art? If we take ambiguity to mean a lack of coherence between human thought and action, perception and behaviour, and apply these disconnected and unrelated concepts to a painting, it implies that the work can be interpreted on two levels. On the one hand the special textural qualities of Masson's paintings convey emotions, moods and a particular atmosphere. On the other, we have a linear drawing which appears abstract but which also contains recognisable figures and objects. It seems as if these figurative elements have been created without the conscious control of the artist, in line with André Breton's definition of *dessin automatique* – an automatic method of drawing capable of producing seismographic images without any rational control by the artist.

André Masson's drawings bearing the title *Automatic Drawing* consist of interwoven lines, which at first sight look like a net created quite fortuitously. Only on closer examination do we perceive nameable forms. We can make out limbs, feet, hands and, here and there, eyes, faces and genitalia. The uncontrolled, spontaneous creative process gives the impression of a composition that changes under the eyes of the spectator, opening up a whole series of new and different perceptions.

At least as influential as Surrealism on Masson's work were his own earlier education and his interest in Nietzsche's philosophy, classical literature and mythology. His passion for these subjects led to his great themes – wars, massacres and heroism. His compositions always deal with figures who, unaware of the fate awaiting them, defenceless against the tides of life and relying on their instincts, are simply swept away. This is true of the villagers in the picture *The Villagers*. A line drawn in the sandy ground demarcates the whole world in which they live. The line leading from the eye of the crude figure in the centre also embraces elements arbitrarily chosen from his surroundings: a cockerel, a bird's head, a broad foot that casts a tangible red shadow suggesting death and violence. The earthy colours and the texture of the sand also symbolise village life. The villagers are part of the natural world that has shaped them, the environment from which the artist has created an image of their lives, even going so far as to scatter sand on the canvas.

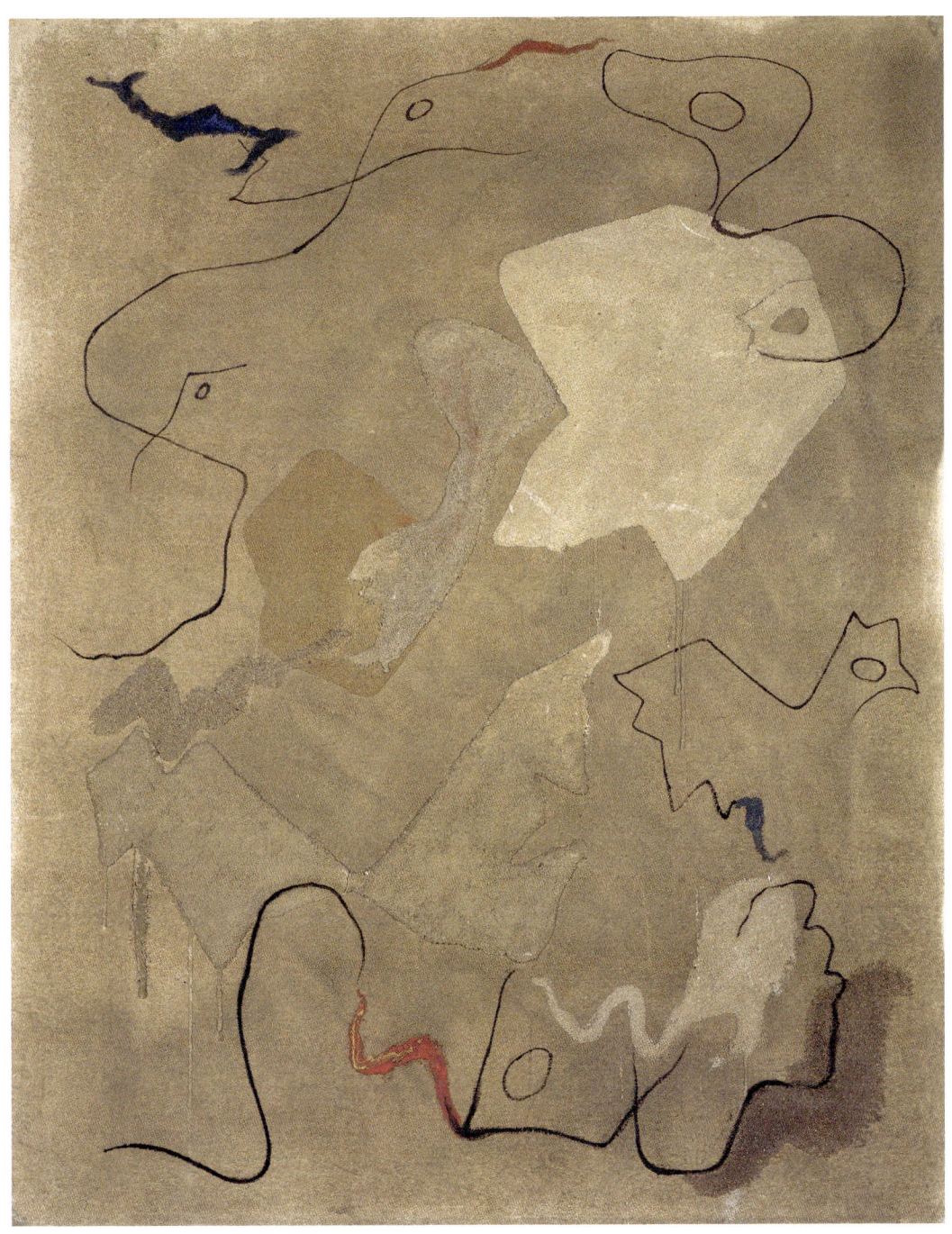

The Villagers, 1927
Oil and sand on canvas, 80.5 x 64.5 cm (31¾ x 25½ in.)
Paris, Musée national d'art moderne, Centre Pompidou

Roberto Matta
Year 44, 1942

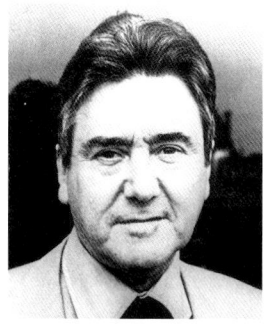

b. 1911 in Santiago de Chile
d. 2002 in Civitavecchia, Italy

It was in 1937, relatively late in the history of the Paris Surrealists, that Matta (Roberto Sebastián Antonio Matta Echaurren) met André Breton and his circle. Matta had worked in Le Corbusier's studio in the city. "I met them and I was so ignorant that they were not interested in me. But then they looked at my drawings and said 'You are a Surrealist.'" In an interview, Matta described his first encounter with a group of artists who would permanently influence his development as a painter. Their support would also help him deal with intellectual problems resulting from his unsatisfactory attempts at architecture. "The question was 'how can we find out more about what a house should actually be, who it should be built for?' In short, who is the guy I am building it for? … Instead of designing houses I designed a state of being – you could call it psychology. I wanted to grasp how the human mind worked. That's why I began to paint without being a painter. I had never been to art school. But how could I represent psychological function? I called the first paintings *morphologie psychologique* – psychological morphology – morphology of desire, morphology of fear, morphology of pain … We simply do not have the language to express these things …"

Matta's paintings present people in space. His figures, seemingly deprived of their outer covering, with their nerves and emotions laid bare, appear in a space that affords them no refuge or protection and bears absolutely no relation to what we would term a house, room or building. In an 1946 article for Société anonyme, Marcel Duchamp wrote that Matta's most important contribution to Surrealist painting was his discovery of spaces that art had so far left unexplored. Matta, said Duchamp, followed modern physicists in their search for this new space which, although represented on canvas, could not be mistaken for yet another three-dimensional illusion.

Year 44, painted in 1942, does not depict space but merely lets the spectator experience it. It conveys the feeling of a person enclosed in a space that echoes his emotions. Matta combines different painterly effects to create that impression – bright draughtsman-like structures on an iridescent red and black background. Floating particles of colour alternate with precisely drawn details, vaguely anatomical fragments seem to interact with the surrounding space, letting it dictate their movements.

Year 44, 1942
Oil on canvas, 127 x 97 cm (50 x 38¼ in.)
Staatliche Museen zu Berlin,
Neue Nationalgalerie

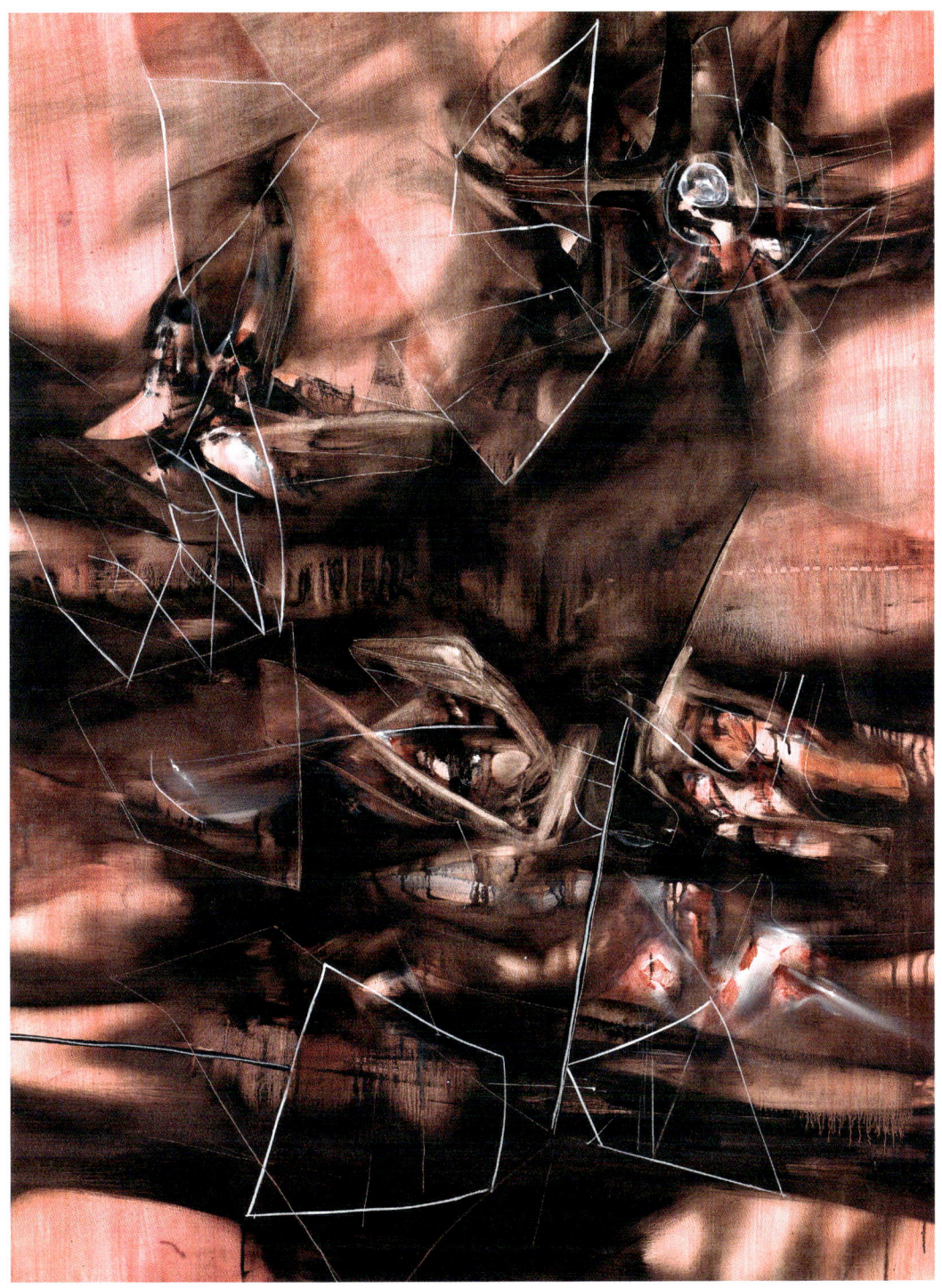

Joan Miró
Stars in the Sexual Organs of Snails, 1925

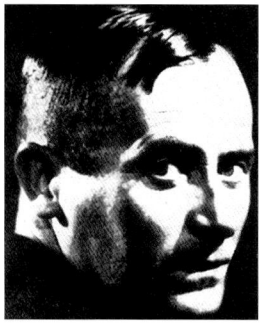

b. 1893 in Barcelona
d. 1983 in Palma de Mallorca

From 1924 onwards, Joan Miró played an active role in the Surrealists' exhibitions and manifestations. This period also marked a turning point in his work. After an initial phase heavily influenced by Cubism and several paintings that could well be described as "magic realism" Joan Miró turned to a style of painting that would truly express what he called the "sparks of the soul". Enthusiastically, he flung himself into paintings in which monstrous or angelic animals, trees with ears and eyes, and even the odd Catalonian peasant with the cap and rifle typical of the region, stand side by side, but without any apparent connection between them. The element that binds them is an atmosphere far beyond any normal perception of reality. Miró's paintings dating from that era might be termed "visions", namely works that open up a space in which dream, poetry and painting meet. In them, concrete forms melt into cloudy areas of colour over which hover magical signs that mingle with lines of poetry to create a dreamlike image.

Stars in the Sexual Organs of Snails is not only a title added to a painting, the lines of script are also an integral part of the composition. The phrase is written in three lines over spirals of soft, blue paint whose shape and colour carry vague associations with snail shells. The letter "t" of the word "escargot" – snail – is caught up in the large red circle in the upper centre of the painting. The soft rounded shape is penetrated by a shooting star, while its lower section is crossed by a black line that links together several of the soft, blurred forms in the bottom half of the painting. The peculiar content and the irregular lettering recall the process of *écriture automatique.* The painting alternates between hard and soft, precision and fluidity, evoking the indefinable sensation of dreaming with its vague awareness that strange, irrational things are happening.

Meanwhile, *Photo: This Is the Colour of My Dreams*, painted in the same year, explores the divergence between rationality and dreams in a quite different way. This is, once again, a "picture poem" in which the writing is an essential ingredient. Conscientiously, like a little boy in his first year at primary school, Miró has written the black letters on the pale canvas: top left in large letters, "Photo", bottom right "ceci est la couleur de mes rêves". The phrase is illustrated by a hazy blue cloud, setting off a seemingly endless series of questions. Do dreams have colours? Can they be photographed? What is hidden behind the blue cloud? Or are the strange remarks written under the inkblot just a bored schoolboy's joke?

Stars in the Sexual Organs of Snails, 1925
Oil on canvas, 129.5 x 97 cm (51 x 38¼ in.)
Düsseldorf, Kunstsammlung
Nordrhein-Westfalen

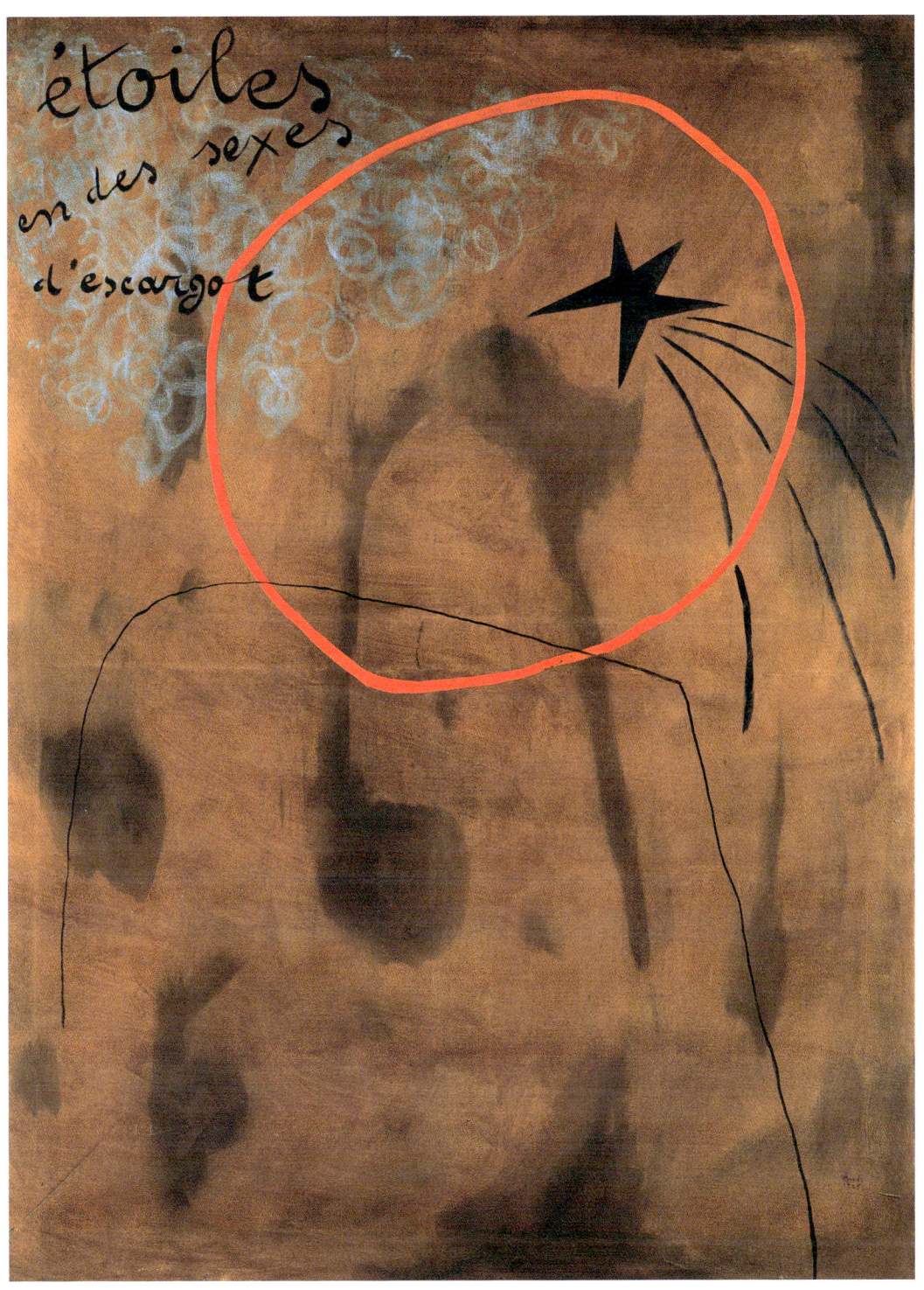

Joan Miró
Collage, 1928

From 1926 onwards, Joan Miró's artistic activities extended beyond painting. He designed stage sets and made objects combining the most incongruous elements and materials. He then went on to create a series of collages, of which this has to be one of the most impressive examples. While in his paintings Miró had already developed succinct formal language, reduced to a few abstract shapes in brown, black and white, Miró's 1928 *Collage* combines simplicity of form with poverty of materials to almost shocking effect. Thick bars of oil paper and old wallpaper lie like a grid over the pale oval background framed with roofing felt. Were this compact composition not overlaid with the delicate and graceful drawing of a female dancer, the work would be dark and heavy, rather than the playful piece that it is. The drawing is like a fragile fabric draped over the grid. The nailed-down background remains empty. The crudity of the material is emphasised by the fragility and elegance of the drawing, which is the focal point of the image. The dancer's body is covered by areas of shadow and the materiality of the collage elements appears to dissolve into thin air. This paradoxical effect make the words of Louis Aragon, poet and friend of Miró, on his Surrealist colleague's work all the more telling: "No matter what it is, however transient it may be, this painter uses everything to express himself, and the more worthless and repulsive it is to those around him, the better."

Meanwhile, other collages are less concerned with the ordinariness and banality of the materials used than with the poetic effect of the clash between different levels of reality. In a *Papier collé* of 1929 Miró cuts two circles out of roofing felt mounted on coarse paper, filling them out in turn with other paper in beige and gray-brown, along with wires and scraps of cloth, and introduces one of his typical drawings. The circles form a universe which, full of motion, also involves the "heavy" elements, integrating them into the circulatory movement.

Collage, 1928
Charcoal on paper, roofing felt,
wallpaper, 99 x 69.5 cm (39 x 27¼ in.)
Munich, Museum Brandhorst

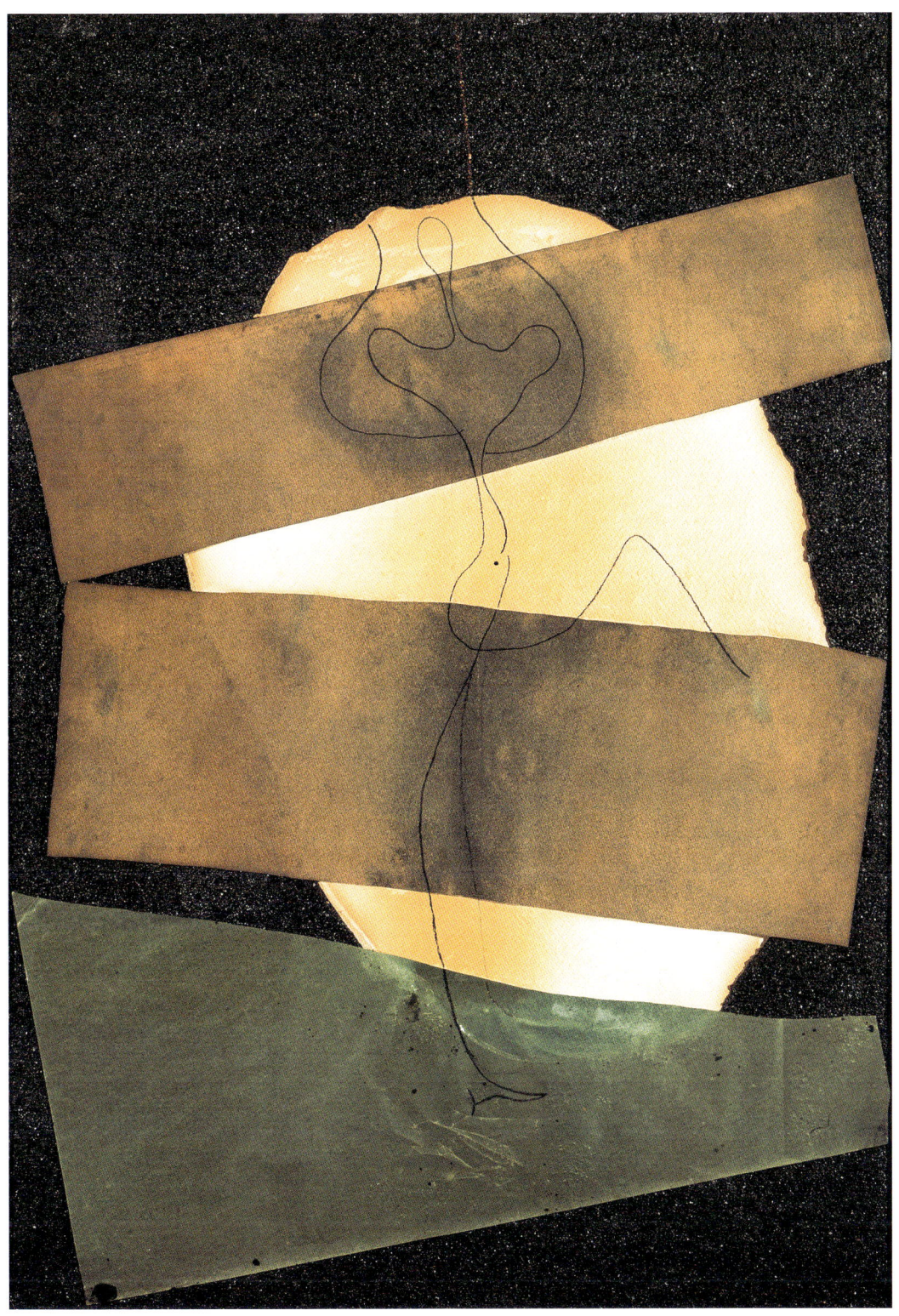

Joan Miró
Woman, 1934

From 1934, when Joan Miró's work entered its so-called "savage" period, there was both cruelty and desperation in his depictions of the human figure. This was a reflection of the historical situation, with the rise of Fascism in Europe and the growing threat of a Second World War. At the same time, there was obvious misogyny in Miró's representations of women as distorted, caricatured figures, every bit as striking as the female creatures that cropped up in Picasso's works of the same period.

Miró, who at this stage frequently used soft, coloured paper and pastels, not only put his subjects through the same horrific metamorphoses as Picasso; he went further still, stressing their ungainliness by using strident colours, whose glowing intensity was underlined by his pastel technique. To the spectator, the woman's body appears soft and bloated, except for the firm horizontal axis, on the left and right of which are tied claw-like hands. In terms of materiality and structure, she is similar to the bone-like forms from which Picasso shaped his *Bathers* in the early 1930s.

As with Picasso's figures, the head is small in relation to the body, and Miró's use of bright colours gives her a birdlike appearance. However, she could also be a huge insect with feelers, like a female praying mantis, which devours the male after sex and which so fascinated the Surrealists. Miró's *Woman (Femme)* is also depicted as a dangerous seductress. Despite the ugliness of her massive body she sends out signals to men who seem to be completely in her thrall. Her breasts, her sex, her rounded hips and large, horizontal orifices blur their vision, leaving them vulnerable to her dangerous allure.

While Miró's 1934 woman is frightening and obsessive, the one portrayed in his 1937 pencil drawing *Naked Woman Climbing a Staircase* is pure caricature. Perched on top of a more or less normally proportioned but thoroughly unappealing body is a bald head with a huge nose, which is also dragged downwards by the weight dangling from it. The naked woman is climbing a staircase and this artificial pose is vaguely reminiscent of an academic nude study. Miró's woman, however, has been robbed of any beauty or idealisation. All that remains is her sexuality.

Picasso's extremely negative perception of women in the early 1930s can be explained by his tense relationship with his first wife Olga. In Miró's case there is no such real-life justification. "The word 'love' as opposed to 'understanding' is an abstract idea," he told Georges Raillard in 1977 during a conversation about the relationship between the sexes. "Lovers are creatures who fight, who consume one another. But I instinctively mistrust abstract ideas."

Woman, 1934
Pastel, 109 x 73 cm (43 x 28¾ in.)
Private collection

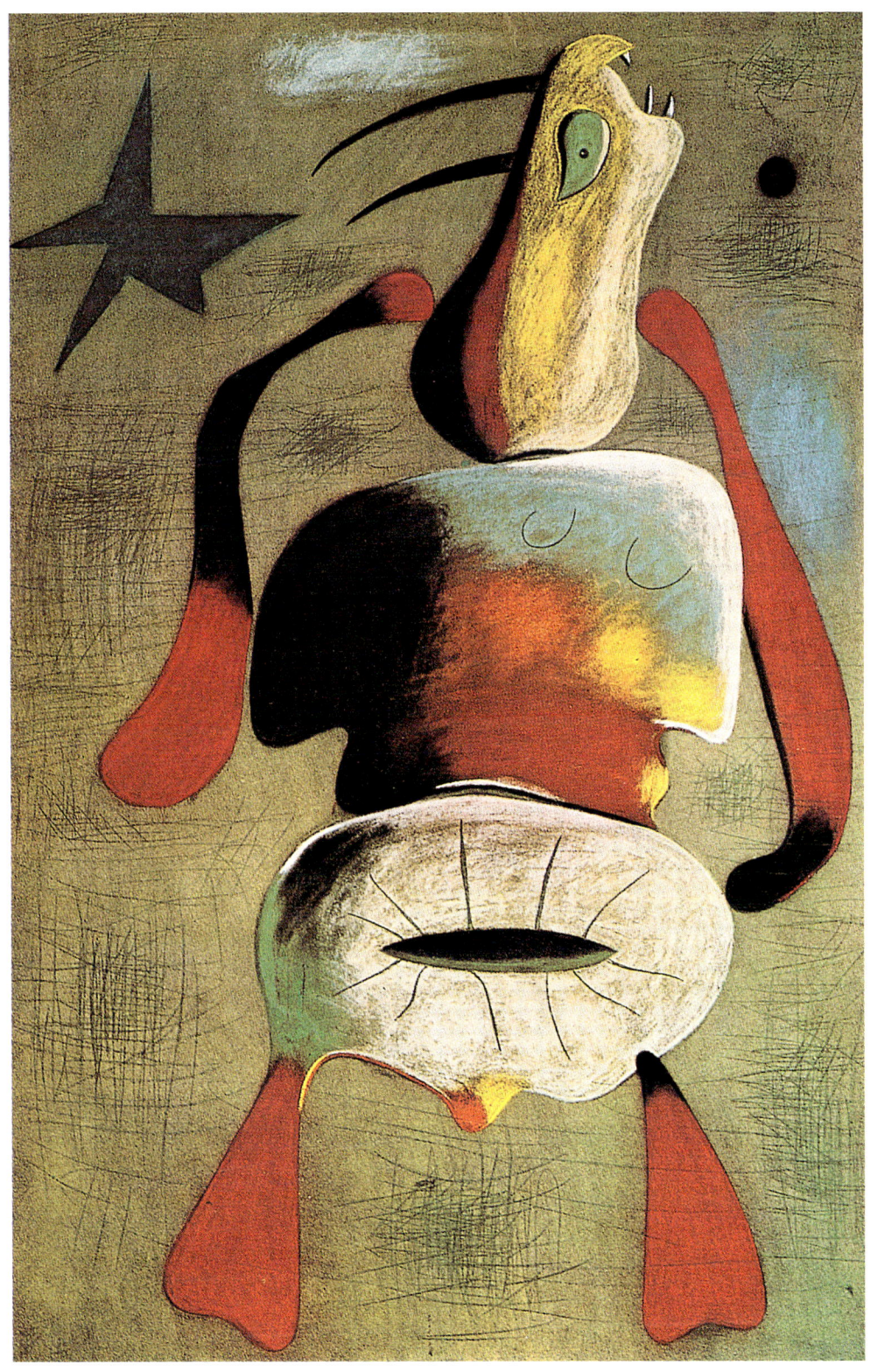

Meret Oppenheim
Fur Breakfast, 1936

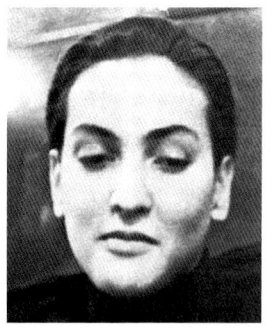

b. 1913 in Berlin
d. 1985 in Basel, Switzerland

Meret Oppenheim was 18 years old when she went to Paris to become an artist in May 1932. Through her friendship with Hans Arp and Alberto Giacometti she quickly made contact with André Breton and the Surrealists. They invited her to take part in a group exhibition and – largely because of a brief love affair with Max Ernst in 1934 – she was accepted into a circle of writers, thinkers and artists with Surrealist sympathies.

She appears to have been a member of that circle until 1935, but after she completed the work that came to symbolise her association with the Surrealists, her ties with them seem to have loosened. *Fur Breakfast (Déjeuner en fourrure)*, shown at the 1936 exhibition of Surrealist objects along with other works by Oppenheim, met with a very positive response from the Surrealists. It was André Breton who came up with a title for the fur-covered cup, saucer and spoon. It was an ironic reference to Manet's famous painting *The Luncheon on the Grass (Le déjeuner sur l'herbe)*. Oppenheim, meanwhile, simply called her object *Cup, Saucer and Spoon Covered with Fur*. The Surrealists' high regard for *Fur Breakfast* seems to have been due mainly to the fact that, in creating this object, Oppenheim succeeded in transforming Surrealist theories into art. In his essay "The Crisis of the Object", published shortly after the exhibition at Galerie Ratton, André Breton demanded that, as a sign of rebellion, everyday things should be given different functions and utilitarian objects should undergo a process of mystification, the objective being to "traquer la bête folle de l'usage" – "hunt down the mad beast of habit". *Fur Breakfast* translates the concept of alienating objects and distancing them from reality in a style that goes way beyond the absurdity and the element of surprise that the Surrealists sought.

Oppenheim's comments about the origins of *Fur Breakfast* were as down-to-earth as her choice of title for the piece. She seemed to be trying to trivialise her work and in so doing tone down its effect, which, while enigmatic, appealed to a popular audience. According to the artist, it all began with a conversation with Picasso, whom she met by chance in a café. They talked about the special role of the café, to which *Fur Breakfast* is a very direct reference, as a meeting place. To the Surrealists, the café not only meant conviviality and the continuation of the bohemian tradition, it was also the ideal setting in which to conspire and collaborate.

At the famous "Fantastic Art, Dada, Surrealism" exhibition that took place in winter 1936/37 at the Museum of Modern Art in New York, the reaction to *Fur Breakfast* was perhaps even more positive than it had been at the recent Surrealist event in Paris. Alfred H. Barr, who organised the New York show in collaboration with the Surrealists and who, when the exhibition closed, bought the work for MoMA, wrote that few works of art had so captured the public imagination in the same way as Oppenheim's Surrealist object, the fur-covered cup, saucer and spoon. Like Lautréamont's famous metaphor of the encounter of a sewing machine and an umbrella or Dalí's soft watches, the fur cup turned the most bizarre impossibility into tangible reality. The feeling of excitement aroused by this object in tens of thousands of Americans was expressed in angry outbursts, laughter, disgust and delight, Barr reported.

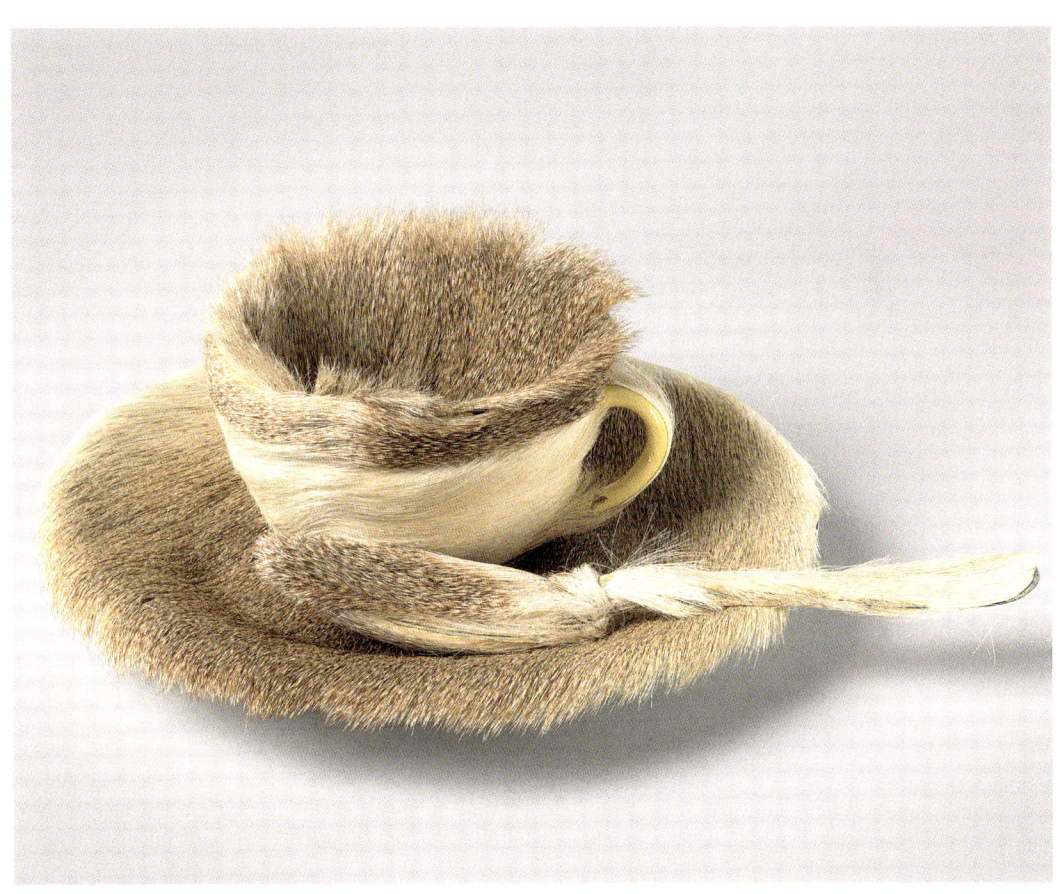

Fur Breakfast, 1936
Fur-covered cup, saucer and spoon,
height 7.3 cm (2⅞ in.)
New York, The Museum of Modern Art

Pablo Picasso
Composition with Glove, 1930

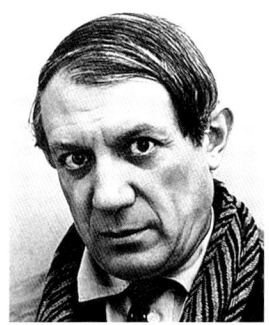

b. 1881 in Málaga, Spain
d. 1973 in Mougins, France

In its Surrealist phase, Pablo Picasso's work transcends every kind of boundary. The human body is turned into a stone skeleton, graceful bathers adopt acrobatically contorted poses and the face of the painter's young lover appears as a configuration of bits of iron. Not only does the physical nature of his subjects undergo unexpected transformation, the line between different media and genres always remains extremely fluid – painting imitates sculpture, sculptures consist of everyday objects, drawings and prints simulate every imaginable surface structure resulting from the use of hugely varying techniques.

The starting point for all these transformations and experiments was the traditional panel painting whose function was both imaginative and illustrative. The stylistic and formal unity of the work of art was broken down, conventional ways of seeing were blocked off so that the spectator was forced into a new, more direct engagement with the work of art.

Few works present such a head-on challenge to traditional assumptions as the sand-coated reliefs that Picasso executed in 1930, among them *Composition with Glove*. Here, the artist turned the canvas over and arranged the various elements of his relief in the hollow space created by the frame. But once again, the limits are overstepped. A bulging glove resembling a hand and shreds of cloth that look like seaweed spill over the edge and create a bizarre face in the middle.

Cut out of sturdy cardboard, the mask is similar to the faces in Picasso's paintings of the period – the openings for mouth, eyes and nose are neither symmetrical nor in their usual places, but are scattered in a seemingly arbitrary way. The configuration conveys the vague idea of a face and body, of a human presence. However, it is covered by a layer of grey sand, which distances it from the spectator. Under its ash-like coating, the relief could be an archaeological find, a long-buried relic of a bygone age, a fragment that has re-emerged from the ashes of Pompeii.

The 1932 *Composition with Butterfly* exudes an air of decay. A dried leaf whose filigree structure is visibly disintegrating and a butterfly whose lifeless state intensifies our sense of its fragility, are flanked by two matchstick men, one made from string, the other from cloth, a drawing pin and matches. Here, too, the whole configuration – including the leaf and the butterfly – is covered with a unifying and simultaneously alienating layer of milky colour. Like the tide, it seems to have swept the things along with it, snatching them away from the flow of time and bringing them together.

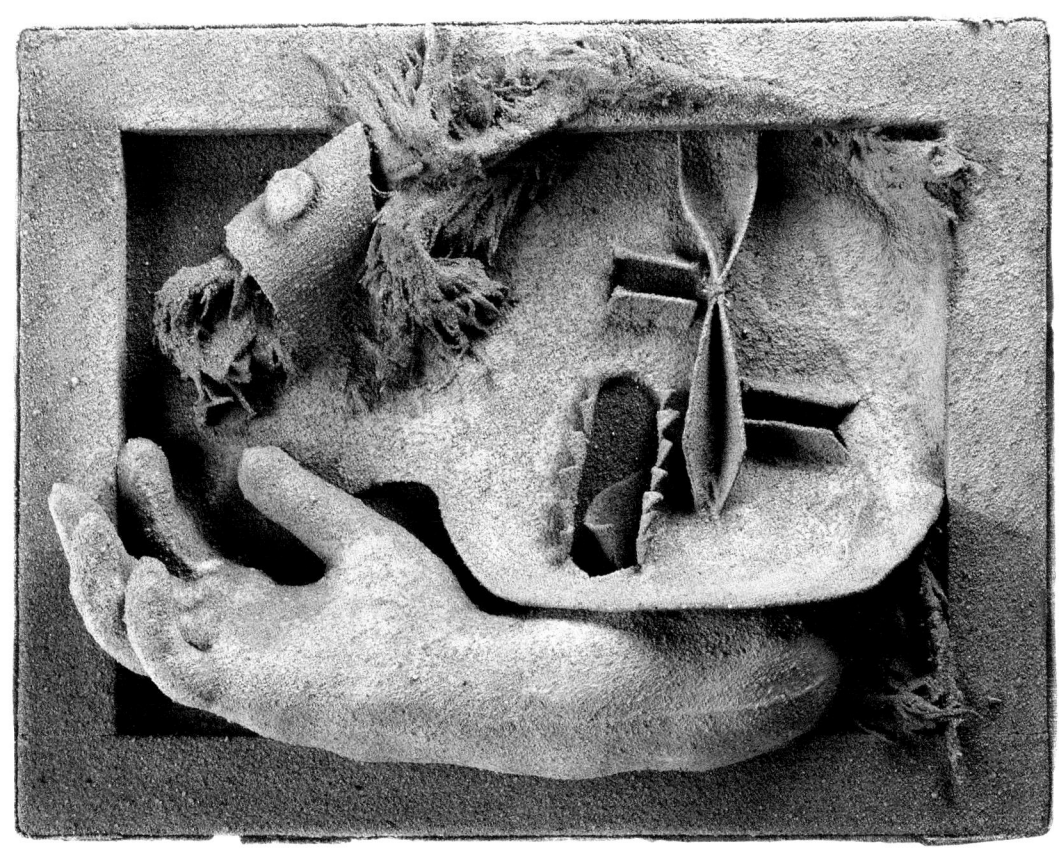

Composition with Glove, 1930
Sand on reverse of framed canvas, glove,
cardboard and plant material on canvas,
27.5 x 35.5 cm (11 x 14 in.)
Paris, Musée Picasso

Pablo Picasso
Woman in a Red Armchair, 1932

Only with difficulty do we recognise the *Woman in a Red Armchair* as a human being. And we only come to this conclusion because we associate the idea of an armchair occupied by an amorphous mass with that of a portrait. However, if we compare the work with Pablo Picasso's other sketches, drawings, sculptures and paintings produced in the same period, we can see it as part of a stylistic development process during which he explored the connections between painting and sculpture. It was also the last in a series of portraits of Marie-Thérèse Walter, completed within a matter of days.

On 14 January 1932 he began by painting a picture of his lover, which showed the young woman elegantly leaning back in an armchair. Picasso constructed the portrait using soft lines extending ornamentally over the canvas. Then, on 26 January, it became the starting point for a work of a completely different nature, for which *Woman in a Red Armchair* can be seen as a preliminary sketch. The painter transformed the separate parts of the woman's body – head, arms, neck, breasts and belly – into abstract sculptural elements which he fitted together to form a bizarre skeleton, mirroring the basic structure of the earlier portrait.

In the early 1920s, Picasso went through a distinctly classical phase, experimenting with orthodox styles of painting and traditional subjects. In 1926 he adopted a completely new approach. His beautiful, carefully balanced figures underwent a metamorphosis, evolving step by step into monstrous, distorted, fragmented bodies, like those in the series of *Bathers* painted in the summer of 1927. For these, Picasso chose two different modes of representation. Either the bodies looked like cut-outs flattened onto the surface of the canvas so that the individual parts appear to be lined up side by side rather than belonging to an organic whole. Alternatively, the artist produced distinctly sculptural forms which fitted together to create a thoroughly ill-proportioned and often very ugly whole.

In Picasso's paintings and sculptures, this approach is combined with dramatic emphasis on materiality, either conveying an impression of soft fleshiness or simulating hard substances like stone or bone. In his experiments with the representation of the human body, Picasso not only thought analytically about its internal structure; he also tried to express the feelings, desires and projections associated with the female body, especially its sexual magnetism. It was this aspect of his work that specifically aligned him with the Surrealists at that period.

Woman in a Red Armchair, 1932
Oil on canvas, 130.2 x 97 cm (51¼ x 38¼ in.)
Paris, Musée Picasso

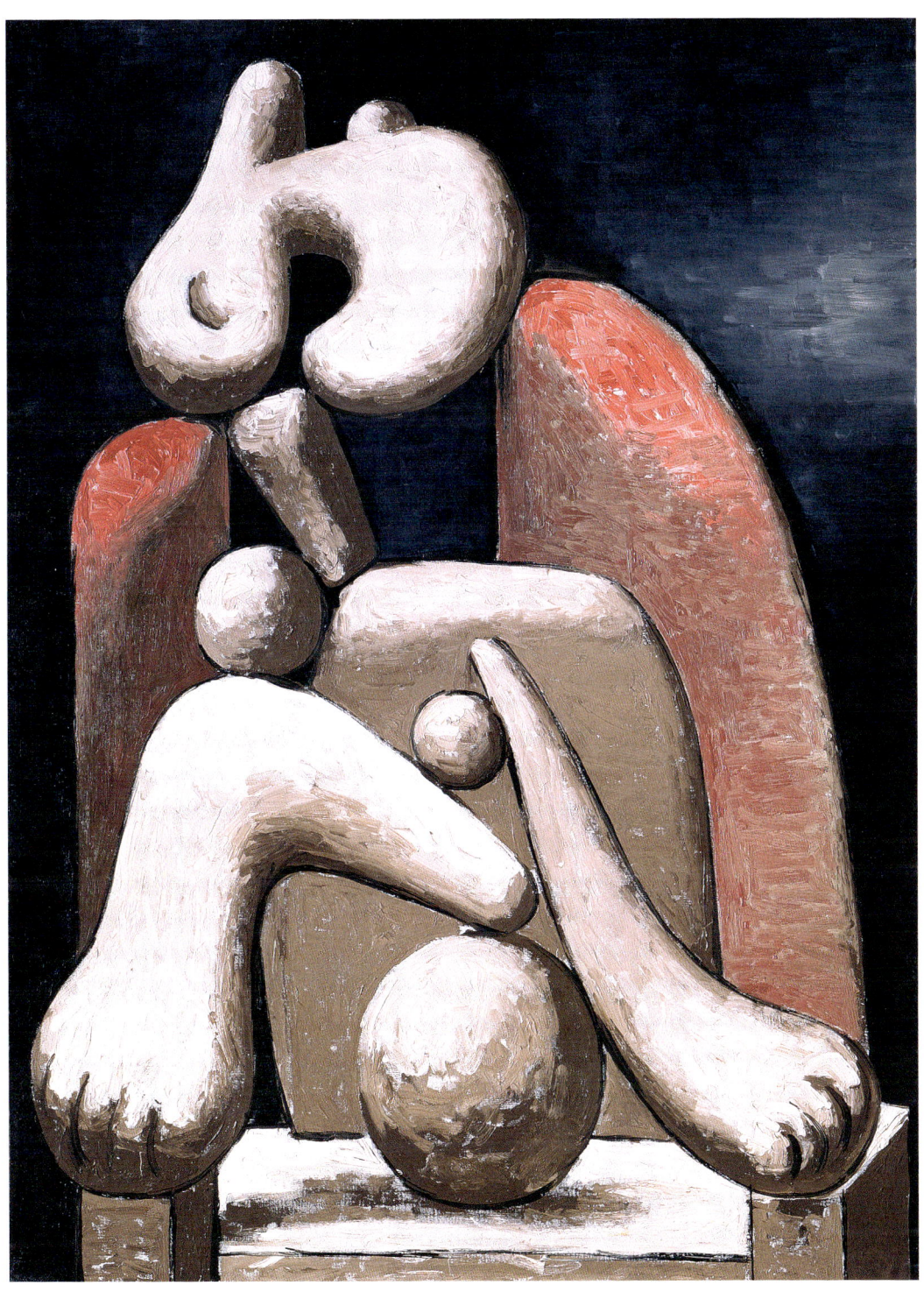

Pablo Picasso
Corrida, 1934

In 1934 Picasso took the *corrida* as the subject of a series of works ranging from quasi-naturalistic representations to extremely stylised versions of the bullfight. However, none of these works directly depict what happens in the bullring. They are more like allegories, a mythical vision that also found expression in Picasso's poetry of the period. The artist saw the bullfight as a ritual sacrifice and placed it on the same level as the cult of Mithras or the Crusades. The artist's visual images are echoed in his Surrealist poetry, in such lines as "when the bull with its horn opens the door of the horse's belly" (15 November 1935), or "the horse spills its entrails like flowers that bend the arena, like sand crashing from clocks" (18 April 1935). Picasso wrote of "pain written in large letters all around the arena" (7 November 1935), and "the fine, delicate banquet of death" (20 January 1936). The bull-fight reveals a mystery that can be read in the entrails of the horse. It is Holy Communion: "the scent, the stench and the horror of the entrails exploding between the murderer's hands, blood gushes over the horse's belly and the Mass begins …, the love feast of a whole race which plunges its hand into the entrails and searches for the heart from which the bull's life drains away" (7 November 1935).

The 1934 painting *Corrida* is also full of contrasting concepts and emotions – unbridled brutality and carefully thought-out stylisation, the cruelty of nature and its sublimation in the beauty of art. Strong colours, black and white, yellow, red and green, spill into each other in the fight between horse and bull. The drama reaches its culmination in the great wound in the body of the horse, gaping and bleeding in the centre of the picture. The bodies of the two animals are interwoven, the heavy shape of the bull obviously representing evil, while the white body of the horse symbolises innocence. This allocation of roles not only runs though all Picasso's works whose protagonists are the bull and the horse.

In *Bull and Horse*, a drawing dating from the following year, it appears even more precise. The bull, whose head shows anthropomorphic features, disembowels the horse and stands with its two forelegs planted in the open wound. While Picasso draws rage and brutality on the bull's face with exquisite precision, he merely sketches the contours of the dead horse, so downgrading it to no more than an anonymous victim.

In this configuration, horse and bull are not only victim and perpetrator; they also stand for woman and man and, ultimately, for innocence and evil, two opposing concepts on which Picasso was to construct his masterpiece *Guernica*. In that monumental painting, the artist's response to the brutal bombardment of the little Spanish town of Guernica, one of the last centres of Republican resistance, the horse and the bull are central figures, the bull portrayed as the ferocious embodiment of evil.

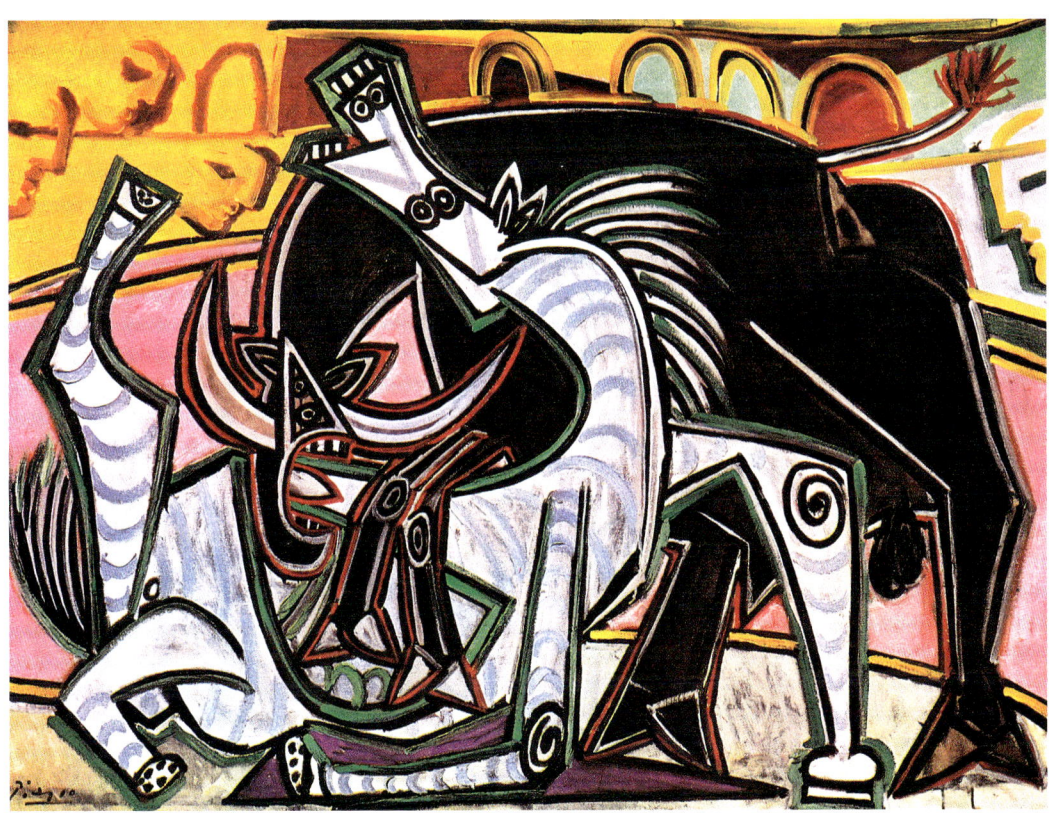

Corrida, 1934
Oil on canvas, 50 x 61 cm (19¾ x 24 in.)
Private collection

Pablo Picasso
Woman with Foliage, 1934

During his Surrealist period, Pablo Picasso took a particularly intense interest in literature and sculpture. In 1930, Picasso bought the Château Boisgeloup, near Gisors in the French *département* of Eure, which offered huge spaces where he could work on his sculptures. Contemporary photographs of the château give some clue of the magical, surreal atmosphere of the place, in which various materials – scrap iron, kitchen utensils and everyday objects – were collected and then combined with finished sculptures to create total works of art from the most diverse bits and pieces.

The Surrealist, collage-like nature of Picasso's sculptures and the wide variety of materials used by the artist are reflected in the small statue *Woman with Foliage.* The spectator is immediately struck by two very different elements: the leafy branch that the woman holds in her right hand and the small, rectangular box which Picasso uses as her face. It is precisely this everyday object worn like a mask that gives her such a deeply dramatic appearance.

She seems to be the mouthpiece for some alien power, a prophetess like Cassandra who, despite her awareness of future disaster, cannot turn away. Such classical associations are underpinned by the figure's sweeping, rhetorical gestures and her long, pleated garment, the pleated effect achieved by pressing corrugated cardboard against the plaster. The extremely naturalistic surfaces of the leaves are the result of a similar transfer process. Like palm branches or laurel leaves, they seem to have some symbolic significance. Nevertheless, their exact meaning remains unfathomable, for we do not know which myth or tragedy the *Woman with Foliage* refers to. Thus her words are incomprehensible, her gestures empty. This complete lack of meaning reduces her from an imposing presence to a figure of fun.

Four years previously, in 1930, with *Woman's Head,* Picasso created a portrait of a woman that was ludicrous in quite a different way. This is also a collage combining all kinds of objects whose original function and meaning remain obvious but which, when put together, create a quite new and unexpected effect. The various pieces of iron, including a very recognisable colander, are welded together to form an aggressive and monstrous face, so absurd that it leaves the spectator with a stale aftertaste.

The act of breaking the human face into pieces and adding what are manifestly spare parts from the material world marks a new departure, opening up immense possibilities for the exploration of the realms of the irrational and the world of dreams.

Woman with Foliage, 1934
Plaster, 39.5 x 21.5 x 26.5 cm
(15½ x 8½ x 10½ in.)
Private collection

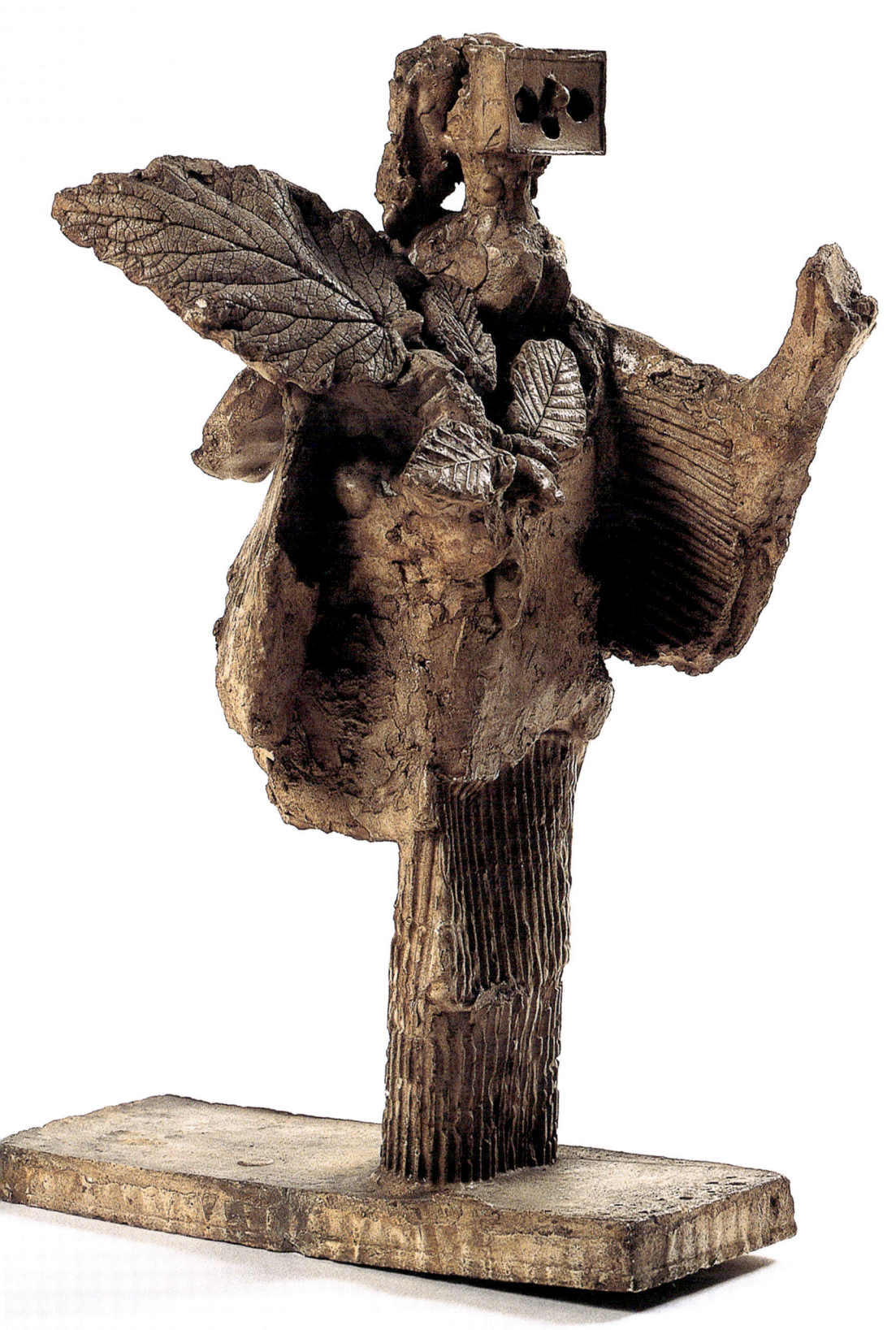

Man Ray
Le Violon d'Ingres, 1924

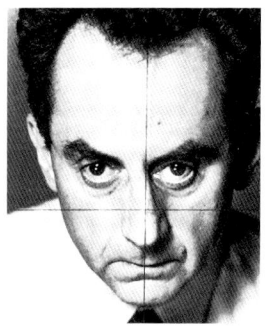

b. 1890 in Philadelphia
d. 1976 in Paris

Man Ray was one of the founders of Dadaism in the United States. He got to know the Surrealists in Paris when he moved to the city in the summer of 1921. Initially he devoted himself to photography, taking portraits of friends and colleagues, in which he created a magical atmosphere through special lighting effects. With the help of Jean Cocteau, Man Ray became portrait photographer to Paris's leading intellectuals and artists, his subjects including Gertrude Stein, Constantin Brancusi and Marcel Proust. After moving to rue Campagne-Première, where the photographer Eugène Atget also lived, Man Ray discovered a kind of ready-made form of photography, a process that created images without the intervention of the artist or even a camera. His "Rayographs" – outlines of objects on light-sensitive photographic paper – were exhibited for the first time in spring 1922.

To create a Rayograph, an object only had to be exposed to the light. This meant that a Rayograph was a work of pure chance that simply created itself. It was an image of transformation and alienation, a concept that fitted to perfection into the intellectual world of the Surrealists. One of the first published works to contain this new photographic process was a portfolio of twelve images by Man Ray, accompanied by Tristan Tzara's essay "Les champs délicieux" (Delicious Fields), which appeared in 1922.

On the other hand, the feeling of alienation produced by other photographs by Man Ray was based on the interplay between image and title. *The Enigma of Isidore Ducasse* is the title of a photograph of an object wrapped in a blanket and tied up with rope, while *Le Violon d'Ingres (Ingres's Violin)* alludes to the two f-holes that Man Ray has drawn on the back of a female nude. He reinterprets the rounded shape of the young woman, transforming it into the soundbox of a musical instrument, so unleashing a whole chain of associations, largely inspired by the title of the picture.

We instinctively think of the importance of stringed instruments to the Cubists, who incorporated mandolins, violins and guitars into their complex still lifes. While in Analytic Cubism they were merely lifeless, sexless objects, Man Ray's "violin" gives the photo an erotic aura. This is underlined by the reference to the classicist painter Jean Auguste Dominique Ingres and his famous *Turkish Bath*, in which the central figure is a nude with her back to the spectator. It is precisely because Ingres has drawn her with such cold precision that she radiates such sensuality. The turban worn by Man Ray's model picks up on Ingres's oriental ambience, but is also an ironic comment on the chilly eroticism of the Turkish bath scene. The title *Le Violon d'Ingres* also alludes to the long tradition of music-making as an allegory for loveplay. From Man Ray's perspective the instrument is simply ready and waiting for the soloist.

Le Violon d'Ingres, 1924
Gelatin silver print, retouched with pencil and Indian ink, 31 x 24.7 cm (12¼ x 9¾ in.)
Paris, Musée national d'art moderne, Centre Pompidou

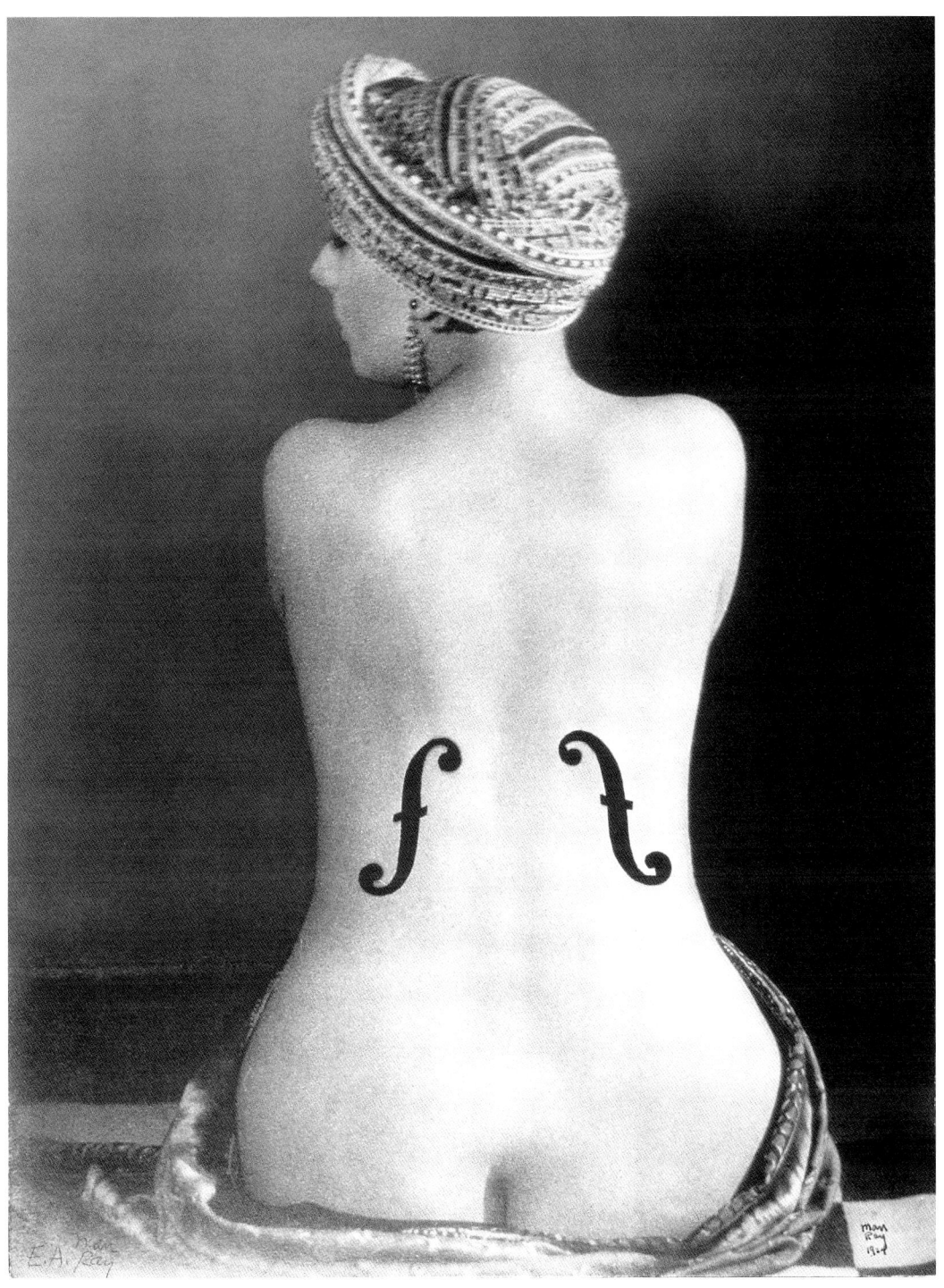

Yves Tanguy
The Dark Garden, 1928

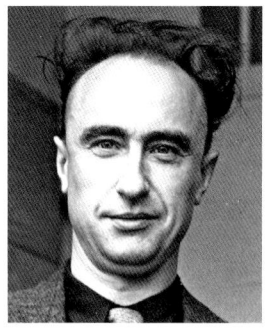

b. 1900 in Paris
d. 1955 in Woodbury,
Connecticut

Yves Tanguy felt his vocation as a painter at the age of 22. From the open platform of a Paris bus he saw two paintings by Giorgio de Chirico displayed in the window of the Galerie Paul Guillaume on the rue de la Boétie. One of them was *The Child's Brain*. Shortly after that experience, without having undergone any formal training, he began to paint in watercolours and oils. Tanguy was a purely self-taught painter who developed his own style and techniques in association with other artists. In the early days, the work of Giorgio de Chirico and Max Ernst were particularly significant.

His relationship with the Surrealist group and particularly with André Breton also proved crucial and until his departure for the USA in 1939 he remained Breton's loyal supporter. He was a close friend of Jacques Prévert and Marcel Duhamel, with whom he shared a house on the rue du Château, where in the early 1920s many of the Surrealists would meet regularly to enjoy long drawn-out games of *Cadavre exquis*.

Tanguy's early paintings adopt motifs from de Chirico and Ernst, but these are surrounded by an atmosphere more akin to Miró's abstract, light-filled backgrounds. The same, indefinable, supernatural light dominated Tanguy's paintings from the outset, imbuing them with a mysterious chill. In the course of the 1920s, Tanguy completely abandoned figurative elements in his painting and set off in a completely opposite direction. As a setting he used a bizarre, other-worldly landscape which he populated with organic forms.

The damply shining surfaces of these figures and the impression they give of softness and malleability are reminiscent of Dalí, whose paintings of boneless limbs probably inspired Tanguy. *The Dark Garden* is also occupied by these faceless beings which nevertheless appear too mobile to be identified with the standing stones found on the coast of Tanguy's native Brittany. As they move in from the left of the painting, these mostly phallus-like creatures are like a mob overrunning and disturbing the orderly structure of the composition, which consists of mechanically drawn wavy lines, creating a deep, dark surface to the sea that merges with the striped pattern of the turquoise sky.

Although these structures rendered on canvas using different techniques reflect the real relationship between sea and sky, it is precisely the artificiality of their appearance that creates the picture's overwhelmingly strange and threatening atmosphere. Tanguy lets the spectator see into a universe far removed from the real world, where there is room for neither Miró's poetically twinkling eye nor Dalí's solid nightmare vision.

The Dark Garden, 1928
Oil on canvas, 91.4 x 71.1 cm (36 x 28 in.)
Düsseldorf, Kunstsammlung
Nordrhein-Westfalen

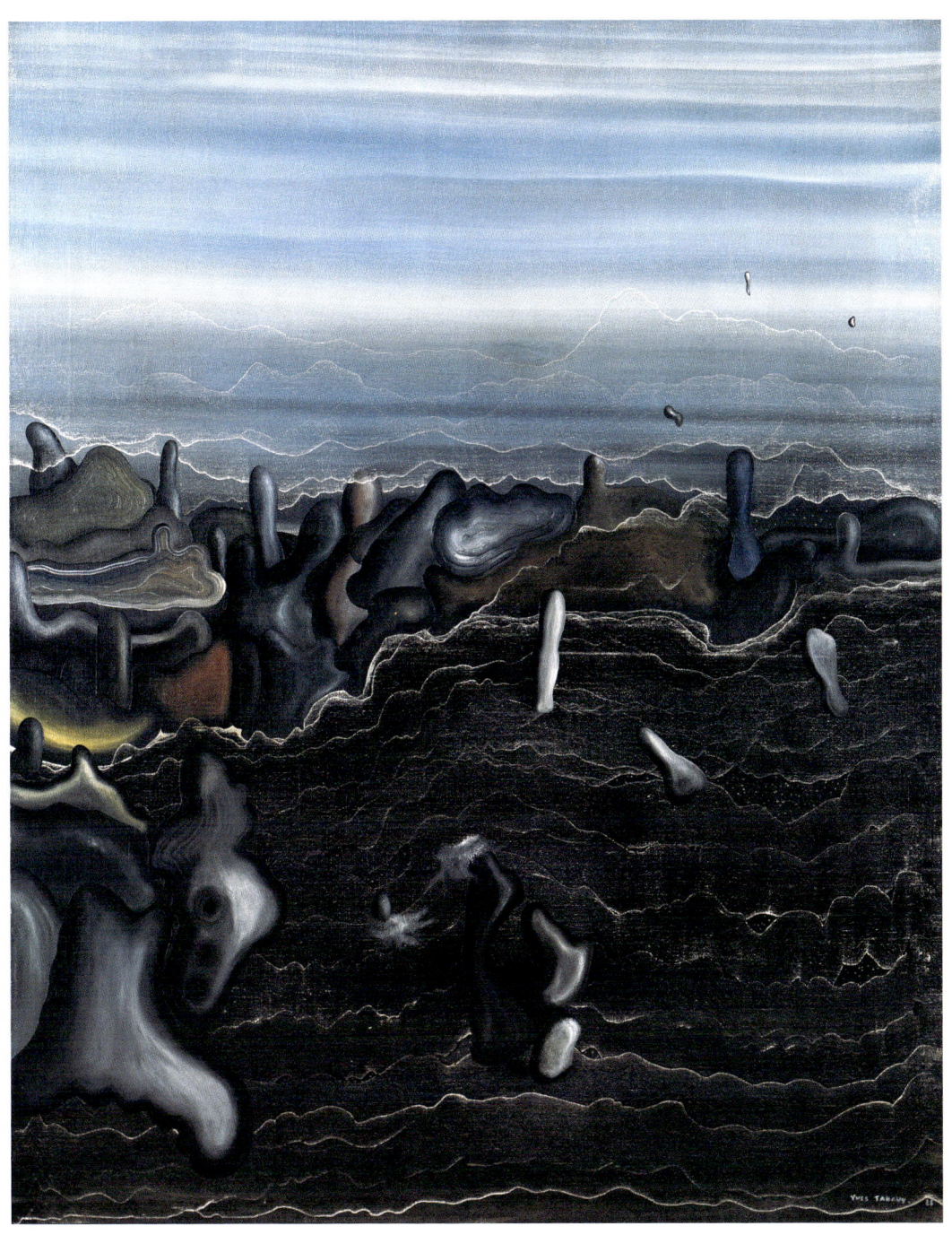

Yves Tanguy
Day of Slowness, 1937

There is a tendency to compare Yves Tanguy's landscapes to photographs of an alien planet, since it is hard to find words to describe the magical chill and latent menace of his invented scenery. The world he depicts, in which composition and use of light are often surprisingly close to those in the paintings of Salvador Dalí, have one decisive difference. While Dalí captures his personal obsessions in very precise visions, Tanguy's art is detached and passionless.

His dream paintings, which only on closer examination are revealed as nightmare visions, produce a vague unease in the spectator. André Breton claimed that it would take the next generation to decipher Tanguy's work. For Breton, Tanguy's significance lay in his refusal to compromise. He made absolutely no concession to anything approaching reality and this is what gave his painting its surreal and mysterious character.

The novelty and uniqueness of Tanguy's painting lies in its elegance and the artist's ability to turn ugliness into eccentric beauty. This quality became increasingly evident in his work in the late 1930s, the period to which *Day of Slowness* belongs. With great precision, Tanguy isolates the individual figurative elements from their background. He reintroduces the bizarrely shaped objects apparently sprouting from water, or other soft substances, that featured so strongly in his earlier paintings.

In his later works the surreal figures also cast deep shadows, so creating space that is in fact non-existent. The lines in the background, floating as though caught by the soft-focus lens of a camera, are transformed into flat, abstract structures. The line marking the transition from darkness to light could be the horizon, giving the impression that this is a landscape.

Against this abstract background, Tanguy sets two main figures. One recalls a knight on horseback brandishing a weapon, while another warrior sits astride the creature approaching snail-like from the right and resembling a tower. In the background, a third small figure on a red pedestal glides by. The whole scene is as silent as it is weird. We do not know whether it is set deep in the past or in the far distant future.

Which brings us back to the integrity of Tanguy's art, so highly esteemed by André Breton, poet and chief spokesman of Surrealism. Certainly, Breton was not just thinking about the painter's honesty as an artist. In the 1930s Tanguy was one of his most loyal friends who stood by him throughout all the conflicts within the Surrealist movement. However, in 1939 they went their separate ways, as Tanguy left for the USA in order to marry the American artist Kay Sage and to reach safety before the outbreak of the Second World War.

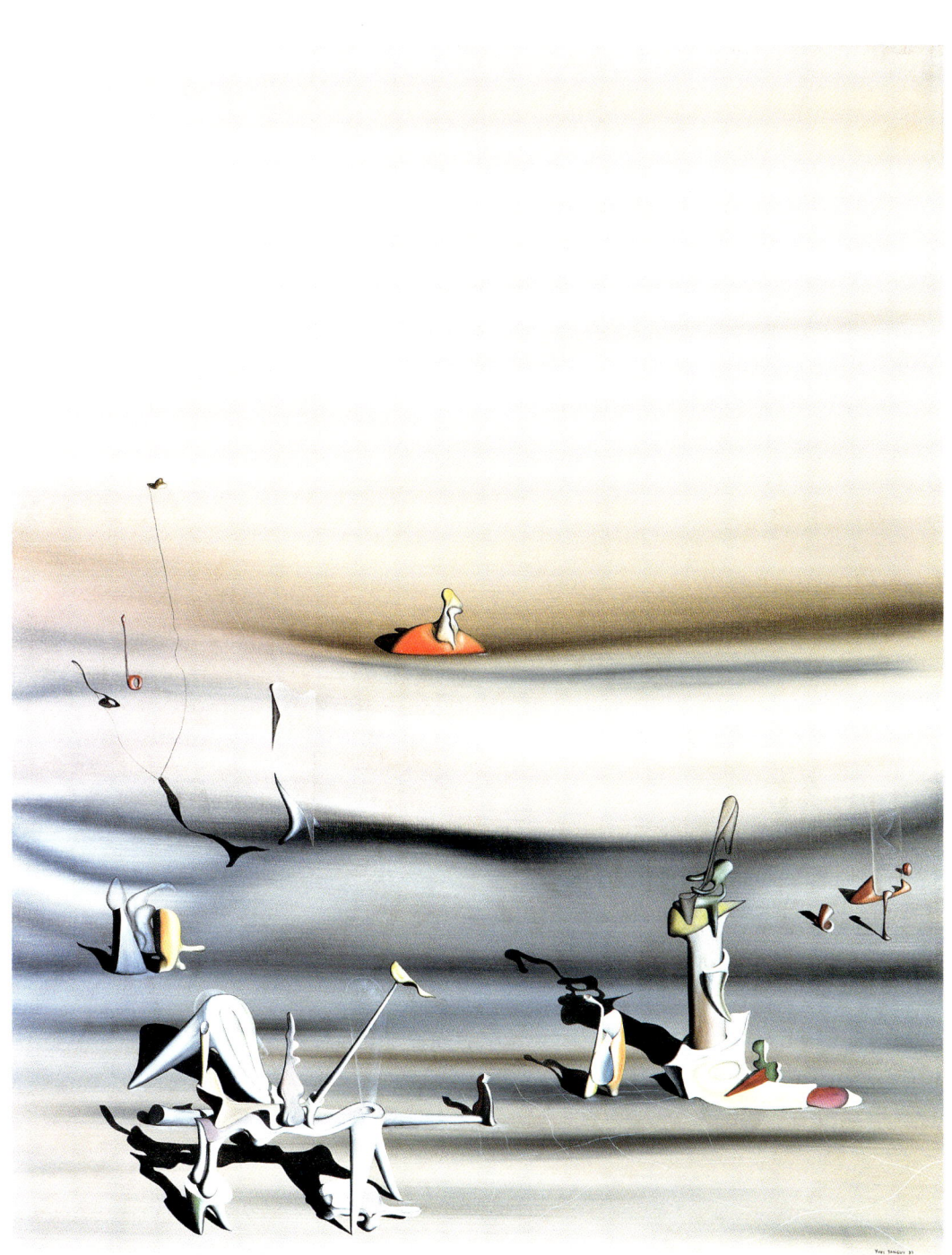

Day of Slowness, 1937
Oil on canvas, 92 x 73 cm (36¼ x 28¾ in.)
Paris, Musée national d'art moderne,
Centre Pompidou

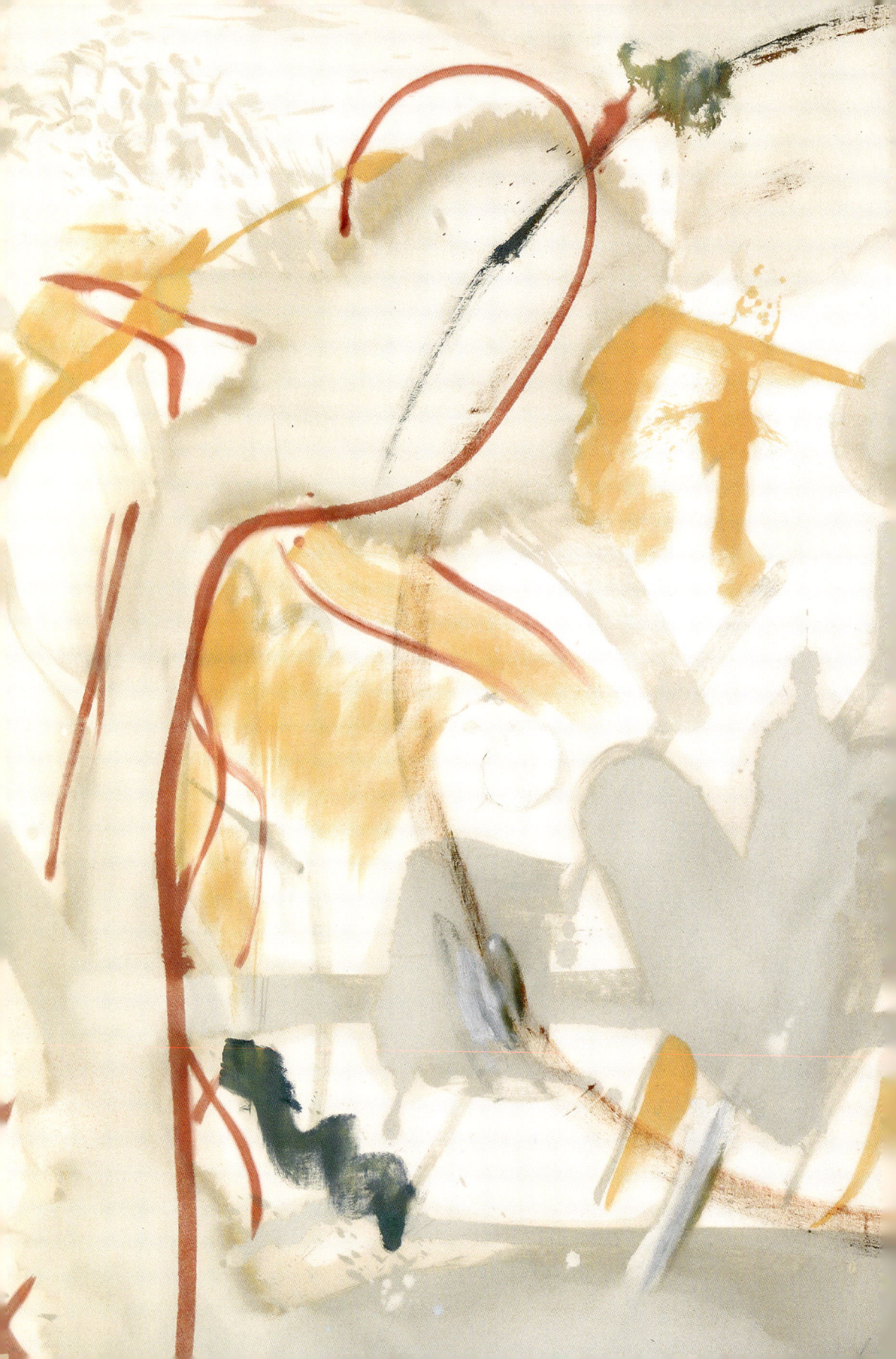

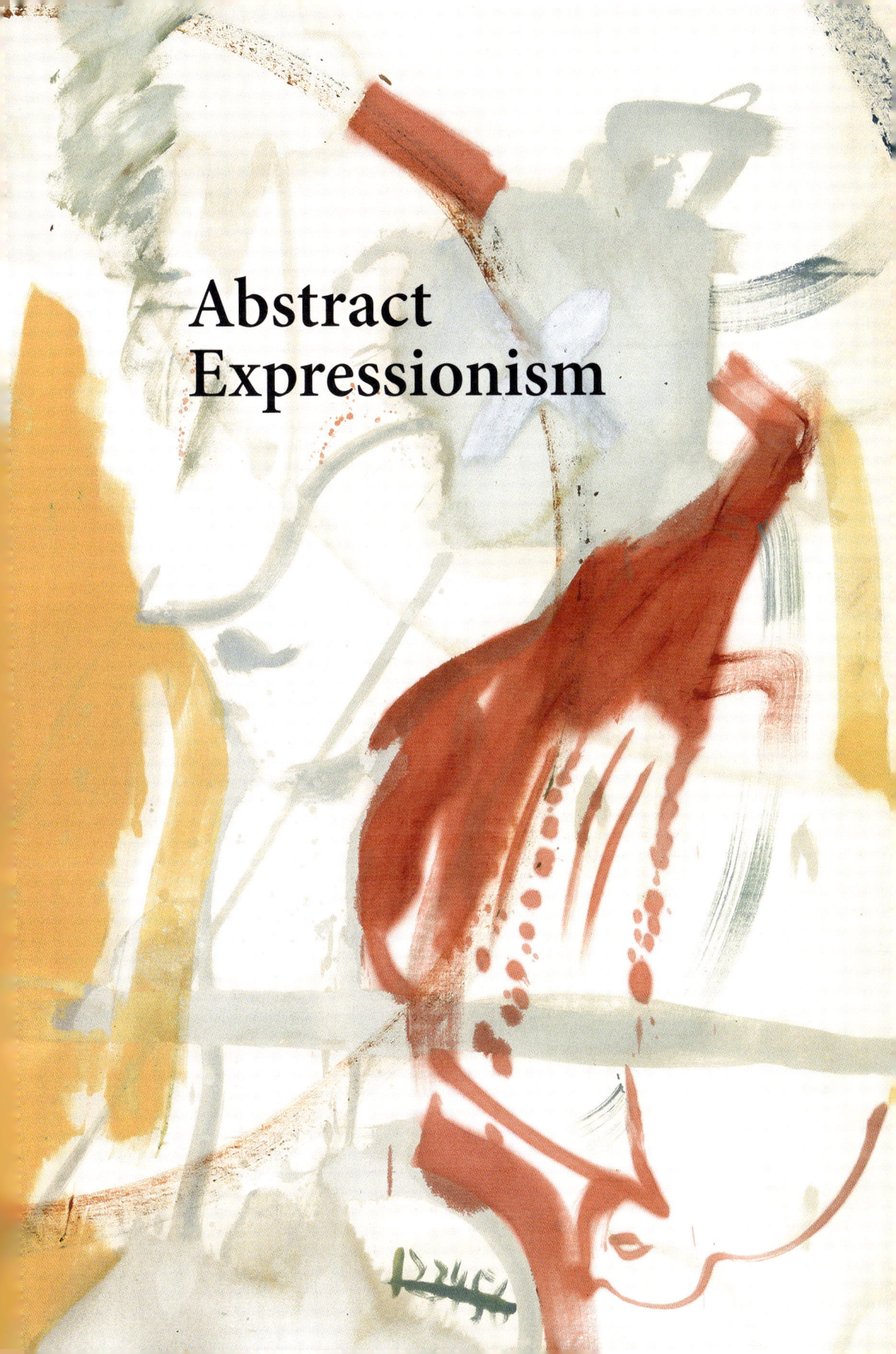

Abstract
Expressionism

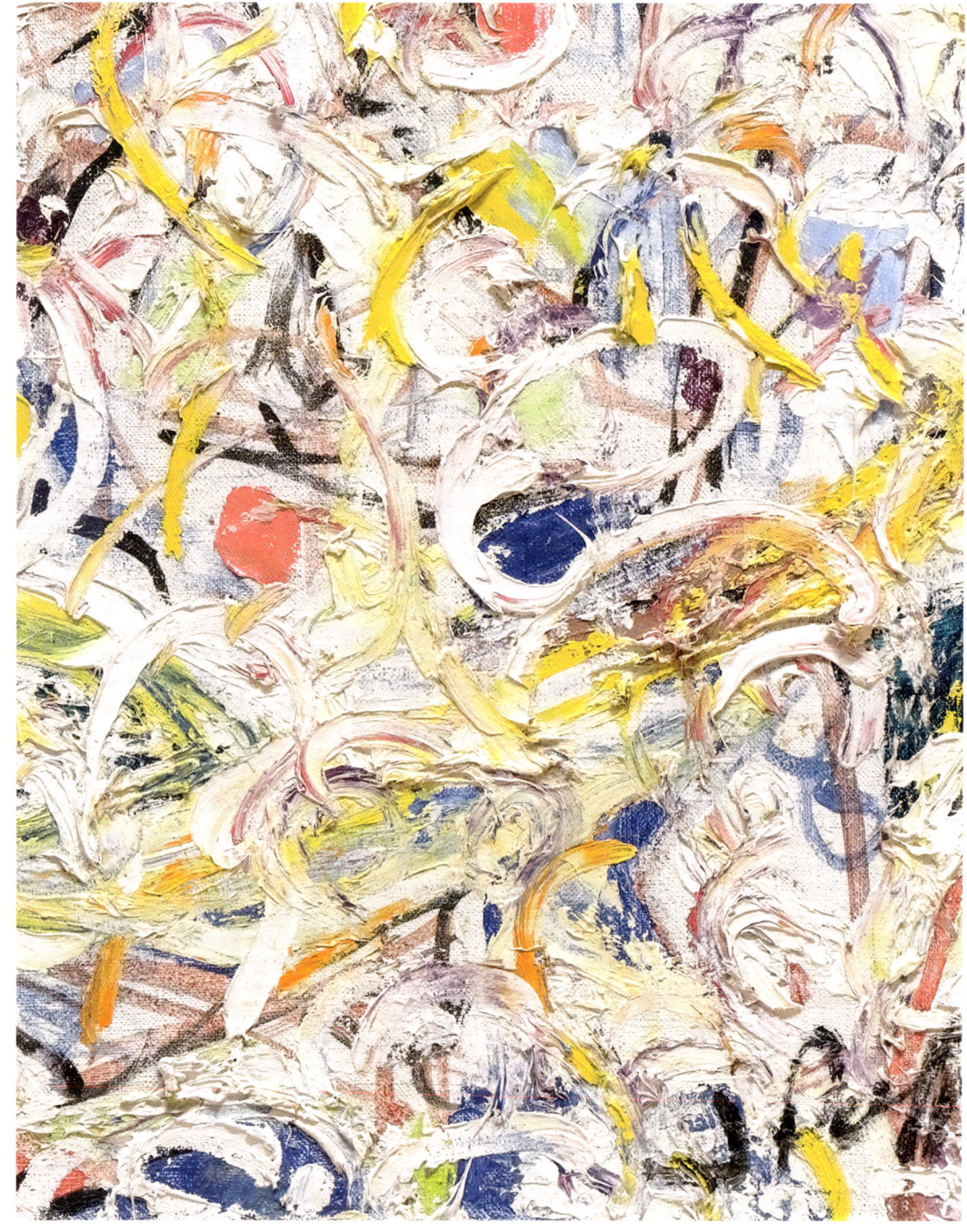

Barbara Hess
Uta Grosenick (Ed.)

Abstract Expressionism

The Painterly Gestures
of Personal Feelings

"The painting has a life of its own."
Jackson Pollock

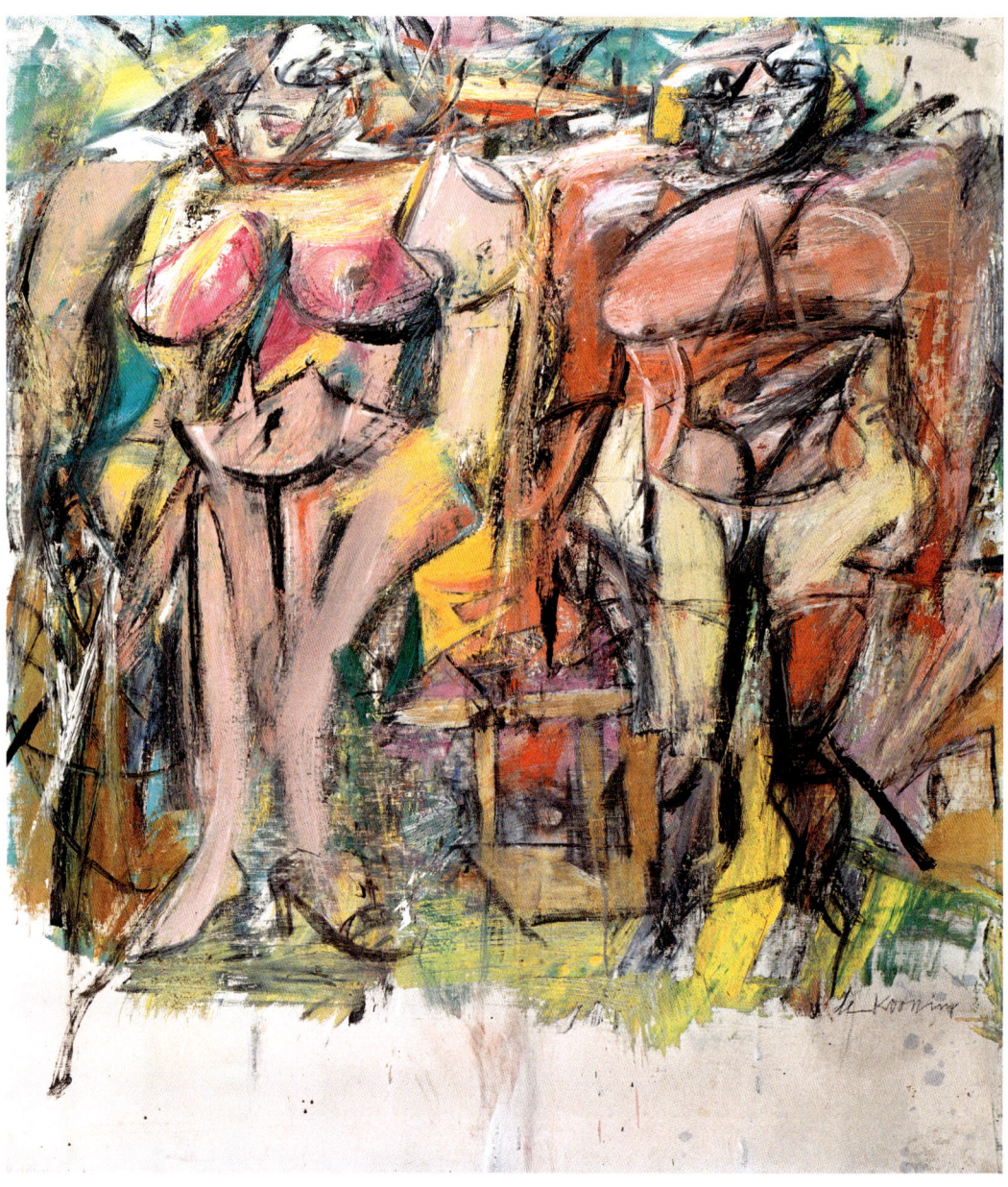

PAGES 302/303: Helen Frankenthaler
Seven Types of Ambiguity (detail), 1957
Oil on unprimed canvas,
242.6 x 178.1 cm (95⅝ x 70⅛ in.)
Bentonville, Crystal Bridges Museum
of American Art

PAGE 304: Jackson Pollock
Shimmering Substance, 1946
Oil on canvas,
76.3 x 61.6 cm (30 x 24¼ in.)
New York, The Museum of Modern Art,
Mr. and Mrs. Albert Lewin and
Mrs. Sam A. Lewisohn Funds

ABOVE: Willem de Kooning
Two Women in the Country, 1954
Oil, enamel and charcoal on canvas,
117 x 103.5 cm (46 x 40¾ in.)
Washington, D.C., Hirshhorn
Museum and Sculpture Garden,
Smithsonian Institution

Contents

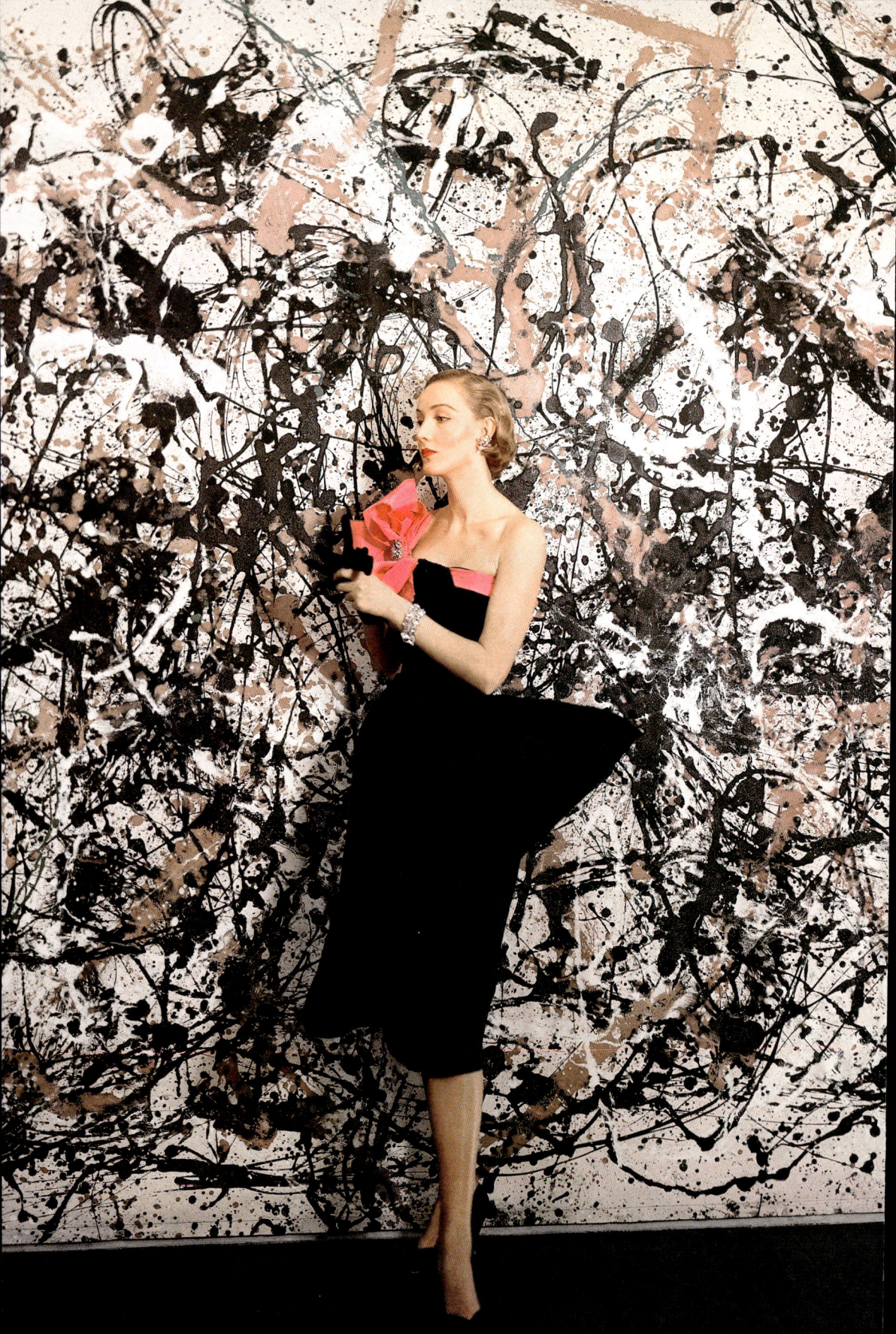

"A Constant Searching of Oneself"

"We agree only to disagree." According to Irving Sandler, writer and observer of the art scene, this was the unwritten motto of that loose grouping of artists in New York in the 1940s and 50s who are generally known as "Abstract Expressionists" or "the first generation of the New York School". In their statements and writings, insofar as they have been preserved, the artists usually considered to have belonged to this school resist being lumped together in this way, fearing that their very different views on art and aesthetic production would be suffocated if subsumed under a single stylistic description or group name. "It is disastrous to name ourselves," answered the painter Willem de Kooning in a panel discussion in 1950 when the former director of the New York Museum of Modern Art, Alfred H. Barr, Jr., demanded: "We should have a name for which we can blame the artists – for once in history!" Barr's remark was an allusion to the fact that most artistic "isms" – such as for example Impressionism and Cubism – were coined by critics and often originally applied derisively.

"It is a widely accepted notion among painters that it does not matter what one paints as long as it is well painted. This is the essence of academicism. There is no such thing as good painting about nothing."
MARK ROTHKO

"Abstract Expressionism" is no exception. On 30 March 1946 there appeared in the *New Yorker* a discussion of an exhibition in the Mortimer Brandt Gallery, the first comprehensive presentation of works by the painter Hans Hofmann, who had emigrated to the USA from Germany in 1932. The author of the review, Robert Coates, observed that until then the artist had been accorded little attention, and explained this in part by his painting technique: "For he is certainly one of the most uncompromising representatives of what some people have called the spatter-and-daub school of painting and I, more politely, have christened Abstract Expressionism."

Coates himself had borrowed this description from another author, probably Alfred Barr. The expression "Abstract Expressionism" had first turned up (in German) as far back as 1919 in the magazine *Der Sturm*, which appeared in Berlin from 1910 to 1932 and was especially well known for its reproductions of Expressionist prints. In the USA, Alfred Barr first used this description in 1929 in relation to works by Wassily Kandinsky, who in about 1911 had abandoned any pretence at copying the world of objects. A few years later, in the catalogue to the 1936 "Cubism and Abstract Art" exhibition, Barr, from a formal perspective, distinguished between two traditions in abstract art: the first, more strongly geometric-structural tendency, in his view led from Georges Seurat and Paul Cézanne, via Cubism, to the various geometric and Constructivist movements in Russia

"The New Soft Look", 1951 Photograph by Cecil Beaton during Pollock's exhibition at the Betty Parsosns Gallery

and Holland, and had, since the First World War, become international. "The second – and, until recently, secondary – current," Barr continued, "has its principal source in the art and theories of Gauguin and his circle, flows through the Fauvisme of Matisse to the Abstract Expressionism of the pre-war paintings of Kandinsky. After running under ground for a few years it reappears vigorously among the masters of abstract art associated with Surrealism. This tradition, by contrast with the first, is intuitive and emotional rather than intellectual; organic and biomorphic rather than geometrical in its form; curvilinear rather than rectilinear, decorative rather than structural, and romantic rather than classical in its exaltation of the mystical, the spontaneous and the irrational."

"The Unwanted Title"

In a certain sense, Barr's article was prophetic for many artists who, in the next two decades, were to attract increasing attention as the "New York School". Surrealism was one of the influential trends with which American artists were coming to terms, in particular when the coming-to-power of the National Socialists in Germany and the outbreak of the Second World War forced numerous exponents of the Surrealist movement to emigrate to the United States. New Yorkers were also acquainted with Wassily Kandinsky's early abstract works through the collection in the Museum of Non-Objective Art, the future Solomon R. Guggenheim Museum. And so the term coined by Alfred Barr and reintroduced by Robert Coates gradually found currency. Among artists, though, it was always "The unwanted title", the motto of a symposium organized by the painter Phillip Pavia in 1952 for that celebrated association of New York artists known simply as The Club.

The more neutral geographical description New York School – in allusion and in contrast to the École de Paris, which until the 1940s had been regarded as the world leader – was first applied primarily on account of New York's being the most important work and exhibition location for a new generation of artists. The name can be traced back to "The School of New York" exhibition which the artist Robert Motherwell organized in 1951 at the Frank Perls Gallery in Beverly Hills, and which included works by, among others, William Baziotes, Willem de Kooning, Adolph Gottlieb, Hans Hofmann, Robert Motherwell, Jackson Pollock, Richard Pousette-Dart, Ad

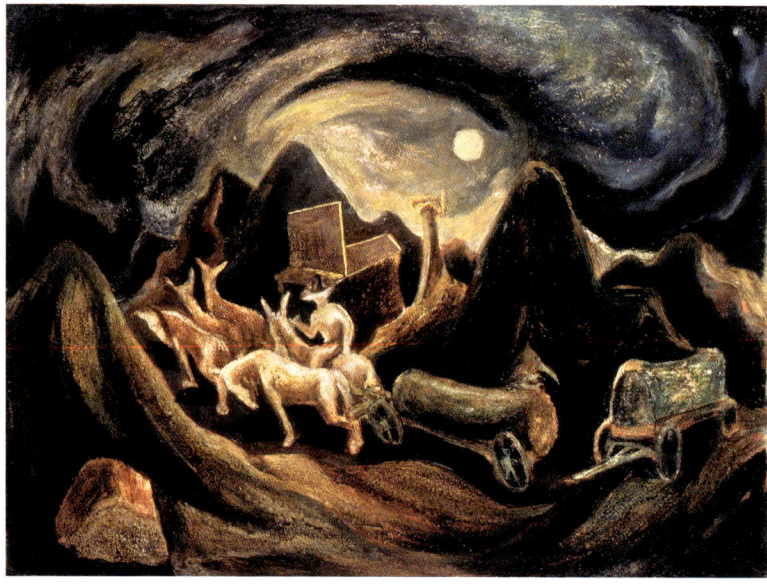

Jackson Pollock
Going West, *c.* 1934/35
Oil and plaster on canvas,
38.3 x 52.7 cm (15 x 20¾ in.)
Washington, D.C.,
Smithsonian American
Art Museum, Gift of
Thomas Hart Benton

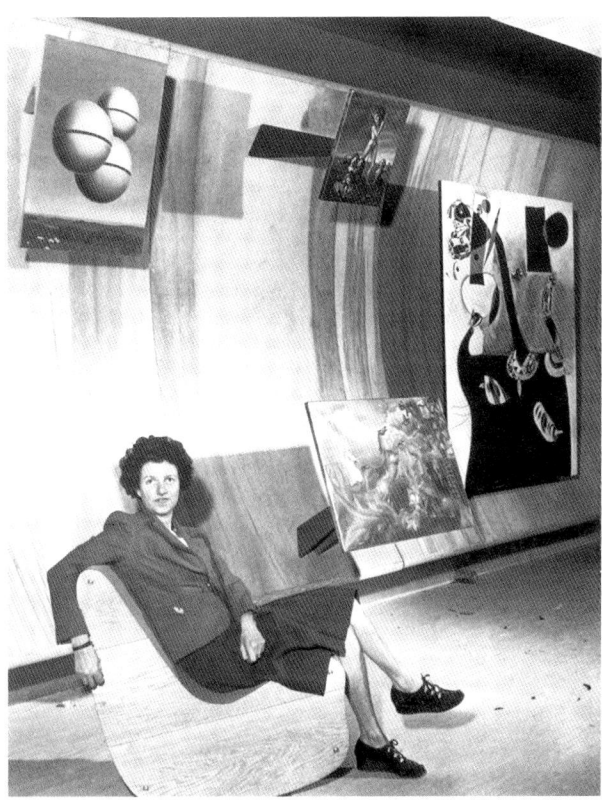

Peggy Guggenheim
in her gallery, 1952

Reinhardt, Mark Rothko, Theodoros Stamos, Hedda Sterne, Clyfford Still, Mark Tobey and Bradley Walker Tomlin.

The aesthetic content of what generally goes by the name of Abstract Expressionism occupies a singularly broad spectrum, and this proviso, with its reference to the decided "individualism" within the New York School, has been a kind of critical platitude since as long ago as the late 1950s. The visual differences range from the – in some cases – transparently overlaid colour veils such as those seen in Mark Rothko's paintings – their "abstractness" clear enough, their "expressiveness" less obviously so – via Willem de Kooning's series *Women* – "expressive" enough with their visible deployment of the body, but indisputably "figurative" in their adherence to the tradition of the female nude – right up to the legendary gestural "drip-paintings" of Jackson Pollock, in whose (literal) outpourings figurative elements can also sometimes be discerned.

The use of paint in the austerely composed, non-figurative pictures of Ad Reinhardt and Barnett Newman appears by contrast reticent and controlled. In his 1955 essay "'American-Type' Painting", the influential critic Clement Greenberg noted, in respect of the large-format canvases employed by Rothko, Newman and Clyfford Still, a "more emphatically flat surface"; in their case, one also speaks of "Color Field Painting" – a term that, in addition, is used of the painting of the 1960s and 70s by such artists as Morris Louis, Kenneth Noland, Jules Olitski and Frank Stella, who worked in the aftermath of Abstract Expressionism.

It seems, then, to be neither possible nor productive to try to pin Abstract Expressionism down to a single aesthetic programme or a stable group identity. Accordingly, there seems little purpose in defining which artists are to be counted as "Abstract Expressionists", even though art historians

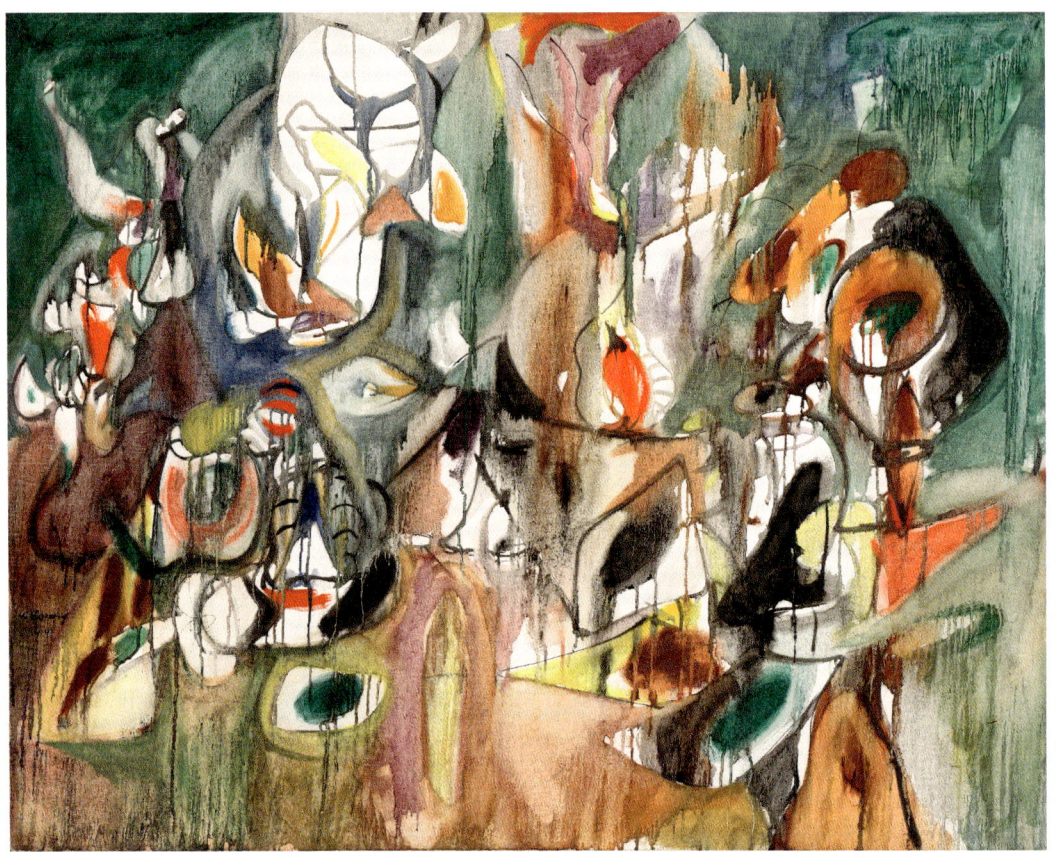

Arshile Gorky
One Year the Milkweed, 1944
Oil on canvas,
94.2 x 119.3 cm (37 x 47 in.)
Washington, D.C.,
National Gallery of Art

OPPOSITE
Mark Rothko
Untitled (Subway), c. 1937
Oil on canvas,
51.1 x 76.2 cm (20 x 30 in.)
Washington, D.C., National Gallery
of Art, Gift of The Mark Rothko
Foundation, Inc.

have tried time and again to do so, with varying results. Alongside the figures already mentioned, we have included James Brooks, Arshile Gorky, Philip Guston, Franz Kline, Elaine de Kooning, Lee Krasner, the sculptor David Smith, and Mark Tobey among the "first generation of Abstract Expressionism"; while the "second generation" of younger artists, or of those who only developed their characteristic techniques in the 1950s, is supposed to include Friedel Dzubas, Sam Francis, Helen Frankenthaler, Grace Hartigan and Joan Mitchell. Like every canon in which works and interpretations defined as "worthy of being handed down" are listed, that of Abstract Expressionism is subject to historico-cultural revision. Without a doubt, the female Abstract Expressionists play a special role in this connection. The American art historian Marcia Brennan tellingly noted that women in Abstract Expressionism were "at the same time selectively present and strategically absent"; not until recently has greater attention been paid to the works and working conditions of artists such as Lee Krasner, Elaine de Kooning, Joan Mitchell or Janet Sobel.

"Myth-Makers" and "Ideographic Pictures"

The prehistory of Abstract Expressionism begins in the late 1920s and early 1930s. After "Black Friday", the notorious Wall Street Crash of 25 October 1929, which triggered off a world economic crisis that was to last many years, America's economic strength fell to a historical low, and unemployment climbed to more than 30 percent. American art at this time was determined by two figurative tendencies: Regionalism, which took its motifs from the lives of the rural population, and Social Realism, which critically

"The stuff of thought is the seed of the artist. Dreams form the bristles of the artist's brush. And, as the eye functions as the brain's sentry, I communicate my innermost perceptions through the art, my worldview."
ARSHILE GORKY

portrayed the darker sides of big-city life such as unemployment and isolation. The future Abstract Expressionists such as Mark Rothko and Jackson Pollock were influenced by these trends in the 1930s. Since the start of the decade, Pollock, for example, had been studying at the Art Students League with the Regionalist Thomas Hart Benton, whose influence is apparent in works like *Going West*; meanwhile Rothko was formulating his melancholy view of human existence in figurative symbolic big-city motifs such as subway and street scenes.

In order to counter the economic distress being suffered by artists, President Franklin D. Roosevelt's Works Progress Administration (WPA) instituted the Federal Arts Project (FAP) in 1935. This enabled numerous artists, including William Baziotes, Willem de Kooning, Arshile Gorky, Philip Guston, Lee Krasner, Jackson Pollock and David Smith, to earn a living from their art for the first time, while also promoting closer links between those involved. One important undertaking by the Federal Arts Project was the commissioning of works of art for public spaces, primarily exterior murals, whose execution was supervised by, among others, major representatives of the Mexican Muralist movement such as Diego Rivera, José Clemente Orozco and David Alfaro Siqueiros. While it is true that an artist like Arshile Gorky ironically described the social-critical orientation of the FAP's figurative wall-painting as "poor art for poor people", it was later to point the

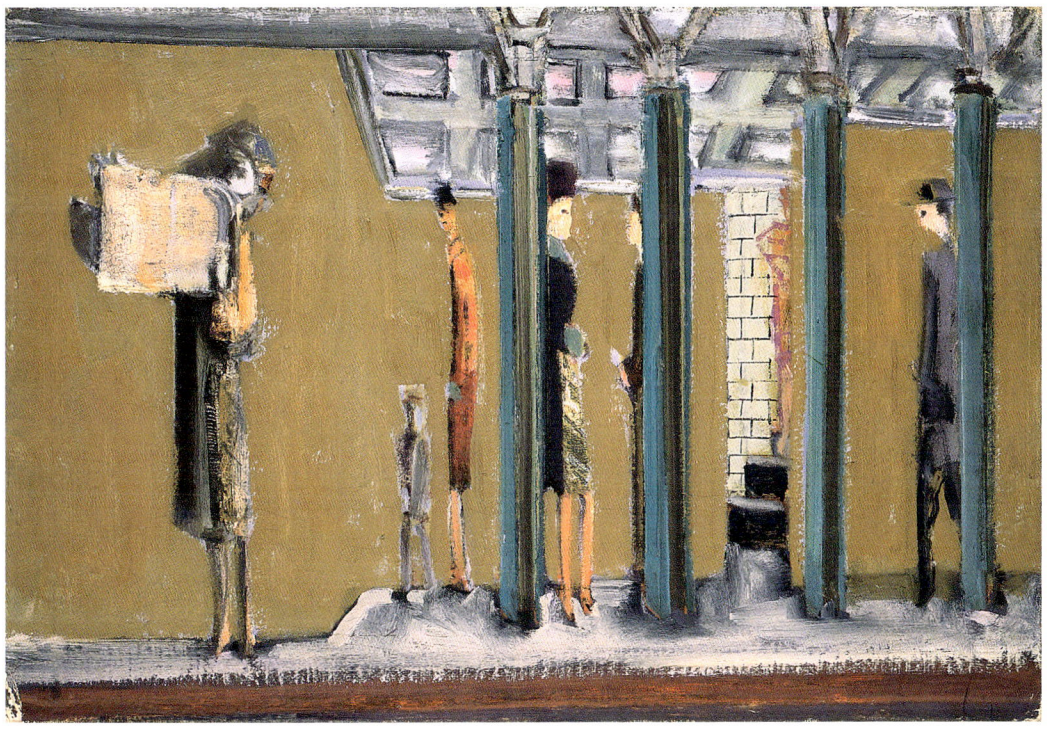

"The ability to simplify means to eliminate the unnecessary so that the necessary may speak."
HANS HOFMANN

way ahead for the Abstract Expressionists' working methods using large-format canvases. Thus, with his 1943/44 *Mural*, Pollock created a painting of wall-filling size for the living quarters of the collector and gallery owner Peggy Guggenheim, and at the beginning of 1947, in his application for a grant from the Guggenheim Foundation, declared: "I believe easel painting to be a dying form, and the tendency of modern feeling is toward the wall picture or mural."

In the years 1936/37 the Museum of Modern Art staged two exhibitions which provided strong impulses for the younger generation of New York artists: "Cubism and Abstract Art" and "Fantastic Art, Dada, Surrealism". The latter, in particular, aroused an interest in the unconscious as a source of artistic expression, and in Surrealist artistic techniques such as "écriture automatique", a form of pictorial or written expression free of any censorship by the rational mind or the conscious will. Following the example of écriture automatique, the self-dynamic of the paint itself came to be increasingly important in the painting techniques of a number of Abstract Expressionists, for example through the use of highly diluted paint in Arshile Gorky's 1944 picture *One Year the Milkweed*, or in Jackson Pollock's drip-paintings. Pollock in addition emphasized his studies of the theories of Sigmund Freud and Carl Gustav Jung, who at the time enjoyed a broad following in the United States. In an interview with Selden Rodman in 1956, he remarked: "I'm very representational some of the time, and a little all of the time. But when you're painting out of your unconscious, figures are bound to emerge. We're all of us influenced by Freud, I guess. I've been a Jungian for a long time… Painting is a state of being… Painting is self-discovery. Every good artist paints what he is."

This view of painting as "self-examination, self-reassurance and self-expression" – a quotation from a panel discussion initiated by *Life* magazine on the subject of "modern art" in 1948 – was definitive for the Abstract Expressionists and their public alike. Mark Rothko, Adolph Gottlieb and Barnett Newman saw themselves, especially during the 1940s, as modern "myth-makers" who, by having recourse to "primitive" and archaic cultures – for example Native American or pre-Columbian art – hoped to create timeless and immediately accessible metaphors and symbols for the condition of "modern man", which was perceived as tragic. Thus Newman, in his preface to the 1947 exhibition "The Ideographic Picture" at the Betty Parsons Gallery, referred to the art of the native peoples of North America and drew a direct parallel between their works and those of his fellow artists such as Hofmann, Rothko, Stamos and Still: "Spontaneous, and emerging from several points, there has arisen during the war years a new force in American painting that is the modern counterpart of the primitive art impulse."

In the early 1990s the American art historian Michael Leja drew attention to the importance, for the appearance of Abstract Expressionism, of the discourse concerning "modern man", which in 1930s and 40s America was being carried on in numerous popular science books and magazines: following the experience of the world economic crisis, social injustice and racial disturbances, the appearance of totalitarian regimes, the holocaust and the lapse into barbarity which it implied, the devastation wrought by the Second World War in general and the atomic bomb in particular, American society was dominated by a feeling of crisis concerning the image of humanity, doubt over what was meant by progress, and a questioning of the value of science and rational thought. In the discourse concerning "modern man" – who was implicitly seen as male, white and heterosexual – this crisis was not analysed as historically determined, but rather interpreted as pointing back to so-called "primitive cultures" as an anthropological constant. In this reference system, Abstract Expressionism could be seen – by its publicists such as gallery owners, curators and critics, but

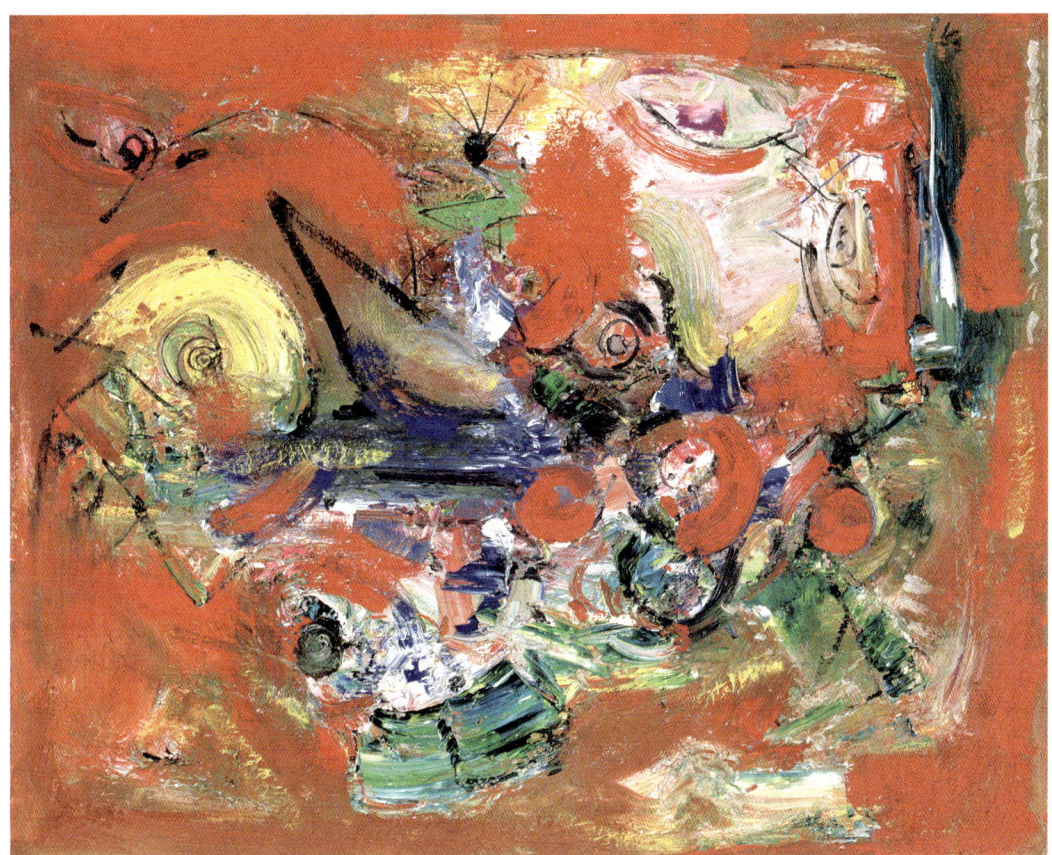

also by collectors and a broader public – as a valid expression of this crisis of "modern man", and as a result, according to Leja, took on a central role in the cultural debate of the time.

Hans Hofmann
Autumn, 1949
Oil on canvas,
61 x 76.2 cm (24 x 30 in.)
New York, Brooklyn Museum of Art,
Bequest of William K. Jacobs, Jr.

An Art Scene Comes Into Being

The gradual rise of Abstract Expressionism in the 1940s cannot be seen in isolation from the appearance of the New York art world, a dense network of new galleries, magazines, art schools and artist meeting places. The story of an avant-garde art movement like Abstract Expressionism, would, according to the sociologist Diana Crane, have taken a fundamentally different course without the continuous expansion of this infrastructure – an expansion, which took place against the background of general growth in the American economy during the 1940s. Thus the painter Max Weber could still observe, in 1936, on the occasion of the "First American Artists' Congress Against War and Fascism" in New York, that artists were advised, at the start of their careers, to make contacts, but that at the end of their lives their only contact was mostly with the workhouse. Up till then, the demand for contemporary American art was not particularly strong; the market was dominated by European art.

Peggy Guggenheim, niece of the collector Solomon R. Guggenheim, had fled to New York from Europe in the company of Max Ernst in 1941 and opened her Art of This Century gallery in October 1943. There were, according to her colleague Sidney Janis, "maybe a dozen galleries in all of

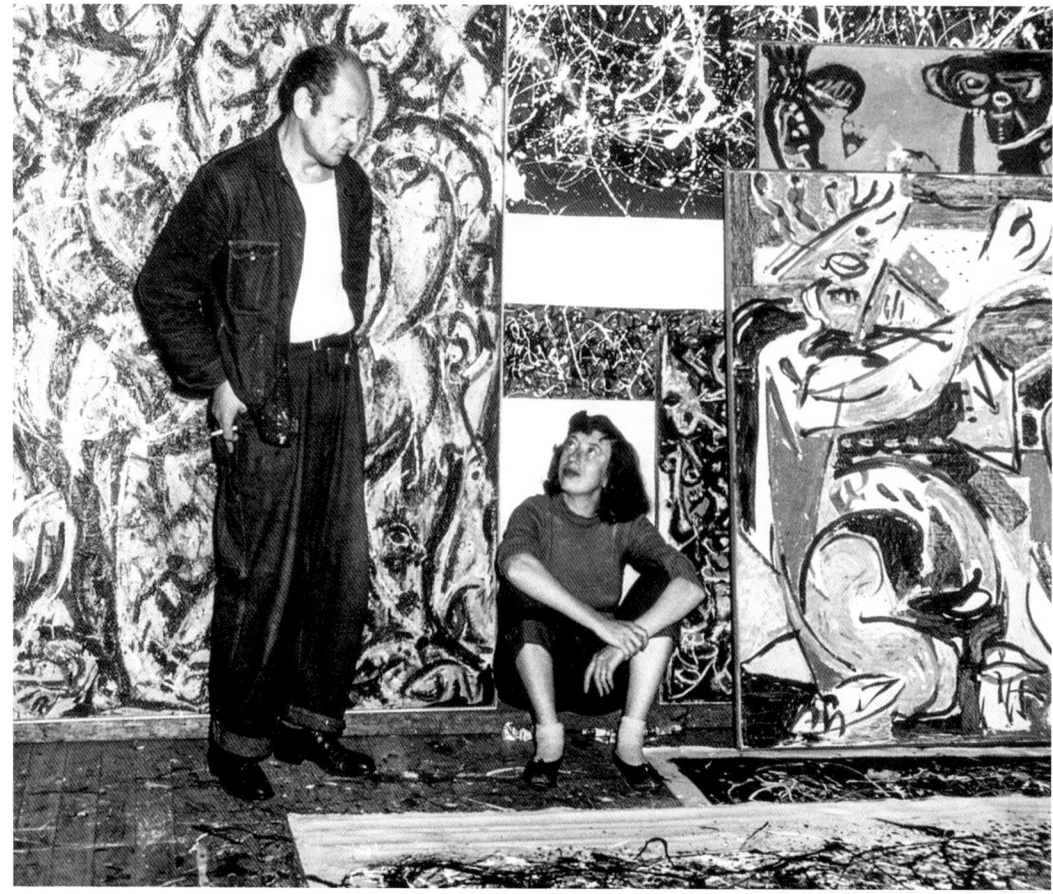

Jackson Pollock and Lee
Krasner in the atelier, 1949

New York". By the early 1950s, according to the art historian and observer of the scene Dore Ashton, about thirty, and ten years later this figure had already increased more than tenfold.

In the Art of This Century exhibition rooms – designed by architect Frederick Kiesler as Surrealist environments capable of continual alteration – Peggy Guggenheim displayed not only her own collection of European Abstract and Surrealist art but, by the time of her return to Europe in 1947 had also staged the first solo exhibitions of the works of numerous American Abstract Expressionists, including Jackson Pollock, Hans Hofmann, Mark Rothko, Clyfford Still, William Baziotes and Robert Motherwell. Guggenheim supported the artists by buying their works and commissioning others, and also sold their works to major collections such as that of the Museum of Modern Art. On the occasion of the closing of Art of This Century, Clement Greenberg wrote: "I am convinced that Peggy Guggenheim's place in the history of American art will grow larger as time passes and as the artists she encouraged mature." He was to prove right.

The artist and dealer Betty Parsons, who opened her gallery in September 1946, took over some of the positions of Peggy Guggenheim's programme following the closure of Art of This Century, among them Pollock, Rothko and Still; in addition Barnett Newman curated exhibitions for her gallery. Parsons came from a patrician New York family, and in her youth had studied sculpture in Paris under Émile-Antoine Bourdelle and Ossip Zadkine, and in California under Alexander

Archipenko. Since the mid-1930s, she had exhibited her own works in New York galleries together with artists such as Theodore Stamos, Hedda Sterne and Adolph Gottlieb. Enthusiastic but not particularly businesslike, she lost many of her artists – one exception was Ad Reinhardt – to other dealers. In his preface to the catalogue for the Parsons Gallery tenth anniversary, Greenberg summed up as follows: "Mrs. Parsons is an artist's – and critic's – gallery: a place where art goes on and is not just shown and sold."

Another dealer widely appreciated by artists was Charles Egan. He had gathered his experience by dealing in works by the German Expressionists and the École de Paris before opening his own gallery at the start of 1946; here, in 1948, he helped Willem de Kooning, who was by then already in his mid-forties, to stage his first successful solo exhibition. Two other influential protagonists of the up-and-coming New York gallery scene were Samuel Kootz and Sidney Janis. Before Kootz set up his gallery in April 1945, he had written a book about *New Frontiers in American Painting* (1943). His programme encompassed both European and American art; for example his inaugural exhibition included works by the French artist Fernand Léger, then living in American exile, along with others by William Baziotes and Robert Motherwell. By dealing in the works of established and high-priced Europeans, above all Picasso, Kootz was able to build up a market for young and unknown American artists.

A similar strategy was pursued by Sidney Janis, whose gallery opened in the autumn of 1948. Janis's career in the art world began as a collector of modern European art, including Pablo Picasso, Paul Klee, Fernand Léger, Henri Matisse, Giorgio de Chirico, Salvador Dalí and Henri Rousseau. In 1944, together with his wife, Harriet Grossman, he published a book on *Abstract and Surrealist Art in America*, in which Pollock, Rothko, Motherwell and de Kooning were also included – artists whose works were later to feature in his gallery.

Alongside the galleries there appeared in the 1930s and 40s a series of non-commercial exhibition rooms, some of them organized by the artists themselves. An important location for an exchange of views was the art school set up in 1933 by the German émigré painter Hans Hofmann. Hofmann had lived in Paris between 1904 and 1914, and he put across to his pupils the basics of new European painting, in particular Cubism and Fauvism.

In the autumn of 1948 William Baziotes, the sculptor David Hare, Robert Motherwell, Mark Rothko and Clyfford Still founded an art school under the name of The Subjects of the Artists, with the aim of distancing themselves from their attribution to "abstract" art and investigating the subjects of the "modern artist": "what his subjects are, how they are arrived at, methods of inspiration and transformation, moral attitudes, possibilities for further explorations, what is being done now and what might be done, and so on". After the financial collapse of The Subjects of the Artists, the activities of the school were continued by Studio 35, founded in the autumn of 1949.

Doubtless the most celebrated rendezvous was the artists' association known as the Eighth Street Club, called into being in the autumn of 1949 by twenty founder members, including Charles Egan, Franz Kline, Willem de Kooning and Ad Reinhardt. Until it closed in the spring of 1962, but in particular up until the early 1950s, it was a venue for discussions and lectures, some of which were published, promoting a lively exchange between a variety of protagonists: critics and writers, American and European artists, dealers and museum curators. They reinforced the conviction, in both the participants and their public, that the visual art created in America was of universal significance: a conviction which was also fired by the attention of the mass media, museums, and a new nouveau-riche class of collector starting to get interested in contemporary American art, and thus also Abstract Expressionist painting. As the critic Aline B. Louchheim put it in July 1944 in the magazine *ARTnews*:

"American paintings are cheaper, they are more plentiful, it is easier to find good ones, and it is seen as 'patriotic' to support American artists."

"Artists: Man and Wife"

In October 1949, the Sidney Janis Gallery organized an exhibition with the title "Artists: Man and Wife". Among the artist couples represented were Lee Krasner and Jackson Pollock, and Elaine and Willem de Kooning, along with the Europeans Ben Nicholson and Barbara Hepworth, and Hans Arp and Sophie Taeuber-Arp. The exhibition was thus a mise-en-scène, on two planes, of a kind of equality within a complicated situation of rivalry: both in the relationship between American and European art, and also within heterosexual artist relationships. In retrospect, however, Elaine de Kooning was, if anything, sceptical concerning the emancipatory impetus behind the idea of the exhibition: "There was something about the show that sort of attached women – wives – to the real artists. Well, maybe it was just too cute. You know, a cute idea; something to get attention for the gallery." As Elaine Fried, she had been a pupil of Willem de Kooning's in the late 1930s; they married in 1943. In spite of a number of joint and solo exhibitions in the 1950s, Elaine de Kooning was at the time best known as a critic; in 1948 she joined the editorial staff of *ARTnews*, the magazine which, under its new editor Thomas B. Hess, was devoting itself to the success of Abstract Expressionism.

A photograph of Rudolph Burckhardt dating from 1950 provides a visual image of the division of labour between the two married partners, though it is not difficult to imagine that in her role as critic Elaine de Kooning was certainly able to exert an influence on the work of the artist: Willem de Kooning seems to be hesitating as to which tube of paint to choose, while Elaine de Kooning watches him, pencil in hand. By contrast, in a later shot of the couple, by Hans Namuth, the artist's wife is literally in the background in relation to the artist: the centre of the photograph – and of the picture on the wall, from the series *Women*, a sequence of female nudes – seems to be taken up by no one apart from the painter himself.

In the same way, the emphatic placement of Hedda Sterne in the famous group photo of the Abstract Expressionists by Nina Leen comes across above all – in Elaine de Kooning's words – as a "cute idea": as the female exception, Sterne seems to lord it (so to speak) over her fourteen exclusively male fellow artists like a figurehead of the avant-garde, drawing all eyes to herself. The picture appeared in January 1951 in the popular magazine *Life* on the occasion of a protest letter by eighteen artists directed at the "American Painting Today – 1950" exhibition at the New York Metropolitan Museum. The signatories, known thenceforth as "The Irascibles", criticized the jury for not yet having given sufficient attention to "advanced art" in the planned exhibition. With their protest against the cultural establishment in the institutions, the "Irascibles" achieved their admission into the tradition of the avant-garde and, in addition, influenced the greater importance given to up-to-the-minute art in the exhibition: but works by female artists such as Hedda Sterne or Lee Krasner were still not included.

"Primarily a Housewife": a Re-evaluation of the Female Artists

In its search for the "greatest living painter in the United States", by contrast, *Life* magazine had, only two years earlier, already directed public attention, as though it went without saying, to a male figure: Jackson Pollock. As late as 1958, his wife Lee Krasner was, as Marcia Brennan has pointed out, still being referred to in the same publication as "Mrs. Jackson Pollock", while in the same breath being designated "Hans Hofmann's best pupil" and at the same time described as "primarily a housewife". Artistic autonomy at that time, according to Marcia Brennan, was considered incompatible with female identity. The rivalry between the male Abstract Expressionists was fixated on individualism, and in this situation the female artists seemed predestined to a marginal role. "In each and every one of them," recalled Lee Krasner in an interview with Grace Glueck in 1982, "you knew how threatened he felt: the hostility was physically palpable. The whole culture's like that." The fact that Pollock respected her art was "the most you could ask for. But to expect that he would stand up to the whole culture and also to his fellow artists, that was going too far. Life was difficult enough as it was." And as late as 1961, five years after Pollock's death, Anita Brookner wrote in the respected *Burlington Magazine* in a discussion of the exhibition "The New York Scene" at the Marlborough New London Gallery: "Lee Krasner paints rather more spontaneously: the man is clearly a romantic." The absence of women in the area of Abstract Expressionism seemed at that time to be so self-evident that it never even occurred to the author to actually check the identity of Lee Krasner.

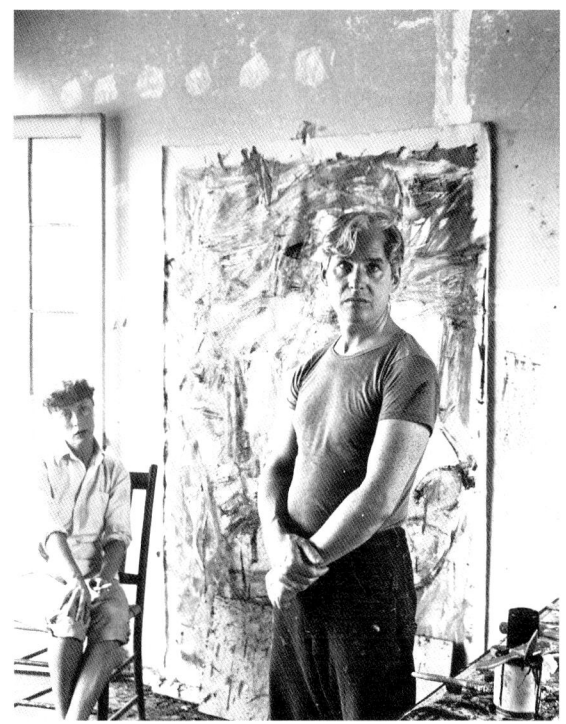

Willem and Elaine de Kooning, 1953

But for all that, Hedda Sterne, Elaine de Kooning and Lee Krasner, to name three female representatives of the first generation of Abstract Expressionism, had long been regularly exhibiting in New York galleries: Hedda Sterne had been represented by the Betty Parsons Gallery since 1947, where she had had regular solo exhibitions, and had also taken part in international group exhibitions, for example at the 1956 Venice Biennale; works by Elaine de Kooning were present in the 1950s not only in galleries, but also in museum exhibitions; Lee Krasner had been exhibiting regularly in New York since 1937, and had had her first solo exhibition at the Betty Parsons Gallery in 1951.

But anyone looking down the indexes of the anthologies of exhibition discussions and critical essays from these decades will find it difficult to discover any mention, let alone detailed discussion, of their works. In the public perception, they took a back seat to their male colleagues; this was especially true, when, like Elaine de Kooning or Lee Krasner, they promoted their husbands' careers and were reduced time and again to the role of eye-witnesses to the latter's production processes. But from this "testimony" it is nonetheless always possible also to discern their own contributions to the process by which the art of their male partners was created: for example, when, in 1969, Lee Krasner reported that in the summer of 1950 Jackson Pollock had, with reference to a new work, posed the legendary question: "Is this a painting?"

In this connection, a certain special role is played by Helen Frankenthaler. She is perhaps the only female artist of the second generation of Abstract Expressionists who was admitted to have had a decisive influence on the subsequent development of non-figurative art. When the great definer Clement Greenberg was writing about the painting of Morris Louis and Kenneth Noland in the magazine *Art International* in 1960, he observed that Louis, having encountered the paintings of

Jackson Pollock and Helen Frankenthaler's picture *Mountains and Sea*, had overcome the influence of Cubism and struck out on a new artistic course. Like Frankenthaler, from then on Louis worked on unprimed, unsealed canvases, which absorbed the runny paint, leaving the weave of the cloth visible. Kenneth Noland also left his canvases unprimed, concentrating on a non-gestural, non-figurative use of paint, which emphasized the visual over the haptic. Not long after, Greenberg described Frankenthaler's characteristic "soak-stain" painting technique using unprimed canvas (a technique reminiscent of watercolour) as pointing the way in a direction that he had christened "Post-Painterly Abstraction" in 1964. It was only after Abstract Expressionism had ended its formative period in the mid-1950s, when its art-historical significance was no longer disputed and its market value was established, that the contributions of the female exponents were given rather more attention in hindsight, and their ongoing productions were also more frequently exhibited – a continuous process of re-evaluation, which is still going on today.

Art in the Cold War

The history of Abstract Expressionism is closely bound up with that phase of post-war history known as the "Cold War". By the end of the Second World War at the latest, America – after a period of isolationism in the 1930s – was beginning to define herself as an economic and military power operating on the international stage, whose task was to defend the "free world" against the threat represented by the communist states of the Eastern bloc.

At this stage, America still had a monopoly on nuclear weapons, whose destructive power was manifested, and engraved on the collective consciousness, by the atomic bombs dropped on Hiroshima and Nagasaki in 1945; this power was perceived as a potential threat of global dimensions. The widespread fear of imminent extinction was reflected in different ways, also, in the artistic production of the Abstract Expressionists. Thus the "abstract" Jackson Pollock was expressly striving to take account, in his art, of the concrete situation of the age he was living in. In an interview with William Wright in 1950 he stressed: "It seems to me that the modern painter cannot express his age, the airplane, the atom bomb, the radio, in the old forms of the Renaissance or of any other past culture. Each age finds its own technique."

The role which Abstract Expressionism played in the complex domestic and foreign politics of the post-war period is extraordinarily multilayered. Thus in the international exhibition business it functioned on the one hand as the official advertisement of a modern, liberal America, while at home it had no shortage of bitter opponents. Sections of the conservative nationalistic camp berated it as un-American, communist, or mentally sick. The most frequently quoted representative of this faction is probably the Republican congressman George Dondero, who in 1949 told the House of Representatives: "All these isms are of foreign origin, and truly should have no place in American art. While not all are the media of social or political protest, all are instruments and weapons of destruction." Dondero had certainly enough political clout to bring about the cancellation, in 1947, of an exhibition which had been touring Europe since 1946 under the title "Advancing American Art", alleging that some of the artists involved had formerly been communist sympathizers.

With the onset of the Cold War and in particular during the early 1950s, when the Republican Senator Joseph McCarthy was waging his notorious crusade against (in most cases, allegedly) communist artists and intellectuals, the debates of the Abstract Expressionists, their adherents and sponsors, seemed however to become largely depoliticized. "Oblique references abounded," remarked Dore Ashton, "but the fifties were not hospitable to art discussions with political orientation." This

Helen Frankenthaler
April, 1963
Acrylic on canvas,
178.4 x 125 cm (70¼ x 49¼ in.)
Private collection

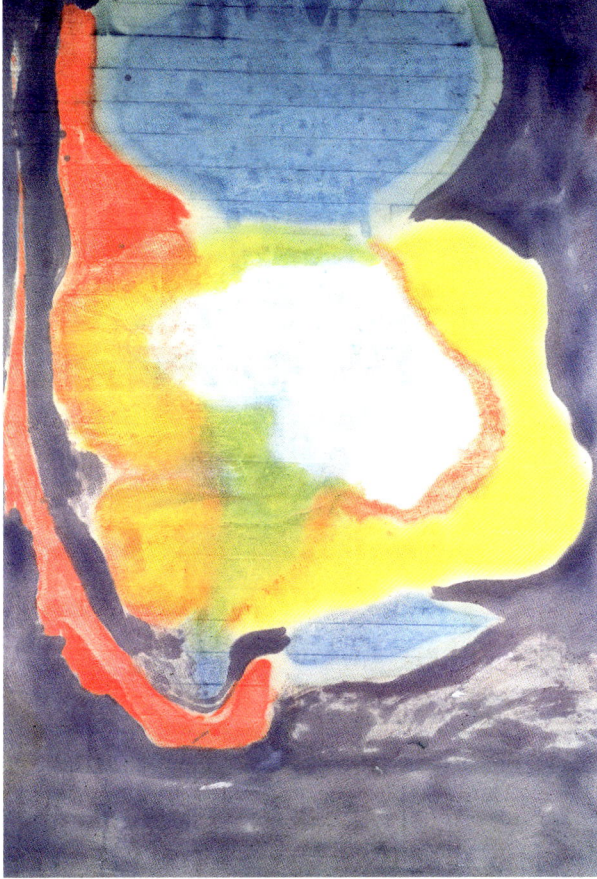

"I've explored a variety of directions and themes over the years. But I think in my painting you can see the signature of one artist, the work of one wrist."

HELEN FRANKENTHALER

retreat on the part of artists was seen by art historians such as Serge Guilbaut as one of the reasons why their art could be reforged as a propaganda weapon in the Cold War, and why, to use Guilbaut's polemical expression, "New York was able to steal the idea of modern art": "The avant-garde artist who categorically refused to participate in political discourse and tried to isolate himself by accentuating his individuality was co-opted by liberalism, which viewed the artist's individualism as an excellent weapon with which to combat Soviet authoritarianism. The depoliticization of the avant-garde was necessary before it could be put to political use, confronting the avant-garde with an inescapable dilemma."

A New American Style of Painting?

In the mid-1930s, the art historian Meyer Schapiro, who taught in New York, could still observe that the term "American art" was necessarily inexact, feigning a fictitious unity. In the art criticism of the 1940s and 50s, by contrast, more intensive efforts were made to assert the aesthetic overcoming of European models and the superiority of modern American painting. Thus in January 1948 Clement Greenberg proclaimed, in "The Situation at the Moment" in the magazine *Partisan Review*: "As dark as the situation still is for us, American painting in its most advanced aspects – that is, American abstract painting – has in the last several years shown here and there a capacity for fresh content that does not seem to be matched either in France or Great Britain."

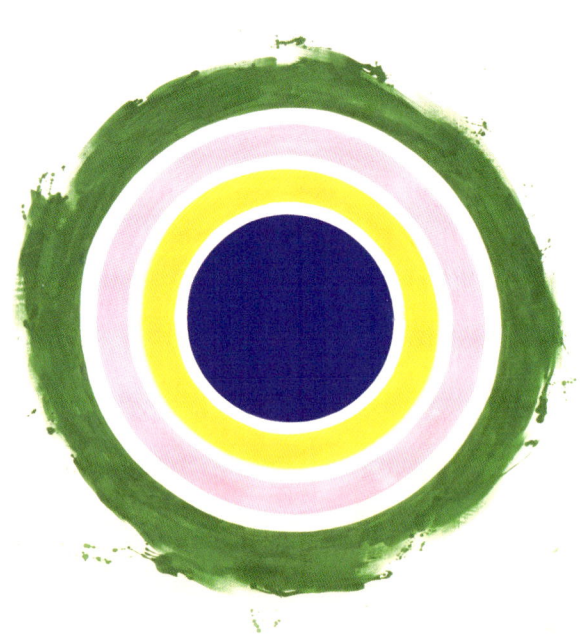

Kenneth Noland
Half, 1959
Acrylic on canvas,
174.3 x 174.3 cm (68⅝ x 68⅝ in.)
Houston, Museum of Fine Arts

OPPOSITE
Morris Louis
Gamma Gamma, 1960
Acrylic on canvas,
260 x 384.5 cm (102¼ x 151½ in.)
Düsseldorf, K20 – Kunstsammlung
Nordrhein-Westfalen

One logical problem in this debate, however, consisted precisely in the difficulty of discerning the specifically "American" aspect of the new painting in the face of its broad spectrum of artistic positions. Greenberg tried to resolve this in his 1955 essay "American-Type Painting". His thesis was that modern painting had made it its goal to investigate its own material conditions and to filter out "the expendable conventions" of the medium, "in order to maintain the irreplaceability and renew the vitality of art": indeed, in order to ensure its viability. And this attack on the conventions of painting – such as three-dimensionality, illusionism, figure-background relationships – Greenberg saw successfully implemented above all in Abstract Expressionist painting, which at the same time was the first American art movement that was not only respected in Paris, but even imitated.

The message that Abstract Expressionism had overturned European models was still being enthusiastically proclaimed in the early 1960s, when the battles had already long been fought and the overwhelming importance of American art at home and abroad was no longer in dispute. In his 1961 essay "The Abstract Sublime", the American art historian Robert Rosenblum took it upon himself to yet again position Jackson Pollock, Clyfford Still, Mark Rothko and Barnett Newman, with their large-format canvases, inviting the beholder to contemplation, as the challengers of the "international domination of the French tradition, with its family values of reason, intellect, and objectivity", and to establish them as the legitimate successors of the Romantic tradition of the 19th century.

In so doing, critics like Greenberg in no way overlooked the fact that Abstract Expressionism in America owed its development since the early 1940s to numerous international interactions. The question "Have We an American Art?", which the art critic of the *New York Times*, Edward Alden Jewell, posed in a 1939 book of that title, could not be answered in a single sentence. Numerous artists in the field of Abstract Expressionism, such as Arshile Gorky, John Graham, Hans Hofmann, Willem de Kooning, Mark Rothko and Hedda Sterne, were European émigrés, as were Rudolph Burckhardt (from Switzerland) and Hans Namuth (from Germany), whose photographs and films created the public image of the Abstract Expressionists that we still have today.

Other protagonists, such as Betty Parsons and Sam Francis, studied or worked at least for a time in Europe. And alongside the numerous works by European artists in New York galleries and museums, it was in particular the presence of international artists, especially after the outbreak of the Second World War, that promoted an intensive cultural dialogue.

Nevertheless, the mostly positive reactions to Abstract Expressionism in the Europe of the late 1950s were often celebrated back home as an American "triumph". Among the places in which the new American painting was effectively staged were the Venice Biennale: its architectural structure with individual national pavilions in a spacious garden setting continues even today to promote the perception of art on the nation-state principle. In 1950 there could be seen here, selected by the Museum of Modern Art, exhibitions by, among others, Arshile Gorky, Willem de Kooning and Jackson Pollock; in 1958 Mark Rothko exhibited in the American pavilion.

Pathbreaking in terms of its creation of international recognition of American painting as a new and significant artistic phenomenon was, not least, a comprehensive touring exhibition entitled "The New American Painting", with works by Baziotes, Brooks, Francis, Gorky, Gottlieb, Guston, Hartigan, Kline, de Kooning, Motherwell, Newman, Pollock, Rothko, Stamos, Still, Tomlin and Tworkow from the collection of the Museum of Modern Art. It was shown in 1958/59 in Basel, Milan, Madrid, Berlin, Amsterdam, Brussels, Paris and London, and finally, in a sense as a climax of a successful mission, presented in the Museum of Modern Art itself.

This "triumph" of the new American painting was finally sealed at the second documenta in Kassel in 1959, which was then, geographically, close to the border of the former (communist) East Germany. Both the American documenta contribution and the touring exhibition had been organized by the Museum of Modern Art's "International Program", which in the 1950s started a cultural-policy offensive directed not only towards Europe, but also other continents, at the centre

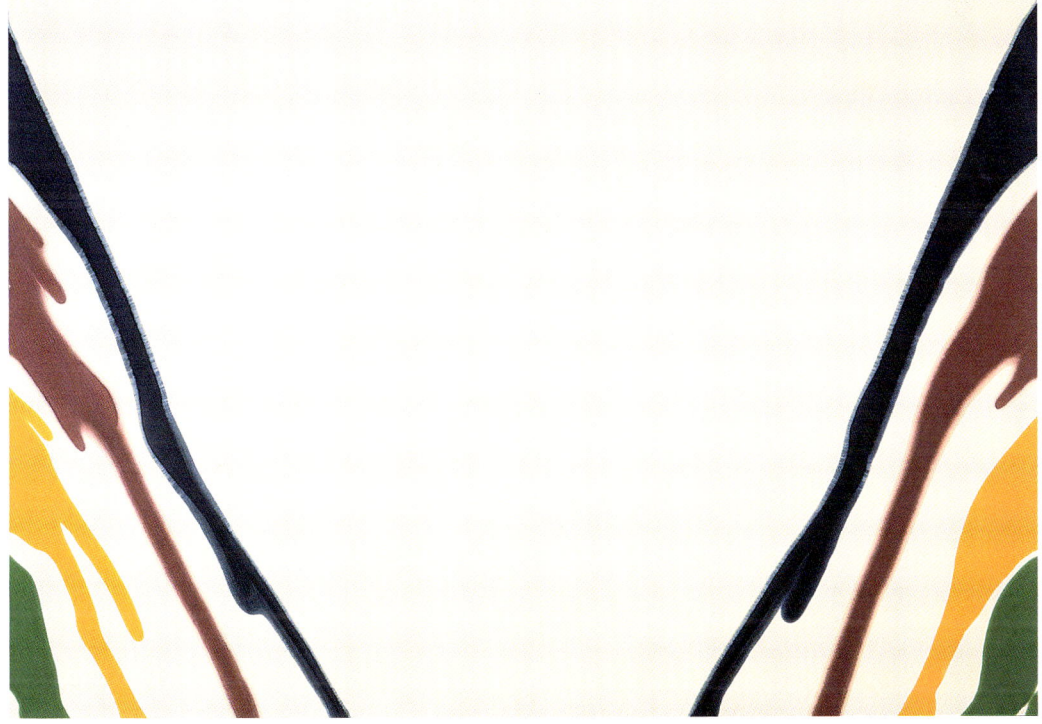

"Aesthetics is for the artist like ornithology is for the birds."

BARNETT NEWMAN

of which Abstract Expressionism stood as the hallmark of the Western world's freedom of expression. When the art historian Eva Cockcroft, in an article published in 1974 in the magazine *Artforum* under the title "Abstract Expressionism, Weapon of the Cold War", questioned the ideological, economic and political background that had contributed to the success of Abstract Expressionism, the cover of the catalogue *The New American Painting, as Shown in Eight European Countries, 1958–1959* served to illustrate her thesis. In the same spirit, the German art historian Will Grohmann, in his 1958 review of this exhibition, had already described the Americans as "world-travellers and conquerors" and asked, rhetorically, whether Europe was already in a state of cultural defensiveness. And indeed the exhibitions organized by the "International Program" not only made a major contribution to America's being accorded a dominant role in the cultural sphere, but also sketched out an image of the artist as an individual struggling with social conventions, but ultimately apolitical. Thus Alfred Barr, in his preface to *The New American Painting*, wrote: "They defiantly reject the conventional values of the society which surrounds them, but they are not politically *engagés* even though their paintings have been praised and condemned as symbolic demonstrations of freedom in a world in which freedom connotes a political attitude." While abstraction was identified with the artistic language of a "free world", Realism was indiscriminately equated with the art form of the totalitarian regimes of National Socialism and Communism. Just as misleading was Barr's assertion that the Abstract Expressionist artists were all apolitical; in fact, some of them, including Philip Guston, Elaine de Kooning, Ad Reinhardt and Mark Rothko, supported the civil rights and anti-war movements.

Even though, as mentioned at the outset, the identity of the first generation of Abstract Expressionists as an artist group, stylistic trend or representatives of a genuinely "American" art cannot be summed up by any one term, they do have at least one thing in common: their international institutional and economic success. "An older generation of major [artists] […] may have made American painting exportable in the first place," was Greenberg's résumé in 1960.

"Apocalypse and Wallpaper"

The point in time from which Abstract Expressionism can be counted as a recognized art movement – whether already from the late 1940s, or from about 1952 with the exhibition "Fifteen Americans" at the New York Museum of Modern Art, or only in the mid-1950s – is debatable. Serge Guilbaut, for example, sees Abstract Expressionism as being established as early as 1948, when, following the American presidential election of that year, the "New Liberalism" established itself, an ideology whose values – freedom, risk, humanism – accorded with the ideals which the avant-garde works of the Abstract Expressionists seemed to embody. A later important caesura for the institutional and economic success of Abstract Expressionism was undoubtedly Jackson Pollock's fatal accident in August 1956; the death of the major protagonist seemed to mark an endpoint in the development of the movement, which was reflected in the art market by a drastic increase in prices for Pollock's works and for those of some of his contemporaries. If, however, the integration of Abstract Expressionism into the cultural mainstream, and into the output of the mass media, is to be regarded as an indicator of its broad acceptance, then March 1951 surely marks an important milestone in this process. That was the month in which the American fashion magazine *Vogue* published fashion photographs taken by Cecil Beaton at the end of 1950 at Jackson Pollock's exhibition at the Betty Parsons Gallery – against a background of pictures considered to be Pollock's "major works". It can easily be imagined that Harold Rosenberg had these photographs in his mind's eye

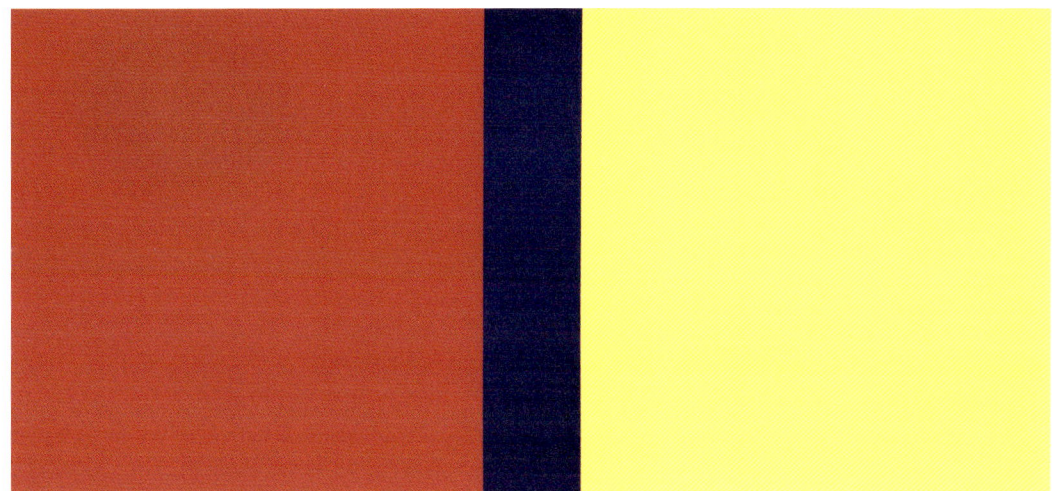

Barnett Newman
Who's Afraid of Red, Yellow and Blue IV, 1969/70
Oil on canvas,
274 x 603 cm (108 x 237½ in.)
Staatliche Museen zu Berlin,
Neue Nationalgalerie

when he wrote his article about "The American Action Painters", which appeared in *ARTnews* in November 1952. Rosenberg's essay is often quoted, because he coined the term "Action Painting" and disseminated Pollock's metaphor of the canvas as "an arena in which to act" – ideas that, to this day, are associated above all with the pictures of Franz Kline, Willem de Kooning and Jackson Pollock himself. In fact Rosenberg avoided mentioning any artists' names in his article, perhaps because he did not wish to push their market value any higher. Rosenberg was influenced by Existentialism and, in his view, painting ought to be a place of free expression for an individual alienated from society; in a climate of increasing material consumption, however, it had become a commodity like any other. "Here the common phrase, 'I have bought an O' (rather than a painting by O) becomes literally true," noted Rosenberg. "The man who started to remake himself has made himself into a commodity with a trademark."

Particularly for a series of younger artists, who by now were almost mechanically reproducing the painterly idiom of the first generation, and also for their public, Abstract Expressionism was threatening to become a decorative cliché. "The result," noted a chastened Rosenberg, "is an apocalyptic wallpaper." The rise of Abstract Expressionist painting to vogue status is veritably incarnated in Cecil Beaton's photographs for *Vogue* magazine: his staging of elegant photographic models against Pollock's drip-paintings did indeed transform the latter in a sense into an "apocalyptic wallpaper" – although it should be said that Pollock himself did not object to the presence either of his person or of his works in the mass media.

The following years saw a rise in warnings that Abstract Expressionism was threatening to become academic. The Club was the venue in 1954 and 1958/59 for a number of panel discussions under the titles "Has the Situation Changed?" and "What is the New Academy?". In this connection Alfred Barr even called in 1958 for a "revolution" on the part of the rising generation against the "young academy", as Dore Ashton recalls.

The fact that Barr, as the former director of the Museum of Modern Art, and still very much involved with the place, was at that time handing down judgement, as it were, from the summit of the Olympus of modernism, evokes the ambivalent picture of an aesthetic revolution from above.

In addition, it soon became clear that Alfred Barr had not only called on younger artists to stage a "revolution" against Abstract Expressionism, but that the Museum of Modern Art was supporting this revolution through its exhibitions, purchases and symposia.

In fact some younger artists had already long since declared their attitude towards the generation of the Abstract Expressionists. Thus Robert Rauschenberg, who had exhibited at the Betty Parsons Gallery in 1951, asked Willem de Kooning in 1953 for a drawing which he could erase and present as his own work – a multiple ambiguous strategy in which the eradication of the famous original, intervention in its creative process, and a new aesthetic are combined. And also in Rauschenberg's famous statement, "Painting relates to both art and life. Neither can be made (I try to act in that gap between the two)", we still hear the echo of Harold Rosenberg, who in 1952 had declared: "The new painting has broken down every distinction between art and life."

It was in particular the relationship between high art and everyday culture that was the object of revision in many ways during the late 1950s, and in this connection, the view of art inherent in Abstract Expressionism was also subjected to close examination. Thus the English critic Lawrence Alloway, in his 1958 article "The Arts and the Mass Media", suggested dropping the rigid distinction between authentic avant-garde art and mass media "ersatz culture", a distinction insisted upon by modernist critics such as Clement Greenberg. In this article, Alloway coined a term that was soon to be adopted for a new, internationally successful movement: Pop Art.

If one attempts to explain what the importance and fascination of Abstract Expressionism are based on today, one factor is certainly its wide-ranging and hitherto ongoing effect on succeeding artistic developments. Indeed, the relationship between the first generation of the New York School and the art of the 1960s and 70s – from Pop and Minimal Art via Happenings, Action Art and Body Art – right up to the present day can be described not primarily as a rupture, but rather as a productive confrontation. The artistic works which point expressly to Abstract Expressionism, in order to transcend it, are extraordinarily numerous. In painting, they extend from Roy Lichtenstein's series of *Brushstrokes* and Andy Warhol's *Piss Paintings* (1961) and *Oxydation Paintings* (1977/78) to Frank Stella's *Die Fahne Hoch!* (1959), to name only a few of the best known examples.

"After the first burst of anti-Abstract Expressionist diatribes in 1962," noted the critic Lucy Lippard in 1970, "it became evident that this withdrawal from the principles of Abstract Expressionism was largely based on admiration and respect for that movement: it had been done too well to continue." In view of the ongoing art-historical and artistic concern with Abstract Expressionism, it could just as well conversely be maintained, however, that "it had been done too well" to end.

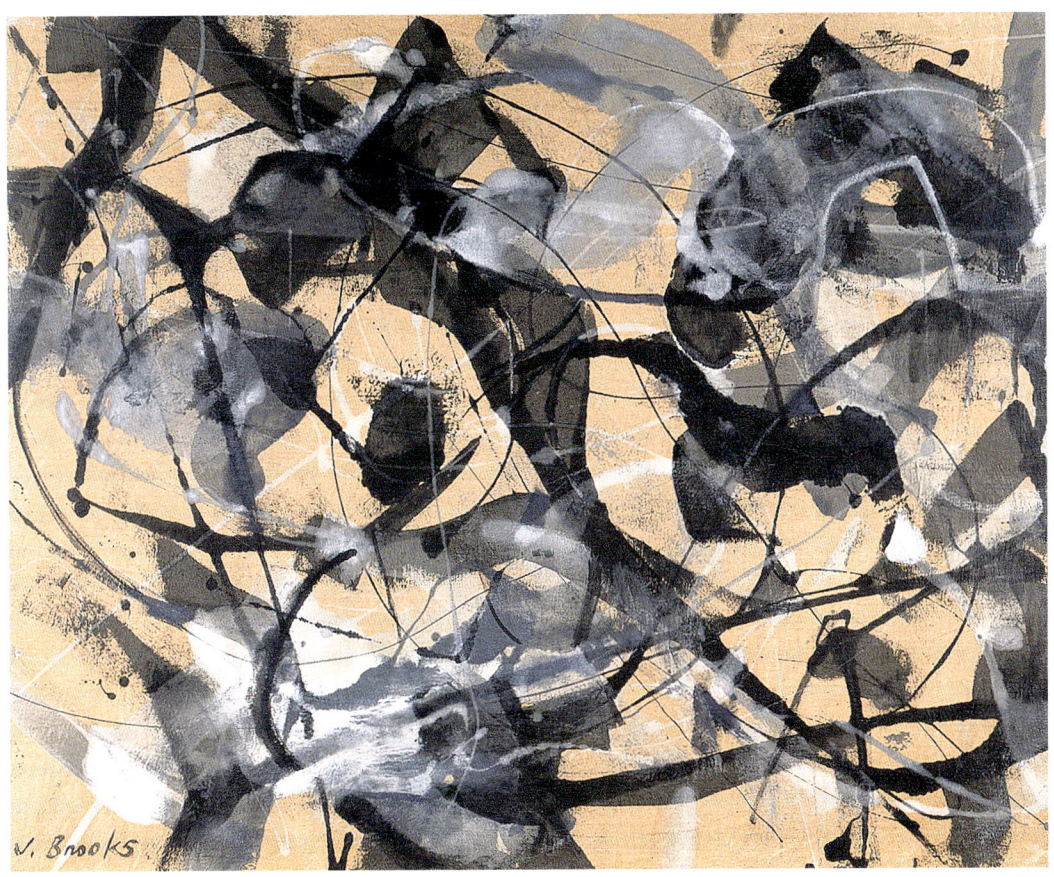

James Brooks
Number 27, 1950
Oil on canvas,
95.4 x 118.4 cm (37½ x 46½ in.)
New York, Whitney Museum of
American Art, Purchase with funds
from Mr. and Mrs. Roy R. Neuberger

PAGES 328/329
Nina Leen
The Irascibles, 1951
Group picture of American artists

FROM LEFT TO RIGHT, SEATED
Theodoros Stamos, Jimmy Ernst,
Jackson Pollock, Barnett Newman,
James Brooks, Mark Rothko;
STANDING
Richard Pousette-Dart, William Baziotes,
Willem de Kooning, Adolph Gottlieb,
Ad Reinhardt, Hedda Sterne, Clyfford Still,
Robert Motherwell, Bradley Walker Tomlin

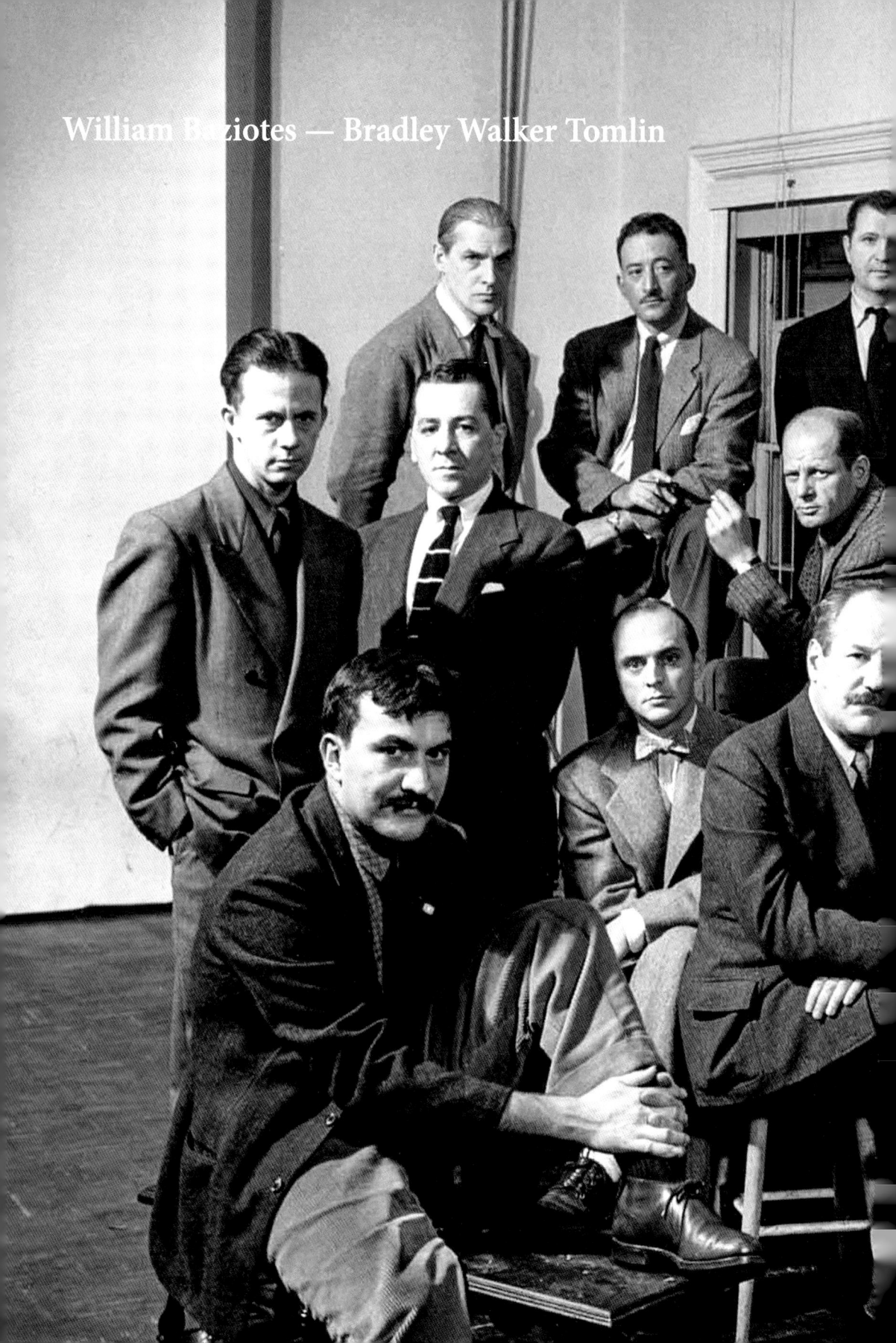

William Baziotes — Bradley Walker Tomlin

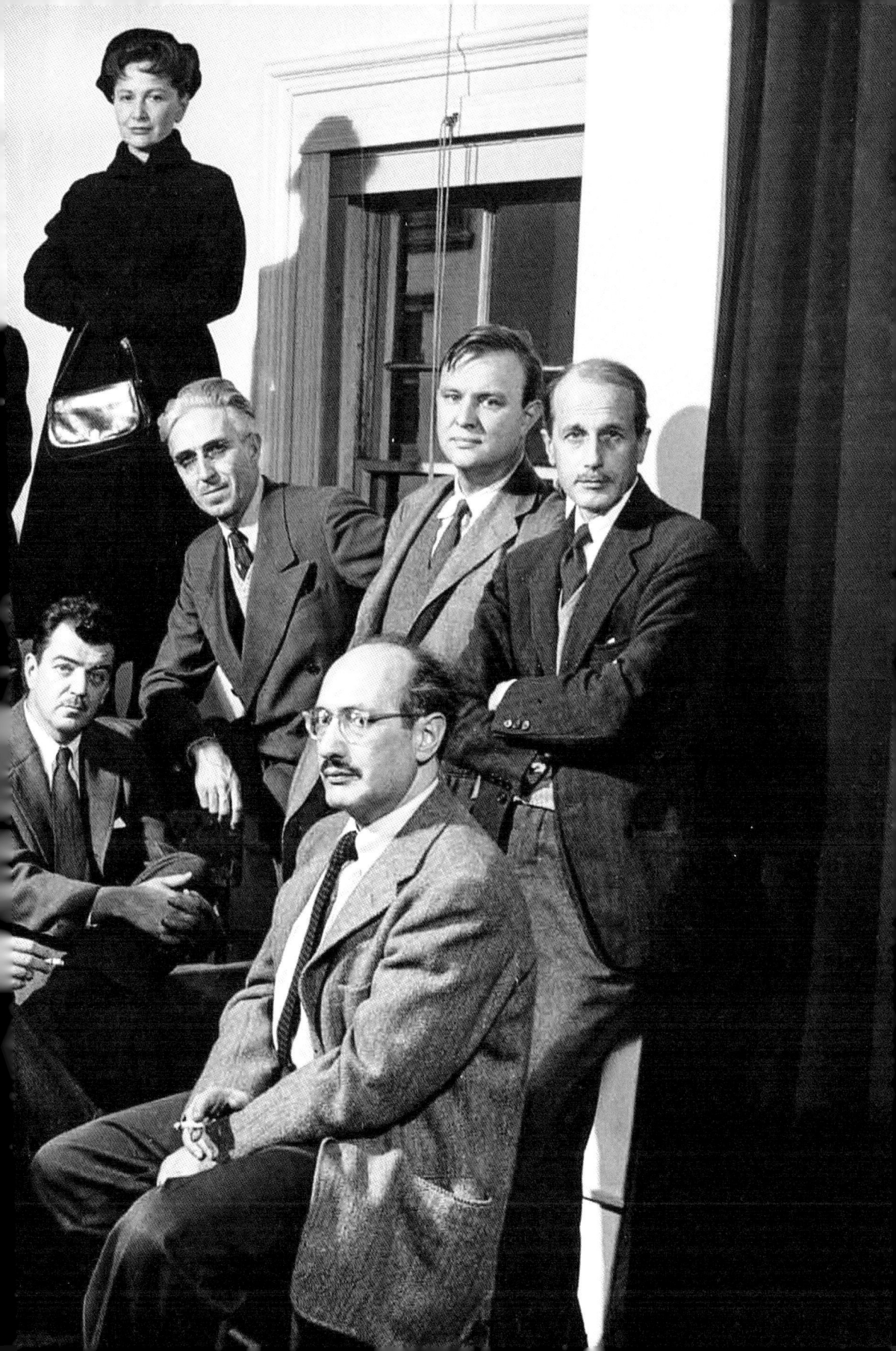

William Baziotes
Cyclops, 1947

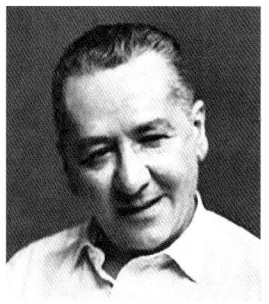

b. 1912 in Pittsburgh
d. 1963 in New York City

"Today it's possible to paint one canvas with the calmness of an ancient Greek, and the next with the anxiety of a Van Gogh," wrote William Baziotes in 1947. This makes him seem almost like a post-modernist artist, open to all kinds of influences without respect to period. Thus indirectly he also rejected ideas – frequently associated with modern art – concerning the "originality" and "uniqueness" of the artist, when, in 1954, he observed: "The painter who imagines himself a Robinson Crusoe is either a primitive or a fool." Baziotes was born the son of Greek immigrants and grew up in poor circumstances; from 1933 to 1936 he studied at the National Academy of Design in New York and subsequently worked until the early 1940s for the Works Progress Administration, a state-sponsored art promotion programme whose socially committed orientation was, however, alien to him.

In 1941 Baziotes became friends with Robert Motherwell, whose interest in French Symbolism and Surrealism he shared; thus we can find in Baziotes' pictures colouration and motifs inspired by the poetry of Charles Baudelaire. Contacts with Surrealist exiles in New York, but in particular his friendship with the Chilean painter Roberto Matta, helped Baziotes to develop his own personal version of "écriture automatique", which the art historian Lawrence Alloway hit the nail on the head by describing as "slow automatism". At the same time, figurative hints are never absent from his pictures, conjuring up ideas of mysterious, archaic organisms; in contrast to most of the other painters regarded as Abstract Expressionists, large formats and the forcing of the gestural play no role in his painting.

"The emphasis on flora, fauna and beings makes the exhibit a most intriguing and artistic one for it brings forth those strange memories and psychic feelings that mystify and fascinate all of us," remarked Baziotes in 1957. An interest in "primitive" cultures and the processes of the unconscious, as was to be expressed in artistic techniques like the écriture automatique of Surrealism, was widespread in the culture of 1940s America. Thus there was a trend to search for parallels between early cultural witnesses – for example, classical mythology – and contemporary consciousness, which was perceived as desperate and tragic. Arguments for this view could be found for example in the writings of Sigmund Freud and C. G. Jung, translations of which were avidly devoured in the USA during the 1940s.

Baziotes often went beyond Surrealism to older traditions of fantastic art. For example, the eponymous motif of the painting *Cyclops* points among other things to the work of the French Symbolist Odilon Redon (1840–1916), in whose pictures the motif of one-eyed figures is not infrequent; Baziotes was also inspired by a visit to the Bronx zoo, where he observed a rhinoceros, for him a descendant of some primeval race. According to Greek mythology, the cyclopes were one-eyed giants who could summon up thunder and lightning, and so we can also see in Baziotes's interest in this figure an autobiographical aspect – a reference to his own Greek heritage.

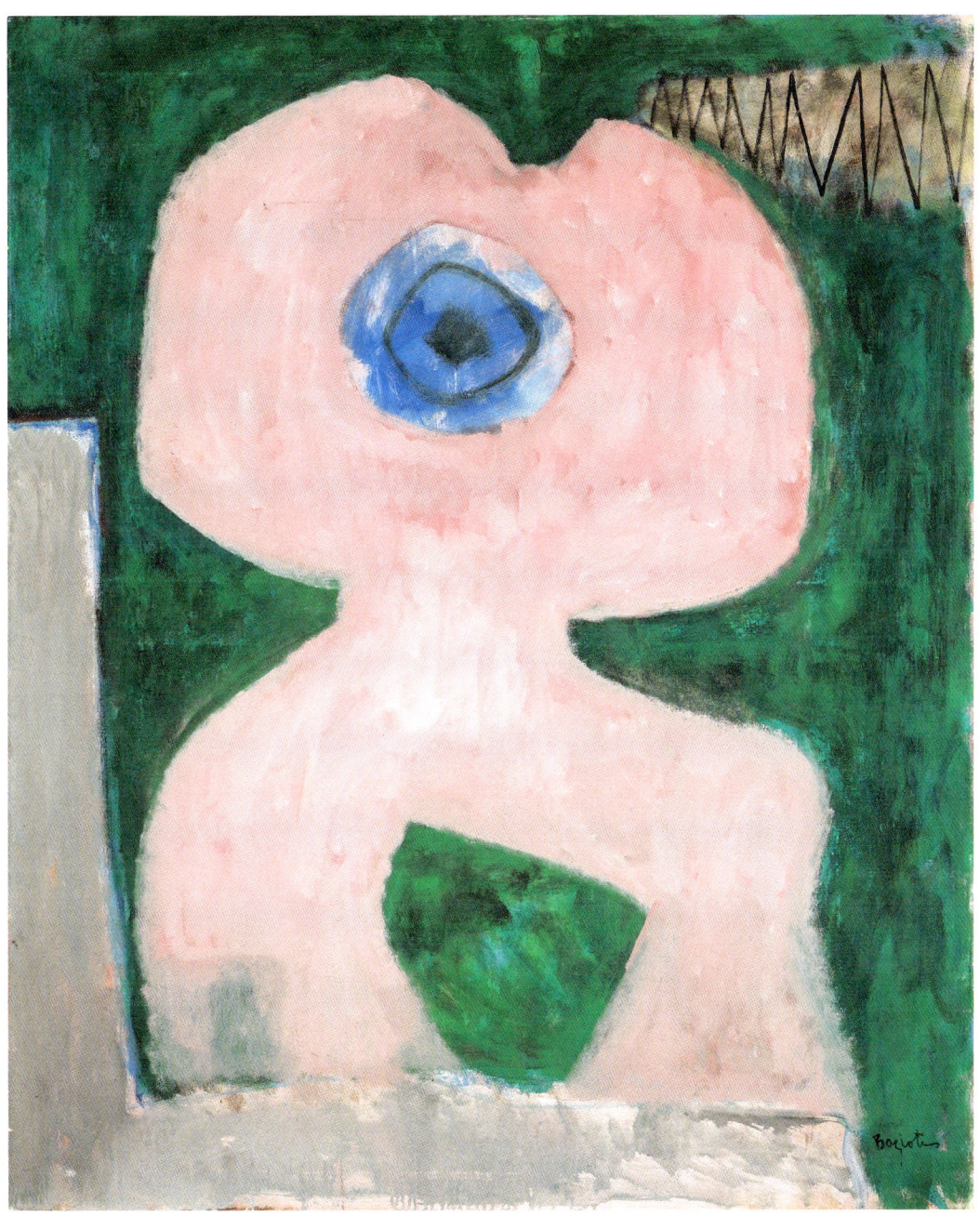

Cyclops, 1947
Oil on canvas, 121.9 x 101.6 cm (48 x 40 in.)
The Art Institute of Chicago,
Walter M. Campana Memorial Prize Fund

Richard Diebenkorn
Urbana No. 6, 1953

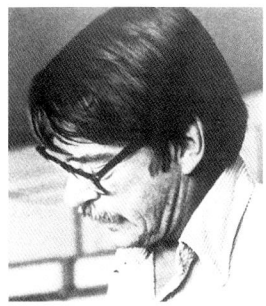

b. 1922 in Portland, Oregon
d. 1993 in Berkeley, California

"On the farther shore of Abstract Expressionism" was the title in 1996 of the first chapter of a catalogue relating to the San Francisco School. The Abstract art which arose from the 1940s to the mid-1960s in the Bay Area was for a long time largely regarded as a reflection and further development of influences emanating from the New York School, not least because Mark Rothko and Clyfford Still had taught at the California School of Fine Arts in San Francisco in the late 1940s. Here, though, the question of the autonomy of a West Coast variant of Abstract Expressionism was indeed raised, a variant which was seen to be in itself no less varied and heterogeneous than its East Coast relation.

It is true that artists on both sides of the continent were reacting to a broader international cultural and political situation, and that mutual exchange was promoted by their teaching activities and by joint exhibitions. At the same time, though, a number of local factors have to be taken into consideration, such as the influence of the beatnik sub-culture in San Francisco, the characteristic West Coast orientation towards Asia, and a greater artistic confrontation with the landscape.

Richard Diebenkorn grew up in San Francisco, and after a period of service with the navy during the Second World War, returned there in 1946. He studied at the California School of Fine Arts, where he took up a teaching post himself in 1947. His painting style, which hitherto had been strongly influenced by Still, among others, changed when he continued his studies in Albuquerque, New Mexico, in 1950/51; encouraged by the distance he had put between himself and his earlier influences, his application of paint became more fluid, the nuances brighter.

In Albuquerque Diebenkorn also began to take a greater interest in the landscape, as hinted at by the titles of his picture series dating from the first half of the 1950s – *Albuquerque, Urbana, Berkeley*: "Temperamentally, perhaps, I had always been a landscape painter," noted Diebenkorn, "but I was fighting the landscape feeling. For years I didn't have the colour blue on my palette because it reminded me too much of the spatial qualities in conventional landscape. But in Albuquerque I relaxed and began to think of natural forms in relation to my own feelings." This lyrically tinted confrontation with impressions of nature and the landscape was incidentally something Diebenkorn shared with other artists of the second generation of Abstract Expressionism, such as Helen Frankenthaler or Joan Mitchell.

Diebenkorn's *Urbana* series, with its colour-fields crisscrossed by lines, was also influenced by two further decisive experiences: the visit of a Matisse retrospective to Los Angeles in 1952 and a flight from Albuquerque to San Francisco the previous year, both of which opened up to the artist a new, abstract way of looking at the landscape, as he recalled in a conversation with Gerald Nordland in 1986: "The aerial view showed me a rich variety of ways of treating a flat plane – like flattened mud or paint. Forms operating in shallow depth reveal a huge range of possibilities available to the painter."

After a figurative intermezzo from 1955 to 1967, Diebenkorn returned in the late 1960s, with his doubtless best-known and most extensive series *Ocean Park,* to the genre of "abstract landscape", a label which *Life* magazine had coined for his work back in 1954.

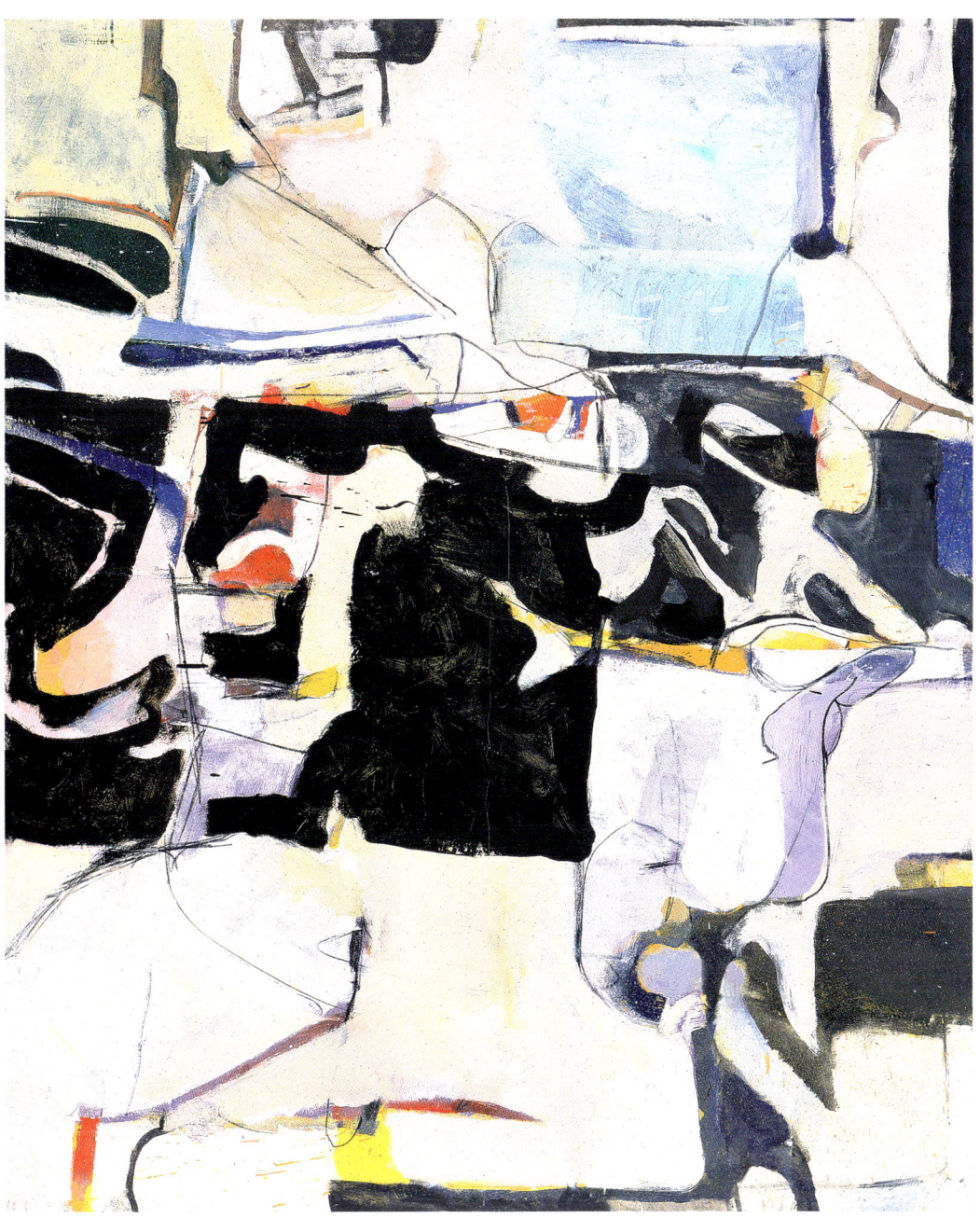

Urbana No. 6, 1953
Oil on canvas, 173.5 x 147 cm (68¼ x 58 in.)
Modern Art Museum of Fort Worth,
Museum purchase, Sid W. Richardson
Foundation Endowment Fund

Sam Francis
Saint Honoré, 1952

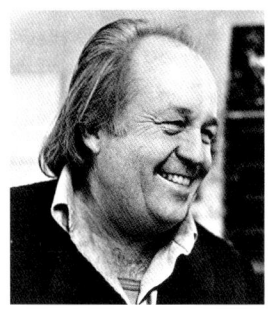

b. 1923 in San Mateo, California
d. 1994 in Santa Monica,
California

Sam Francis began to develop his painterly position in the first half of the 1950s. He thus belonged, to use Clement Greenberg's phrase, to the period "after Abstract Expressionism" and to an artist generation which had to confront the dominant influence of artists such as Barnett Newman, Jackson Pollock and Clyfford Still in order to create an independent profile for themselves.

In 1947 Francis enrolled to study painting at the University of California at Berkeley. At this time, Clyfford Still and Mark Rothko were teaching at the California School of Fine Arts in nearby San Francisco; in spite of what one often reads, Francis was not one of their students, but was certainly familiar with their works through exhibitions in the region.

Unlike most of the representatives of the first generation of the New York School, Francis did not reject the European tradition. His decision in 1950 to go to Paris, where he lived until 1957, he explained in an interview in 1988: "I simply wanted to go to Paris; I didn't know what I wanted to do. I went my way. I wanted to be away from the USA. I had the impression that it was a prison and I wanted to see European art. I wanted to see true painting, no matter which." His primary interest in colourism, in light and colour, received major impetus through the encounter with French painting, in particular with Claude Monet's water-lily pictures, and the painting of Henri Matisse and Pierre Bonnard.

Francis developed his characteristic early-1950s painting technique in 1949/50: following the all-over principle, the whole surface of the picture is covered in biomorphous forms reminiscent of cells or petals executed in semi-transparent, runny paint. The diaphanous nature of the paint application points to the superimposed colour veils of Rothko's pictures, while the dripping streaks of paint develop Arshile Gorky's technique of the 1940s. In early-1950s pictures such as *Saint Honoré*, which Francis included in a successful exhibition held at the Galerie du Dragon in Paris, he reduced his colour spectrum to dully glowing white and grey hues, recalling the characteristic milky light of the French capital.

Francis himself, however, was less interested in the descriptive function of colour, but constantly raised the question, in his aphorisms, of its spiritual and meditative dimension. According to the art historian Pontus Hulten, Francis, in allusion to Herman Melville's famous 1851 novel *Moby Dick*, had described his brush as the harpoon with which Captain Ahab hunted the white whale. In his later work too, the colour white, in particular as the empty middle of the picture, continued to be of great importance for his painting.

Saint Honoré, 1952
Oil on canvas, 201 x 134.5 cm (79¼ x 53 in.)
Düsseldorf, K20 – Kunstsammlung
Nordrhein-Westfalen

Helen Frankenthaler
Seven Types of Ambiguity, 1957

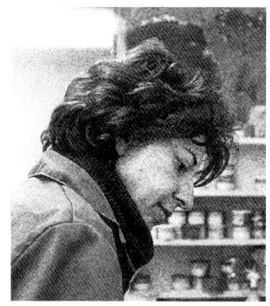

b. 1928 in New York City
d. 2011 in Darien, Connecticut

Helen Frankenthaler, a central figure of the second generation of Abstract Expressionists, established a new approach to painting with her characteristic "soak-stain technique", which also defined the aesthetic relevance of the work shown here, *Seven Types of Ambiguity*. In this technique the paint is applied to unprimed canvas on the floor. Oil paints, heavily diluted with turpentine or paraffin, penetrate the fibres of the canvas and produce a watercolour effect. The unity of paint and canvas conspicuously emphasizes the flatness of painting as a medium, and thus fulfils a central criterion of modern painting as formulated by influential critic Clement Greenberg (1909–1994), who was among her earliest and most consistent supporters.

Frankenthaler had begun to study painting while at Bennington College in 1946. When she took part in a group exhibition at the Jacques Seligmann & Co. gallery in New York in 1950, one of those she invited was Greenberg, who soon became a close friend and introduced her to many artists. Already in early works such as *Great Meadows* (1951, Museum of Modern Art, New York), a watercolour on paper, her interest in uniting paint and background was apparent.

The breakthrough point for her method was the monumental 1952 painting *Mountains and Sea* (National Gallery of Art, Washington, D.C.). Frankenthaler recalled in 1997: "I painted *Mountains and Sea* after seeing the cliffs of Nova Scotia. It's a hilly landscape with wild surf rolling against the rocks. Though it was painted in a windowless loft, the memory of the landscape is in the painting." She also described the work as a synthesis of Cubism, Pollock, Kandinsky and Arshile Gorky.

Her technique of pouring paint from containers onto canvas spread on the floor and working it into the fabric was inspired by Jackson Pollock's drip paintings. Seeing his paintings at the Betty Parsons Gallery in 1950 and visits to his studio in 1951 were a decisive impetus. Frankenthaler, however, always stressed the difference between Pollock's approach to the act of painting and her own: "I had no desire to copy Pollock. I didn't want to take a stick and dip it in a can of enamel. I needed something more liquid, watery, thinner. All my life, I have been drawn to water and translucency. I love the water; I love to swim, to watch changing seascapes. One of my favourite childhood games was to fill a sink with water and put nail polish into it to see what happened when the colours burst upon the surface, merging into each other as floating, changing shapes."

The innovation apparent in *Mountains and Sea* was consistently carried on by the artist in later works such as *Seven Types of Ambiguity*. This picture illustrates how she refined her technique and found a new balance between spontaneity and control. *Seven Types of Ambiguity* may exemplify how Frankenthaler uses forms of ambiguity to enrich Abstract Expressionism with a multifaceted dimension, thus increasing the complexity of the work of art. Artists such as Morris Louis and Kenneth Noland found an important source of inspiration in her methods.

Seven Types of Ambiguity, 1957
Oil on unprimed canvas,
242.6 x 178.1 cm (95½ x 70 in.)
Bentonville, Crystal Bridges
Museum of American Art

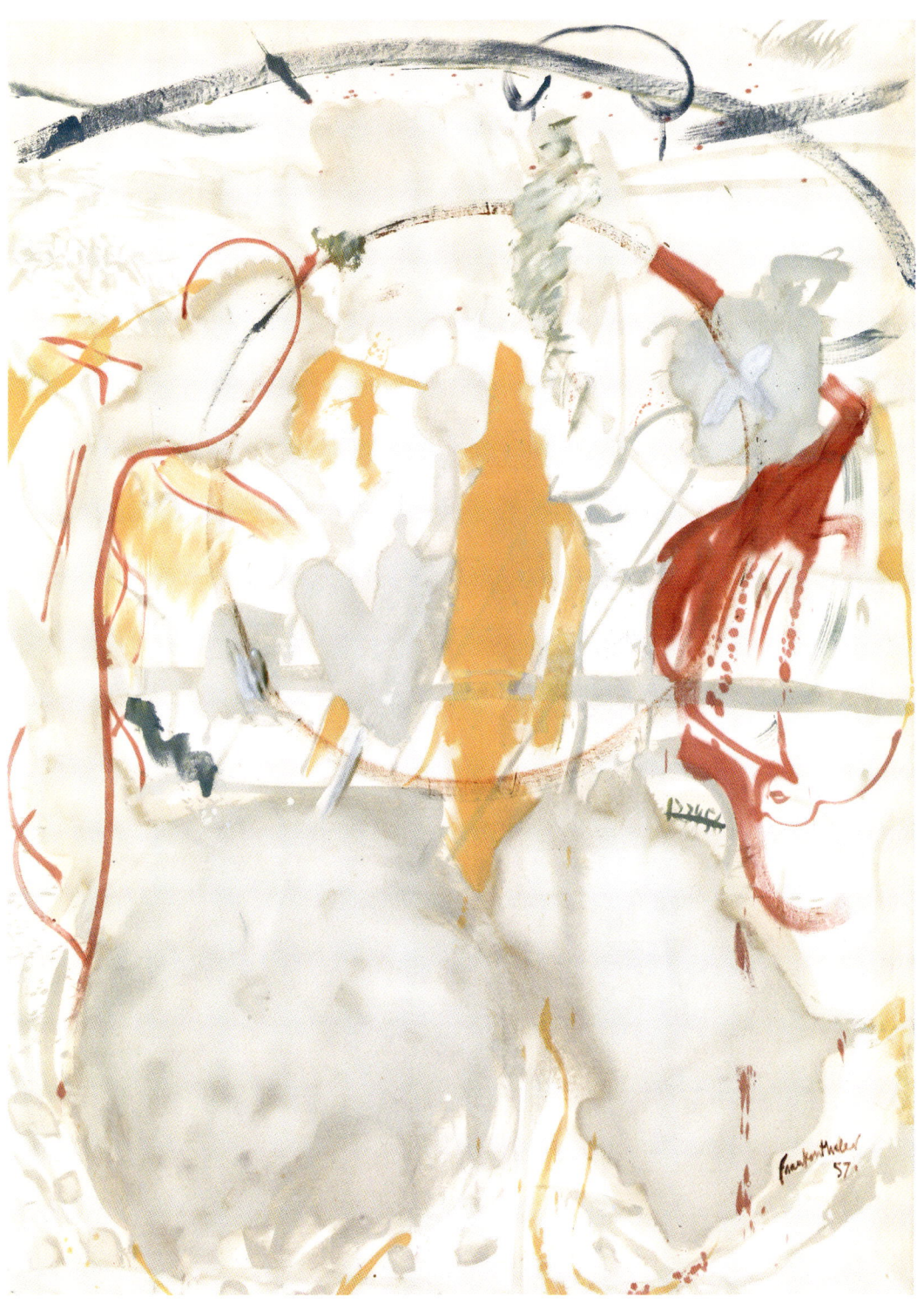

Arshile Gorky
Water of the Flowery Mill, 1944

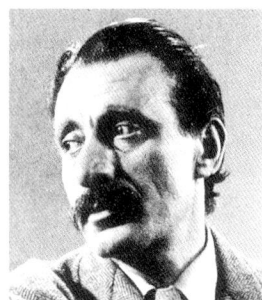

b. 1904 in Khorkom, Armenia
d. 1948 in Sherman,
Connecticut

Thomas M. Messer waxed eloquent in 1981 on the occasion of an Arshile Gorky retrospective at the New York Guggenheim Museum, stressing his key artistic position at the interface between Surrealism and Abstract Expressionism: "Arshile Gorky, seen as the end product of a historical evolution, becomes the last link in a chain of modern painters who have compelled our vision since the late nineteenth century. But at the same time and not inconsistent with such a view, we endow Gorky today with the attributes of a pioneer. For it was his painterly insights and attributes that helped shape the generation of Americans who, having waged their first decisive battles at about the time of his death, were carried to prominence and victory in the 1950s as the martyrs or heroes of the New York School."

Messer's rhetoric would doubtless have assigned Gorky, who hanged himself in his studio in 1948, to the camp of martyrs. Born in Armenia as Vosdanik Adoian, he emigrated to the USA with his sister in 1920 as a consequence of the Turkish government's policy of persecution and expulsion. In the spring of 1924 he painted his first picture, which he signed with the pseudonym Arshile Gorky; the forename alluded to the great hero of ancient Greece, Achilles, and the surname to the Russian writer Maxim Gorki. A few months later, Adoian alias Gorky moved to New York – the same year as André Breton's first *Manifesto of Surrealism* appeared in Paris. In 1944 he met Breton and became friends with other émigré Surrealists.

Gorky worked in the late 1920s at first under the influence of the Synthetic Cubism of Georges Braque and Pablo Picasso. In the 1930s he oriented himself in his figurative work towards Picasso's neo-classical figures of the 1920s. But from the middle of the decade Gorky's own artistic development came to be dominated by Surrealism, in particular the works of André Masson and Joan Miró. "Art," he commented in 1945 on his intensive confrontation with modern trends, "is a language that must be mastered before it can be conveyed."

Likewise in 1945 Gorky presented the first of his solo exhibitions at the Julien Levy Gallery in New York, which continued to exhibit his work regularly right up to his death (his first solo exhibition of all was at the Mellon Galleries in Philadelphia in 1931, his first in New York at the Boyer Galleries in 1938). From now on, Gorky was able for the first time in his career to lead a life free of financial worries. For the catalogue, Breton wrote a contribution entitled "The Eye-Spring", in which he emphasized both Gorky's closeness to Surrealism and the fact that his method of presenting pictures deviated from that of the Surrealists.

While the latter put their trust in "psychological automatism" as an artistic process, Gorky, in pictures like *Water of the Flowery Mill* started out from the observation of nature. In summer 1942 he had begun, as he said, to "look into the grass" on his parents-in-law's farm in Virginia, sketching, from nature, the forms and movements of plants and insects in the summer heat. "Here for the first time nature is treated as cryptogram," remarked Breton in "The Eye-Spring": from the link between memories and associations, studies of nature and other forms, which Gorky obtained from art, not least from traditional Armenian culture, he created "hybrids", which allowed him "to decode nature to reveal the very rhythm of life".

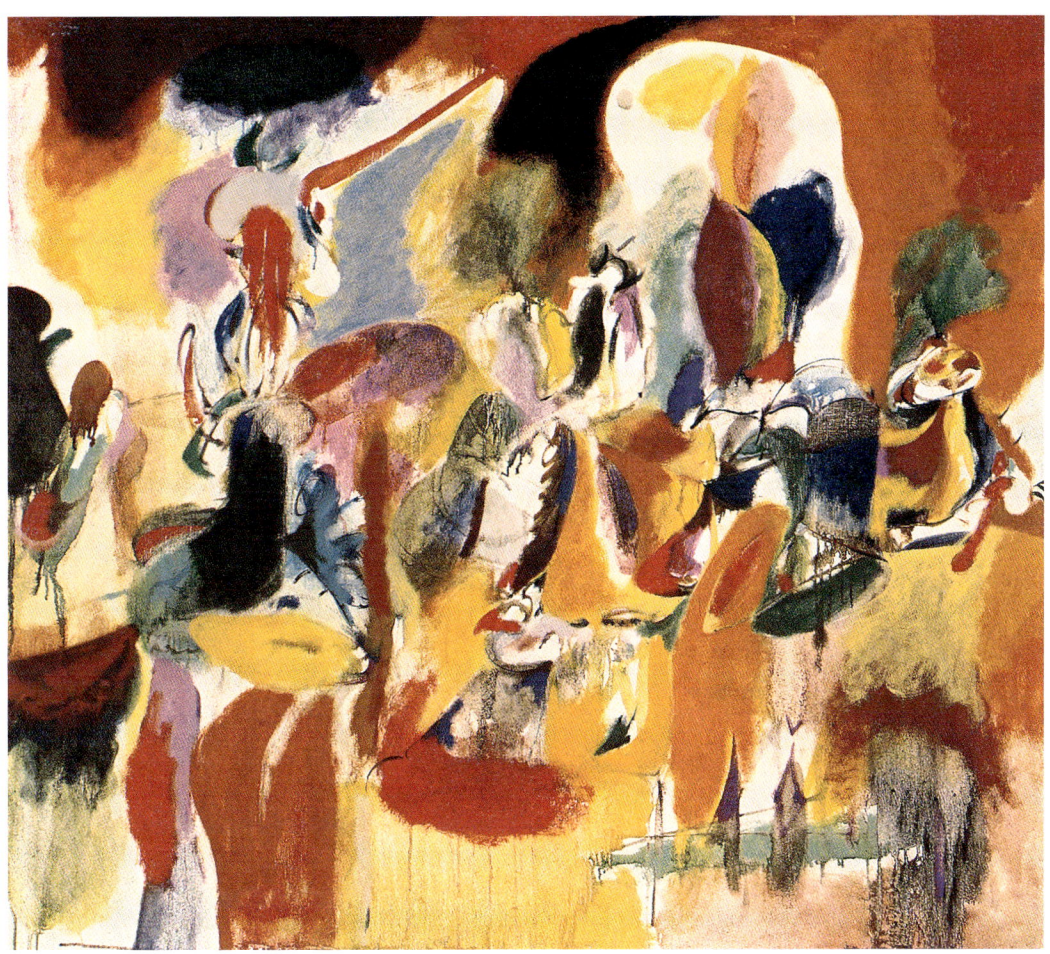

Water of the Flowery Mill, 1944
Oil on canvas, 107.3 x 123.8 cm (42¼ x 48¾ in.)
New York, Metropolitan Museum of Art,
George A. Hearn Fund, 1956

Adolph Gottlieb
Blast, I, 1957

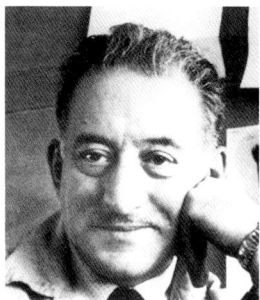

b. 1903 in New York City
d. 1974 in New York City

When the *New York Times* art critic Edward Alden Jewell expressed his "befuddlement" concerning the pictures of Adolph Gottlieb and Mark Rothko, the two artists, in collaboration with Barnett Newman, replied in a letter to the editor, which was published in the paper on 13 June 1943. This reply is still regarded as a kind of manifesto of American painting in the early 1940s. In it, the authors stressed the following aesthetic convictions:

"1. To us art is an adventure into an unknown world, which can be explored only by those willing to take the risk.

2. This world of imagination is fancy-free and violently opposed to common sense.

3. It is our function as artists to make the spectator see our way, not his way.

4. We favor the simple expression of the complex thought. We are for the large shape because it has the impact of the unequivocal. We wish to reassert the picture plane. We are for flat forms because they destroy illusion and reveal truth.

5. It is a widely accepted notion among painters that it does not matter what one paints as long as it is well painted. This is the essence of academism. There is no such thing as a good painting about nothing. We assert that the subject is crucial and only that subject-matter is valid which is tragic and timeless. That is why we profess spiritual kinship with primitive and archaic art."

During the 1920s, Gottlieb had studied at the Art Students League and the Parsons School of Design (among other places) in New York, as well as at the Académie de la Grande Chaumière in Paris. During this decade he travelled around Germany and France. His contacts with the European Surrealists confirmed him in his opinion that art could be an expression of the unconscious, and reinforced his interest in archetypal motifs. Against this background, from 1941 he developed the first of his two extensive groups of works, the so-called "Pictographs". These go back to an "archaic" or "primitive" imagery, such as the pictograms of the native Americans, which they embed in grid compositions, which likewise were inspired by narrative pictorial schemas of the Italian early Renaissance as well as by Giorgio de Chirico's *Pittura metafisica.*

In 1956/57 Gottlieb struck out on a new path: the extensive series known as *Bursts* marked the start of a major simplification in the motifs of his painting. On vertical-format canvases, against a spatially undefined, atmospheric background, two vertically arranged shapes, the top one round and more clearly contoured, the bottom one if anything chaotically eruptive, confront each other. The configuration of the two shapes allows numerous interpretations, extending from abstract landscapes to symbols of rival forces. It is revealing that Gottlieb gave the pictures in the *Bursts* series different names – such as *Blast, I* (1957), *The Crest* (1959), *Counterpoise* (1959) or *Bullet* (1971) – and thus suggested constantly new interpretations of the motif himself.

Gottlieb also translated the motif of the bursts into a series of sculptures, which represent some of the few contributions of this medium to Abstract Expressionism.

Blast, I, 1957
Oil on canvas, 228.7 x 114.4 cm (90 x 45 in.)
New York, The Museum of Modern Art,
Philip Johnson Fund

Philip Guston
The Tormentors, 1947/48

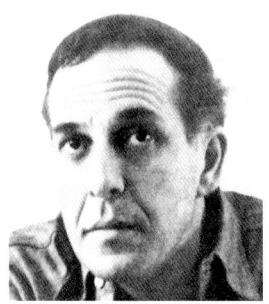

b. 1913 in Montreal
d. 1980 in Woodstock, New York

Philip Guston grew up in Montreal and Los Angeles as the child of Russian immigrants from Odessa. Even as a teenager he started to draw cartoons, and enrolled in a correspondence course at the Cleveland School of Cartooning. As a student during the 1930s, Guston took an interest in, among other things, Giorgio de Chirico's *Pittura metafisica* and its older historical precursors, including the frescoes of Italian Renaissance artists such as Masaccio, Andrea Mantegna and Paolo Uccello. In the late 1930s, Guston himself was painting murals for the state-sponsored art promotion project known as the Works Progress Administration: it was a medium which he hoped would create a broader public for his politically committed figurative painting. In the early 1940s, he returned to easel painting.

It is characteristic of Guston's works that they are often linked by a family tree; many pictures were developed from elements contained in earlier works. "To paint is always to start at the beginning again, yet being unable to avoid the familiar arguments about what you see yourself painting. The canvas you are working on modifies the previous ones in an unending, baffling chain which never seems to finish," was how he described his working method in the magazine *ARTnews* in 1966.

The Tormentors, considered to be Guston's first abstract picture, was painted at a time when most of the artists regarded as Abstract Expressionists were giving up the figurative elements in their painting. The composition of *The Tormentors* takes up motifs from an earlier, still figurative work, *Porch No. 2* (1947), a picture which also reveals Guston's confrontation with the Expressionist painting of Max Beckmann (1884–1950); both artists worked for a time under the influence of world war: the First in Beckmann's case, the Second in Guston's. Among the important impulses for Guston's pictures in the immediate post-war period are thought to be the photographs taken by Margaret Bourke-White during the liberation of concentration-camp prisoners from Buchenwald; these pictures appeared in *Life* magazine in May 1945.

Porch No. 2, now at the Munson-Williams-Proctor Institute in New York, shows, in a kind of theatrical setting, a row of children on a stage-like veranda: Disjointed body parts and a headless body suspended as if by its feet evoke ideas of violence. In *The Tormentors* the figurative allusions are much less in evidence, but the title points to a traumatic situation. Guston insisted on the narrative aspect of his painting, even while his work tended towards the abstract during the 1940s and 50s. At a panel discussion in 1960, a time when new figurative art movements such as Nouveau Réalisme and Pop Art were about to make their breakthrough, he said: "There is something ridiculous and miserly in the myth we inherit from abstract art: That painting is autonomous, pure and for itself, therefore we habitually analyse its ingredients and define its limits. But painting is 'impure'. It is the adjustment of 'impurities' which forces its continuity. We are image-makers and image-ridden."

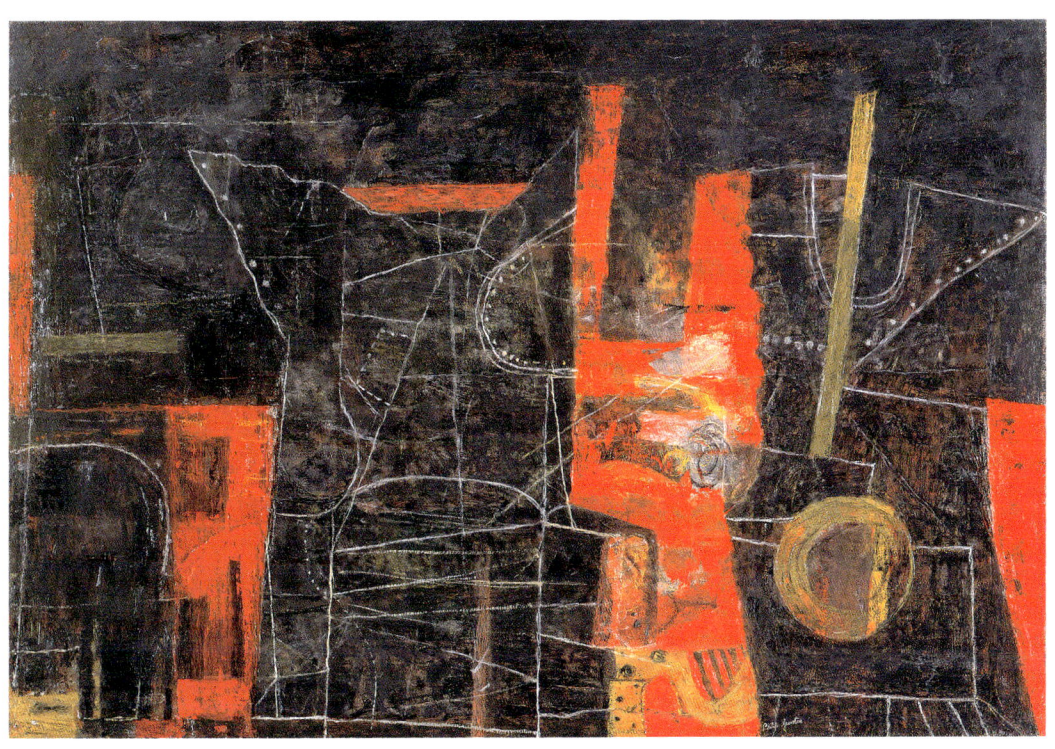

The Tormentors, 1947/48
Oil on canvas, 103.8 x 153.7 cm (40⅞ x 60⅝ in.)
San Francisco Museum of Modern Art,
Gift of the artist

Philip Guston
For M, 1955

In the work of Philip Guston, abstraction was an episode which was largely confined to the late 1940s and the 1950s. Like most fellow artists of his generation, he was averse to being called an Abstract Expressionist or to the idea that painting could be fulfilled in a simple self-investigation of the medium. "As a matter of fact, I don't remember in any of the get-togethers I had with painters of that period that that word was exchanged. Nobody ever said, you so-and-so abstract-expressionist, you," recalled Guston in the 1960s.

In the early 1950s, Guston developed a type of picture, new in his work: this consisted of vertical and horizontal brushstrokes, thickly applied, either crossing or cancelling each other out, getting denser towards the centre of the picture and increasing in colour intensity. It is as though a kind of moving veil, "a fog of muted tones", had been laid over the motif. The axial orientation of the brushstrokes has often been compared to Piet Mondrian's "plus-minus-pictures" of the mid-1910s. Starting from the motif of a clear starry night over the sea, the crossing lines hinting at its glittering reflections, Mondrian's *Compositions* stand at the transition from Cubism to his abstract grid compositions. In addition, Guston's choice of pastel shades in works such as *For M* recalled for many a beholder, on a formal plane, the painting of the Impressionists, so that Louis Finkelstein in a 1956 article in *ARTnews* could speak of Guston's "Abstract Impressionism".

Guston himself described the – figurative or abstract – works of artists who stimulated him as "living organisms" and the painting process as a dialogue with the picture, whose significance was not easily accessible even to the painter. As he explained in 1966: "So as I was going to say, for reasons that I do not understand, the late 1940s, early 1950s, when I went into non-figurative painting, although I felt I was even involved with imagery even though I didn't understand the imagery completely myself, but I thought it was imagery, and for some reasons that's not quite clear to me yet and maybe I don't want to be clear about it either…"

This gesture of refusal was interpreted by some critics as a form of repression of traumatic experiences, either private or social, which were vividly present in Guston's painting of the 1930s and 40s, and which returned with a vengeance in the late 60s. Thus in the 1930s Guston's pictures were full of the gruesome deeds of the masked members of the racist Ku Klux Klan – a motif from his southern Californian environment, which in the late 1960s turned up again in his paintings and drawings. Guston shocked sections of the public with his grotesque figures and everyday objects, recalling his early enthusiasm for comics, such as nail-studded shoe soles. From the orthodox perspective of Abstract Expressionism, the return to pictorial narrative was a breach of taboo, "like I had left the Church, and had been excommunicated," he remarked.

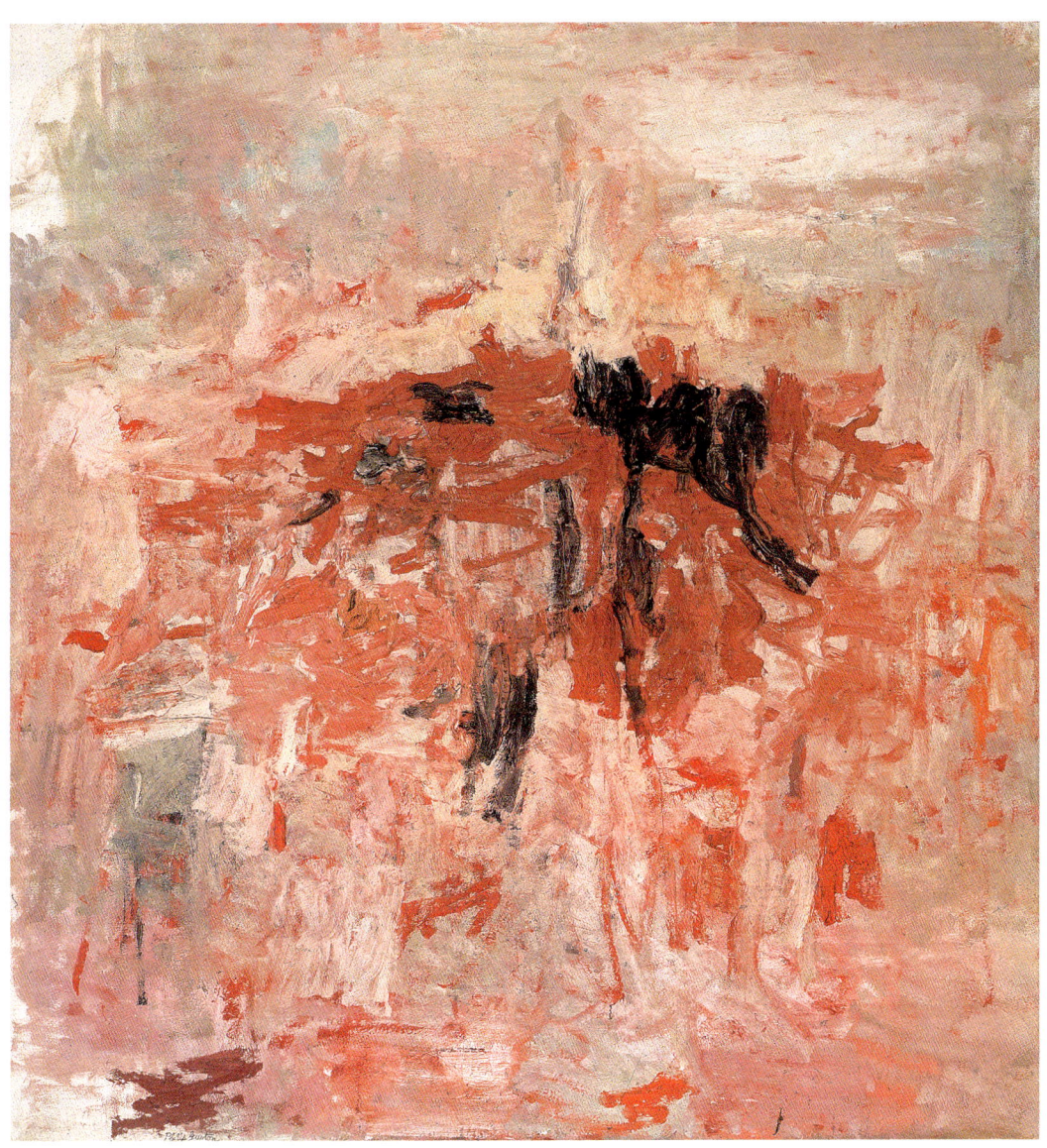

For M, 1955
Oil on canvas, 194 x 183.5 cm (76½ x 72¼ in.)
San Francisco Museum of Modern Art,
Anonymous gift

Hans Hofmann
Bacchanale, 1946

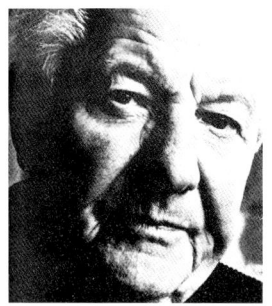

b. 1880 in Weissenburg,
Germany
d. 1966 in New York City

"I would maintain," wrote Clement Greenberg in 1961 about Hans Hofmann, "that the only way to begin placing Hofmann's art is by taking cognizance of the uniqueness of his life's course, which has cut across as many art movements as national boundaries, and put him in several different centers of art at the precise time of their most fruitful activity. On top of that, his career as an artist has cut across at least three artists' generations."

Hofmann had attended a private art school in Munich from 1898. Between 1904 and the outbreak of the Great War in 1914 – the period which saw the appearance of Fauvism and Cubism – he lived in Paris; like Henri Matisse, one of the places he studied at was the Académie de la Grande Chaumière, and he was friendly with artists such as Sonia and Robert Delaunay. Exempted on medical grounds from military service, in 1915 he opened an art school in Munich, where one of the students was the future head of the art department at the University of California in Berkeley, Worth Ryder.

At Ryder's invitation, Hofmann paid his first visit to the USA in 1930, and moved there permanently in 1932. He taught at the Art Students League in New York, among other places, and the following year opened an art school of his own in the city. Its numerous prominent alumni included Ray Eames, Allan Kaprow and Lee Krasner. The latter introduced him to her husband Jackson Pollock in 1942, and it was due to Pollock's mediation that Hofmann was able to hold his first New York solo exhibition at Peggy Guggenheim's influential Art of This Century gallery in 1944.

In Hofmann's pictures dating from this period, which include alongside *Bacchanale* also *Idolatress I* (1944) and *Ecstasy* (1947), we find dionysiac motifs, transcending the rational, which come close to abstraction. In a 1948 article, "The Search for the Real in the Visual Arts", Hofmann explained his conviction that painting and sculpture were an expression of the surreal in material form. In his exuberant, gestural painting technique, Hofmann squeezed some of the paint directly from the tube on to the canvas; "The weight and density of his paint," in Greenberg's view; "launched the 'heavy' surface in abstract art," both visually and physically.

Hofmann occupies a particular role in Abstract Expressionism not only by reason of belonging to an older generation, but also because he was the first painter of the New York School to be identified by this description. The critic Robert Coates reviewed Hofmann's comprehensive solo exhibition at the Mortimer Brandt Gallery for *New Yorker* in 1946 and spoke here for the first time of a current artistic trend which he christened "Abstract Expressionism". In addition, Coates commented on the squirts of paint in Hofmann's pictures, in a sense a prototype of Jackson Pollock's dripping technique, which was developed in 1947.

"There's no doubt," observed Coates in respect of Hofmann's exhibition, and not without a hint of smugness, "that his painting is 'difficult', and there are four or five of the eighteen canvases in the show in which the emphasis on accidental effects (that is, spatters and daubs) is so strong that I'd be willing to dismiss them as sheer nonsense if in some of the others he didn't display a combination of subtlety and power which argues an over-all intention too well developed to be brushed aside so lightly."

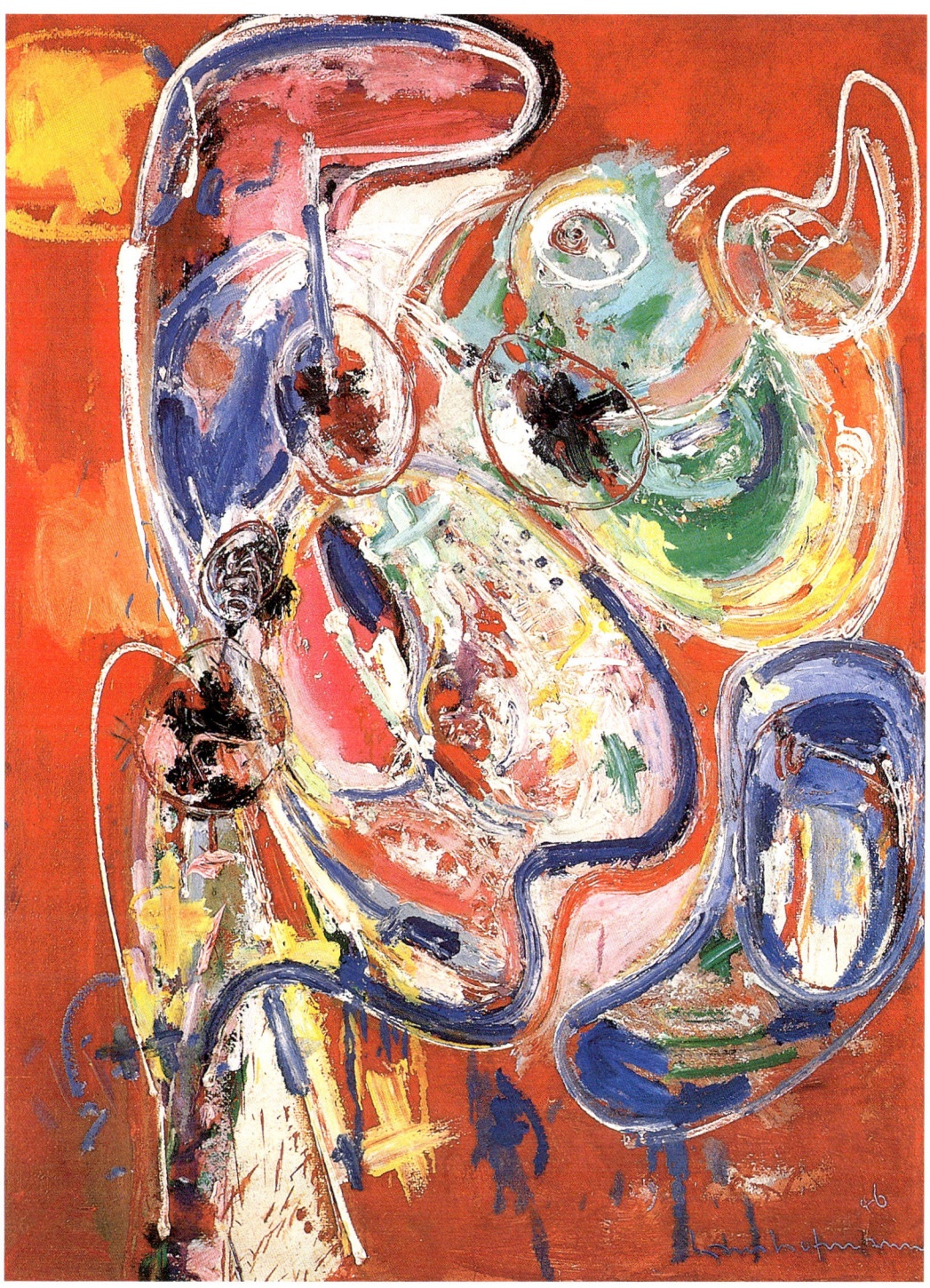

Bacchanale, 1946
Oil on cardboard,
162.6 x 121.9 cm (64 x 48 in.)
Private collection

Hans Hofmann
Pompeii, 1959

After more than forty years teaching art, in, among other places, renowned colleges in New York and Provincetown, Massachusetts, in 1958 Hans Hofmann closed down his institutes and began to devote himself primarily to his own painting. In the Abstract Expressionist art scene Hofmann was perceived as an influential teacher rather than as an artist, which may have contributed to the fact that only when he was in his sixties was his work to be seen more frequently in solo exhibitions.

Irving Sandler has pointed to the fact that this delayed reception was also due to the cultural climate in New York during the 1940s and 50s: for one thing, Hofmann's painting in the eyes of curators and younger fellow artists betrayed too much of the influence of the French legacy of Cubism and Fauvism; for another, his optimistic artistic and textual statements hardly fit into a context in which artists such as Adolph Gottlieb, Barnett Newman and Mark Rothko were continually emphasizing that the subjects of their art were "tragic and timeless". "Throughout his long career as a painter, teacher, and theorist, one would be hard pressed to find a stroke or word that is melancholy, bitter, ironic, or disenchanted," remarked William Seitz, the curator of a comprehensive Hofmann retrospective in the Museum of Modern Art in 1963. Hofmann was "*the* hedonist of Abstract Expressionism, robust and generous", a description which Irving Sandler doubtless used in allusion to another European "hedonist": Henri Matisse, with whom Hofmann had studied in Paris.

In his 1948 essay "Search for the Real in the Visual Arts" Hofmann created the painterly principle with which his name is still linked today: "Depth, in a pictorial sense, is not created by the arrangement of objects one after another toward a vanishing point, in the sense of the Renaissance perspective, but on the contrary (and in absolute denial of this doctrine) by the creation of forces in the sense of *push and pull*." As there was no way of creating "real depth" in painting by boring a hole in the canvas, Hofmann rejected any perspective illusionism and demanded instead that the flatness of the two-dimensional canvas be emphasized. Spatial effects should be generated exclusively through colour contrasts, as in *Pompeii*: flat rectangles in dissonant red, orange and magenta hues contrast with accents in green, blue, and turquoise, and create a visual dynamic without disturbing the impression of a wall-like surface. The title of the picture and the dominance of the warm colour tones point to the ancient city on the Mediterranean which was covered in volcanic ash when Mount Vesuvius erupted in 79 AD.

One of the most important sources for Hofmann's view of art was an 1893 text by the German sculptor Adolf von Hildebrand, "Das Problem der Form in der bildenden Kunst" (The Problem of Form in the Visual Arts), which Hofmann introduced to his American public. Hofmann's teaching activities not only exerted an influence on the practice of a younger generation of American artists, but also largely shaped formalistic art criticism, which found its most pronounced expression in the writings of Clement Greenberg. Greenberg pointed expressly on a number of occasions to the inspirations he had derived from Hofmann's lectures.

Pompeii, 1959
Oil on canvas,
214 x 132.7 cm (84¼ x 52¼ in.)
London, Tate

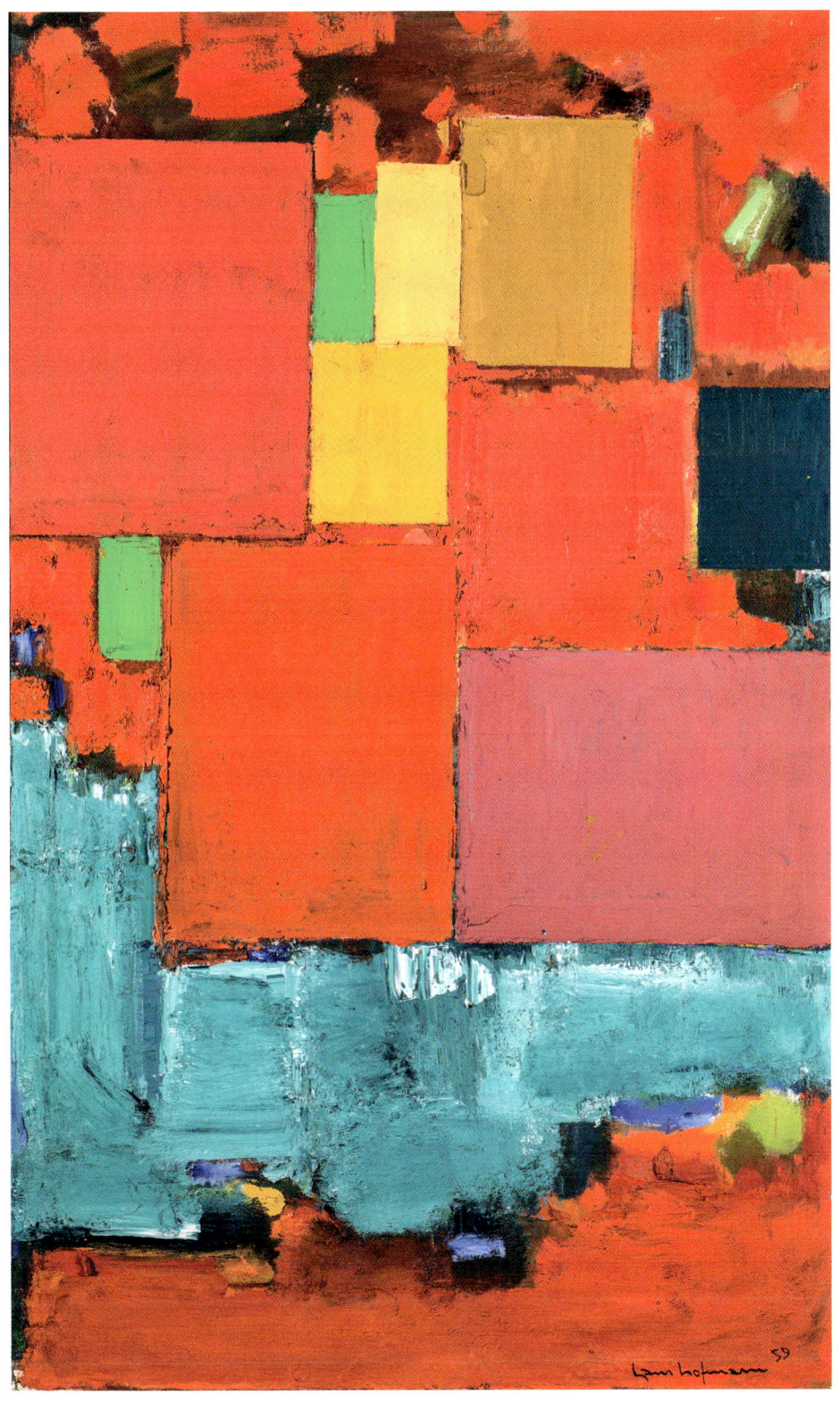

Franz Kline
Untitled, 1957

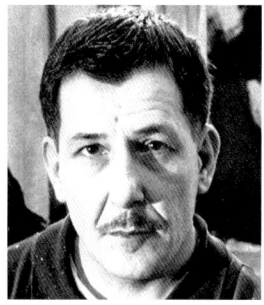

b. 1910 in Wilkes-Barre,
Pennsylvania
d. 1962 in New York City

From the late 1930s until the mid-1940s Franz Kline often derived the motifs of his then still figurative pictures from his home region, a mining district in eastern Pennsylvania. And the dynamic compositions of his later abstract works, painted after the mid-1940s, are often reminiscent of the characteristic colliery winding towers of this region, known there as "tipples", their wooden structures coming across as rickety and not built to last. These regional references are further underlined by the titles of the pictures, which refer to the names of towns or railways in the region.

Even though Kline broadened his colour spectrum during the course of the 1950s, in particular after his arrangement with the Sidney Janis Gallery in 1956, he is known above all for his black-and-white pictures. *Cardinal* – according to Kline the name of a railway – was first exhibited on the occasion of his first one-man show at Charles Egan's gallery in the autumn of 1950. At this time, other painters of the New York School, in particular Willem de Kooning and Jackson Pollock, were reducing their colours to black and white. Clement Greenberg explained this choice in his 1955 essay "'American-Type' Painting" as an art historically important further development of chiaroscuro, which in his view constituted the basis of painting. "And the new emphasis on black and white has to do with something that is perhaps more crucial to Western painting than to any other kind."

It is true that Kline had also concerned himself with Oriental art, and as an art student in London in the late 1930s he had collected Japanese prints; for this reason, his black-and-white pictures were often linked to Japanese calligraphy, as with *Untitled* in 1957. Kline himself explicitly rejected any such comparison, as he did not work only with black paint on a white ground, but also overpainted black with white and white with black, thus building up his motifs step by step. His working method, which involved taking weeks or months over a picture, during which time he would work on a number of canvases in parallel, is also not comparable with the rapid execution of an Indian-ink drawing on paper. "The Oriental idea of space is an infinite space; it is not painted space, and ours is," said Kline in an interview in 1962. "In the first place, calligraphy is writing, and I'm not writing. People sometimes think I take a white canvas and paint a black sign on it, but this is not true. I paint the white as well as the black, and the white is just as important."

The starting point for Kline's pictures was often a spontaneous sketch, which for reasons of expense he often executed on the pages of telephone directories or on newspaper. In about 1948, in de Kooning's studio, Kline learnt about the potential applications of the Bell-Opticon, an enlargement appliance which allowed drawings to be projected on to a wall. It was when projecting some of his black-and-white drawings that Kline came upon his characteristic technique: transferring the configurations of the drawings – but without the help of a projector – on to large-format canvases.

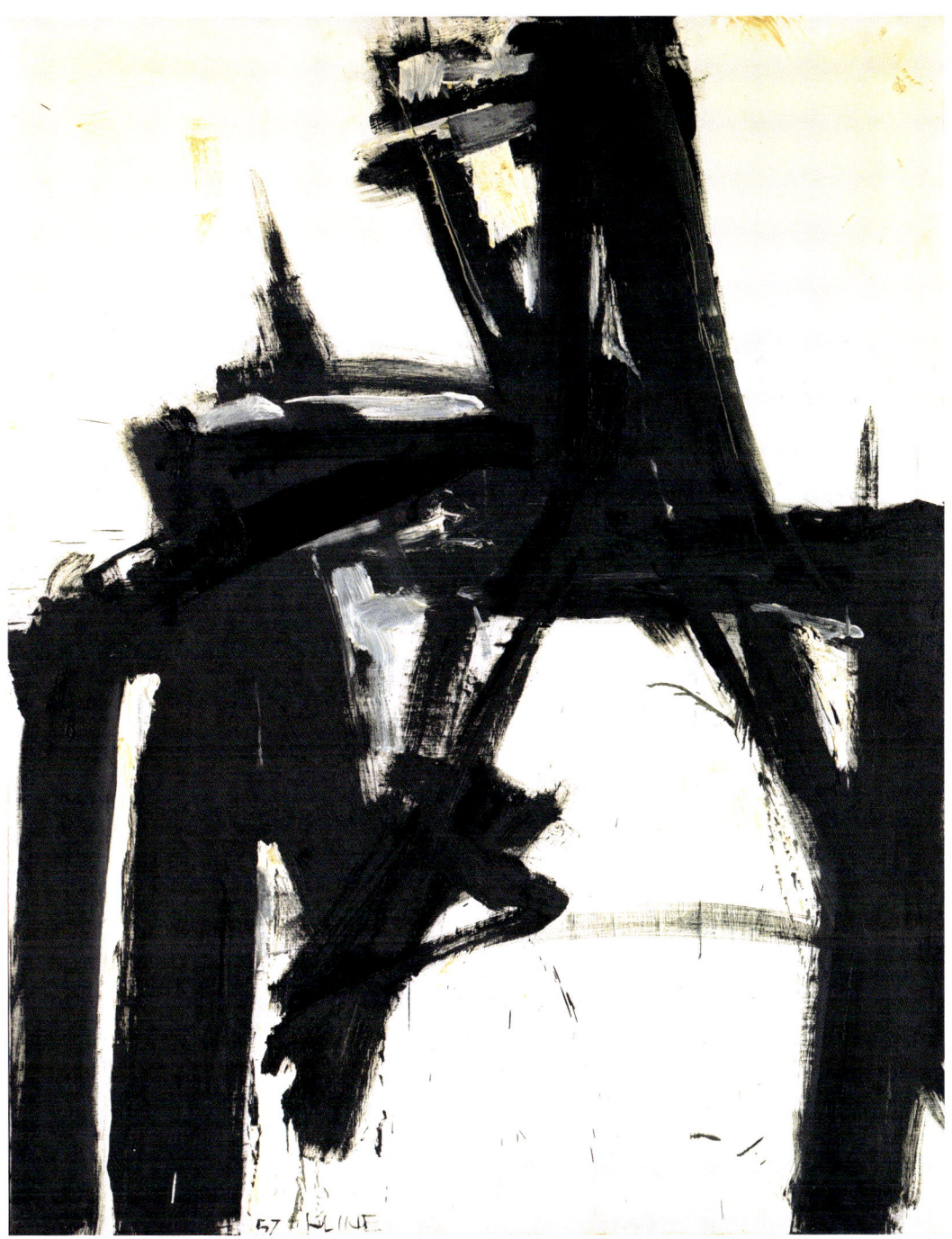

Untitled, 1957
Oil on canvas, 200 x 158.5 cm (78¾ x 62½ in.)
Düsseldorf, K20 – Kunstsammlung
Nordrhein-Westfalen

Willem de Kooning
Excavation, 1950

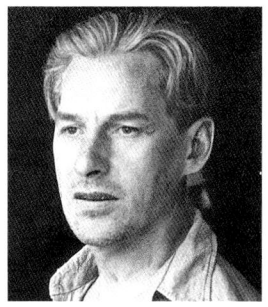

b. 1904 in Rotterdam
d. 1997 in Long Island, New York

"De Kooning's is a slippery universe made of expanding numbers of indications and changing points of view," observed Thomas B. Hess in the first monograph about the artist, which appeared in 1959. The number of "allusions and changing standpoints" that Hess observed in Willem de Kooning points not least to the legacy of Cubism, which de Kooning confronted in numerous works. In a lecture on abstract art at the New York Museum of Modern Art in 1951, where *Excavation* was currently on display, he emphasized: "Of all movements, I liked Cubism most."

Born in the Netherlands, de Kooning obtained an artistic training at, among other places, the Rotterdam Academy of Art and Technology and in 1926, at the age of 22, went to New York; where, from 1936, he devoted himself exclusively to painting. In spite of an obvious concern with the Cubists and the work of Pablo Picasso, he described himself in an interview with Harold Rosenberg in 1972 as "an eclectic painter by chance; I can open almost any book of reproductions and find a painting I could be influenced by." The reference system in which *Excavation* can be located is correspondingly many-layered. Apart from a stage set dating from 1946, it is de Kooning's largest picture. The format and the broken off-white colouration make it look like a wall, which, as it were with graffiti, is covered with a tangled weave of black-contoured, fragmented depictions of bodies. And in fact in the mid-1930s de Kooning had indeed gathered experience in the sphere of mural painting in the framework of the state arts sponsorship project, the Works Progress Administration.

The sketchily reduced wide-open eyes and mouths are reminiscent of a tumult or a struggle. As one possible input to *Excavation*, Picasso's famous 1937 anti-war picture *Guernica* is often quoted, but another is a spectacular scene from Giuseppe de Santis's 1949 neo-realist black-and-white film *Riso amaro* (Bitter Rice), in which a group of women fight with each other in a rice field. In addition, de Kooning obtained his inspirations for motifs and colouration often from the everyday world: the construction pit alluded to in the title was a common sight in New York. "Excavation" awakens the impression that it is a pre-existent picture, a historic find, a witness to some human catastrophe, and all that the artist has done is to uncover it. Many exponents of Abstract Expressionism interested themselves, as a result of devastating experiences in the Second World War, in so-called "primitive" art, such as prehistoric cave painting: de Kooning's title suggests such a retrospective reference.

De Kooning ended his work on *Excavation* in June 1950, when the picture was due to be presented at the American Pavilion at the Venice Biennale – his first important participation at an exhibition abroad. In November 1951 he was awarded the Purchase Prize of the Art Institute of Chicago. *Excavation* did not just mark a moment of institutional recognition in de Kooning's career, however, but at the same time a turning point in his artistic development: immediately after the work on *Excavation* was finished, de Kooning started on the figurative series *Women*, which was to occupy him until March 1953.

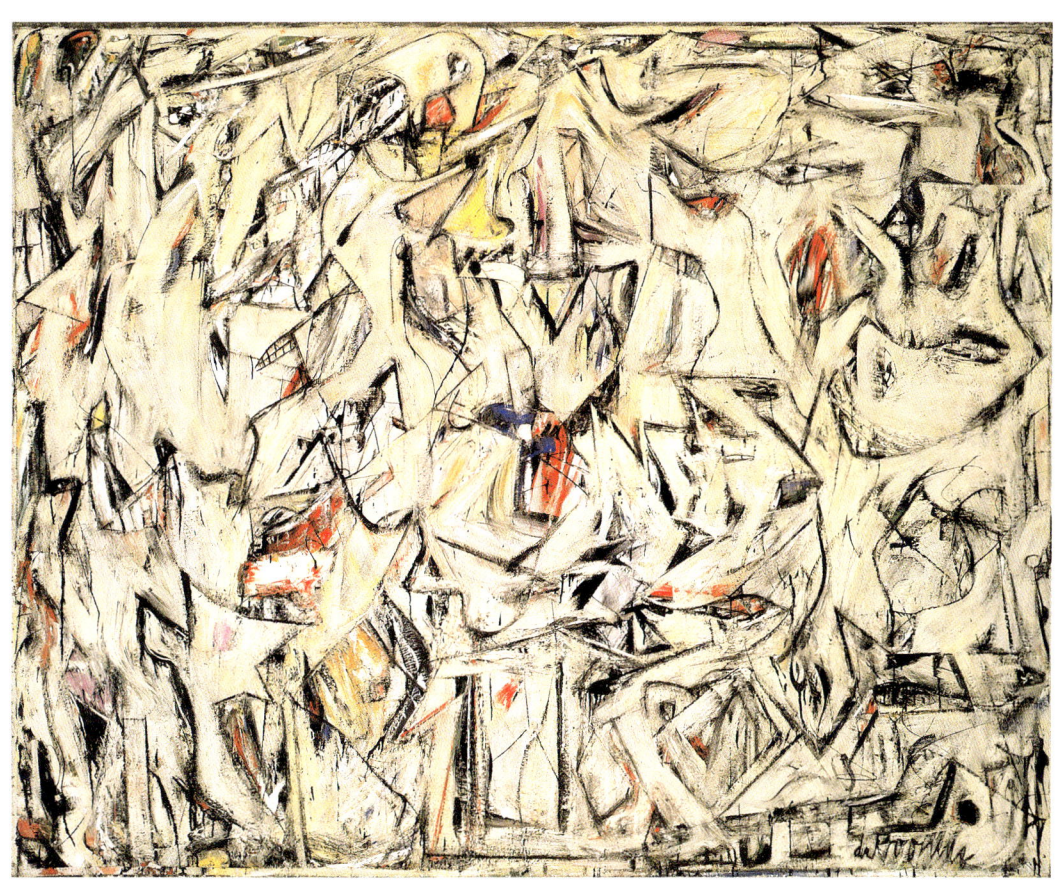

Excavation, 1950
Oil and gloss-paint on canvas,
205.7 x 254.6 cm (81 x 100¼ in.)
The Art Institute of Chicago, Mr. and Mrs. Frank
G. Logan Purchase Prize Fund, Gift of Mr. Edgar
Kaufman, Jr., and Mr. and Mrs. Noah Goldowsky

Willem de Kooning
Woman, I, 1950–52

If we are to believe what we have been told, Willem de Kooning's doubtless best-known and at the same time most controversial work almost failed to see the light of day. In June 1950 de Kooning, who usually composed his pictures directly on the canvas, had begun work on preparatory drawings for *Woman, I.* When the respected art historian Meyer Schapiro visited him in his studio in March 1952, de Kooning had rejected the picture as a definitive failure, and already resignedly removed the canvas from the stretcher. With Schapiro's encouragement de Kooning re-worked the painting, however, and soon brought the work to completion.

In March 1953 the picture was exhibited at the influential Sidney Janis Gallery together with five other works from the series entitled *Paintings on the Theme of the Woman.* The magazine *ARTnews* provided flanking support for the event by publishing the same month a lengthy article about the artist, among other things documenting in photographs the various stages in the difficult gestation process of *Woman, I.* The same year as it was exhibited at the Sidney Janis Gallery, the picture was acquired by the Museum of Modern Art.

In spite of this success, de Kooning's *Women* came across to many beholders in the artistic and art-critical penumbra of the New York School, in which abstraction was being celebrated as a progressive achievement in the evolution of contemporary American painting, quite literally as a foreign body. In the oeuvre of the artist, the motif of the human figure, by contrast, had been present from the very beginning, and kept turning up, with interruptions during which abstract works came more to the fore, time and again, as for example in *Woman* (1948), which already heralded the later series.

De Kooning attempted to escape being pinned down to abstraction or figuration, and in 1960 declared in an interview: "Certain artists and critics attacked me for painting the *Women*, but I felt that this was their problem, not mine. I don't really feel like a non-objective painter at all. Today, some artists feel they have to go back to the figure, and that word 'figure' becomes such a ridiculous omen – if you pick up some paint with your brush and make somebody's nose with it, this is rather ridiculous when you think of it, theoretically or philosophically. It's really absurd to make an image, like a human image, with paint, today, when you think about it, since we have this problem of doing it or not doing it. But then all of a sudden it was even more absurd not to do it. So I fear that I have to follow my desires."

The series *Women* was and is controversial not least on account of the seemingly negative image of woman which it presents, in which the depiction of the female figure functions as a projection surface for male aggression. In a wide-ranging discussion, the feminist art historian Linda Nochlin pleaded in 1998 above all for people to view the group of works with a discriminating eye: "I am not sure I can agree with any single evaluation of the *Women* series from the viewpoint of 'positive' or 'negative' gender representation. There is too much ambivalence here. And what, precisely, constitutes 'positive' or 'negative' when a cultural concept like 'woman' (in general) is at stake?"

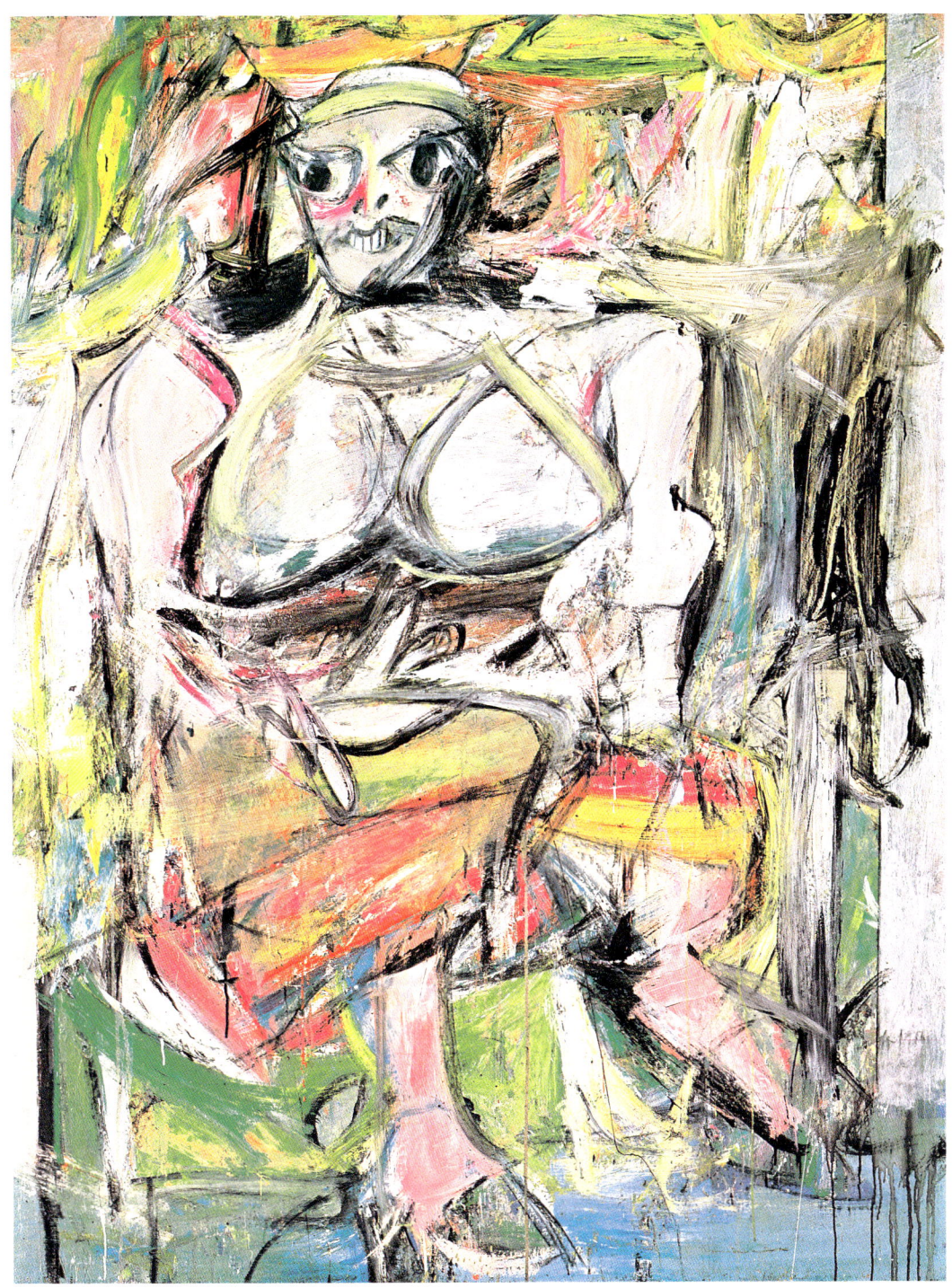

Woman, I, 1950–52
Oil on canvas, 192.7 x 147.3 cm (76 x 58 in.)
New York, The Museum of Modern Art

Lee Krasner
Untitled, 1949

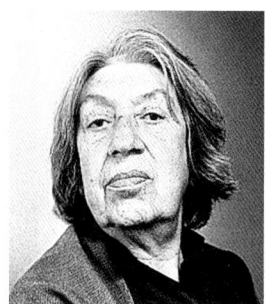

b. 1908 in New York City
d. 1984 in New York City

Of all the Abstract Expressionist artist-couples, the private and professional partnership between Lee Krasner and Jackson Pollock is doubtless the best known and most investigated. This widely practised approach to Krasner's work – only seeing it in relation to Pollock's – is in itself enough to point up her dilemma as an artist: her difficulty consisted largely in being taken notice of without her work being reduced on the one hand to her being a woman, or on the other to her relationship with Pollock, the leading figure of Abstract Expressionism. This was less an individual than a historically conditioned situation, which Krasner shared with other female artists in the field of Abstract Expressionism, as the American art historian Michael Leja emphasized in 1993: namely the "exclusion from the experience of and the power to represent the self of Modern Man discourse, as that self was embodied in Abstract Expressionist painting and aesthetics." "Modern Man" in the prevailing view was always male, white and heterosexual.

Lee Krasner, whose real name was Lena Krassner, was the child of Ukrainian immigrants. She started her artistic training in 1929 at the age of 21, and between 1937 and 1940 she took lessons at Hans Hofmann's renowned School of Fine Arts, which familiarized young American artists with the formal achievements of modern European painting. It was here that Krasner began to paint in an abstract style; regular exhibitions followed, for example with the group known as American Abstract Artists.

From the start of her relationship with Pollock, Krasner's work took a back seat to his, both in respect of her own productivity, and of her public presence. The period between 1942 and 1945, during which Krasner and Pollock shared a studio on Eighth Street, she once described as her "blackout period", in which very few works were painted or preserved. Pictures which Krasner called "grey slabs" were constantly being scraped off the canvas and covered with dense new layers of paint, as though the motifs beneath were not to come to the surface.

After the couple settled in The Springs on Long Island in 1946, living a somewhat reclusive life, Krasner painted her first important group of abstract works, entitled *Little Images* (1946–50), in which she moved on from the Cubist schemes of composition taught by Hofmann, and started to work on the all-over principle. Barbara Rose has divided this group of works into three series: (1) mosaic (divisionist); (2) webbed, 1947–49; and (3) grid (hieroglyph). Krasner herself summarized all these works under the heading "hieroglyphs". Krasner shared an interest in the calligraphic and in the Surrealist "écriture automatique" with artists such as Mark Tobey and Bradley Walker Tomlin.

The fact that in some of the *Little Images* – whose title sounds like a demonstrative, maybe ironic gesture of humility – she used the technique of dripping is mostly interpreted as a reaction to Pollock's current experiments in this technique. However Krasner's dripping, unlike Pollock's, comes across not as an expression of an uninhibited breaking-down of barriers, but as a reaction to the constraints of the grid-structure. This process has often been interpreted negatively as the expression of some sort of mental block or of exaggerated self-control. Krasner herself, by contrast, described it in positive terms, as the attempt at union of opposites such as male and female, organic and geometric, mind and matter.

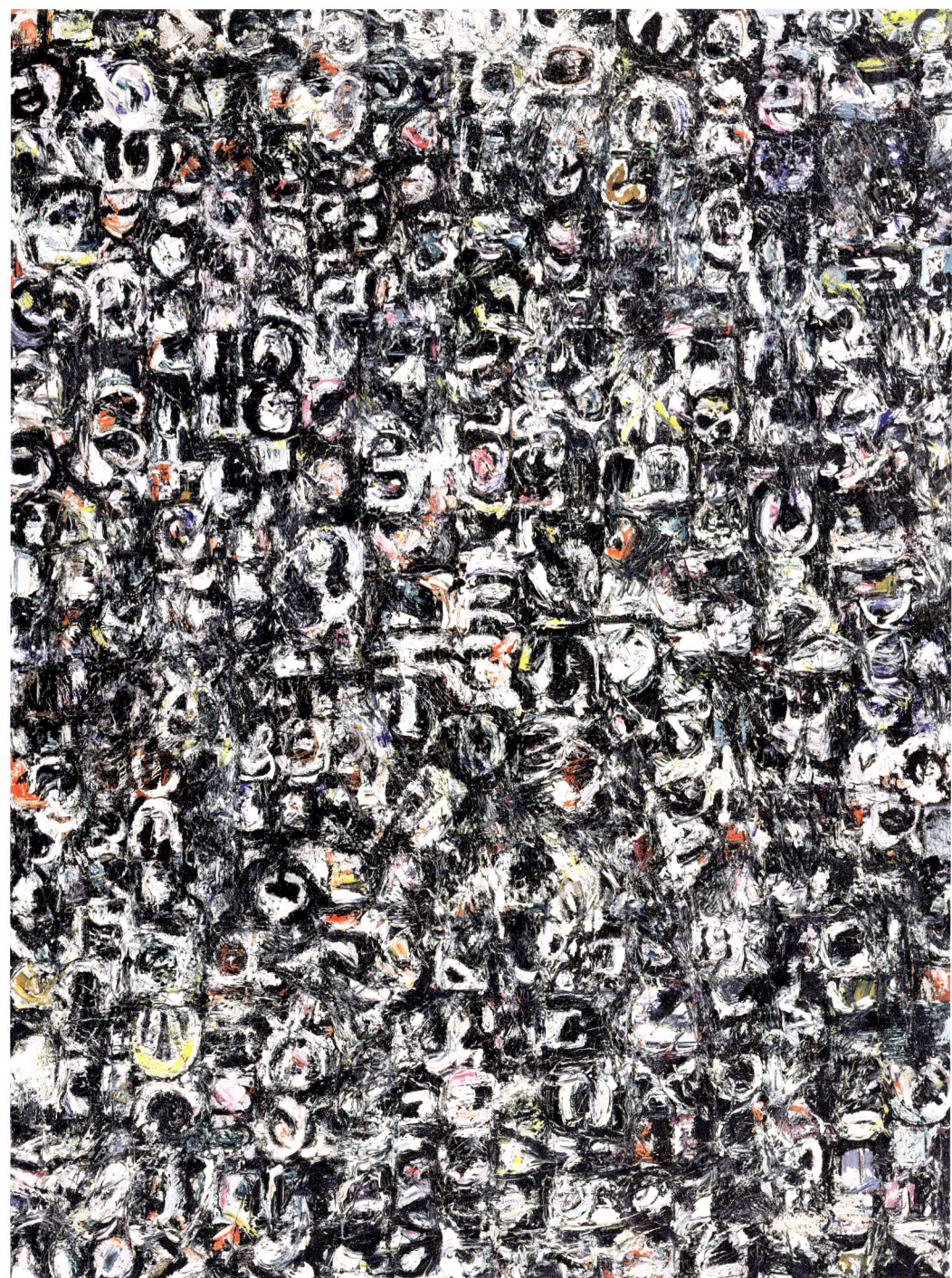

Untitled, 1949
From the series *Little Images*, 1946–50
Oil on composition board, 121.9 x 94 cm (48 x 37 in.)
New York, The Museum of Modern Art,
Gift of Alfonso A. Ossorio

Lee Krasner
Bald Eagle, 1955

Following the *Little Images* series of the late 1940s, Lee Krasner's collages of the years 1953 to 1955 form her second extensive group of works. Krasner's break with the working method employed in *Little Images* cannot simply be explained by a series of critical reactions to these works. Even so, they offer a penetrating insight into the public perception of the relationship between Krasner's work and that of Jackson Pollock. The couple had taken part in the "Artists: Man and Wife" group exhibition at the Sidney Janis Gallery in 1949, where Krasner displayed one of her *Little Images*. In the magazine *ARTnews*, the publication that set the tone for Abstract Expressionism at this period, Gretchen T. Munson wrote in a review of October 1949: "There is also a tendency among some of these wives to 'tidy up' their husbands' styles. Lee Krasner (Mrs. Jackson Pollock) takes her husband's paints and enamels and changes his unrestrained, sweeping lines into neat little squares and rectangles."

Rhetorically, Krasner was thus reduced – by another woman, mark! – to the stereotype of the house-proud housewife, something to which other critics were also not averse. A more complex interaction between Krasner's and Pollock's painting techniques and their respective particularities was faded out in favour of the idea of a one-sided influencing of Krasner's work by her husband.

In October 1951, Krasner had her first solo exhibition at the Betty Parsons Gallery; from the point of view of sales, it was a failure. When Pollock left the Betty Parsons Gallery that same year for the commercially more successful Sidney Janis, Krasner had also to leave the gallery at Parsons's behest. Of the 14 pictures that she had shown there in 1951, she overpainted twelve and used some of them as canvases for new works, a series of collages. After the fiasco at the Parsons Gallery, Krasner had at first completed a few black-and-white works on paper in 1953. Dissatisfied with the result, she took the drawings off the wall, tore them up, and threw the shreds on the floor. Not until a few weeks later did she return to her studio, as she recalled in an interview given in 1980: "When I opened the door and walked in, the floor was solidly covered with these torn drawings that I had left and they began to interest me and I started collaging. Well, it started with drawings. Then I took my canvases and cut and began doing the same thing, and that ended in my collage show in 1955." This show took place in the renowned Stable Gallery to critical applause, at a time when Pollock was producing no new work.

In *Bald Eagle* Krasner uses not only her own canvases; the elements with squirts of black paint, including the piece in the centre of the picture, whose shape is reminiscent of an eagle's head, obviously derive from a rejected picture of Pollock's. Among the inspirations for Krasner's collages are considered to be the "découpages", or cut-outs, by Henri Matisse, of which she thought highly, and works by Anne Ryan, an artist friend. What seems remarkable about Krasner's approach to her large-format collages is that like Pollock's drip-paintings of 1950 they are in a sense painted from a horizontal perception, insofar as Krasner saw the arrangement of the torn-up drawings as in an "all-over" on the floor of her studio.

Bald Eagle, 1955
Oil, paper and canvas on linen,
195.6 x 130.8 cm (77 x 51½ in.)
Los Angeles, Collection Audrey and
Sidney Irmas, Courtesy Robert Miller
Gallery, New York

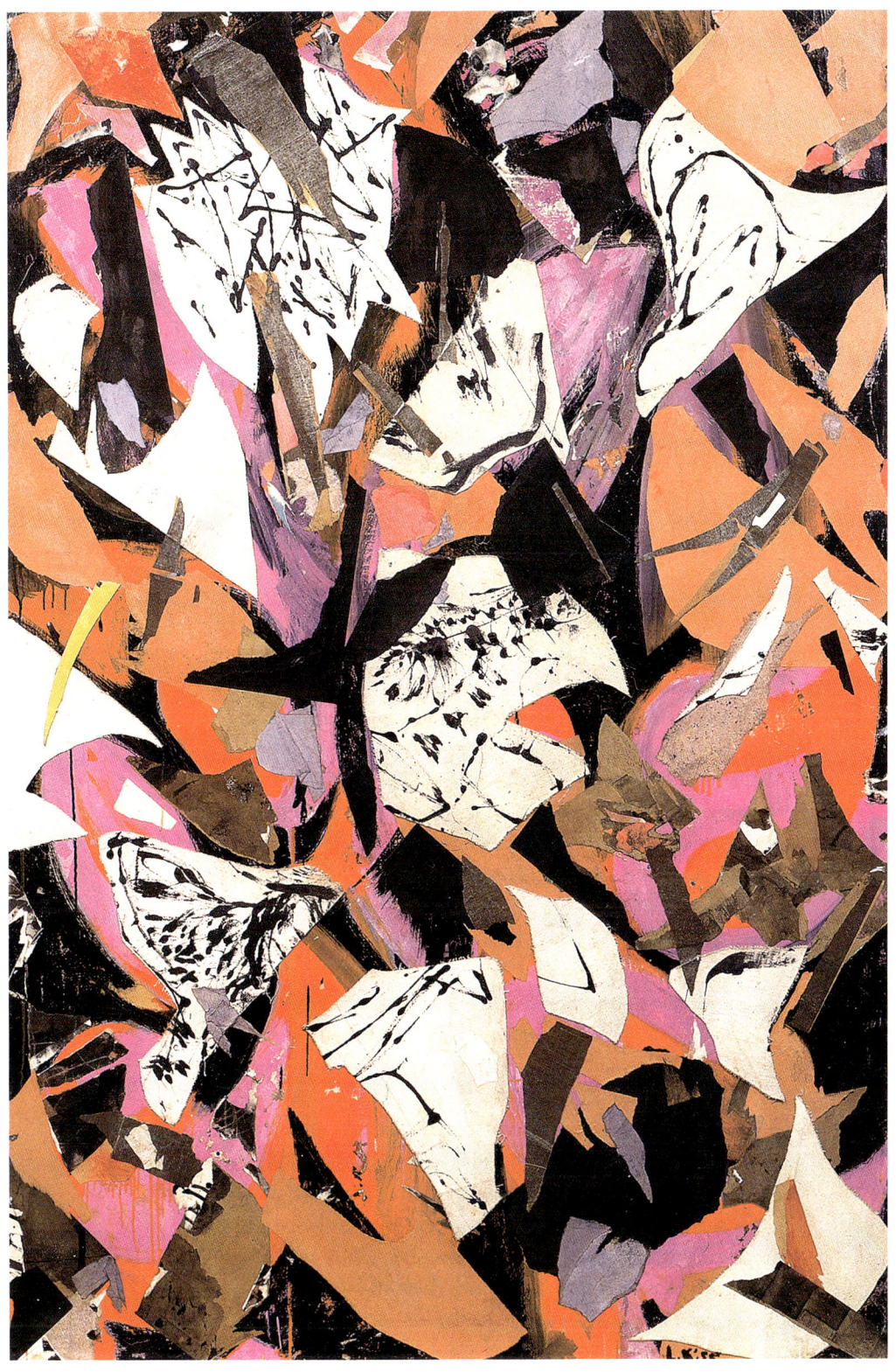

Joan Mitchell
Hemlock, 1956

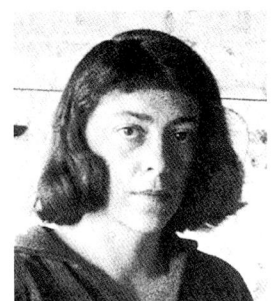

b. 1925 in Chicago
d. 1992 in Paris

"My painting is not an allegory, it is not a story. It is more like a poem," declared Joan Mitchell in the 1980s. Mitchell was born into a home that promoted and encouraged her literary and artistic ambitions from her childhood onwards. Her father was a respected doctor who painted and sketched in his spare time; her mother was a poet and published the noted literary magazine *Poetry*.

At an early age, Mitchell herself got to know important works of European art in the collection of the Art Institute of Chicago. In 1947, she moved to New York; in 1948/49 she was awarded a travel grant, which enabled her to work as an artist both in Paris and in the south of France. After her return to New York, in 1951 she became, alongside Lee Krasner, Elaine de Kooning and Helen Frankenthaler, one of the few women members of the Eighth Street Club, and participated in major group exhibitions such as the "Ninth Street Show" organized by Leo Castelli in 1951.

Not only experiences of the countryside and the natural world, but also literary texts, often form the reference points for Mitchell's gestural abstractions. The title *Hemlock* (it refers to the conifer) she took from a poem by Wallace Stevens, "Domination of Black", but only supplied it once the picture was finished. The title invites us to interpret the brushstrokes in green and blue – which seem to be hurled outwards from the middle of the picture by some centrifugal force – as the branches of a conifer in a snowstorm.

For Mitchell herself, the colour white, which was often dominant in her pictures at this period, had a series of negative meanings, which go beyond its descriptive characteristics: "It's death. It's hospitals. It's my terrible nurses. You can add in Melville, *Moby Dick*, a chapter on white. White is absolute horror, just horror. It is the worst."

In the late 1950s, Mitchell's work came to enjoy increasing recognition. 1957 saw the appearance of the first detailed monograph on her work in *ARTnews*; in 1958, *Hemlock* was displayed at the exhibition "Nature in Abstraction: The Relation of Abstract Painting and Sculpture to Nature in Twentieth Century American Art" at the Whitney Museum in New York, and in this context purchased by the museum.

Unlike most New York artists considered "Abstract Expressionists", Mitchell did not attempt to distance herself from European painting tradition. On the contrary, she lived and worked from 1955 to 1959 both in the USA and in Paris. In 1959 she finally settled in France; thenceforth, her pictures were painted exclusively there, in spite of regular trips to the USA. This point of time, the late 1950s, also marked a caesura in the post-war art scene. Thus in 1959 Mitchell also took part in the documenta II exhibition in Kassel, which finally sealed the international acceptance of Abstract Expressionism, laying the foundations for American art's claim to world leadership in the coming decade.

Meanwhile, on the New York art scene, criticism was increasingly being voiced that Abstract Expressionism's painterly language, especially its interpretation by the second generation, to which Mitchell belonged, and their successors, was threatening to become an academic commonplace. The rise of new art movements was casting its shadow: "Pop Art, Op Art, Flop Art and Slop Art," observed Mitchell ironically in the mid-1970s. "I fall into the last two categories."

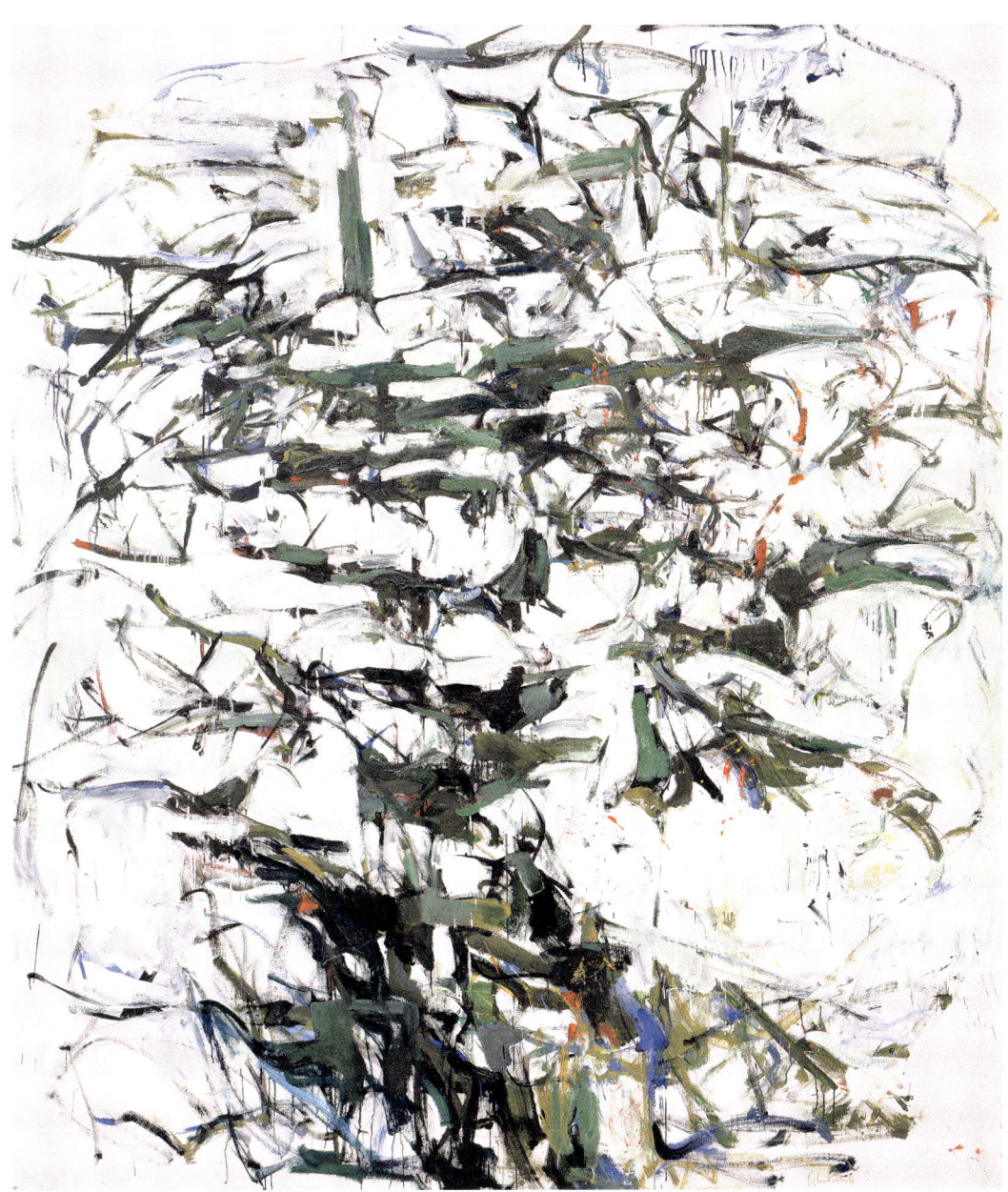

Hemlock, 1956
Oil on canvas, 231.1 x 203.2 cm (91 x 80 in.)
New York, Whitney Museum of American Art,
Purchase, with funds from the Friends
of the Whitney Museum of American Art

Robert Motherwell
Elegy to the Spanish Republic, No. 34, 1953/54

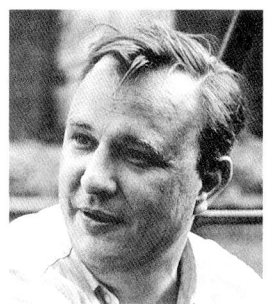

b. 1915 in Aberdeen,
Washington
d. 1991 in Provincetown,
Massachusetts

Consisting of more than two hundred paintings, the *Elegies to the Spanish Republic* represent one of Robert Motherwell's most extensive group of works. It occupied the artist for more than thirty years. The end of the young Spanish Republic had been sealed in 1939 with the victory of the fascist dictator Francisco Franco following the devastating three-year civil war. The *Elegies* series was not begun until a good ten years later.

The occasion for the black-and-white Indian-ink drawing *Ink Sketch (Elegy No. 1)* was a poem by Harold Rosenberg, "The Bird for Every Bird", which appeared in 1948 in the first and only edition of the magazine *Possibilities* – a project on which Motherwell, Rosenberg, John Cage and Pierre Chareau formed the editorial staff. On the model of the French magazine *Verve*, Motherwell wrote the poem, which has nothing to do with the Spanish Civil War, out by hand and "illustrated" it with an abstract drawing.

The basic elements which were to characterize the whole series are already apparent in the first sketch: the picture surface is rhythmatized by vertical elements, between which oval forms are enclosed. Motherwell was employing the Surrealist technique of "écriture automatique", to the extent that the first thing he did was apply a spontaneous arrangement of Indian-ink lines to the paper. Unlike Surrealists, however, he did not seek as a next step to create a figurative design from the result, but rather an abstract composition. It was not until an exhibition at the Samuel Kootz Gallery in December 1950, where Motherwell displayed a number of pictures from the series, that he gave them the title *Elegies (to the Spanish Republic)*.

Elegy to the Spanish Republic, No. 34 was described by Motherwell as "one of the half-dozen most realized of the *Spanish Elegy* series", having been created during what the artist described as a "painting block", in which he spent a lot of time "realizing" details. The background colours are a reference to the flag of the Spanish Republic in yellow, red and blue.

In a 1963 interview, Motherwell commented on the *Elegies* as follows: "I take an elegy to be a funeral song for something one cared about. The *Spanish Elegies* are not 'political', but are my private insistence that a terrible death happened that should not be forgot. They are as eloquent as I could make them. But the pictures are also general metaphors of the contrast between life and death and their interrelation." The colours white and black, which play a central role in the *Elegies* series, symbolize according to Motherwell this universal dualism of life and death. Even though Motherwell himself said that the *Elegies* were not political, the topic nevertheless had a political currency, as Spain remained a dictatorship until Franco's death in 1975, and only adopted a democratic constitution in 1978.

Another widespread, quasi-psychological reading of the *Elegies* is the interpretation of their organic, oval and vertical forms as symbols of the male and female sexes, or as the phallus and testicles of a slaughtered bull on a white wall.

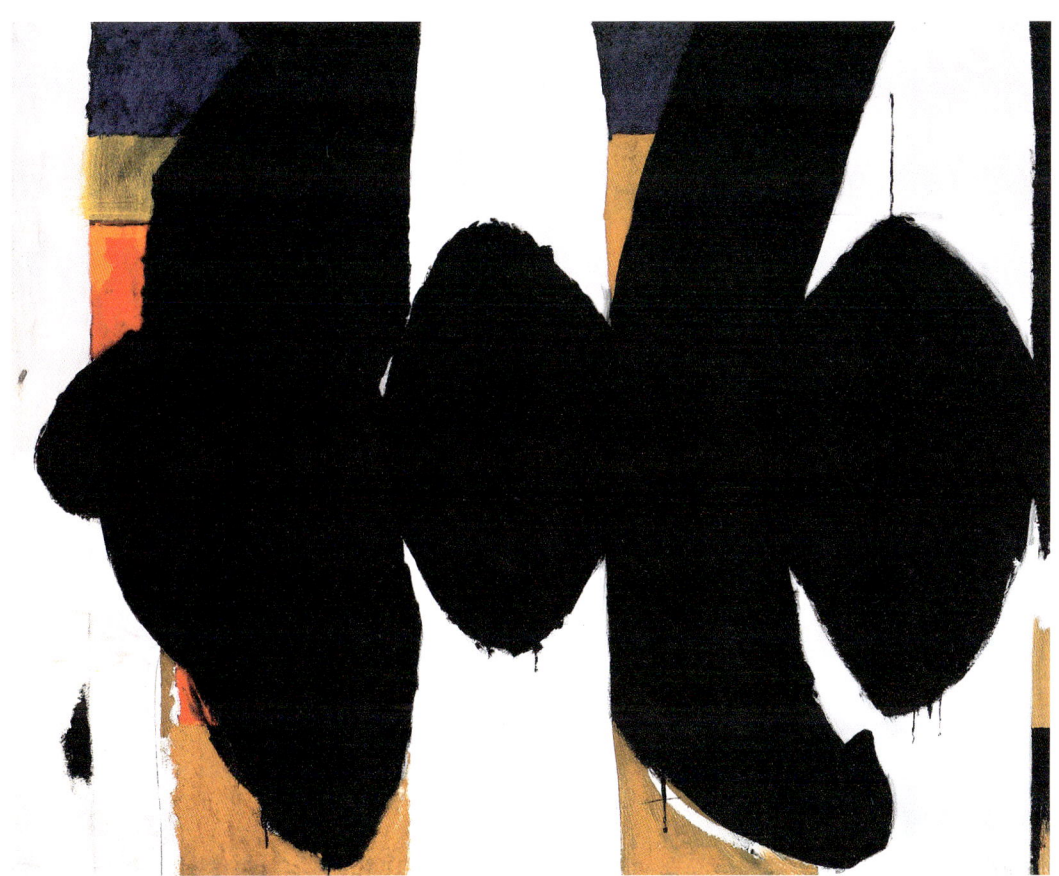

Elegy to the Spanish Republic, No. 34, 1953/54
Oil on canvas, 208.3 x 259.1 cm (82 x 102 in.)
Buffalo, Albright-Knox Art Gallery,
Gift of Seymour H. Knox, Jr., 1957

Barnett Newman
Onement, I, 1948

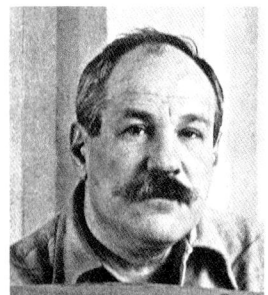

b. 1905 in New York City
d. 1970 in New York City

In April 1945 Barnett Newman wrote in an article on Rufino Tamayo and Adolph Gottlieb: "Man is a tragic being, and the heart of this tragedy is the metaphysical problem of part and whole. This dichotomy of our nature, from which we can never escape and which because of its nature impels us helplessly to try to resolve it, motivates our struggle for perfection and seals our inevitable doom. For man is one, he is single, he is alone; and yet he belongs, he is part of an other. This conflict is the greatest of our tragedies…" In the New York art world, Newman was, until well into the 1950s, known above all to many contemporaries as a curator and (often polemical) author. Thus in 1944 and 1946 he had organized exhibitions of pre-Columbian painting for the Betty Parsons Gallery. In these projects, as also in his earlier writings, Newman indicated his interest in "primitive" art – to which his own art was supposed to be the modern equivalent – as the expression of the human search for metaphysical insight.

The birth of *Onement, I* was dated by the artist to 20 January 1948, his own 43rd birthday. A rectangular canvas in vertical format, with a partly translucent application of russet paint, is divided down the middle by a narrow orange-red strip, or stripe, of painted adhesive tape with irregular edges. The vertical stripe Newman called a "zip" and indeed, it does both divide and reunite the two halves of the picture like a zip fastener. For Newman it was "a field that brings life to the other fields, just as the other fields bring life to this so-called line."

The first zips had already appeared in 1946 in a number of pictures such as *Moment* or *Genesis – The Break*. Even so, *Onement, I* is regarded as a decisive turning-point in Newman's artistic development. In 1965, he described it as the new beginning of his existence: "I realized that I'd made a statement which was affecting me and which was, I suppose, the beginning of my present life, because from then on I had to give up any relation to nature, as seen." In fact Newman referred to *Onement, I* having, in his view, a kind of independent existence: "The painting itself had a life of its own in a way that I don't think the others did, as much."

The importance of this image-creation can be seen not least in the fact that *Onement, I* was followed by about a year of unusual productivity, in which seventeen other works appeared. Thus in *Onement, III* (1949) Newman used the same compositional principle as in *Onement, I*, while increasing the dimensions of the picture to 182.5 x 84.9 cm (72 x 33½ in.), so that it could be viewed by beholders even more strongly as something with which they were physically confronted. To this extent, *Onement, I* and the invention of the zip can be understood as the painterly expression of what Newman already in 1945 was calling the "metaphysical problem of part and whole". And indeed, when one views Newman's compositions from close up, as the artist demanded on the occasion of his second exhibition at the Betty Parsons Gallery in 1951, "man is one, he is single, he is alone; and yet he belongs, he is part of an other."

Onement, I, 1948
Oil on canvas, 69.2 x 41.2 cm (27¼ x 16¼ in.)
New York, The Museum of Modern Art,
Gift of Annalee Newman

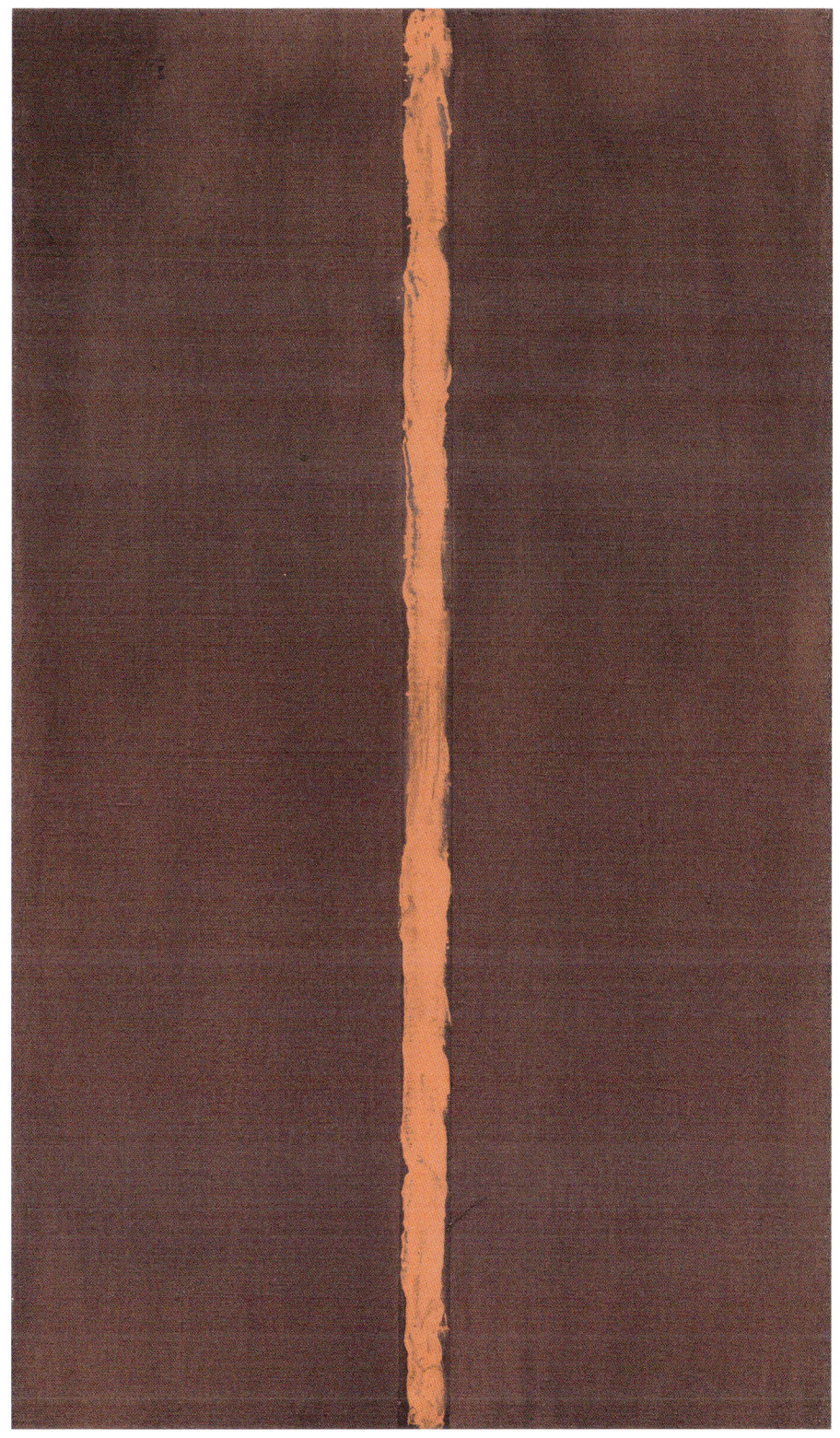

Barnett Newman
The Wild, 1950

In about 1950, Barnett Newman began to work on a series of unusual picture formats. At one end of the spectrum there are horizontal pictures more than five metres broad, such as *Vir Heroicus Sublimis* (1950/51) and *Cathedra* (1951), and at the other end, some narrow vertical pictures just a few centimetres across, of which *The Wild* represents an extreme case. On a blue-grey background, a red stripe, about two centimetres across, painted twice over, covers almost the whole picture. Its upper layer is somewhat blurred at the edges. With *The Wild* Newman directed the beholder's attention to the zip, which both divides and unites the monochrome fields of his pictures, making it clear that this was the decisive element in his paintings. According to Thomas B. Hess, Newman was reacting to the opinion of a curator that all that mattered in Newman's pictures were the mutual proportions of the colour fields, placing him in the Bauhaus tradition. In addition, Newman wanted to make it clear that in his painting it was not so much the format as the scale that was important. Thus in 1966 he declared in an interview, with reference to *The Wild*: "I think it holds up as well as any big one I have ever done. The issue is one of scale, and scale is a felt thing."

If Newman, with the isolated zip of *The Wild*, was expressly appealing to the feeling for scale – which is bound up with the physical presence of the work and the beholder in the room – this is all the more explicit in his first sculpture, *Here I*, which likewise dates from 1950 and was exhibited together with *The Wild* in 1951 at the artist's one-man show at the Betty Parsons Gallery. Clearly the principle of the isolated zip in *Here I* has been transferred to the third dimension. The sculpture was first executed in plaster of Paris; only in 1962 were two copies cast in bronze; it was followed in 1965/66 by the two related sculptures *Here II* and *Here III*. In the case of *Here I* we have a impermanent-looking almost square plinth – a wooden crate for milk bottles – on which there are two amorphous heaps of plaster, from each of which projects a flat stele, approximately 245 centimetres (ten feet) in height: the narrower of the two has smooth edges, while the broader has ragged edges.

Newman's unusual work, which marks a location, inspired contemporary interpreters to think up a series of symbolic readings, for example with reference to the Jewish religion, or as a metaphor for New York, the city of immigrants and the artistic focus of the Western world. As a possible inspiration for the concept behind *Here I*, an exhibition of stele-like plaster sculptures by Alberto Giacometti was often mentioned, which Newman saw at the Pierre Matisse Gallery in New York in 1948.

Also of great importance was his visit to Native American cultic sites in Ohio in 1949, which he regarded as sites of enhanced self-awareness; thus in retrospect he wrote: "Looking at the site you feel, Here I am, *here*… and out beyond there (beyond the limits of the site) there is chaos, nature, rivers, landscapes… But here you get a sense of your own presence… I became involved with the idea of making the viewer present: the idea that 'Man is Present'."

The Wild, 1950
Oil on canvas, 243 x 4.1 cm (95¾ x 1½ in.)
New York, The Museum of Modern Art,
Gift of the Kulicke Family, 1969

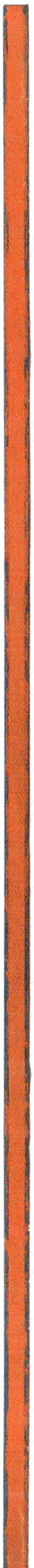

Barnett Newman
First Station, 1958

"If the 1930s and early 1940s were 'limbo' for him, 1955 through 1960 was his inferno," remarked Thomas B. Hess in the catalogue that appeared in 1971 to accompany the posthumous Barnett Newman retrospective in the Museum of Modern Art. Both in the general public attention given to his works, and also in respect of their sale, Newman at the time was well behind such fellow artists as Franz Kline, Jackson Pollock, Mark Rothko or Willem de Kooning – a situation which did not begin to change until 1959, and then only gradually. The years 1956 and 1957 were in addition years of crisis as far as his creativity were concerned, giving rise to no new works. Finally in November 1957 he suffered a heart attack, a decisive experience which he likened to "instant psychoanalysis".

The first picture to appear after this collapse, at the beginning of 1958, was a narrow vertical format measuring 219 by 15 cm (86¼ x 6 in.), and entitled *Outcry*, which took up where *The Wild* left off. With this picture Newman laid the foundation of the group of works entitled *Stations of the Cross – Lema Sabachthani*, which is regarded as one of his most important works, and which the art historian Franz Meyer went as far as to describe as the "Sistine Chapel of the 20th century".

In February 1958, Newman began work on the first two pictures, before they were actually thought of as parts of a cycle or "a theme with variations", as he wrote in 1966: "I began these paintings eight years ago the way I begin all my paintings – by painting. It was while painting them that it came to me (it was the fourth one) that I had something particular here. It was at that moment that the intensity that I felt the paintings had, made me think of them as the Stations of the Cross. It is as I work that the work itself begins to have an effect on me. Just as I affect the canvas, so does the canvas affect me."

In Christian iconography, the Stations of the Cross, from the Condemnation to the Entombment, have since the 17th century numbered 14 scenes of suffering, and Newman followed this tradition with his own 14-part version, without illustrating the stations individually. Newman reduced his media to the colours black, and in three of the Stations, white, in addition to the unprimed identically sized canvas and adhesive tape, in order to create sharp-edged or frayed zips. From this limited instrumentarium Newman obtained a broad spectrum of aesthetic effects. In 1966 he extended the cycle with the addition of a final work, *Be II* (1961–64); this had already been exhibited at the Allan Stone Gallery in 1962 under the title *Resurrection*, and attributed to Newman's friend Tony Smith; however it was only completed in 1964.

The subtitle of the group of works points back to Newman's *Outcry* of 1958. In a statement issued on the occasion of the presentation of *Stations of the Cross*, Newman wrote: "*Lema Sabachthani* – why? Why did you forsake me? To what purpose? Why? This is the Passion. This outcry of Jesus. Not the terrible walk up the Via Dolorosa, but the question that has no answer." This was a renewed defence by the artist of the claim made by the content of his artistic project. At the same time, he emphasized the autobiographical and self-reflexive dimension of the cycle by declaring that the title was not to be understood literally, but as a metaphor for his feelings while painting the pictures: every Station of the Cross was also a station in his personal life and his life as an artist.

First Station, 1958
From the series *Stations of the Cross –
Lema Sabachthani*, 1956–58
Magna on canvas, 197.8 x 153.7 cm (78 x 60½ in.)
Washington, D.C., National Gallery of Art,
Robert and Jane Meyerhoff Collection

Jackson Pollock
The Moon-Woman Cuts the Circle, 1943

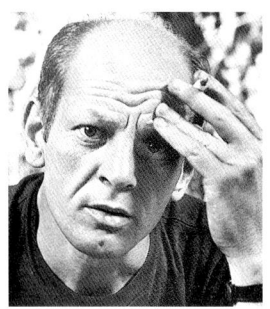

b. 1912 in Cody, Wyoming
d. 1956 in East Hampton,
New York

"Pollock was not a 'born' painter. He started out as a sculptor, at sixteen, but before he was eighteen had changed over to painting. He had to learn with effort to draw and paint." This was how in 1967 Clement Greenberg, on the occasion of a posthumous retrospective at the Museum of Modern Art, outlined the start of the career of Jackson Pollock, who died in 1956 as a legend in his own lifetime.

Pollock studied from 1930 to 1933 at the New York Art Students League. His teachers included the Regionalist Thomas Hart Benton, who put his stamp on Pollock's early, figurative style of the 1930s. In a 1944 questionnaire, Pollock described his work with Benton as "important as something to react upon very strongly, later on; in this, it was much better to have worked with him than with a less resistant personality who would have provided a much less strong opposition". In the same questionnaire, Pollock emphasized the influence on his work of his origins in the American West, the broad horizontal expanse of the country as well as the art of the Native American peoples: "The Indians have the true painter's approach in their capacity to get hold of appropriate images, and in their understanding of what constitutes painterly subject-matter. Their colour is essentially Western, their vision has the basic universality of all real art." To the question concerning the importance of the famous European artists living at that time in the USA, Pollock answered: "I am particularly impressed with their concept of the source of art being the unconscious. This idea interests me more than these specific painters do, since the two artists I admire most, Picasso and Miró, are still abroad."

The Moon-Woman Cuts the Circle, dating from 1943, is, together with *Mad Moon-Woman* (1941), and *The Moon-Woman* (1942), one of three pictures painted in the early 1940s in which Pollock concerned himself with the motif of the Moon-Woman; all three were exhibited at his first solo exhibition at Peggy Guggenheim's Art of This Century gallery in November 1943. The figure's head-dress points to Native American culture, details like the silhouette and the eyes to Pablo Picasso's 1937 anti-war picture *Guernica*, the contrast-rich colouration to paintings by Joan Miró.

Pollock's mention in 1944 of the "basic universality of all real art" which he saw in the Native American cultures of the American West recalls C. G. Jung's idea of a "collective unconscious" transcending cultures and common to all human beings. Pollock had undergone psychotherapy at the hands of a Jungian from 1939 to 1942, primarily on account of his alcoholism. In Jung's theory, the moon is a symbol of the female principle, which is active in both genders; it stands for the unconscious, intuitive, emotional and subjective.

The title of the picture *The Moon-Woman Cuts the Circle* is however, according to Michael Leja, difficult to interpret by reference to Jung's writings. "Perhaps she cuts the circle of the full moon to produce the crescent, or she may so appear in her character as Opener of the Womb, or as the deity to whom circumcisions were dedicated." All the same, Leja sees Pollock's use of Jungian symbolism not as an unconscious, but rather as a deliberate act in a social context which, since the late 1930s, had turned away from political and sociological models to explain crisis situations, and increasingly preferred the approach of psychological theories.

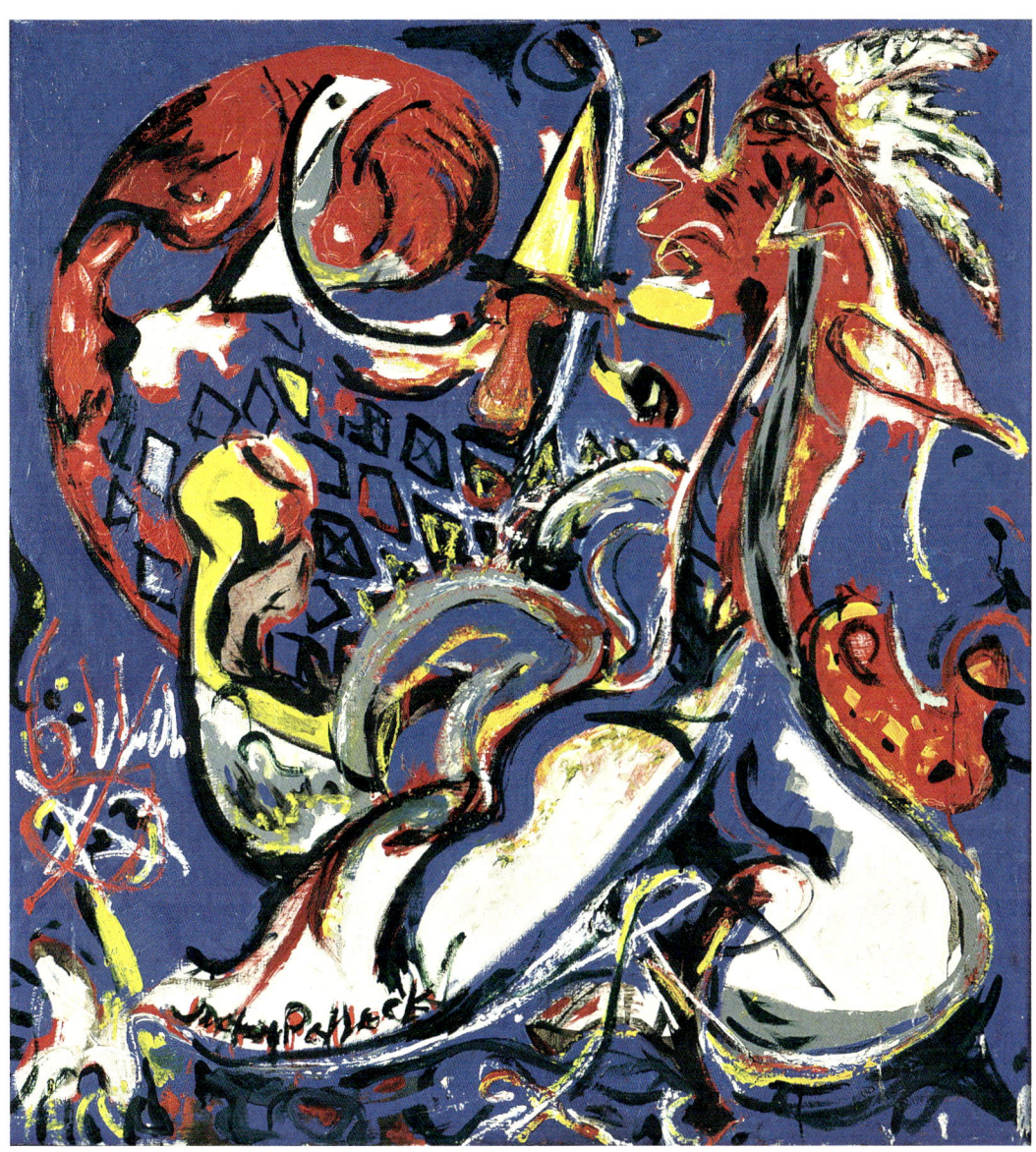

The Moon-Woman Cuts the Circle, 1943
Oil on canvas, 109.5 x 104 cm (43 x 41 in.)
Paris, Musée national d'art moderne,
Centre Pompidou

Jackson Pollock
Full Fathom Five, 1947

The winter of 1946/47 marks a decisive change in the work of Jackson Pollock: a turning away from traditional easel-painting and the start of his work on large-format canvases spread out on the floor. Pollock had come across the dripping technique in 1936 at the "Experimental Workshop" of the Mexican painter David Alfaro Siqueiros (1896–1974), also described as "a laboratory of modern techniques in art", and he had already applied it in 1943 in *Composition with Pouring II*. It is true that Hans Hofmann and Surrealists like André Masson and Max Ernst had already experimented with this form of paint application before Pollock, but "it was not the dripping, pouring or spattering *per se*, but what Pollock *did* with them that counted," as William Rubin observed in 1967.

In a statement for the magazine *Possibilities*, whose one and only edition came out in the winter of 1947/48, Pollock described his painting process in detail: "My painting does not come from the easel. I hardly ever stretch my canvas before painting. I prefer to tack the unstretched canvas to the hard wall or the floor. I need the resistance of a hard surface. On the floor I am more at ease. I feel nearer, more a part of the painting, since this way I can walk around it, work from the four sides and literally be *in* the painting. This is akin to the method of the Indian sand painters of the West." Instead of the ordinary tools of the painter's trade, such as easel, palette and brush, Pollock's techniques of dripping and pouring used objects such as sticks, spatulas, knives, or vessels with which the paint could be dripped or hurled on to the canvas, without directly touching the latter; sometimes the paint was mixed with other materials such as sand or splinters of glass.

While the interest of today's interpreters is now more strongly oriented towards the share of conscious control of the painting process, Pollock emphasized the automatism of his approach, which points to the influence of the Surrealist "dessin automatique": "When I am in my painting, I'm not aware of what I'm doing. It is only after a sort of 'get acquainted' period that I see what I have been about. I have no fears about making changes, destroying the image, etc., because the painting has a life of its own. I try to let it come through. It is only when I lose contact with the painting that the result is a mess. Otherwise there is pure harmony, an easy give and take, and the painting comes out well."

As was revealed by an X-ray examination carried out by the Museum of Modern Art's restoration workshop in the late 1990s, the weave of the top colour-layers in *Full Fathom Five* veils a figure in lead paint. The objects worked into the picture, such as keys or buttons, are placed with reference to this hidden figure, as could be demonstrated by the X-ray pictures.

The title *Full Fathom Five* was suggested by the writer Ralph Mannheim: it is a line from a song in Shakespeare's *The Tempest*, and here it alludes to the figure "submerged" beneath the smears of paint: "Full fathom five thy father lies/Of his bones are coral made/Those are pearls that were his eyes/Nothing of him that doth fade/But doth suffer a sea-change/Into something rich and strange."

Full Fathom Five, 1947
Oil on canvas, nails, drawing pins,
buttons, keys, coins, cigarettes, matches etc.,
129.2 x 76.5 cm (51 x 30 in.)
New York, The Museum of Modern Art,
Gift of Peggy Guggenheim

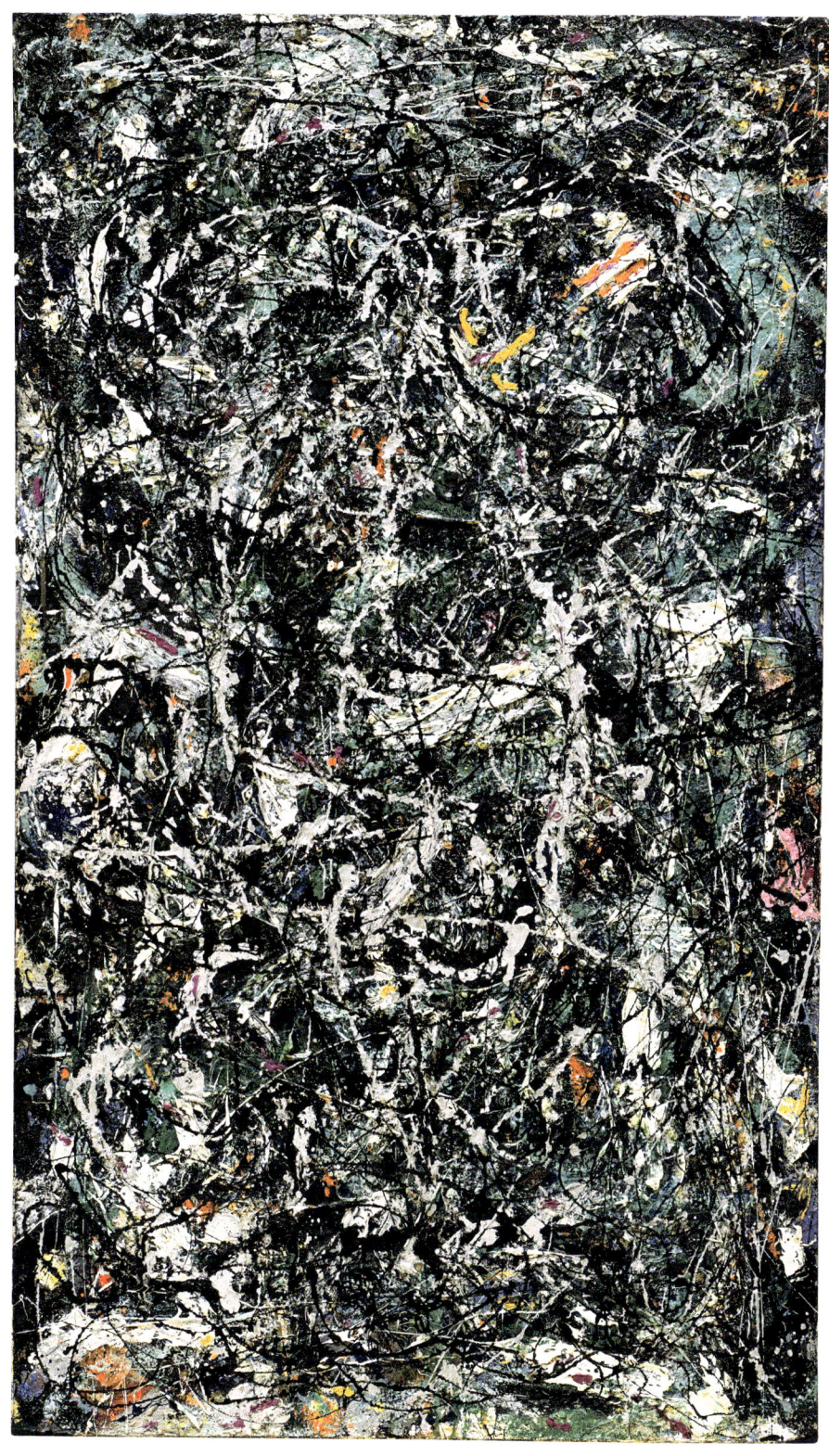

Jackson Pollock
Number 1, 1950 (Lavender Mist), 1950

With the creation of more than 50 works, 1950 was the most productive year in Jackson Pollock's career. *Number 1, 1950 (Lavender Mist)*, which appeared in the spring of that year, marks the start of a series of large-format drip-paintings. Together with the three monumental horizontal canvases *Number 32, One: Number 31*, and *Autumn Rhythm: Number 30*, all of which also date from 1950, this is often spoken of as one of Pollock's "classic" works: "They are 'classic' in their thorough use of the pouring application and the uncompromising unity which resulted," as an art critic observed in the late 1970s. Their radical formal innovation of a non-perspective spatiality, which arose as the result of the layering of hurled or dripped streaks of paint, had the potential to seriously destabilize the position of the beholder. Parker Tyler in his review of March 1950 coined the metaphor of "the infinite labyrinth" – albeit one with no way out, and to which, as Tyler noted, not even its creator seemed to possess the key: a complex structure of numerous labyrinths, one on top of the other, crossing each other, each consisting exclusively of dead ends.

The 1950 paintings are still today at the focus of considerations of Pollock's work not least because at the time they were painted they were the objects of increased media interest. When in November/December 1950 *Number 1, 1950 (Lavender Mist)* and other pictures of this period were exhibited at the Betty Parsons Gallery, the prominent society photographer Cecil Beaton used them as the background for a series of fashion photos which were intended to proclaim the "new soft look" in the March 1951 edition of *Vogue*. Above all, however, Pollock himself became a public figure when Rudolph Burckhardt and Hans Namuth photographed and filmed him at work from July to October 1950. Their pictures created the mythic, sexually charged image of Pollock as "Jack the Dripper" and hero of "Action Painting", making it available to a broad public; the films shot by Namuth were already being shown the following year at the Museum of Modern Art.

The year 1950 represents a caesura in Pollock's career in numerous ways. After the end of Namuth's filming in October 1950, Pollock started drinking again after four years' abstinence. To his friend Alfonso Ossorio, he described his psychological situation after the Betty Parsons exhibition as an "all-time low". Even though it is problematic in principle to relate biographical and artistic developments directly as through they were cause and effect, the crisis at the end of 1950 does point to a fundamental change in Pollock's work, which went hand-in-hand with a restriction, for a while, to the colour black, and a return to recognizably figurative elements. A whole variety of factors may have played a role.

Krasner, who had been married to Pollock since 1945, thought that he had reached the end point of his artistic development in 1950, and was not satisfied with thenceforth continually repeating himself. But the change in his working method may well have been a reaction to the media image (and the expectations that this involved) which had been created during this year. In June 1951 Pollock commented on his new black-and-white pictures to Alfonso Ossorio and Ted Dragon, emphasizing among other things his technical virtuosity as a draughtsman. "I've had a period of drawing on canvas in black – with some of my early images coming thru – think the non-objectivists will find them disturbing – and the kids who think it simple to splash a Pollock out."

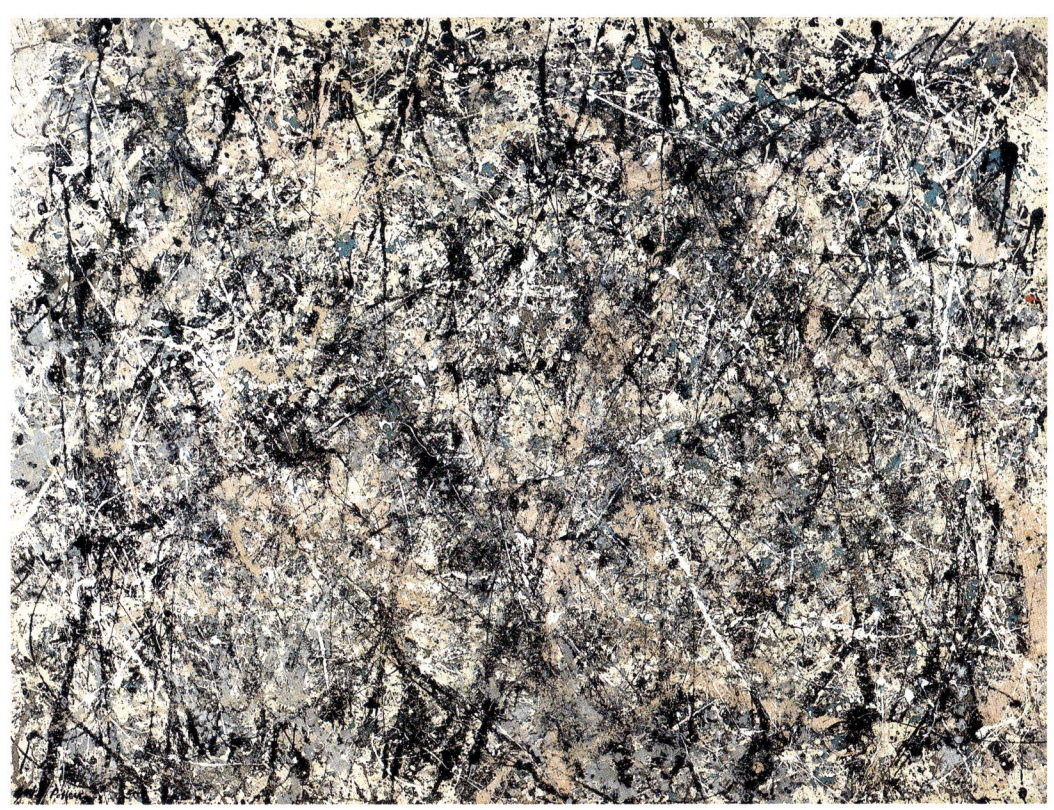

Number 1, 1950 (Lavender Mist), 1950
Oil, gloss-paint, and aluminium paint
on canvas, 221 x 299.7 cm (87 x 118 in.)
Washington, D.C., National Gallery of Art,
Ailsa Mellon Bruce Fund, 1976

Jackson Pollock
Easter and the Totem, 1953

Jackson Pollock's final period, between 1952 and 1954, saw the appearance of few pictures, and these not uniform in style. They convey the impression of a search for possible directions to pursue. In the process, Pollock had recourse to elements of his own work that preceded the "classic" drip-paintings of the years 1947 to 1950, but at the same time integrated influences from other sources, including his favourite European "rivals" Pablo Picasso and Henri Matisse. Thus *Easter and the Totem*, painted conventionally with a brush, recalls in point of composition and colouration two pictures by Matisse, *Bathers by the River* (1916) and *The Moroccans* (1915/16), which were exhibited at the Museum of Modern Art in 1951. Clement Greenberg, who in the late 1940s and early 1950s had doubtless been Pollock's most influential supporter, criticized these late works for what he saw as their self-imposed restriction to technical virtuosity. In 1967 Greenberg described the years between 1952 and 1954 as a phase, in which "he [Pollock] displayed proficiency in an obvious enough way to win admission to any guild of 'good' painters". Pollock himself, by contrast, in a 1956 interview, stressed his identification with a figurative style of painting which he described as psychologically motivated: "I'm very representational some of the time, and a little all of the time. But when you're painting out of your unconscious, figures are bound to emerge. We're all of us influenced by Freud, I guess. I've been a Jungian for a long time… Painting is a state of being… Painting is self-discovery. Every good artist paints what he is."

With the motif of the totem, a pillar cut off by the left-hand edge of the picture, Pollock was using a symbolism which had interested him since the late 1930s after undergoing psychotherapy with Joseph Henderson, a pupil of C. G. Jung. In Jung's opinion, the contents of the collective unconscious, which were forged at the beginning of human history, have been reborn in every individual ever since. Already in the late 1930s Pollock had thematized the motif of birth in an eponymous painting dating from *c.* 1938–41, which makes use of the forms of Native American masks. Several visits to the exhibition "Indian Art of the United States" at the Museum of Modern Art in 1941 reinforced Pollock's interest in Native American culture and its basic features, such as totemism.

With the reference to the Native American totem – an animal, bird, plant or force of nature, which is regarded as the ancestor of a social group and which is believed to have magical powers – and to Easter as the Christian festival of the Resurrection, Pollock seems to be taking up the motif of birth once more as "rebirth". His personal crisis and reduced artistic creativity in the years after 1952, which followed a relapse into alcoholism in November 1950, were in inverse proportion to his rapid rise to international artistic fame. Even Pollock's last exhibition during his lifetime, at the gallery of the successful dealer Sidney Janis in November 1955, was presented as a retrospective by reason of his inability to paint. The financial magazine *Fortune* recommended his works in 1955 as investments with growth potential, a prognosis that was to be fulfilled soon after Pollock's death in August 1956.

Easter and the Totem, 1953
Oil on canvas, 208.6 x 147.3 cm (82¼ x 58 in.)
New York, The Museum of Modern Art,
Gift of Lee Krasner in memory of
Jackson Pollock, 1980

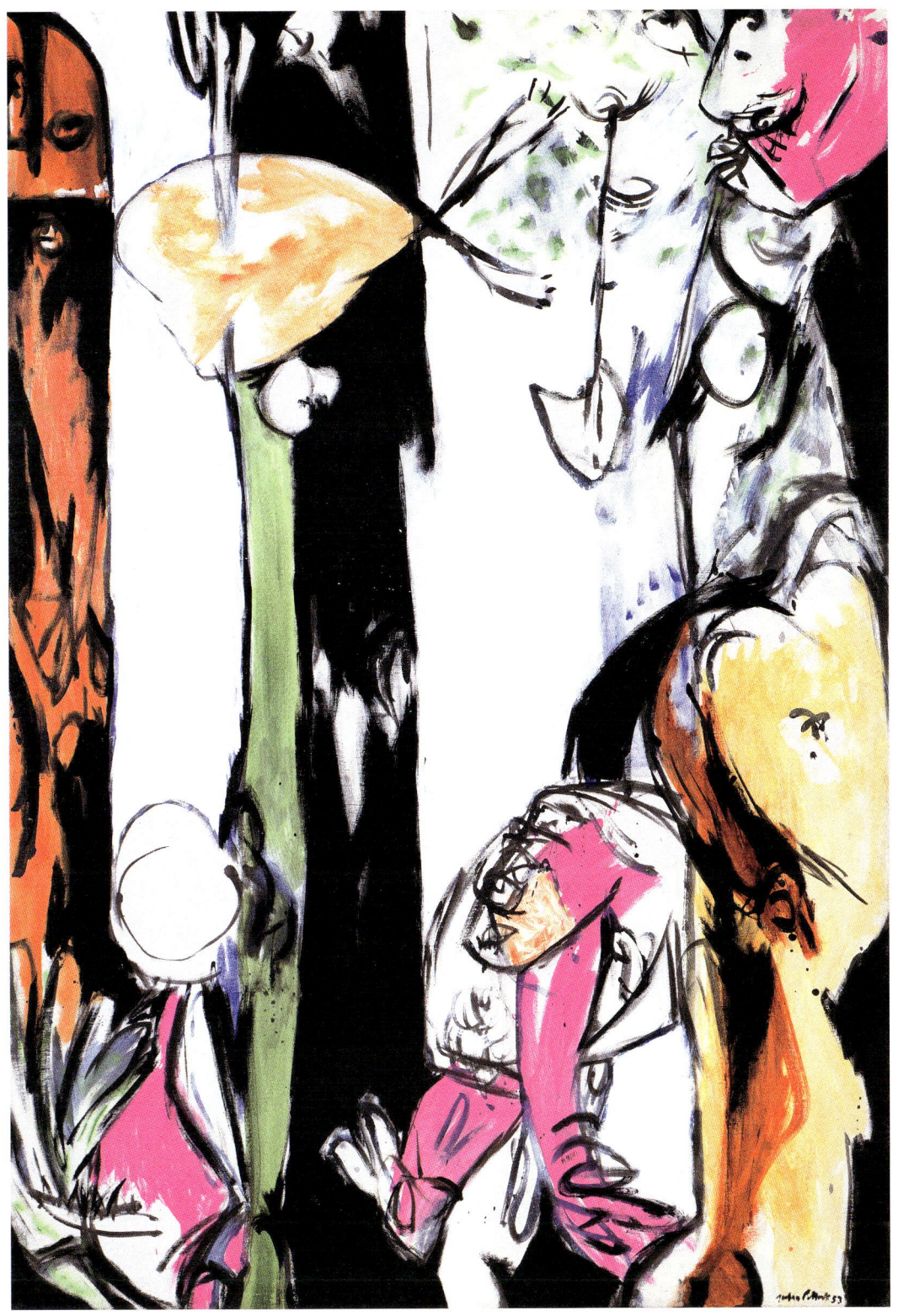

Ad Reinhardt
How to Look at Modern Art in America, 1946

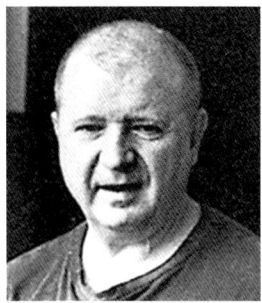

b. 1913 in Buffalo, New York
d. 1967 in New York City

The chronology which Ad Reinhardt compiled for his retrospective in the New York Jewish Museum in 1966 combines personal, political and art-historical information with double-edged observations. It reads like an experimental autobiography: "1913 Born, New York, Christmas Eve, nine months after Armory Show. (Father leaves 'old country' for America in 1907 after serving in Tsar Nicholas' army. Mother leaves Germany in 1909.)" Even this very first entry relating to the year of the artist's birth resembles the opening paragraph of a novel. Reinhardt describes himself in a sense as a "child" of the Armory Show, that legendary major exhibition of modern art which in 1913 first acquainted the American public with post-Impressionist avant-garde art; in addition, by noting that he was born on Christmas Eve, Reinhardt confers on his self-presentation a tongue-in-cheek messianic undertone. And finally the year of his birth also seems to anticipate his artistic programme: "1913 Malevich paints first geometric-abstract painting."

In fact, the composing of texts and the production of pictures are inseparable in Reinhardt's artistic practice. While he saw the strict division of art and life as fundamental to his painting, in his highly allusive "Art Comics" he subjected the intricacies of the post-1945 booming New York art market to mercilessly ironic criticism. Most of these cartoons, which were created between 1945 and 1956, first appeared in the left-liberal, anti-fascist and anti-communist magazine *PM* and later in *ARTnews*; the aesthetic techniques used are free-hand drawings and collages, for which latter Reinhardt often used illustrations from nineteenth-century books and magazines.

The early cartoon *How to Look at Modern Art in America*, dating from 1946, was described by Reinhardt in the accompanying text as a "gallery guide – the art-world in a nutshell". He gave visual metaphorical expression – in the form of a tree in a field of maize – to a spectrum of painting which from Reinhardt's point of view ranged from "pure (abstract) 'paintings'" on the left-hand side to "pure (illustrative) 'pictures'" on the right-hand side. The leaves stand for the individual artists – a few empty pages can be filled and inserted in by readers themselves; the trunk and roots represent their historical precursors. In the accompanying text, Reinhardt writes that the most inaccessible artists are to be found on the left-hand side, the easiest and most familiar on the right; at the same time he criticizes artists like Philip Guston, "who somehow regard themselves as abstract and illustrative at the same time (as though one could be both nowadays)".

Fifteen years later, in the summer of 1961, Reinhardt published an updated version of the cartoon in *ARTnews*, in which many names appeared in new positions. Reinhardt was drawing a picture of decline: the whole left-hand half of the tree, including the branch representing "pure (abstract) 'painting'", has gone, while the most overloaded branch, with the names of artists whose pictures Reinhardt saw as "pure (illustrative)", continues to hang down heavily towards the ground. Reinhardt's laconic solution approach remains unchanged: "The best way to escape from all this is to paint yourself."

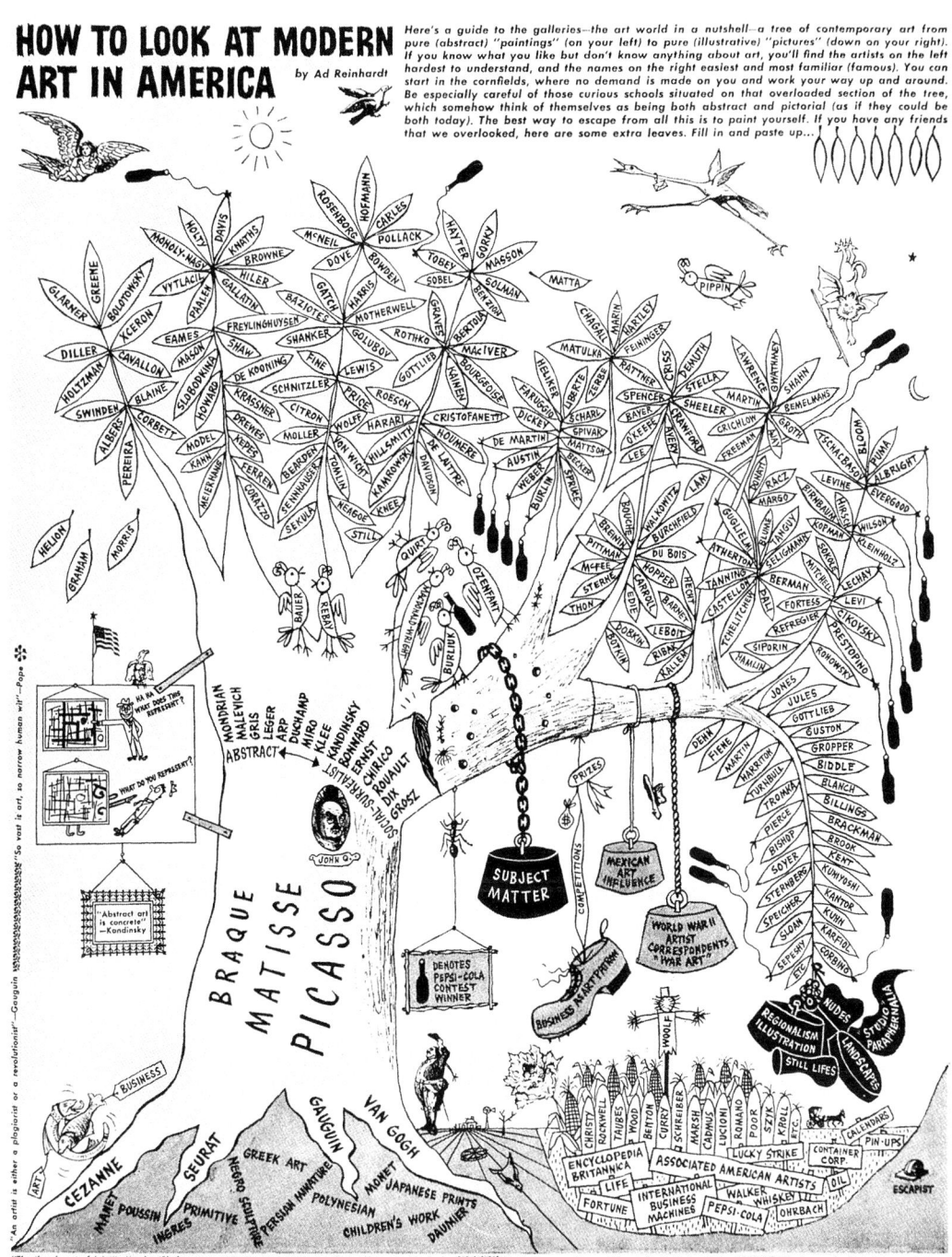

How to Look at Modern Art in America, 1946
For the magazine *PM*, 2 June 1946

Ad Reinhardt
Number 5 (Red Wall), 1952

Unlike the Abstract Expressionist artists Willem de Kooning, Jackson Pollock or Mark Rothko (with whose circle Ad Reinhardt maintained contact, in spite of continually railing against their art) Reinhardt's own work was at no time figurative. From the outset in the 1930s, Reinhardt placed his early post-Cubist collages and his painting strictly in the tradition of abstract art. "It's been said many times in world-art writing that one can find some of painting's meanings by looking not only at what painters do but at what they refuse to do," he observed in 1952. For Reinhardt the ultimate resistance consisted in "not confusing painting with everything that is not painting". References to the world of objects or the world of the artist's imagination were thus, for Reinhardt, programmatically excluded. In the painting of Abstract Expressionism, by contrast, he discerned an internal contradiction, which he summed up in 1966 as follows: "The tension between the abstract painters and the Surrealists was clear in the 1930s. Abstract Expressionism mixed them all up."

From 1950 to 1953, Reinhardt worked on series of red and blue pictures in a spectrum of closely similar colour tones, a principle which already points to the barely differentiated, monotone colour-ation of his extensive series of "black" pictures, which are regarded as Reinhardt's most important achievement. The vertical-format canvas *Number 5 (Red Wall)* is, on the all-over principle, covered with rectangular, in some cases overlapping shapes. The loose arrangement of forms is reminiscent of a collage, a medium in which Reinhardt had taken an intense interest in the 1930s.

It would be inaccurate to describe Reinhardt's red and blue pictures as monochrome, and yet Reinhardt, through his use of minimal tonal differentiation, avoided an "interaction of colour", thus achieving a more complex form of unity. Reinhardt taught in 1952/53 in the art department of Yale University, where one of his colleagues was the German émigré, the former Bauhaus teacher Josef Albers (1888–1976). In 1950, Albers had begun his best-known and most extensive group of works *Homage to the Square*, square pictures in which he investigated the perception of the interaction of three or four square colour fields, in echelon one behind the other. Albers published the results of this investigation in 1963 in the book *Interaction of Color*.

Reinhardt's red and blue pictures of the early 1950s and the transformation that his painting underwent in 1953 are to be seen not least with reference to a confrontation with Albers's project. Thus in his "Chronology", dating from 1966, he writes: "1953 Gives up principles of asymmetry and irregularity in painting", and "1953 Paints last paintings in bright colours." While the first change could be seen as a tribute to Albers's *Homage to the Square* (where the pictures are symmetrical and regular), the second decision, namely the renunciation of bright colours, represents a turning-away from Albers's painterly investigations of colour. When the red and blue paintings were publicly exhibited, critics noticed such characteristics as their decorative quality and "beauty", characteristics that Reinhardt sought to remove in his "black" paintings.

Number 5 (Red Wall), 1952
Oil on canvas, 203.2 x 106.7 cm (80 x 42 in.)
Washington, D.C., Corcoran Gallery of Art,
Gift of Gilbert H. Kinney

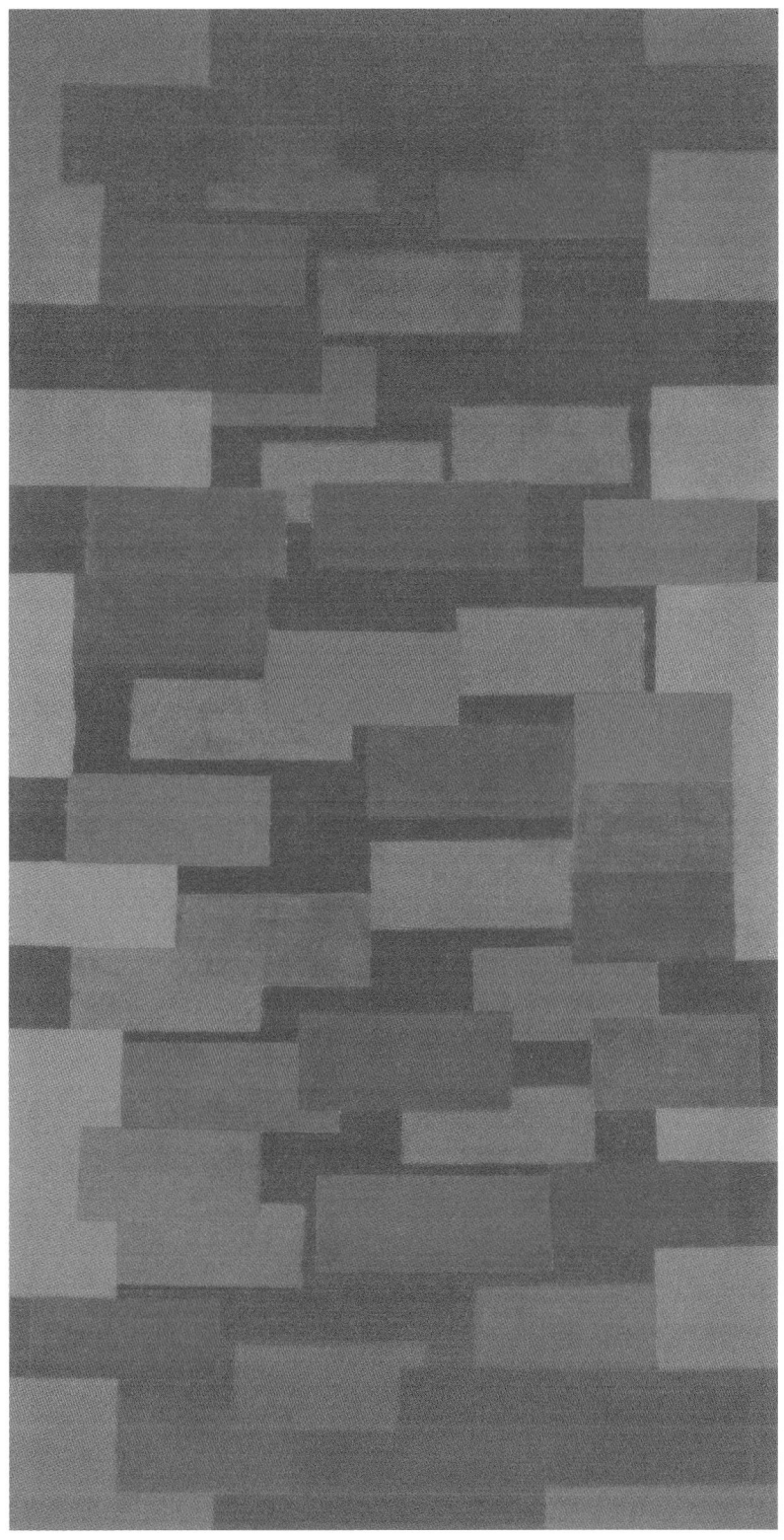

Ad Reinhardt
Abstract Painting No. 34, 1964

From 1954, Ad Reinhardt definitively reduced the colouration of his geometric abstractions to shades of black. In 1960 he finally arrived at a pictorial design to which he was to devote himself exclusively until his death in 1967: square canvases measuring sixty by sixty inches (152.4 cm), whose surface is divided into nine equal squares – a composition, which Reinhardt regarded as "no composition". Reinhardt related the format to the approximate body measurements of a beholder standing in front of the canvas with outstretched arms.

The lightless, contrastless colouration of the fields is minimally differentiated by additions of green, blue and brown; the matt quality of the paint excludes any reflection of the surroundings in the surface of the picture. *Abstract Painting No. 34* is one of the paintings to be based on a grid of differently coloured squares, divided by a horizontal green stripe. The oil-paint was applied manually with a brush in such a way that no brushstrokes can be discerned. If pictures were damaged at exhibitions, Reinhardt overpainted them, with the result that they can no longer be unambiguously dated.

When the New York Museum of Modern Art acquired one of the "black paintings" in 1963, Reinhardt received from the museum a questionnaire with the request to give his views on the importance of this group of works. Reinhardt defined this in a detailed statement as "the most extreme, ultimate, climactic reaction to and negation of" a tradition of Abstract art, which embraces Cubism and the work of Piet Mondrian, Kasimir Malevich, Josef Albers and Burgoyne Diller. Through his insistence on what his painting was not, Reinhardt tried to get the partly contradictory interpretations of his pictures as "neo-Classical", "Romantic", "purist", "avant-garde", "religious" and so on to run into the sand.

While Reinhardt declared that he was leading an artistic tradition to its climax through negation, at the same time with his "black paintings" he was exerting pioneering influence on a younger generation of artists and was assigned in this connection the controversial role of a "forerunner" of Minimal Art and Concept Art. Thus the philosopher of art Richard Wollheim, for example, in his 1965 essay "Minimal Art" asserted that in Reinhardt's works, the art content was minimal, as the works in question were to a very high degree undifferentiated. In 1969 Joseph Kosuth, in his essay "Art After Philosophy", which is regarded as the manifesto of an analytical tendency within Concept Art, quoted the first lines of Reinhardt's 1962 text "Art as Art": "The one thing to say about art is that it is one thing. Art is art-as-art and everything else is everything else. Art-as-art is nothing but art. Art is not what is not art."

Kosuth's use of the short quote taken out of context, which is followed by quotes from other artists and theoreticians, is nothing less than a productive "mistaken interpretation" of Reinhardt's utterances: unlike Kosuth, he was concerned solely with a negative definition of Abstract painting. "Art can be corrected, but, alas, the public cannot." This bon mot was attributed by the critic and artist Elaine de Kooning in a 1957 article for *ARTnews* to a fictitious artist named Adolf M. Pure, doubtless Ad Reinhardt's alter ego.

Abstract Painting No. 34, 1964
Oil on canvas, 153 x 152.6 cm (60¼ x 60 in.)
Washington, D.C., National Gallery of Art,
Gift of Mr. and Mrs. Burton Tremaine

Mark Rothko
Untitled, 1948

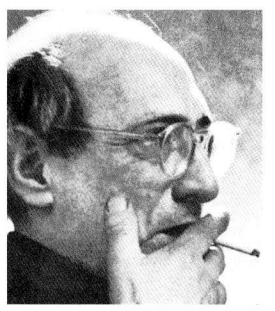

b. 1903 in Dvinsk, Russian
Empire (now Daugavpils, Latvia)
d. 1970 in New York City

"One might say that Rothko and his friends constituted the theological sector of Abstract Expressionism," observed Harold Rosenberg two years after Rothko's death in 1970. "Together with Still, Newman, Reinhardt, Gottlieb (the names suddenly translate themselves into characters of a miracle play), Rothko sought to arrive at an ultimate sign."

Indeed, Mark Rothko had given expression to his religious attitude in numerous articles, for example in a statement in 1945 on the occasion of his participation in the group exhibition "A Painting Prophecy", he stressed his belief that alongside everyday reality there existed both a world generated in human consciousness as well as one created by God outside human consciousness.

Marcus Rothkowitz, who abbreviated his name to Mark Rothko in 1940, emigrated with his family to the USA in 1913 on account of the political and economic pressure being applied to Russian Jews. He lived in America thereafter, moving in 1923 from Portland, Oregon, to New York, where he enrolled at art college. In the 1920s and 1930s, he worked in a figurative style, which sometimes recalls the Italian *Pittura metafisica*: among his 1930s' cityscapes there are numerous street and subway scenes reflecting the isolation of big-city existence. In the early 1940s, Rothko, influenced by Surrealism, largely painted mythological motifs.

In about 1946 he began to put this style behind him and to develop an abstract formal language of his own from colour fields which come across as partly transparent or floating in an atmospheric pictorial space, such as *Untitled*, dating from 1948. The large-format works of the period 1946 to 1949, which Rothko saw as a transition to his later working technique, are often described as "multiforms", a term not coined by Rothko himself. The artist saw his pictures as the living "counterpart" of the beholder, which could be hurt by the latter's ignorance. Thus in 1947 he wrote in "The Romantics Were Prompted": "On shapes: They are unique elements in a unique situation. They are organisms with volition and a passion for self-assertion. They move with internal freedom, and without need to conform with or to violate what is probable in the familiar world. They have no direct association with any particular visible experience, but in them one recognizes the principle and passion of organisms."

The art historian Eliza E. Rathbone emphasized, tellingly, that Rothko's work possessed "an aspect of self-portraiture", which makes his pronounced desire to exercise as much control as possible over the reception of his pictures all the more plausible. Thus in March 1948, in a letter to his long-standing dealer Betty Parsons, he wrote that his pictures should not be accessible to every visitor, but only to those who understood something of their value. In particular, no one was to be allowed to write about them. These were demands that, with Rothko's increasing success from the mid-1950s, due not least to his new dealer Sidney Janis, were hardly enforceable.

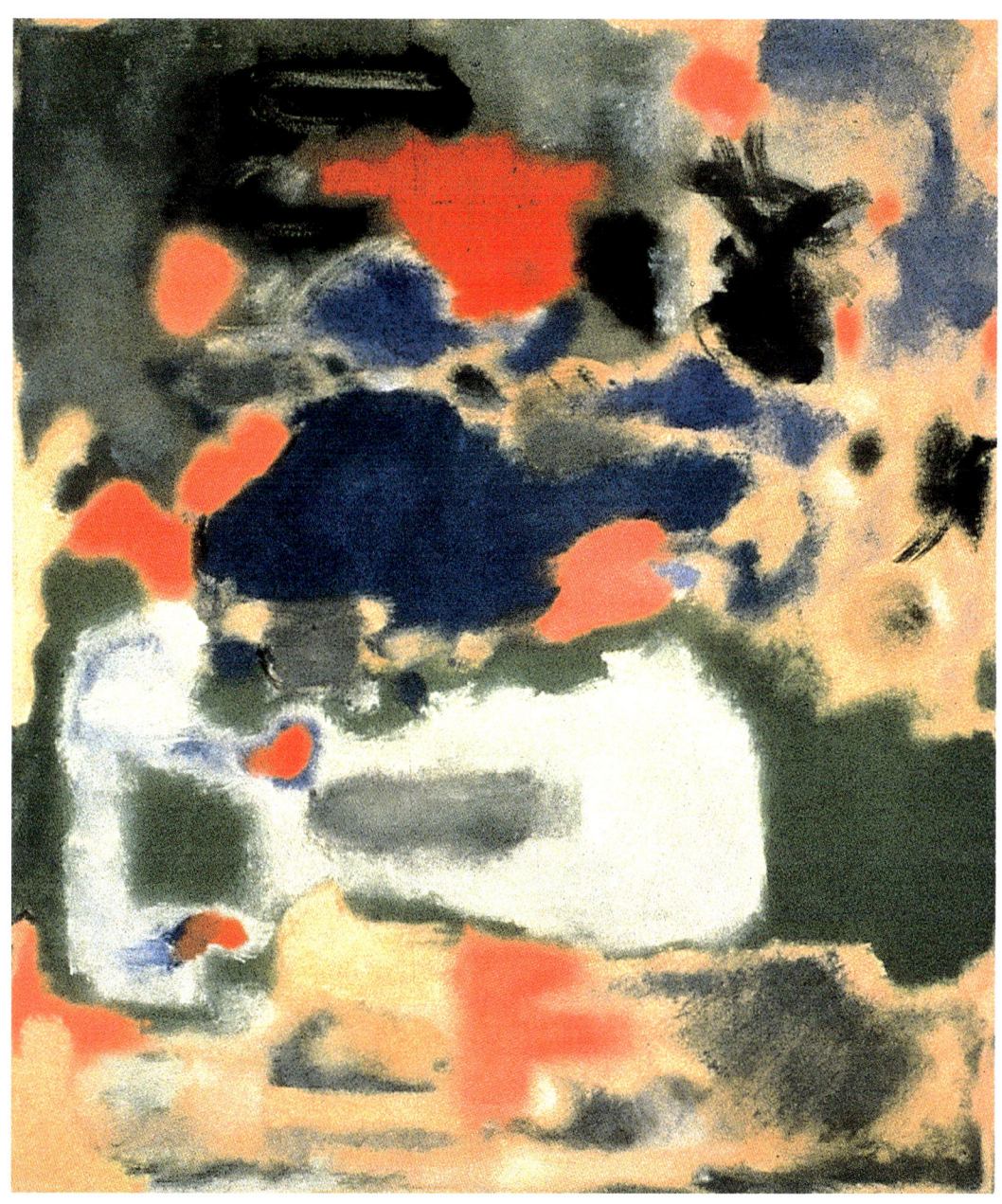

Untitled, 1948
From the *Multiforms* series, 1946–49
Oil on canvas, 127.6 x 109.9 cm (50¼ x 43¼ in.)
Collection Kate Rothko-Prizel

Mark Rothko
Ochre and Red on Red, 1954

In 1949, after the transitional phase of the so-called "multiforms", Mark Rothko settled down to his characteristic, horizontal arrangement of colour-fields on a monochrome background, which he retained with a few variations until the end of his painting career. His decision to work with large formats, already apparent in earlier phases of his work, was explained by Rothko in 1951 on the occasion of a symposium on the potential of a link-up between architecture, painting and sculpture: "I paint very large pictures. I realize that historically the function of painting large pictures is painting something very grandiose and pompous. The reason I paint them, however – I think it applies to other painters I know – is precisely because I want to be very intimate and human. To paint a small picture is to place yourself outside your experience, to look upon an experience as a stereopticon view or with a reducing glass. However you paint the larger picture, you are in it. It isn't something you command."

Subsequently Rothko tried to determine as far as possible for himself how his pictures were to be presented: the selection, the hang, the illumination. Thus Philip Guston recalled going to an exhibition of Rothko's work at the Sidney Janis Gallery, in which Rothko had switched off half the lamps in order to create a dim light: "I'm positive that Mark sneaked up there every day and turned the lights down – without ever complaining or explaining."

Rothko's sensitivity in the matter of how his works were to be treated required a relationship of close trust to his collectors and curators, who had to be ready to accept the unmistakable conditions laid down by the artist. Thus he succeeded, on the occasion of the "Fifteen Americans" exhibition at the Museum of Modern Art in 1952, which was curated by Dorothy Miller, in being assigned a room of his own in which to exhibit nine pictures. In numerous other cases, he refused to take part in group exhibitions or to submit proposals to purchasing committees if he regarded the expected presentation as inappropriate.

Against this background the collaboration between Rothko and the Washington collectors Marjorie and Duncan Phillips has a model character. The collectors, who had acquired two of his works as early as 1957, had their home enlarged in 1960 by the addition of a museum wing. Here, one room was devoted to three large-format pictures by Rothko, the first permanently installed Rothko room in collection open to the public. One of these pictures was *Ochre and Red on Red*. Rothko viewed it a year later, corrected the lighting conditions, and asked for the inclusion of a bench for visitors to sit on. In 1966, the museum was rebuilt, which involved a rehang of the Rothko collection, which has since comprised four pictures.

As early as 1952, Rothko, in a letter to the co-director of the New Yorker Whitney Museum, had explained his feeling of responsibility for "the life my pictures will lead out in the world"; from the late 1950s he was to place the space-centred working method already hinted at in the permanent hang of the Phillips Collection, at the focus of his artistic activity.

Ochre and Red on Red, 1954
Oil on canvas, 235.5 x 162 cm (92¾ x 63¾ in.)
Washington, D.C., The Phillips Collection

Mark Rothko
Rothko Chapel, 1965/66

From the late 1950s, Mark Rothko's struggle for "the life my pictures will lead out in the world" took a new course. By the time of his death in 1970, Rothko had developed three (commissioned) room-related groups of works. For his one-man show at the Sidney Janis Gallery in 1955 he had already arranged for the formats of his pictures so that in height they matched that of the wall, and in breadth partly blocked the doorways. The close relationship between the dimension of the picture and the pictorial design of the walls or of whole rooms can be traced right back to Rothko's early work. In 1932 he painted a small panel entitled *Interior*, which depicts a view of a two-storey wall, divided into six colour-fields; in 1938 and 1940 Rothko designed murals for a post office in Rochelle, New York, and for the Social Security Building in Washington, D.C., which however were never executed.

In June 1958 Rothko was commissioned to execute murals for the Four Seasons Restaurant in New York's Seagram Building, designed by the architects Philip Johnson and Mies van der Rohe. In his studio, Rothko had a wooden structure built, which corresponded to the spatial situation in the restaurant, and developed a type of picture that was new for him: approximately square or horizontal rectangular canvases in dark red and brown tones. Standing out against monochrome backgrounds are frames with single or double vertical openings, which, according to Rothko, are supposed to be reminiscent of closed doors or windows; as one exemplar, he named the blind windows in Michelangelo's Biblioteca Laurenziana in Florence. In the summer of 1959, Rothko interrupted work on the project to undertake a journey to Europe; in the ancient murals of Pompeii he discovered a close relationship with his own art. After his return, he visited the Four Seasons Restaurant in 1960 and because he thought the ambience would reduce his art to mere decoration, saw himself constrained to turn down the commission; the pictures already executed were later exhibited in different arrangements and contexts.

The only time Rothko himself installed pictures in a particular room was when he presented the *Harvard Murals* in 1962/63 to the oldest university in the United States, which he conceived for the Dining Hall at the Holyoke Center. The group consists of a triptych and two single pictures with uniform deep-red backgrounds. Rothko explained to the President of Harvard, Nathan Pusey, that the triptych referred to the Passion of Christ on Good Friday, while the two lighter pictures referred to Easter and the Resurrection. In this case too, Rothko ultimately found the circumstance that the Dining Hall was furnished to be a disturbing factor. In addition, there was no satisfactory way of regulating the sunlight, which over the years led to the light-sensitive pigments fading, so that in 1979 the pictures were removed.

As early as 1957 Rothko had begun increasingly to work with darker colours; a year later, he emphasized that "a clear preoccupation with death" was one of the "ingredients" of his painting. A dark palette also characterizes Rothko's last major group of works, which was commissioned by the collectors Dominique and John de Menil: the interdenominational *Rothko Chapel*, which was built according to his ideas and belongs to Rice University in Houston, Texas. The pictures are his first to evince sharp outlines for the colour fields; these, and the similarly new monochrome panels enhance the aesthetic austerity of the design. The chapel was consecrated posthumously in 1971 after Rothko's suicide.

Rothko Chapel, 1965/66
3 of 14 paintings (including 3 triptychs), west, north-west and north wall paintings, oil on canvas
Houston, The Menil Collection

David Smith
Hudson River Landscape, 1951

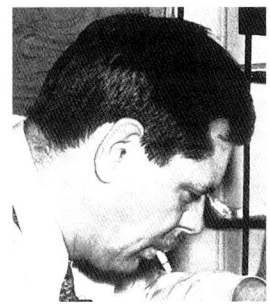

b. 1906 in Decatur, Indiana
d. 1965 in Bennington, Vermont

In Abstract Expressionism, sculpture played a subordinate role. Or, as Ad Reinhardt put it in 1957: "Sculpture is no problem. Nobody likes sculpture." The most prominent exponent of this medium in the context of the New York School is without a doubt David Smith, and Reinhardt's mordant observation is in tune with the fact that from the 1930s to the 1950s, Smith was able to sell very few works. It took a grant from the Guggenheim Foundation in the early 1950s to improve his situation. Smith gathered his first experiences in metalworking outside the field of art: as a student in 1925, he worked as a welder in a Studebaker car factory in South Bend, Indiana. In 1926 he moved to New York, where he studied painting and drawing at the Art Students League from 1927 to 1932. He obtained his knowledge of European avant-garde sculpture primarily from his acquaintanceship with the Russian exile John Graham, who played an important role among the Abstract Expressionists as a conduit of information concerning European art.

Inspired by illustrations of the wrought-metal sculptures of Pablo Picasso and Julio González in the French magazine *Cahiers d'Art*, Smith created his first sculpture of welded metal in 1933. A welding shop in Brooklyn placed rooms, appliances, materials and technical expertise at Smith's disposal for the production of his sculptures. When Smith moved in 1940 to the neighbourhood of Bolton Landing, New York, a remote township in the Adirondack Mountains, and there built a workshop to his own design, he named it "Terminal Iron Works" after the factory in New York. Smith described his workplace as "an industrial factory type… because the change in my sculpture required a factory more than an 'atelier'".

On his death in a car accident, Smith left a comprehensive oeuvre comprising more than 700 sculptures; his productivity, which increased in the final decades of his life, is regarded as partly due to strict organization of the production process and quasi-industrial form of manufacture. He often described his early employment in the car and railway industry as an important influence, an attitude which was also to become typical of a succeeding generation of American sculptors in the context of Minimal Art.

The process by which *Hudson River Landscape* was created was described by Smith in 1951 as follows: the design "started from drawings made on a train between Albany and Poughkeepsie… On this basis I started a drawing for a sculpture. As I began I shook a quart bottle of India ink, it flew over my hand, it looked like my landscape. I placed my hand on paper and from the image this left I travelled with the landscape to other landscapes. Is my work… the Hudson River, or is it the travel, the vision, the ink spot, or does it matter?"

A landscape is actually a rather unusual subject for a sculptor. Early beholders were surprised by the *Hudson River Landscape* with its, as Rosalind E. Krauss recalls, "insubstantiality of a paper cut-out". And indeed, Smith's innovative work can also be described as a calligraphic drawing in three dimensions, bringing together various different elements – hints of bridges, steps, waves and a bird's skeleton   which do not allow the beholder countless views of equal status, but are best seen from the front.

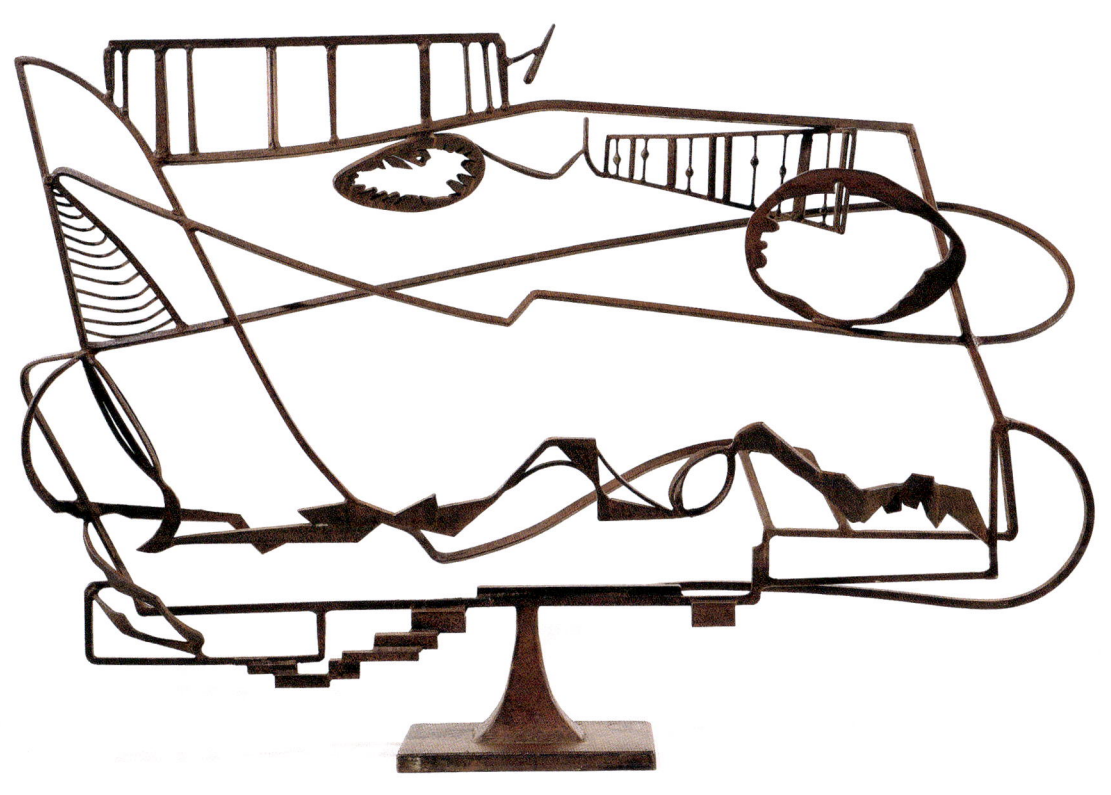

Hudson River Landscape, 1951
Carbon steel and stainless steel,
123.8 x 183.2 x 44 cm (48¾ x 72¼ x 17¼ in.)
New York, Whitney Museum of American Art

Theodoros Stamos
documenta II, 1959

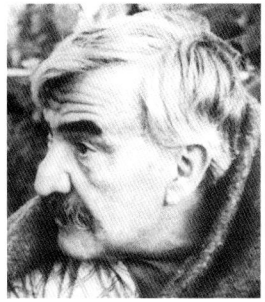

b. 1922 in New York City
d. 1997 in Ioannina, Greece

On what must be the most famous group photograph of the Abstract Expressionists, taken by Nina Leen and published in January 1951 in *Life* magazine, Theodoros Stamos can be seen sitting as the youngest protagonist among the so-called "Irascibles" in the front row on the left. They were protesting against a planned survey exhibition of American painting at the Metropolitan Museum, which they regarded as excluding "advanced art".

The son of Greek immigrants, Stamos had at first studied sculpture at the American Artists School, but in 1939, self-taught, had begun to devote himself entirely to painting. His first solo exhibition took place in 1943 at the Wakefield Gallery, which at the time was run by Betty Parsons, and brought him into contact with artists such as Adolph Gottlieb and Barnett Newman, in whose circle his work was to develop in the succeeding years. Thus Stamos, together with Hans Hofmann, Ad Reinhardt, Mark Rothko and Clyfford Still, took part in the 1947 group exhibition "The Ideographic Picture", which Newman curated for the Betty Parsons Gallery. "Spontaneous, and emerging from several points," declared Newman in his introductory text to the exhibition, "there has arisen during the war years a new force in American painting that is the modern counterpart of the primitive art impulse." This "modern counterpart of the primitive art impulse" manifested itself during the 1940s not least through the choice of mythological motifs, such as we see in Stamos's 1947 picture *Ancestral Worship*.

The 1959 painting *documenta II* is part of Stamos's extensive *Field* series (1954–61). The term "field" refers to one of the two main currents within Abstract Expressionism, Action Painting and Color Field Painting; the latter was boosted in particular by Clement Greenberg's influential 1955 essay "'American-Type' Painting". The large format *documenta II* is characterized by a simplified, almost geometric composition, which divides the surface of the picture vertically into two monochrome halves. The swirling atmospherically translucent application of paint is reminiscent of elements such as fire and air. Stamos himself emphasized in 1958: "There is a strong and conscious relationship between my work and nature, which finally manifests itself in an impersonal expression."

Unusually, Stamos named his picture after the important documenta II exhibition of international contemporary art held in the German city of Kassel in 1959, at which he was represented. The year before he had taken part in the international touring exhibition "The New American Painting" (1958/59), which had been organized by the Museum of Modern Art in order to demonstrate the superiority of American painting over its contemporary European rivals. Also in 1959, Mark Tobey became the first 20th-century American painter to win the Painting Prize at the Venice Biennale.

At the second documenta, the International Program of the Museum of Modern Art presented numerous exponents of Abstract Expressionism, who attracted lively – and overwhelmingly positive – attention. There were some critical voices, however, who noted that the majority of the exhibits had only been produced immediately before (and on the occasion of) the influential major international exhibition, and saw this as evidence of increasing entanglement between public art institutions and the art market.

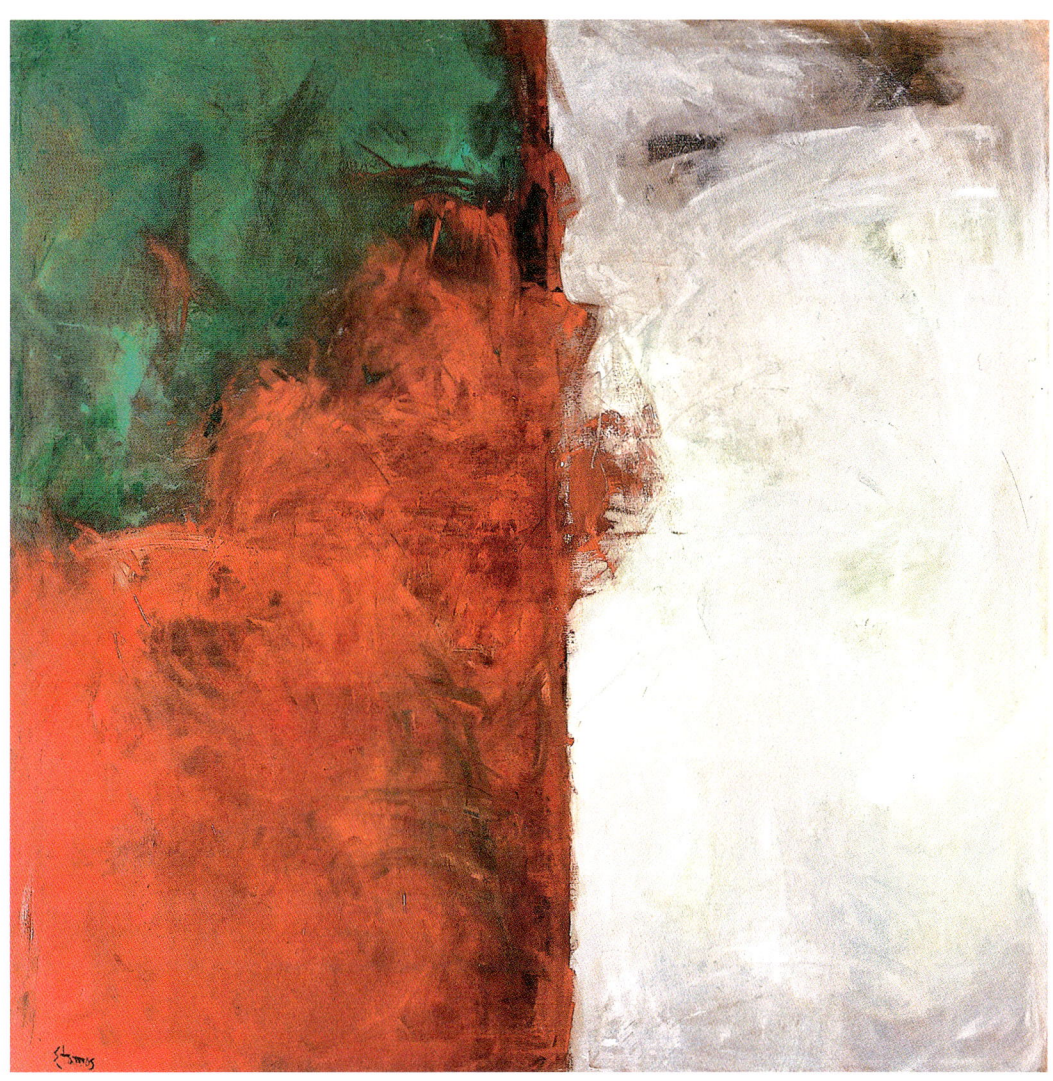

documenta II, 1959
Oil and acrylic on cotton,
174 x 176.3 cm (68½ x 69½ in.)
Private collection

Clyfford Still
1949-H, 1949

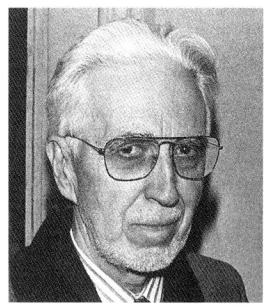

b. 1904 in Grandin,
North Dakota
d. 1980 in Baltimore, Maryland

In 1966 Ethel Moore wrote in the biographical notes for the catalogue of an exhibition by Clyfford Still: "When he was twenty he made the first trip to New York, arriving at the Metropolitan Museum of Art before the doors opened. He was, however, disappointed in what he saw. He found something missing, some statement that he felt profoundly and did not find in the work of the European masters. Having decided that he should pursue a more formal art education, he enrolled in a class at the Art Students League but found that disappointing also, and left after 45 minutes." Still remained in the city – this was in 1924 – for a few more weeks, in order to visit more museums and galleries, but the first impression seemed only to be confirmed. "Disillusioned, he shortened his stay in New York and returned West."

These few sentences sketch out the picture of the eccentric American artist in an almost idealizing fashion. His "disillusionment" with and rejection of European art, which he saw as "decadent", the fact of his being self-taught, his distancing himself from the big city – New York – and its "corrupt" art scene, and finally his departure and return to the American West. In 1945, twenty years after his early "disappointment", Still returned however to New York and was living there – with interruptions – during the period of the "triumph of American painting", as Irving Sandler put it. In the mid-1950s, while he refused to take part in exhibitions in New York, this gesture of withdrawal was rewarded by the public, who interpreted it as a sign of his particular artistic authenticity, and it certainly did nothing to diminish his renown. In 1961 Still finally retired to the rural isolation of Maryland.

During the final years of the war, Still had concerned himself, like many of his fellow artists, with myth-laden motifs, but in 1946/47 he developed his characteristic form of colour-field abstraction, with mostly vertically oriented forms and abrupt, irregular contours, as seen in *1949-H*. The oil paint, applied to the canvas with a spatula, comes across as cracked and intentionally "uncultivated". Within the colour zones there is no shading, and between them there are no figure-to-ground relationships. Still's all-over compositions come across as details of a larger field extending beyond the borders of the picture, which in turn contributes to the unfinished appearance of the picture.

Interpreters of Still's pictures have seen in them time and again references to the wide-open landscape of North Dakota where he was brought up, or to the American West Coast, where he lived and taught in the late 1940s. This brings the aesthetic concept of the "sublime" into play, which was also central for other artists such as Barnett Newman and Mark Rothko: the confrontation of the subject with the idea of infinite size or infinite power in the face of an overwhelming experience (of nature). Still himself promoted this view of things, for example when he wrote in 1963: "The sublime? A paramount consideration in my studies and work from my earliest student days. In essence it is most elusive of capture or definition – only surely found least in the lives and works of those who babble of it the most."

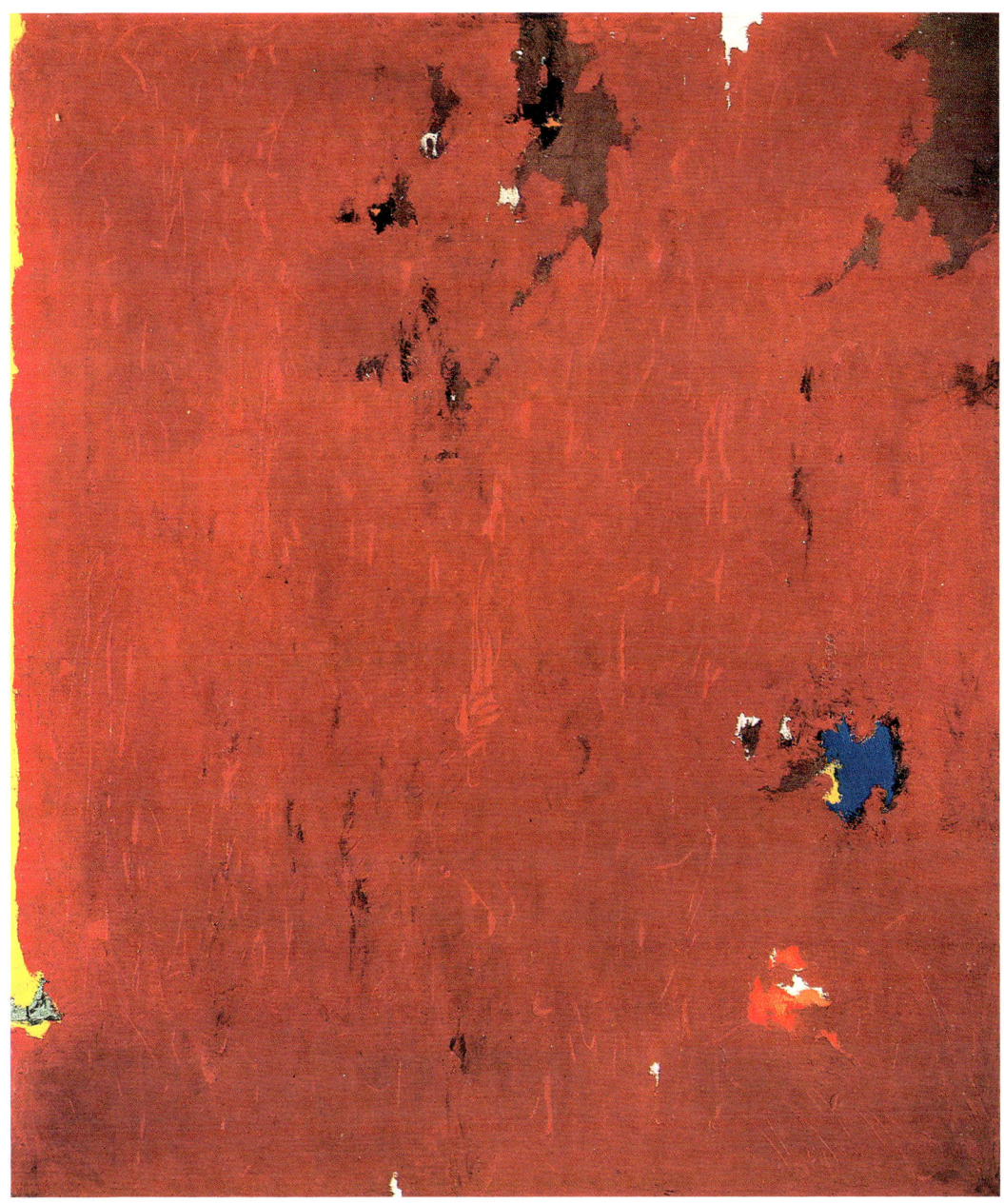

1949-H, 1949
Oil on canvas, 210.2 x 180.7 cm (82¾ x 71¼ in.)
Buffalo, Albright-Knox Art Gallery,
Gift of the artist, 1964

Mark Tobey
Universal City, 1951

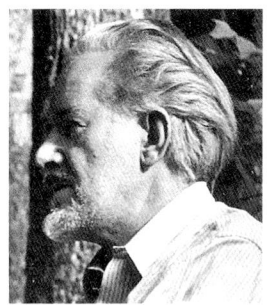

b. 1890 in Centerville, Wisconsin
d. 1976 in Basel, Switzerland

"It may be a chronological fact," declared Clement Greenberg in his much-quoted 1955 essay "'American-Type' Painting", "that Mark Tobey was the first to make, and succeed with, easel pictures whose design was 'all-over' – that is, filled from edge to edge with evenly spaced motifs that repeated themselves uniformly like the elements in a wallpaper pattern, and therefore seemed capable of repeating the picture beyond its frame to infinity. Tobey first showed his 'white writings' in New York in 1944, but Pollock had not seen them when he did his own first 'all-over' pictures in the late summer of 1946, in dabs and ribbons of thick paint that were to change at the end of the year into liquid spatters and trickles." As so often in Greenberg's writings, the mention of a particular artist – here Mark Tobey – serves as a foil against which he can all the more clearly bring out the originality of his favourite Jackson Pollock. Since then, the comparison between Pollock's and Tobey's all-over structures – and the question of their mutual influence – has returned time and again in debates on the New York School, for example when John Canaday, the art critic of *The New York Times*, mentioned the two very different artists in one breath in 1960: "Mark Tobey and Jackson Pollock (a philosopher and an athlete)."

Although the work of Tobey is often discussed using art-historical labels such as Abstract Expressionism, it is impossible to pin down to simple categories. Tobey, born in 1890, was markedly older than the inner circle of the New York School. He moved to the city in 1911, and exhibited there for the first time in 1917. In 1918 he took a decision which was to have a decisive influence on his later work, namely to join the Baha'i Faith, whose principles and influences on his work he described in 1934: "The root of all religions, from the Baha'i point of view, is based on the theory that man will gradually come to understand the unity of the world and the oneness of mankind. It teaches that all the prophets are one – that science and religion are the two great powers which must be balanced if man is to become mature. I feel my work has been influenced by these beliefs. I've tried to decentralize and interpenetrate so that all parts of a painting are of related value."

During numerous stays abroad, including Japan and the Middle East, Tobey also took an interest in oriental calligraphy. In 1935, a year after he had spent a month in a Zen monastery near Kyoto, he started on his *White Writing* series: calligraphic signs painted on top of each other in white or pale colours on an abstract colour-field; the signs consist of countless enmeshed brushstrokes. At first, as in *Broadway* (1935), Tobey still based his work on specific places, but later he developed the motif of the city into symbolically abstract depictions of the *Universal City* in the spirit of Baha'i.

It was with a pronounced critical undertone that Greenberg, in his 1947 article "The Present Prospects of American Painting and Sculpture", said of Tobey that he had "turned out so narrow as to cease even to be interesting. Sensibility confined, intensified, and repeated […]": aesthetic qualities which in the 1960s were to enjoy a decisive re-evaluation and which have thus also contributed indirectly to Tobey's increasing appreciation since.

Universal City, 1951
Watercolour on paper, mounted on hardboard, 95.3 x 63.5 cm (37½ x 25 in.)
Seattle Art Museum, Gift of Mr. and Mrs. Dan Johnson

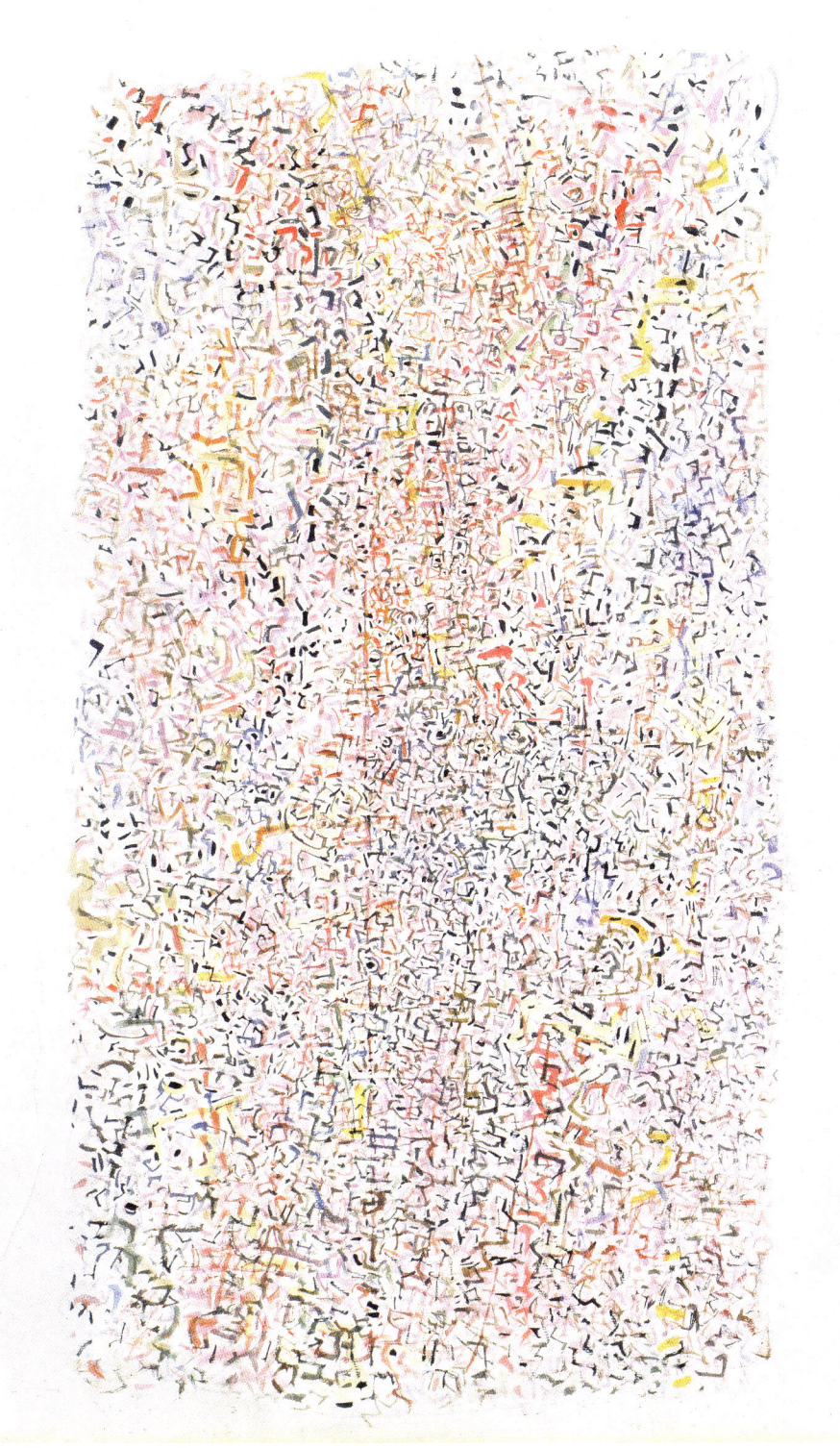

Bradley Walker Tomlin
All Souls' Night, No. 2, 1949

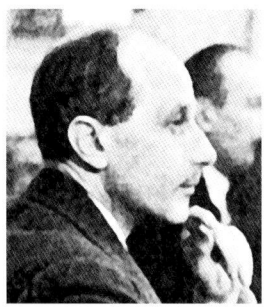

b. 1899 in Syracuse, New York
d. 1953 in New York City

The critic John Ashbery once described Bradley Walker Tomlin as "the gentleman Abstract Expressionist" – a double-edged compliment, which did its subject no favours. In a context that defined masculinity rather in terms of extroversion, aggressiveness and competitiveness, Tomlin found himself in the role of outsider.

Like many of his generation in the New York School, Tomlin began with figurative work before shifting to abstraction in 1946. He then became a regular exhibitor at the Betty Parsons Gallery, a key venue for Abstract Expressionism. In the fall of 1949, Tomlin took part in the group exhibition entitled "The Intrasubjectives", by which the Samuel Kootz Gallery hoped to establish a kind of canon of Abstract Expressionism. In addition to a painting by Tomlin, works by William Baziotes, Willem de Kooning, Arshile Gorky, Adolph Gottlieb, Hans Hofmann, Robert Motherwell, Jackson Pollock, Ad Reinhardt, Mark Rothko and Mark Tobey were displayed.

Kootz titled the show "The Intrasubjectives" to reflect the artists' focus on inner exploration over external reality. Tomlin's lyrical *All Souls' Night, No. 2* fits this idea, its title evoking the Christian festival on 2 November and the belief that unredeemed souls return from Purgatory that night.

Tomlin, like many of his fellow artists, was interested in oriental calligraphy and in Surrealist "écriture automatique" as a means of access to the unconscious; unlike Pollock's contemporary drip-paintings or Franz Kline's vehement, beam-like brushstrokes, Tomlin's application of paint comes across, however, as more calculated and recalls the work of Paul Klee.

The voices of the prominent authors who wrote about his work are conspicuously of one mind: thus Thomas B. Hess, on the occasion of Tomlin's first solo exhibition at the Betty Parsons Gallery in 1950: "Here and there are lapses of taste – or, more serious, too great an emphasis on 'good taste'." Philip Guston, who was friends with Tomlin, noted in respect of the latter's posthumous retrospective in 1957, that Tomlin's "temperament insisted on the impossible pleasure of controlling and being free at the same moment". And Dore Ashton commented the same year on his version of the all-over, that by the late 1940s was part of the common artistic stock-in-trade of the New York School: "He used it intelligently, but too intelligently."

Tomlin, like many of his fellow artists, attempted to intervene in the debate about his work. Thus in reaction to a review of his last solo exhibition at the Betty Parsons Gallery in 1953, a review in which he regarded himself as having been inappropriately interpreted, he wrote to the magazine *ARTnews*: "Frankly, at times, I think the art critics have something to do with it… that they stymie things – what with all these different promotions about who is the great American painter, how can they ever get results?"

The fact that Tomlin is one of those Abstract Expressionist artists whose work was less highly regarded in their lifetimes, and is threatened today with oblivion, can also be understood as an effect of art criticism, a fact that Tomlin himself was only too well aware of. The crucial influence of critics on artistic careers was more than clear in the case of Pollock and Clement Greenberg or de Kooning and Harold Rosenberg.

All Souls' Night, **No. 2**, 1949
Oil on canvas, 121.9 x 81.3 cm (48 x 32 in.)
Private collection

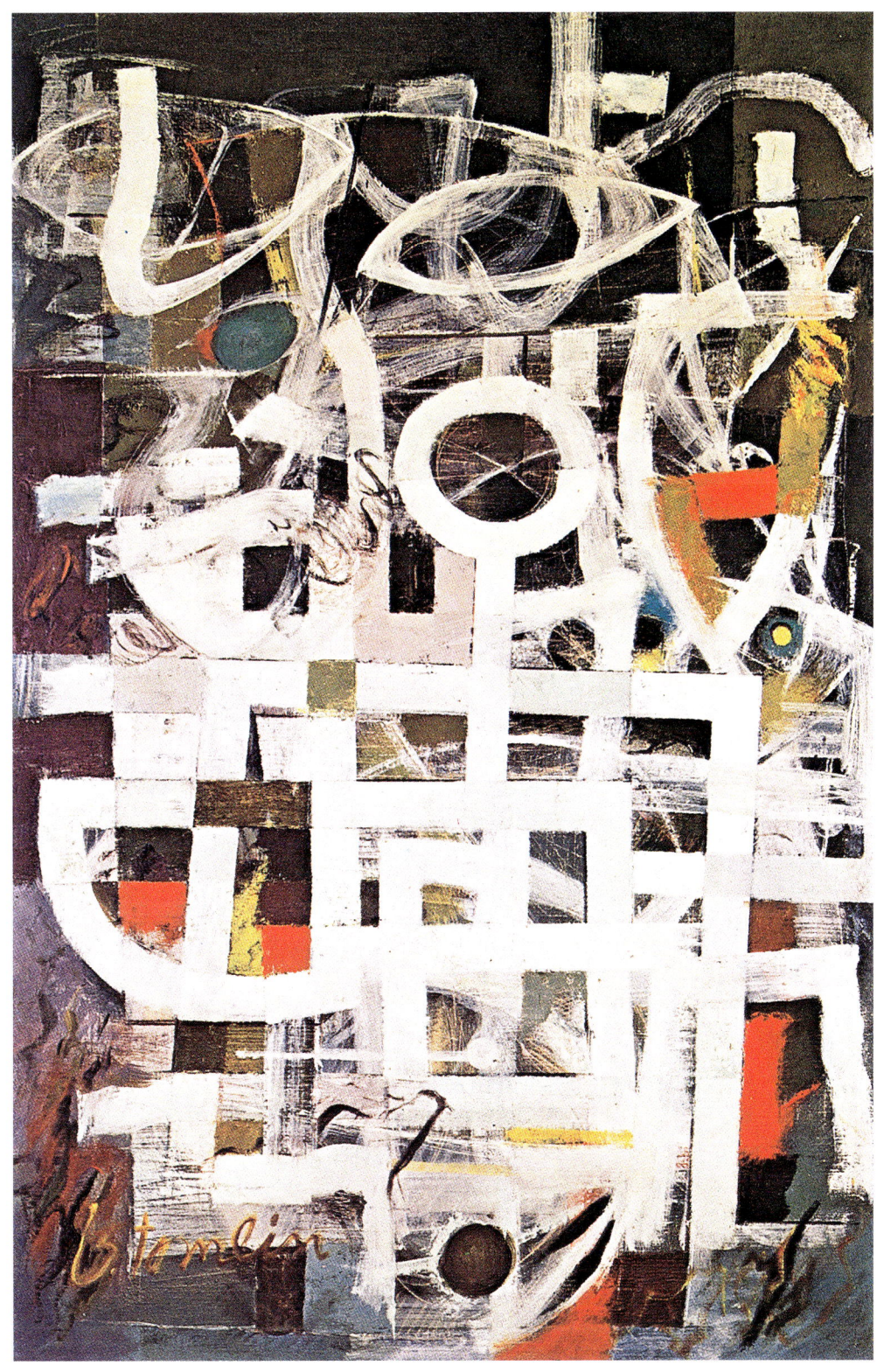

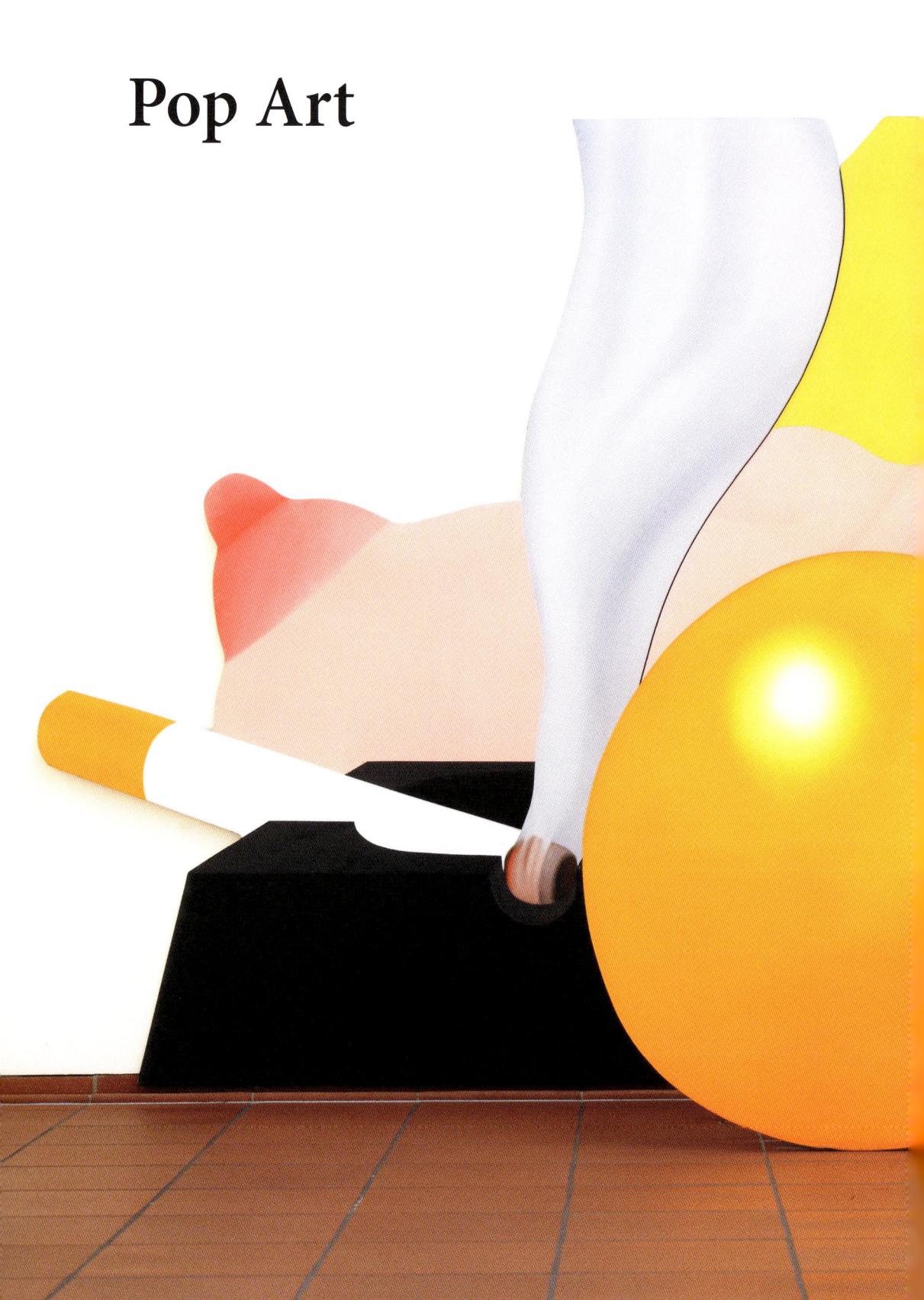

Pop Art

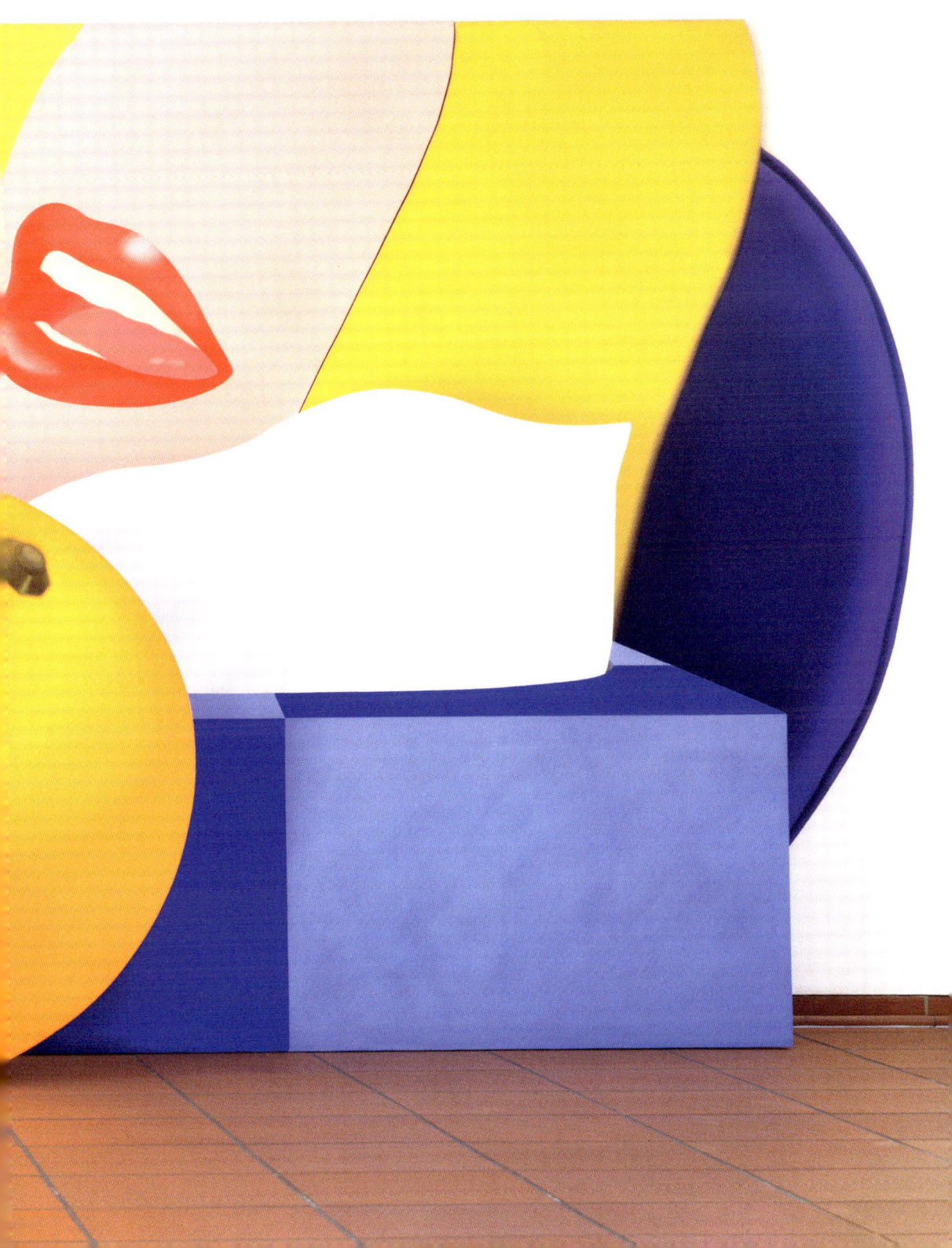

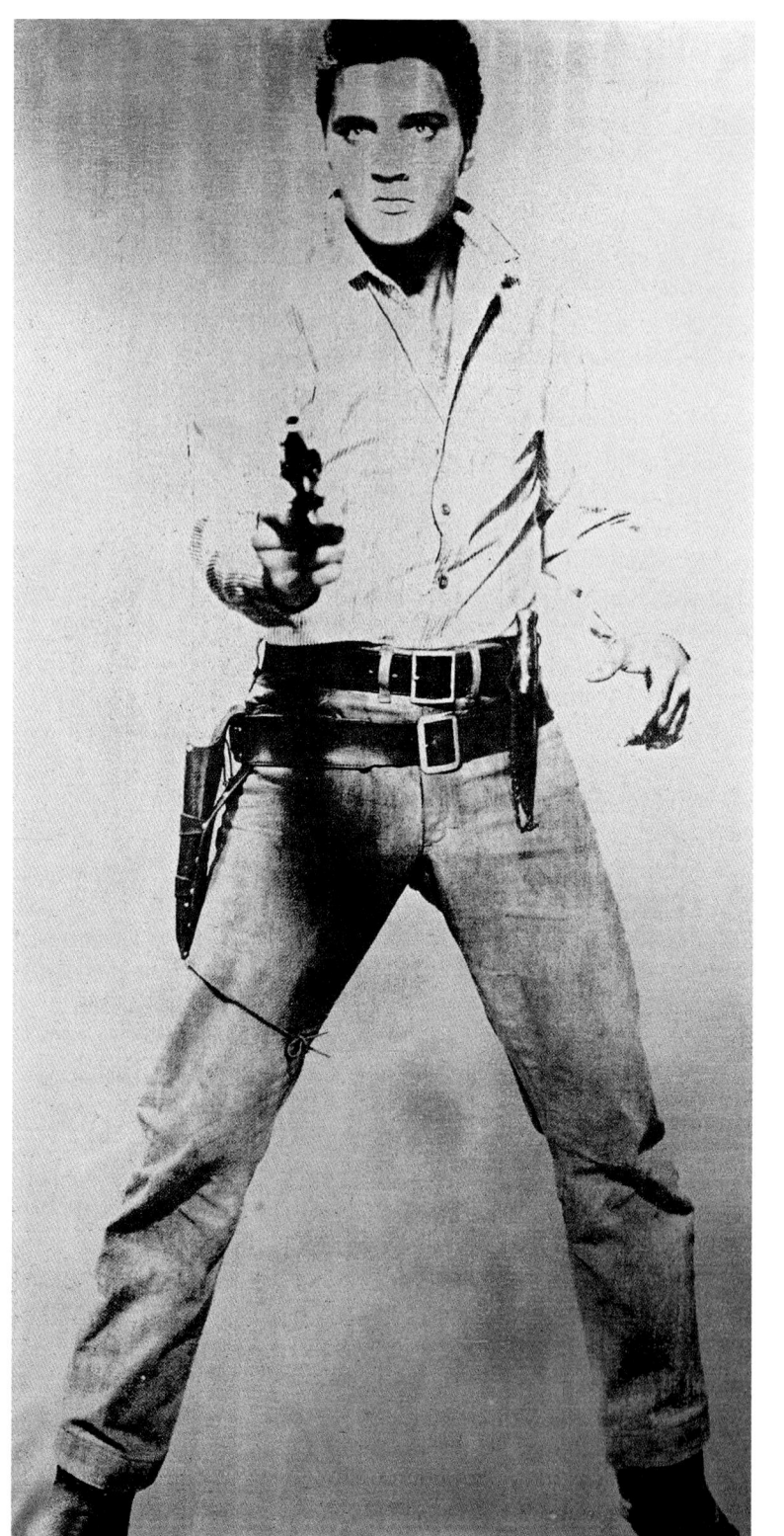

Klaus Honnef
Uta Grosenick (Ed.)

Pop Art

When the Kitschy and Mass-Market Became Art

"Pop Art is popular, transient, young, witty, sexy, gimmicky."
Richard Hamilton

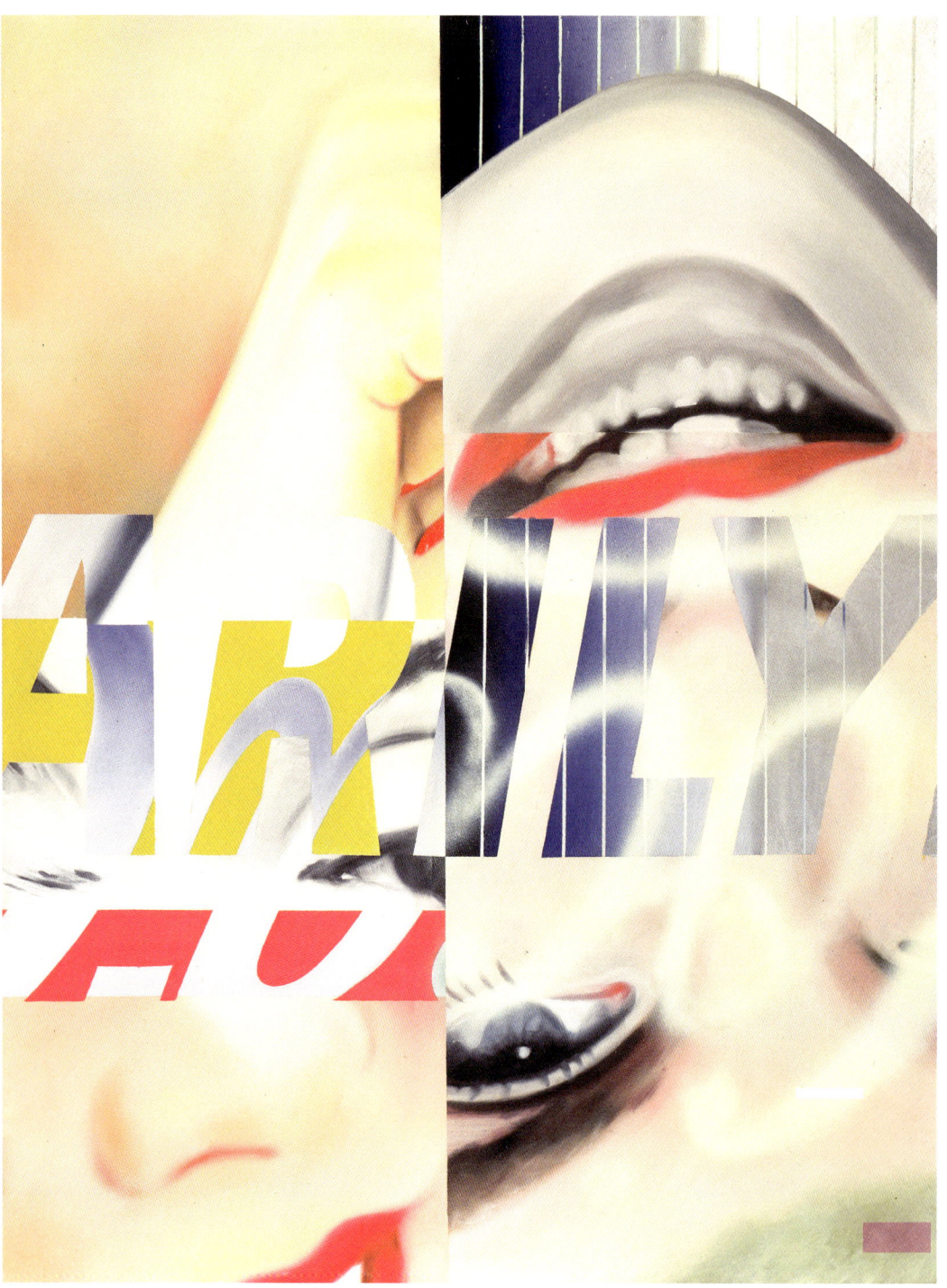

Contents

Pop Art
406

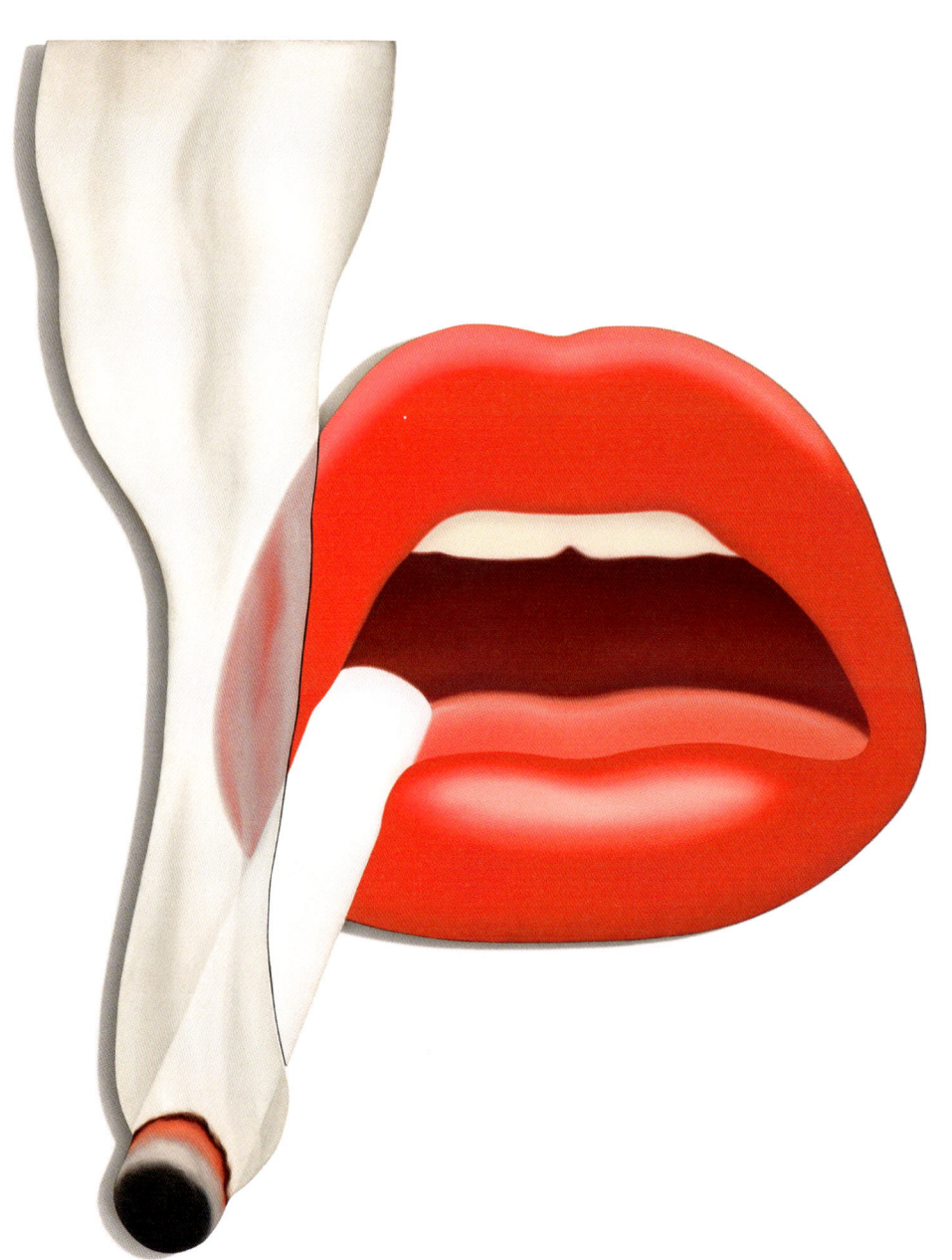

Pop Art

Its godfather demurred, saying he did not suggest the baby's name. At least not in the form that has since become a household name worldwide: Pop Art. Mere modesty, British understatement? Lawrence Alloway, an English art critic who later moved to New York, qualified the statement that he had coined the term Pop Art. "Furthermore, what I meant by it then is not what it means now. I used the term, and also 'Pop Culture', to refer to the products of the mass media, not to works of art that draw upon popular culture. In any case, sometime between the winter of 1954/55 and 1957 the phrase acquired currency in conversation …"[1]

By the time Alloway put this straight it was 1966, and Pop Art had long soared from its launching pad in modest shows at art schools and tiny private galleries into the orbit of the contemporary art sphere. Yet the geographic location of its success was not England, where a handful of young architects, authors, artists and intellectuals had early on discovered the charm of the brash vocabulary of the commercial mass media and established an informal committee, the Independent Group, at the Institute of Contemporary Arts (ICA) in London. The key location was the United States, where, almost simultaneously and with no knowledge of British developments, young artists began to charge the language of art with the visual jargon of the streets.

More precisely, the place was New York, and even more precisely, Manhattan. Names like Roy Lichtenstein, Claes Oldenburg, James Rosenquist, Tom Wesselmann and Andy Warhol were already being bandied about by those in the know, and Robert Rauschenberg, Jasper Johns and Larry Rivers were attracting the attention of serious collectors. Their paintings and sculptures celebrated the idiom of urban culture – advertising, comics, photography, design – with sometimes affirmative, sometimes ironical or critical intent.

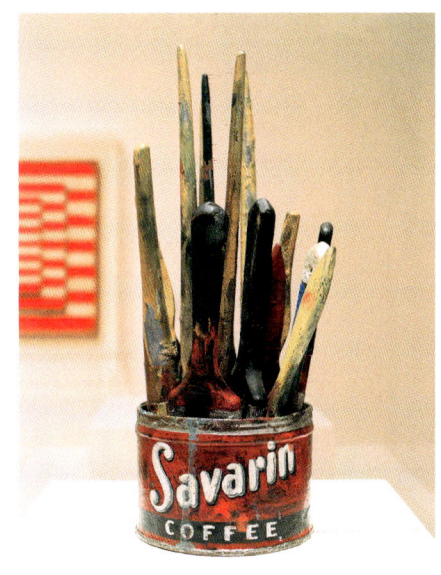

OPPOSITE
Tom Wesselmann
Smoker 1 (Mouth, 12), 1967
Oil on canvas, 2 parts,
277 x 216 cm (109 x 85 in.)
New York, The Museum of Modern Art,
Susan Morse Hilles Fund

TOP
Jasper Johns
Painted Bronze (Savarin Can), 1960
Painted bronze, height 34 cm,
ø 20 cm (height 13½, ø 8 in.)
New York, The Museum of Modern Art,
promised gift of Marie-Josée and
Henry R. Kravis

Suddenly a draught of vulgarity sent shivers through the elitist art scene in the world's financial capital. Yet with the emergence of Pop, New York also became the world's focus of contemporary art, supplanting Paris, which until then had set the tone in the international aesthetic concert. Ever since, the decision whether artists will find international renown, or must content themselves with a lesser reputation, has been made in the galleries and museums of Manhattan. Pop Art, moreover, appeared to be the American art par excellence – much to the chagrin of many supporters of modern art in the U.S.

From the American East Coast the wave of Pop soon spread to the Old World, creating great ripples especially in the western half of divided Germany. Collectors there either acquired entire American Pop collections or built up their own through broad-based buying, then presented them to astonished audiences in prestigious museums, even before this unfamiliar art had found a foothold in the country's galleries. Aachen, Darmstadt, other cities in the cultural provinces, and Cologne were the places where these brash works received the consecration of museum display. German artists sniffed the bracing breezes and drew inspiration from the audacity of Pop imagery. Documenta 4, in 1968, brought final aesthetic legitimation for its poster-coloured pictures and sculptures in cheap materials, and Kassel, a sleepy north Hessian city not far from the demarcation line between the power blocs of West and East, outstripped Venice and its somewhat older Biennale to become the most prestigious international forum for promising tendencies in contemporary art. Probably the finest collection of Pop Art today is to be found in European rather than American museums. Though dispersed among various European nations, it is united under the patronage of its collectors: Peter and Irene Ludwig.

The enthusiasm generated by Pop ever since it first saw the light of day in small exhibitions has still not cooled. On the contrary, it has continually grown. These works still hold an undiminished appeal for young people, despite their now classical look and distance from current concerns. An artist like Andy Warhol is just as much a pop idol as the latest movie or music superstar. And not without reason. In retrospect, Warhol appears to be the most significant, because most consistent, representative of Pop Art. The only surprising thing is that despite the fact that no one seriously questions his artistic rank, he enjoys a popularity accorded to no other visual artist – with the possible exception of Picasso – and otherwise reserved largely for musicians. So one man, at any rate, has evidently succeeded in bridging the still deep chasm between demanding art and wide popularity.

From the start, an abundance of misunderstandings and misconceptions surrounded the development of a group of British and American artists who broke with many of the conventional ideas about art and yet at the same time confirmed many others, because they feared to put themselves beyond the pale of the often-quoted triangle of artist, private collector and museum. On the other hand, by this time the conceptions of art held within this territory had already become relatively flexible. Art itself had ensured this by raising a continual breaking of rules to the status of a system. Accordingly, the recent history of art could be described by its chroniclers as a permanent revolt against the time-worn and obsolete schemes of art, embodied in a long series of "isms".

The designation "avant-garde" lent a spurious uniformity to the seemingly endless sequence of unconventional works that began to shake the serious academic art world in Paris in the last quarter of the nineteenth century, and whose liberating impulses soon spread to neighbouring countries. Although many a later artist thought the term avant-garde, used so loosely as to become meaningless, ought to be given back to the military, whence it derived, it quite aptly described the attitude behind a consciously modern art. In light of this attitude, the course of art appeared to take the form of a virtually endless chain of skirmishes for ascendancy, with links called Impressionism,

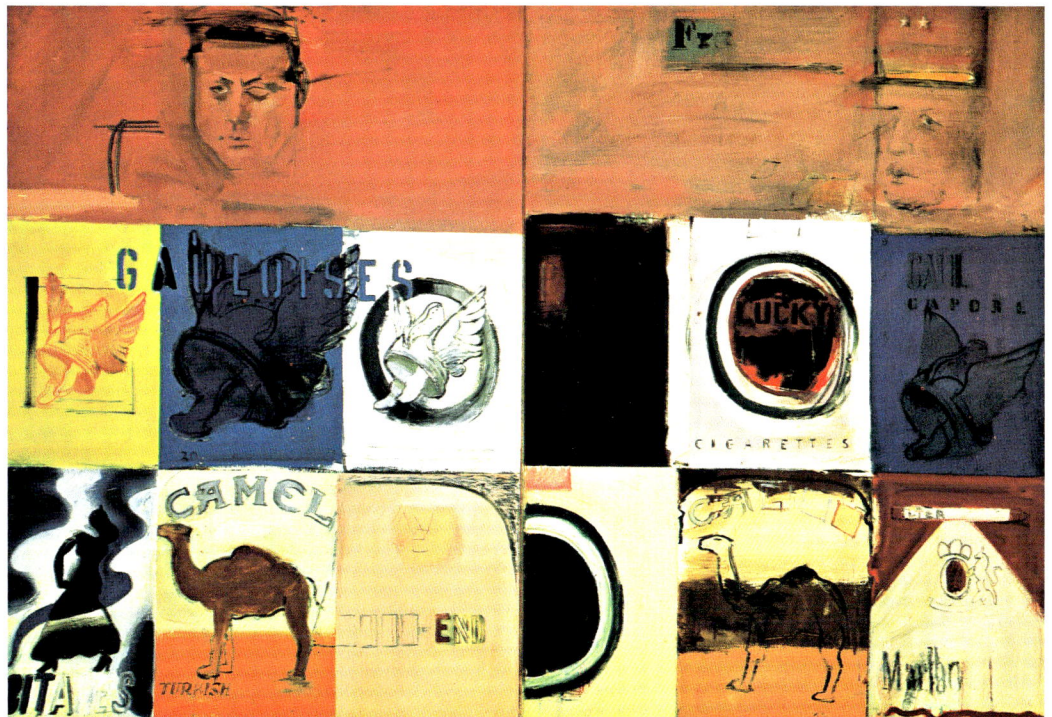

Larry Rivers
*Friendship of America and France
(Kennedy and de Gaulle)*, 1961/62
Oil on canvas, 130 x 194 x 11 cm
(51¼ x 76½ x 4¼ in.)
Courtesy Marlborough Gallery Inc.,
New York

Divisionism, Symbolism, Expressionism, Fauvism, Cubism, Constructivism, Dadaism, Surrealism, all the way down to Abstract Expressionism and L'Art Informel in the immediate forefield of Pop Art.

Art critics and historians have devoted remarkable effort and ingenuity to distilling out the various traits of these different directions and movements and declaring them to be defining stylistic characteristics. In the process they have often overlooked the underlying links between them and ultimately prepared the ground for a view of art oriented primarily to superficialities, trademark traits. In many respects, misinterpretations and misunderstandings have faithfully accompanied every one of these directions in art. And paradoxically, they have even served to markedly augment their effect. The polemics launched against the avant-garde, in particular, have had an extraordinary significance. Not all of these attacks were completely off the mark, and many turned out to be quite productive. It was no coincidence that designations like Impressionism and Cubism were originally meant derogatorily – and nevertheless took root because they pointed to traits in the art that struck the eye as typical. The present essay, too, is bound to extend the list of such actual or apparent errors in judgement.

The source of this dilemma is to be found in the works of art themselves, and it in fact represents their most important capital. The conventional wisdom notwithstanding, ambivalence is a characteristic trait of art. Ambivalence is that multiplicity of meaning which enables art to overcome its ties with its own period. Ambivalence should not be confused with arbitrariness. Works of art would be arbitrary if they provided a clear answer to every conceivable question or challenge. Works of art change their nature depending on the point of view from which they are seen, and yet nevertheless retain a validity that transcends the idiosyncrasies of time. Some people see an aspect of the absolute in this.

Robert Rauschenberg, generally considered one of the forerunners of Pop, is said to have stated that he had never seen a more beautiful sculpture than Marcel Duchamp's urinal, titled *Fountain*. By saying this, of course, Rauschenberg stood the French artist's intention on its head. By presenting a vulgar utilitarian commodity in an art exhibition, the second Armory Show of 1917 in New York, Duchamp hoped to provoke a certain reaction. His aesthetic goal was to replace an art designed to please the eye – he called it "retinal art" – with an art of the intellect. Not the object as such was important to him but the train of thought it would touch off in the context of an unfamiliar environment. Thanks to Rauschenberg's fruitful misunderstanding, the Frenchman and naturalized American was suddenly installed in the geneology of Pop, as if he were interested in the trivial everyday world rather than in challenging the art world. Though obviously misunderstood, Duchamp never protested. And since there is no evidence to prove that the original *Fountain* ever actually existed, or whether the management of the non-juried exhibition who rejected it despite previous agreement might not have been fooled by a rumour launched by Duchamp, he is moreover claimed to be a father of that art of ideas known as Conceptual Art.

It was likely no accident that the hour of birth of the avant-garde coincided with the expansion of the modern press and publication industry. One of the most crucial consequences of this development, as far as art was concerned, was the emergence of the professional art critic, who was no longer an artist and whose activity required neither artistic training nor artistic talent to pursue. The noisy battle that ensued among art critics advancing their arguments pro and con in increasing numbers of periodicals created a bridge to a growing audience. From then on, critics' opinions shaped, even became, public opinion. This development had been preceded by a fundamental change in the structure of public affairs, when the bourgeoisie became their vehicle. If previously the strict rules of an aristocratic *ancien regime* had determined the course of public affairs, now an exchange between citizens who were equal before the law began to shape the social and cultural climate. Although avant-garde artists never wished to, or could, entirely identify with middle-class tastes, they acted on the same cultural terrain, paradoxically tilling it all the more intensively the more violently they reacted against its supposed barrenness.

Leading artists have again and again spoken in simple and clear terms about their works and the ideas they wished to convey through them. Yet they were seldom listened to. In the version of their self-styled interpreters, who soon donned the mantle of expertise, artists' intentions invariably took on a more complicated, profound and mysterious air than in their own explanations. As a result, critics' statements enormously increased the impact of the artistic tendencies in question and attracted the attention necessary to make them topics of public discussion. Sometimes artists defended themselves against all-too-glaring critical misconceptions, but they generally avoided a sharp counterattack when they realized how useful the critics actually could be. Artists are pragmatic people.

His profession of art critic notwithstanding, Lawrence Alloway attempted to defend Pop against the misconceptions and dubious conclusions that had already begun to circulate back then. "Pop Art has been linked to mass communication in facetious ways as well as in straight arguments: references to the mass media in Pop Art have been made the pretext for completely identifying the source with its adaptation … There is a double flaw in the argument: an image in Pop Art is in a new context … and this is a crucial difference; and, in addition, the mass media are more complex and less inert than this view presupposes."[2] For British artists, at least, this held true. Although they discovered a previously almost unexploited repertoire in the visual storehouse of commercial culture, they subjected it to their own personal view and transformed it aesthetically. For the Americans, on the other hand, Alloway's statement holds only with qualifications, and by no means for all of them. Yet the British

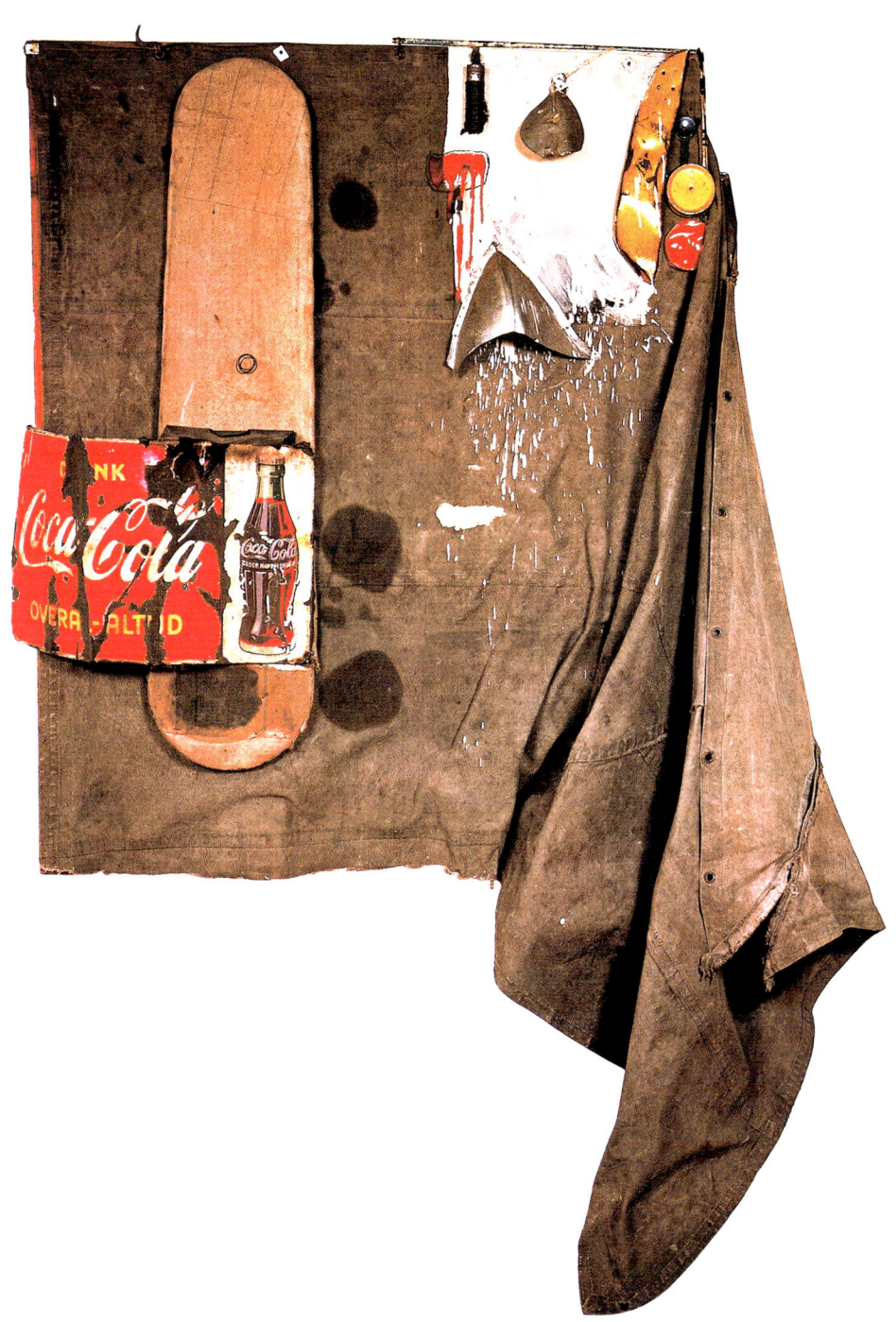

Robert Rauschenberg
Dylaby, 1962
Mixed media, 278.1 x 221 x 38.1 cm
(109½ x 87 x 15 in.)
Private collection

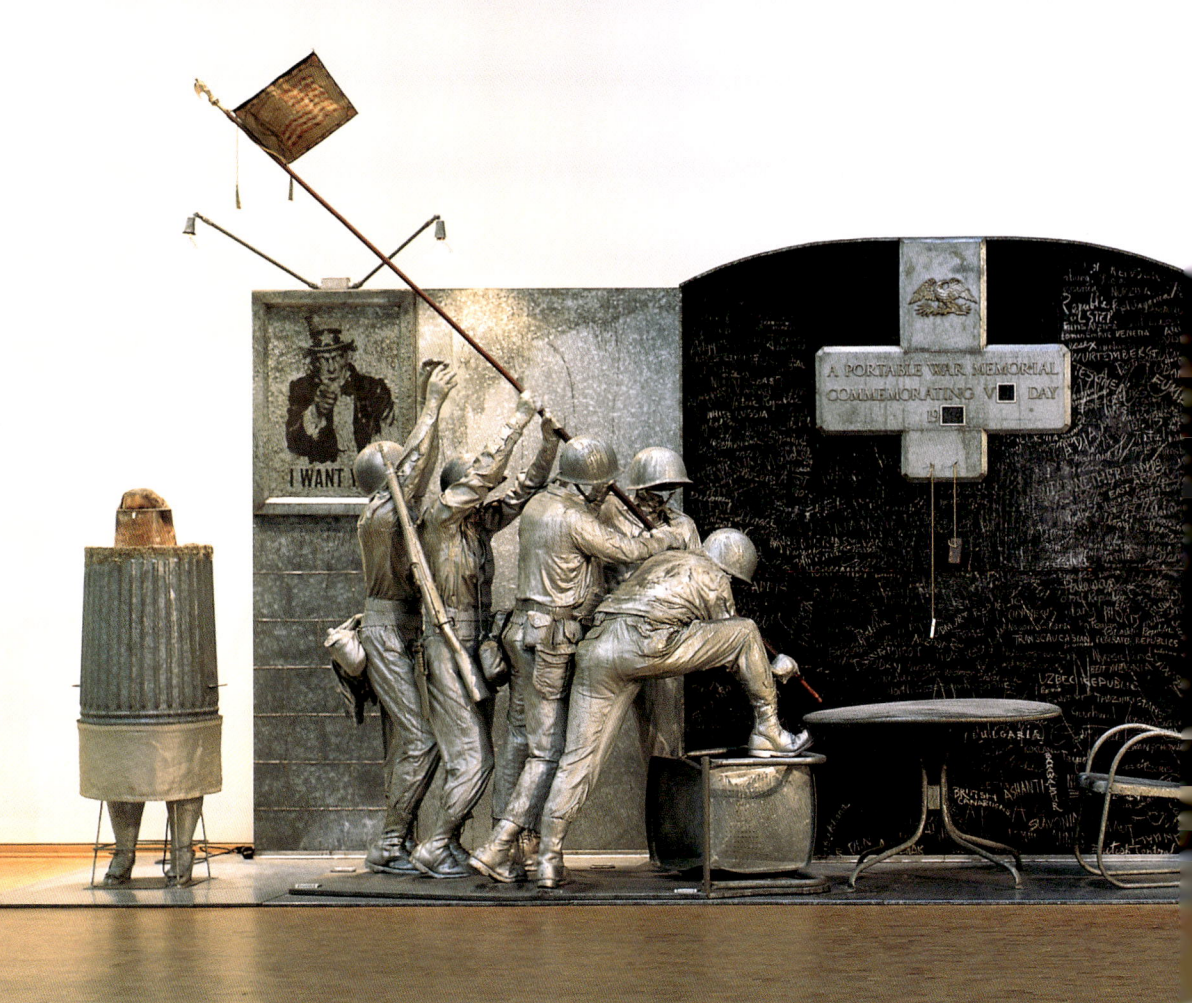

critic's remarks do touch upon the decisive issue. It remains a matter of opinion whether one considers Pop Art just another artistic direction that existed largely within the familiar framework of modern art, or a movement that exploded this framework and opened the door to a new art and a new conception of art. To put the question differently, does Pop represent one of those many variants of modern art which have continually expanded its range into previously unconsidered areas of human life, or does it mark a break with the art of the avant-garde and possibly a conscious or unconscious reversion to artistic ideas against which the avant-garde had formed ranks in the first place?

As clear as the alternatives might seem, it would be naive to assume that an equally clear answer to this question could be derived from the practice of art. Nor has the issue ever been a matter of either-or, neither for artists nor for their contemporary viewers. As regards Pop, the question can only be answered with a clear "both-and". Especially seeing as the great majority of the artists and critics involved agreed, beyond all of their differences, that Pop fit seamlessly into the picture of the avant-garde, a picture marked by baffling leaps and glaring contradictions anyway.

To quote Lucy R. Lippard, one of the most committed advocates of this art shot through with commercial trivialities like comic strips, press photos, movie star clichés, cinema marquees, food stuffs of papier maché and plastic, "Pop Art has more in common with the American 'post-painterly abstraction' of Ellsworth Kelly or Kenneth Noland than with contemporary realism. When Pop first

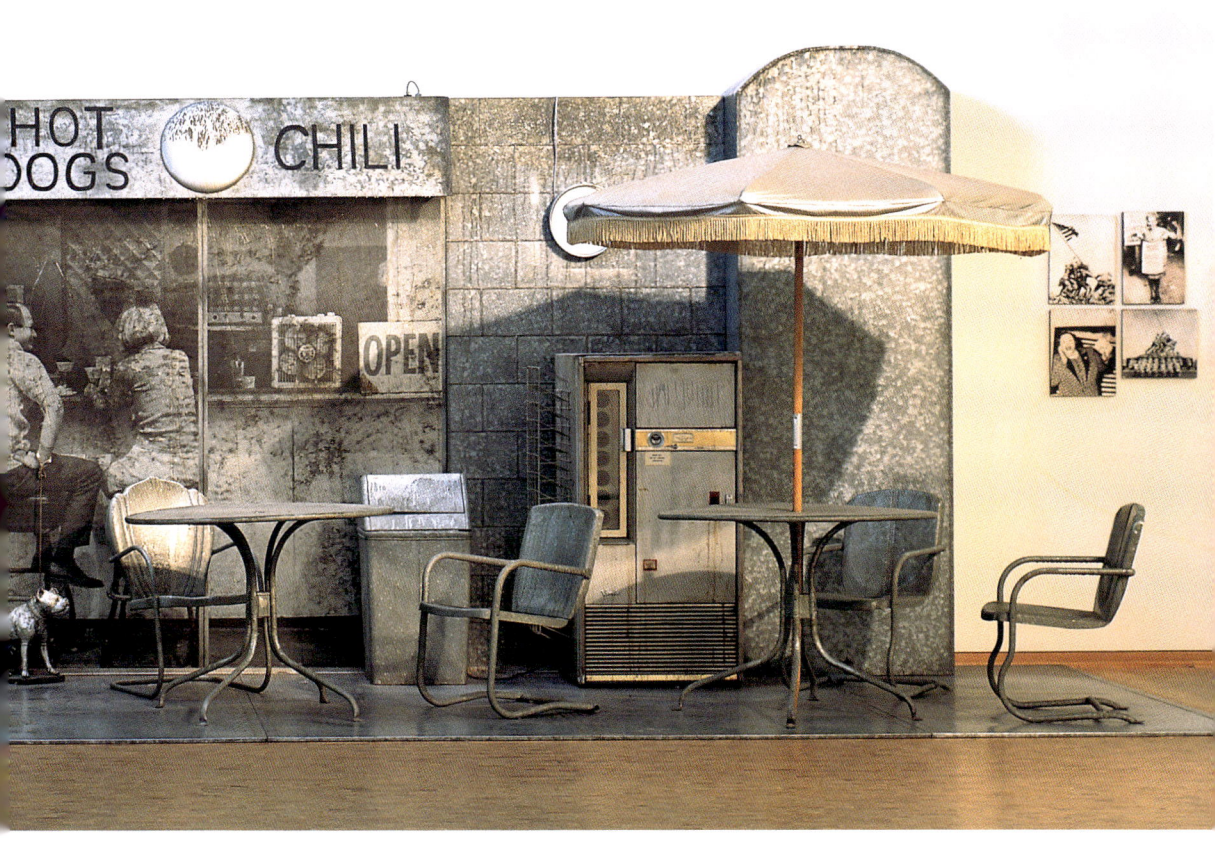

Edward Kienholz
The Portable War Memorial, 1968
Mixed media, 285 x 950 x 240 cm
(112¼ x 374 x 94½ in.)
Cologne, Museum Ludwig

emerged in England, America, and Europe, raised eyebrows and indignation were accompanied by a profound disappointment on the part
of many artists and critics. This unexpected outcome of a decade of
Abstract Expressionism … was hardly a welcome one, since it dashed
hopes for the rise of a 'new humanism', known as the 'New Image of
Man' in America and 'New Figuration' in Europe. Man might make an occasional appearance in Pop
canvases, but only as a robot remotely controlled by the Consumers' Index, or as a sentimentalized
parody of the ideal. For other observers, however, such a brash and uncritical reflection of our environment was a breath of fresh air."[3]

Two aspects of this passage deserve closer attention. The first is Lippard's opinion that Pop possesses a greater affinity with the abstract art of Kelly or Noland than with conventional approaches
such as realism; the second culminates in her characterization of the reaction of the broad masses to
Pop, as one of indignation, frank rejection. Unfortunately Lippard does not give any reasons for this
rejection. It would seem surprising that most people should have rejected Pop despite the fact that its
vocabulary and materials must have been entirely familiar to them from their daily encounters with
things of this sort. Or perhaps this itself was the reason? Might not people's negative reaction to Pop
pictures and sculptures have resulted from their quite different notion of what art should consist of

and convey – whether spiritual edification or a type of aesthetic experience long since schooled on avant-garde art, with which Pop brutally collided? In terms of the then-current model of incessant artistic progress, apparently confirmed by avant-garde developments, the advance of modern art led almost automatically to pure abstraction. Accordingly, Lippard is concerned to place the works of Pop artists, as it were, under the protective aesthetic umbrella of abstraction, so as not to jeopardize their progressive status. It is indicative that she dissociates her protégé from realism in art, but not from the potential temptations of the commercial media, which supplied Pop Art with its subject matter, themes, and in many cases its mode of depiction. Her motive is not hard to understand. If the many, various and often controversial approaches of the avant-garde have any common denominator, it is their innate hostility towards every variant of realism. It should not be forgotten that when Lippard penned her analysis, one of these variants was politically still very much alive. This was the wretched doctrine of "socialist realism". The Soviet Union and its satellites still represented an acute threat to the capitalist hemisphere. The Cold War still cast its shadow over the art scene.

Not surprisingly, in their verbal statements artists of the day confessed their undivided allegiance to the avant-garde. Many of them had tried their hand, without much success, as third-generation Abstract Expressionists, and all of them had enjoyed a formal art education. Jim Dine, whose contacts with Pop Art were on the sporadic side despite his employment of motifs such as giant neckties and the fact that many considered him a Pop artist, demurred when asked in an interview about his links with an art based on a popular repertoire. "I don't feel very pure in that respect", said Dine. "I don't deal exclusively with the popular image. I'm more concerned with it as part of my landscape. I'm sure everyone has always been aware of that landscape, the artistic landscape, the artist's vocabulary, the artist's dictionary." To preclude overhasty conclusions, Dine then added that he did not believe Pop represented a "sharp break" with Abstract Expressionism, nor that it replaced it.

And Roy Lichtenstein, another American, despite his exploitation of the visual impact of popular comic strips in his art, denied any artistic affinity with their makers, instead citing experimental forms of art as his source of inspiration. He was thinking more of the happenings of Oldenburg, Dine, Whitman and Kaprow, Lichtenstein explained. Though he had not seen many happenings, they seemed to him to concern themselves with American industrial development. And Pop Art, he added in another place, was "actually industrial painting … I think the meaning of my work is that it's industrial, it's what all the world will soon become."

Only Warhol, who had begun to produce paintings by a commercial silkscreen process early on, relinquished this defensive stance. He brashly declared, "I think it would be so great if more people took up silk screens, so that no one would know whether my picture was mine or somebody else's." When the interviewer asked whether this would turn art history upside down, Warhol simply replied, "Yes."

The three artists quoted represented different variants of Pop, and Lippard counted only Lichtenstein and Warhol among its hard core, but not the vacillating Dine. "And although he is frequently included in the Pop rosters", she explained, Dine's "every work and statement show him to be worlds apart from that touch iconoclasm and formal emphasis."

All in all, the statements made by most of the artists involved would seem to confirm the findings of Alloway, Lippard and the majority of commentators, who imply that Pop represented merely one of the many mutations of contemporary art. Seen in this light, Pop by no means, as Warhol suggested, subverted the self image of modern art. So it is all the more surprising to find influential critics occasionally railing against this particular variant. Lippard mentioned them only summarily and in passing. Yet these were critics who had proved themselves knowledgeable and courageous advocates of the avant-garde. A podium discussion in New York, in which heavyweights of criticism and art history participated, is a revealing case in point.

On 13 September 1962, the Museum of Modern Art held a symposium on Pop Art, for no visible reason, neither an exhibition nor a purchase having occasioned it. Thanks to its exemplary collection and its groundbreaking modern exhibitions, the museum had long gained an international reputation as an unsinkable avant-garde flagship. The early date of the symposium was nevertheless surprising. At the time, Pop had hardly spread beyond the small, 10th-Street galleries where works of its protagonists had been shown. It had not yet arrived at the better Manhattan galleries. Nor had the term Pop yet entered common usage. It was still vying for acceptance with other names, such as Neo-Dada, New Sign Painting, or New American Dream. The painting and sculpture department of the Museum of Modern Art owned only six works in the genre. Nor did the two curators responsible for painting and sculpture, the legendary Alfred H. Barr Jr., former director of the museum, and the competent Dorothy C. Miller, deem it necessary to attend the symposium. Nevertheless, it was to have far-reaching consequences, not only for the renowned museum on 46th Street.

The camp of Pop enthusiasts was underrepresented on the podium. In truth, it consisted of only a single person: Henry Geldzahler, a young assistant curator at the Metropolitan Museum of Art. Peter Selz, who had organized the meeting and worked at the time as curator in the MoMA exhibitions department, was quite frank about his scepticism regarding Pop. The other participants either took a waiting stance or opened their critical fire on the Pop artists' aesthetic positions. Hilton Kramer, conservative star critic of the New York Times, even imputed that the fact the symposium was even being held reflected a bald-faced bias in favour of Pop. Yet in the crossfire of opposing opinions one key question stood out: Is Pop Art art at all? And by art, the participants meant exclusively modern art, the art of the avant-garde. According to their virtually unanimously held view, the avant-garde represented an art liberated from the mode of depiction, or in expert jargon, "non-representational" art. The standards of

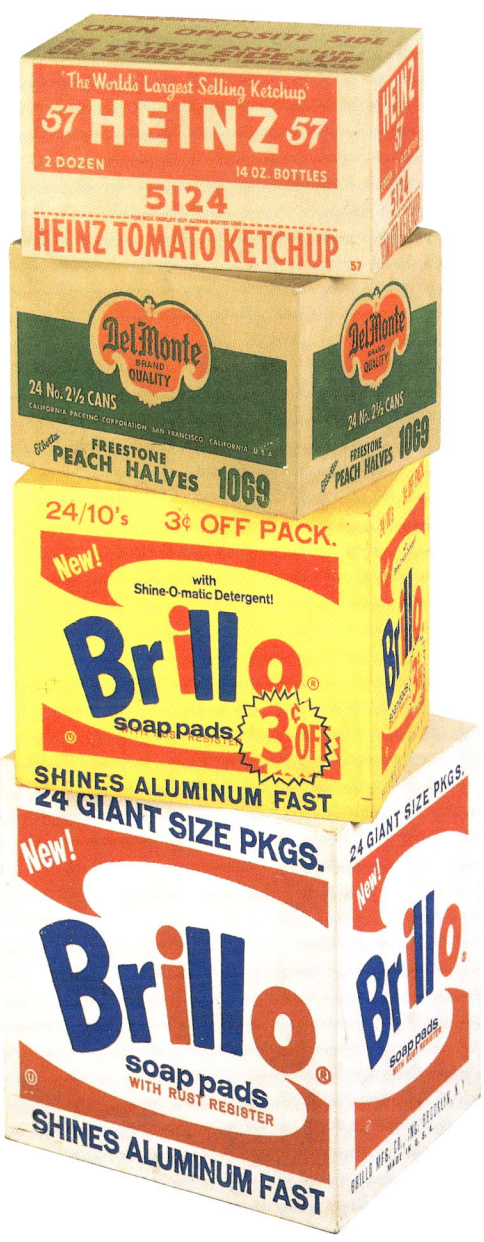

Andy Warhol
Brillo, Del Monte and Heinz Boxes, 1964
Silkscreen on wood, 44 x 43 x 36 cm (17¼ x 17 14¼ in.);
33 x 41 x 30 cm (13 x 16¼ x 11¾ in.);
21 x 40 x 26 cm (8¼ x 15¾ x 10¼ in.)
Private collection

aesthetic expression were set solely by art itself. Artists were precluded from looking at reality, and every attempt to artistically and aesthetically digest real impressions had fallen under the curse of the unartistic and historically outmoded. In the work of a true artist, the outside world had no role to play. While Selz censured Lichtenstein for having supposedly translated comic strips "almost directly" into his paintings,[4] the poet, critic and Pulitzer prizewinner Stanley Kunitz accused Warhol's pictures of Campbell's Soup can labels of having been mechanically reproduced without the aid of a pencil. Geldzahler's objection that Lichtenstein, at least, had made artistic incursions into the structure of his patterns was greeted by general laughter, then countered by the art historian and famous author Dore Ashton, who maliciously replied that he, Geldzahler, could only have observed that through a magnifying glass.

In the eyes of its prominent opponents, Pop lacked revolutionary élan in the artistic sense. Its "signs and slogans and strategems come straight out of the citadel of bourgeois society", averred Kunitz, "the communications stronghold where the images and desires of mass man are produced." Then Selz struck a further blow, alleging that Pop artists represented "the spirit of conformity and the bourgeoisie". Hilton Kramer summed up the objections with a connoisseur's eye, declaring that Pop was "indistinguishable from advertising art". Both ultimately attempted to "reconcile us to a world of commodities, banalities and vulgarities". In view of such intentions, Kramer insisted that Pop Art must be resisted at all costs.

Above the heads of the debaters hovered, like a kind of superfather, the powerful Clement Greenberg. A profound and eloquent critic and man of learning, Greenberg had once provided the theoretical underpinnings for American abstract art and, with his essays and subtle influence, had materially contributed to its worldwide reputation. And though the heyday of Abstract Expressionism was long over, his influence remained unbroken. What Greenberg said and wrote may no longer have had the power of law, but it still carried incredible weight. As early as 1939, in an epoch-making essay titled "Avant Garde and Kitsch",[5] which by the time of the symposium had gone through several reprints, Greenberg had forged the intellectual weapons in defence of an art cleansed of all non-artistic ingredients. His carefully polished and convincing arguments were now repeated, in coarser form, by the opponents of Pop.

But it was not only their acumen that made Greenberg's hypotheses as interesting now as they were when published over half a century ago. It was the circumstance that Pop relegated them to the museum of art theory. Why was this so? While Pop swept Greenberg's definition of art aside, it was only against its background that the fundamentally new and different nature of Pop became graphically apparent. What sounded like a paradox lost its paradoxical character when the areas Greenberg categorically excluded from his definition suddenly became the focus of attention.

With consciously polemical intent, Greenberg projected the German term "kitsch" onto the visual phenomena of mass culture. "Simultaneously with the entrance of the avant-garde", he wrote, "a second new cultural phenomenon appeared in the industrialized West: that thing to which the Germans give the wonderful name of Kitsch: popular, commercial art and literature with their chromeotypes, magazine covers, illustrations, ads, slick and pulp fiction, comics, Tin Pan Alley musicals, tap dancing, Hollywood movies, etc. etc." It was time, Greenberg added, to inquire into the why and wherefore of this long-neglected phenomenon. Disregarding a few of the genres on Greenberg's negative list, its items add up to the preferred repertoire of Pop Art.

Saleability was and still is the mark of Cain of popular culture. The critic admitted it could be tempting even for serious artists: "Kitsch's enormous profits are a source of temptation to the avant-garde itself, and its members have not always resisted this temptation … The net result is always to

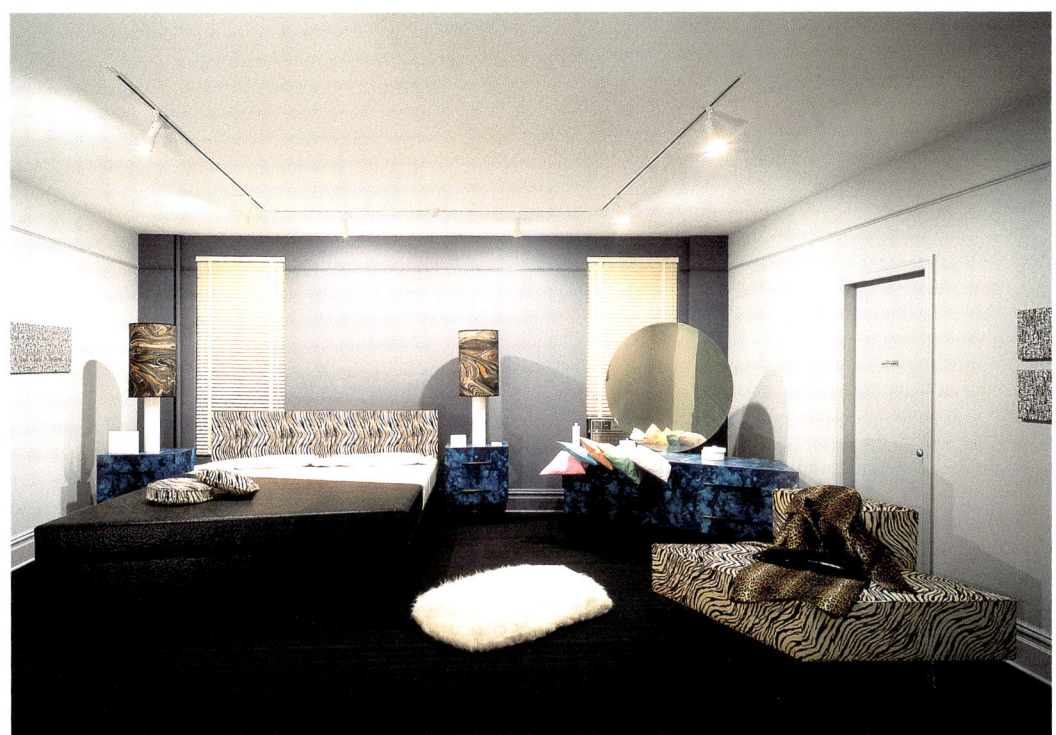

the detriment of true culture, in any case." Though in the leftist political camp at the time his essay was published, Greenberg could not resist swinging the moral cudgel against an art of popular appeal. The true avant-garde artist or writer who remained uninfluenced by the commercialism of his environment would "maintain the high level of his art both by narrowing and raising it to the expression of an absolute in which all relativities and contradictions would be either resolved or beside the point. 'Art for art's sake' and 'pure poetry' appear, and subject matter or content becomes something to be avoided like a plague."

Greenberg always remained faithful to these aesthetic maxims, which were suffused by the sublime light of German idealistic philosophy. And far from being the product of his own private tic, in one form or another they dominated the Western art scene until the appearance of Pop. Whether current aesthetic notions were based on a rigidly grounded theoretical conception of the kind Greenberg formulated or merely on the idea of modern art being a never-resting assembly line that produced innovation after surprising innovation, was immaterial. Everyone had to agree with Greenberg when he declared that "Picasso, Braque, Mondrian, Miró, Kandinsky, Brancusi, even Klee, Matisse and Cézanne, derive their chief inspiration from the medium they work in. The excitement of their art seems to lie most of all in its pure preoccupation with the invention and arrangement of spaces, surfaces, shapes, colours, etc., to the exclusion of whatever is not necessarily implicated in these factors."

Not that Pop artists threw space, plane, form and colour by the wayside – in the beginning, at least, they attempted to transcend this self-referential system and throw open the window of an all-too hermetic art to admit the fresh air of the streets. Nor was this by any means the first time a direction in art had turned to the hustle and bustle of ordinary, everyday life. Long before art had shed the

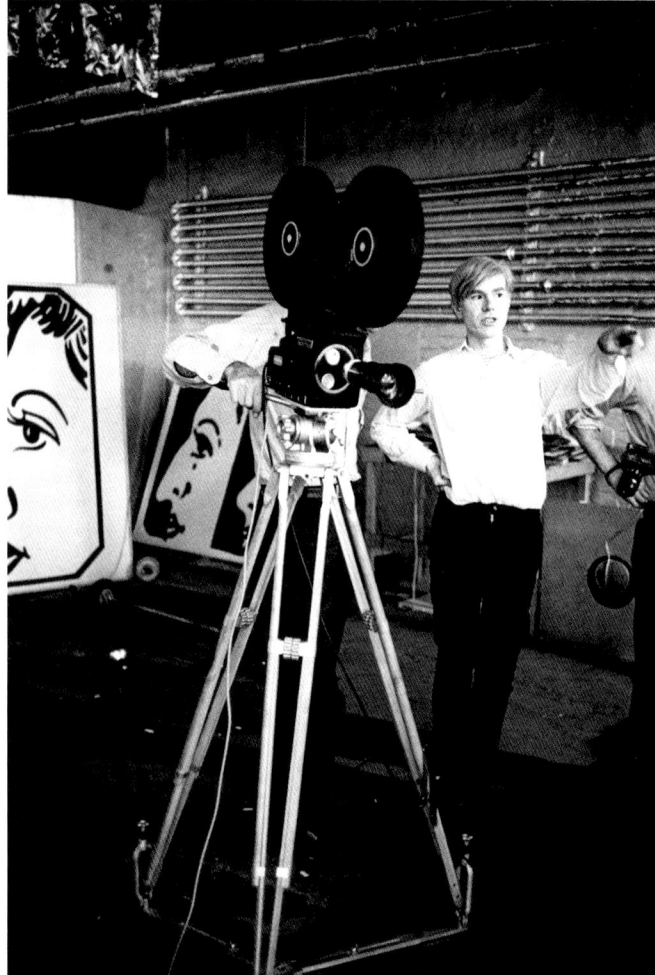

Steve Schapiro
Andy Warhol directing a movie at The Factory, New York, 1965

Andy Warhol
Dick Tracy, 1960
Casein and coloured pencil on canvas, 122 x 86 cm (48 x 34 in.)
Private collection

fetters of purpose and service to be nothing but art, it had turned an eye to the visible and invisible phenomena that existed beyond the picture frame. In each case, admittedly, different levels of risk were involved. While still in the service of the church and the secular aristocracy, art celebrated their attitude towards God and the world. In the service of the bourgeoisie, it depicted the bourgeois view of the world and the things this stratum found essential. Modern art, in turn, derived its reason for being from the certainty of having liberated itself from such strictures, despite the fact that many of its detractors considered this a hypocritical assertion and maintained that art was released from its previous obligations because its tasks could be more effectively performed by technical media such as photography and film, and commercial forms of communication like advertising, illustrated magazines and comic strips. Yet one thing was undeniable: since the emergence of what Greenberg called a "second new cultural phenomenon" and its mass dissemination, art has established itself as an autonomous cultural phenomenon whose involvement in the relationships of visible and experienceable reality is indirect at best.

Anyone who sets out to find a historical point of departure for Pop is bound to arrive at Dada or Duchamp. The parallels are more than obvious. Thanks to intelligently composed snippets, the firmament of commercial imagery already shone in the Dada collages of Raoul Hausmann and Hannah Höch, George Grosz and John Heartfield. Max Ernst's phantasmagorical universe was shaped of cuttings from popular illustrations. Scissors and paste replaced brush and paint, and illustrated magazines supplanted the media of art. Kurt Schwitters, the German Dadaist, built a house of waste and discarded materials inside his Hanover apartment and titled it *Merz*. Evidently Dada targeted the art of the bourgeoisie, especially the kind based on education and good taste. In the minds of its protagonists, Dada was to be a "slap in the face" of self-satisfied respectable citizens. Dada was intended to wipe the slate clean of them and their culture. Was Pop in a comparable cultural situation when it emerged?

Hardly, either in a political or an economic sense. Incidentally, even the most pointed works of the Pop artists reflect a complete absence of political intent. Criticism of the injustices of capitalist society is found only rarely, and even then it does not undermine the social consensus. At best it lays bare the hidden mechanisms of society. On the other hand, the discovery of mass culture by Pop artists was preceded long before by the Cubists, who pasted newspaper clippings into their paintings, or the American artist Stuart Davis, who depicted a bottle of mouthwash in his painting *Odol*, 1924. The list of possible predecessors could be extended without ever once breaking the taboo by mentioning a realist. Nor did any Pop artist in the United States ever dream of singing the praises of anarchy. Only the underground cinema movement, to which Warhol contributed several remarkable works, confessed its allegiance to aesthetic revolt and jettisoned the conventions of narrative and art cinema in the process.

That the works of British Pop artists were dominated by a frank fascination with the brash factory-made imagery of consumption and the culture of commerce, was not surprising. While the United States experienced a phase of economic prosperity in the 1950s and 1960s and private consumption reached record peaks, Great Britain's economy recovered only slowly from the devastating consequences of World War II. The situation improved even less quickly than in West Germany, the land of the vanquished. When the dreary London streets were gradually brightened by the glam-

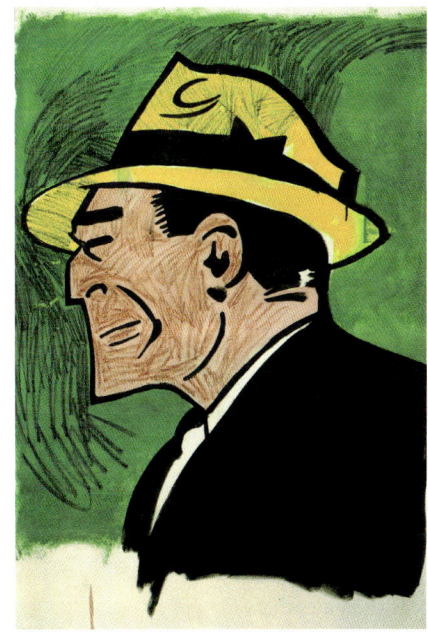

our of commercial advertising and the dreams of Hollywood, artists were as unable to resist their spell as the broad public.

Richard Hamilton, who had made replicas for Duchamp, encountered the visual temptations of consumer culture with mixed feelings. His collage, *Just what is it that makes today's homes so different, so appealing?*, 1956, a wonderful early example of the aesthetic watershed, brought standard figures from the realm of trivial imagery into a modern overfurnished apartment. The work was intended for publication in the catalogue for the exhibition "This is Tomorrow", held at the Whitechapel Gallery, London, in 1956. It also served as the poster motif. Although "This is Tomorrow" was not a show of nascent Pop Art, it provided decisive impulses.

The exhibition consisted of twelve separate displays in which the participants, principally architects and urban planners, were able to realize their ideas at their own discretion. The interesting thing was that they drew attention to the visual environment of contemporary civilization. The results were astonishing, said Hamilton, ranging from purely architectural pavilions through department-store displays to a turbulent, incredibly exciting funfair architecture. The enterprise was a true eye-opener, revealing previously unknown horizons for artistic developments to come. Moreover, "This Is Tomorrow" underscored the increasing significance of exhibitions for the public dissemination of art. Exhibitions were soon to become key loci in which isolated artistic initiatives condensed into manifest trends.

To his way of thinking, Hamilton noted, the point of the exhibition was not so much to find art forms as to test values. The Independent Group opposed those who were primarily concerned with "creating a new style". They rejected the notion that "tomorrow" could be expressed by establishing rigorous formal concepts. "Tomorrow" would merely expand present-day visual experiences. What was needed, Hamilton continued, was not a definition of the serious work of art but the development of a potential perspective, in order to be able "to accept and apply the continual enrichment of visual material". All of the work of British Pop artists, including Hamilton, since the 1950s, said Alloway, showed that they "accepted industrial culture and assimilated aspects of it into their art" in an eclectic and all-embracing way.

The artists had no intention of denying the primacy of art in dealing with the visual challenges of mass culture. Instead, they set out to adapt a largely unexploited repertoire, material, as Hamilton called it, from advertising, movies and television which could be used to infuse new life into "high" art, whose once compelling power seemed on the wane. By so doing, Hamilton, like every likeminded artist, committed a sacrilege on Greenberg's definition of the avant-garde. He focused on the *effects* of artistic possibilities. "If the avant-garde imitates the processes of art, kitsch … imitates its effects", decreed Greenberg. The slightest contact with commercial culture would infect art and irreparably sully the purity of the artist's intentions.

Actually, Hamilton went only a small step beyond Francis Bacon. Bacon had incorporated into his paintings still photos from Sergei Eisenstein's legendary film *The Battleship Potemkin*, 1925, and stop-motion photographs by Eadweard Muybridge. He reworked them without concealing their origin. Bacon's use of such material was highly regarded in the art world. Hamilton, unlike Bacon, did not alter the structure of his photographic material but combined various photographic elements into a different photographic reality from that manifested in the original material.

A case in point is *My Marilyn*, 1964. This series of photos of the film star Marilyn Monroe in a bikini on the beach was based on a sheet of contact prints. A few of these were partially painted over and alienated mechanically or by hand. In other pictures, the photographic originals were modified into soft, painterly forms recalling cosmetic ads. Yet despite appropriating visual clichés, the images of consumer culture, Hamilton retained his detachment. Especially continental European critics tended to imply that British Pop artists were critical of mass media imagery. In general, the actual works do not warrant this view. Admittedly Peter Blake, Richard Smith, Derek Boshier, Patrick Caulfield, David Hockney, Allen Jones and Peter Phillips did address the visual forms of popular culture to varying extents and with different intents, and Eduardo Paolozzi, not a true Pop artist at all, paid tribute to some of the more fantastic aspects of modern civilization with his brightly coloured robots. But they all blended selected set pieces from the commercial idiom into a subjective artistic language and reshaped them in terms of their personal vision, yet without resorting to an expressive approach to package their message. Their gestures were cool and objective, almost abstract, or as if borrowed second-hand. In terms of their artistic procedures, their impersonal and prefabricated touch, they were related to the hardcore American Pop artists Oldenburg, Lichtenstein, Rosenquist, Wesselmann and Warhol.

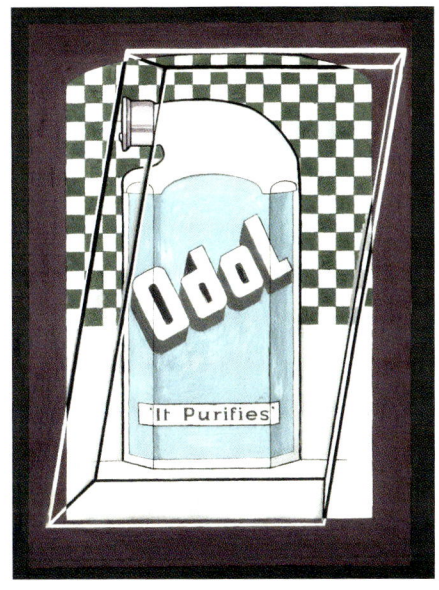

Stuart Davis
Odol, 1924
Oil on canvas, 60.9 x 45.6 cm (24 x 18 in.)
New York, The Museum of Modern Art,
Mary Sisler Bequest

In his painting *On the Balcony*, 1955–57, Peter Blake arrayed the entire arsenal of industrially produced imagery: magazine covers from *Life* and *Weekly Illustrated*, picture postcards, photos of pop stars, a parade of royals, a picture of Sir Winston Churchill with King and Queen, a caricature. On the same level he arranges reproductions of paintings, including Manet's *Balcony*, 1868. These are accompanied by mundane commodities such as a half-empty bottle of mineral water or soda pop, a margarine package, a newspaper, and many others. The provocation lies in the mixture. Everything is painted with equal attention to detail. The result is a painting of extraordinary aesthetic delicacy, a painted collage, and, if you will, a clever retranslation of a "progressive" artistic technique back into Old Masterly terms.

Richard Smith, who would soon move to the U.S., combined the achievements of abstract art with the brash visual impact of consumer imagery. Cigarette packs and shipping cartons for industrially manufactured foods inspired him to gigantic, illusionistic paintings from which direct allusions to the visual vocabulary of the mass media were expunged. Sometimes he trimmed the format of his painted pictures into shapes that, again repainted, suggested three-dimensional objects.

Derek Boshier conserved traces of expressive painting, inoculated with a touch of irony. In *First Tooth Paste Painting*, 1962, he applied the silhouette of a sprawling, apparently male figure onto a toothpaste tube projecting from the left into a light-blue field. On the right, the toothpaste is being squeezed in garish red and white stripes onto a green toothbrush. Like Blake, Boshier is an excellent painter, and it is unlikely that he ever considered sacrificing the qualities of his craft to the power of commercial imagery. According to one commentator, his paintings "might be called visions of negative utopias. The technological achievements and prefabricated models consume or engulf the individual" (Tilman Osterwold). Smith, a friend of Boshier's, took a more down-to-earth view. Though Boshier's pictures were "social comment", he explained, it was in "mad, comic terms. Billy Wilder says, 'One thing I dislike more than being taken too lightly is being taken too seriously.'"

Allen Jones brought the fury of the feminists down upon his head. Like Pop in the cultural arena and the election of John F. Kennedy to the presidency in the political one, the burgeoning of the women's movement was a sign that fossilized structures in the social edifice of the Western world were beginning to break up. When Jones emphasized the breasts, buttocks and legs of his female models to the point of fetish worship, the verdict was clear: sexism. Later he even converted specially fabricated female shop- window dummies into tables and chairs – a dubious invitation, it seemed, to the exploitation of women. Still, Jones' objects did not leave the familiar system of art, they merely stretched it to the breaking point. He denied having been inspired by commercial imagery. A head with a necktie under it, Jones averred, was a "phallic totem image", and thus not a part of "popular iconography".

Private notions and obsessions were likewise the motive force behind David Hockney's artistic universe. His apparently childlike graphic style lent his pictures an aura of carefree innocence, and their often bright illumination a touch of unreality. Geldzahler, a friend to whom Hockney devoted a few portraits – including *Henry Geldzahler and Christopher Scott*, 1969 – doubted that the artist had any affinity with Pop Art. His reasoning was surprising, since it detached Hockney's work from contemporary influence. His "sources and exemplars", said Geldzahler, "are more likely to be the poets George Herbert and Andrew Marvell or Degas and Toulouse-Lautrec than this morning's headlines. Curious as he is intellectually, he has little room in his working aesthetic for the cascade of data that crackles about us like static."[6] Except for a handful of early works, Hockney painted no definitely Pop pictures. *Tea Painting in an Illusionistic Style*, 1961, was one of them, a clever, shaped canvas like a tea box for a race of giants.

None of the British artists of his generation devoted himself more uncompromisingly to the spirit and look of commercial culture than Peter Phillips. With Boshier, Jones and Hockney, Phillips represented the third wave of Pop in England and, taking its cue from the widely respected Hamilton, the second wave with a figurative tendency. Phillips' characteristic paintings adapt the bizarre configurations of the illuminated decor on pinball machines with their lightning flashes and aggressively tempting pin-up girls, and blow them up to a format that veritably blasts the viewer with an incessant fire of visual stimuli. During a two-year stay in New York (1962–64), Phillips bought an airbrush of the kind he had long considered using and began to execute his cool imagery with a technique equally as detached. Using a machine, as Christopher Finch explained, was a logical, almost unavoidable expansion of Phillips' previous painting methods. The even clearer and more intensive immediacy of his visual language was likely one result of this airbrush technique. With his radical waiver of personal touch, his frank idolization of commercial imagery, and his use of unusual formats, Phillips was not only the most rigorous of British Pop artists but the one with the greatest intellectual and visual affinity to the Americans. Only Caulfield was similarly rigorous in approach.

What distinguished the American artists from the British, their unfiltered Pop ideology, was the result of a break between cultural developments in the U.S. and the European tradition. At exactly what point in time this occurred, cannot be said with certainty. At any rate, the break was provoked and furthered by the burgeoning of that commercial culture which Greenberg denounced as "kitsch". By using this polemical label, Greenberg laid as false a trail as Alloway, who preferred the kinder term "folk culture".

Popular culture, which from another point of view figures as mass culture, is neither the result of local cultural traditions nor a growth springing from the midst of the people. It is a product of the increasing industrialization of Western societies, and governs their relationships and mechanisms. Oriented towards the expectations of urban consumers, popular culture reacts seismographically to potential changes in collective moods and behaviour. Its originators are professional designers – artists, if you will – who work on commission and must adjust their individual ideas to conform with those of their clients. They might be compared to artists before the advent of the avant-garde, such

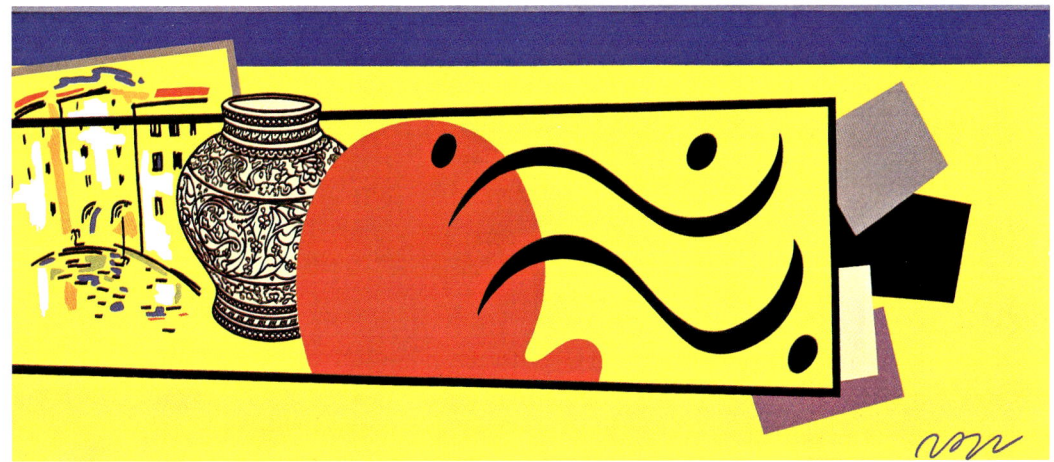

Patrick Caulfield
Artist's Studio, 1964
Oil on wood, 91 x 281 cm
(36 x 110¾ in.)
London, The Arts Council
of Great Britain

as the members of medieval building associations or early modern guilds. Like theirs, the activity of contemporary professionals is conducted on the basis of a division of labour, and they have no control over the final product of their work.

Industrially organized production of culture has always seemed suspect to committed cultural critics. For Max Horkheimer and Theodor W. Adorno, it represented an instrument of subtle oppression in the hands of those who possessed and administrated economic and political power. Its products served only one purpose – to draw people's attention away from their true interests and, by colonizing their minds, divert it towards superficial, surrogate pleasures. Beyond this, the mass production of standardized commodities and ideas, aimed at the lowest common denominator, would lead to a gradual decline in the general intellectual level. Greenberg thought similarly.

In view of commercial movies, René König reached a more differentiated conclusion. "If the effect of the mass nature of film and television presentations is in fact a massing of the audience, then this must be based on the assumption either that their effect falls everywhere on the same soil or that the recipients are completely passive."[7] The first assumption was unfounded, said König, because viewers and their mentalities were integrated in numerous different social spheres and differed in terms of sex, age, occupation, income and cultural attitude; the second assumption was unfounded because only certain people went to the cinema and not even they reacted uniformly to what it offered. By comparison with the traditional arts, moreover, film had the advantage of possessing a considerably greater range. It provided a crystallization point not necessarily for "manifest mental moods and ideas reduced to solid formulae, but, and especially, for the latent, frequently subliminal attitudes and expectations … of the collective unconscious."

Lichtenstein, Oldenburg, Rosenquist, Wesselmann and Warhol were probably more or less avid moviegoers. But they were definitely habitual beneficiaries of the American way of life. In addition, during, after or in parallel with their art studies, all of them practised commercial art, either voluntarily or as a way of earning a living. Lichtenstein gained experience as a technical draughtsman and designer of windows and sheet metal products. Oldenburg, from a well-off family, tried his hand at journalism and published drawings in illustrated magazines. Rosenquist worked as a billboard painter for a time, and Wesselmann studied cartooning. The best-known and most successful commercial artist among them was Warhol, who did brilliant, mannerist drawings for shoe ads. "Yet all of them", as Lucy Lippard explained, "were artists first and foremost, devoting their energies to serious painting … They have all steered away from the slick advertisement that imitates the modern fine arts." Their ambitions helped trigger the abrupt transformation of the art scene known as Pop.

If, in the early modern era, journeymen were furthered by their masters and introduced to potential clients, in the bourgeois period students were helped by their teachers, and in the modern age artists were publicized by writers and critics. Since the advent of the avant-garde, art dealers have had an increasing influence on the vicissitudes of the art scene. Abstract Expressionism owed its overwhelming international resonance not least to a powerful alliance of eloquent artists, intelligent critics like Greenberg, Harold Rosenberg et al., and strategically clever art dealers with a sense of artistic originality and energy, willingness to take risks, and force of character. Under the aegis of the avant-garde, the art trade emerged from its previous role of behind-the-scenes intermediary to become a key player on the stage of art.

In the 1940s and 1950s, young experimental artists and audacious dealers moved into the former industrial lofts in downtown Manhattan, a once vital manufacturing neighbourhood. The rents were affordable. The artists needed a platform from which to become known in the art world; the dealers knew their profit margin would increase the faster their clients advanced from unknown to successful artists. Both profited from the arrangement. In addition, artists' cooperatives and alternative sites funded by patrons gave ambitious artists an opportunity to attract attention and prove their talent outside the commercial gallery scene. Leo Castelli, Ileana Sonnabend, Ivan Karp and Richard Bellamy, who ran small galleries, supported Pop no less than the artists themselves or the first receptive critics and museum curators, such as Alloway, G. R. Swenson, Lucy Lippard, John Coplans, Geldzahler or Walter Hopps.

In the capitalist U.S., success was no stigma – it meant public recognition, even fame, even though this tended not to be openly admitted. Jasper Johns, whose work is generally associated with Pop, was once moved by a derogatory remark Willem de Kooning made about his dealer, Castelli, to cast two

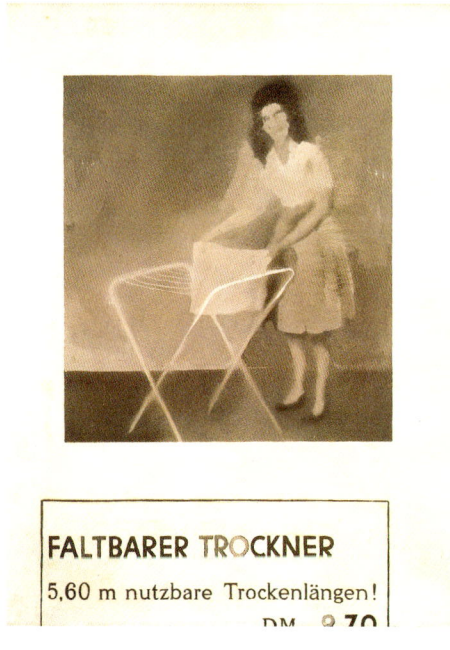

FALTBARER TROCKNER

5,60 m nutzbare Trockenlängen!

DM 8.70

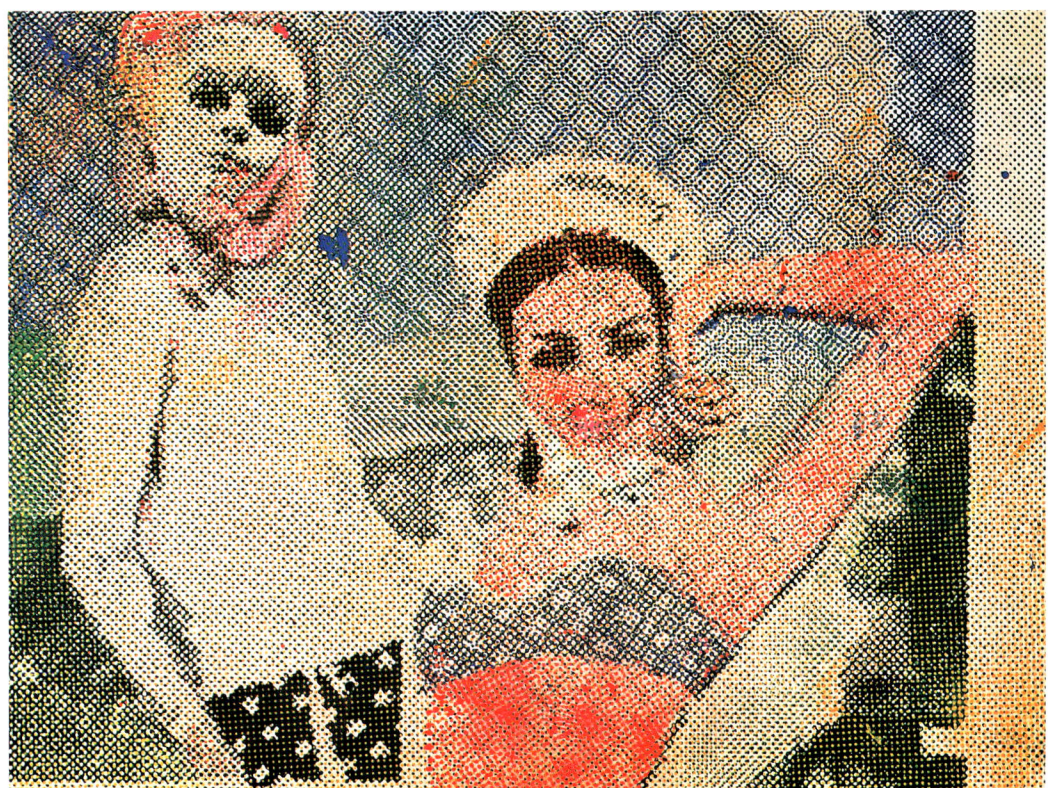

beer cans in bronze, carefully paint labels on them, and place them on a pedestal. De Kooning had maintained that Castelli could sell anything as art, even beer cans. And as Johns amusedly remembered, de Kooning was right.

Castelli had shown Johns as early as 1954. The artist concerned himself with the thorny problem of what works of art really are, and invented paintings that appeared to convey contradictory meanings. Johns selected very special motifs: flags, targets, numbers. The flag and target paintings raised the issue of identity. What did they mean? Were they flags, targets, numerals, or simply value-free works of art? Should the viewer put his hand over his heart in face of a painting of an American flag, or shoot a gun at a target, or simply derive an aesthetic experience from these things? Johns subtly challenged the claim of modern art to radical autonomy, the ideological premise of the avant-garde, and illustrated its fundamental hollowness in face of the flux of changing meanings associated with even the most common things. As he realized, such meanings take on continually new nuances depending on the point of view from which objects are seen and the interests projected into them. In formal terms, Johns cooled down the explosive gestural language of Abstract Expressionism, yet still put great store in masterfully painted finish and individual touch.

"I'm not a Pop artist!" declared Johns, and in fact almost nothing connected him with Pop – apart from the fact that he infringed on the criteria of avant-garde art by opening the aesthetic inner sanctum to the general viewer and included the phenomenon of the effect of art works in his approach. He took the faithful depiction of objects so far that it approached sheer imitation, only the sensitive painterly treatment of the motifs representing the difference. This is why, whether he liked it or not, Johns paved the way for Pop.

While Johns kept the option between art and reality open, Robert Rauschenberg plastered his mostly huge-format paintings with all manner of things from the mundane world and charged them with reality. Reproductions of newspaper articles, press photos and pin-ups, street signs, letters, wire, wood, grass, even stuffed chickens and goats populated his painting surfaces. Heterogeneous found objects were embedded in gesturally painted passages, and what might have been a disorganized jumble was coerced into a disparate aesthetic unity. Yet the selected actual materials did not entirely fuse with the art.

Fields of tension developed between the territories of the artistic and the real. Rauschenberg treated both on a basis of equality, and as a result, the aesthetic factor took on the character of the real. In a certain sense he also raised the question as to the identity of the painted image, seeing as many of the real things he employed were products of mass culture. Rauschenberg used both traditional painting techniques and contemporary artistic processes. The method of transferring printed illustrations onto canvas – decalcomania – was borrowed from the Surrealist Max Ernst, and Rauschenberg, like Warhol, employed the commercial technique of silkscreen, or serigraphy, to reproduce photographic imagery.

Although they did not jettison the postulate of artistic subjectivity, Johns and Rauschenberg lent the sphere of the real more weight in their works than the British Pop artists did. In view of the Americans' paintings, Max Imdahl rightly diagnosed symptoms of an "identity crisis". Shaping reality was something with which these artists were familiar anyway. They had decorated display windows for the upscale department store Bonwit Teller on Fifth Avenue, and had participated in Allan Kaprow's legendary happening *Eighteen Happenings in Six Parts* in 1959.

A mixture of theatrical actions with elements of dance and an informal dramaturgy, unconventional modes of artistic depiction and everyday behaviour, happenings were aesthetic attempts to escape from the self-chosen isolation of the avant-garde. Allan Kaprow in the U.S., Jean-Jacques Lebel and Wolf Vostell in Europe, developed the happening into a highly provocative form of art – and into an opposite pole to popular culture. "Art is life" was their battle cry.

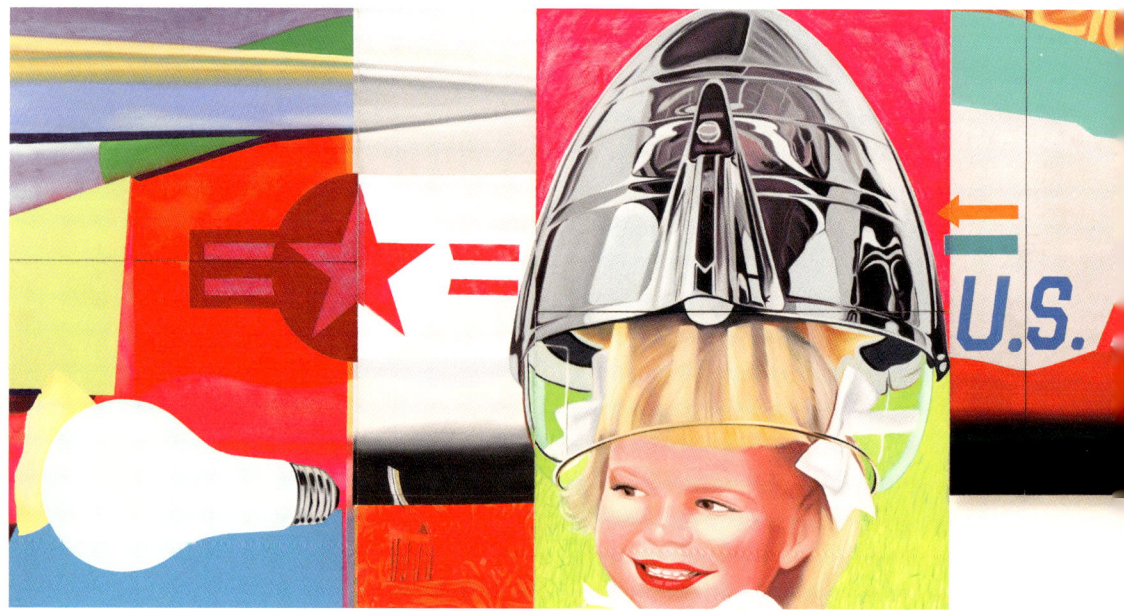

Downtown Manhattan, a vital milieu abounding in talents and eccentrics, was the site of the first group and solo exhibitions of Lichtenstein & Co. The artists knew each other through common projects, friends or goals. Oldenburg, like Dine and Lichtenstein, got on extremely well with Kaprow, for all of them had launched happenings. Rosenquist had gone to school with Oldenburg and Robert Indiana, and took drawing instruction during his postgraduate studies before becoming a prolific billboard painter. Wesselmann, after abandoning attempts in Abstract Expressionism, launched into collages with set-pieces from reality, and Warhol charmed clients and audiences with his shoe designs. Despite their intensive training as fine artists, they were all more deeply rooted in commercial culture than Johns or Rauschenberg, Kaprow or the British Pop artists. Their studies had not been limited to art, nor did they immediately succeed in making their mark on the art scene. They had to first detour through various fields of popular culture. Cinema, design and advertising belonged to their cultural environment like hamburgers and Coke.

So it is not surprising that after their initial halting attempts in an Abstract Expressionist vein, these artists began to search for aesthetically unexploited and visually powerful forms of imagery, and found them in the broad visual repertoire of mass culture. After all, they were experts in the field. Up to that point artists had merely quoted, usually ironically, this incredibly powerful imagery in their works, aesthetically transformed it or alienated it in collages or montages. The artists just listed, in contrast, appropriated this effervescent idiom almost unchanged, merely adapting specific characteristics to their artistic needs and intentions. They were not satisfied with simply transferring comics, food brands, design, photography, film and its personnel into the context of art, à la Duchamp. Instead, they as it were aesthetically improved the products of popular culture and lent them a permanent, if precarious, value.

Pop artists divided up the range of visual popular culture among themselves, and as soon as they had staked their claim to a certain segment, they began to subject it to variation after variation. Lichtenstein voted for the visual schemata

James Rosenquist
F-111 (detail), 1964/65
Oil on canvas, 305 x 2621 cm (120 x 1032 in.)
New York, The Museum of Modern Art,
Mr. and Mrs. Alex L. Hillman and
Lillie P. Bliss bequest

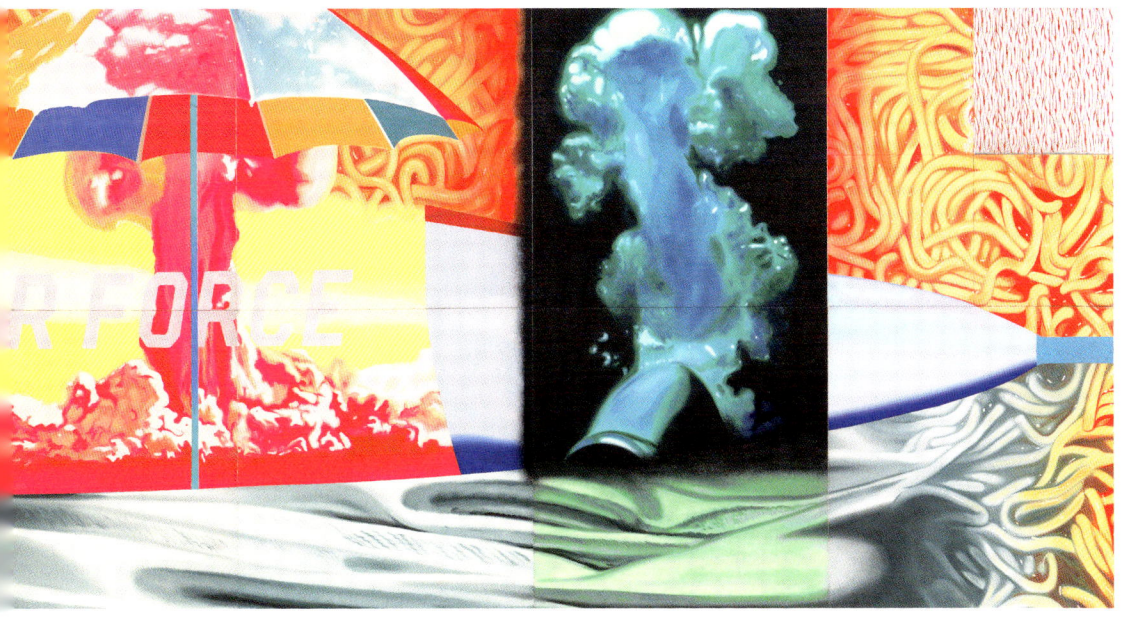

of cartoons. Warhol abandoned comics as soon as he saw Lichtenstein's pictures, turning instead to the compelling emblems on soup cans, detergent boxes and soft-drink bottles, then progressing to photographic reproductions of movie stars, car and airplane crashes, electric chairs, mafiosi and world-famous works of art. Oldenburg produced home appliances and foodstuffs – in unusual materials and on unusually large scales. Wesselmann perfected advertising design, and Rosenquist painted irritating billboard-like images in modish colours of jet fighters, Volkswagens, women's legs and Ford cars garnished with spaghetti in tomato sauce. After rapidly staking their claims, these artists proceeded to shape their prefabricated vocabulary into individual brands that might superficially be described as styles.

A further point of agreement consisted of an impersonal artistic treatment of visual motifs and a cultivation of the smooth, perfect paint application of professional commissioned work. The resulting paintings provided no insight into their makers' mood, mental state, thinking, feelings or aspirations. No one would maintain that Lichtenstein was obsessed with comics, or Warhol with artless photographs. Although most Pop artists favoured hand craftsmanship (only Warhol adopting a technical process), their paintings could just as well have been executed by trained assistants working to their instructions. Assistants indeed began doing the basic work in their studios after the art market had accepted their works and they had attracted the attention of collectors like the taxi entrepreneur Robert Scull (whose Pop collection would be acquired by the German manufacturer Karl Ströher), the architect Philip Johnson, and the publisher Harry Abrams.

Lichtenstein condensed the narrative line of cartoons and its rapid progression from frame to frame into a single, characteristic image, or, more rarely, a double or triple one. He unified the image, honed it to a point. In his vision of comic imagery, Lichtenstein expressed what the photographer Henri Cartier-Bresson called the "decisive moment". The formulaic visual language of his patterns – which were never taken from recent comic books, but already had a certain patina – permitted Lichtenstein to evoke effusive feelings such as fear and horror, love and hate, without drifting into cloying sentimentality. An ironic overtone frequently reverberated in his pictures, especially when Lichtenstein translated outstanding paintings of classical modernism into the terms of his semiotic and chromatic system. "If a commercial advertising firm had a mind to really knock the public out for a hard sell, they might use one of Wesselmann's paintings", said Jill Johnston, a pre-Pop artist of the day, aptly pointing out the narrowness of the gap between commercial and supposedly non-commercial art. Wesselmann, who created Pop icons with his series of *Great American Nudes*, explained, "I use a billboard picture because it is a real, special representation of something, not because it is from a billboard." What might appear puerile and tasteless when seen on a street, takes on an unexpected freshness when encountered in an art gallery or museum.

Rosenquist, too, had no fear of sullying himself by contact with commercial art. He executed his compositions using the same methods he had learned as a billboard painter. His decision to expand the painting area to dimensions that viewers could not take in at a glance likewise went back to sophisticated advertising strategies. The artificial world of Rosenquist's art excluded all ordinary reality, including that of nature, and replaced it with the artificial reality of popular culture, fascinating and threatening in one. In his compositions an F-111 jet fighter plane extends across twenty-six metres of spectacular painting, a gigantic tank appears on diaphanous packaging foil, and a VW Beetle mutates into a horrifying insect.

Oldenburg maintained the greatest distance to the culture industry. His art was shot through with fine irony and a covert love of anarchy. Oldenburg reproduced mass-produced consumer articles in papier-maché and other absurd materials, rendering them useless for any meaningful purpose, or

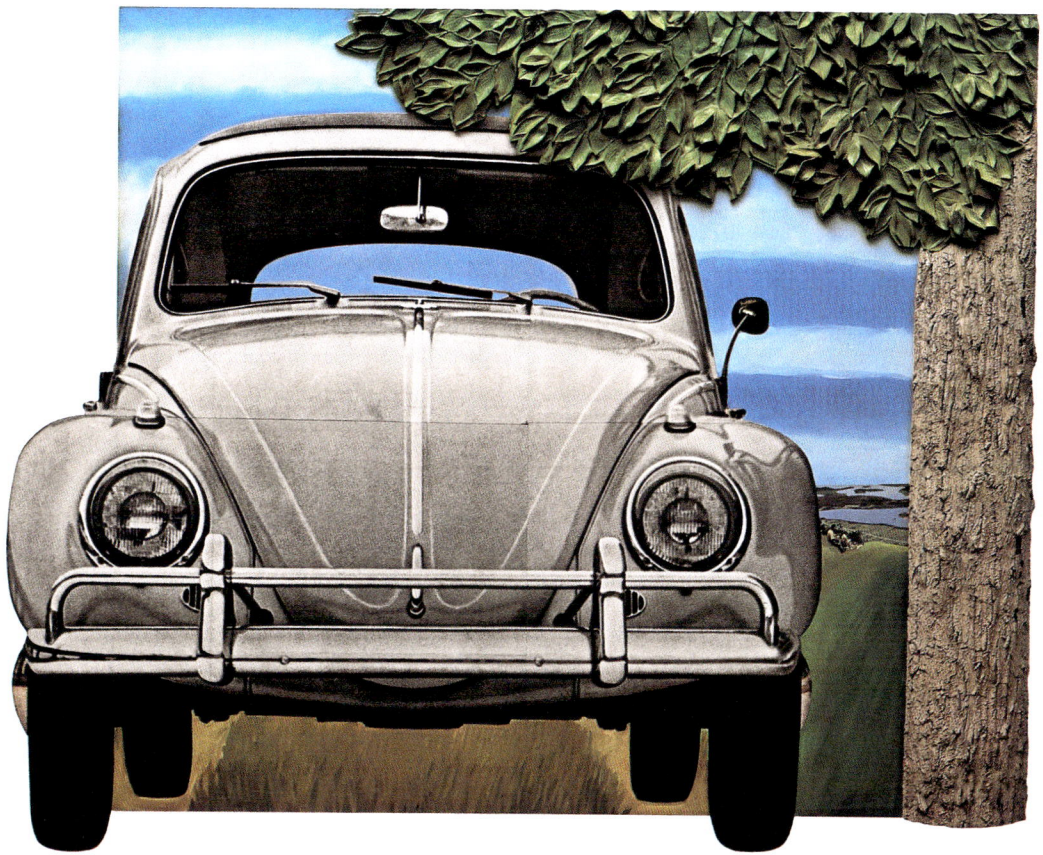

Tom Wesselmann
Landscape No. 2, 1964
Photograph, oil-paint and plastic on canvas, 193 x 239 cm (76 x 94 in.)
Cologne, Museum Ludwig

blew them up to such a monstrous scale that they exploded the familiar context and seemed to rock the foundations of civilization itself. Only in the commercial cinema of Alfred Hitchcock does the insurrection of objects take on a similarly frightening aspect.

The Pop artist par excellence is doubtless Andy Warhol. He represented Pop not only in his art, but in his own person. Everything that made Pop revolutionary was contained in his work. And he rightly rejected the assertion that Pop was a "counter-revolution". He linked up with artistic ideas that involved neither exaggerated individualism nor reflection on aesthetic models. In modern mass media and their technical possibilities he discovered an artistic potential suited to modern mass society.

Warhol transferred their techniques, materials and forms, with slight retouchings, into the aesthetic field of art. By so doing, Warhol intensified the "identity crisis" of painting, which Johns had triggered with his flag and target paintings, into an identity crisis of modern art per se. His posthumous pictures of the movie star Marilyn Monroe – were they painted portraits or mythical icons? As icons, they would visually embody the absent actress, would represent a piece of mythical reality, and thus would not be art in the modernist sense of the term. After all, it was Warhol's *Marilyn* series that spirited the star into the realm of myth.

Warhol's art undermined the remaining bastions of art-as-art and used the popular media to breach its walls. Little by little, photography and film advanced into the galleries and museums, international exhibitions and collections. And in their wake followed fashion, event culture, pop music. Warhol's Pop threw open the doors, and ever since, not only has popular culture been a theme of art but vice versa, art has become an integral part of popular culture. In hindsight, Alloway's reservations appear short-sighted.

In a "Factory" established for the purpose, the indefatigable Warhol oversaw a production of paintings on a division-of-labour, assembly-line basis. The process was half mechanical, half manual, employing the silkscreen technique, which had become a favourite of commercial artists after World War II. That the execution was intentionally sloppy represented a concession to aesthetic reservations regarding the perfection of popular mass-produced imagery. The subjects of Warhol's paintings and objects stemmed from the realm of consumerism and glossy magazines. By repeating the same motifs over and over again in endless series, he reflected the standardization of industrial mass-production. On the other hand, incessant repetition was a time-tested means used by the cultural industry to inculcate the significance of spectacular events.

The camera accompanied Warhol wherever he went. Not coincidentally, his photos mark a key stage in the history of photography. Moreover, as director and producer of documentary and feature films, he catapulted himself into cinema history. Warhol was not only the "cool" producer and observer; he was a virtuoso player on the keyboard of the cultural enterprise and consciously exploited its laws for his own purposes. With his canny and slightly subversive activity, Warhol put an end to the fiction according to which a non-commercial approach was an infallible sign of extraordinary art. "Noncommercial art has given us Seurat's *Grande Jatte* and Shakespeare's sonnets, but also much that is esoteric to the point of incommunicability. Conversely, commercial art has given us much that is vulgar or snobbish (two aspects of the same thing) to the point of loathsomeness, but also Dürer's prints and Shakespeare's plays."[8] And the images of Pop Art, photography, motion pictures …

George Segal
Portrait of Sidney Janis with Mondrian Painting, 1967
Mixed media, 177.3 x 142.8 x 69.1 cm (69⅞ x 56¼ x 27¼ in.)
New York, The Museum of Modern Art,
The Sidney and Harriet Janis Collection

PAGES 432/433
Hans Namuth
Leo Castelli and Artists
The Odeon, 1982

FROM LEFT TO RIGHT, STANDING:
Ellsworth Kelly, Dan Flavin, Joseph Kosuth,
Richard Serra, Lawrence Weiner, Nassos Daphnis,
Jasper Johns, Claes Oldenburg, Salvatore Scarpitta,
Richard Artschwager, Mia Westerlund Roosen,
Cletus Johnson, Keith Sonnier; SEATED:
Andy Warhol, Robert Rauschenberg, Leo Castelli,
Ed Ruscha, James Rosenquist, Robert Barry

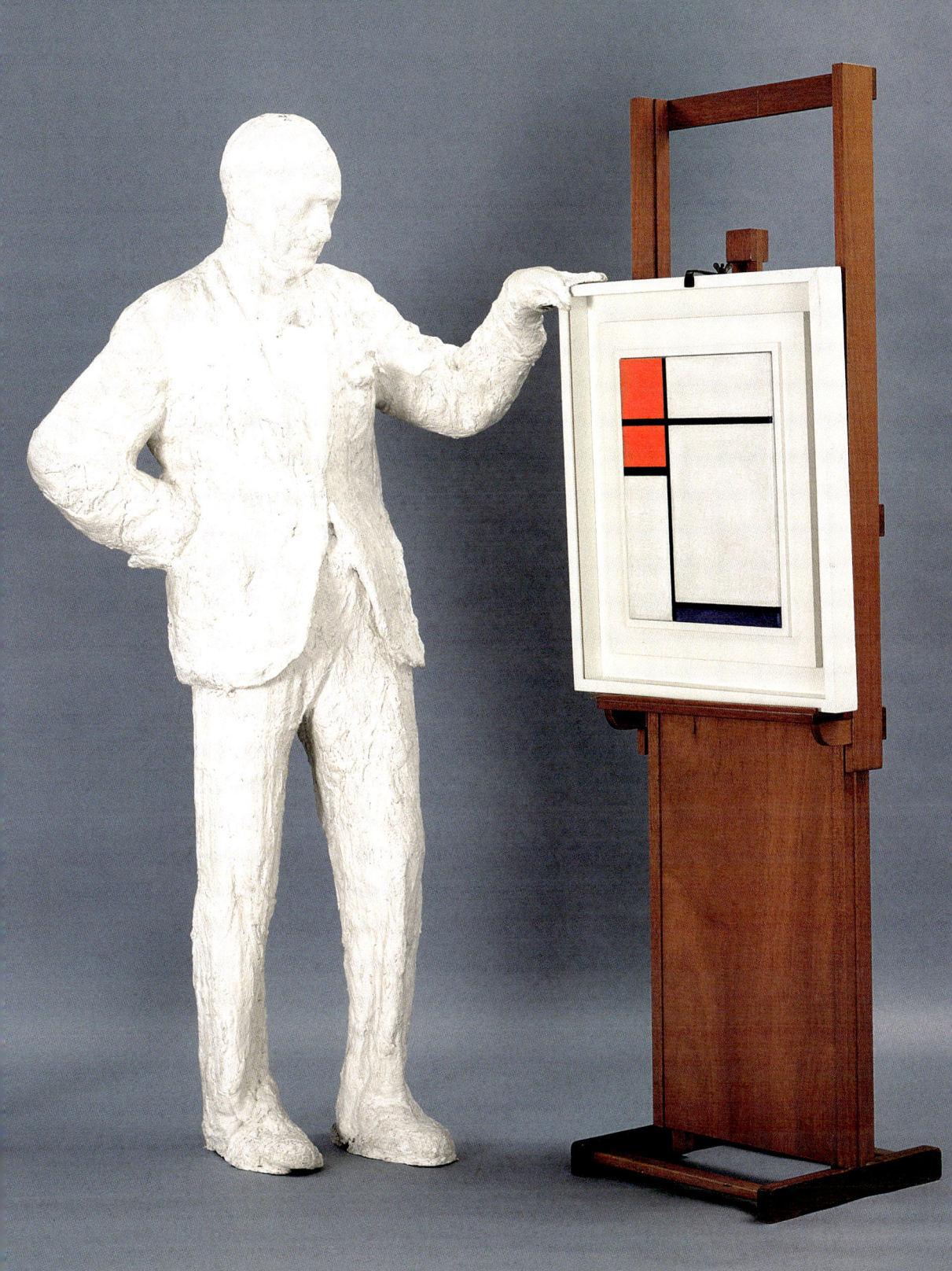

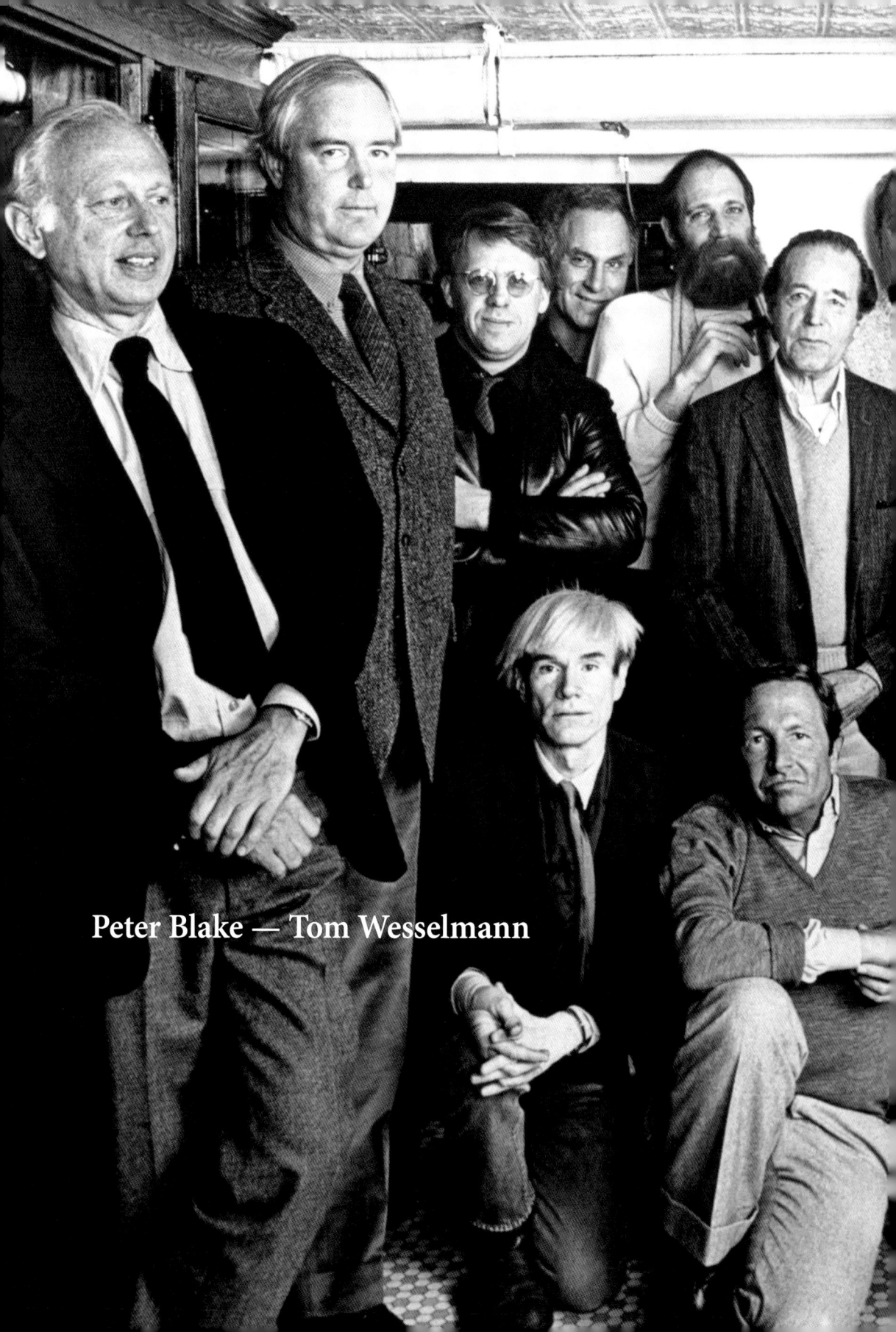

Peter Blake — Tom Wesselmann

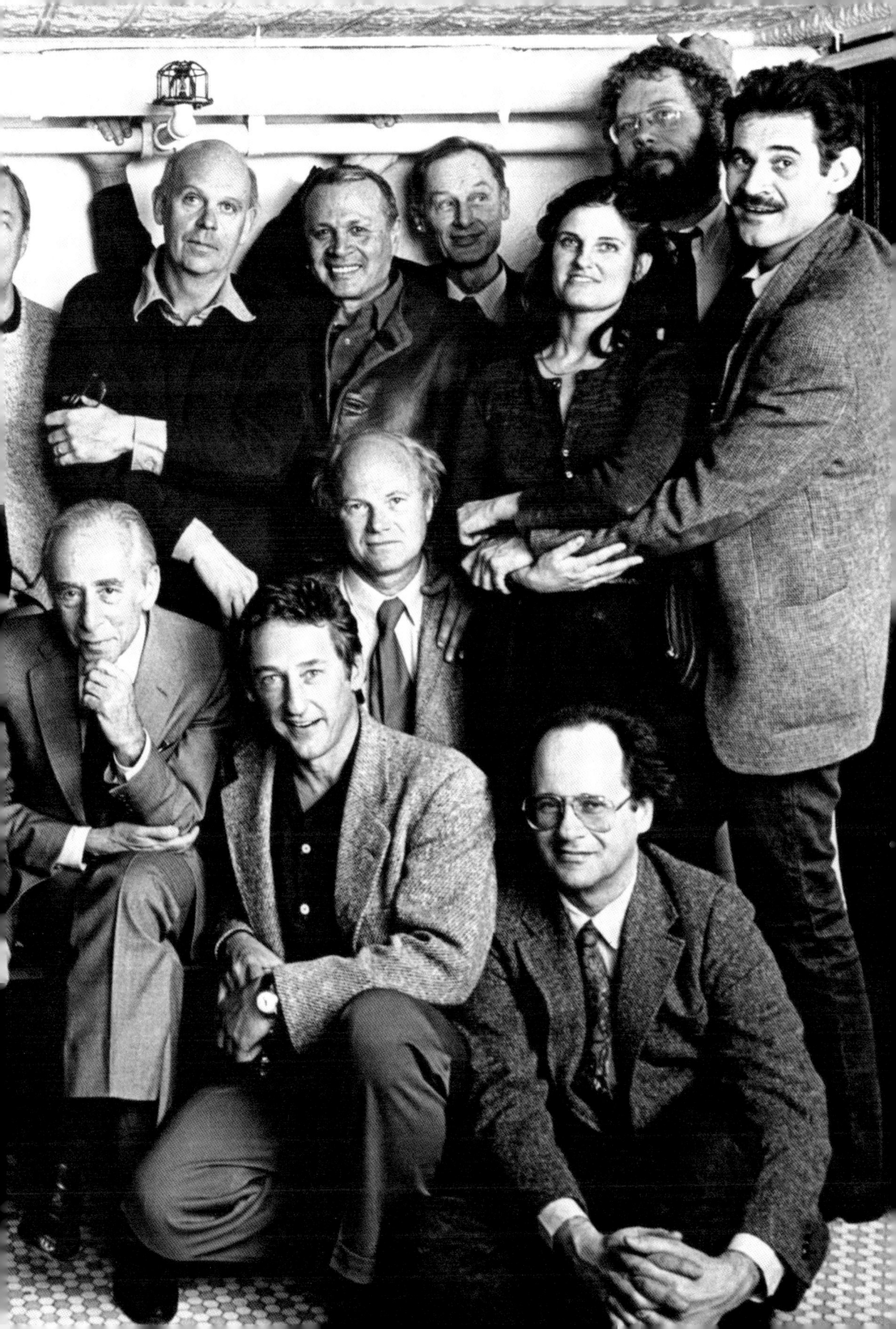

Peter Blake
On the Balcony, 1955–57

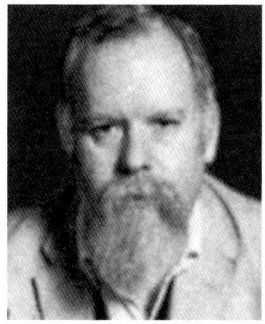

b. 1932 in Dartford,
United Kingdom

Long before contemporary art legitimated the collecting of curios under the name of "clue-finding" or "forensic art", Peter Blake showed himself to be a collector, or at least a painstaking registrar. He presented his collection not in the form of original finds but in painted form, as here, where they are brought together frontally on a green ground. The objects of Blake's collection share the picture with four young people, lined up in pairs on a bench. Also depicted is an angular table, on which stands another girl, only the lower half of whose figure is visible. The character of the things depicted might best be described by the term "miscellaneous". Two-dimensional objects like paintings and drawings of diverse origin – but none over one hundred years old – are in the majority. These are accompanied by covers from the illustrated magazines *Life* and *Weekly Illustrated*, a photograph of Sir Winston Churchill complete with waving royal family, an earlier panorama picture of the royal family with European relatives, a packet of cigarettes, an open book, a third photograph, and a pennant. On the table at the left sit ordinary consumer goods such as a package of margarine, a half-full bottle of pop, a tin of sardines, a newspaper … The list is by no means exhaustive. Probably the artist merely "registered" whatever had happened to accumulate in his studio. Every motif is painstakingly rendered, down to the tiniest detail, with photographic fidelity. Their plasticity contrasts strangely with the schematically depicted, relatively childish faces and figures of the young people. Nothing in the collection seems extraordinary – were it not for the masterpiece by Édouard Manet that crops up almost unnoticed at the left edge and that gave Blake's picture its title: *The Balcony*, 1868. The artist has placed this superb work of art on the same level as the trivia of mass culture. In fact, in this context it becomes an integral part of this culture. For as its small dimensions indicate, the Manet is merely a copy or reproduction in a gilded frame. Although the relationships among the diverse objects remain enigmatic, Blake's painting subliminally raises the issue of the status of the work of art in the age of its technical reproducibility (the subject of a groundbreaking essay by Walter Benjamin), and quite casually demonstrates the change that has taken place in our habits of perception since the French artist's day, the consequences of distracted vision.

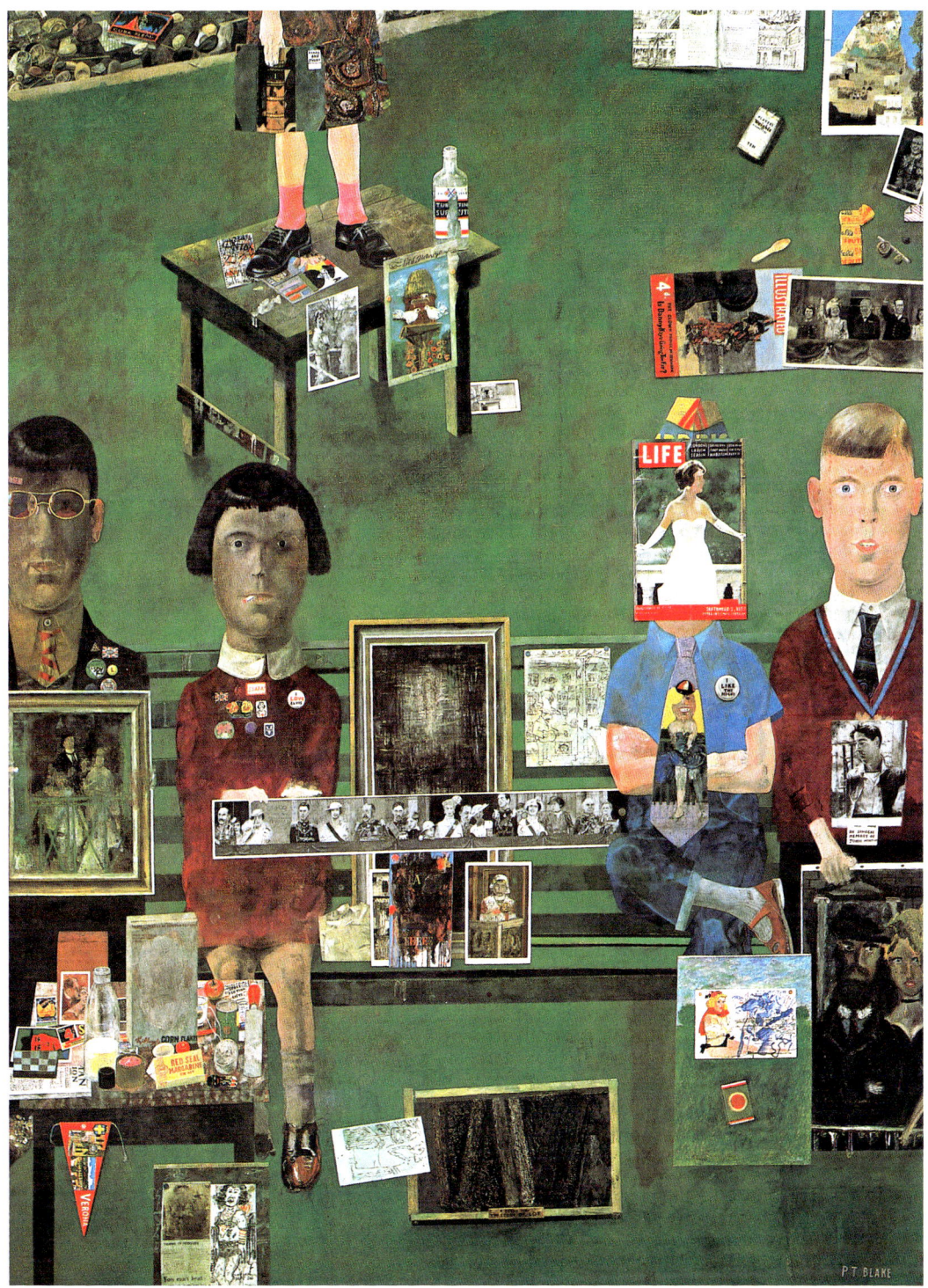

On the Balcony, 1955–57
Oil on canvas, 121 x 91 cm (47¾ x 36 in.)
London, Tate

Allan D'Arcangelo
U.S. Highway 1, Number 5, 1962

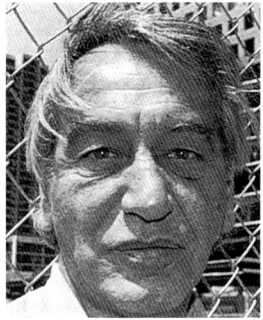

b. 1930 in Buffalo, New York
d. 1998 in New York City

With the exception of meteorite hits from outer space and the long ice ages with their geological displacements, nothing has changed the face of our planet more than the automobile. Neither industry nor the railroad nor the aeroplane. And unlike the railroad and the aeroplane, the automobile is more than just an essential factor in modern civilization and a key motor of economic growth. It is also a symbol of individual freedom – the freedom to move without physical exertion wherever and whenever we like. Yet to do so, a dense network of streets and roads through cities and countryside is required. Private cars mobilize the masses, and as a result, cities burgeon into endless unwieldy megalopolises, beset by an incessant flow of traffic in and out, resulting in the inevitable jams. An independent culture has grown up around the automobile, complete with its own sign system and behavioural code: traffic culture. Allan D'Arcangelo, a painter whose relationship to Pop vacillates, has made a psychological aspect of this culture the subject matter of his art, and graphically developed it in extended series of works. In his large-format paintings, the experience of the landscape from the point of view of a speeding motorist becomes a visual event. The geological, topographical and cultural differences between the stretches of countryside the car rushes through are reduced to a few fleeting, cursorily depicted details: the endless ribbon of road, the changing light, emblems from the repertoire of traffic signage, and the sky over a far horizon. Accordingly, the painter reduces perception of the landscape to elemental forms and a few highly contrasting colours, to the data registered by the motorist's eye. D'Arcangelo is the sole Pop artist to have relinquished the role of detached observer. The composition of *U.S. Highway 1, Number 5*, one of five versions in a series, is marked by an exaggerated perspective that literally pulls the viewer's eye into it and catapults it up to the upper edge, directly linking perception with physical sensation. It mobilizes the eye and draws it over the strongly foreshortened road from the anonymous foreground to the illuminated billboard and the numbering behind it. The painting surface suddenly metamorphoses into a virtual movie screen, on which the image seems to be in motion. An image as if taken by a camera moving precipitously forward. The smooth paint application and constructed composition stand in contrast to the picture's emotional effect. Not even the evocation of the twilight hour awakens romantic feelings. The picture as such, at any rate, is a symbol of the unlimited possibilities of the American dream, as invoked in countless literary works, photographs and above all, in the movies.

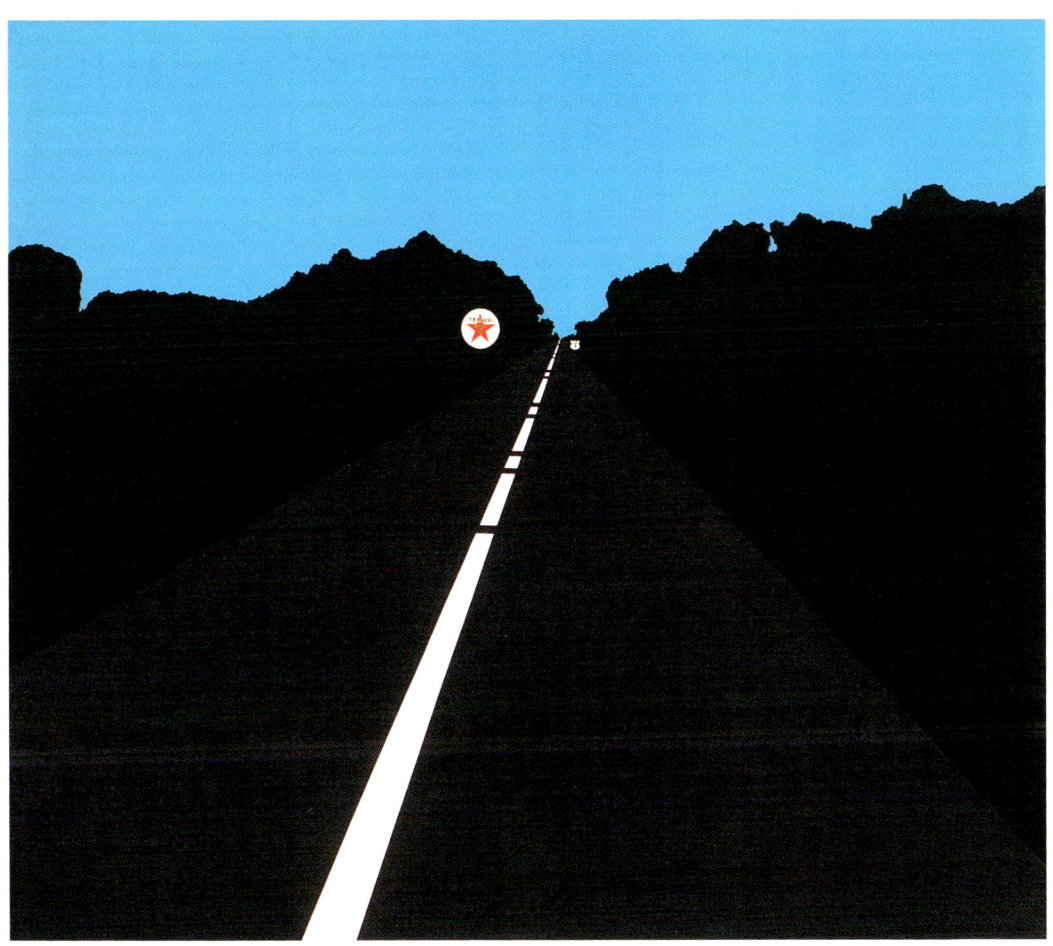

U.S. Highway 1, Number 5, 1962
Synthetic polymer on canvas,
177.6 x 207 cm (70 x 81½ in.)
New York, The Museum of Modern Art,
gift of Mr. and Mrs. Herbert Fischbach

Jim Dine
Double Isometric Self-Portrait (Serape), 1964

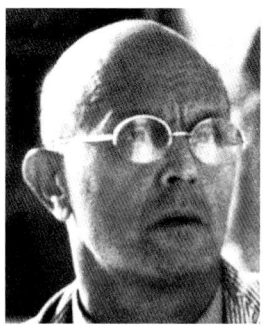

b. 1935 in Cincinnati, Ohio

Although his paintings – more precisely, his painting-objects – have been and still are represented in every important exhibition of Pop Art, Dine has never concealed his scepticism with regard to its significance. Superficially, there would seem to be little difference between his works, especially the earlier ones, and those of Lichtenstein, Warhol, et al. A preference for the everyday and mundane is found in Dine as well, as is a distance from Abstract Expressionism. No less obvious, however, is the artist's inner detachment from popular culture. Still, articles of clothing did play a key role in Dine's work during the emergence of Pop. Trousers, jackets, coats in many variants populated his canvases, and not seldom these functioned as mere backgrounds for the real articles, hung in front of them.

Double Isometric Self-Portrait (Serape) is a double image of a schematically rendered robe. At least on first glance. Soon we realize that these must be two robes, if extraordinarily similar in terms of outline, form and length. That the depictions resemble sewing patterns is no accident, and it would be more correct to describe them as reproductions of patterns for articles of slightly different sizes. Especially as they are composed of a series of separate elements, like collages. This impression is further underscored by the diverse colouring. And just as the artist has built up the robes' form of precisely contoured irregular colour fields, he has structured the two wings of the picture like a mosaic of diversely coloured shapes. As a result, on longer scrutiny the distinction between figure and ground begins to blur, the contours of the robes dissolve into abstract formal puzzles. In front of these dangle chains, one in each half. At the lower edge, the chains end in a ring with a section of wooden dowel.

The world of things in Dine's works is pervaded by personal references and allusions. The articles of clothing are like a second skin to the artist, a second self. On the other hand, in a happening he staged before beginning his painting career, Dine used his own skin as a basis for painting. Still, the artist is concerned most with elementary artistic problems, foremost issues of visual perception, the tension between signified and signifier, simulated and factual.

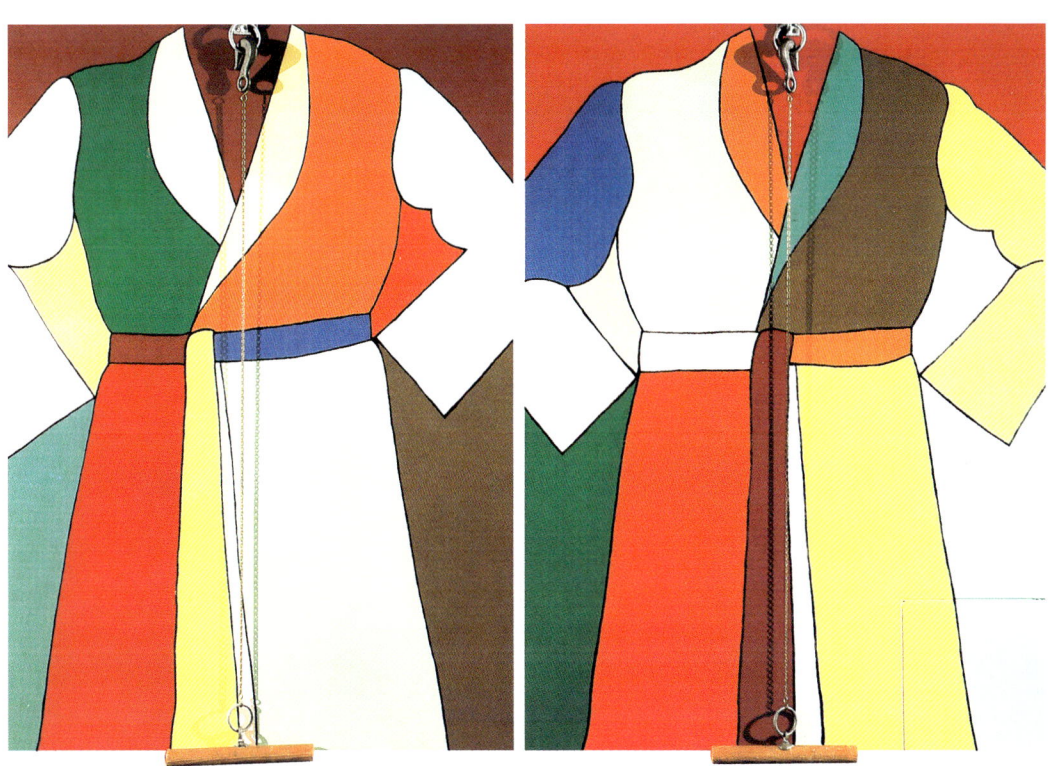

Double Isometric Self-Portrait (Serape), 1964
Oil, wood and metal on canvas, 145 x 215 cm (57 x 84¾ in.)
New York, Whitney Museum of American Art,
gift of Helen W. Benjamin

Red Grooms
Hollywood (Jean Harlow), 1965

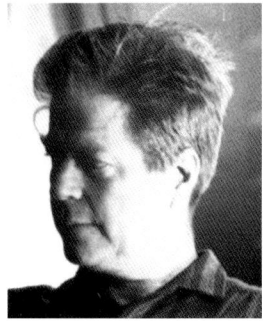

b. 1937 in Nashville, Tennessee

If Ruscha illuminated the Hollywood myth in the form of magical letters and Warhol celebrated it in the form of great divas, Grooms materialized the fleeting glamour of the Dream Factory in three-dimensional plastic shape. Wood and acrylic paint are the stuff of which myths are made. In front of a fanlike semicircle, like Aphrodite receiving one of her numerous suitors, a goddess of the silver screen who died at an early age reclines on a divan with pleated coverlet, beaming with wide eyes and tempting smile at her audience, who stand in for her lover. Everything, every gesture, facial expression, appeal is addressed, as in the movies, not to her fellow actors but solely to her public. With the difference that Grooms, unlike the illusion machine that is cinema, does not hide this circumstance but accentuates it. Her pretty legs raised and bared to over the knee, the platinum blonde Harlow accords us a glance into her magnificent décolleté by lifting her arms to her head. She dominates the scene in the sculpture as she frequently did in her films, despite the fact that a male partner in a black tuxedo sits on the edge of the bed, worshipping her. This is not Clark Gable, into whose arms she fell most often, but probably Franchot Tone, whom Grooms did not find worthy of mentioning by name.

Harlow, who died prematurely in mysterious circumstances, was more than a prototype for the pin-ups Lana Turner and Marilyn Monroe, with whom she had much in common. Yet despite her unusually erotic screen presence and comic talent, she has long descended into the shadow realm of cinema, and even in Grooms' sculpture, she figures as little more than a metaphor for a culture industry that transforms mere shades into deceptive heroines and heroes. In addition to advertising, comics and glossy magazine photos, Hollywood provided much material for the stockpile of Pop imagery. Grooms, however, was no typical Pop artist. Although he had exhibited with Dine, Lichtenstein, Oldenburg and Segal in downtown Manhattan (at the Reuben Gallery) and participated in happenings, unlike them he practised an outspoken social critique, usually with a satirically exaggerated touch.

Harlow's smile in *Hollywood* turns into a distorted grimace, and her obtrusive appeal to the audience only conceals the abysmal loneliness of a former sex symbol, as well as the fact that in the eyes of the culture industry, she was little more than a vehicle for earning money.

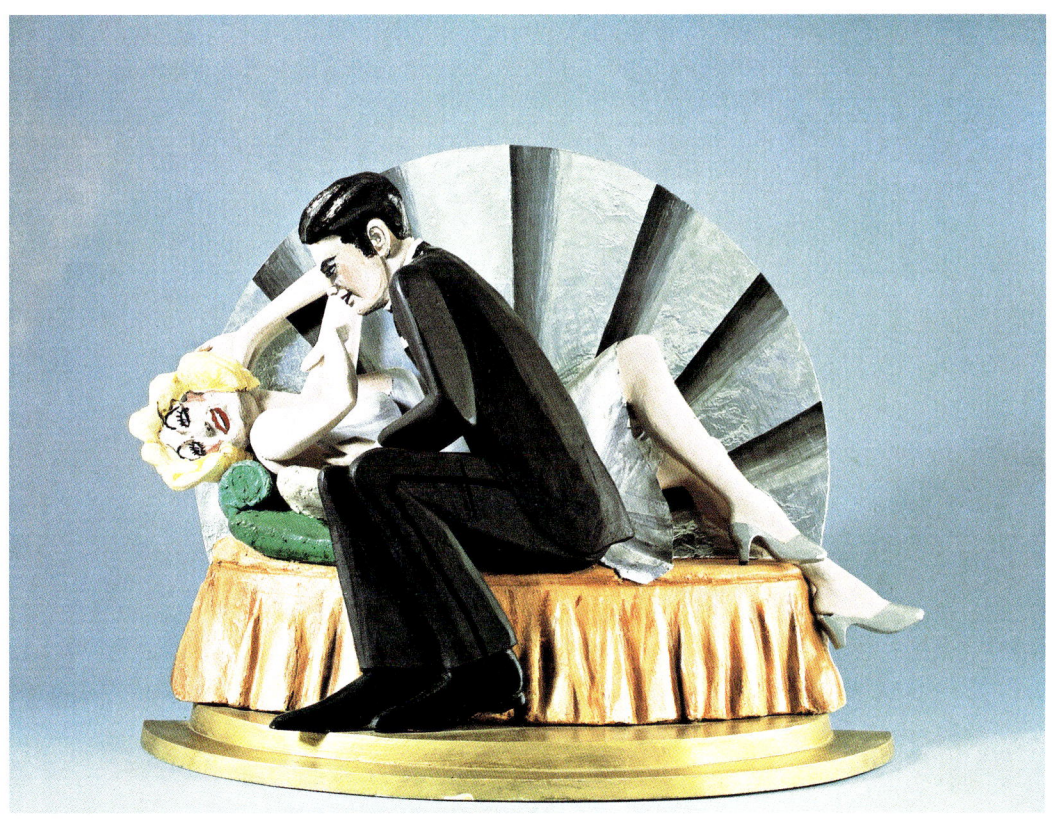

Hollywood (Jean Harlow), 1965
Acrylic on wood, 79 x 91 x 31.5 cm (31 x 36 x 12½ in.)
Washington, D.C., Hirshhorn Museum and
Sculpture Garden, Smithsonian Institution,
gift of Joseph H. Hirshhorn

Richard Hamilton

Just what is it that makes today's homes
so different, so appealing?, 1956

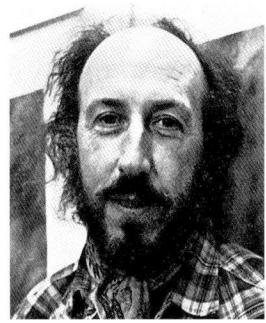

b. 1922 in London
d. 2011 in London

When the critical literature cites one picture as having announced the advent of Pop Art, it is referring to Richard Hamilton's collage with the tricky question, *Just what is it that makes today's homes so different, so appealing?* On the lollipop wrapping being toted for some inscrutable reason by the muscle builder at the left stands the word "POP", in yellow on red. For many people, this collage of cut-out magazine illustrations represents the primary source of the term. Other commentators go so far as to state that every connection between Pop and popular culture was a matter of chance, accidental. Pop, like Dada, was a spontaneous coinage, they say, and cite the British artist's work as proof. What speaks against this argument is the fact that the collage was not originally conceived as an independent work of art, but rather as an illustration for the catalogue to an exhibition with the fine title, *This is Tomorrow*, held in 1956 at the Whitechapel Gallery. Although the show concerned itself with issues of everyday culture, primarily from the point of view of architects and city planners, it was not without influence on the development of Pop Art in Britain, because it looked beyond the confines of fine art to modern urban civilization and its forms of visual expression. Hamilton was one of the designers involved in the presentation, which caused a furore especially because of its "fun-fair architecture". Yet more importantly, the insignia of popular culture had suddenly cropped up in a bona fide art gallery which, like all art galleries, had previously considered itself a bastion against the "visual trash" purveyed by the commercial media. Hamilton's innuendo-filled collage presents some of the key building-blocks of this industrially produced popular culture: sexy, artificially modified human physiques both male and female; contemporary video and audio technologies; and the clinically clean atmosphere of the modern household, complete with its impersonal furnishings. And the composition contains a nearly complete anthology of modern visual media: poster, company emblem, cinema – visible behind the body builder is an ad for what is thought to be the world's first sound movie, *The Jazz Singer* – and television. Not to forget the handicraft of collage, a paste-up of various set pieces from the illustrated press, a technique and form used by the artist to reflect on the nature of the medium itself. Every element from which Pop Art would later grow is present, including a critical undertone. Doubtless this collage stands at the beginning of an artistic revolution, but it does not embody it, merely having served to supply it with motifs. Yet this holds, if at all, only for the British version of Pop, not the American.

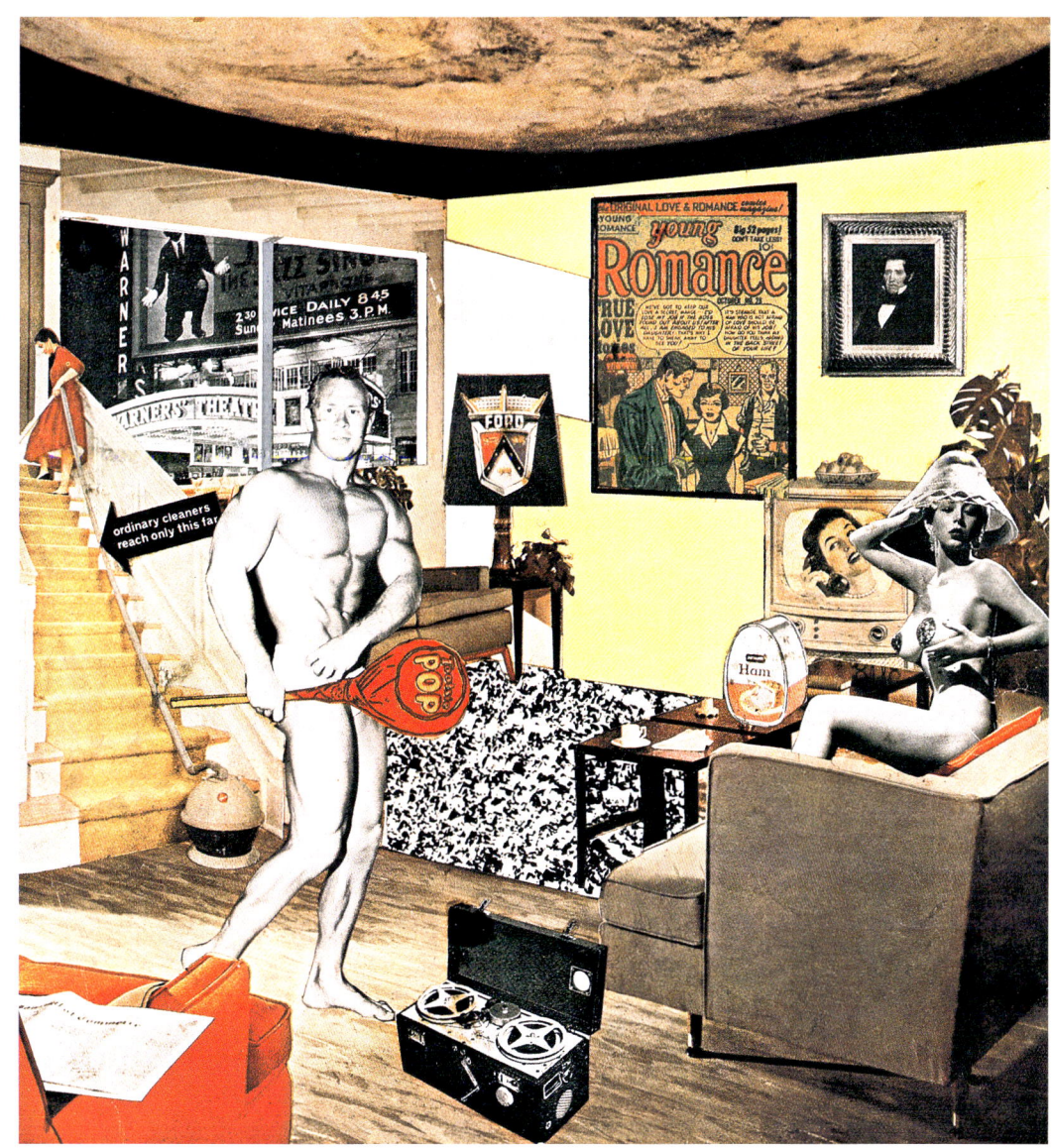

Just what is it that makes today's
homes so different, so appealing?, 1956
Collage, 26 x 25 cm (10¼ x 10 in.)
Kunsthalle Tübingen

Richard Hamilton
My Marilyn (paste up), 1964

Two years after her death, Richard Hamilton created his personal image of Hollywood star Marilyn Monroe in this "paste up", a term used by commercial artists to describe a layout ready for reproduction and printing. This is no homage to the actress who was a great star in the cinematic sky but had not yet reached the mythical status which Warhol helped her achieve. Hamilton's image is more like a brief, graphic analysis of the mechanisms to which she owed her fame. Twelve photos of Monroe are arranged on the canvas, their frames identifying them as contact prints from a photo session on the beach. With few exceptions, Hamilton has coloured or tinted them. The formats of the altered contacts vary, only the last one diverging, and not in terms of size alone. Against a sky divided into purple and orange fields, we see a white fleck instead of a person, only the contours of the figure remaining, like an empty stencil. In the series of shots arranged in two blocks of four, the artist has apparently conducted something in the nature of a successive expungement of a human personality, or the transformation of an individual into an object of consumption. Marilyn Monroe had evidently posed in a bikini for an unnamed photographer, while performing her usual antics. Hamilton used the results for his collage. The best pictures from the session were intended for publication, that is, were not private snapshots. This is indicated by the crosses on the many photos which did not pass muster. One bears the remark "good". It shows the star in her most marketable pose: happily laughing, taken from the slightly raised vantage point of the "American view", that is, revealing deep insight into the top of her bathing suit. *My Marilyn*, of which an earlier, less radical version exists, mercilessly illustrates by the simplest means the price someone from the pin-up school had to pay to become a Hollywood star. In her last interview, published by Enno Patalas, Marilyn confessed that the worst part of being a sex symbol was that it made you into a thing. And she simply hated being a thing.

Hamilton was an unusual artist. Before studying painting at various schools, he devoted himself to a career in commercial design and advertising. As a teacher and co-organizer of groundbreaking exhibitions he figured, alongside Eduardo Paolozzi, as a key figure in British Pop Art, and was a member of the creative Independent Group at the ICA. He became a confidant and friend of Marcel Duchamp, who, with James Joyce, exerted a great influence on him when Hamilton concerned himself intensively with Duchamp's work, including the making of a reconstruction of his masterpiece, *The Large Glass* (1915–23). Hamilton belonged to that exclusive group of artists for artists, who have had a much greater influence on the art of modernism than their sparing presence in the world's museums would suggest. Hamilton himself, by the way, considered himself an "artist in the old style".

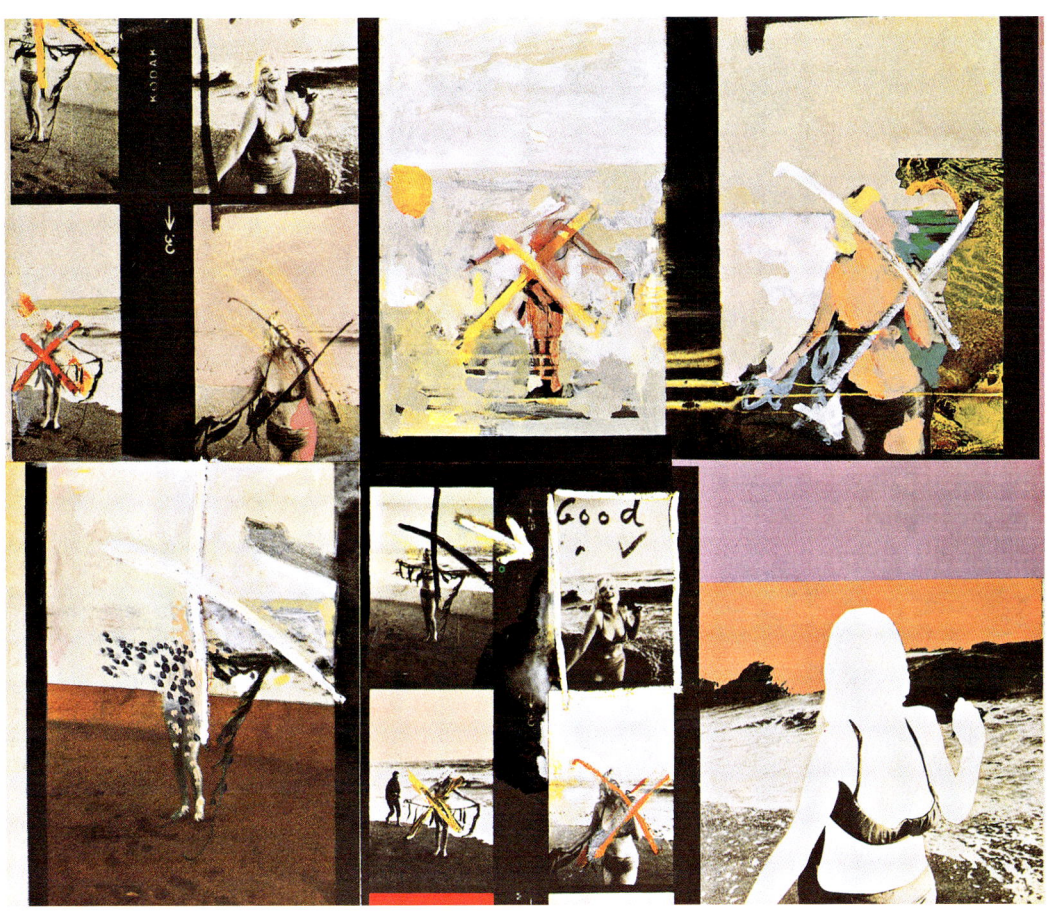

My Marilyn (paste up), 1964
Photos and oil on canvas,
51 x 62 cm (20 x 24½ in.)
Cologne, Museum Ludwig

David Hockney
Tea Painting in an Illusionistic Style, 1961

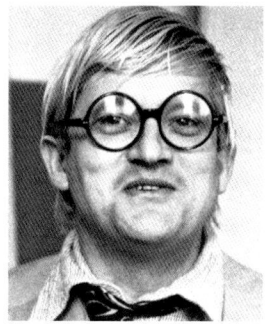

b. 1937 in Bradford,
United Kingdom

The outside contours of this oil painting correspond to a two-dimensional depiction of an open tea box, viewed from above. Yet the shape of the open lid already diverges from the laws of perspective. This form runs counter to the rules of illusionistic representation that govern traditional painting, forcing the upper section of the picture into the actual plane of the canvas. The same is true of the painting approach itself. Although a few details of the label are identifiable and the "image" of the package is conveyed, the arrangement of the lettering and the paint application reveal a certain subjectivity, a carelessness and spontaneity that cannot be explained by evanescent reflections like those in the upper part of the picture. But the seated nude male figure, extending beyond the outlines of the tea box, completely eludes the convention of the "illusionistic style" referred to in the title. This is literally a foreign body, the most disturbing one in the composition. Naturally the title claims just the opposite of what we see, and the apparent lack of mastery of traditional schemes of representation is only feigned.

Although *Tea Painting in an Illusionistic Style* partakes of the spirit of Pop, primarily in terms of motif, David Hockney is anything but a Pop artist. Neither is he interested in the realm of mass consumption and its brazen symbolism, nor is he fascinated by the phenomenon of the reproducibility of the work of art, including its standardized language. Hockney does receive impulses from popular culture, but he reshapes them to conform with his aesthetic ideas. The resulting imagery ultimately remains more beholding to his artistic world than to the reality from which its elements were derived. The apparently childlike drawing, the delicate use of colour, the traces of the painting hand, the suggestions of sexual desire are more important than the elaborately rendered box, despite the fact that tea is for the English what Coca-Cola is for Americans.

The artist's later development illustrated his distance from Pop even more clearly. It was more strongly inspired by the Mediterranean spirit of Matisse and Bonnard, especially in terms of a celebration of light and regardless of choice of motif and palette, than by the spirit of cinema and advertising. And even when Hockney turned to photography, his concern was not so much with its character as a medium as with its specific pictorial qualities.

Tea Painting in an Illusionistic Style, 1961
Oil on canvas, 232.5 x 83 x 3.8 cm (91½ x 32¾ x 1½ in.)
London, Tate

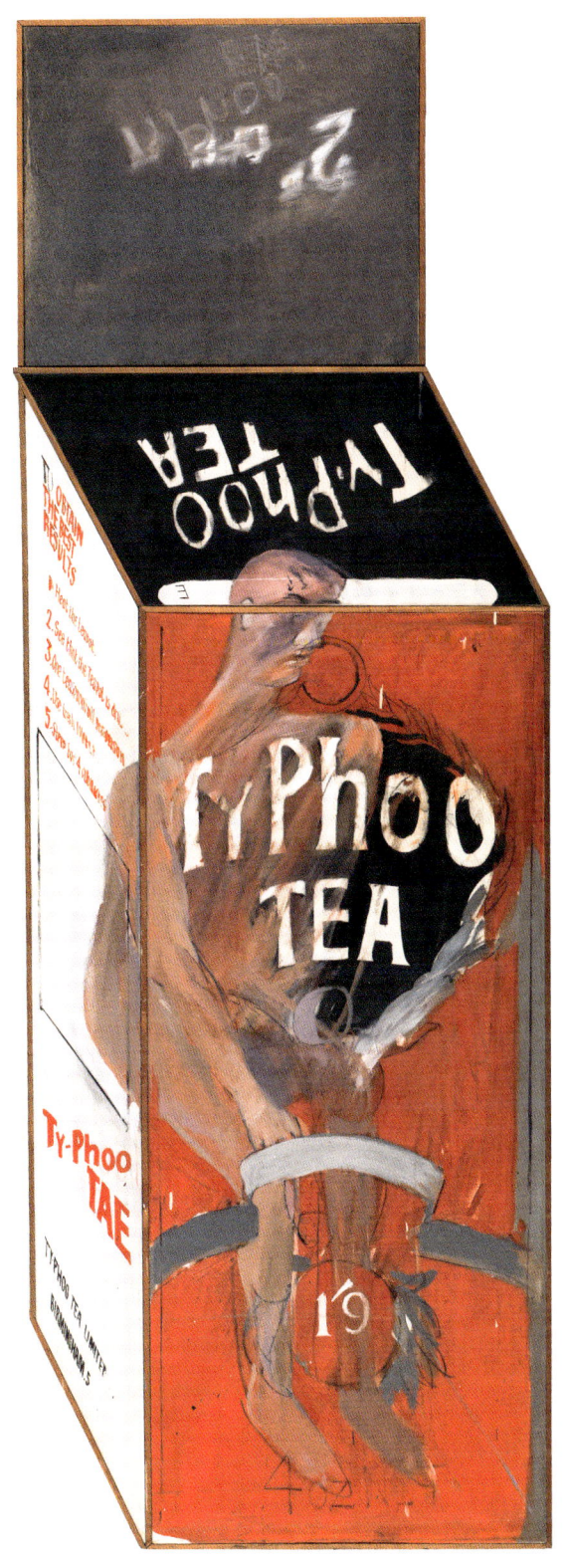

Robert Indiana
The Big Eight, 1961

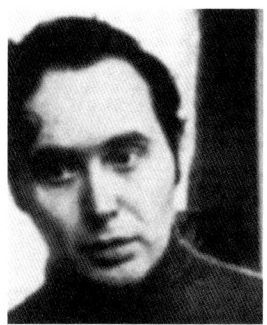

b. 1928 in New Castle, Indiana
as Robert Clark
d. 2018 in Vinalhaven, Maine

Abstract? Figurative? Realistic? Art for art's sake? Somehow all of these questions bounce off this painting with a great, bright red figure eight on a blue ground in the centre. Certainly a number is an abstract symbol representing a certain amount. But here the digit does not indicate an amount, unless it be the circle composed of eight arc segments in white that surrounds it like a nimbus. The title naturally leaves no room for such speculation. It does not go beyond what the eye sees. "What you see is what you see", is the often-quoted maxim of the artist Frank Stella, a contemporary of Robert Indiana. Yet Stella made his mark with abstract, structuralist painting-objects, whereas Indiana is associated with Pop Art. So might the number refer to something beyond the painted canvas which the title conceals? In other works by this artist, numbers refer to the numbers of national highways, which in fact provided the initial inspiration for his concern with numbers. Yet nothing indicates the presence of this reference here. The number, given as a digit rather than being spelled out in letters, seems to represent pure form, as in Jasper Johns' early number paintings. Both artists raised standard numbers to the level of an artistic motif. While Johns qualified the intrinsic value of numbers by embedding them in a gesturally painted field, Indiana presents numbers straightforwardly, like insignia, in all of his paintings and sculptures. Still, the present work cannot be called an abstract painting – the number as an autonomous image, corresponding at most to the eight-part circle whose centre it occupies, with a tendency to three-dimensional emphasis typical of Indiana. Because in terms of form, colour and presentation, the composition has its source in the fund of popular culture. The "8" is a stereotype; the colours, applied in an apparently monochrome way, form a familiar red-blue contrast; and the fact that the "8" appears in a square stood on one corner calls up associations with highway signs. Indiana, who originally wrote poetry, builds a bridge between Pop Art and the hard-edge painting of an Ellsworth Kelly, without making facile compromises. At the same time, he ironically undermines art critics' obsession with classification. This is seen, for instance, in the fine bands in various gradations of blue that make up the seemingly monochrome ground. With his *Number* and *Love* paintings and sculptures, Indiana created true icons of Pop.

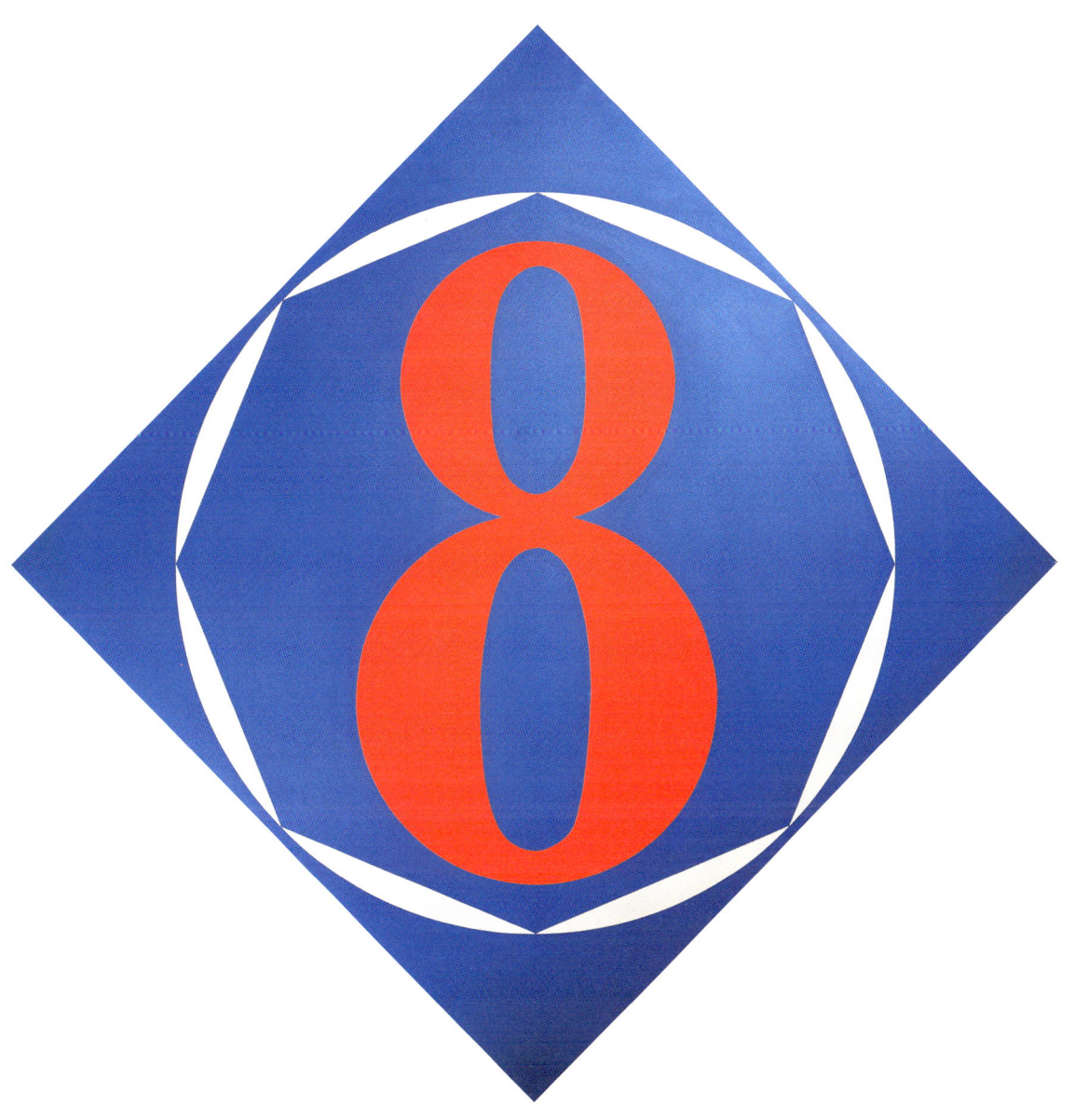

The Big Eight, 1961
Acrylic on canvas,
220 x 220 cm (86½ x 86½ in.)
Cologne, Museum Ludwig

Jasper Johns
Flag, 1954

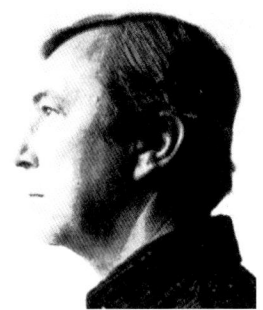

b. 1930 in Augusta, Georgia

The by now inevitable question as to the identity of this painting was not raised until ten years after its completion, when the critic Alan Solomon asked whether it was a flag or a painting that represented a flag. It is both, according to the artist's various answers to this question. On the surface, the work possesses many traits of the American star-spangled banner: appearance, the congruence of ground and motif, proportions. Then, too, the painting, in analogy to the flag, consists of three separate parts fitted together: a field with stars, and adjacent fields with red and white stripes to the right and below. In other words, it is a montage. Each star, as in the original, is a separate piece, adhered to the ground. What initially appears to signal an artistic context turns out to correspond to real circumstances. He dreamed of painting the "Stars and Stripes", the artist explained his baffling decision to treat this subject, and he wasted no time in putting the dream into practice. In fact, he did not depict a flag, but painted the flag. The flag is not the motif of the picture; the picture is a flag. On first view, the subject and painting surface are identical. From this we may conclude that Johns was right when he said that the theme of the painting was painting itself – painting in the physical sense, as brushstroke, colour, object.

The encaustic technique employed is difficult to handle, because the medium, liquid wax, solidifies quickly and immediately fixes every gesture. Its traces remain visible. Johns began with enamel, but since the drying process lasted too long, he changed to encaustic. The translucent strokes reveal loosely collaged pieces of newspaper underneath. These shimmer through the painted surface and serve as the actual background for the flag's stripes. In light of a more precise analysis, various layers of meaning crystallize out of this painting with the laconic title *Flag*, that convey complex relationships between reality and art without any clear statement of position, in analogy to the American flag itself. Viewed soberly, the banner is nothing but a printed or dyed and hemmed piece of cloth. Yet in fact it is a symbol of national and social identity in the United States. When the artist executed this painting, the phenomenon of war influenced his view of the world. War in three variants: the Cold War between East and West, the U.S. and the U.S.S.R. competing for world dominance; the hot war in Korea, which had just come to an end; and Senator McCarthy's witchhunt on intellectuals, which was still underway and poisoning the American cultural climate. *Flag*, in many people's eyes a milestone on the road to Pop Art, was viewed by others as an attack on patriotic feelings.

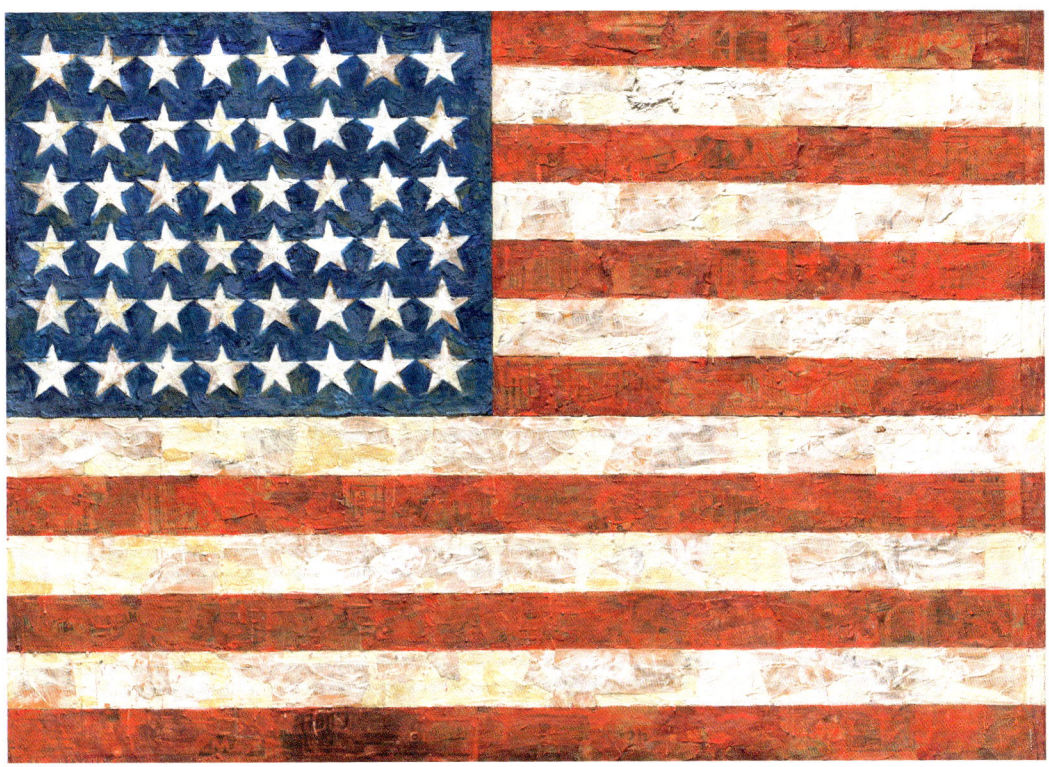

Flag, 1954
Encaustic, oil, collage on cloth, mounted on
plywood, 107.3 x 153.8 cm (42¼ x 60⅝ in.)
New York, The Museum of Modern Art, gift of
Philip Johnson in honour of Alfred H. Barr Jr.

Allen Jones
Perfect Match, 1966/67

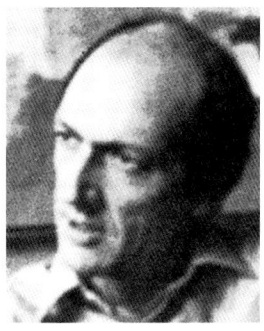

b. 1937 in Southampton,
United Kingdom

Successful careers on Broadway are only a matter of "tits and arses", according to a saucy song in the film musical *A Chorus Line*, 1985, by Sir Richard Attenborough, a reprise of an old, already filmed play with updated lyrics. Allen Jones long since knew this, and threw in slender shapely legs and a sensual mouth for good measure. In three superposed parts, a vertical triptych, he rendered the ideal female image that pre-occupied men's minds in a period of social and cultural transition. At the same time, it is an image of covert anxieties. The figure's parts are so exaggerated to conform with personal tastes or neuroses that they can stand for themselves. Mouth and breasts in the upper field; hips, buttocks, pubic area and thighs in the middle; calves, ankles and feet in the lower field. The sharp, shaded contours underscore the cliché and focus it to the point of caricature. The head is cut off above the mouth by the edge of the picture, as if a woman's face were dispensable. A miniskirt reveals more than it conceals – just as in "real life". The legs are rendered in a Futurist manner, a subtle homage to Marcel Duchamp and his renowned *Nude Descending a Staircase*, 1912. Just as little nuanced as the drawing is the handling of colour. Red predominates. At the top, in a strong contrast with black, in the middle a bit cooler and balanced by blue-grey and yellow, and at the bottom the red explodes in a complementary contrast with toxic green, interspersed with yellow and orange. The palette is like a strident pop concert translated into visual terms. Doubtless Jones has created a modern fetish image here. Yet it conveys not the slightest insight into the thoughts and emotions that moved him. Any attempt at psychological interpretation is bound to miss the point of the painting. Jones stays as cool as Helmut Newton, whose photographs of women were concurrently triggering controversy. Jones' female image is the equivocal product of aesthetic design and commercial insignia. Entirely artificial, all the way to the erect nipples, just as shrill and vulgar as the magazines that were purveying the same image at the time. In the museum context, however, it still embodies an extreme challenge to the aristocratic female image of the classical art around it, a travesty that reveals what these works often conceal beneath a veil of painterly refinement. It was David Hockney who drew Jones' attention to the world of the mass media. In 1978 Jones would design an ad for a stocking manufacturer, which filled an entire wall of a railway station, Schweizer Bahnhof, in Basel. Here the influence of advertising on art was reflected back on advertising.

Perfect Match, 1966/67
Oil on canvas, three parts,
280 x 93 cm (110¼ x 36½ in.) overall
Cologne, Museum Ludwig

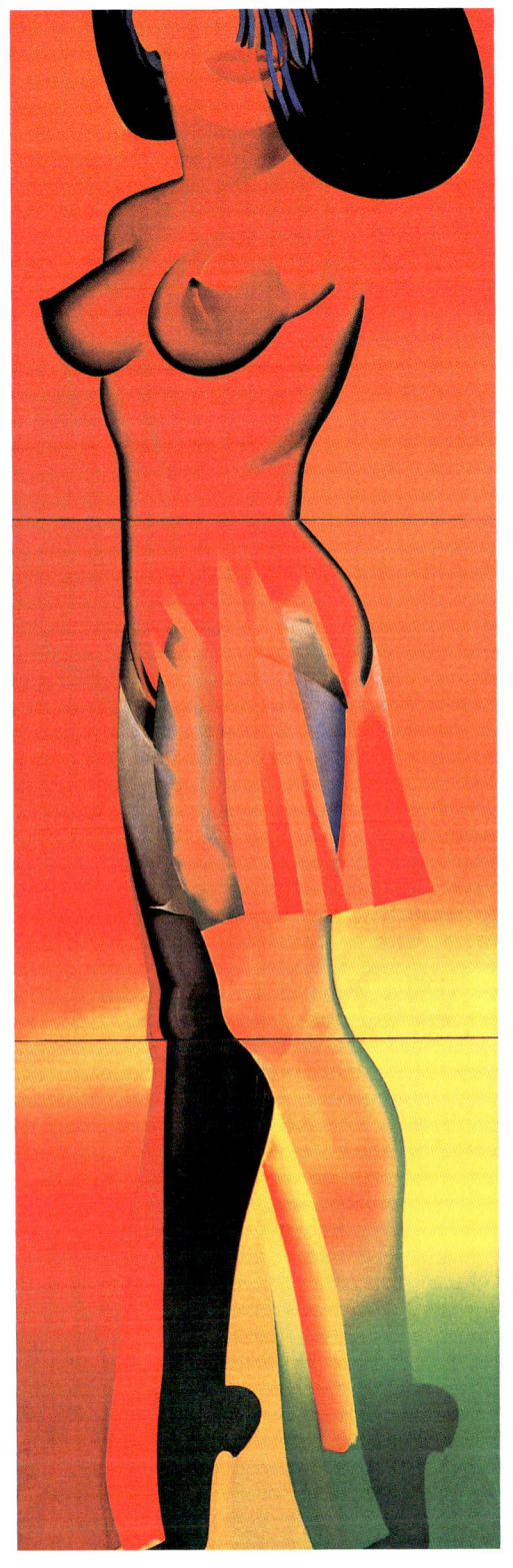

Roy Lichtenstein
Takka Takka, 1962

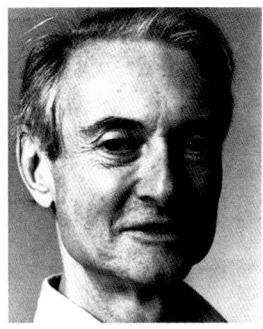

b. 1923 in New York City
d. 1997 in New York City

Pablo Picasso's painting *Massacre in Korea* drew harsh criticism. Yet the many aesthetic arguments marshalled against it basically reflected a doubt as to the ability of painting in general to adequately depict the horrors of war. Hardly twenty years after Picasso's canvas *Guernica*, 1937, which was immediately accepted as an icon of critical art, photography had far outstripped painting as a medium to convey the effects of war. Roy Lichtenstein's *Takka Takka*, an outstanding Pop contribution to art history, proves how baseless such distinctions are. Precisely the coarsening effects of the cartoon idiom, in combination with elements of written language, lend the painting an overwhelming force and, at the same time, give it a disturbing ambivalence. The threatening muzzles of the barking machine gun in harsh black and white above the dark green jungle leaves, underscored by the echoic "TAKKA TAKKA" in blood red capitals and the shamelessly heroicizing text on a yellow ground in the upper third of the composition, convey a more unforgettable impression of the violence of war than all of the noncommital television images taken by cameramen "embedded" with troops in a real war thirty years after this painting was completed. And not only this – Lichtenstein's work provides insight into the role which images have played and will continue to play in war. The artist initially limits himself to showing guns at the moment they fulfil their purpose, as if automatically and only because this is what they are manufactured in great numbers to do. Neither a gunner nor his potential victim is visible. This considerably increases the aggressiveness of the image. There is no shallow psychology, no dubious human touch, to mitigate the challenge. The gunner is mentioned only in the cloyingly heroic texts, which sound as hollow as most justifications of violent acts and the commentaries of war reporters. Victims, on the other hand, do not fit into the picture of triumphant violence, and never have. By condensing aspects of artificiality – poster-like colour and formal systematization – to an extreme point, Lichtenstein creates room for an invasion of the real into the world of fiction, by way of the bridge of the imagination. By these means he conveys an idea of the consequences of an outbreak of brute violence, even though it takes shape primarily in the mind of the viewer – thanks to the sheer power of the medium.

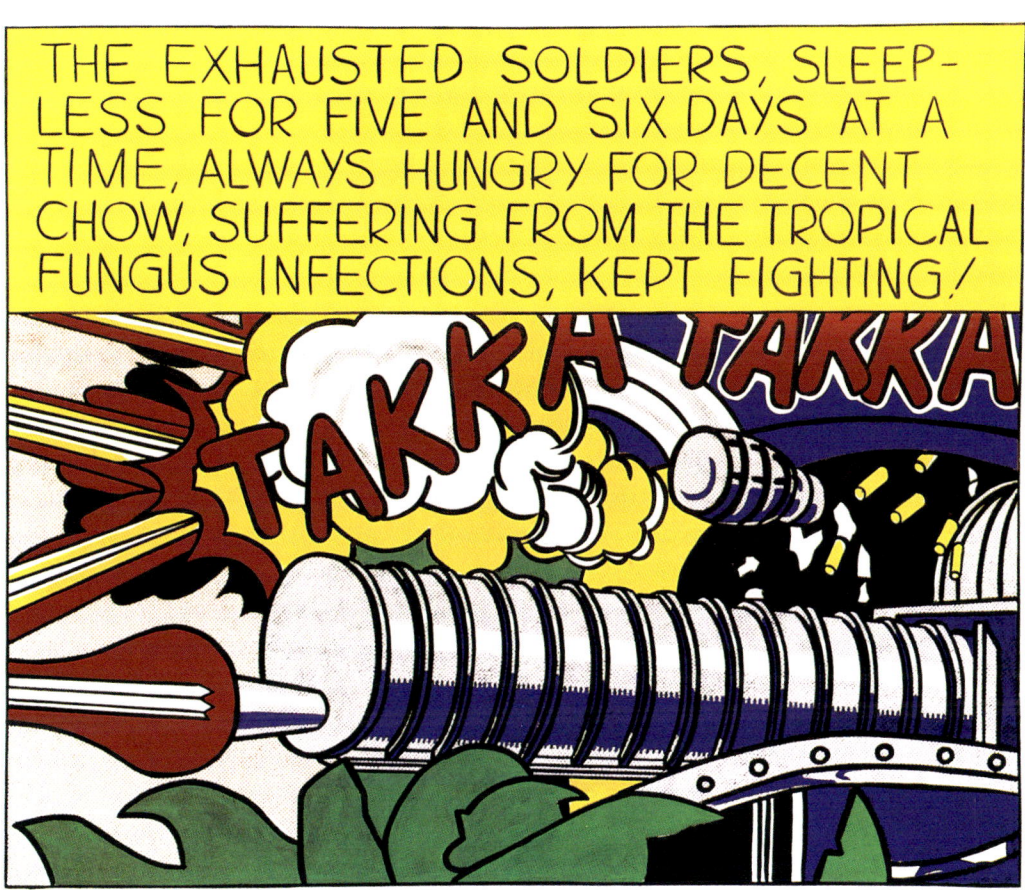

Takka Takka, 1962
Magna on canvas,
173 x 143 cm (68 x 56¼ in.)
Cologne, Museum Ludwig

Roy Lichtenstein
M-Maybe, 1965

What especially stimulated his interest in cartoons, the artist once said in an interview with critic, curator and photographer John Coplans, was the contrast between highly emotional content and "cool" means of depiction. Especially in the many paintings of young women done during the first half of the 1960s, Lichtenstein staged this contrast with amazing virtuosity, lending the compositions a vibrant tension. In *M-Maybe*, an attractive blonde directs her blue-eyed gaze at us, yet seems to look past us, preoccupied with her own thoughts. Head resting in her left, white-gloved hand – a traditional visual metaphor for melancholy – she wonders, as the balloon reveals, why she has been made to wait in vain. Apparently some man has stood her up. The everyday nature of this situation immediately triggers empathy on our part. It is certainly not hard to identify with this girl – were it not for the standardized way in which the artist depicts her. This puts the despondent girl at an undefinable, vague distance, in view of which our budding empathy turns out to be a special form of hypocrisy. The relationship between picture and viewer suddenly seems based on false premises. The artificiality of the style corresponds to the stereotyped female image derived from comic books. And also to the cheap sensations this image was designed to elicit in us, which suddenly put us in the role of Pavlov's dogs. The artist skilfully exploits the gap between the world and individual consciousness. He heightens comic-book clichés by honing his technique to an apex of forcefulness: primary colours, strong contrasts, and striking, unifying drawing. This amounts, so to speak, to an optimization of the popular aesthetic. Lichtenstein always emphasized that he aesthetically improved the vulgar aesthetic of cartoons. His first step in making a painting was to project the original on canvas with the aid of a slide projector, thus creating an analogy on the technical level between mechanical production and the world of trivial feelings. Then the face was covered with a dot pattern – a relic of the printed original, divested of its function to take on an aesthetic life of its own in the work of art.

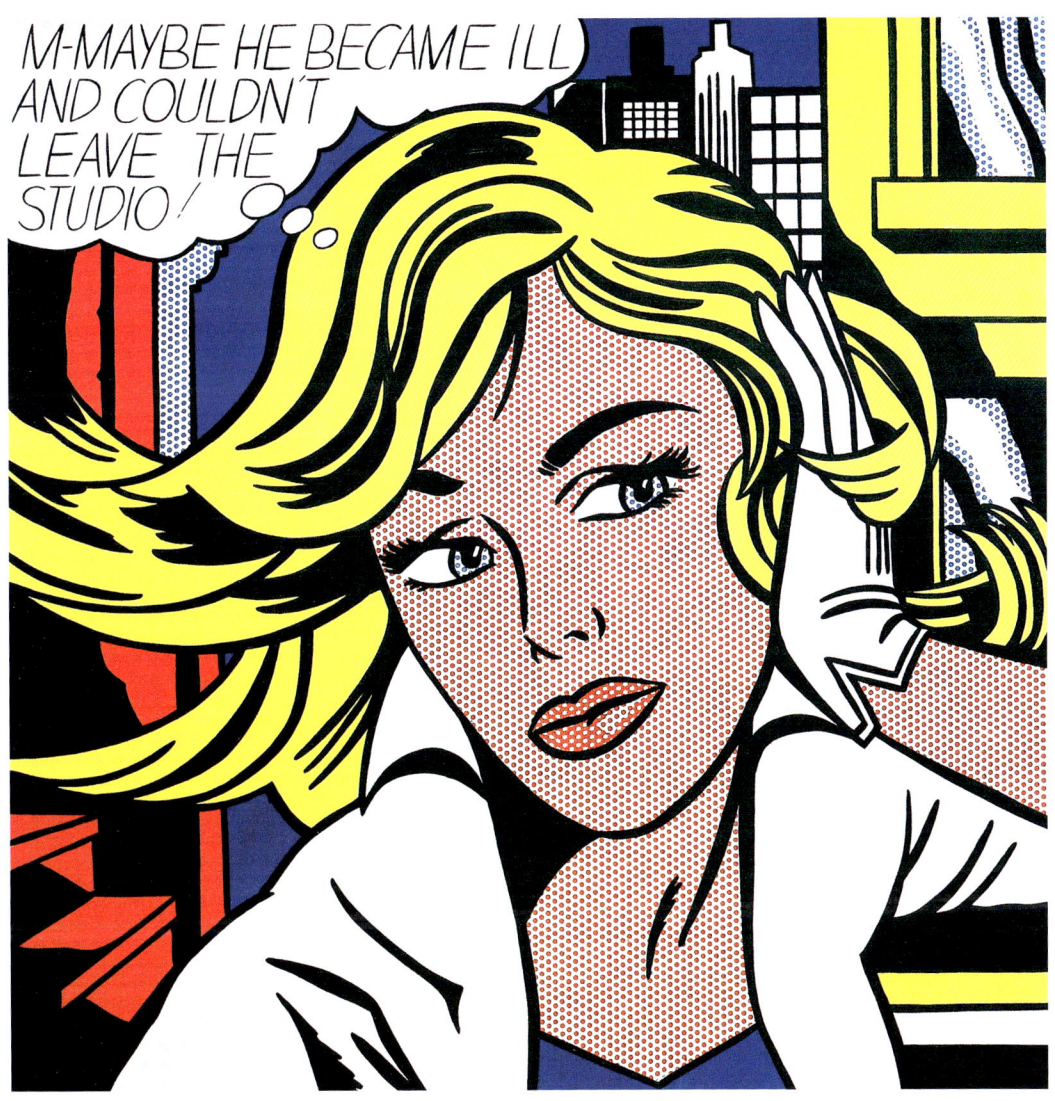

M-Maybe, 1965
Magna on canvas,
152 x 152 cm (60 x 60 in.)
Cologne, Museum Ludwig

Roy Lichtenstein
Yellow and Green Brushstrokes, 1966

Every type of painting consists of an abundance of brushstrokes. The way these are executed is not unimportant, since it determines the visual effect of the motifs to which they add up, whether these motifs be objective or abstract. In other words, the visual effect of a finished painting depends on the process used to make it. As art became more and more individual and artists' subjective vision began to appear just as, if not more, important for the aesthetic judgement than the depiction itself, the psychological aspect of brushstrokes was discovered, and they began to be read as notations of artists' states of mind during the creative process. Expressionist tendencies augmented this development, to the point that the gestural strokes in Abstract Expressionist paintings were thought by many to completely reveal their maker's psyche. In his series of *Brushstroke* paintings, Lichtenstein shed ironic light on this cult of the brushstroke, prompted by the work of Jackson Pollock and others. At the same time he undermined the very definition of modern art, which rests on artistic originality and the potential uniqueness of every work of art. Lichtenstein has isolated the brushstroke from its painterly context, enlarged and simplified it by means of projection, and reproduced the result in the standardized language of the mass-produced printed cartoon. *Yellow and Green Brushstrokes*

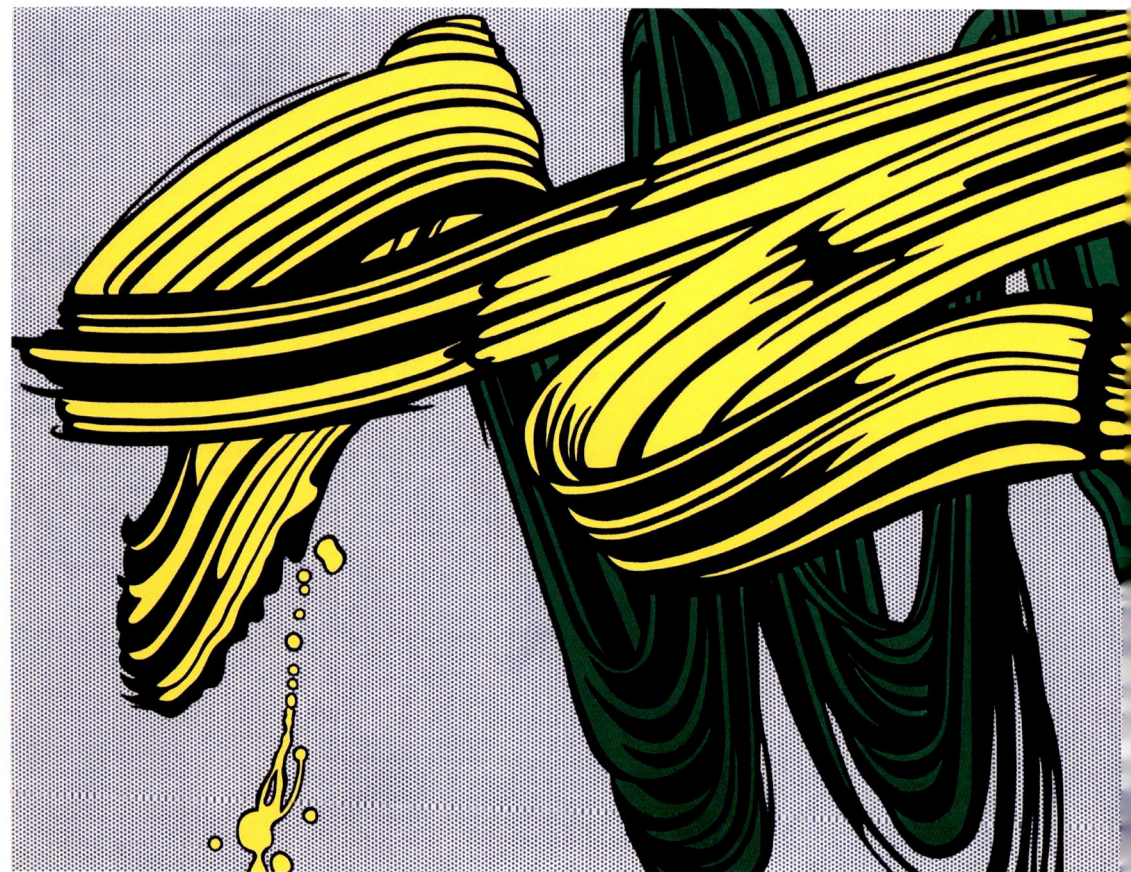

presents two superimposed swaths of the brush, including a few drips. As simple as the composition may seem, its structure is actually quite complex. It is one version of the subject among many. The source of the first version in the series was actually a comic drawing. Yet every further variant was the result of exhaustive experimentation, a process of trying, testing and inventing until the definitive form had been found. What appears to be a spontaneous, dynamic, well-nigh accidental configuration is actually the product of an ambitious mechanized procedure. Yet the images in this series find their true fulfilment only in printed form, as silkscreens. The silkscreen technique replicates the symbol of individuality. In these works, moreover, Lichtenstein raises the question of the difference between commercial trademark and artistic style. The *Brushstrokes* obviously blur the distinction to the point of unrecognizability. How, one might ask, does an incessantly repeated, identifiable mark in art differ from a standardized, industrially produced symbol?

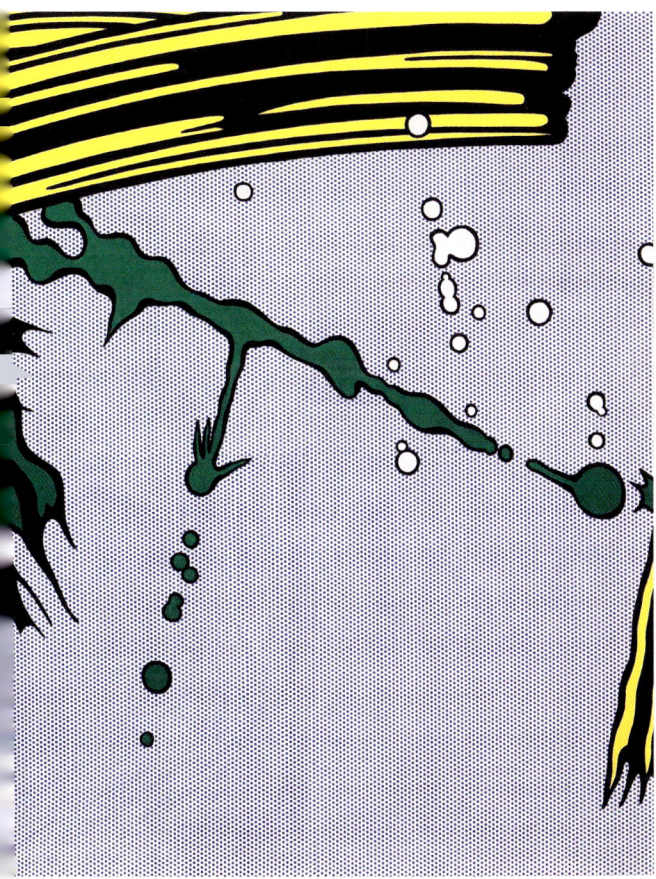

Yellow and Green Brushstrokes, 1966
Oil and magna on canvas, 215 x 460 cm (84¾ x 181 in.)
Frankfurt am Main, Museum für Moderne Kunst

Claes Oldenburg
Pastry Case I, 1961/62

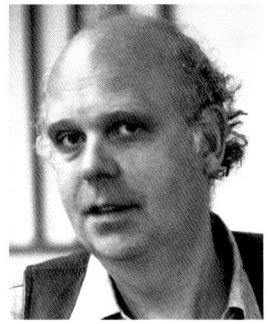

b. 1929 in Stockholm
d. 2022 in New York City

Oldenburg objected to all too high-flown interpretations of his work. The foodstuffs, he wrote about this collection of pastries in a showcase, were naturally not edible. A little thought was enough to reveal that they were not real but manifestations of art that were self-sufficient rather than serving purposes of any kind. Oldenburg took nine different products of an average pastrycook's imagination, made plaster versions of them, and painted some in an Expressionist manner. A blueberry pie, a few scoops of ice cream, a toffee apple, a banana split, arranged on plates or platters – traditional products often advertised as "homemade", yet mostly straight from the factory. In the present case, however, they are truly "handmade", by the artist. Most of these supposed delicacies were shaped of coarse canvas or muslin, dipped in plaster, spread over a wire framework, and finally painted. The difference from the originals is immediately obvious. Neither in terms of form nor colour is any exact resemblance to food strived for, quite unlike, say, the astonishingly real-looking wax displays in Japanese restaurants. Rather, we gain the impression that the artist's miniature sculptures were primarily intended as parodies of Expressionist painting and sculpture. On the other hand, he alludes to the great tradition of Netherlandish still-life painting, those magnificent depictions of poultry, fish, hams, vegetables and fruit which, apart from physical enjoyment, celebrate the skill of the artists and moreover, in the manner of conspicuous consumption, shed light on the hedonism of their clients and the shadow of *memento mori* it casts. Yet Oldenburg's acid humour warns us against overestimating such links: "I am for the art of … sat-on bananas", he once declared. By the way, *Pastry Case I* is a key document in the history of Pop Art. It is a re-creation of a work in the legendary show "The Store", held in the Green Gallery in Manhattan in 1962. The dealer Sidney Janis purchased it there for $324.98 and included it in his renowned Pop exhibition "New Realists", which opened on 1 November of the same year. This exhibition brought together American and European Pop artists such as Lichtenstein, Oldenburg, Warhol, Klein, Arman and Niki de Saint Phalle. It is generally considered to have marked the international breakthrough of Pop.

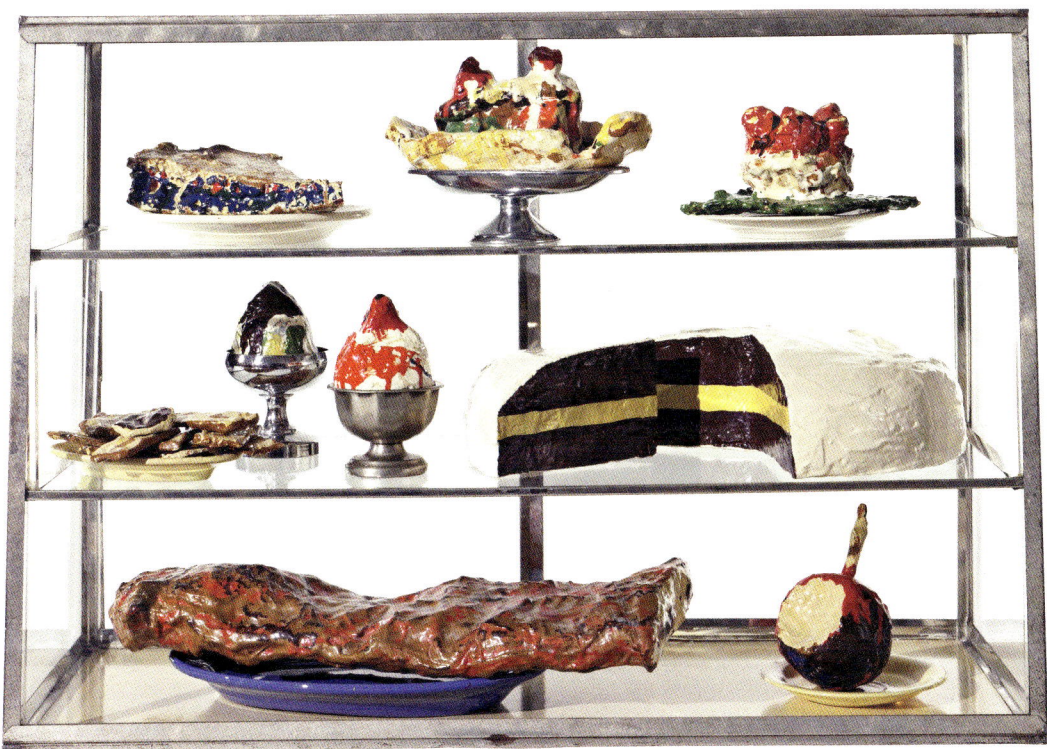

Pastry Case I, 1961/62
Burlap and muslin soaked in plaster, painted
with enamel, in glass-and-metal case,
52.7 x 76.5 x 37.3 cm (20¾ x 30 x 14¾ in.)
New York, The Museum of Modern Art,
The Sidney and Harriet Janis Collection

Claes Oldenburg
Soft Washstand, 1965

The associations suggested by the title of this piece and its actual appearance lie worlds apart. Anyone who has neglected to read the description will have to be very imaginative to recognize what this object represents. Using linen, wood, kapok (an upholstery material), and paint, the artist has created something normally made of porcelain, plastic and metal which serves mundane hygienic purposes: a wash basin on a stand. Instead of a compact, polished object with rounded or square corners, hard and solid in consistency, the viewer is confronted with a limp, rather grimy-looking configuration that could never hold water if one tried to fill it. Only the faucets appear substantial, although they are made of wood rather than metal. The supplement to the title indicates that this soft sculpture is a version in cloth. Other versions exist as well, for instance in vinyl and painted plywood. Although modelled on an ubiquitous home fixture and feature of modern civilization, Oldenburg's consciously imperfect imitation was not intended to address social or cultural aspects or relationships. It was intended as an aesthetic object whose effect owes solely to the circumstance that it is a work of art. Thus the gap between designation and function. While the explanatory adjective in the title aptly describes the character of the object, the noun is misleading, since it conveys the impression that the object fulfils a practical function. Already on this semantic level, a contradiction arises which suffuses the entire work. A soft washstand can never fulfil its designated task, just as little as a work of art can fulfil a practical function. It is no coincidence that Oldenburg is viewed as one of the precursors of Conceptual Art. Yet because his complex works aim at an effect involving a confusion of opposing sensations – what is hard becomes soft, solid things begin to flow – they form a bridge to an art beyond the avant-garde. A tendency underscored by his veritably Old Masterly drawings. In addition to home appliances, food represented one of the main sources of inspiration for this artist, who collected his first experiences as an initiator of and actor in happenings.

Soft Washstand, 1965
Vinyl filled with kapok, on metal
stand painted with acrylic,
137 x 88 x 55 cm (54 x 34¾ x 21¾ in.)
Cologne, Museum Ludwig

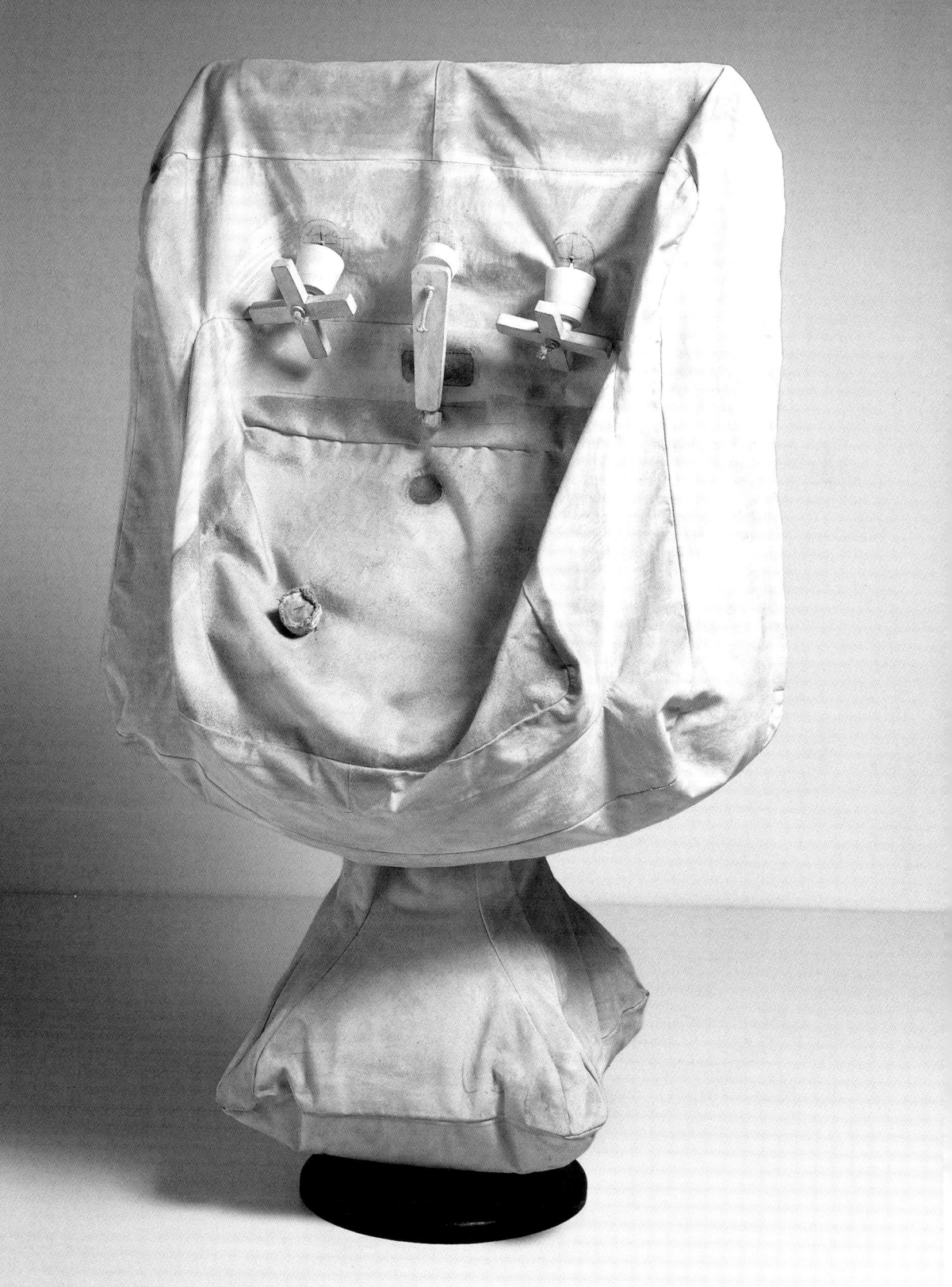

Claes Oldenburg
Giant Fagends, 1967

Evidently Oldenburg is an artist who is moved to reveal the monstrous traits of ordinary mundane objects and common consumer goods. To this end he employs various yet analogous artistic devices, either replacing the original material of the object by one of a quite different character, or blowing it up to gigantic proportions, which automatically entails an alteration in material. Foods metamorphose into plaster lumps, sanitary fixtures into limp cloth hangings, and household appliances into instruments for a race of giants. A type of plastic, urethane foam, was used to make the crushed-out filter cigarette butts in *Giant Fagends*, which the artist piled on an inclined polygonal base measuring two-and-a-half by two-and-a-half metres. Altered in terms of form, substance and dimensions, these tobacco products are divorced from their normal everyday context and raised with the aid of a pedestal to the status of autonomous object of art. When viewed from close quarters, the object is not immediately recognizable as an enlarged rendering of a full ashtray. Not even the colours, ranging from white through ochre to blackish-brown, suggest the presence of waste; rather, they have a subtle, well-nigh elegant, elegiac effect which stands in strange contrast to the subject depicted. The sculptural perfection of the object does not jibe with the notion of smelly, dirty cigarette stubs. Such contradictions are the elixir on which Oldenburg's works thrive. Material and meaning conform as little with each other as form and content. This incongruence reveals the contradictions of modern civilization in a flash. While it infuses intellectual and aesthetic values into cheap consumer goods, Oldenburg ennobles trivial things to the rank of art.

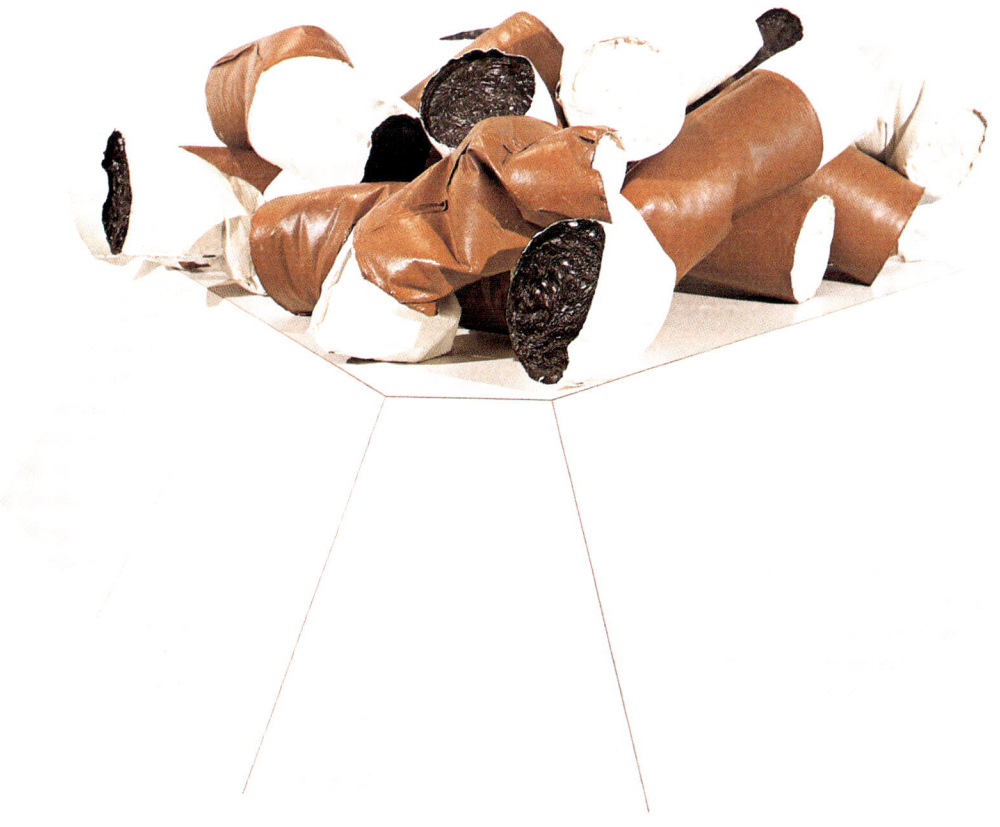

Giant Fagends, 1967
Canvas, urethane foam, wire, painted with
latex in "ashtray" of wood covered with formica,
132 x 244 x 244 cm (52 x 96 x 96 in.)
New York, Whitney Museum of American Art,
purchased through the Fund of the Friends
of the Whitney Museum of American Art

Peter Phillips
Lions Versus Eagles, 1962

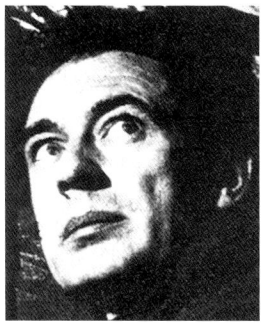

b. 1939 in Birmingham,
United Kingdom
d. 2025 in Sunshine Coast,
Queensland, Australia

Although he was considered the most American of British Pop artists, Phillips took the European tradition as the framework for his paintings. He looked far back into history, to a period before the renewal of art brought about by the Renaissance. In view of the formal nature of his preferred iconography – as in the present combination of lion and eagle, two mythological creatures, in a single visual context – Phillip's explanation seems surprising. Obviously his visual language was derived from the storehouse of popular culture. The stereotypical character of the depiction, drawing and palette leave no doubt about this. On the other hand, he has arranged the elements in this early composition in the way that medieval artists used to tell the stories of the Bible, in simple, separate fields that occasionally overlap at the edges. Phillips described his pictures as combinations of spatial, iconographic and technical factors working together in a single motif. In pre-Renaissance painting, he added, there is a complex visual situation with a central image and other, related scenes depicting a story or a phenomenon. The centre of the present composition is occupied by two lion's heads in a circle. They are approached by an eagle with mighty wings, depicted against a dark-green background. These are likely familiar manufacturing trademarks that consciously allude to the mythological significance of the animals and their symbolism of courage and power. Today mythology no longer serves its erstwhile function of explaining the world, but is merely exploited to create an effective image for commercial products. The ensemble is topped by schematically rendered rays in alternating red and yellow, and two discs enclosed in triangles, below them two stars, yellow and black on a white ground, both labelled "STAR". Despite its figurative forms the painting has an abstract appearance. It is executed like a blueprint, yet the things depicted do not go with one another. It is solely their arrangement, repetitions and correspondences that lends them aesthetic plausibility. In *Lions Versus Eagles* – a title, incidentally, that reverses the visible fact – a sort of integrative visual model of narration comes into effect which is quite different from that of Renaissance art. A model whose content, rather than being conveyed by a sequence of images, results from a merger and interweave of heterogeneous visual elements.

Lions Versus Eagles, 1962
Oil on canvas, 213 x 153 cm (84 x 60¼ in.)
Ghent, Stedelijk Museum voor Actuele Kunst

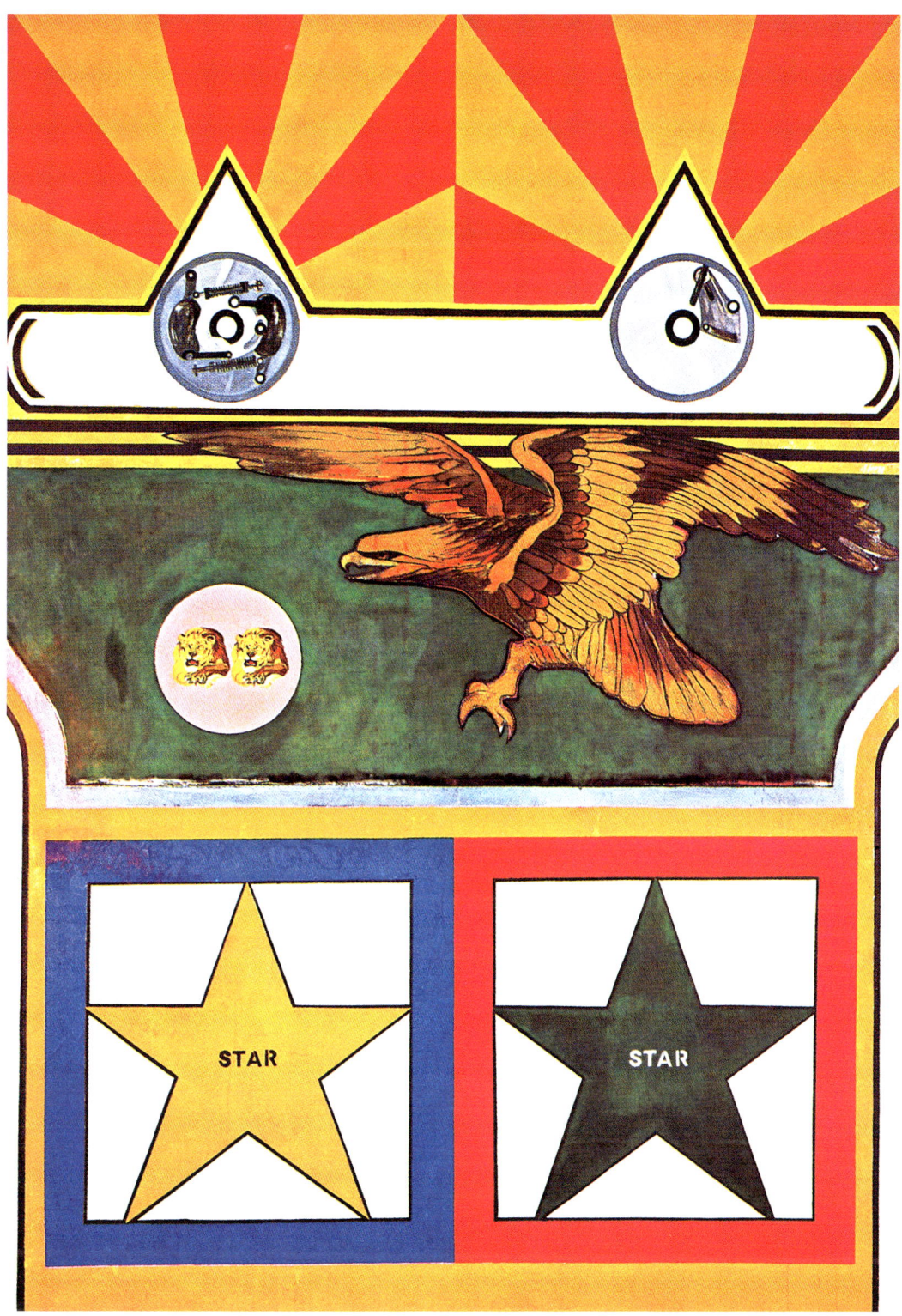

Peter Phillips
Custom Painting No. 5, 1965

The unusual format of this painting itself suggests that the artist had mass-media effects in mind when designing it. Cinemas of the day resorted to similarly oversized pictures in an attempt to retain audiences in the face of the rapid spread of television. As if from a projection screen, an abundance of heterogeneous visual impressions storms the viewer, a tangle of rotating shapes that at the same time seems to form a visual correspondence to the high-volume sound of the cinema experience. Yet the visual context here was not determined by the time dimension of film. The British painter juxtaposed and superimposed the separate elements of the composition on the two-dimensional plane of painting, whose laws govern the plausibility of the result. At the upper left, admittedly, the point of a high-heeled shoe, on the foot of a pin-up girl whose figure descends diagonally to the right, disturbs the integrity of the rectangular plane and simultaneously emphasizes the object character of the painting. The girl glances at us out of the corner of her eye, as if in passing. The rest of the surface is occupied by all sorts of things – a sectioned turbine, the grille of an American car, a technical drawing of a spark plug. Plus an orange octagon, a wavy band in the complementary contrast of red-green, a purple zigzag, and a

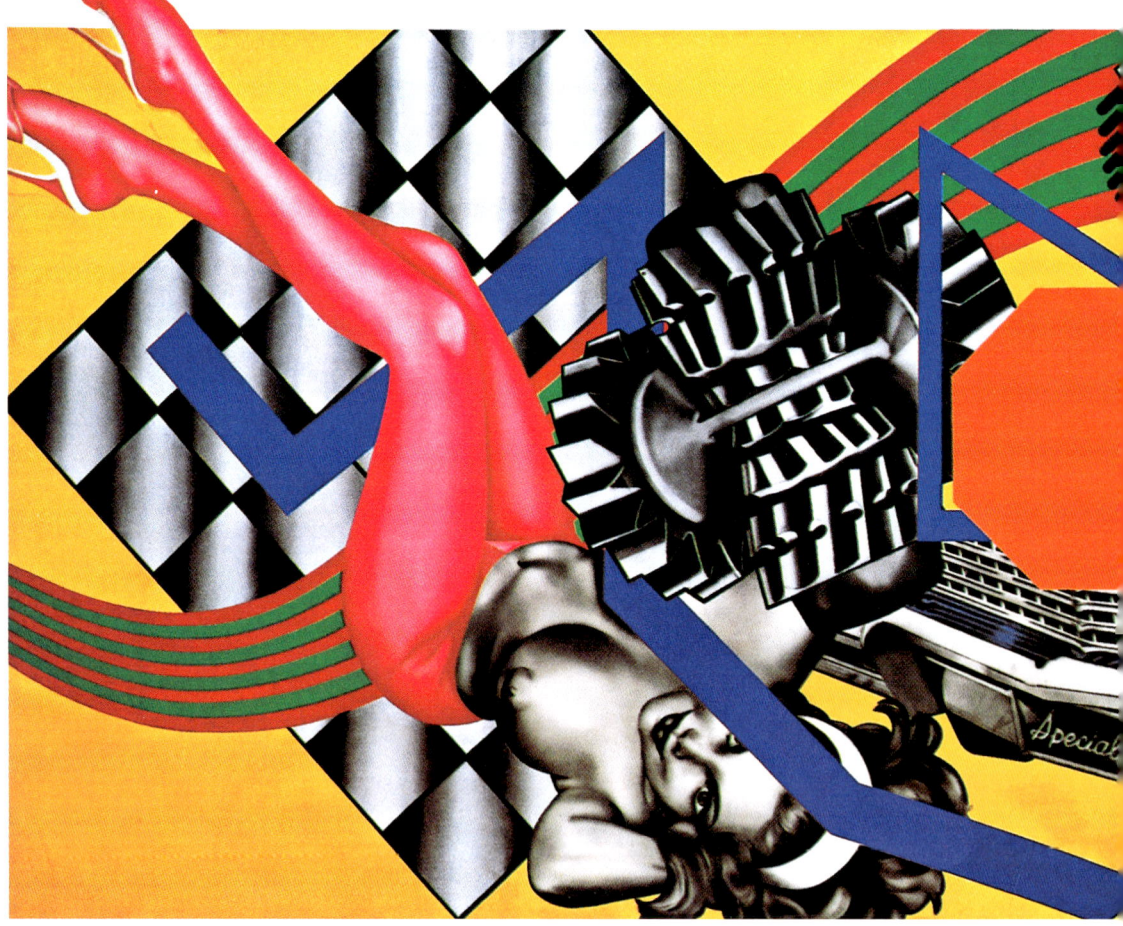

square stood on one corner with an oscillating chequerboard pattern. All of these diverse motifs are brought together on a ground rendered in gradations of yellow. Flatness and plasticity interweave – with the exception of the pin-up girl, the swelling volumes of whose body are depicted with the naturalism expected of a professional illustrator, head and torso in photographic black-and-white, legs in white and red. The puzzle of motifs and their montage-like interlock recall the game window of a pinball machine, with the complementary contrasts of red-green, violet-orange and blue-yellow evoking the flickering lights behind it. Fun, sex, technology, the trademarks of consumer society, are all concatenated in this turbulent picture. During his second period of study at the Royal College of Art in London, Phillips met Allen Jones (with whom he would later travel to the U.S.), Boshier, Caulfield and Hockney, who would form the third and best-known phalanx of British Pop artists.

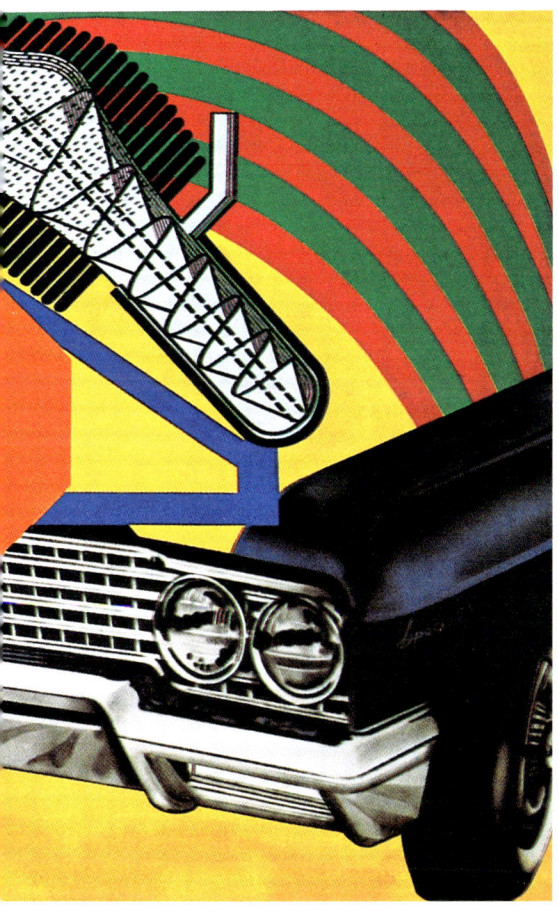

Custom Painting No. 5, 1965
Oil on canvas, 175 x 300 cm (69 x 118 in.)
Private collection

Mel Ramos
Velveeta, 1965

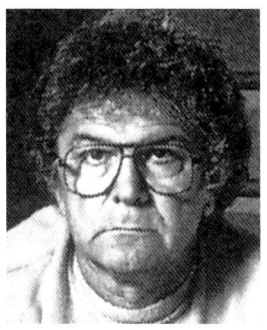

b. 1935 in Sacramento, California
d. 2018 in Oakland, California

The term "pin-up" derives from the practice of factory workers, soldiers, or truck drivers of mounting pictures of pretty girls in their lockers or cabs, to bring a little pleasure into their mundane lives. The painted versions of these are invariably based on photographs. Marilyn Monroe, too, began her career as a pin-up girl. The clientele for pin-ups is male, and mostly lower-middle class. A girl with an inviting look in her eye, sensually open mouth, long legs and ample breasts is one stereotype of the genre, and her counterpart is the apparently shy girl attempting to conceal her charms from unwanted glances. Both are products of male sexual fantasies, and tailored to a man's world. In the hierarchy of visual arts, pin-ups are considered a bit more vulgar than sentimental or martial comics, the sources Lichtenstein exploited, or labels on detergent boxes or soup cans, which Warhol reduplicated dozens of times. Yet they, too, received artistic honors in Pop Art.

It was a painter from California who paved pin-ups' way into the museum. Mel Ramos, alongside Thiebaud and Ruscha, is a representative of Californian Pop, and in terms of attitude, he is no less radical than Ruscha or Warhol. In his eyes, there is no basic aesthetic difference between serious and trivial art. Nor does he make any distinction between commercial and non-commercial art. After beginning, like Warhol, with an apotheosis of comic-book heroes such as Batman, Ramos turned to the female denizens of calendars and glossy magazines. With his paintings, sex at long last re-entered the field of fine art, ending an abstinence caused by abstraction. At the dawning of the "sexual revolution" and in the shape of aseptic sex, there began a renaissance of lust that was mobilized by advertising to sell products.

In *Velveeta*, a package of processed cheese serves the svelte nude model as a pedestal. The figure's treatment recalls a nude by Canova, presenting her comely back as she turns her perfectly coiffured head to give the viewer a languorous glance. The precisely reproduced label of the commodity and its form possess the same aesthetic value as the smoothly rendered body with its dimpled buttocks. Thanks to this combination of disparate elements, the image creates an absurd frame of reference with a slightly surreal flavour, and subliminally conveys the cynical message that personal happiness can be had only through an incessant consumption of surrogates, like pin-ups or factory-made foodstuffs.

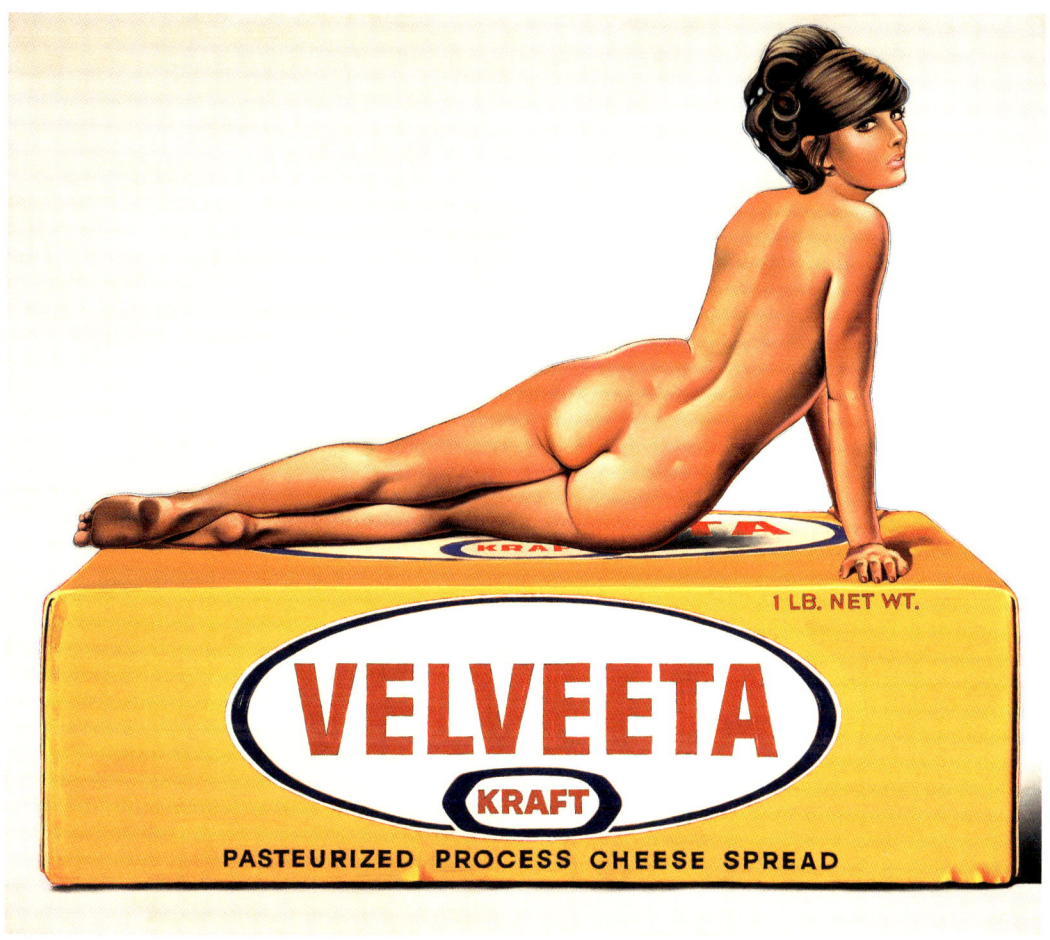

Velveeta, 1965
Oil on canvas, 152 x 178 cm (60 x 70 in.)
New York, Collection Louis K. Meisel

Robert Rauschenberg
Black Market, 1961

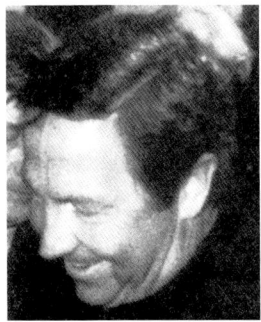

b. 1925 in Port Arthur, Texas
d. 2008 in Captiva Island, Florida

Attached to the point of the traffic sign reading "ONE WAY" is a cord that connects the canvas with a dark, wooden box lettered "OPEN" on the floor. Painting was equally a part of life and art, Rauschenberg once declared, and established his position as an artist in the gap between them. The cord might be seen to embody his stance. It connects heterogeneous things, both actually and symbolically. Various mundane objects are affixed to the canvas in an aesthetically interesting way. The central horizontal axis is emphasized by four notebooks with painted metal covers. These vie for attention with the street sign that literally leads the eye "one way". The surface also contains a photograph of the dome of the Capitol in Washington, D.C., a car licence plate, and scattered digits and letters. These things are overlapped, tied together and accentuated by passages of spontaneous brushwork, which perform the same function as the cord for the three-dimensional objects. Rauschenberg aptly called the series of works to which *Black Market* belongs "combine paintings". He brought art, which had been spirited into the realm of the sublime and absolute under the aegis of Clement Greenberg and abstract painting, back down to earth by subverting the rigid categories and aesthetic theory of the avant-garde. Just the fact that his works were neither pure paintings nor pure sculptures, but united both disciplines, reflected the tendency of Rauschenberg's intentions. A friend of the composer John Cage and the dancer Merce Cunningham, and a former student of Josef Albers at Black Mountain College, Rauschenberg organized key happenings and participated in others before beginning to concentrate on space and plane. He is considered one of the forerunners of Pop Art. Yet although his art incorporated much of what would be exhaustively treated by Pop – such as the symbols of transportation and typography – its thrust was different. It was not on the glamorous aspects of urban civilization that the artist cast his eye but on the used and discarded, things whose glamour had been tarnished, if they ever possessed it at all. His works lend new dignity to the unspectacular, and in retrospect they appear to have much more in common with Abstract Expressionism than with Pop Art.

Black Market, 1961
Canvas, wood, metal, oil paint,
152 x 127 cm (60 x 50 in.)
Cologne, Museum Ludwig

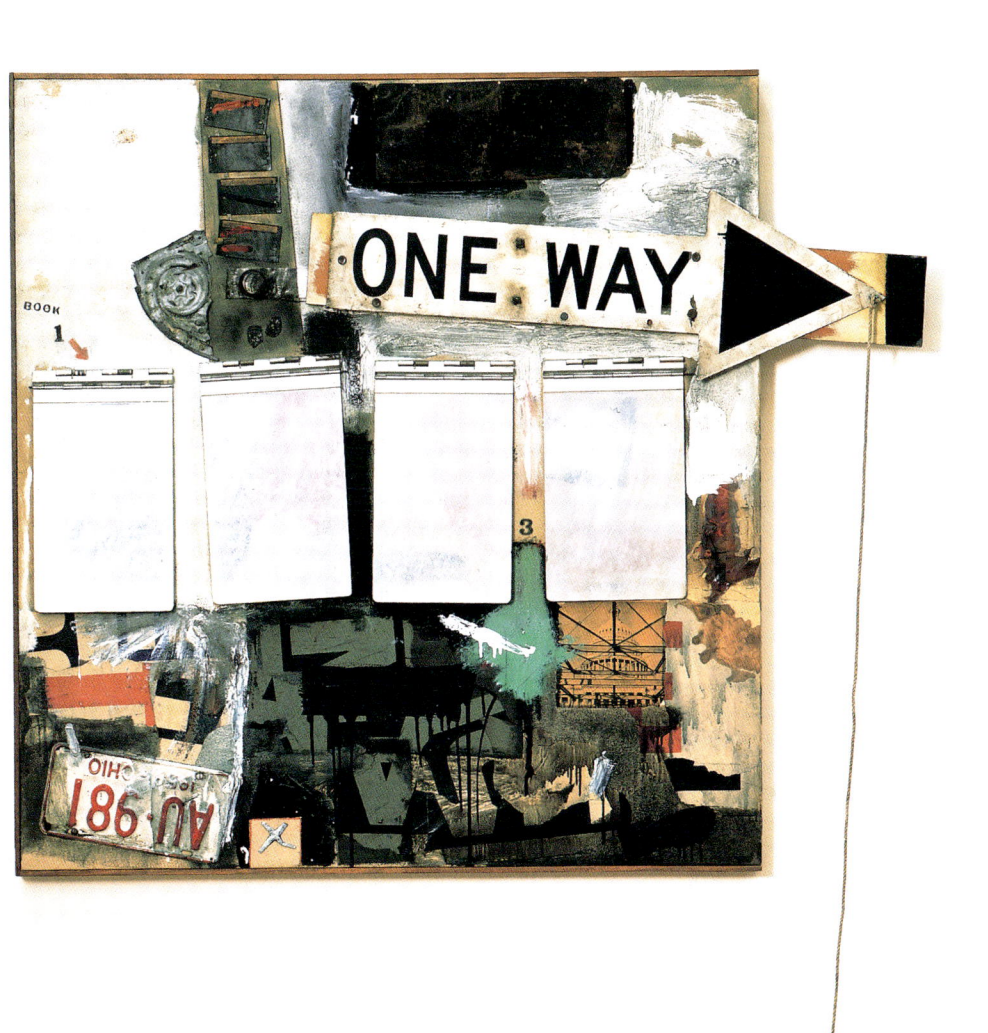

James Rosenquist
Untitled (Joan Crawford), 1964

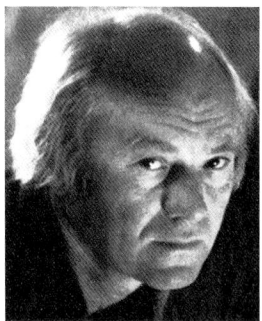

b. 1933 in Grand Forks,
North Dakota
d. 2017 in New York City

The shadow that fell on the great movie star's reputation was cast by her own daughter, who posthumously described Joan Crawford as a "bad mother" in a detailed book. Everything was secondary to her career, she stated, not only her private life but her little daughter. Crawford had often played career women on screen, hard, goal-oriented and successful, in a strange symbiosis of art and life, thirty years before Rosenquist portrayed her. But is this really a portrait, or just the opposite? The painting was based on a magazine illustration, which was probably itself done from a photograph. In this image Crawford's external trademarks have hardened into an almost caricatural cliché: the wide-open eyes with plucked eyebrows and false eyelashes, the routine smile congealed into a lopsided grimace, the permanent-waved hair. Her face is a mask that stares beyond the viewer into the distance. The original ad was apparently for a "mild" cigarette, but the artist has cut off the text, leaving a likewise truncated cigarette in the star's left hand as an indication. In fact, Rosenquist has robbed the ad of its effect, its message and function. It surprisingly turns out to be a purely aesthetic phenomenon, a painted montage of various typefaces, positive and negative, a poster-like autograph card rendered in carefully gradated colours of the kind often found in soap ads. Various red and ochre tones against a background of grey and greenish bands set the colouristic scene. Rosenquist's canvas is doubtless a counterpart to Warhol's more famous depictions of Marilyn Monroe, from which it basically differs only in terms of a more painstaking rendering and the lesser degree of attention it attracted. The reason for this lies in the model. In art, Crawford's persona never underwent the transformation into an icon that Monroe's did, despite the fact that the two actresses occupied the same level in the Hollywood pantheon. Admittedly, Crawford was of an earlier generation. Her last great box-office success, *Whatever Happened to Baby Jane*, 1962, directed by Robert Aldrich and with Bette Davis playing her rival, already lay two years in the past when Rosenquist picked up his brush. In the meantime, the diva had switched to a managerial career in the beverage business. And unlike Monroe's, her career was for the most part of her own making rather than being determined from outside. Crawford embodied the type of the emancipated woman – in both fiction and reality. And because Rosenquist's painting is not a portrait, it tells more about the mechanisms of the entertainment industry that transforms human beings into images than about the psychology of its sitter.

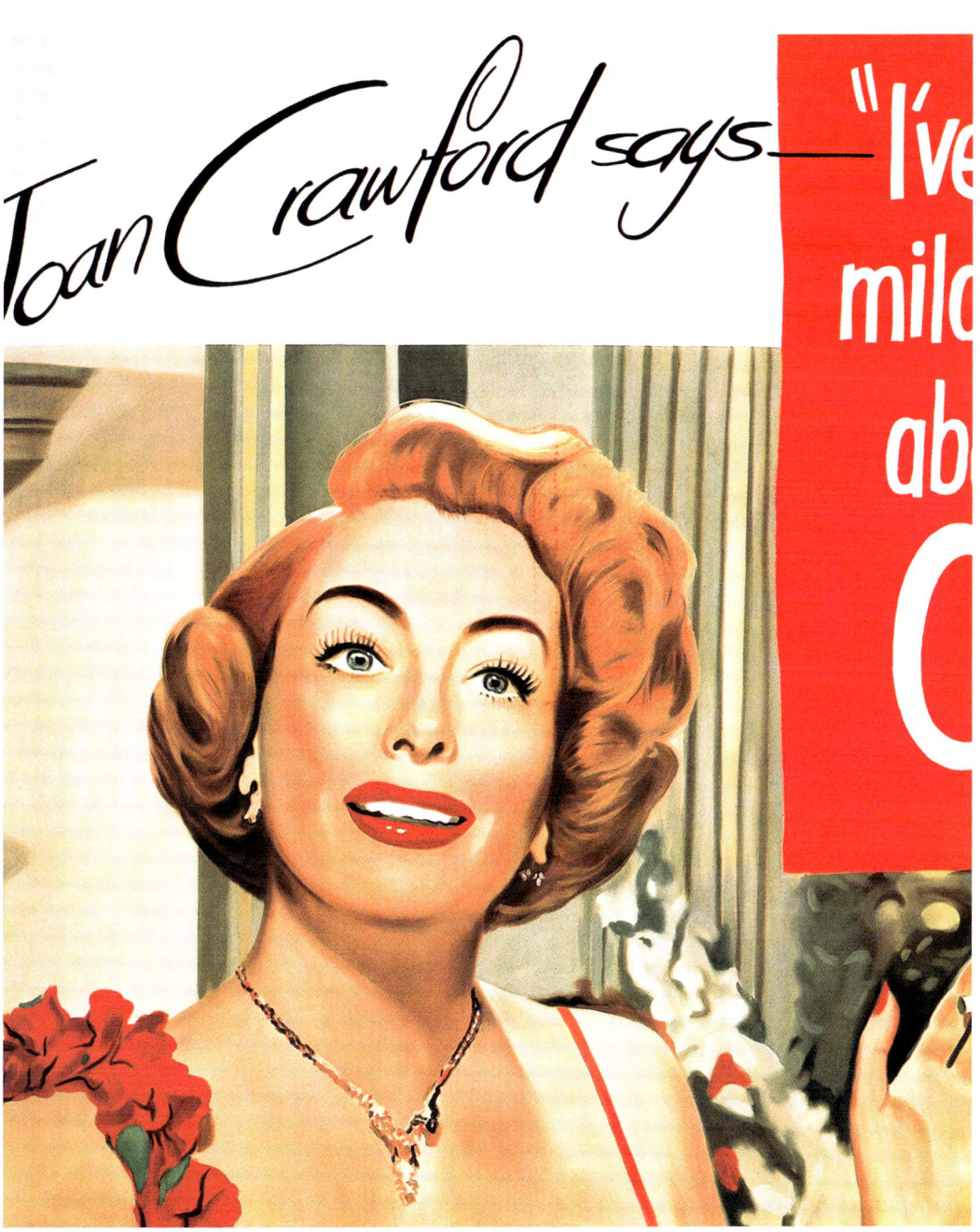

Untitled (Joan Crawford), 1964
Oil on canvas, 242 x 196 cm (95¼ x 77¼ in.)
Cologne, Museum Ludwig

Edward Ruscha
Standard Station, 1966

When he arrived in Los Angeles from Oklahoma City, Ed Ruscha was bent on acquiring the skills that would qualify him for a career in commercial art. He enrolled in the Chouinard Art Institute, a renowned school that had produced many illustrators for the Walt Disney Studio, but also had artists like Robert Irwin and Billy Al Bengston on its teaching staff. As Ruscha often recounted, it was seeing a reproduction of one of Jasper Johns' *Target* paintings in the journal *Print* that caused him to turn to fine art. Yet his interest continued to focus on the world of commerce, and he transferred the techniques and means of depiction of the standardized, mass-produced insignia of popular culture into the field of serious art. Besides Warhol, Ruscha is one of the most significant of Pop artists. The two share more than superficial formal links in common. *Standard Station* represents the sum total of all of the filling stations along Route 66, which runs between Ruscha's home town and the centre of the entertainment industry. While driving this highway several times, he made very straightforward, unpretentious black-and-white photos of the stations and published them in a slim volume called *Twentysix Gasoline Stations*, in a limited edition of 400. According to the artist, it was

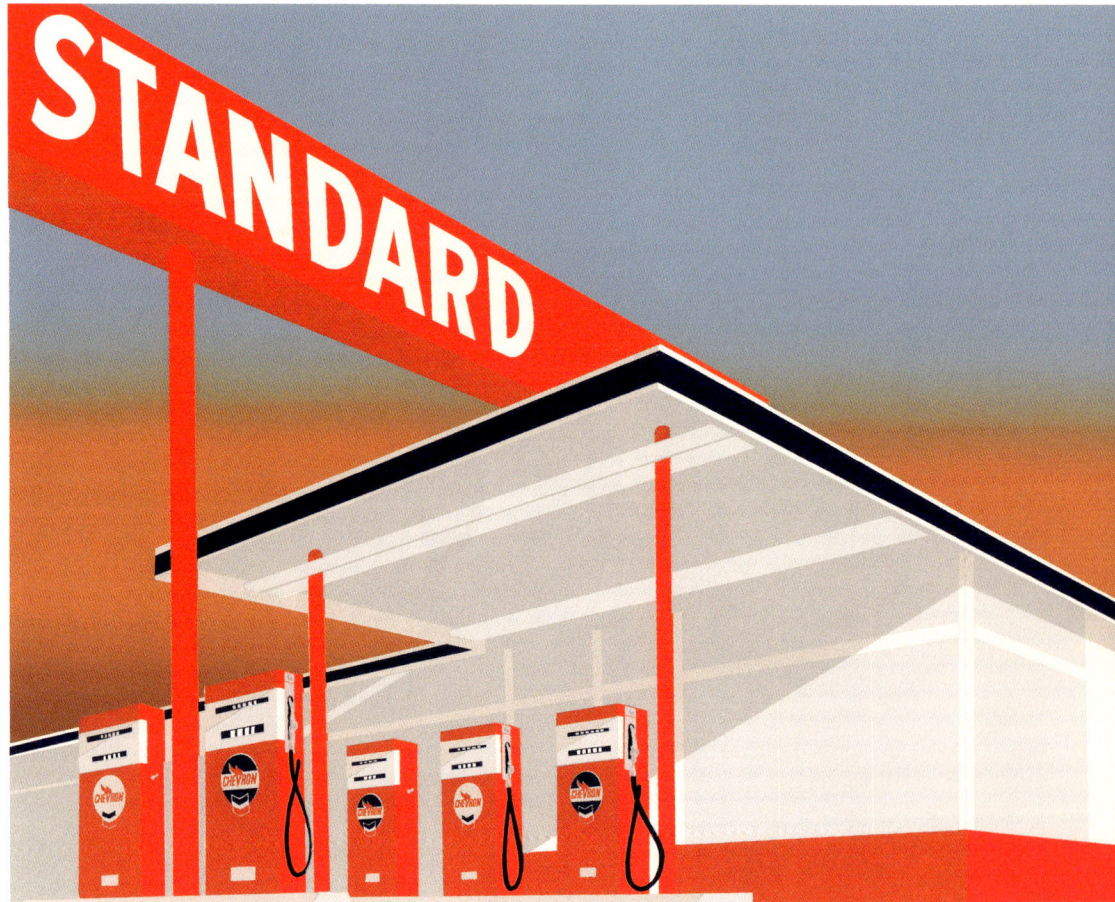

a wordplay that gave him the idea for the title, especially the combination of the number "twenty-six" with the term "gasoline". Ruscha is the only Pop artist to have used the medium of photography without altering it to his own ends – in the form best suited to it, namely the illustrated book. A mechanical reproduction technique also underlies the colour print on the canvas *Standard Station*. The concept of "standard" takes on an ambivalent meaning here, since it applies both to the subject depicted and its industrial character, as well as to contemporary art in general. The word hovers as a brand name over the roof of a standardized gas station and five equally standardized red pumps. The hard-edge contours of the architecture stand in sharp contrast to the soft transition between horizon and sky – one of the most common, standard devices of traditional painting. Using the simplest means, the artist condenses the visual clichés of the everyday environment and the clichés of art into an exemplary Pop image on the most advanced technical level.

Standard Station, 1966
Screenprint, 49.5 x 93.8 cm (19½ x 37 in.)
New York, Modern Museum of Art,
John B. Turner Fund

Edward Ruscha
Hollywood, 1968

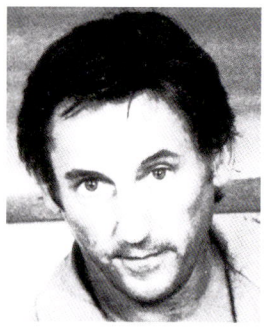

b. 1937 in Omaha, Nebraska

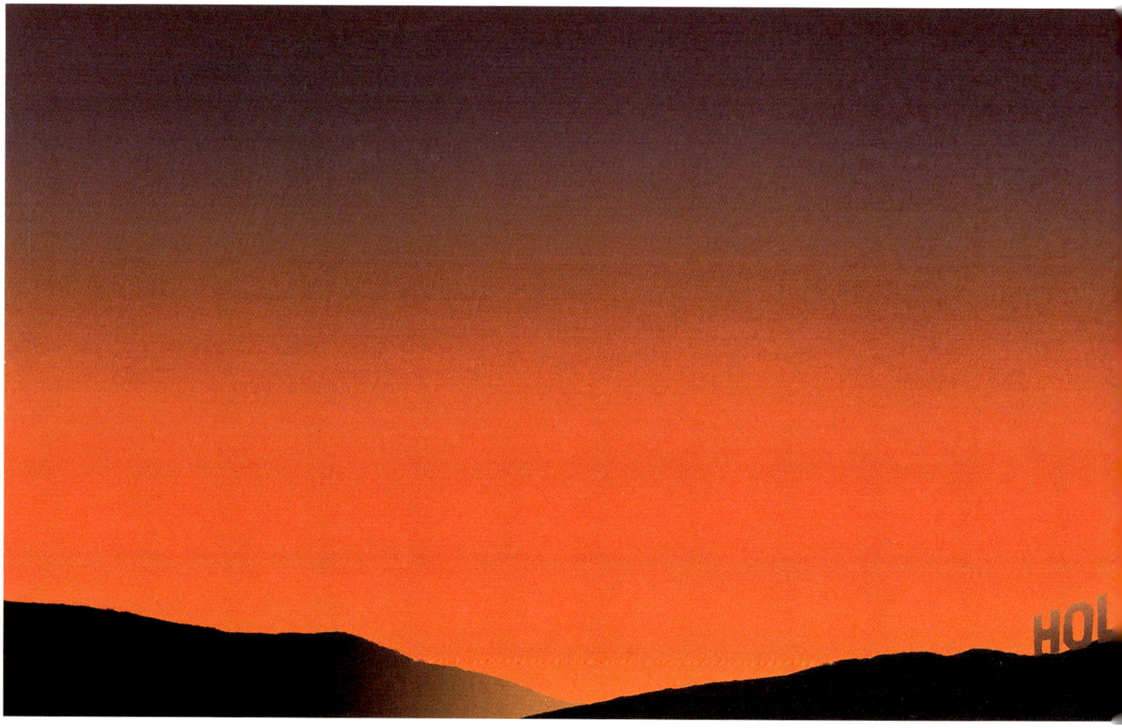

Myths elude depiction in visual art. Yet sometimes myths crystallize around visual images, and sometimes they engender them – as in the case of icons, which are believed by the faithful to truly embody the figure depicted, or in the case of movies, with their sheer visual power to convince. Ancient myths actually represent collective memories formed in ages prior to the invention of writing. They belong to the realm of oral narration. Modern myths, in contrast, are collective fabrications of an industrial character. They form around manufactured commodities, automobiles, ships, railways, and occasionally around places or regions. But above all they form around the Dream Factory, as motion pictures were once known. Some film stars have taken on virtually mythical proportions – Greta Garbo, Gloria Swanson, Marlene Dietrich, Humphrey Bogart, Ava Gardner, Marlon Brando, James Dean, and Marilyn Monroe, following her premature death. Yet most Hollywood stars have merely reached the status of idols. Pop Art is the art that has intensively concerned itself with modern myths. Warhol contributed to the nimbus that now surrounds Monroe; Wesselmann and Rosenquist augmented the cult status of the VW Beetle. Ruscha, who lives quite near Hollywood, set out to visualize the myth of the movie metropolis. He produced several versions, for instance reproducing the animated trademark of one of the great studios, 20th Century Fox, or depicting the illuminated letters "HOLLYWOOD" jutting over a dark, hilly horizon before a morning (or evening) sky, both nearby and distant, as if surrounded by an aura. At the upper edges the letters shine so brightly that they almost merge with the dazzlingly bright sky, only fine shading setting them off. The artist is a specialist for the visual effect of lettering and onomatopoeic words. By means of refined rendering, he gives these a resounding meaning they do not actually possess. Hollywood! Hollywood! In view of Ruscha's picture, one speaks the name softly, with a measure of awe. *Hollywood*, this silkscreen print in an unusual cinemascope format, calls up all the fantasies we associate with the movies. Quite in keeping with long-forgotten aesthetic theories, Ruscha mobilizes the viewer's imagination, knowing that art takes place in our own minds. It is no coincidence that he is considered a leading figure in Conceptual Art, which only goes to show that many differences between classical and modern art are really no more than superficial.

Hollywood, 1968
Silkscreen print, edition of 100,
31.6 x 103.5 cm (12½ x 40¾ in.)
Private collection

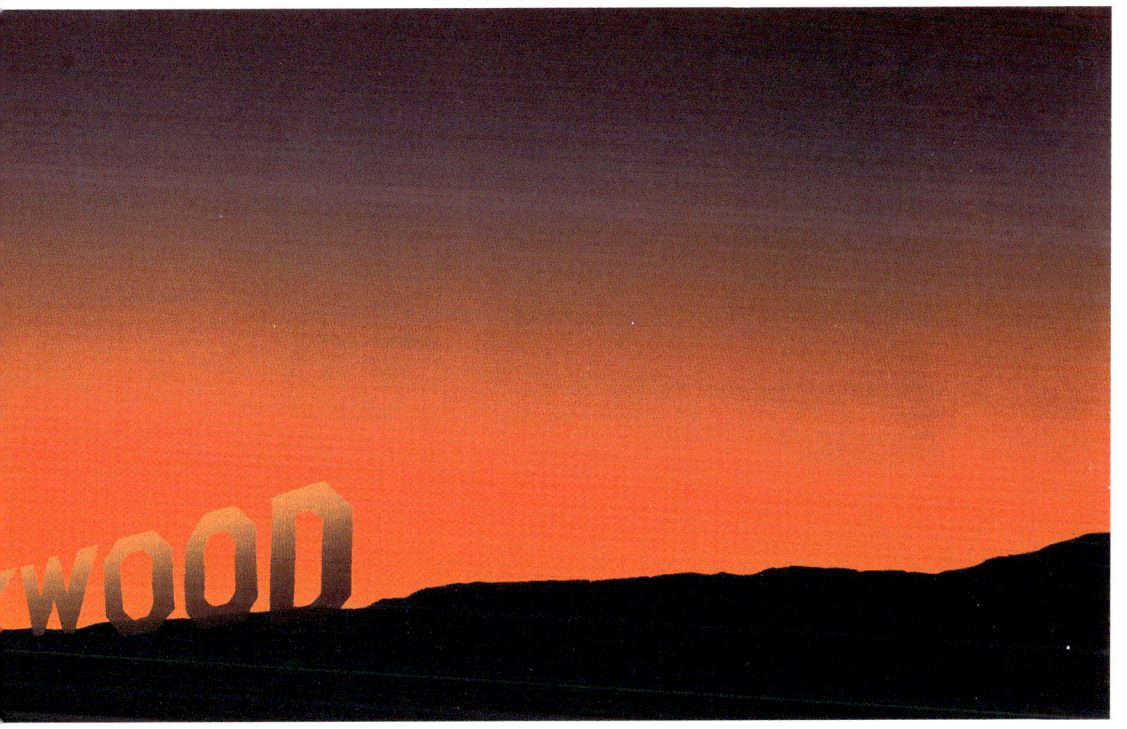

George Segal
Woman Washing her Feet in a Sink, 1964/65

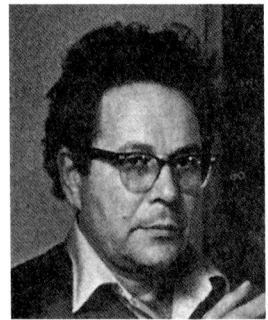

b. 1924 in New York City
d. 2000 in South Brunswick,
New Jersey

Originally Segal was a painter, for ten years. Disappointed by the limited possibilities of painting to evoke three dimensions, he turned to sculpture. The impulse to change his field of art leaves little room for speculation as to what sort of painting Segal practised. At any rate, he remained true to his artistic convictions, in sculpture, too, adhering to an empirical approach. It would nevertheless be misleading to associate him with that current which, primarily in Europe, is known as realism. Realism is merely one of many frameworks within which an artist can deal with reality. Segal, in contrast, is more interested in reality pure and simple than in a vision that manifests itself in the form of an artistic statement. His attitude is shaped by the pragmatism of American culture. He had created a space, Segal once said, and that which strived to fill the space with a volume, which was known as sculpture. There could be no more concise statement of his aims. Segal made his first sculpture in the year 1958. *Woman Washing her Feet in a Sink* is another of his earliest works. It contains every trait that is typical of his art: a plaster figure, the immediate surroundings that define its existence in space, the real objects that anchor it in reality. Instead of artistically modifying things based on a certain notion of reality, Segal presents them in combination with the figure of the title, the only element subjected to aesthetic transformation. The figure was created from a living model, with the aid of plaster-soaked bandages. But rather than using the resulting hollow mould to create the final figure, as in conventional sculpture, Segal lent the provisional stage of the modelling process the seal of finality. The traces of the process of making remain visible. In consequence, a subtle relationship of tension develops between the plaster figures and real objects in Segal's sculptural ensembles, comparable to that between photographic image and photographed motif. Beyond this, a sense of oppressive loneliness engraves itself in our visual memory – the image of a woman of uncertain age in shabby surroundings, doing something in which nobody is particularly interested. Not a motif for voyeurs, and therefore not especially photogenic.

Woman Washing her Feet in a Sink, 1964/65
Plaster, wash basin, chair, height 158 cm (62¼ in.)
Cologne, Museum Ludwig

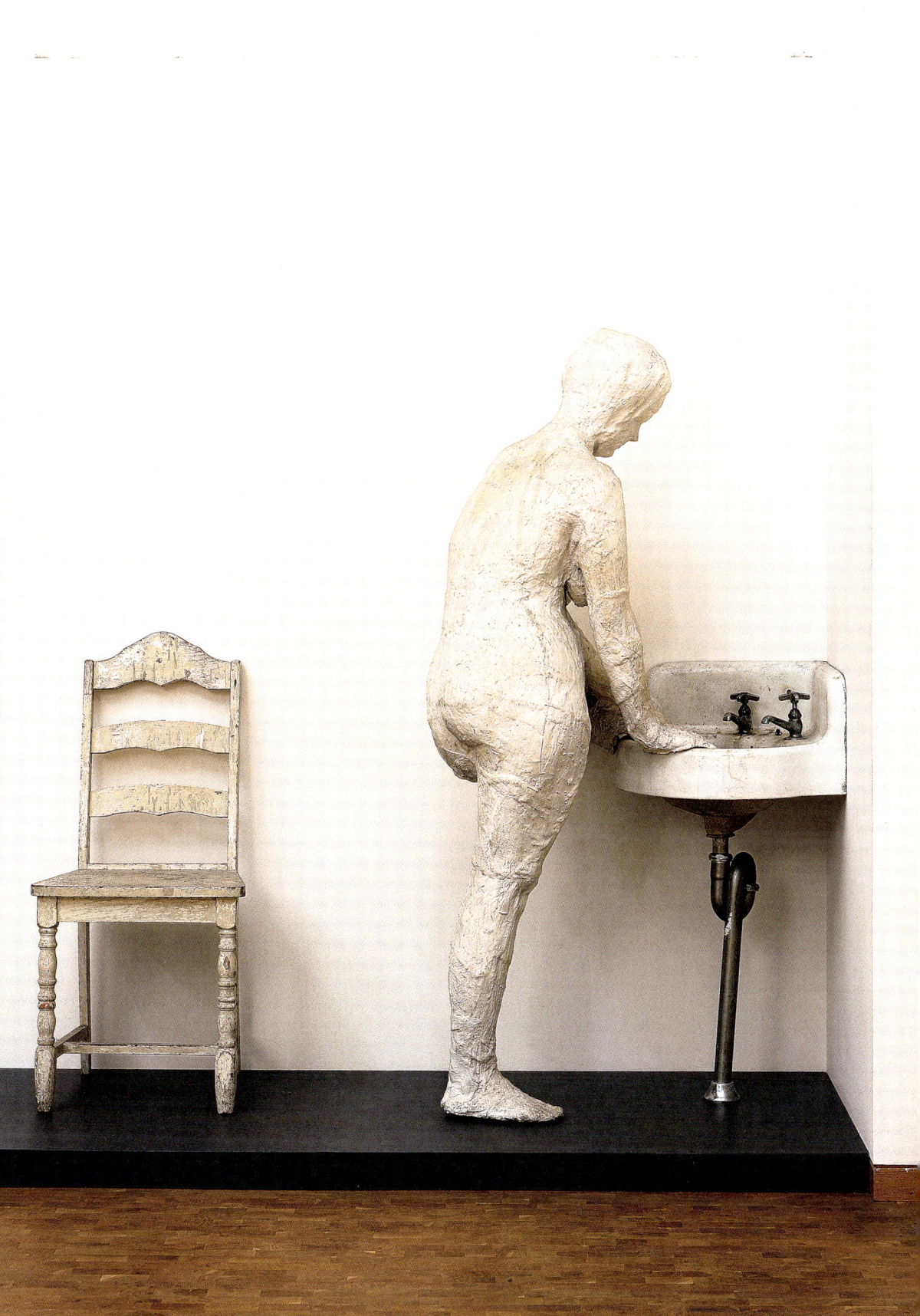

George Segal
The Restaurant Window I, 1967

A woman sits alone at an empty table in the window of a restaurant, as a man, lost in thought and hands thrust into his coat pockets, walks by. He has not yet passed the woman, but it seems unlikely that he will notice her, despite the fact that she sits in the restaurant window as if on display. The artist created the two plaster figures from living models. The remainder of the piece, as generally in his art, consists of real things – window, table, chair. The scene sends shivers down one's back. In a single "decisive moment", everything that contradicts the promise of commercial culture that happiness and fulfilment can be had through consumption comes together: the piercing loneliness of the individual in the shadow of the world of glamour and glitter. If the work can be said to have a connection with Pop Art at all, it is as a hollow or negative form, that is, due to its demonstrative lack of all the traits that characterize Pop. Within the Pop context, Segal's work is like a foreign body. It is rooted instead in a specific tradition of American art. The reference of the present piece to Edward Hopper's famous painting *The Nighthawks*, 1942, which likewise depicts a restaurant in the hours after dark, is obvious. The artist has merely reduced the number of figures and condensed the painting's ambivalent atmosphere to its naked core. On the other hand, the diner is one of the most significant institutions in American culture. Not the restaurant in the European sense, but what in the U.S. goes under the name of drugstore, bar, diner or drive-in. As sites of social intercourse, these places play an essential role in Hollywood movies. Paradoxically, Segal's version of Pop possesses a covert connection with its more typical manifestations in terms of technique. Most of his works have what can be called a photographic structure, being, as it were, materializations of ambitious photographers' mass-disseminated pictures. Like the man behind the camera, Segal freezes typical situations and constellations, and out of this condensation develops the crystallization point for a story that begins to unfold in the viewer's mind. He draws our attention to the dark side of a supposedly incessantly fun-loving consumer society, to people who cannot or will not participate in its diversions, the counter-image to the world evoked by advertising and glossy life-style magazines. At the same time, Segal gives convincing proof of the power of art to keep the gap between illusion and reality open. A retrospective of Segal's oeuvre, one imagines, would be no less than a nightmare.

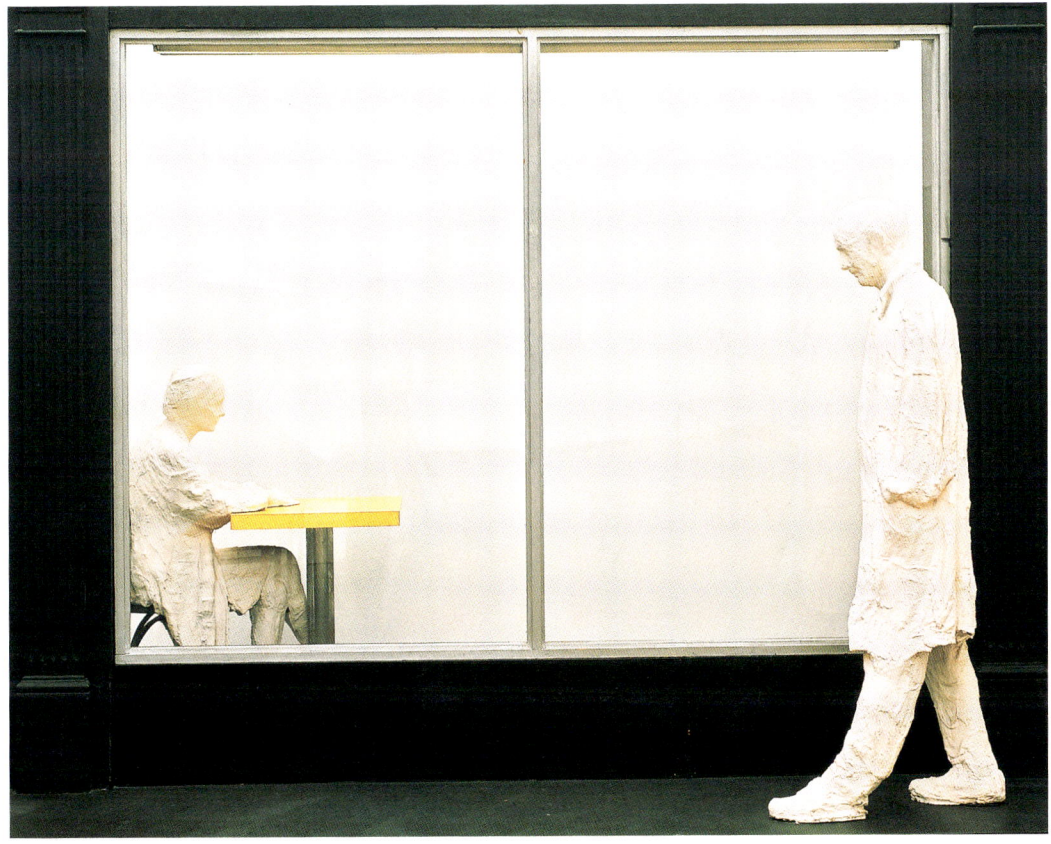

The Restaurant Window I, 1967
Plaster, restaurant window, wood, metal,
Plexiglas, neon tubing, chair, table,
244 x 340 x 206 cm (96 x 134 x 81 in.)
Cologne, Museum Ludwig

Wayne Thiebaud
Cake Counter, 1963

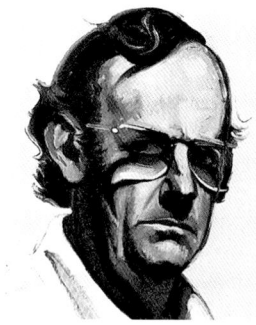

b. 1920 in Mesa, Arizona
d. 2021 in Sacramento,
California

As in a bakery window, cakes of various sizes and shapes are arranged to catch the observer's eye. The upper of the two shelves contains cakes with four layers, carefully decorated with off-white frosting. They recall the temples in the historical Hollywood movies of Cecil B. De Mille. Smaller versions with greater colour variations are displayed on the lower shelf, some of them already cut to reveal their luscious inside. Cut off by the picture edge on right and left, the two ranks of cakes seem to extend indefinitely beyond the frame. Their various hues emphasize the specific quality of the goods, and even though the blue may seem extravagant, it is not beyond a confectioner's skills. Creamy tones predominate, and of course the deep brown of chocolate and the bright white of whipped cream. The painting could be described entirely in gastronomical terms. At any rate, it re-establishes the lost ambivalence of the outmoded term "taste", once an aesthetic category, and subliminally recalls the loss to art which its reduction solely to visual stimuli has caused.

Thiebaud is a representative of the Californian variant of Pop. The surface of his paintings reflects the process of making, for the brushstrokes remain clearly visible. The paint is not applied in a slick, anonymous, commercial-art manner, yet nor does it approach the subjective character of Abstract Expressionism. It creates an illusion of cakes and pies in a dual sense: by means of imitation (local colour) and through a heavy impasto that emphasizes, a bit obviously, the creamy physical consistency of cake frosting. Apart from the objects, the illumination plays a key role here. The light seems to cast almost no shadows. As the artist once said, he was interested in what happens when the similarity of colour and pictorial content was as great as possible, as when viscous brilliant white was applied to a painted cake like frosting. Thiebaud is a sort of Californian Chardin who has cut his piece from the cake of art, and a Pop artist primarily by virtue of his choice of subject matter. That he is also a virtuoso painter can be seen from *Cake Counter*, which is bisected horizontally as if by a visual barrier. This lends the objects an incredible plasticity. Yet the formal unity of the composition is by no means prejudiced by this canny disturbance.

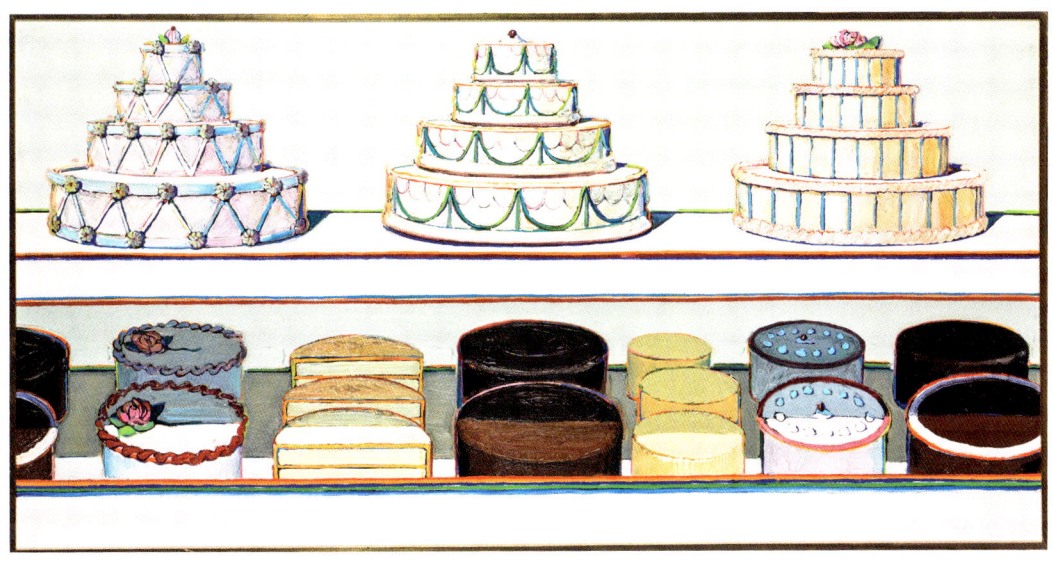

Cake Counter, 1963
Oil on canvas, 92 x 183 cm (36¼ x 72 in.)
Cologne, Museum Ludwig

Andy Warhol
129 *Die in Jet*, 1962

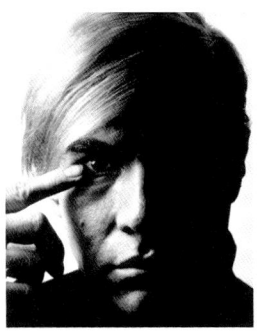

b. 1928 in Pittsburgh,
Pennsylvania
d. 1987 in New York City

On 4 June 1962, a Monday, the front page of the *New York Mirror* carried the screaming headline "129 DIE IN JET!" Between the capitalized lines appeared a press photo, twice as large as the headline, showing a half-destroyed wing jutting into a cloudless sky, with a few policemen or rescue workers silhouetted in the foreground. Shortly after the disaster, Warhol used a slide projector to transfer the page to a canvas measuring 254.5 by 182.5 cm, and rendered it with brush and paint. Newspaper title, headline and illustration (complete with byline) make up a composition with which Warhol introduced the series of what he termed "death paintings". These, in contrast to the celebration of the American way of life in many of his other works, shed glaring light on its seamier side. The letters of the headline have a tremendous visual impact. In subsequent works Warhol would create a similar effect by repeating a single image over and over again. The suggestive force of the capital letters and painted photograph are difficult to resist. Both get under our skin despite the fact that airline disasters have since become an almost daily occurrence. Warhol's treatment of the press photo adapts it to the graphic presence of the lettering, and reduces the details of the photo reproduction to a few characteristic abbreviations. This increases the tendency to abstraction already present in the enlargement. The few artistic incursions create a distance to the original, and to the event itself, divesting the painting of any suggestion of embarrassing realism and raising its message to an exemplary level. At the same time, they heighten the print-image combination into a timeless symbol. The mediated reality of the yellow press is sublimated into the reality of art, leaving mental associations to the viewer's imagination. The idea for the picture was suggested by Henry Geldzahler, then curator at the Metropolitan Museum of Art in New York and one of the few advocates of Pop on a museum level at the time. Warhol was having breakfast with Geldzahler in a Manhattan restaurant. The curator was reading the *New York Mirror*, whose title page, Geldzahler reputedly said, would make a good subject for a painting. Warhol was always receptive to suggestions from others; in fact, they were an integral part of his aesthetic principles. His founding of a "Factory" to produce pictures a short time later was not only prompted by commercial considerations but reflected an aesthetic stance in which the contemporary artist figured not as a lone genius but as a sort of catalyst for diverse outside influences.

*129 **Die in Jet***, 1962
Acrylic on canvas,
254.5 x 182.5 cm (100¼ x 72 in.)
Cologne, Museum Ludwig

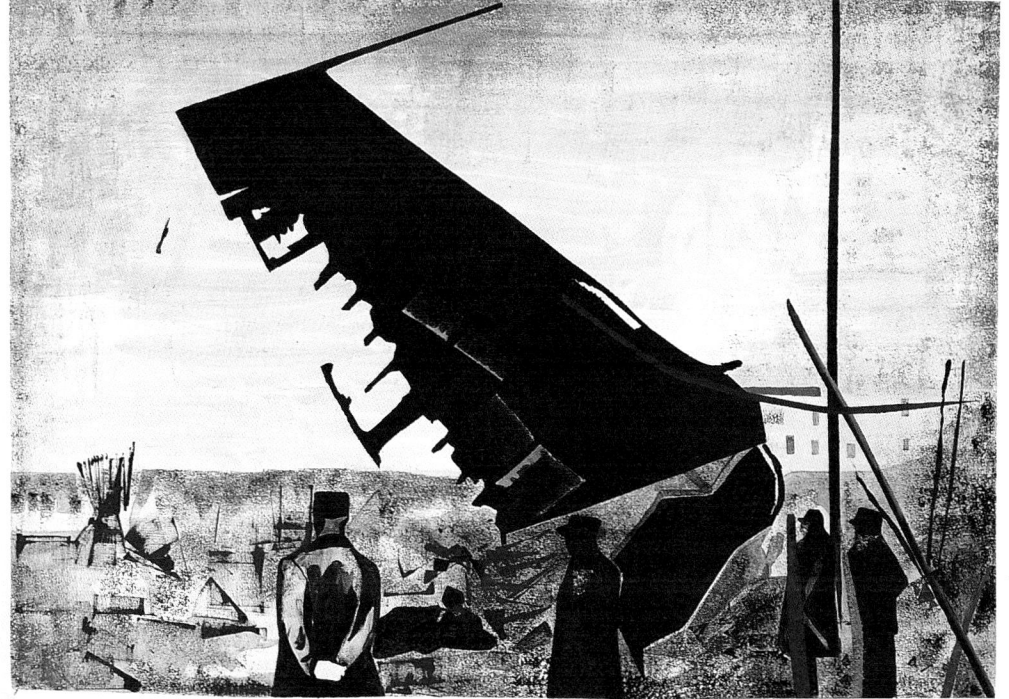

Andy Warhol
Gold Marilyn Monroe, 1962

Andy Warhol may have contributed more to Marilyn Monroe's myth than Hollywood and the glossy magazines put together. Commerical movies and their public relations campaigns merely made her into a sex symbol and the prototype of the dumb blonde. She suffered under this image, as her various biographies, both fictitious and authentic, have since made clear. People laughed at Marilyn's ambition to be taken seriously as a thinking and feeling person, with only few exceptions. Her desire to play dramatic roles after successfully taking courses at the famous Actor's Studio in New York was looked upon as an infringement of the rules by the movie industry. Shortly after her death in 1962, possibly as a result of a fateful error, Warhol transformed a quite mundane publicity photo, taken by the American photographer Frank Powolny in the early 1950s, into an icon of popular culture. When the picture was taken, Monroe had just managed to escape the pin-up calendars and postcards, much appreciated by G. I.s, for which she had posed while working in the armament industry. Thanks to notable minor roles in John Huston's *Asphalt Jungle*, 1950, and Joseph L. Mankiewicz's *All about Eve*, 1950, she had made her mark in ambitious Hollywood films. Yet Monroe was never entirely able to escape the label of sex bomb. Apart from her attractive figure, the movie industry merely exploited her comic talent, but continued to deny her the honour of being a serious actress. *Bus Stop*, 1956, by Joshua Logan, and *The Misfits*, 1960, another Huston film, were the only major roles that gave Monroe a chance to prove her dramatic talent. Many contemporary movie stars enjoyed greater reputations, in public as well as on screen, than she. It was only after her death that her true fame began; in fact, death seems to have been a condition for it. By placing the uninteresting photographic portrait with its forced, stereotypical smile in an expansive space that surrounds it like a dignified frame, and covering the whole field with gold – the colour of the Heavenly Jerusalem, which lends icons their supernatural effect – Warhol idolized it. The arched lips, the eyes, curly hair and face, deprived of volume and realism by the silkscreen technique, detach themselves from the background and float in front of and above it like stars in a golden sky. In many later versions, Warhol secularized the idol by constantly repeating or isolating the smile, and linked the myth of the star with the methods used by the mass media to make a star. By means of continually new variations and incessant sequences, as an industrialized product, a consumer commodity.

Gold Marilyn Monroe, 1962
Polymer, silkscreen, oil on canvas,
211.4 x 144.7 cm (83¼ x 57 in.)
New York, The Museum of Modern Art,
gift of Philip Johnson

Andy Warhol
Two Dollar Bills (Front and Rear), 1962

Put in the simplest terms, the content of this picture is 80 dollars. This is its subject, and nothing else. Represented are 80 dollars, in units of 40, worth two dollars each. The artist has depicted their obverse and reverse sides, in ten rows comprising four bills each. To decode the work's content, we need only perform a little simple addition. Apart from this exercise, it demands no particular intellectual acumen, and the process of understanding runs a clear, rational course. Possible misreadings are excluded from the start. Nor need we fear that any potential observer might not be familiar with the motif of the printed canvas. It is as omnipresent as God in theocratic states. To this extent, the comparison with icons, which is used *ad nauseam* with respect to Warhol's pictures, would apply best to his long and varied series of dollar-bill depictions. God has merely been replaced by the material phenomenon of money – likewise a magical system based on faith. The dollar bills, too, embody – in the truest sense of the word – that which they represent: money. There is no fundamental gap between original and image, between real bills and the "counterfeit" bills applied to canvas with the aid of a silkscreen. Both represent an abstract system, a mercantile value that far transcends their actual, material value. With the difference that the mercantile value of Warhol's dollar-bill works is considerably greater than that of the value of the banknotes depicted. To realize this value, only a commercial exchange is necessary. No artist before him more mercilessly exposed the fiction of the incompatibility of intellectual and material values in the sphere of art than Warhol. At the same time, he shed harsh light on the interdependence of economic and cultural mechanisms in the art trade, and recognized this to be constituitive for the substance of a contemporary work of art. Contrary to legend, in other words, the value of a work of art is not measured by its aesthetic quality alone, whatever that may be, but equally by the price it can command and – not to be forgotten – by the prestige of its author. Successful circulation in the commercial art trade is an integral part of the artistic (not aesthetic) quality of a work. And every sale of one of Warhol's dollar-bill paintings fills its content with new life.

Two Dollar Bills (Front and Rear), 1962
Silkscreen on canvas,
210 x 96 cm (82¾ x 37¾ in.)
Cologne, Museum Ludwig

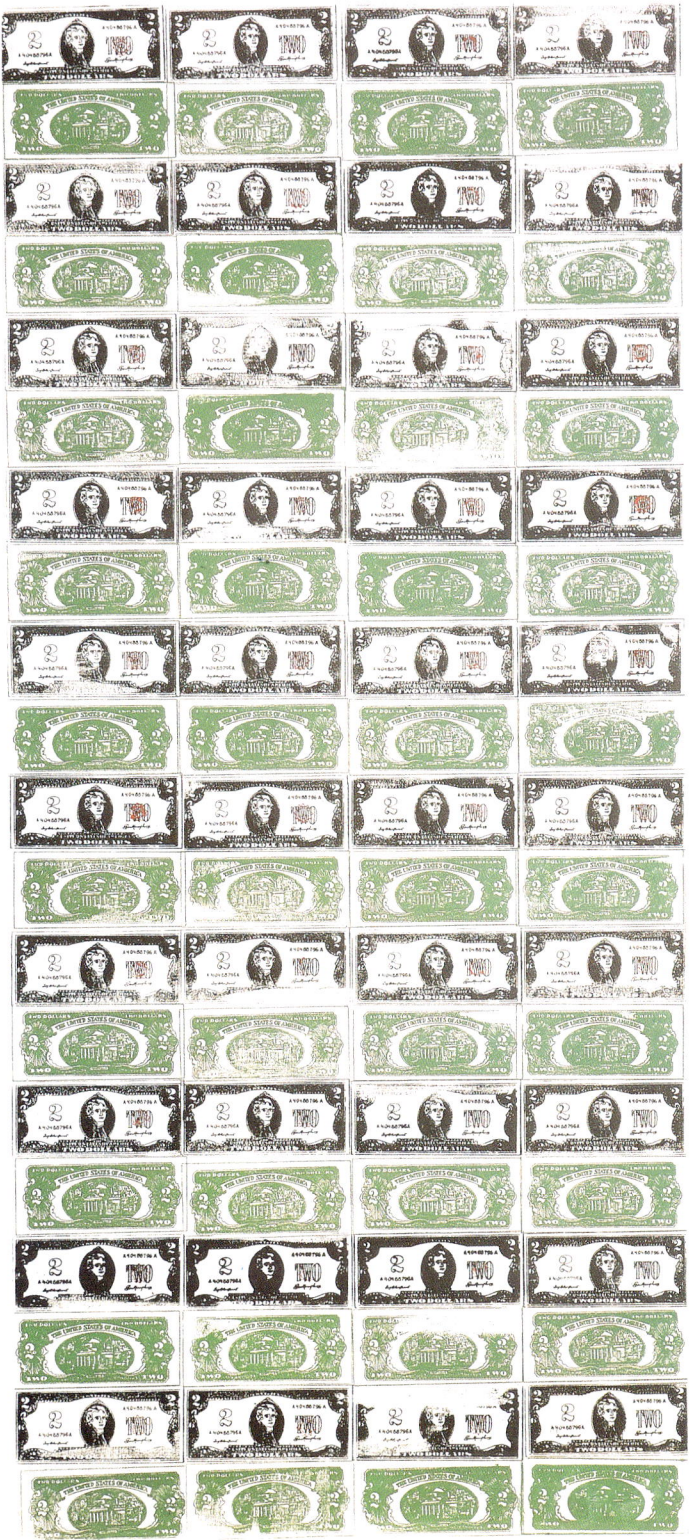

Andy Warhol
Campbell's Soup Can I, 1968

When Warhol first exhibited his pictures of Campbell's soup cans in July and August 1962 – thirty-two all told – he presented them in the way tinned foods are offered for sale in a supermarket, in orderly, evenly spaced rows. Quite in keeping with the guidelines of "product placement", in other words, commercially oriented aesthetic considerations. The site of the demonstration, however, was no ordinary supermarket in Los Angeles, but the Ferus Gallery, a pioneer in the propagation of Pop Art. The paintings cost 100 dollars each, compared with 29 cents for the original. In terms of technique, the pictures were a semi-mechanical product – a mixture of painting, silkscreen and a stamp process, practices partly manual and partly industrial in nature. Although a superficial glance revealed no differences between the individual, 50.8 x 40.6 cm images, they in fact differed in a key detail, each representing a different kind of soup, an individual taste beneath the monotony of the packaging.

The exhibition represented a conscious provocation, triggered not only by the mundane motif and its stereotyped depiction, but by the parallels purposely suggested between art gallery and supermarket, art trade and food trade. For Warhol, who had studied sociology, the social context in which a work of art is presented was just as important as its specific subject, and the subject itself invariably reflected its social background. Campbell's soups, Coca-Cola, Kellogg's Cornflakes and Brillo detergent, industrially produced commodities of American civilization, lent the dignity of art by Warhol, shaped the life of the American middle class, of which he was part, as much as sex and death.

Campbell's Soup Can, a later, enlarged, and isolated version of the tomato soup can, might convey the erroneous impression that Warhol was out solely to apotheosize the idiom of popular culture. In fact its social effects were equally important to him. What made America fabulous, Warhol once explained, was that it established a tradition in which the richest consumers basically bought the same products as the poorest. You could watch television and drink a Coca-Cola, and you knew the president drank Coke, Liz Taylor drank Coke, and there you were, drinking Coke, too. A Coke was a Coke, concluded Warhol, and no amount of money could buy you a better one.

This insight perhaps explains why he set out to achieve something similar in the field of art. With the aid of standardized production methods, Warhol infused art with the magic of the perpetually same. After photography had entered the cultural scene as the "great leveller" (Jonathan Crary), Warhol followed its cue in the field of art.

Campbell's Soup Can I, 1968
Acrylic, Liquitex, silkscreen
on canvas, 92 x 61 cm (36¼ x 24 in.)
Aachen, Ludwig Forum für
Internationale Kunst

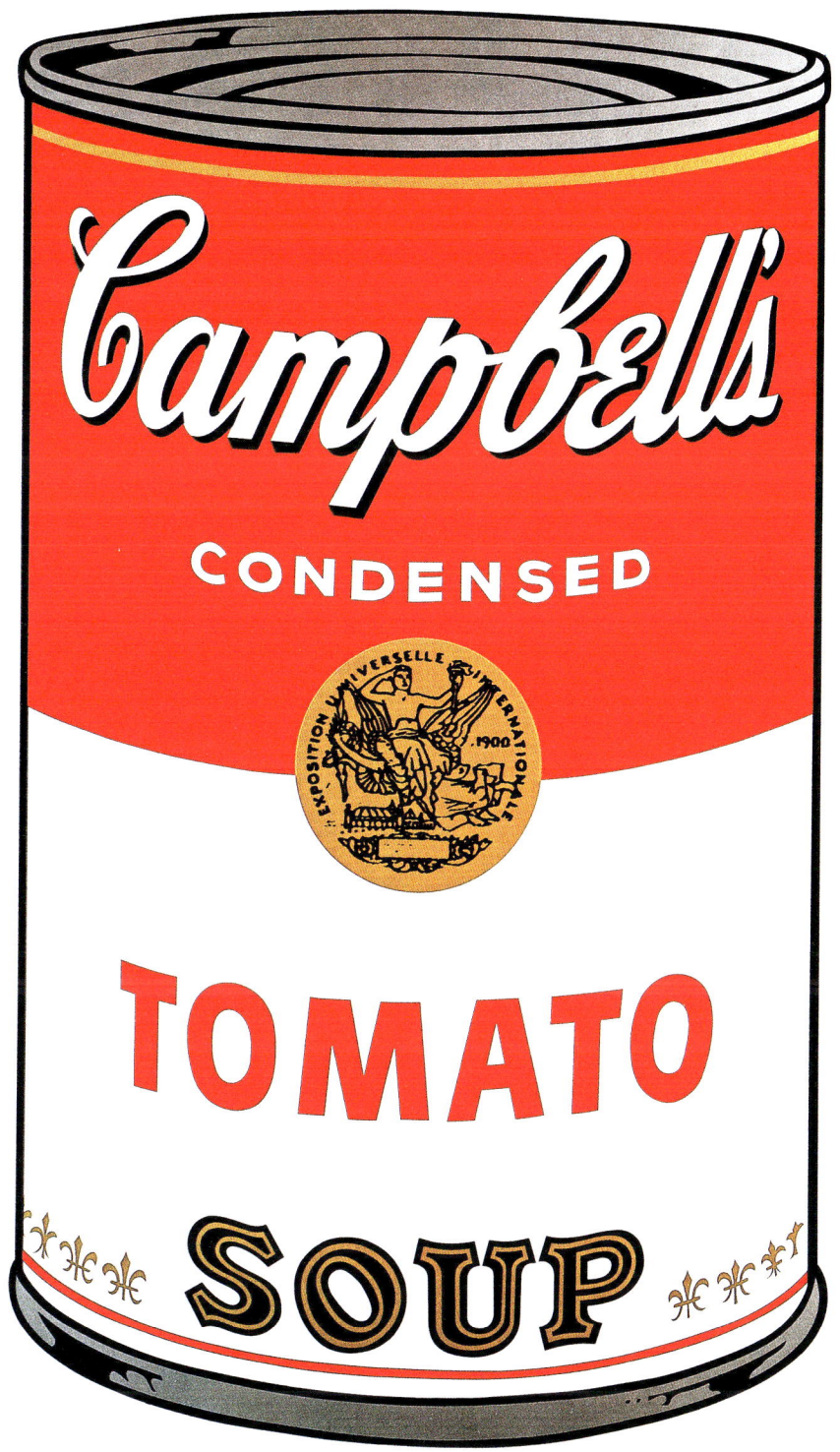

Tom Wesselmann
Still Life No. 20, 1962

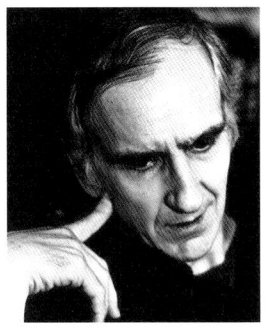

b. 1931 in Cincinnati, Ohio
d. 2004 in New York City

The Mondrian is a copy. The bottles, toast, bananas, apple, glass of Coke and table expand the chapter of *trompe l'oeil* in the field of art. Real, on the other hand, are the cabinet, its contents, the fluorescent tube, and the faucet with soap and soap dish. Out of paint, paper, wood and these consumer commodities, Wesselman has fabricated a cross between a kitchen and bathroom. Three levels of the real are interlocked in this assemblage: reality *per se*, photography and painting. However, photographic elements turn out to be painted, painted elements turn out to be coloured prints, and real things turn out to be elements of an art work, at least in light of the modernist definition of art. As soon as something is shown in a museum, the spotlights of art fall upon it and illuminate it as a work of art. On the other hand, the work of art included in *Still Life*, a framed copy of a Mondrian painting, takes on an aspect of the real, since its use as an item of interior decoration reduces its artistic meaning, causes its intellectual dimension to pale. The photographically rendered foodstuffs, finally, have the character of hallucinations, and the remaining things that of trivial pieces of decor, like the Mondrian copy.

Pop Art was never as linear as many critics maintain. The context in which works of art are perceived was often the underlying theme. The conditions in which a work is manifested influence its perception. Such tensions between the levels of the real are reflected in the formal tensions in Wesselmann's assemblage – the tension between illusionistic painting and actual object, between plane and space, between art and decor. After his *Nudes* Wesselmann turned to the subject of still life. And as there, he veritably conjugated this genre in an extended series of works. The focus of this series was no longer woman as object, but her domestic environment, the kitchens and bathrooms of middle-class suburban homes. The sexual connotations were toned down, but not eliminated, as the chance encounter of pointed bananas and round apples indicates. As a rule, fruit stands for male and female, phallus and breast, in Wesselmann's art, including *Still Life No. 20*. The sexual obsessions seep through the façade of respectable, prudish American life like butter through waxed paper.

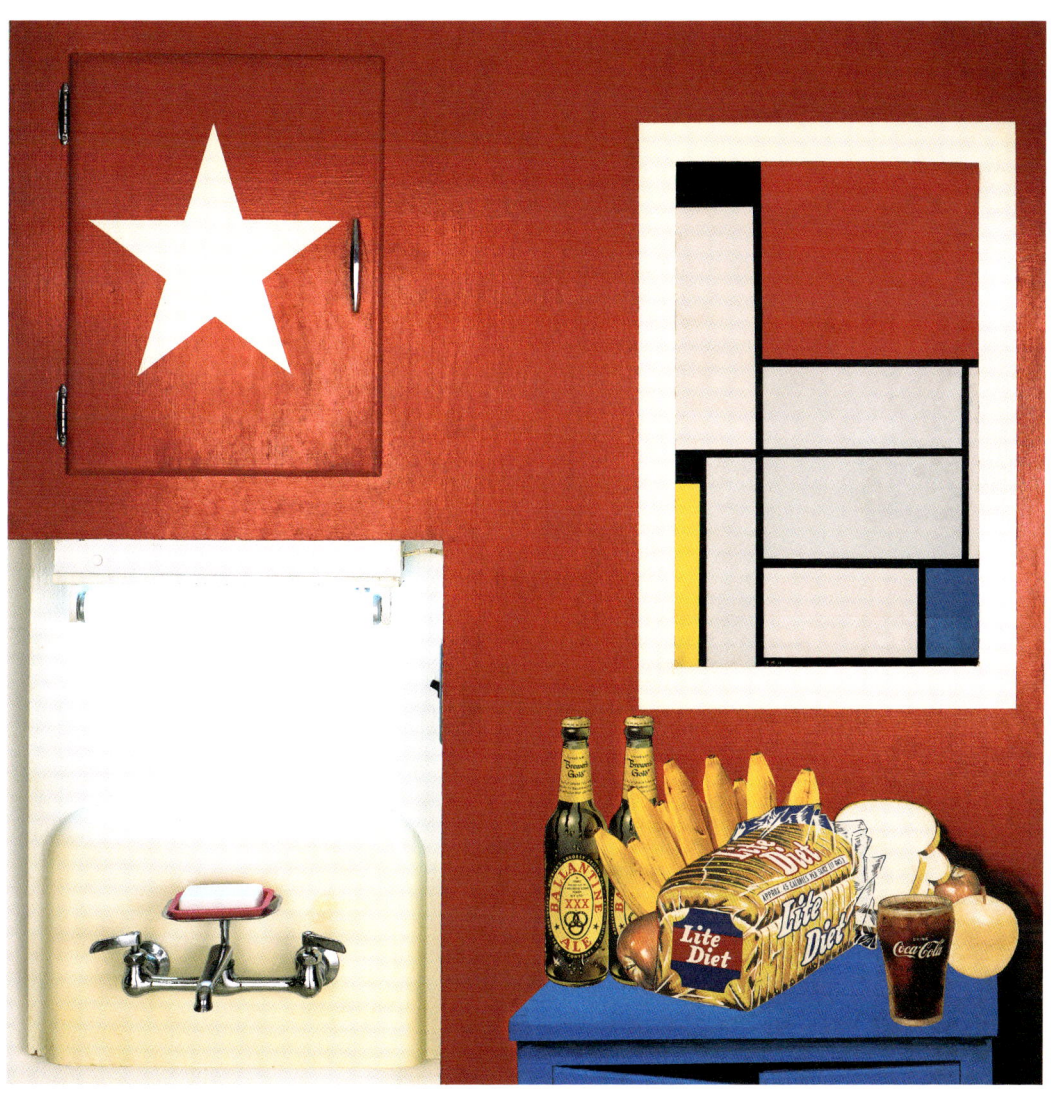

Still Life No. 20, 1962
Mixed media, 104 x 122 x 14 cm (41 x 48 x 5½ in.)
Buffalo, Albright-Knox Art Gallery,
gift of Seymour H. Knox Jr.

Tom Wesselmann
Bathtub No. 3, 1963

It would be hard to imagine a better ad for a bathroom for singles. Yet the only thing this picture advertises is the skill of its maker. An unusual work – a combination of painted and real things, including a door, towel, bathmat, laundry basket, shower curtain. In modern art such montages generally serve the purpose of counteracting any sense of illusion, as in Cubism. Here, this aesthetic principle serves just the opposite purpose – to increase the sense of illusion. The reality of the photographic rendering glosses over the difference between painting and reality. Only the flat silhouette of the naked blonde woman drying her back with a red-and-white striped towel indicates the artificial character of the arrangement. Her nakedness is in fact largely the product of the viewer's imagination, since it is only suggested by subtly rendered nipples and pubic triangle. Wesselmann plays a canny game with various levels of reality, bringing products of the real world as counters into the game. Not even the bather's silhouette corresponds to a conventional silhouette, being white instead of black. In fact, the supposed silhouette is a template, equipped with obvious sexual attributes: blonde hair, nipples, pubic hair, those neuralgic symbols which the male imagination invariably tends to flesh out. Yet the artist has set limits on the imagination by his choice of ambience. Sexual fantasies are confined to a clinically clean terrain. Nothing is present that would be prohibited in advertising. Once again, Wesselmann proves himself a skilled exploiter of the erotic world of Henri Matisse in the commercial climate of sexualized American popular culture. By entirely expunging the dark aspects of sexuality that reverberate in some of the French artist's paintings, he outdoes the art of his idol in terms of sheer artificiality. Paradoxically, he finds support in the set pieces he has lifted from reality. The real flips over into the sphere of the artificial.

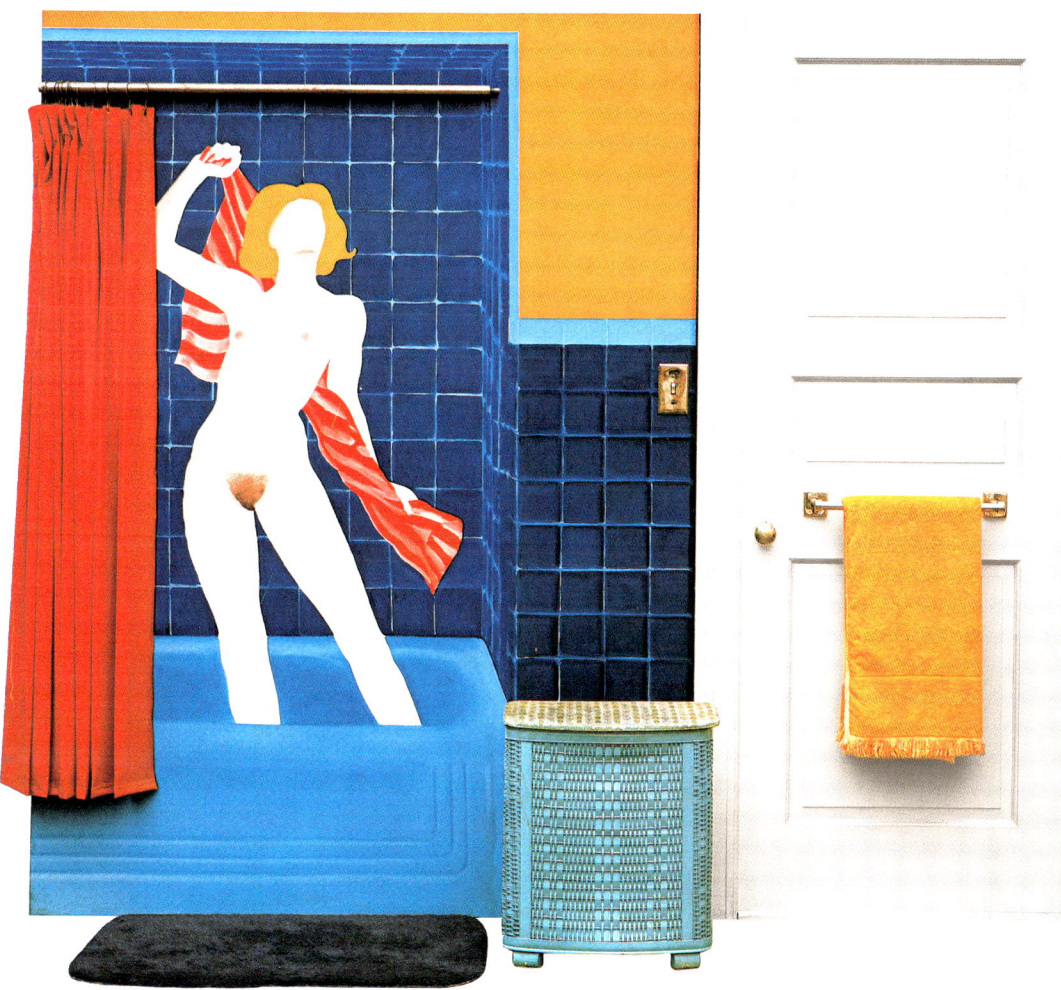

Bathtub No. 3, 1963
Oil on canvas, plastic, various objects,
213 x 270 x 45 cm (84 x 106¼ x 17¾ in.)
Cologne, Museum Ludwig

Tom Wesselmann
Great American Nude No. 98, 1967

Jean-Pierre Melville, the great French film author, once scoffed in conversation with Rui Nogueira that the female ideal of American men was "a woman who wears her behind on her chest". Tom Wesselmann frequently paid tribute to this notorious obsession with big breasts, which feature in a highly visible way in this picture-object consisting of five canvases. He has added a few related attributes: the model's long blonde hair, a temptingly open red mouth with brilliant white teeth and pink tongue, a luminous reddish- yellow orange with highlight in the foreground, and a smoking cigarette immediately in front of the jutting breast in the middle ground. A rectangular blue box of Kleenex tissues, a black ashtray and a semicircular cushion complete the ensemble. Thanks to the compressed arrangement of the three superimposed pictorial levels, the sexual attributes immediately strike the eye. And they are rendered in a highly schematic manner. The lack of individuality of the woman's face, and the smooth paint application lacking every trace of personal touch, signal the source of the artist's inspiration – advertising. Yet although his straightforward effects were derived from its vocabulary, Wesselmann has altered the strategy of advertising in a decisive way. By means

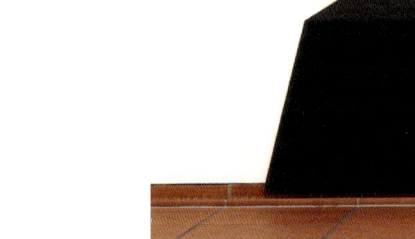

Great American Nude No. 98, 1967
Oil on canvas, 250 x 380 x 130 cm
(98½ x 149½ x 51¼ in.)
Cologne, Museum Ludwig

of exaggeration, instead of using sex to draw the viewer's attention to the surrogate satisfactions of consumption he presents it pure, and transforms the consumer goods depicted into sexual symbols in their own right. The incredibly refined colours lend the work a seductive force and gloss over the all-too-obvious clichés. The result is a provocative tension, sensed just above the threshold of perception, which the artist has purposely factored into the equation. Before he arrived at his typical style, Wesselmann experimented with Abstract Expressionism à la Willem de Kooning, with collages based on abstract and mass-media sources, and with relatively conventional depictions of objects and landscapes. His experience with the collage technique – instead of painting from existing material like most Pop artists, he employed it unaltered – is immediately apparent in the characteristic structure of Wesselmann's brand of Pop.

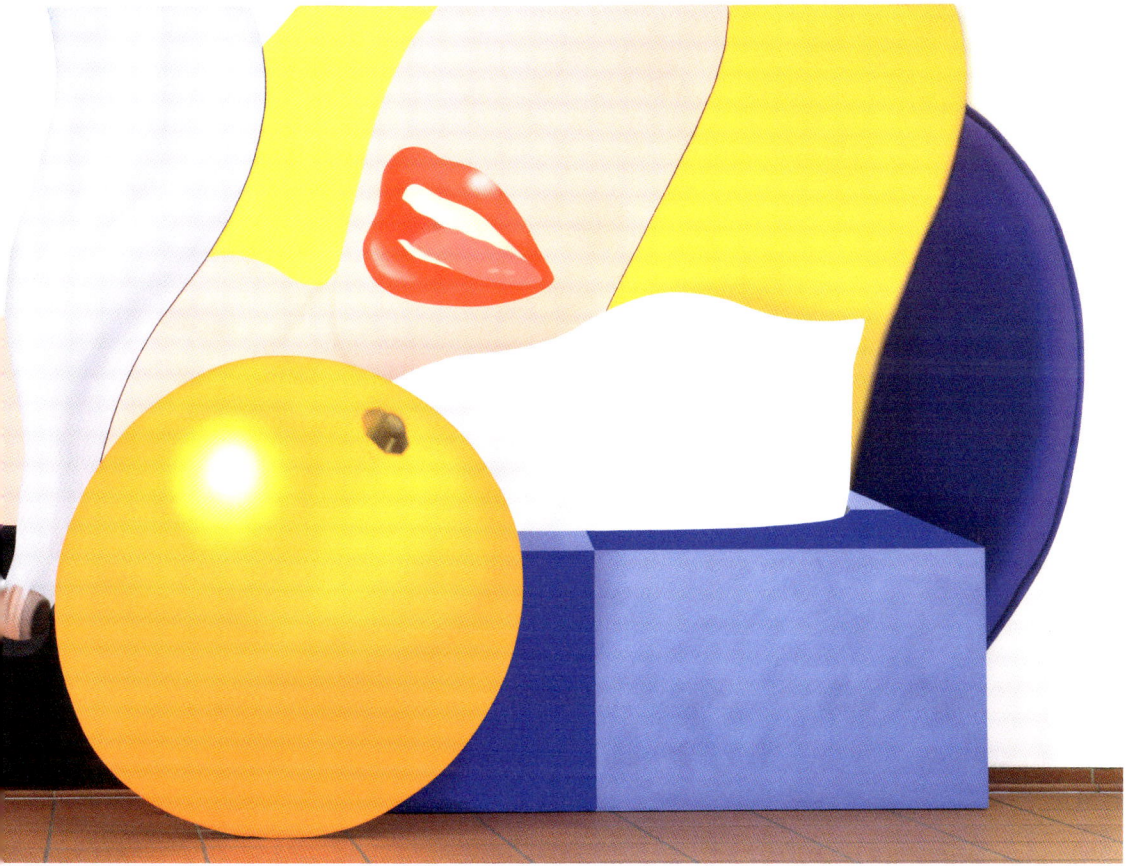

Appendix
Photo credits, copyrights, authors, notes

The publisher wishes to thank the museums, collections, photographers and other institutions mentioned in the captions and in the credits who granted permission to reproduce works and supported the making of this book. Where not otherwise indicated, the reproductions were based on material in the publisher's archive. Any omissions are unintentional and appropriate credit will be given in future editions should such copyright holders contact the publisher.

Impressionism
Photo credits

akg-images: pp. 32, 35, 52, 82, 83, 89, 92; Laurent Lecat: pp. 38, 66; Erich Lessing: p. 42; National Gallery Global Limited: pp. 93; © Sotheby's: p. 53
ARTOTHEK: p. 101; Blauel / Gnamm: p. 21; Christie's Images: p. 69
bpk | The Metropolitan Museum of Art: p. 31
Bridgeman Images: pp. 30, 47, 65; © The Henry Barber Trust, The Barber Institute of Fine Arts, University of Birmingham: p. 33; Kunsthalle, Bremen: p. 99; Musée Marmottan Monet, Paris: p. 63; Musée d'Orsay, Paris: p. 71; Musée d'Orsay, Paris © Photo Josse: p. 12; Museum of Fine Arts, Boston, Massachusetts / Photograph © 2025. All rights reserved. / M. Theresa B. Hopkins Fund: p. 15; Roger-Viollet, Paris:

pp. 36/37; Worcester Art Museum, Massachusetts: p. 10
Detroit Institute of Arts: p. 39
Fine Arts Museums of San Francisco, Legion of Honor and de Young Museums: p. 79
© Musée Rodin, photo Jean de Calan: front cover, p. 57
Museo de Bellas Artes de Bilbao: p. 51
© 2025 Museo Nacional Thyssen-Bornemisza / Scala, Florence: p. 67
Museum Folkwang, Essen, Photo J. Nober: p. 76
The National Gallery, London: pp. 85, 95
National Gallery of Art, Washington, D.C., Ailsa Mellon Bruce Collection: p. 29
National Museums Liverpool: p. 87
Niedersächsisches Landesmuseum Hannover: pp. 60, 97
© 2025 Photo The Philadelphia Museum of Art / Art Resource / Scala, Florence: pp. 4/5, 49, 81
Rheinisches Bildarchiv, Cologne: p. 8
RMN – Photo Bulloz: p. 22; Photo Hervé Lewandowski: pp. 16, 17, 19, 41, 43, 45, 55, 91;Photo René-Gabriel Ojéda: pp. 25, 59
© 2025 Photo Scala, Florence: pp. 18, 26, 75; Courtesy of the Ministero Beni e Att. Culturali e del Turismo: p. 34

The author

Berlin-based Karin H. Grimme works as a historian, art historian, and author for museums, exhibitions, and media, focusing on the history of the 19th and 20th

centuries and in particular on the history of the Jews in Europe. She is the author of numerous journalistic and academic publications in the press, in broadcasting, and in the multimedia sphere; as author and editor she has produced works on, among other things, the Jewish bourgeoisie in the 19th century.

Expressionism
Copyright

© for the work of Ernst Barlach: Ernst Barlach Lizenzverwaltung, Ratzeburg
© for the works of Heinrich Campendonk, Otto Dix, Lyonel Feininger, Conrad Felixmüller, Gabriele Münter, Karl Schmidt-Rottluff, and Kees van Dongen: VG Bild-Kunst, Bonn 2026
© for the works of George Grosz: Estate of George Grosz, Princeton, New Jersey / VG Bild-Kunst, Bonn 2026
© for the works of Ernst Ludwig Kirchner: Dr. Wolfgang und Ingeborg Henze-Ketterer, Wichtrach/Berne
© for the works of Oskar Kokoschka: Fondation Oskar Kokoschka / VG Bild-Kunst, Bonn 2026
© for the work of Edvard Munch: The Munch Museum / The Munch Ellingsen Group
© for the works of Emil Nolde: Nolde Stiftung, Seebüll
© for the works of Max Pechstein: Pechstein – Hamburg/Tökendorf

The author

Norbert Wolf graduated in art
history, linguistics, and medieval
studies from the Universities of
Regensburg and Munich, and
earned his PhD in 1983. He held
visiting professorships in Marburg,
Frankfurt, Leipzig, Düsseldorf,
Nuremberg-Erlangen, and
Innsbruck. His extensive writings
on art history include many
TASCHEN titles, such as *Diego
Velázquez, Ernst Ludwig Kirchner,
Caspar David Friedrich, Roman-
esque, Landscape Painting,*
and *Symbolism.*

Surrealism

The author

Cathrin Klingsöhr-Leroy studied art history, archaeology and German literature in Regensburg, Bonn and Paris. She wrote her doctoral thesis on "The Artist Portrait in the French Grand Siècle". Previously curator of the Fritz Winter Foundation at the Bayerische Staatsgemälde-sammlungen in Munich, she is currently director of the Franz Marc Museum in Kochel am See. She has published works on Lyonel Feininger, Lovis Corinth, Franz Marc and the Blue Rider and in particular on Paul Klee.

Abstract Expressionism

Copyright

Photo credits

The author

Barbara Hess is an art historian, critic, and translator and resides in Cologne. Her numerous articles on contemporary art have been featured in *Camera Austria*, *Flash Art*, *Kunst-Bulletin*, and *Texte zur Kunst*. She co-curated the touring exhibition *Ready to Shoot: Fernsehgalerie Gerry Schum/videogalerie schum* at the Kunsthalle Düsseldorf and the Musée d'Art Moderne de la Ville de Paris.

Pop Art

The author

Klaus Honnef was honorary professor of photography theory at the Kassel Art Academy. He was one of the organizers of documenta 5 and documenta 6 in Kassel, and has been the curator of more than 500 exhibitions in Germany and abroad. He has written numerous books, including TASCHEN's *Contemporary Art* and *Andy Warhol*.

Notes

1 Lawrence Alloway, "The Development of British Pop", in Lucy R. Lippard, *Pop Art* (1966), 1970, p. 27.

2 Ibid.

3 Ibid., p. 9.

4 Peter Selz, quoted in Anna Umland, "Pop Art and the Museum of Modern Art: An Ongoing Affair", in *Pop Art – Selections from The Museum of Modern Art*, exh. cat., The Museum of Modern Art in collaboration with the High Museum of Art, ed. by Harriet Schoenholz Bee, New York, 1988, p. 13.

5 Clement Greenberg, "Avant-Garde and Kitsch" (1939), in *Pollock* and *After*, ed. by Francis Frascina, London, 1985.

6 Henry Geldzahler, "Hockney: Young and Older", in *David Hockney. A Retrospective*, exh. cat., Los Angeles County Museum of Art, Metropolitan Museum of Art, Tate Gallery, organized by Maurice Tuchman and Stephanie Barron, Los Angeles, 1988, p. 19.

7 René König, *Soziologische Orientierungen, Vorträge und Aufsätze*, Cologne and Berlin, 1965, p. 544.

8 Erwin Panofsky, "Style and Medium in the Motion Pictures", in *Three Essays on Style*, ed. by Irving Lavin, MIT Press, Cambridge, Mass. and London, 1995, p. 119. This essay was first published in 1936.

Imprint

**EACH AND EVERY TASCHEN BOOK
PLANTS A SEED!**

Each year, we offset our annual carbon emissions with
carbon credits at the Instituto Terra, a reforestation
program in Minas Gerais, Brazil, founded by Lélia
and Sebastião Salgado. To find out more about this
ecological partnership, please check:
www.taschen.com/institutoterra.
Inspiration: unlimited.
Carbon footprint: (almost) zero.

Want to see more? Visit taschen.com to view our
current publications, browse our latest magazine,
and subscribe to our newsletter.

© 2026 TASCHEN GmbH
Hohenzollernring 53, D–50672 Köln
www.taschen.com

English translations: John Gabriel, Worpswede
(Expressionism, Pop Art); Michael Scuffil,
Leverkusen (Impressionism, Abstract Expressionism);
Isabel Varea for Grapevine Publishing Services,
London (Surrealism)

Printed in Bosnia-Herzegovina
ISBN 978-3-7544-0145-3

FRONT COVER
Vincent van Gogh
Portrait of Père Tanguy, 1887
Oil on canvas, 92 x 73 cm (36¼ x 28¾ in.)
Paris, Musée Rodin

BACK COVER AND PAGE 1
Andy Warhol
Gold Marilyn Monroe, 1962
Polymer, silkscreen, oil on canvas,
211 x 145 cm (83 x 57 in.)
New York, The Museum of Modern Art,
gift of Philip Johnson

PAGES 2/3
Wassily Kandinsky
St Ludwig's Church in Munich, 1908
Oil on cardboard, 67.3 x 96 cm (26½ x 37¾ in.)
Madrid, Museo Thyssen-Bornemisza,
on loan from the Collection of Carmen
Thyssen-Bornemisza

PAGES 4/5
John Singer Sargent
In the Luxembourg Gardens, 1879
Oil on canvas, 65.7 x 92.4 cm (25¾ x 36¼ in.)
Philadelphia Museum of Art